P9-DZN-584

understanding
Psychology
second edition

understanding
Psychology
second edition

ACADEMIC ADVISERS

Dr. George Fuller
*City College of
San Francisco*

Dr. James Calhoun
SUNY, Stony Brook

Dr. Martin Schulman
Essex Community College

WRITER: Ann Levine

CRM
Random House

Second Edition
987654321

Copyright ©1974, 1977 by Random House, Inc.

Library of Congress Cataloging in Publication Data

Levine, Ann.
    Understanding psychology.

    First ed. published in (1974) entered under title.
    Includes bibliographies and index.
    1. Psychology. I. Fuller, George. II. Moreland,
Henry. III. Title.
BF131.U48 1977   150   76-45363
ISBN 0-394-31195-7

Manufactured in the United States of America.
Composed by Westminster Graphic, Inc. Woodside,
N.Y. Printed and bound by Rand McNally & Co.,
Versailles, Ky.

Cover and title page art: © Glen Heller 1976
Cover design: Susan Gebel
Text design: Meryl Sussman Levavi
Photo research: R. Lynn Goldberg and Helena Frost

Preface

Revising a successful textbook is always a risky project, as change does not necessarily bring improvement. We believe this revision maintains all the outstanding features of the first edition and provides significant new attractive features.

When we decided to revise *Understanding Psychology* we also decided that the surest way to improve the text was to ask the people who use it how they would like to see it changed. We did a large survey, and over 200 instructors who used the first edition answered our questionnaire. The responses to the questionnaires provided our guidelines for this edition, and we see this edition as a tailor-made one.

Those who responded to the questionnaire clearly identified the most important strengths of the book. These strengths are:

- Clear, straightforward writing style that is not at all condescending to students

- Attractive and informative graphics

- Concise, yet broad coverage of the field of psychology

- Up-to-date coverage of this quickly changing field

The second edition has these same strengths, and it is an even more effective teaching tool. The changes have truly made a good book better.

Here is a brief sketch of the most important changes and additions in this revision:

- While as readable as the first edition, the revised text has greater depth. Students will receive fuller, more precise, and up-to-date accounts of important topics, with research findings supporting statements that would otherwise seem too general.

- There is now even greater emphasis on the practical applications of research findings to students' own lives, so that students can see psychology as a means of understanding and affecting their own lives, not just as a subject to be studied. For example,

  □ In Chapter 2: Learning: Principles and Applications, we discuss how to improve study habits.

  □ In Chapter 3: Memory and Thought, we suggest ways to improve one's memory.

☐ In Chapter 6: Motivation and Emotion, we discuss achievement motivation and fear of success.

☐ In Chapter 9: Adolescence, Adulthood, and Old Age, the challenges of each of these stages are explored in a way that will help students to think about the coming stages in their own lives and in the lives of those around them.

☐ Chapter 14: Adjustment in Contemporary Society examines a number of important life adjustments students may have to make or may have made—adjustments to school, work, love, marriage, and even social change.

☐ Chapter 18: Applying Psychology is about specific ways psychology can be applied to the real world. It covers such things as the effects of television, crowding, jury selection, and evaluation of social improvement programs.

• We have added four new chapters that give better coverage of some areas of growing importance.

☐ Chapter 6: Motivation and Emotion
This chapter represents an expansion of the material in the first edition. Instructors felt it was necessary to have more discussion of these two closely associated areas and to have this discussion as a separate chapter.

☐ Chapter 9: Adolescence, Adulthood, and Old Age
The inclusion of this chapter reflects a significant shift in the study of development from an interest in childhood and adolescence to an interest in the entire life span.

☐ Chapter 14: Adjustment in Contemporary Society
This chapter has been added because of the interest in the normal adjustments that almost everyone experiences as opposed to the more serious disturbances, which are discussed in Chapter 15: Disturbance and Breakdown.

☐ Chapter 18: Applying Psychology
Many instructors have indicated that they and their students are interested in exploring the practical applications of psychology. Given the present concern that disciplines address themselves to the problems of the human condition as well as to pressing social problems, we think this chapter is an exciting addition to our book.

• We have strengthened the pedagogical devices in the text.

☐ There is now an outline of the headings in the chapter to provide an overview of the topics to be covered in that chapter.

☐ There is now a *Glossary* of important terms at the end of each chapter. These glossaries are a helpful review of the chapter.

☐ New *Activities* have been added and many have been revised. Many instructors indicated that they found these projects useful for classroom activities and for outside assignments. We believe that the revision will make them even more appealing.

☐ There are also *References* at the end of the chapter to allow students to follow up on any topics of interest.

☐ The *Suggested Readings* have been updated and enhanced by the addition of magazine articles.

☐ Of course, the other pedagogical devices have been revised and will serve students and instructors as well in this edition as in the last. We believe the chapter organization, the main headings and sub-headings, the illustrations and captions, and the summaries at the end of each chapter are again superior features in this text.

• Our total package is revised and should serve even more as an asset to your teaching

☐ *Student Handbook: A Review Guide, Activities Manual, and Reader.* Each chapter of the handbook has systematic review questions, student projects, and one or two readings from *Psychology Today* magazine. We see this handbook as both a review aid to students and as a teaching aid for instructors. The review questions are well thought out, the projects imaginative, and the readings are engaging and enrich the material in the text.

☐ The *Instructors Manual* has been revised and expanded to compliment the text. Most of the test questions have been pretested. We are sure you will find the test items intelligent and appropriate.

All of this adds up to a very fine revision that provides you with a first-rate teaching tool, enhanced by excellent supplements.

Many people deserve credit for the planning and execution of what we believe to be a successful revision. Roberta Bauer Meyer, one of our most talented editors, organized and coordinated the entire project. Her intelligence and good judgment are an asset to any project. Jan Carr analyzed the survey data and prepared a very useful summary of recommendations for revising the text. Other people at Random House who contributed to the project are Paul Shensa, Executive Editor; Meryl Levavi, Designer; and Debbie Conner, Editorial Assistant. Thomas Flagg, our researcher on the project, was absolutely indispensable. He is a discriminating researcher, who is always clever and thorough.

Our Academic Advisers, George Fuller, Martin Schulman, and James Calhoun, were very hard working and conscientious about contributing material and reviewing drafts. Our Editorial Review Board, Henry Moreland, John Reibsamen, Frank Sjursen, and Robert Smith, gave us valuable feedback on chapters. And our Specialist Reviewers commented on particular chapters in their area of specialization. We certainly appreciate the time and thought our advisers and reviewers put into their work on this book.

Probably the most important person of all is our gifted writer Ann Levine. Ann is a professional writer in every sense of the word. She has extensive writing experience, particularly with textbooks. She is serious about wanting texts to be appealing and readable, and she has the imagination, intelligence, and the sense of organization that makes a text truly teach.

One final note of thanks to instructors who responded to our questionnaire. Your constructive comments and suggestions were our guides every step of the way. For that reason, we hope you will find using this edition doubly rewarding.

Much work and thought has gone into the revision. We think we have given you a text that will work for you and for your students, one that will provide an engaging and clear introduction to the fascinating subject of psychology. We hope you will find it both useful and enjoyable to use this text.

VIRGINIA L. HOITSMA
PSYCHOLOGY EDITOR

To the Student

Since around the beginning of the twentieth century, the body of psychological knowledge has grown immensely. In the last three-quarters of a century, psychologists have discovered a vast number of facts and developed a variety of theories about human development, mental processes, behavior, and interaction. The purpose of this book is to pass along to you some of the knowledge that has been gained. To accomplish this purpose, we have made a special effort to explore as many facets of psychology as possible, without emphasizing a particular subject area or point of view to the exclusion of any others.

To enhance this approach, we prepared this book with three broad objectives in mind: first, to provide an introduction to the terms and concepts psychologists use; second, to present these topics in a clearly written, interesting style; and third, to explain the significance of psychological findings for the reader's own life.

This text will serve as your handbook to the understanding of psychology, and as such it contains a number of aids designed to make the information it presents as clear and as useful as possible. These aids include:

1. *Organization.* The book is divided into eighteen chapters, which are grouped into six units. Each unit roughly corresponds to a major field of psychology. The unit openings give you an overview of what each section and chapter contains.

2. *Text and Illustrations.* The text, captions, and illustrations work well together to present the research, theories, and ideas central to psychology. Chapters are divided by numerous subheadings that describe the subject of each section, and key terms and concepts are italicized when they are first introduced to draw them to your attention. The illustrations and captions are designed to clarify important ideas, to add interesting information, and to provoke thought.

3. *Outlines and Summaries.* Brief outlines at the beginning of each chapter prepare you for what you are about to read. Summaries at the end of the chapters help you locate the important points and to review them.

4. *Glossaries.* Definitions of key terms follow every chapter summary. These lists will help you to review important ideas.

5. *Activities.* The activities that follow each chapter are intended to help you relate the ideas in the chapter to experiences of your own.

6. *Suggested Readings.* Each chapter contains a description of several interesting and readable books and magazine articles related to the topics presented in the chapter.

7. *References.* After each chapter you will find a list of books and articles that provide in-depth coverage of some of the subjects explored in the chapters. These sources are useful for pursuing an interest in a particular topic.

All these aids have been developed to help make the field of psychology come alive for you. This is a book you can study from, but it is also one you can browse through, read for enjoyment, and refer to when trying to understand psychological aspects of the world you live in, the people you know, and your own personality.

Contents

understanding
Psychology
second edition

1

Introducing Psychology

Psychology is one of the classes students genuinely look forward to taking. And no wonder. All of us want to know "what makes people tick." We've had experiences and done things we find difficult to explain, even to ourselves. We hear about people doing, saying, and believing things we can't imagine—some "crazy" or "sick," some wonderful, almost superhuman. Most people expect psychology to solve these riddles, and in many cases it does.

But the vast majority of psychologists are concerned with everyday, commonplace behavior and feelings—not with the unusual and bizarre. Everyone learns, remembers, and solves problems. Everyone develops intellectually and socially, from infancy to adulthood. Everyone perceives environmental stimuli (sounds, sights, smells, and the like) and interprets this information from their senses. Everyone's behavior depends on physiological functions—on signals darting to and from the central nervous system. We all feel emotions and engage in motivated behavior. Everyone has a personality, and most of us are curious about where it came from and where it is going. And everyone's behavior is affected by the many formal and informal groups to which he or she belongs. Not everyone is psychologically disturbed or in need of therapy, but many people have a friend or relative who is. (According to one estimate, about one American in four develops a problem serious enough to warrant treatment at some point in life.) These everyday things are the focus of psychology.

We can make two promises in this book: first, to answer some of the questions readers have about themselves and other people; and second, to show that everyday behavior is far more complex—and interesting—than most people imagine.

PSYCHOLOGY AND EVERYDAY LIFE

What is it that fascinates psychologists about ordinary behavior? What exactly do they study? The clearest way to answer this question is to look at a slice of life through a psychologist's eyes.

A young, female student decides to have lunch at the school cafeteria. She walks to the cafeteria, joins the food line, selects her meal, and pays for it. She looks around for someone to sit with. Seeing no one she knows well, she chooses an empty table, sits down, and begins to eat. A shadow falls across her plate. It is a young man from her English

Figure 1.1
This bookstore display suggests the diversity of topics psychologists study. Each of these areas will be discussed in the chapters that follow.

class. Her spirits sink. Although she finds him quite attractive, he never speaks to her unless he has missed a class and wants to borrow her notes. She greets him coolly but he sits down anyway, launching into a rambling tale of an all-night party that left him with a nagging headache. The young woman recalls that he missed this morning's class and notices that he is eyeing her notebook as he talks. Annoyed, she hurriedly finishes eating and begins to collect her things. Attempting a casual smile, the young man asks for her notes. Now she is more than annoyed. Although her English notebook is in plain sight, she tells him curtly that she is sorry but she left her notes in the library—to which, as a matter of fact, she must return right away. As she leaves the cafeteria, she glances back and sees the young man still sitting at the table, nervously smoking a cigarette. He looks depressed. Suddenly, she feels a bit depressed herself.

This is a simple story, but from a psychologist's point of view, the behavior we witnessed was complex. First of all, the young woman decided to have lunch because of her *physiological state* (she was hungry). She may also have been *motivated by cognitive* elements (she knew it was noon, her habitual lunchtime). When she entered the cafeteria, she *perceived sensory stimuli* different from those outside. But she paid little attention to the new sights, sounds, and smells, except to note that the food smelled good and the line was mercifully short. She went through the line and paid for her food—*learned behavior not too* different from that of a hungry rat that runs a maze for a food reward.

The young woman looked for a *social group* to join, but found none to which she belonged. She sat alone until the young man joined her. He felt free to do so because in most schools there is an informal rule, or *norm,* that students who have a class together may approach each other socially. (This rule usually does not hold for members of a looser group, such as commuters who ride the same bus.) The young woman *remembered* how the young man had behaved toward her in the past and realized that he seemed to be embarking on the same note-borrowing course. This triggered the *emotional reaction of* anger. However, she did not throw a tantrum, as a two-year-old might, but acted in a way that was more appropriate to her stage of *development.* We can presume that her response was characteristic of her *personality:* She told the young man that she didn't have the notes (even though he had seen them) and left.

In the example above, if such situations occurred often, and if they were always followed by depression, either student's behavior could indicate psychological *disturbance.* If the young man always relied on others for help and manipulated people to get his way, his behavior might be a sign of disorder. So might the young woman's, since she interprets simple requests as demands but finds herself unable to either meet or refuse the request in a direct way. However, in this context, neither student's behavior seems abnormal.

Viewed in this way, an apparently simple event raises numerous questions about why people behave and feel as they do. How do physiological states influence behavior? What motivates people to choose one action instead of another? Nearly all the topics covered in this book's table of contents appear in this brief story.

WHY STUDY PSYCHOLOGY?

As the example above suggests, one advantage of learning about psychology is that it offers a new framework for viewing daily events: The things we take for granted come to life. There are other advantages as well.

Insight

Understanding psychology can provide useful insights into your own and other people's behavior. Suppose, for example, that a student is convinced that he is hopelessly shy and doomed forever to feel uncomfortable in groups. Then he learns from social psychology that different kinds of groups tend to have different effects on their members. He thinks about this for a while and notes that although he is miserable at parties, he feels fine at meetings of the school newspaper staff and with the group he works with in the biology laboratory. (In technical terms, he is much more uncomfortable in unstructured, social groups than in structured, task-oriented groups.) Realizing that he is only uncomfortable in some groups brings a flood of relief. He isn't paralyzingly shy, he just doesn't like unstructured groups. And he is not alone in his feelings. There is something about each of us in this book. You, too, may find that one chapter or another makes you see yourself in a new way.

Practical Information

Some of the chapters in this book include material that has practical application to everyday life. You will read, in concrete and detailed form, how to carry out a number of useful procedures psychologists have developed.

For example, Chapter 3 includes a description of several *mnemonic*

FIGURE 1.2
A knowledge of psychology would help this young man understand that he is affected differently by different kinds of groups. Although uneasy in unstructured group situations, like parties, he feels fine in structured meetings with other students.

FIGURE 1.3
Kissing is a response that is subject to shaping. Here the response is emitted tentatively and would probably be repeated only after a considerable time interval if it produced no result. The kiss is reinforced, however, and immediately the response increases in frequency. Note that the operant behavior increases in vigor, as well as frequency, after reinforcement.

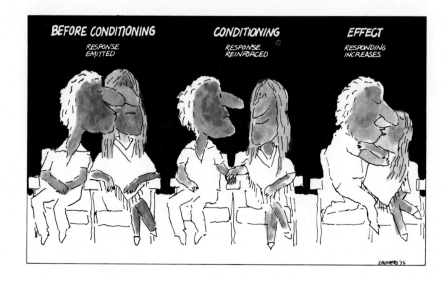

devices, or memory aids, which will help you to learn information by rote. The rhyme beginning, "Thirty days has September," which helps many people to remember the number of days in each month, is an example. Mnemonic devices usually require you to associate each item on a list with some sort of mental picture. Although this in itself may require time and effort (especially the first time), memory experts have shown it is worth the trouble. The techniques described may help you to memorize almost any list of words or numbers—the names of the presidents of the United States and their dates in office (for a history course), the authors and titles of books (for an English course), telephone numbers, shopping lists, and so on.

Chapter 2 describes the systematic way of dispensing rewards and punishments that psychologists call *shaping*. You will definitely find this useful if you ever have to train a puppy, and you may find yourself wondering how you shape the behavior of people around you. Perhaps you have a friend who is always happy to join you for coffee or a movie but who never brings any money along. You've loaned him money many times, and just as many times he's failed to pay you back. You know he can afford to pay his share, and you have told him so repeatedly. But he's a good friend, so you end up paying his way again and again. In doing so you are rewarding or reinforcing an undesirable behavior pattern. Is that what you really want to do?

In the chapter on child development you will recognize some of the experiences you had in your own childhood. The chapter on disturbance and breakdown may help you understand the more difficult periods in your own life and in the lives of those around you. And Chapter 16 will tell you about the different kinds of therapy available to people who are experiencing severe or chronic difficulties. Of course, you should not jump to conclusions on the basis of this introduction to psychology. It takes a trained professional to diagnose and treat developmental and psychological problems (as Chapter 16 explains).

1. The behavior of most lower animals—insects, reptiles and amphibians, most rodents, and birds—is instinctive and unaffected by learning.
2. For the first week of life, a baby sees nothing but a gray blur regardless of what he or she "looks at."
3. A child learns to talk more quickly if the adults around the child habitually repeat the word he or she is trying to say, using proper pronunciation.
4. The best way to get a chronically noisy schoolchild to settle down and pay attention is to punish him or her.
5. Slow learners remember more of what they learn than fast learners.
6. Highly intelligent people— "geniuses"—tend to be physically frail and socially isolated.
7. On the average, you cannot predict from a person's grades at school and college whether he or she will do well in a career.
8. Most national and ethnic stereotypes are completely false.
9. In small amounts, alcohol is a stimulant.
10. LSD causes chromosome damage.
11. The largest drug problem in the United States, in terms of the number of people affected, is marijuana.
12. Psychiatry is a subdivision of psychology.
13. Most mentally retarded people are also mentally ill.
14. A third or more of the people suffering from severe mental disorder are potentially dangerous.
15. Electroshock therapy is an outmoded technique rarely used in today's mental hospitals.
16. The more severe the disorder, the more intensive the therapy required to cure it; for example, schizophrenics usually respond best to psychoanalysis.
17. Quite a few psychological characteristics of men and women appear to be inborn; in all cultures, for example, women are more emotional and sexually less aggressive than men.
18. No reputable psychologist "believes in" such irrational phenomena as ESP, hypnosis, or the bizarre mental and physical achievements of Eastern yogis.

Testing Beliefs

This book will also enable you to check some of your assumptions about human behavior and feelings. Psychologists have put common sense to the test, to find out whether things many of us take for granted are true or false. The statements about behavior printed on this page represent a small fraction of the beliefs psychologists have examined. How many of these statements do you think are true?

Before telling you the answers, we ask you to consider the implications of these opinions. An employer who believes that retarded people are mentally ill (item 13) and that most mentally ill people are dangerous (item 14) will undoubtedly refuse to hire a retarded person, even though he or she may be perfectly suited for the job. Parents who believe that extremely bright people are usually "social failures" (item 6) will probably suppress signs of unusual intelligence in their child—perhaps turning down a request for a chemistry set or the complete works of Shakespeare. Both of these reactions would be unfortunate, for psychologists have found that all the statements in this list are false.

In short, you will find this book useful in a number of ways. You will probably gain insights, practical information, and evaluations of popular beliefs about yourself and others. But our main goal is to introduce psychology as a basic science.

BASIC AND APPLIED PSYCHOLOGY

People often describe psychology as a "basic science." *Basic science* is the pursuit of knowledge for its own sake, in order to satisfy curiosity about the nature of things. The immediate "usefulness" of the knowledge is not an issue. *Applied science,* on the other hand, involves finding ways to use basic science to accomplish practical goals. Biologists and physicists nearly always practice basic science; physicians and engineers practice applied science.

Psychologists may practice both. A developmental psychologist who is studying the ability of infants to perceive visual patterns is doing basic research. He is not concerned with the implications his findings may have for the design of a crib. A psychologist who does applied science, perhaps as a consultant to a toy manufacturer, would be. Similarly, a social psychologist who is studying friendships in an office—who likes whom, how much, and why—is doing basic science. If she discovers that one individual has no friends in the office and another has so many he hardly has time to work, she will try to understand and explain the situation. But she will not try to correct it. This is a job for applied scientists, such as clinical or industrial psychologists.

Why is this distinction so important? Because transferring findings from basic to applied science is a tricky business. For example, psychologists doing basic research have found that babies raised in sterile institutional environments are seriously retarded in their physical, intellectual, and emotional development. Wayne Dennis (1960), among others, traces this to the fact that these babies have nothing to look at but a blank white ceiling and white crib cushions, and are only handled when they need to be fed or changed. However, we have to be very careful not to apply this finding too broadly. Because children who lack stimulation tend to develop poorly, we can't jump to the conclusion that by providing a child with maximum stimulation—by playing with him continually, having music piped into his room, surrounding him with fancy toys—we can guarantee that he will grow up emotionally sound and intellectually brilliant. On the contrary, it appears that most babies do best with a medium level of stimulation (White, 1969).

In short, what basic science gives us are specific findings: what happened in one study conducted at one time and in one place. To generalize these specific findings into a list of general rules is dangerous.

On the other hand, scientists can also make mistakes by being *too* specific when they move from basic to applied psychology. For example, pediatrician Lee Salk suspected that unborn babies associate their mother's heartbeat with the security and comfort of the womb. If this is true, Salk reasoned, newborn infants should find the sound of a heartbeat soothing. He tested this idea by placing infants in two separate nurseries and playing the sound of an amplified heartbeat in one. It turned out that the babies in this nursery slept more, cried less, and gained weight faster than babies in the quiet nursery. Salk concluded that his original idea was correct (1962).

Yvonne Brackbill and several of her colleagues were not entirely convinced, however (1966). In a preliminary study they found that two different rhythmic sounds—a metronome and a lullaby—were just as effective in quieting babies as the heartbeat. Thus it appeared that infants were responding to the constant, monotonous rhythm, not to the heartbeat

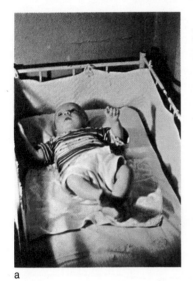
a

b

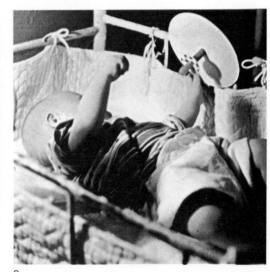
c

FIGURE 1.4

In an experiment by White, infants in institutions were reared under three conditions of environmental enrichment. (a) The normal institutional environment, little opportunity for visual or tactual exploration is provided. (b) A massive enrichment of the environment. (c) A slightly enriched environment; there is a single toy that can be looked at and grasped. To the surprise of many, White found that infants reared in environment (c) developed reaching behavior sooner than infants reared under either of the other conditions. By systematically exploring the full range of possible levels of stimulation, White discovered that there could be too much stimulation as well as too little.

itself. Brackbill went on to test whether newborn infants responded favorably to other monotonous sensations—constant light, increased heat, and snug swaddling. She found that *all* of these seemed to comfort babies (1971). Thus Salk's conclusions weren't entirely wrong, but neither were they entirely right. He had simply been too specific. Newborn babies seem to find a wide variety of monotonous, constant sensations reassuring.

In other cases the findings of basic science flatly contradict each other. As a result, scientists wishing to apply these findings have to decide for themselves who to believe.

Consider, for example, the question of whether violence on television and in the movies is bad for children. Some psychologists say it is, because children imitate what they see. Others say no, that watching crime stories and Westerns provides a substitute outlet for children's aggressive feelings, and that identifying with the characters in such shows makes children less inclined to behave violently. The reason for this conflict is that there are psychological studies—basic research—supporting both sides. This is probably because the experiments themselves were different. Perhaps the researchers showed children different forms of violence; perhaps they measured the children's reactions in different ways. As basic science, these studies are a good beginning. However, as guides for parents and social reformers, they leave a lot to be desired. The question of whether seeing violence on television or in the movies is bad for children remains to be answered.

As the above example suggests, psychologists can and do disagree. This strikes many people as strange. Psychology calls itself a science, and science is supposed to offer proofs, not opinions. But no science, not even chemistry or physics, consists solely of demonstrated facts. There are unanswered questions in all sciences. And psychology probably has more than its share, partly because the workings of the human mind are difficult to pin down and partly because the study of psychological processes is less than one hundred years old. But sometimes questions are as valuable as answers. To the scientist, for example, the conflicting findings of different studies are a spur to further research. But what about the student who simply takes a psychology course and goes on to some other kind of work? Here too the questions that psychology raises can be valuable. Any science that encourages you to challenge accepted notions—to look carefully at what actual human beings do, rather than rush to conclusions about "people in general"—is bound to sharpen your perceptions and add richness to your life.

THEORETICAL APPROACHES TO PSYCHOLOGICAL QUESTIONS

One reason psychologists disagree is that, like other scientists, they have different ways of approaching their subject—different ideas as to what is most important. To use the technical term, every psychologist starts out with a particular *theoretical orientation,* that is, an overall view of human psychology, a specific set of beliefs about why we behave as we do.

In this section we will examine three major theoretical orientations: the social-learning approach, the psychoanalytic approach, and the cognitive approach. As we shall see in later chapters, these three theoretical approaches have been used to interpret many aspects of human behavior, from learning (Chapter 2) to childhood development (Chapter 8) to personality structure (Chapter 13). And because each theoretical orientation approaches human behavior from a different angle, each ends up with a different interpretation. To illustrate this fact, let us apply the social-learning, psychoanalytic, and cognitive approaches to a topic that never fails to generate dispute: sex roles.

The Question

Turn back to the beginning of this chapter and reread the story about the two students, reversing the sexes of the main characters. Does their behavior seem as natural to you as it did the first time you read this account? Is it likely that a young woman—even one with as few social skills as the young woman in the story—would brag to a male acquaintance about all-night parties? Or that a young man who has been asked several times for his notes by an attractive female would become annoyed with her? Possibly, but probably not.

Babies are not born knowing their sex. In fact, until they are two or three years old, most children cannot say for sure whether they are boys or girls. Many three- and four-year-olds think that people can change their sex if they want to. However, by the time they enter school, most children have clear ideas about sex differences. Children of five know that girls are expected to play with dolls, boys with trucks. Most feel that men have more power and prestige than women. And many firmly believe that fathers are supposed to work outside the home while mothers are supposed to stay home. The question is, How do children develop these behaviors and beliefs?

FIGURE 1.5
Dolls like Barbie and her recently created male counterpart Big Jim serve to teach and reinforce traditional sex-role stereotypes. For Barbie, there is an enormous wardrobe of stylish clothes, jewelry, equipment for hairdressing, and the like. Big Jim has athletic costumes for football and baseball, and he has sports cars. Because of Big Jim's sex-appropriate furnishings and activities, some parents might not object to their son playing with such a doll—ordinarily behavior believed to be inappropriate for boys.

The Social-learning Approach

According to social-learning theorists, children are taught, in daily interaction, to behave in ways society considers appropriate for their sex.
This is called modeling. Parents, teachers, and friends shape behavior by
dispensing rewards and punishments and by acting as models for a child
to imitate. For example, a girl realizes that her parents praise her for
taking good care of her dolls but ignore or actively discourage her attempts to learn how to play football. So she plays with dolls. A boy sees
that his parents are proud when he excels on the football field but are
downright horrified when they find him dressing a doll. He never touches
dolls again.

A girl hears her mother's friends praising her cooking and committee
work. She sees that certain older girls who are friendly and outgoing and
pay attention to their appearance receive a great deal of attention. She
tries to imitate these people, in the hope of winning the same sorts of
rewards. Similarly, a boy models himself after the older boys and men
other people seem to admire. Sex-typed behavior, then, results from seeking rewards and avoiding punishments by modeling behavior after the
parent and other adults of the same sex.

The Psychoanalytic Approach

The psychoanalytic explanation of sex roles, based on Freud's theory of
personality development (described in Chapter 13), is far more dramatic.
According to this approach, every child goes through a series of crises
in his or her early years. At about age three, the child forms a deep attachment to the opposite-sex parent. When this happens, the child begins to
see the same-sex parent as a rival and has vivid fantasies of getting rid
of him or her. However, children perceive adults as enormously powerful
and fear the same-sex parent will punish them for these thoughts. Eventually the child resolves these conflicts unconsciously by *identifying* with
the same-sex parent.

Identification is more than simple imitation or modeling. A boy uncrit-
ically *internalizes* his father's beliefs and attitudes in a single gulp, so
to speak. They become an integral part of his personality, as if his father
were inside him. Similarly, girls identify with their mothers. Identification
enables a child to avoid the same-sex parent's anger and at the same time
to possess the opposite-sex parent indirectly.

Psychoanalytic theorists believe these changes are largely unconscious,
in contrast to social-learning theorists, who emphasize more or less deliberate and conscious imitation.

The Cognitive Approach

The cognitive approach to psychology derives from Jean Piaget's theory
of mental development, which we will describe in some detail in Chapter
8. Piaget demonstrated that children perceive the world quite differently
than adults do. For example, a baby does not realize that a ball that has
rolled behind a chair is still there. As far as he knows, it is gone—forever.

FIGURE 1.6
The three major theories of how sex-typed identities are acquired. All such theories must account for certain accepted facts: that children form strong attachments to their parents, that children typically choose to model themselves on the parent of the same sex, and that children acquire a clear sense of the sexual behavior that is appropriate for them at a fairly early age. The three theories give quite different accounts of how these facts are related and of what other factors are important in the process.

If an adult pours water from a short, wide glass into a tall, thin glass, a child of three will say that the second glass contains more water, even though she has watched the operation. Similarly, children of this age think that a person can change his or her sex simply by changing their clothes and hair style.

It is only at about age six that children learn that some things are permanent, even though they may change in appearance—among them, sex. At this point they begin to reorganize their mental picture of the world around the fact that they are a boy or girl, and to seek out "boy things" or "girl things." In other words, they try to make their behavior match their newly perceived identity as girl or boy. They are motivated not so much by a desire for rewards as by a desire for mental consistency.

Each of these three explanations of how sex-typed behavior develops emphasizes a different aspect of the person. Social-learning theorists stress behavior; psychoanalytic theorists stress feelings; cognitive theorists stress mental operations.

In short, different theoretical approaches can give different answers to the question, Who (or what) controls a person's behavior? According to social-learning theory, human behavior is shaped by outside agents—parents, teachers, and so on. Psychoanalytic theory maintains that unconscious psychological forces determine how a person will behave. That is, the crucial processes go on inside the person, and for the most part they are not under his or her conscious control. Cognitive theory falls between the two: what happens inside a person (mental development) changes the way he or she perceives and deals with what happens outside.

As we have mentioned, these different approaches help to explain why psychologists often disagree. Because they focus on different aspects of the person and have different ideas about "what makes people tick," they ask different questions and arrive at different answers. But as we noted

FIGURE 1.7
This engraving depicts a forest scene, doesn't it? If you answer yes, the reason may be that you only looked at the "framed area." If we had said, "Look at the muddy road," you would have seen that the forest is simply a reflection in a puddle. The same thing happens in psychology. There are various ways of viewing psychological processes, such as sex-role development, each supported by research. Attending to one theoretical view tends to prevent one from seeing others. Hence psychologists often disagree.

FIGURE 1.8 (*opposite*)
Psychologists at work.
(a) A psychotherapist talks with a woman, helping her sort out the difficulties she is having in her personal life. (b) Using an automated instructional system designed by educational psychologists, a child learns to make letter and word combinations as first steps in learning to read and write. (c) A psychologist administers a standard intelligence test to a young girl to find out how she compares intellectually to other children her age. (d) A mentally disturbed boy is coaxed, prompted, and rewarded by a psychotherapist who is trying to increase the boy's responsiveness to the world around him. (e) Psychologists have contributed to solving engineering problems related to man's behavior in the unique conditions present in a space vehicle. (f) Two psychological researchers gather information about sleep and dreaming by examining the brain-wave patterns of a person sleeping in another room. (g) Family interaction is videotaped and later observed by the family and by psychotherapists in order to help family members understand their problems. (h) A researcher operates on a rat's brain. Later, the rat is placed in a controlled situation where the effects of chemical brain stimulation on its behavior can be measured.

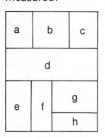

earlier, disagreement can be helpful. Each perspective generates more research, either to confirm one point of view or to challenge alternative points of view. And whether helpful or not, disagreement is inevitable. Like any other combined human effort, the study of psychology proceeds dispute by dispute. The existence of different theoretical orientations gives us a fuller, more complete picture than we might have otherwise.

We have seen, in brief, how different psychologists think. What do psychologists do?

PSYCHOLOGY AS A PROFESSION

Psychology today covers an enormous range. There are psychologists working in advertising, education, and criminology; psychologists studying death, art, and robots. Psychological themes and terminology have penetrated all areas of life and have become integral parts of novels, films, and television programs.

In the process of growing, psychology has divided into a number of subfields. *Clinical* and *counseling psychology* are the most popular areas of specialization today. Both involve applied science. Most clinical psychologists are psychotherapists. They work in mental hospitals, prisons, schools, clinics, and private offices, helping people with psychological problems. Some specialize in administering and interpreting personality tests that are designed to determine whether or not a person needs treatment, and what kind. Counseling psychologists usually work in schools, industrial firms, and the like, advising and assisting people who would be classified as normal rather than disturbed.

Personality, social, and *developmental psychology* also attract large numbers of specialists. These psychologists are usually involved in basic rather than applied science. Personality psychologists study personality development and traits, and devise personality tests. Social psychologists study groups and the way groups influence individual behavior. Some are particularly interested in public opinion and devote much of their time to conducting polls and surveys. Most developmental psychologists focus on children from birth to age fifteen or thereabouts. However, in recent years a number have been leaning toward the "cradle to grave" approach—that is, studying development as something that extends from birth to old age.

Educational psychologists deal with topics related to teaching children and young adults, such as intelligence, memory, problem-solving, and motivation. They are concerned with evaluating teaching methods, devising tests, and developing new instructional devices such as films and television. One of their major contributions to education is the teaching machine, which allows each individual to proceed through a subject at his or her own rate. The machine provides information, asks questions, and tells the student whether his or her answers are right or wrong.

Industrial psychology is another area of specialization. Psychological methods have been used to boost production, improve working conditions, place applicants in the jobs for which they are best suited, devise

methods for training people, and reduce accidents. Psychologists have also been involved in improving machines, for example, by making control panels more readable. Industrial psychologists generally work as consultants to private firms or government agencies.

Finally, about a fourth of all psychologists are engaged in *experimental psychology*. These psychologists do everything from testing how electrical stimulation of a rat's brain affects its behavior, to studying how disturbed people think, to observing how different socioeconomic groups vote in elections. They are basic scientists. Many work in colleges and universities, teaching and writing as well as conducting experiments.

All psychologists have an area of special interest, but most participate in diverse activities. A busy psychologist might divide her time between doing research, teaching, administering psychological tests, providing therapy or counseling, writing books and research papers, serving on college committees, figuring departmental budgets, and attending professional conventions.

The business lives of psychologists are not the subject of this book, however. Rather, this text describes what psychologists think about, what they know, what experiments they have done, what observations they have made, what conclusions they have drawn, and what their work means to a person who is not a psychologist. Psychology is a science dedicated to answering some of the most interesting questions of everyday life:

What happens during sleep?
How can bad habits be broken?
Is there a way to measure intelligence?
Why do crowds sometimes turn into mobs?
What does the world look like to other animals?
Do dreams mean anything?
How does punishment affect a child?
Can memory be improved?
What causes psychological breakdowns?

In trying to answer such questions, psychology ties together all that has been discovered about human behavior and feelings in order to look at the total human being. The picture is far from complete, but much of what is known will be found in the chapters that follow.

SUMMARY

1. The primary focus of psychology is the complexity of everyday behavior.

2. An apparently simple and ordinary meeting in a college cafeteria illustrates the topics psychologists study: physiological states, perception, cognition, motivation, memory, learned behavior, development, social groups, emotions, personality, disturbances, and breakdowns.

3. This introduction to psychology may pro-

vide insights, practical information, and an objective test of your beliefs. However, the major portion of the book is devoted to psychology as a basic science.

4. Basic science is the pursuit of knowledge for its own sake—in contrast to applied science, which is the search for ways to put basic science to use in accomplishing practical goals.

5. Basic science thrives on debate. The results of a single study should not be mistaken for "the final answer" or for authoritative advice on how to handle everyday situations.

6. A psychologist's theoretical orientation is the angle from which he or she approaches the study of behavior and feelings.

7. Social-learning theorists take the position that people essentially are what they do. They focus on outside influences on behavior.

8. Psychoanalytic theorists imply that people are what they feel. They emphasize internal but unconscious controls on behavior.

9. Cognitive theorists stress the interaction between internal, mental development and external forces.

10. Psychology is subdivided in practice as well as in theory. Major areas of specialization in psychology today include: clinical and counseling psychology; personality, social, and developmental psychology; educational psychology; industrial psychology; and experimental psychology.

11. In the course of describing what psychologists think about and what they have learned in the chapters that follow, we hope to show what their work means to people who are not psychologists.

GLOSSARY

applied science: Finding ways to use scientific findings to accomplish practical goals.

basic science: The pursuit of knowledge about natural phenomena for its own sake.

cognitive theory: An approach to psychology that emphasizes the role of learning and conscious mental processes in shaping behavior.

psychoanalytic theory: An approach to psychology derived from Freud's theories of the role of childhood conflicts and the unconscious in shaping behavior.

psychology: The study of mental processes and the behavior of organisms.

social-learning theory: An approach to psychology that emphasizes the role of imitation, modeling, reward, and punishment in shaping behavior.

ACTIVITIES

1. Write your own definition of psychology. How different is your definition from one you would have written before reading the chapter? Put the definition away, and at the end of the course take it out and reread it.

2. How is psychology involved in your life? Considering the information at the end of the chapter regarding the various areas of psychology, make a list of all the ways that psychology affects your life. (Hint: Traffic signs and classroom interiors are often designed by psychologists.)

3. Psychology is generally thought of as being a benevolent science, and it is expected to produce such results as happier people, accident-free and more productive workers, and greater

understanding in interpersonal relationships. But well-meaning people throughout history have also applied what they considered to be sound "psychological" techniques that have actually served to increase the torment of or to totally destroy their intended beneficiaries. Can you see any possibilities today that psychological knowledge could be used against the best interests of an individual or society?

4. Much of psychology is in effect an attempt to articulate the nature of human nature. Make a list of characteristics or behavioral tendencies that you think apply to all people. Compare your list to the lists of other students in the class. Do you think there are any characteristics or "laws," comparable to established physical attributes and physical laws in physics, that are universally valid for all of us?

5. List some of the child-rearing practices that were differentially applied to girls and boys when you were growing up. How have they influenced your present behavior in terms of sex roles and your attitudes toward them? Do you see any changes in these practices today?

6. Make a list of various professions or occupations. List the ways one or another type of psychologist might contribute to the better functioning within the occupation or profession. What kind of psychologist do you think would be most helpful in performing each job?

SUGGESTED READINGS

AMERICAN PSYCHOLOGICAL ASSOCIATION. *Careers in Psychology*. Washington, D.C.: American Psychological Association, 1975. This useful booklet provides information on the various kinds of careers open to students interested in pursuing their study of psychology, and describes the type of education required for each career.

BAKER, ROBERT A. (ED.). *Psychology in the Wry*. New York: Van Nostrand, 1963 (paper). A collection of amusing, satirical articles in which psychologists make fun of their own pomposity and other shortcomings.

EYSENCK, HANS J. *Fact and Fiction in Psychology*. Baltimore: Penguin, 1965. Eysenck delves into popular notions of psychology and applies the scientific method to come up with some witty and entertaining conclusions. Topics range from criminal personality and the four temperaments to accident proneness. Also of interest are two other books by Eysenck that, together with this one, make up a trilogy: *Uses and Abuses of Psychology* (1953) and *Sense and Nonsense in Psychology* (1957).

GOLDENSON, R. M. *Mysteries of the Mind*. Garden City, N.Y.: Doubleday, 1973. Goldenson has gathered together a wide variety of unusual case studies in human behavior. He discusses such things as child prodigies, voodoo deaths, photographic memory, mass hysteria, and multiple personalities, and tries to find explanations for these fascinating phenomena.

JAMES, WILLIAM. *Psychology (Briefer Course)*. New York: Macmillan, 1962 (paper). Published originally in two volumes in 1890 this is the abridgement of James' *Principles of Psychology*, the first major classic in the field of psychology. This book, which remains highly readable and thought-provoking today, attracted many eminent psychologists to the field and has influenced innumerable others in their thinking and research.

MACKAY, CHARLES. *Extraordinary Popular Delusions and the Madness of Crowds*. New York: Farrar, Straus & Giroux, 1932; originally published, 1841. A remarkable book describing in vivid detail cases of human folly throughout the ages. Special emphasis is given to mass movements and the psychology of crowds, which will be discussed in detail in Chapter 10.

SARGENT, D. S., AND STAFFORD, K. R. *Basic Teachings of the Great Psychologists*. New York: Dolphin, 1965 (paper). A good introduction to the major areas of psychology. The authors trace the historical and present-day explorations of such questions as: How can human abilities be measured? What is instinct? How does the nervous system work? What is personality?

SHAPIRO, EVELYN (ED.). *PsychoSources: A Psychology Resource Catalog*. New York: Bantam, 1973 (paper). This large-format paperback is a treasurehouse of information about psychology. It contains book and film reviews, access information, and comments and essays about current trends on everything from identity crisis to health care in China.

WILSON, J. *The Mind*. New York: Time-Life Books, 1964. A beautifully illustrated and easy-to-read book about the past, present, and possible future of psychological investigation.

BIBLIOGRAPHY

BRACKBILL, YVONNE. "Cumulative Effects of Continuous Stimulation on Arousal Level in Infants." *Child Development*, 42 (1971): 17–26.

BRACKBILL, YVONNE, ET AL. "Arousal Level in Neonates and Preschool Children Under Continuous Auditory Stimulation." *Journal of Experimental Child Psychology*, 4 (1966): 177–188.

CATES, JUDITH. "Baccalaureates in Psychology: 1969 and 1970." *American Psychologist*, 28 (1973): 262–264.

DENNIS, WAYNE. "Causes of Retardation among Institutional Children: Iran." *Journal of Genetic Psychology*, 96 (1960): 47–59.

EYSENCK, HANS J., ARNOLD, W., AND MEILI, RICHARD. *Encyclopedia of Psychology*. 3 vols. New York: Herder & Herder, 1972.

HEBB, D. O. "What Psychology Is About." *American Psychologist*, 29 (1974): 71–79.

MARX, MELVIN H., AND HILLIX, WILLIAM A. *Systems and Theories in Psychology*. 2nd ed. New York: McGraw-Hill, 1973.

SALK, LEE. "Mother's Heartbeat as an Imprinting Stimulus." *Transactions of the New York Academy of Sciences*, 24 (1962): 753–763.

WHITE, BURTON L. "Child Development Research: An Edifice Without a Foundation." *Merrill-Palmer Quarterly of Behavior and Development*, 15 (1969): 49–79.

WOLMAN, BENJAMIN B. (ED.). *Handbook of General Psychology*. Englewood Cliffs, N.J.: Prentice-Hall, 1973.

UNIT I

Learning and Cognitive Processes

One of the main distinctions between humans and other animals is our dependence on learning. We are not the only species that is capable of learning. Other animals can be taught to work for people, to perform all sorts of tricks, and even (in the case of chimpanzees) to communicate with sign language. Recent experiments suggest that chimpanzees, our nearest relatives in the animal kingdom, are able to think on about the level of a three-year-old child.

But no other species *depends* on learning to the extent that ours does. Most animal behavior is guided by instincts—by genetically programed "knowledge" of how to obtain food, cope with danger, and relate to other members of the species. In contrast, almost all human behavior is the result of learning.

This unit describes what psychologists have discovered about learning, memory, and thought, and how they made these discoveries. Chapter 2 focuses on what psychologists call "conditioning"—on techniques for changing behavior through the use of rewards and punishments. Chapter 3 details the ways in which people acquire, organize, store, and use information to solve problems and to create.

In this unit you will find a number of useful suggestions for improving your memory and study habits, and for changing behavior you do not consider desirable. You may also gain new insight into the way you shape or influence other people's behavior toward you.

2 Learning: Principles and Applications

FIGURE 2.1
These children are demonstrating their skill at applying previous learning to a new set of problems. They must know how to handle symbols. They must also be skilled at attending to the task and at performing it in a wide variety of environments. To understand such a complex process, psychologists must discover the nature of the interactions between people and their environment that lead to learning. Then they must show how these processes are organized into more complex behaviors.

Most people define learning as acquiring a new skill (such as speaking French) and new information, but this definition is only partly correct. Nearly all human behavior involves learning. We have to learn to hold ourselves upright, to walk, and to use our hands, as well as to dance, play tennis, or operate machinery. We learn to flip a switch to turn on the lights; to read and memorize information to pass an exam; to get what we want by asking, bargaining, or pouting. We may learn to be afraid of people in positions of authority, to make speeches, or to take exams—and perhaps to overcome those fears. We also learn how to learn. A more complete definition of *learning* is a lasting change in behavior that results from experience.

In this chapter we are concerned with learning in the broad sense of the term, not just schooling. We will discuss various kinds of learning, including classical conditioning, operant conditioning, and the learning of complex forms of behavior. We will also suggest some practical applications for what psychologists have discovered about learning. (We discuss memory and thought in Chapter 3.)

THE BASIC ELEMENTS OF LEARNING: STIMULUS AND RESPONSE

All learning involves changing one's behavior under the influence of one's environment. *Stimuli* are "pieces" of the environment that we can analyze, such as events or objects. *Responses* are units of behavior. When you learn to swim, for example, you must adjust to a new environment, one in which your previous behaviors will not move you around efficiently. The properties of water—quite different from the properties of solid ground—are the stimuli; the way you move your arms and legs are the responses.

Nonswimmers usually respond to the water in disorganized and useless ways. Most of them become quite tense, splash about aimlessly, and try to keep their heads out of the water. However, after much experimentation and practice the relationship between the person's behavior and the new environment changes. He responds to the stimulus of water in a coordinated and relaxed manner, breathing and moving efficiently. He has learned to swim.

The environment-behavior relationship is the basis of all learning.

23

FIGURE 2.2
The process of habituation is shown in this sequence of illustrations featuring a hypothetical medieval character, Emmett Cerf. At first Emmett is frightened (response) by the growling and barking of an angry watchdog (the stimulus). As the stimulus continues to be presented, Emmett's fear responses (sweating, trembling) gradually die out. Emmett is featured in several other learning situations in the following pages.

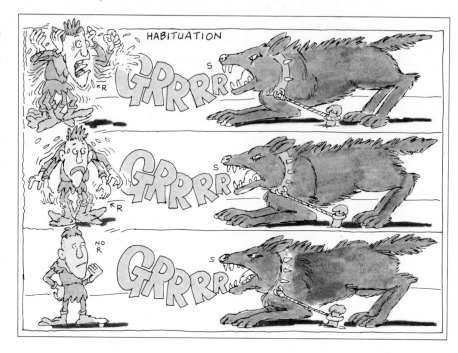

Whether you are trying to "get the knack" of swimming or algebra, you are acquiring patterns of responding to stimuli in new ways.

Habituation

One of the first and most fundamental things we learn is *not* to respond to all stimuli. A newborn baby is startled or frightened by almost every loud noise he or she hears. In time, however, many of these sounds become familiar, and the baby learns to ignore them. This process of learning *not* to respond to familiar stimuli is called *habituation*. An adult example of habituation is the way people who live near railroad tracks stop responding to the vibrations, screeching, and clanking of trains going by. However, a stimulus to which you are habituated may be made to produce a response if it is associated with something meaningful—as Ivan Pavlov discovered.

CLASSICAL CONDITIONING: LEARNING BY ASSOCIATION

Like many great discoveries, Ivan Pavlov's discovery of the principle of classical conditioning was accidental. Pavlov was a Russian physiologist whose primary area of interest was the digestive system. In the 1890's he began a series of experiments with dogs, focusing on the secretion of juices into the mouth. By attaching a tube directly to a dog's salivary gland, Pavlov could measure the flow of saliva from the dog's mouth. At first, the dog salivated after a meat powder had been put into its mouth. Later, it began to salivate as soon as the food was placed in its dish. Then it began to salivate at the first sight of the meat powder and even at the sound of an experimenter entering the room. Eventually, the dog began to salivate as soon as it was placed in the testing apparatus.

Pavlov began to wonder if any stimulus, paired with food, would bring about this response. Abandoning his original work, he set out to explore this phenomenon.

Pavlov's Experiment

Pavlov (1927) began his experiments by ringing a tuning fork and then immediately placing some meat powder on the dog's tongue. He chose the tuning fork because it was a *neutral stimulus*—that is, one that had nothing to do with the response (salivation). After only a few times the dog started salivating as soon as it heard the sound, even if food was not placed in its mouth. Pavlov went on to demonstrate that any neutral stimulus will elicit an unrelated response (cause it to happen) if it is presented regularly just before the stimulus that normally induces that response (here, food).

Pavlov distinguished among the different elements of the experiment as follows. He used the term "unconditioned" to refer to natural stimuli and to automatic, involuntary responses, such as blushing, shivering, being startled, or salivating. In the experiment, food was an *unconditioned stimulus (UCS)*: a stimulus that causes a certain response without previous training. (A dog doesn't have to be taught to like meat.) Food normally causes salivation. This is an *unconditioned response (UCR)*: a response that occurs naturally and automatically.

Under normal conditions the sound of a tuning fork would not cause salivation. The dog had to be taught or *conditioned* to associate this sound with food. A neutral stimulus that, after training, causes a response such as salivation is termed a *conditioned stimulus (CS)*. The salivation it causes is a *conditioned response (CR)*. A conditioned response is learned.

FIGURE 2.3
The apparatus used by Ivan Pavlov to study conditioned salivation in dogs. The harness held the dog steady, while the tube leading from the dog's mouth deposited saliva on an arm connected to the recorder on the left. Drops of saliva moved the pen, making a permanent record of the dog's salivation response to such stimuli as food and sights or sounds that had been associated with food.

A wide variety of stimuli may serve as conditioned stimuli for salivation: the sight of food, an experimenter entering the room, the sound of a tone, the flash of a light. Controlling an animal's or a person's responses in this way so that an old response becomes attached to a new stimulus is called *classical conditioning*.

In the same set of experiments, Pavlov also explored the phenomena of generalization and discrimination. Generalization happens when a range of stimuli similar to the original conditioned stimulus elicits a conditioned response. When Pavlov conditioned a dog to salivate at the sight of a circle (the CS), he found that the dog would salivate when it saw an oval shape as well. The dog had generalized its response to a similar stimulus. Pavlov was able to teach the dog to respond only to the circle by always pairing meat powder with the circle but never pairing it with the oval. He thus taught the dog *discrimination*: the ability to respond differently to similar but distinct stimuli.

A number of different responses may be conditioned. But for each such response there must be an unconditioned stimulus; one that elicits the response automatically, either because it does so innately or because the stimulus is already a strong conditioned stimulus. Most such responses are "reflex" responses; that is, ones that occur automatically whenever the correct unconditioned stimulus occurs. These include responses produced by the glands, such as salivation or weeping, and responses of our internal muscles, such as those of the stomach. In general these responses are controlled by the autonomic nervous system, and, as we will see in Chapter 4, Body and Behavior, they are very much involved in our emotions. As you might expect then, our emotional lives tend to be greatly affected by classical conditioning.

Classical Conditioning in Children

John B. Watson (1920) showed how conditioning could work on a human infant. Watson experimented with a normal eleven-month-old child named Albert. He presented Albert with many objects, including a white rat, a rabbit, blocks, a fur coat, and a hairy Santa Claus mask. Albert showed no fear of any of these objects—they were all neutral stimuli for the fear response.

Watson decided that he would attempt to condition Albert to fear rats. He began by placing a rat in front of Albert. Albert would reach out to touch it, and each time he did, one of Watson's assistants would strike a metal bar with a hammer behind Albert's head. The first time the metal bar was struck, Albert fell forward and buried his head in a pillow. The next time that he reached for the rat and the bar was struck, Albert began to whimper. The noise, the unconditioned stimulus (UCS), brought about a natural, unconditioned response (UCR), fear. After only a few such pairings, the rat became a conditioned stimulus that elicited a conditioned response, crying and cringing.

After Watson conditioned Albert to fear rats, he presented him with a furry white rabbit. Albert now reacted fearfully to the rabbit. Watson found that the degree of fear Albert felt toward other neutral stimuli depended upon how much they resembled the furry white rat. His conditioned fear response had generalized to the sight of the rabbit. Other furry white objects, such as a fur coat and a Santa Claus mask, also caused Albert to cry and try to escape whenever Watson presented them, although the response was not as great as when the rabbit was presented.

Extinction

Albert learned to respond emotionally to the sight of the rat in the same way that Pavlov's dogs learned to respond with their salivary glands to the sound of a tone. Pavlov discovered, though, that if he stopped presenting food after the sound of the tuning fork, the sound gradually lost its effect on the dogs. After repeatedly striking the tuning fork without giving food, Pavlov found that a previously conditioned dog no longer associated the sound with the arrival of food—the tuning fork lost its power to elicit the salivation response. Pavlov called this effect _extinction_ because the conditioned response had gradually died out. Similarly, Watson could have extinguished fear of rats in Albert by presenting the rats without the jarring sound. Unfortunately, Albert's mother took her son away before such extinction could be accomplished.

This example shows how classical conditioning works with emotional responses, either because someone deliberately pairs stimuli or because the stimuli are paired in the environment (such as the CS of lightning and the UCS of thunder). These sorts of responses are not under our voluntary control. But classical conditioning is much less useful in analyzing our "voluntary" responses, those we use to control or change our environment in some way. When we walk from one place to another, manipulate tools, or speak to others, we are engaging in behavior for which there is no obvious UCS. We may speak only in the presence of a certain stimulus, namely, other people, but the presence of others does not _elicit_ speaking; we may choose to remain silent. Speaking is not a reflex, automatic behavior, as salivation is. Another kind of learning must be responsible for modifying behavior which is not under the control of unconditioned stimuli.

makes a clear point about what responses can be conditioned.

OPERANT CONDITIONING

Suppose a dog is wandering around the neighborhood, sniffing trees, checking garbage cans, looking for a squirrel to chase. A kindly old lady sees the dog and tosses a bone out the kitchen door. The next day the dog is likely to stop at her door on its rounds—if not going to her house directly. The kindly lady produces another bone, and another the next day. The dog becomes a regular visitor.

Suppose a baby is crawling around a room, vigorously exploring the world as babies will as soon as they are able to crawl. She discovers a large, shiny white box and touches it. The baby pulls back, squealing in alarm. She has touched a hot stove. A short time later she tries again—and gets burned again. From that day forward, she avoids the stove.

FIGURE 2.4

Rats are used a great deal in psychological research because they are small, cheap, and sturdy. In addition, learning can be studied more simply and objectively in rats than in humans. This particular rat is pressing a bar in an apparatus commonly called a Skinner box, named for its designer, B. F. Skinner. The Skinner box is an artificial environment in which lights, sounds, rewards (food or water), and punishments (electric shock) can be delivered and controlled and in which some of the animal's behaviors (such as bar pressing) can be recorded by automatic switches.

Both of these stories are examples of *operant conditioning*—so named because it occurs when the subject operates on the environment and produces a result that influences whether he or she will operate in the same way in the future. Operant conditioning involves learning from the consequences of your actions.

In the laboratory, operant conditioning might take the form of allowing an experimental animal to explore a cage at random until it happens to press a bar that releases a food pellet or perhaps one that produces an electric shock. In time, the animal will become conditioned to approach or avoid the bar. Operant conditioning constantly occurs in "real life," as the examples above suggest.

Reinforcement

B. F. Skinner (1974) is the psychologist most closely associated with operant conditioning. He and his colleagues believe that most behavior is influenced by one's past history of *rewards* and *punishments*. Suppose you want to teach a dog to shake hands. One way would be to give the animal a pat on the head or a biscuit every time it reaches up to you with its paw. The biscuit or pat is called a *positive reinforcement*. When such a reinforcement follows some response, that response (or one like it) is likely to occur more frequently. In this example, the dog will "get the message" and shake hands to get its reward. Learning from rewards is one kind of operant conditioning. Reinforcement makes the operant behavior more likely to occur again.

On the other hand, if you want to break a dog of the habit of pawing at you and others when it wants attention, you issue a sharp no and perhaps a smack on the rump each time it reaches up with its paw. If you are consistent about this, the dog will eventually stop pawing people. In this example, the consequences of the behavior decrease the likelihood of its occurring again. Negative consequences are called *punishments*.

FIGURE 2.5

Pigeons are another species commonly used in learning research. This pigeon is showing signs of emotional upset common in extinction of an operantly conditioned response. The bird was trained to obtain food from the square hole by pecking at the key in the round hole. When the experimenter switched off the circuit that made this arrangement work, the bird pecked the key for a while and then, finding no food, began to jump around and flap its wings.

The nature of the consequences, then, influences the organism's tendency to engage in the same behavior in the future. Behavior that is reinforced tends to be repeated; behavior that is not reinforced or results in punishment tends not to be repeated.

Extinction does not occur as smoothly after operant conditioning as it does after classical conditioning. The novelty of your dog shaking hands wears off and you stop rewarding it for the trick—you withdraw reinforcement. Eventually, the dog will stop reaching up to shake hands. But it takes time. In fact, for a while the dog will probably become impatient, bark, and paw even more insistently than it did before when you stop rewarding it.

Schedules of Reinforcement

One might suppose that behavior would best be maintained by reinforcing every response. This is called a *continuous schedule* of reinforcement. A continuous schedule does not produce the best results. When reinforcement occurs only intermittently, responding is more stable and more persistent. Consider, for example, a man who has two cigarette lighters; one lights immediately every time (continuous reinforcement), whereas the other must be flicked four or five times before it lights (intermittent reinforcement). Next, suppose that both lighters stop lighting completely. Which lighter will he give up on first? Most likely, he will discard the first one immediately because it is now functioning differently from his expectations for it. But he will probably not consider it at all unusual for the second lighter to fail for the first five or six attempts.

Although intermittent reinforcement may be arranged in a number of ways, four basic methods, or schedules, have been studied in the laboratory. Schedules of reinforcement may be based either on the number of correct responses that the organism makes between reinforcements (*ratio* schedules) or on the amount of time that elapses before reinforcement is made available (*interval* schedules). In either case, reinforcement may appear on a regular, or *fixed*, schedule or an irregular, or *variable*, schedule. The four basic schedules result from the combination of these four possibilities. People respond differently to each type.

On a *fixed-interval schedule*, reinforcement is available at a predetermined time. Workers who are paid at the end of each week or month are operating on a fixed-interval schedule, at least in respect to their check-seeking behavior. Instructors who base students' grades on one final examination are using a fixed-interval schedule regarding studying behavior. In general this type of schedule does not generate a great deal of enthusiasm or extra-hard work, because no matter how much they produce, people cannot increase the frequency of their rewards. Students being graded on the basis of a single examination are likely to do most of their studying at the end of the course, cramming the night before the exam. This kind of behavior—responding slowly until just before reinforcement time—is typical of a fixed-interval schedule.

On a *variable-interval schedule*, the time at which reinforcement will be available varies around some average, rather than being fixed. An example would be studying for a course with a professor who gives surprise quizzes at irregular intervals. Students in such a professor's course would be much more likely to distribute their studying behavior evenly throughout the term than would students working under the fixed-interval schedule described above.

In *fixed-ratio schedules*, reinforcement depends on a certain amount of behavior being emitted, for example, rewarding every fourth response. The student who receives a grade after completing a paper of a specified length, the salesperson who is paid a commission for each sale, and the typist who is paid every time he finishes a certain number of pages are all on fixed-ratio schedules. People tend to work hard on fixed-ratio schedules, pausing briefly after each reward. However, if the amount of work or number of responses to be completed before the next reward is large, the student, salesperson, or pieceworker is likely to show low morale at the beginning of each new cycle because there is a long way to go before the next reinforcement.

On *variable-ratio schedules*, the number of required responses varies around some average, rather than being fixed. For example, a door-to-door salesperson may make a sale at the fourth house, the tenth house, and not again until the twentieth house. People on variable-ratio schedules tend to work or respond at a steady high rate. Why? Because the more the organism produces, the more reinforcement is obtained. Since the next reinforcement may follow the very next response, there is no pausing. The classic example of this is a gambler at a slot machine. The faster he puts money into the machine, the closer he feels to a payoff—since he never knows just when the reward will come.

Thus in general, responses are learned better and are more resistant to extinction when reinforced on a variable-interval or variable-ratio schedule.

Signals

In operant conditioning, stimuli that are associated with getting rewards or punishment become signals for particular behaviors. For example, everyone learns to cross a street only when the green light signals safety and to answer the phone only when it rings. These signals simply indicate that if one crosses the street or answers the phone, reinforcement is likely to follow, in the form of safe arrival on the other side of the street or a voice on the phone.

Just as organisms generalize among and discriminate between conditioned stimuli in classical conditioning, they also generalize and discriminate stimuli that serve as signals in operant conditioning. For example, the child who has been rewarded for saying "doggie" every time he or she sees the family's basset hound may generalize and say "doggie" when he or she sees a sheep, a cow, or a horse. These animals are similar enough to the hound for them to become signals that "doggie" will produce a reward. Discrimination results when "doggie" fails to produce a reward in these other cases. The child learns to confine the use of this word to dogs and to respond differently when seeing horses, cattle, or sheep.

Because signals are guides to future rewards and punishments, they often become rewards or punishments in and of themselves. In this case, the signal is called a *conditioned reinforcer*, because without the conditioning process, it would have no positive or negative value to a person. With conditioning, almost any stimulus can acquire almost any value.

One experimenter (Wolfe, 1936) demonstrated this with chimpanzees. Poker chips have no value for chimps—they aren't edible and they aren't very much fun to play with. However, this experimenter used operant conditioning to teach the chimps to value poker chips as much as humans value money. He provided the animals with a "Chimp-O-Mat" that dispensed peanuts or bananas, which are *primary reinforcers*, or natural rewards. (All chimps like these foods.) However, to obtain food the chimps had to first pull down on a heavily weighted bar to obtain poker chips, then insert the chips in a slot in the machine. In time, the poker chips became conditioned reinforcers. The value of the poker chips to the chimpanzees was evident from the fact that they would work for them, save them, and sometimes try to steal them from one another.

But we needn't look to animals for examples of this phenomenon. Smiles have little value for a newborn baby, and words of approval have no meaning. However, in time a baby learns that these expressions and sounds mean he or she is about to be picked up, cuddled, perhaps fed (primary reinforcers). They signal the fact that he or she is about to be rewarded. In time, the child begins to value smiles, praise, and other forms of social approval in and of themselves. They become conditioned reinforcers. Social approval is one of the most important conditioned reinforcers for almost all human beings.

Aversive Control: The Effects of Pain

Pleasant consequences are one way of influencing behavior. But unpleasant consequences also occur in life. There are two ways in which unpleasant events, or *aversive stimuli*, can affect behavior: as punishers and as negative reinforcers. In punishment, an unpleasant consequence *decreases* the frequency of the behavior that produced it. In negative reinforcement, the removal of unpleasant consequences *increases* the frequency of the behavior that removed the aversive stimuli. Two examples of negatively reinforced behaviors are avoidance and escape. *Escape* involves shutting off the aversive stimulus after it starts. *Avoidance* involves postponing or preventing the recurrence of the stimulus before it starts. A child who feels anxious around strangers may learn to escape this unpleasant feeling by hiding in her room or avoid it by visiting a friend whenever guests are expected.

Anything that brings pain can serve as an aversive stimulus, whether inflicted physically (shocks or blows) or psychologically (isolation or disapproval). A child whose mother becomes angry when he is noisy or messy may learn that if he apologizes he will escape this punishment. He may also become an extremely apologetic, self-effacing person. The child who hides from strangers may grow up to be a loner who avoids social gatherings—if these childhood strategies work. Indeed, the child

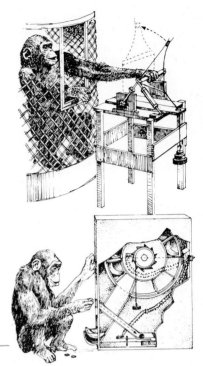

FIGURE 2.6

A strong conditioned reinforcer in daily human life is money. Wolfe showed in an important series of experiments that chimpanzees, too, could learn to use "money." Wolfe showed that they could be conditioned to pull down a heavily weighted handle in order to obtain tokens (poker chips), which could then be inserted into a machine that vended peanuts or bananas. The value of the tokens to the chimps was evident from the fact that they would work for them and save them—and would sometimes try to steal them from one another.

FIGURE 2.7

A rat in a Skinner box jumps clear of the grid through which it is receiving electric shock, an aversive stimulus. Psychologists perform experiments such as this one to find out how rewards and punishments control behavior. They have found that behavior can be changed more effectively by reinforcing what is desirable than by punishing what is undesirable.

may be so successful at never meeting strangers that she will never discover the positive reinforcement that may follow. Thus, avoidance behavior may be very long lasting, even after it has become inappropriate.

As another example, suppose that a child wants to play in the mud. When his parents respond with an emphatic "No!" the child throws a temper tantrum. Exasperated, his parents give in and let him have his way. The parents have positively reinforced the child's tantrums by letting him play in the mud—that is, his tantrum produced the desired event, playing in the mud, and so has been reinforced. At the same time, the child has negatively reinforced the parents' giving in—that is, giving in has escaped the aversive stimulus (the tantrum) and so has been reinforced. (It may help you to understand negative reinforcement if you remember that it *follows* and takes away, or *negates*, an aversive stimulus.) Also, the parents tried to prevent the child from playing in the mud, but he punished their efforts with a tantrum. In this way he reduced the likelihood that his parents would attempt to keep him out of mud puddles in the future. (See the illustration opposite.)

Psychologists have found several disadvantages to using aversive stimuli to change behavior. For one thing, aversive stimuli can produce side effects such as rage, aggression, and fear. For another, the whole situation may become a *conditioned aversive stimulus*, in the same way that signals for reward situations become conditioned reinforcers. For example, if a parent tries to control a child by punishing her, the child may try to escape and avoid the whole family situation.

Punishment may often achieve the opposite effect of what is desired—the person who is punished may actually increase the punished behavior. This occurs when what one person thinks is punishment is actually a reinforcement for the person receiving it. For example, teachers may find that the more they reprimand a disruptive child, the more he or she will misbehave. What such children really want is some sort of attention, and even punishment will provide this type of reward.

Psychologists thus often recommend to parents and teachers that they try to pay more attention to a child's good behavior than to his or her misbehavior.

FACTORS THAT AFFECT LEARNING

Several factors can help or hinder the learning process. Among them are feedback, transfer, and practice.

Feedback

Finding out the results of an action or performance is called feedback. Without feedback, you might repeat the same mistakes so many times that you develop a skill incorrectly—you would never learn what you were doing wrong. Even if you were performing correctly, you would not be receiving reinforcement for continuing.

FIGURE 2.8

An analysis of the relationship between the behavior of a child and the behavior of his parents. To follow the analysis it is important to remember that one person's response may at the same time be another person's consequence. (from left to right and from top to bottom) The child is about to engage in a positively reinforcing activity (playing in the mud), but his parents are emitting a behavior (forbidding him to play in the mud) that threatens to block his access to that reinforcer. He punishes their forbidding behavior with an aversive stimulus (a violent tantrum). Their forbidding behavior decreases in strength and is replaced by a new behavior: They give in. The parents' giving-in behavior is now negatively reinforced by the removal of the aversive tantrum. The child's tantrum is positively reinforced with the consequence: playing in the mud. The results of this conditioning process are that tantrums are now more likely, forbidding is less likely, and giving in is more likely. The new behavior may generalize to any new situation that is similar enough to the situation in which the conditioning originally occurred.

Transfer

Often a skill that you have already learned can help you to learn a new skill. If you have learned to play the saxophone, it will be much easier for you to learn to play the clarinet. You can transfer skills you already have such as reading notes and converting them into responses in your lips, tongue, and fingers to the clarinet. When previously learned responses help you to learn a new task, it is called *positive transfer*.

When a previously learned task hinders learning, *negative transfer* has occurred. An American may find driving in England to be more difficult than it is for an Englishman who is learning to drive for the first time. In England the steering wheel is on the opposite side of the car, and people drive on the opposite side of the road. The learned skill of driving American-style makes it difficult to perform the necessary new mental and motor tasks. An American's responses are often the exact opposite of what is needed.

Practice

Practice, the repetition of a task, is the only way to bind responses together. It is the key element that makes for smooth and fluent movement from response to response.

Because practice takes time, psychologists have been interested in determining how to use that time most efficiently. They have found that whatever type of skill a person is learning, it is better to space out practice rather than do it all at once.

It is possible to practice by imagining oneself performing a skill. Athletes imagine themselves making golf swings over and over again or mentally shooting free throws in basketball to improve their performance. Psychologists call such effort *mental practice.* Although it is not as effective as the real thing, it is better than nothing at all.

LEARNING STRATEGIES

It would be difficult to solve problems if people had to relearn the solution process each time a problem occurred. Fortunately, when you learn to solve one problem, some of the problem-solving experience may transfer to other, similar problems. Once you learn certain *strategies* for solving problems and learning tasks, you can be assured of an easier time on your next attempts. (Such problem-solving strategies are also discussed in Chapter 3.) Strategies are affected by their consequences just as less complex responses are. If a strategy works, the person or animal is likely to use it again. Many learned principles for dealing with life are valuable; others may actually be handicaps.

Learning to Learn

Harry Harlow (1949) has shown that animals can learn to learn: They can learn to use strategies for solving similar problems and tasks. He gave monkeys the problem of finding a raisin under one of two wooden lids, one red and one green. The raisin was always hidden under the green lid, but because the experimenter kept changing the position of the lids the monkey took a while to realize that color was important, not location.

When the monkey had learned to always pick the green lid, the experimenter changed the problem. Now the monkey had to choose between triangular and circular lids. The raisin was always placed under the circular lid, and the experimenter again changed the location of the lids on each trial. As before, it took several tries for the monkey to learn that the shape of the lid, not its location, indicated where the raisin would

FIGURE 2.9

Harry Harlow presented monkeys with pairs of lids like those shown here and required them to learn strategies for determining which lid in each pair covered a morsel of food. After being presented with a few hundred such problems, the monkeys learned to use the same strategy for dealing with each new pair.

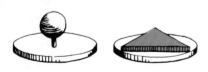

be. After doing a number of problems like these, the monkey began to learn that the difference between the two lids always contained the key to the problem. Eventually the monkey could solve any similar two-choice problem with, at most, one error.

The learning of strategies and principles is extremely important in human behavior. In school you get practice in such skills as reading books, writing essays, and taking tests. In many cases the particular things you have learned will be less important in the long run than what you have learned about learning generally. Learning to extract information from a book, for example, will be helpful whether the book is about physics, grammar, or cooking. Just as Harlow's monkey acquired a general method for quickly solving particular problems, you are acquiring a general strategy for learning particular pieces of information.

Helplessness and Laziness

Psychologists have shown that general learning strategies can affect a person's whole relationship to the environment. For example, if a person has numerous experiences in which his actions have no effect on his world, he may learn a general strategy of helplessness or laziness.

Learned helplessness was demonstrated in an experiment with dogs (Seligman, 1973). The dogs were strapped into a harness from which they could not escape and were then given electric shocks at unexpected intervals. After days of shock treatment, the dogs were unharnessed. Now they could escape the shocks or avoid them entirely simply by jumping over a hurdle into a safe compartment. But more than half the dogs failed to learn to jump. When several dogs that had not had the experience of being shocked were also tested, almost all of them quickly learned to jump to safety. Apparently, many of the dogs in the first group had learned to stand and endure the shocks, resigned to the fact that any effort to escape would be useless.

It is not hard to see how these results can apply to human situations. In order to be able to try hard and to be full of energy, people must learn that their actions *do* make a difference. If rewards come without effort, a person never learns to work (learned laziness). If pain comes no matter how hard one tries, a person gives up (learned helplessness).

LEARNING COMPLICATED SKILLS

When you acquire a skill such as knitting, photography, shooting a basketball, or talking persuasively, you learn more than just a single new stimulus-response relationship. You learn a large number of them, and you learn how to put them together into a large, smooth-flowing unit. Psychologists have devoted considerable attention to how new responses are acquired and to how they are put together in complex skills.

Shaping is a process in which reinforcement is used to sculpture new responses out of old. An experimenter can use this method to teach a rat to do something it has never done before and would never do if left to itself. He can shape it, for example, to raise a miniature flag. The rat is physically capable of standing on its hind legs and using its mouth to pull a miniature flag-raising cord, but at present it does not do so. The rat probably will not perform this unusual action by accident, so the experimenter begins by rewarding the rat for any action similar to the wanted responses, using reinforcement to produce successive, or closer and closer, approximations of the desired behavior.

shaping

Imagine the rat roaming around on a table with the flag apparatus in the middle. The rat inspects everything and finally sniffs at the flagpole. The experimenter immediately reinforces this response by giving the rat a food pellet. Now the rat frequently sniffs the flagpole, hoping to get another pellet, but the experimenter waits until the rat lifts a paw before he gives it another reward. This process continues, with the experimenter reinforcing close responses and then waiting for even closer ones. Eventually, he has the rat on its hind legs nibbling at the cord. Suddenly the rat seizes the cord in its teeth and yanks it. Immediately the rat is rewarded, and it begins pulling rapidly on the cord; a new response has been shaped.

Shaping has been used to teach language skills to impaired children. Psychologists at first reward the children for simple sounds, such as "bah." Later the children are only rewarded for complete words, such as "beans," and later for complete sentences such as "Beans, please." Many such children have successfully learned to use some language by this method (Lovaas, 1967).

Combining Responses: Chaining

In order to learn a skill, a person must be able to put various new responses together. Responses that follow one another in a sequence are put together in *chains*. Each response produces the signal for the next one. For example, to hammer in a nail, one would have to put together the following chain of responses: pick up hammer, pick up nail, position nail, swing hammer, hit nail, swing hammer, hit nail, and so on until the nail is completely sunk in. Each hit of the nail signals that one is striking it correctly, and the nail's being flush with the board's surface signals that no further responses are required.

In learning, chains of responses are organized into larger response patterns. For example, the complex skill of swimming has three major chains that are combined to make up the whole swimming pattern: an arm-stroke chain, a breathing chain, and a leg-kicking chain. After much practice, you no longer have to think about the different steps involved. The behavior takes on a rhythm of its own: the chains of responses flow naturally as soon as you dive into the water.

It is necessary to learn simpler responses first before mastering the complex pattern. If you cannot hit a nail with a hammer, you certainly cannot build a house. Therefore, before a person can learn to perform a particular skill he or she must learn all the subordinate skills that make the larger skill possible.

FIGURE 2.10
When a skilled carpenter engages in a task such as shingling a roof, he is actually combining a number of simultaneous response chains into a single coordinated movement pattern. Each response chain is composed of smaller response units, which originally had to be shaped by themselves. To perform this roofing task, the carpenter first had to learn to balance himself on sloping surfaces, to hold objects with his toes, his hands, and his mouth, and to coordinate his hands and eyes.

MODELING

Up to this point it would seem that there are two types of learning: Emotional responding is conditioned by the close association of neutral and unconditioned stimuli, and operant responses are learned either by reward or punishment. But the informal observations you have been making all your life concerning learning probably suggest to you that there is more to learning than this; that in fact we most often learn by imitating others. This is especially true of social responses—when we learn how to behave in a new situation by watching how others behave. When you go to a concert for the first time, you may be very hesitant about where to go, when to enter (especially if you are late), when to clap, how to get a better seat after the first intermission, and so on. So you observe others, and follow them, and soon you are an "old hand."

We would expect imitation to be responsible for more basic forms of behavior as well, when the proper response is essential to life. Trial-and-error learning is not useful if the punishment for failure to emit the response is being eaten by a predator. If correct avoidance behavior is not innate it must be learned by imitating.

The general term for this kind of learning is *modeling*. It includes three different types of effects. In the simplest case the behavior of others simply facilitates our performance of a similar behavior, already learned by us. We clap when others do, look up at a building if everyone else is looking there, and copy the styles and verbal expressions of our peers. But no learning occurs in this case, in the sense of acquiring new responses; we simply perform old responses that we otherwise might not be using.

The second type of modeling is usually called observational learning, or simply, imitation. In this sort of learning an observer watches a model perform a behavior and is later able to reproduce it closely, though the observer was unable to do this before observing the model. An example is watching someone use an unfamiliar tool, either live or on film, and afterwards being able to handle the tool yourself.

A third type of modeling involves disinhibition. When an observer watches someone else engage in a threatening activity without being punished, the observer may find it easier to engage in that behavior later. For example, someone with a snake phobia may watch another person handling snakes; such observation may help to alleviate the phobia. This procedure is used in clinical work, as we will see in the chapter on therapies.

The second type of modeling is most relevant to this chapter. E. R. John and his associates (1968) were able to show this kind of learning dramatically in a nonverbal animal: the cat. In their experiment a naive cat watched a well-trained cat press a lever to avoid an unpleasant shock. Later, the naive cat learned to press the lever to avoid shock, and learned much more quickly than cats who never watched a model perform the act. In fact the learning was almost immediate.

What happens when an observer learns by watching? Early theorists believed that we have some sort of "instinct" for imitation, and indeed it is probable that some animals do imitate automatically, especially when they are very young and have good models constantly around them: their parents. Operant conditioning theorists such as Skinner have suggested that imitation itself is a kind of response, one which is often reinforced because it works so well. That is, the behavior of others comes to function as a discriminative stimulus for a sort of matching behavior, which is then reinforced because it works on the environment, or because other persons tend to reinforce such matching (as when a mother praises her child for correctly imitating her words). The trouble with this theory is that it is hard to explain what happens during the acquisition period, when the observer is simply watching and not performing any overt behavior. At this time there is no response to reinforce, and no reinforcement. Later (perhaps even days later) the observer may perform the behavior and get reinforcement, but how was the delay bridged? The reinforcement interpretation may explain why the behavior finally did come out (because of reinforcement), but it does not explain how the behavior was acquired observationally in the first place.

Most psychologists working in this area (such as Bandura, 1971) believe that during the observation phase the model's responses are coded symbolically by the observer; later the symbolic code directs the observer's new behavior. An experiment illustrating this was performed by Gerst (1971). The subjects in this study observed a film of a model exhibiting some of the hand signs used by the deaf in their visual language. Immediately after each response was shown, the subjects did one of four things. One group tried to remember the hand sign visually, using vivid imagery. A second group tried to convert the response into words describing the hand sign very specifically. A third group was instructed to create a concise verbal label or picture that would help to recall the general nature of the response ("like the fist-waving of an angry cabbie"). The fourth group did mental calculations unrelated to the hand sign, and thus did not code the motor response at all. All subjects attempted to reproduce the signs fifteen minutes later. As might be expected, the noncoding fourth group did very poorly. The first and second groups did better, but the third group, using the concise labels, did twice as well as they did, when asked to reproduce exactly the type and order of movements in each hand sign. Yet from the standpoint of reward and punishment, all these groups received identical forms of training! Thus it is clear that coding of some kind must occur during observation. Exactly how the coding works and how we learn to use it is not yet clear.

APPLICATIONS OF LEARNING PRINCIPLES

In the preceding pages we largely avoided classroom examples in order to emphasize the point made at the beginning of the chapter—namely, that learning is a by-product of all kinds of experiences, not just schooling. However, in this section we want to see how the principles we have been discussing can be applied to school-related learning. We will show how teachers have consciously and deliberately used reinforcement in the classroom, and how you might use the same techniques to affect your own behavior.

Classroom Management

A number of experiments have shown that operant conditioning—reinforcing desirable behavior through systematic rewards—can be used to improve the teaching atmosphere of the classroom and even make students enjoy school more.

Praise.   How does a teacher get students to sit in their seats, pay attention, and study their assignments? One way is to reinforce good behavior and good work with praise. This may seem obvious, but research has shown that most teachers spend more time reprimanding students than they do praising them. This is probably because verbal disapproval produces an immediate reward for the teacher. The teacher tells a student to stop talking or leave the room; the student quiets down; the teacher's behavior has been *reinforced*. Praise does not produce such immediate effects. It may take many days of encouragement to have a positive effect on a class. The "payoff" for the teacher lies in the distant future, so many resort to repeated verbal disapproval. As a result many students become disenchanted with schools; teachers, in turn, become increasingly disenchanted with students and deliver more punishment creating more disenchantment. Students and teachers become locked in a vicious cycle. Each party gives the other fewer and fewer rewards, less and less reinforcement (White, 1975).

Token Economies.   Psychologists tried an experiment with a group of extremely disenchanted boys in Washington, D.C. In fact, the boys had been labeled "uneducable" and placed in the National Training School. The experimenters used what is known as a *token economy* to motivate the boys. The youngsters received points for good grades on tests. They could "cash" these points in for such rewards as snacks, lounge privileges, or items in a mail order catalog. In other words, they created a system that worked like the Chimp-O-Mat discussed earlier. Within a few months, a majority of the students showed a significant increase in IQ scores (an average gain of 12½ points). The boys continued to improve in the months that followed—showing that they were, indeed, educable (Cohen and Filipczak, 1971).

In another experiment teachers used a token economy to teach preschoolers in a Head Start program to write, and compared their scores on writing tests with those achieved by children who did not participate in a token economy. The youngsters who received tokens which they could exchange for food, movies, and other rewards improved dramatically. Equally important, they seemed to be developing a very positive attitude toward school. The youngsters who did not receive tokens made very little progress (Miller and Schneider, 1970).

Giving Students a Break.   What if a school doesn't have extra money for such rewards? Some teachers have used free time to reinforce good behavior. In one class students were given a five-minute break if, and only if, they sat quietly and paid attention for fifteen minutes. They could use the break to go to the water fountain, play, or do whatever they liked. This strategy worked for two reasons. Children who disliked the

FIGURE 2.11
Allowing students free time to spend as they wish often serves as an effective reinforcer for performing appropriate classroom behavior. A teacher who has interesting exhibits and materials in the classroom can make this time, even if brief, a rich learning experience in itself.

classroom (children for whom the classroom had become a conditioned aversive stimulus) were allowed to *escape* periodically. At the same time, the free time offered such *positive reinforcements* as a cool drink or a chance to run around (Osborne, 1974).

In general, attempts to reinforce good behavior and good schoolwork with tokens or points that can be exchanged for rewards, rest periods, and verbal praise have proven quite effective. Thus learning and applying the principles of operant conditioning help a teacher to manage a classroom and do more teaching.

Individualized Instruction

So far, we have been talking primarily about younger children. The *personalized system of instruction,* or PSI, was developed at universities for college students. It, too, is based on the principles of operant conditioning.

In PSI the course material is broken down into a series of small units. Each unit is clearly defined so that students know exactly what skills they have to master and what information they must absorb to complete the unit. Students are allowed to proceed from unit to unit at their own pace. Instead of lecturing each hour, the instructors deliver only a few lectures and leave the other hours open for study or question periods. (A number of instructors are available to individual students for this purpose.) When a student feels he has mastered a unit, he asks to take the test. If he passes, he moves on to the next unit. If he fails, he may go back over the unit and ask for another test—and another and another, until he passes. A student who completes all the units in the course receives an A, no matter how many tests he failed along the way. A student who completes most of the units receives a B, and so on.

PSI has a number of advantages. First, students receive immediate *reinforcement* for learning each unit. They do not have to wait for a midterm or final exam to learn how well they are doing. Discussions with instructors also provide immediate reinforcement: Students can identify what confuses them, grasp the material, and see that the instructor knows they have grasped it. Second, PSI eliminates some of the *aversive aspects* of traditional classes. Students do not have a schedule forced on them. They do not have to sit through lectures on material they already know or lectures on material they cannot understand because they haven't read an assignment yet. Indeed, they do not have to attend lectures at all. Finally, students are on a *fixed-ratio reinforcement schedule*—they know that they will get an A if they complete all the units. In addition, the instructor can teach later concepts knowing that earlier ones have already been mastered.

PSI has proven to be an effective way of teaching and learning. Students who take courses structured in this way generally do better than students in traditional classes. One problem, however, seems to be a relatively high percentage of incompletes. For this reason one group of psychologists recommends that professors who use PSI set target dates for completion of units and allow students only three chances to pass the test for a unit.

If the student passes the test before the target date, he or she may move ahead. If the student fails to pass the test in this time period, he or she will be required to drop the course (Miller, Weaver, and Semb, 1974).

PSI should not be considered the ideal teaching method for all kinds of courses. It works best for subjects that stress factual learning. If the instructor does not wish to structure the subject of his teaching so thoroughly, but would rather have students present their own ideas, then PSI is inappropriate. For example, in a course in seventeenth-century English drama, PSI would not be appropriate if an instructor wanted the class to discuss their own interpretations of a play. But he might use some PSI techniques to make sure that all of his students have adequate background knowledge in the area.

Behavior Modification

Perhaps the most interesting techniques psychologists have developed for applying operant conditioning to schooling are those you can use yourself to modify your own behavior.

Improving Your Study Habits.   One psychologist designed a program to help students improve their study habits and tried it on a group of volunteers. The students were told to set a time when they would go to a small room in the library they had not used before, taking only the materials they wanted to study. They were then to work for as long as they remained interested—and *only* as long as they were interested. As soon as they found themselves fidgeting, daydreaming, becoming drowsy or bored, they were to make the decision to stop studying. There was only one condition. They had to read one more page, or solve one more simple problem, before they left. But even if this made them want to study longer, they were instructed to hold to their decision to leave the library, go for a cup of coffee, call a friend, or do whatever they wanted to do.

The next day they were asked to repeat the same procedure, adding one page to the amount they read between the time they decided to leave and the time they actually left the library. The third day they added a third page, and so on. Students who followed this procedure found that in time they were able to study for longer periods than before; that they were studying more effectively; and that they didn't mind studying so much.

Why did this procedure work? Many students force themselves to study. One common technique is to go to the library to avoid distractions. The result may be hours spent staring at a book without really learning anything. Repeated failures to get anything accomplished and sheer discomfort turn studying into a dreaded chore. The library becomes a *conditioned aversive stimulus*—you hate it because you've spent so many uncomfortable hours there. The procedure was designed to change these feelings.

Requiring students to leave as soon as they felt distracted helped to reduce the negative, punishing emotions associated with studying. The students stopped when these feelings began. Studying in a new place removed the conditioned aversive stimulus. Thus aversive responses were not conditioned to the subject matter or the room, as they are when students force themselves to work.

Second, the procedure made use of *successive approximations*. The students began by reading just one page after they became bored, and only gradually increased the assignment. This also reduced the aversive response to studying. The task no longer seemed so difficult.

Finally, when they left their work the students received two kinds of *positive reinforcement*. First, they had the satisfaction of knowing they had followed the procedure and completed an assignment (namely, one more page). Second, they were free to do something they enjoyed. Thus they rewarded or reinforced themselves for however much studying they did (Fox, 1966). You might try this procedure.

The SQ3R Method.   Many people define studying as reading, underlining important passages, and taking notes. Once students have done this they believe they have "discharged their duties"—and many feel cheated if they do not receive positive reinforcement in the form of good grades. The SQ3R method is an alternative. SQ3R stands for Survey, Question, Read, Recite, and Review.

SURVEY: First flip through the chapter, reading the headings, to see what the chapter is about, what material it covers.

QUESTION: Go back through the chapter a second time and formulate questions about each major section. (For example, what does this term mean? What do psychologists know about this? Does this apply to me?)

READ: Now read the chapter *without* underlining or taking notes. Look for the answers to your questions.

RECITE: Close the book (sit on it if you have to) and outline the chapter from memory.

REVIEW: Now reopen the book and check your outline. Did you leave out any important points? Misunderstand some of the material?

Changing Personal Behavior.   You can also use conditioning to change patterns of behavior that you don't like in yourself. The basic idea behind self-modification is to make a *contract* with yourself. You set a goal for yourself, decide on realistic steps (or successive approximations) toward that goal, and either reward yourself for completing each step or punish yourself for failing.

For example, one college sophomore was annoyed with herself for never talking to professors. They scared her so much she had only spoken to one, Professor A. She began by examining her current behavior and thinking about how she *wanted* to behave. (A person's current behavior is called a *baseline*. The way he wants to act is the *target behavior*.) She wrote out a contract with herself and decided she would not eat lunch unless she lived up to the terms. The contract read as follows:

FIGURE 2.12
This student may have developed a conditioned aversive response to studying in the library. A program which gradually increases the amount of studying she must do before she leaves the library could help her to study more effectively.

Step 1.   Go up to Prof. A while he is talking to another professor and say hello to both of them.

Step 2.   Go up and talk to Prof. A while he is talking with another professor and talk with the other one for at least one sentence.

Step 3.   Talk with the other one for five seconds.

Step 4.   Ten seconds talking with the other one.

Step 5.   Fifteen seconds.

Step 6.   Thirty seconds, then on up from there by fifteen-second jumps.

The student gave herself plenty of time for each step, and the plan worked.

Another student worked out a contract with himself to overcome his fear of participating in class discussions. He set a goal of constant participation, then designed a schedule that began with saying anything to another class member and progressed to talking about the class with a fellow student, occasionally addressing the class as a whole, and finally participating regularly in class discussions. He used the band he played with as a *reinforcer* because of two effects. First, he loved the band; second, if he didn't show up for a job, the other five members of the band would be furious with him. His contract made playing in the band contingent on living up to his schedule (Watson and Tharp, 1972).

SUMMARY

1. Learning is a lasting change in behavior that results from experience and involves pairing stimuli and responses in a new way.

2. One simple form of learning is habituation, in which a response to a stimulus that is repeated disappears.

3. Classical conditioning, another form of learning, was discovered by Ivan Pavlov. In this process, a previously neutral stimulus comes to elicit a response because it has been paired with a stimulus that already elicited a response. Extinction of a classically conditioned response occurs when it is no longer associated with the stimulus.

4. Operant conditioning occurs when an organism's spontaneous activities are either reinforced or punished. Any consequence that increases the likelihood of a response is called a reinforcement. Extinction of a response occurs when it is no longer reinforced.

5. Different schedules of reinforcement produce different patterns of behavior. When reinforcement depends on number of responses (ratio schedules), the organism tends to respond faster than it does if reinforcement is dependent on time (interval schedules). When responses are reinforced on a highly regular basis (fixed schedules), the organism will tend to pause after a reward. If reinforcement appears irregularly (variable schedules), the organism will keep going at a steady rate. Intermittently reinforced responses are more resistant to extinction than are continuously reinforced ones. Therefore, a response is learned better if it is only reinforced some of the time.

6. Signals are stimuli that come to be associated with getting rewards or punishments. Organisms have the ability to generalize among and discriminate between signals. A signal becomes a conditioned reinforcer when the signal itself serves as a reward or punishment.

7. Aversive control means using unpleasant influences on behavior. In punishment, the unpleasant event comes as a consequence of a response; in avoidance and escape condition-

ing, the response has the effect of removing the unpleasant event; in negative reinforcement, the frequency of a response that terminates an unpleasant event increases.

8. Factors that influence learning include attention, feedback, transfer, and practice.

9. Organisms can learn to learn by discovering certain strategies. A strategy for solving problems or learning tasks can be applied to subsequent, similar situations. Organisms learn strategies of laziness or helplessness if they experience situations in which their behavior has no consequences.

10. To learn a complicated skill, a person must acquire and coordinate a number of new responses. Skills require continuous coordination of stimulus-response relationships in order to produce a smooth-flowing action. Learning of skills may be facilitated by imitation and shaping. Learning a skill requires putting new responses together in chains, which are then organized into response patterns.

11. Modeling is a kind of learning that results from imitation. Experimental evidence suggests that when we observe a model performing a behavior that is new to us, we code the model's responses. Later, we decode our observations to perform the behavior. Exactly how the coding process occurs is unclear.

12. The use of praise rather than disapproval, token economies, giving students free time, and personalized systems of instruction are some of the ways in which teachers have used learning principles in the classroom. It is also possible to change one's own habits through reinforcement.

GLOSSARY

aversive control: The process of influencing behavior by means of aversive, or unpleasant, stimuli.

avoidance: Postponing or preventing the recurrence of a painful stimulus before it starts.

classical conditioning: A learning procedure in which a stimulus that normally elicits a given response is repeatedly preceded by a neutral stimulus (one that usually does not elicit the response). Eventually, the neutral stimulus will evoke the response when presented by itself.

conditioned reinforcer: A stimulus that increases the frequency of a response because it has become a signal for a stimulus which is reinforcing.

conditioned response (CR): In classical conditioning, the learned response to a conditioned stimulus.

conditioned stimulus (CS): In classical conditioning, a once-neutral stimulus that has come to elicit a given response after a period of training in which it has been paired with an unconditioned stimulus (UCS).

discrimination: The ability to respond differently to similar but distinct stimuli.

escape: Performing a behavior that removes the organism from a painful stimulus or otherwise terminates the stimulus.

extinction: The gradual disappearance of a conditioned response because the reinforcement is withheld or because the conditioned stimulus is repeatedly presented without the unconditioned stimulus.

feedback: Information received after an action as to its effectiveness or correctness.

fixed-interval schedule: A schedule of reinforcement in which a specific amount of time must elapse before a response will elicit reinforcement.

fixed-ratio schedule: A schedule of reinforcement in which a specific number of correct responses is required before reinforcement can be obtained.

generalization: Responding similarly to a range of similar stimuli.

habituation: The process of learning not to respond to familiar stimuli.

learning: A lasting change in behavior that results from experience.

negative reinforcement: Increasing the strength of a given response by removing a painful stimulus when the response occurs.

neutral stimulus: A stimulus which does not initially elicit a response.

operant conditioning: A form of conditioning in which a certain action is rewarded or punished, resulting in corresponding increases or decreases in the likelihood that similar actions will occur again.

personalized systems of instruction (PSI): Breaking course material down into a number of small units and allowing students to proceed from unit to unit at their own pace.

primary reinforcers: Natural rewards.

punishment: The procedure of imposing a penalty on an organism in response to certain behavior, with a resulting decrease in the frequency of such behavior.

reinforcement: Immediately following a particular response with a reward in order to strengthen that response.

response: A unit of behavior.

response chains: Learned responses that follow one another in sequence, each response producing the signal for the next.

shaping: A technique of operant conditioning in which the desired behavior is "molded" by first rewarding any act similar to that behavior and then requiring closer and closer approximations to the desired behavior before giving the reward.

signals: In operant conditioning, behavioral cues (or stimuli) that are associated with reward or punishment.

stimulus: Any environmental event or circumstance to which an organism can respond.

token economy: A form of conditioning in which desirable behavior is reinforced with tokens, which can be accumulated and exchanged for various rewards.

transfer: The effects of past learning on the ability to learn new tasks.

unconditioned response (UCR): In classical conditioning, an organism's automatic (or natural) reaction to a stimulus.

unconditioned stimulus (UCS): A stimulus that elicits a certain response without previous training.

variable-interval schedule: A schedule of reinforcement in which varying amounts of time must elapse before a response will obtain reinforcement.

variable-ratio schedule: A schedule of reinforcement in which a variable number of responses are required before reinforcement can be obtained.

ACTIVITIES

1. Here's a simple experiment to show habituation. Locate a friend or family member who is willing to be your subject. Puff gently through a straw at his or her eye, causing it to blink. Keep puffing. If the eye blink eventually ceases, habituation has occurred.

2. Try this experiment in classical conditioning: Sit at a table with a lamp you can switch on and off. Place a glass of water and a spoon within easy reach. Have your subject sit across from you so you can observe his or her eyes. First, turn off the lamp to observe how much

your subject's eyes dilate under normal conditions. Then switch on the lamp and begin your conditioning trials. Take the spoon and tap the glass of water, and then immediately turn off the lamp. Let the subject's eyes adjust, then switch the lamp on and repeat the process several times. Be sure to allow time in each case for the eyes to dilate. After several trials, tap the glass but leave the lamp on. What happened to your subject's eyes? Why?

3. Businesses often make use of conditioning techniques in their commercials. They associate the name of their product with pleasant tunes or exciting scenes, so that the name alone will elicit conditioned relaxation or excitement. Think of specific ads that use these techniques. Can you think of selling methods that use operant conditioning?

4. Using the principles outlined in the skill-learning section of the chapter, how would you go about learning to do a simple dance step; to make an omelet; to drive a car; to pitch a baseball?

5. Which of the schedules of reinforcement do your instructors generally use in conducting their classes? How would your classes be different if they used the other schedules? Give examples for your answers and justify your reasoning.

6. Can you condition yourself? Select a subject in which you have difficulty. Set up a schedule of study for yourself in which you feel comfortable. For example, fifteen minutes for English or history or five problems in math. Work for the time allotted or on the number of problems, but add five more minutes or one more problem. When you have achieved this goal reward yourself with some token. As you work along, increase the time or number of problems, but always try to surpass the limit you set. Each time you do, reward yourself with a token. When you have earned five tokens, reward yourself with a treat. How successful were you in carrying out this schedule of learning? Which do you believe was more influential on your behavior: the conditioning or the motivation

you established by creating this experiment for yourself?

7. If you have a dog or a cat, or have access to one, try a simple conditioning experiment on it. Using Pavlov's techniques of classical conditioning as discussed in the chapter, teach the animal to like a neutral stimulus by pairing it with a pleasing stimulus. After the animal is sufficiently conditioned, apply extinction techniques.

8. If you take a moment to sit in a room, listening for sounds and concentrating on looking around, you will undoubtedly hear and see things that you usually ignore. Why? Give five examples of habituation that occur in your everyday experiences.

9. Conduct an operant-conditioning experiment of your own to modify the behavior of a member of your family or a friend. Tell him or her as much or as little as you choose, but carefully record everything that you do tell this person. Use positive reinforcement only, and record all results. Using the procedures described in the chapter, write a paper describing your experiment in behavior modification.

10. In the experiment on learned helplessness, the animals who were unable to change their situation for long periods of time seemed unable or unwilling to change when the possibility was opened to them. What implications do such experiments have for humans? Can you think of situations in your life that have had the effect of learned helplessness?

11. Take a real-life situation, such as waiting for an elevator, eating a sandwich, or climbing a tree, and analyze the stimuli, responses, rewards, punishments, and signals in the situation.

12. Select some particular subject of study that you find difficult or unpleasant. Whenever you sit down to study this subject, play one of your favorite records or tapes as you study. In time, the favorable feelings toward this music may become associated with the subject of study, making it easier to learn and remember.

SUGGESTED READINGS

BANDURA, A. (ED.). *Psychological Modeling: Conflicting Theories*. Chicago: Aldine-Atherton, 1971. Discusses the theories behind modeling and observational learning; discusses research on modeling as a therapeutic technique.

BARBER, T. X. (ED.). *Biofeedback and Self-Control*. Chicago: Aldine-Atherton, 1970. An excellent collection of papers on biofeedback. The readings cover experiments on meditation, hypnosis, drug states, EEG feedback, and other such topics.

CARMAN, ROBERT A., AND ADAMS, W. ROYCE. *Study Skills: A Student's Guide for Survival*. New York: Wiley, 1972. This paperback is in a programed format. It gives specific instruction on improving reading abilities, how to approach textbooks, how to take exams, and how to write papers. It offers advice on how to use the SQ3R technique, and it is written in a chatty and humorous vein.

MCINTIRE, ROGER. *For Love of Children: Behavioral Psychology for Parents*. Del Mar, Calif.: CRM Books, 1970. As the title suggests, this book is a guide to child rearing based on the principles of operant conditioning. The author's premise is that children (and everyone) behave in ways that have been reinforced. Parents can therefore control their child's behavior by making themselves aware of why behavior is occurring and by shaping desired behavior in accordance with conditioning principles.

SKINNER, B. F. *Walden Two*. New York: Macmillan, 1948. Skinner's best-known work is a novel of an ideal, behaviorally engineered community. It is readable, interesting, and instructive.

———. *Science and Human Behavior*. New York: Free Press, 1953 (paper). This widely read book discusses the relationship between a science of behavior and everyday ways of talking about personality, self, and culture. Skinner begins with an explanation of the scientific principles of behavior and then goes on to explain his analysis of "self-control," thinking, social interaction, psychotherapy, economics, and religion.

WHALEY, D. *Contingency Management*. Behaviordelia, P. O. Box 1044, Kalamazoo, Mich. 49001. A 250-page comic book created by Whaley and some of his graduate students. A painless and humorous introduction to the conditioning approach to learning.

WHALEY, D., AND MALLOTT, R. *Elementary Principles of Behavior*. New York: Appleton-Century-Crofts, 1971. One of the most readable introductory texts on Skinnerian behaviorism and the principles of behavior modification. It puts behavioral techniques to practice by pacing and rewarding the reader throughout the text.

BIBLIOGRAPHY

BANDURA, A. "Analysis of Modeling Processes." In *Psychological Modeling: Conflicting Theories*, edited by A. Bandura. Chicago: Aldine-Atherton, 1971, pp. 1–62.

COHEN, H., AND FILIPCZAK, J. *A New Learning Environment*. San Francisco: Jossey-Bass, 1971.

ENGBERG, L. A., ET AL. "Acquisition of Key-Pecking via Autoshaping as a Function of Prior Experience: 'Learned Laziness?'" *Science*, 178 (1972): 1002–1004.

FISCHER, K. W. *The Organization of Simple Learning*. Chicago: Markham, 1973.

FOX, L. JUNGBERG. "Effecting the Use of Efficient Study Habits," In *Control of Human Behavior*, edited by R. Ulrich, T. Stachnik, and J. Mabry. Glenview, Ill.: Scott, Foresman, 1966, Vol. 1.

GERST, M. S. "Symbolic Coding Processes in Observational Learning." *Journal of Personality and Social Psychology*, 19 (1971): 9–17.

HARLOW, H. F. "The Formation of Learning Sets."

Psychological Review, 56 (1949): 51–65.

HONIG, W. H. (ED.). *Operant Behavior: Areas of Research and Application.* New York: Appleton-Century-Crofts, 1966.

JOHN, E. R., ET AL. "Observation Learning in Cats." *Science,* 159 (1968): 1489–1491.

LOVAAS, O. I., ET AL. "Establishment of Imitation and Its Use for the Development of Complex Behavior in Schizophrenic Children." *Behavior Research and Therapy,* 5 (August 1967): 171–181.

MILLER, L. K., AND SCHNEIDER, R. "The Use of a Token System in Project Headstart." *Journal of Applied Behavior Analysis,* 3 (1970): 213–220.

MILLER, L. KEITH, WEAVER, F. HAL, AND SEMB, GEORGE. "A Procedure for Maintaining Student Progress in a Personalized University Course." *Journal of Applied Behavior Analysis,* 7 (1974): 87–91.

OSBORNE, J. G. "Free-Time as a Reinforcer in the Management of Classroom Behavior." *Journal of Applied Behavior Analysis,* 7 (1974): 87–91.

PAVLOV, IVAN P. *Conditioned Reflexes.* Translated by G. V. Anrep. London: Oxford University Press, 1927.

REYNOLDS, G. S. *A Primer of Operant Condition-ing.* Glenview, Ill.: Scott, Foresman, 1968.

SAHAKIAN, WILLIAM S. *Psychology of Learning.* Chicago: Markam, 1970.

SELIGMAN, MARTIN E. P. "Fall into Helplessness." *Psychology Today,* 7 (June 1973): 43–48.

SKINNER, B. F. *The Behavior of Organisms.* New York: Appleton-Century-Crofts, 1961.

——. *About Behaviorism.* New York: Knopf, 1974.

WATSON, DAVID L., AND THARP, RONALD G. *Self-directed Behavior: Self-modification for Personal Adjustment.* Monterey, Calif.: Brooks/Cole, 1972.

WATSON, J. B., AND RAYNER, ROSALIE. "Conditioned Emotional Reactions." *Journal of Experimental Psychology,* 3 (1920): 1–14.

WHITE, MARY ALICE. "Natural Rates of Teacher Approval and Disapproval in the Classroom." *Journal of Applied Behavior Analysis,* 8 (1975): 367–372.

WOLFE, JOHN B. "Effectiveness of Token-Rewards for Chimpanzees." *Comparative Psychological Monographs,* 12 (1936): whole no. 5.

3 Memory and Thought

Taking Information In
Selective Attention / Feature Extraction
Storing Information
Sensory Storage / Short-term Memory / Long-term Memory / Theories of Memory
Retrieving Information
Recognition / Recall / Forgetting / Improving Memory
Central Processing of Information
Thinking / Problem-solving / Creativity

Understanding how the mind works—how human beings think, remember, solve problems, and create ideas—is one of the most fascinating and challenging goals of psychology. For simplicity's sake, psychologists treat all cognitive or mental activities—from memorizing lists of numbers to writing poems and inventing new technologies—as *information processing*. This involves three steps: input, central processing, and output. *Input* refers to the information people receive from their senses. *Central processing* refers to the storing (in memory) and sorting (by thought) of this information in the brain. *Output* refers to the actions that result from processing.

Psychologists know a great deal about how the senses take in information (see Chapter 5). They also know a great deal about how people behave. However, exactly what happens between sensory input and behavior output remains something of a mystery. In this chapter we will focus on this mystery, describing what psychologists have learned so far about information processing.

TAKING INFORMATION IN

Input comes through the senses in many forms—voices, musical sounds, sweet tastes, pungent odors, colorful images, rough textures, painful stings. At any given moment a confusing array of sights, sounds, smells, and other sensations compete for your attention. If you accepted *all* these inputs, you would be completely overwhelmed. Two processes help people to narrow sensory inputs down to a manageable number: selective attention and feature extraction.

Selective Attention

The ability to pick and choose among the various available inputs is called *selective attention*. For example, if you are at a large party where the music is turned up and everyone is talking, you can focus on a friend's voice and ignore all other sounds. In a way, selective attention is like tuning in a specific television channel.

Unlike a television dial, however, selective attention does not completely block out the other programs or stimuli. You may be listening

FIGURE 3.1
Few of us ever have to memorize anything on so grand a scale as a major part in a Shakespearean play. Exactly how actors accomplish this is not entirely understood, but psychologists do know quite a bit about the brain's ability to store and retrieve information.

FIGURE 3.2

While staring at this figure, quickly flip the page so that you see the black frame on page 54 for just a moment. What letters and numbers did you see in the third row? The purpose of this experiment will be explained in the text.

attentively to what a friend is saying, but at the same time you are unconsciously monitoring information that is coming in over other channels. If your name is mentioned in a conversation going on three feet away, you will notice it and tune into that input. If someone strolls by dressed in a bathing suit, snorkel, and fins, you will notice him. The "cocktail-party phenomenon," as selective attention is sometimes called, allows you to concentrate on one thing without tuning out everything else that is happening.

Laboratory experiments have shown how selective attention works (Hernández-Peón, 1961). For example, if people are asked to pay attention to an auditory stimulus, the brain waves that record their response to sound will get larger. While this is happening, the brain waves that record their response to what they see will get smaller because they are not paying close attention to visual stimuli. If the same people are asked to pay attention to visual stimuli, the reverse occurs: Visual brain waves increase while auditory brain waves decrease. A similar experiment showed that a certain kind of brain wave diminished but did not disappear when people were given a problem to solve or were drawn into conversation. Such experiments seem to indicate that the brain somehow evaluates the importance of the information that comes in over different channels. Top-priority information is allowed to reach the highest brain centers, whereas unimportant information is suppressed.

What makes one input more important than another? Information leading to the satisfaction of such needs as hunger and thirst has top priority. (A person who is very hungry, for example, will pay more attention to his dinner than to the dinner table chitchat.) We also give priority to inputs that are strange and novel, such as an individual who comes to a party dressed for snorkeling. A third director of attention is interest: The more interested you are in something, the more likely you are to notice it. For example, most people "tune in" when they hear their name mentioned; we're all interested in what other people have to say about us. Likewise, if you become interested in chess, you will suddenly begin to notice newspaper articles about chess, chess sets in store windows, and references to chess moves in everyday speech (for example, "stalemate"). These inputs are not new. They were there last year and the year before, but you simply weren't interested enough to notice them.

Feature Extraction

Selective attention is only the first step in narrowing down input. The second step is to decide which aspects of the selected channel you will focus on. This process, called *feature extraction*, involves locating the outstanding characteristics of incoming information. For example, if you want to identify the make of a car, you look for distinctive features—the shape of the fenders, the proportion of height to length, and so on. For the most part, you ignore such features as color, upholstery, and tires, which tell you little about the make of the car. Similarly, when you read, you focus on the important words, skimming over such words as "the," "and," or "for example."

Being able to extract the significant features of an input helps a person to identify it and compare it to other inputs. For example, you are able to distinguish faces from one another, and at the same time see resemblances. You may notice that all the members of a family have similar noses, yet you are able to recognize each person on the basis of other features.

Obviously, feature extraction depends to some extent on experience—on knowing what to look for. This is especially true where fine distinctions must be made. It takes considerable expertise to distinguish an original Rembrandt from a skillful forgery. Most of us cannot say what vineyard produced the wine we are drinking in what year, but a gourmet who knows what to look for can.

Like selective attention, feature extraction is an evaluative process. If you are reading a novel for pleasure, you may look for the "juicy" parts; if you're reading an historical biography to prepare for an exam, you concentrate on the facts.

STORING INFORMATION

In order to be used, the inputs that reach the brain must be registered, held onto, perhaps "filed" for future reference. We call the storage of inputs memory. Psychologists distinguish among three kinds of memory, each of which has a different purpose and time span. Sensory storage holds information for only an instant; short-term memory keeps it in mind for about twenty seconds; long term memory stores it indefinitely.

Sensory Storage

The senses seem to be able to hold an input for a fraction of a second before it disappears. For example, when you watch a movie you do not notice the gaps between frames—the actions seem smooth because each frame is held in sensory storage until the next frame arrives.

Psychologists have measured the length of sensory storage by testing subjects with inputs such as that shown in Figure 3.4. This image is flashed on a screen for one-fiftieth of a second, and immediately afterward the subject is signaled to recite one of the lines he or she has seen. The subject is usually able to report all four items on the required line if the signal is sounded within a quarter of a second after the exposure. (However, they cannot do this if the signal is delayed for a second or more.) It is therefore thought that the subject retains a brief image of the whole picture so that he or she can still read off the items in the correct row *after* the picture has left the screen (Sperling, 1960).

The information held momentarily by the senses has not yet been narrowed down or analyzed. It is like a short-lived but highly detailed photograph or tape recording. However, by the time information gets to the next stage—short-term memory—it has been analyzed, identified, and simplified so that it can be conveniently stored and handled for a long time.

FIGURE 3.3
Can you spot the hidden faces in this picture? To find them, it is necessary for you to extract those features that define a human face from a large amount of irrelevant and misleading information.

FIGURE 3.4
A pattern of letters and numbers used to investigate information storage. Psychologists use a machine called a tachistoscope to flash such patterns on a screen in front of a subject. The subject is then asked to report what he or she has seen. By such methods, experimenters can determine how much information a person stores in the fraction of a second after he or she has seen something.

Short-term Memory

The things you have in your conscious mind at any one moment are being held in short-term memory. Short-term memory does not necessarily involve paying close attention. You have probably had the experience of listening to someone only partially and then having that person accuse you of not paying attention. You deny it, in order to prove your innocence, and you repeat to him, word for word, the last words he said. You can do this because you are holding the words in short-term memory. However, in all probability, the sense of what he was saying does not register on you until you repeat the words out loud. Repeating the words makes you pay attention to them. This is what psychologists mean by rehearsal.

Rehearsal.   To keep information in short-term memory for more than a few seconds, you have to repeat it to yourself, in your mind or out loud. When you look up a telephone number, for example, you can remember the seven digits long enough to dial them *if* you repeat them several times. If you are distracted or make a mistake in dialing, the chances are you will have to look the number up again. It has been lost from short-term memory.

Psychologists have measured short-term memory by seeing how long a subject can retain a piece of information without rehearsal. The experimenter shows the subject a card with three letters on it, such as CPQ. However, at the same time the experimenter makes the subject think about something else in order to prevent her from rehearsing the letters. For example, she might ask the subject to start counting backward by threes from 798 as soon as she flashes the card. If the subject performs this task for only a short time, she will usually remember the letters. But if she is kept from rehearsing for more than eighteen seconds, the information is gone forever. Thus short-term memory seems to last for less than twenty seconds without rehearsal.

Chunking.   Short-term memory is limited not only in its duration, but in its capacity as well. It can hold only about seven unrelated items. If, for example, someone quickly reels off a series of digits to you, you will be able to keep only about seven or eight of them in your immediate memory. Beyond that, confusion among them will set in. The same would be true if the unrelated items were a random set of words. We may not notice this limit to our capacity because we usually do not have to store so many unrelated items in our immediate memory. Either the items are related (as when we listen to someone speak) or they are rehearsed and placed in long-term memory.

The most interesting aspect of this limit, discovered by George Miller (1956), is that it involves seven items of any kind. Each item may consist of a collection of many other items, but if they are all packaged into one "chunk" then there is still only one item. Thus we can remember about seven unrelated sets of initials, such as COMSAT, DDT, SST, or the initials of our favorite radio stations, even though we could not remember all the letters separately. This occurs because we have connected or

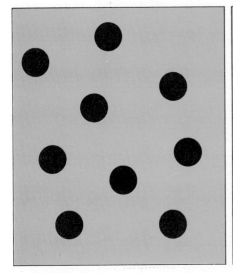 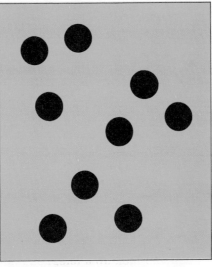

FIGURE 3.5
Glance quickly at the left figure in this pair, then look away. How many dots did you see? Now do the same with the right figure. You were probably more sure and more accurate in your answer for the right figure because the organization of the dots into a small number of chunks makes it easier to process the information.

"chunked" them together previously, so that DDT is one item, not three.

One of the tricks of memorizing much information quickly is to chunk together the items as fast as they come in, by making up connections with them, so that, in effect, they become fewer. As Figure 3.5 illustrates, we use chunking to remember visual as well as verbal inputs.

Even with chunking, short-term memory is only a temporary device. It contains information labeled "of possible interest." If the information is worth holding onto, it must be transferred to long-term memory.

Long-term Memory

Long-term memory is where we store information for future use. It can be thought of as a kind of filing cabinet or storage bin for names, dates, words, faces, and the like. When we say someone has a good memory, we usually mean he or she can recall a great deal of this type of information. But long-term memory also contains representations of countless experiences and sensations. For example, you may not have thought about your childhood home for years, but you can probably still visualize it.

Long-term memory involves all the processes we have been describing. Suppose a person goes to see a play. As the actors say their lines, the sounds flow through sensory storage. Selective attention screens out other sounds, and feature extraction turns sounds into words. These words accumulate in short-term memory and form meaningful phrases and sentences.

The viewer attends to the action and changing scenery in much the same way. Together, they form chunks in her memory. An hour or two later, she will have forgotten all but the most striking lines, but she has stored the meaning of the lines and actions in long-term memory. The next day, she may be able to give a scene-by-scene description of the play. Throughout this process, the least important information is dropped and only the essentials are retained. A month or two later, the woman may only remember a brief outline of the plot and perhaps a few vivid images of

FIGURE 3.6
The flow of information processing. Input to the senses is stored temporarily, and some of it is passed on into short-term memory. Information may be kept in short-term memory by rehearsal or it may be passed on to long-term memory. Material stored in both short- and long-term memory is used in making decisions. The decision process results in outputs such as talking, writing, or moving. This chapter focuses on those stages that occur between input and output.

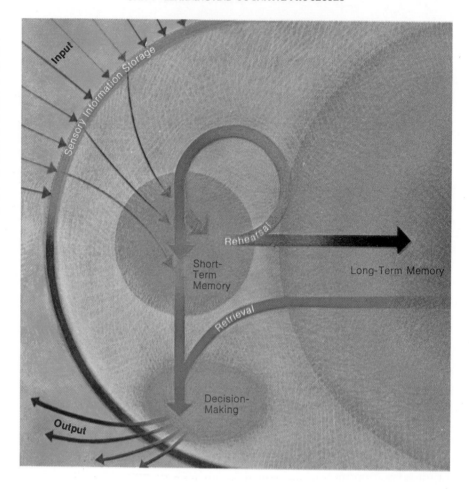

particularly impressive moments. In time she may not remember anything about the play. Other, more recently stored items block access to earlier memories, or may even replace them. But if she sees the play again, she will probably recognize the lines of the play and anticipate the actions. Although it has become less accessible, it is still stored in long-term memory.

Theories of Memory

What happens in the brain when something is stored in long-term memory? This question is highly controversial. Although psychologists agree that some physiological changes must occur in the brain, they do not always know what these changes are.

One theory is that memory is due to changes in the form of protein molecules in the brain. In one experiment, a number of mice were trained to run through a maze, avoiding alleys where they would receive an electric shock. Then the mice were injected with a chemical known to disrupt protein production in the brain. Afterward the mice could no longer remember the safe way out of the maze (Flexner, 1967). Recently researchers (Flood, 1975) have been able to control the amount of "amnesia" in mice by injecting varying amounts of the chemical for certain time periods after the training task. The more of the protein-blocking chemical the mice receive, the more forgetful they become. It may be that senility is related to the cessation of protein production in the brain.

Another theory focuses on chemical-electrical changes in the brain. It may be that memory develops when the characteristics of the synapses change chemically. When information is learned, some pathways in the brain are facilitated, others inhibited. To date, it is impossible to say which of these theories is closer to the truth.

To complicate matters further, memories seem to be distributed over wide areas of the brain, rather than located in particular areas. No one cell, or group of cells, can be removed to destroy a memory. Indeed, Karl Lashley (1929) found that he had to destroy most of the upper part of a rat's brain to erase memory of a problem it had learned to solve. As a result, many psychologists believe that memories may be stored in the brain in multiples, so that destroying one area of the brain simply removes one copy.

All these ideas remain highly speculative. Many psychologists believe, however, that a better understanding of the processes underlying memory will be reached in the near future.

RETRIEVING INFORMATION

Stored information is useless unless it can be retrieved from memory. If you've ever tried to find a lost pen or key in a room you haven't bothered to clean up for some time, you have an idea of how difficult retrieval can be. Also, trying to remember a name by closing your eyes and concentrating on dragging the name out of your memory is often futile. However, if you give up and go off to do something else, the name may well come to you.

The problem of memory is to store many thousands of items in such a way that you can find the one you need when you need it. The solution is *organization*. The fact that human memory is extraordinarily efficient suggests that it must be extremely well-organized. Psychologists do not yet know how it is organized, but they are studying the processes involved in retrieval for clues.

Recognition

The organization of human memory seems to be designed to make recognition quite easy—people can say with great accuracy whether or not something is familiar to them. If someone asked you the name of your first-grade teacher, for example, you probably would say you don't remember it. But chances are that you would recognize the name if you heard it. Similarly, a multiple-choice test may bring out knowledge that a student might not be able to show on an essay test. The ability to recognize suggests that much more information is stored in memory than one might think.

The process of recognition provides insight into how information is stored in memory. People can recognize the sound of a particular musical instrument (say, the piano) no matter what tune is being played on it. We can also recognize a tune no matter what instrument it is being played on. This pattern of recognition indicates that a single item of information may be "indexed" under several "headings" so that it can be reached in a number of ways. Thus "Mr. Stevens leading a class discussion on memory" may be indexed under "Mr. Stevens," under "memory," under "Introduction to Psychology," and possibly under other headings as well. The more categories an item is filed in the more easily it can be retrieved.

Recall

More remarkable than the ability to recognize information is the ability to recall it. *Recall is the active reconstruction of information*. Just think about the amount of recall involved in a simple conversation: Each person uses hundreds of words involving all kinds of information, even though each word and bit of information must be retrieved separately from the storehouse of memory.

Recall involves more than searching for and finding pieces of information, however. This was demonstrated in an experiment. The researcher showed a group of young children a bottle of colored water, tilted as shown in Figure 3.7. The children were then asked to draw what they had seen from memory. Most of their drawings showed marked changes from the original arrangement. However, six months later, when the same children were asked to draw the bottle they had seen, many did much better. Apparently they now had a better idea of what the tilted bottle *should* look like (Inhelder, 1969).

Because of this process of reconstruction, memories may change over time. They may be simplified, enriched, or distorted, depending on the individual's experiences and attitudes. This is why we sometimes make mistakes in memory. One type of mistake is called *confabulation*: a person "remembers" information that was never stored in memory. Confabulation generally occurs when an individual remembers parts of a situation and fills in the gaps by making up the rest.

Confabulation can create problems. Suppose a witness is testifying in court about a robbery he witnessed a year earlier. He may only have seen the getaway car parked on the corner and the defendant standing near the bank. But in court he unconsciously distorts the reality and "remembers" seeing the accused person jump into the car and speed away. His attitude toward the defendant may have caused him to fill in the gaps in his memory incorrectly. Or perhaps he simply wants to tell a more interesting story, so he unconsciously adds whatever details he needs.

Some people do not need to reconstruct information, because they have an *eidetic memory*, usually referred to as a "photographic memory." People with eidetic memories can remember with amazing accuracy all the details of a photograph, or pages of a text, or an experience on the

FIGURE 3.7
Children between the ages of five and seven were shown a bottle half filled with colored water and suspended at an angle, such as is shown in this drawing. After each child had seen this arrangement he was asked to draw it from memory. Some of the results of this experiment are shown in Figure 3.8a, b.

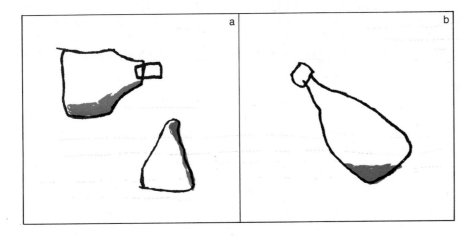

FIGURE 3.8
Drawings produced by children who had been shown an arrangement like that depicted in Figure 3.7. (a) The five- to seven-year-old children were not too successful in reproducing this arrangement from memory. (b) A drawing done by one of these children six months later. Even though the child had had half a year to forget what he had seen, his reproduction of the arrangement actually improved because he had developed a better idea of what bottles look like and of how water behaves. Such experiments demonstrate that memory for how things *are* depends greatly on one's conception of how things *should be*.

basis of short-term exposure. Interestingly, children seem to possess this ability to a far greater degree than adults. As people grow up and come to rely on their verbal memory much more than on their visual memory, most of their eidetic ability seems to disappear.

Forgetting

Everyone experiences a loss of memory from time to time. You're sure you've seen that person before but can't quite place her; you have the word on the tip of your tongue, but. . . . When information that once entered long-term memory cannot be retrieved, it is said to be forgotten. Forgetting may involve decay, interference, or repression.

Some inputs may fade away, or *decay*, over time. Items quickly decay in sensory storage and short-term memory, as indicated above. It is not certain, however, whether long-term memories can ever decay. We know that a blow to the head or electrical stimulation of certain parts of the brain can cause loss of memory. The memories lost are the most recent ones, however; older memories seem to remain. The fact that apparently forgotten information can be recovered through meditation, hypnosis, or brain stimulation suggests that at least some memories never decay. Rather, interference or repression causes people to lose track of them.

Interference refers to a memory being blocked or erased by previous or subsequent memories. In *proactive interference* an earlier memory does the blocking; in *retroactive interference* a later memory does the blocking. Suppose you move to a new home. You now have to remember a new address and phone number. At first you may have trouble remembering them because the memory of your old address and phone number gets in the way (proactive interference). Later, you know the new information, but have trouble remembering the old data (retroactive interference).

It may be that interference actually does erase some memories permanently. In other cases the old data have not been lost. The information is in your memory somewhere, if only you could find it. Sometimes blocking is no accident. A person may "intentionally" block memories of an *intentionally blo...* embarrassing or frightening experience. This kind of forgetting is called *repression*. The material still exists in the person's memory, but it has unconsciously been made inaccessible because it is so disturbing. (We discuss repression further in Chapter 13.)

Improving Memory

Techniques for improving memory are based on efficient organization of the things you learn and on chunking information into easily handled packages. Meaningfulness, association, lack of interference, and degree of original learning all influence your ability to retrieve data from memory.

The more *meaningful* something is, the easier it will be to remember. For example, you would be more likely to remember the six letters DFIRNE if they were arranged to form the word FRIEND. Similarly, you remember things more vividly if you *associate* them with things already stored in memory or with a strong emotional experience. As pointed out earlier, the more categories a memory is indexed under, the more accessible it is. If an input is analyzed and indexed under many categories, each association can serve as a trigger for the memory. If you associate the new information with strong sounds, smells, tastes, textures, and so on, encountering any of these stimuli could trigger the memory. The more senses you use when trying to memorize something, the more likely it is that you will be able to retrieve it. This is a key to improving your memory.

For similar reasons, a good way to protect a memory from interference is to *overlearn* it—to keep on rehearsing it even after you think you know it well. Another way to prevent interference while learning new material is to avoid studying similar material sequentially. For example, instead of studying history right after political science, study biology in between. Still another method is to space out your learning. Trying to absorb large amounts of information at one sitting results in a great deal of interference. It is far more effective to study a little at a time.

Mnemonic Devices. Mnemonic devices are techniques for using associations to memorize information. The ancient Greeks memorized speeches by mentally walking around their homes or neighborhoods and "placing" each line of a speech in a different spot. Once they made the associations, they could recall the speech by mentally retracing their steps and "picking up" each line. A more familiar mnemonic device is the rhyme we use to recall the number of days in each month ("Thirty days has September"). Another is the phrase, "Every Good Boy Does Fine," in which the first letters of the words are the same as the names of the musical notes on the lines of a staff (E, G, B, D, and F); the notes between the lines spell FACE (see Figure 3.9).

Another useful mnemonic device is to form mental pictures containing the information you want to remember—the sillier the better. Suppose you have trouble remembering the authors and titles of books, or which artists belong to different schools of painting. To plant the fact that John Updike

FIGURE 3.9
Memorization of the locations of musical notes on the staff has long been aided by this popular mnemonic device. The notes that fall in the spaces spell the word "face," and the notes that fall on the lines provide the initial letters for the sentence, "Every good boy does fine."

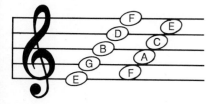

wrote *Rabbit Run* in your mind you might picture a RABBIT RUNning UP a DIKE. To remember that Picasso was a Cubist, picture someone attacking a giant CUBE with a PICKAX (which sounds like Picasso) (Lorayne and Lucas, 1974: 166-169).

Mnemonic devices are not magical. Indeed, they involve extra work—making up words, stories, and so on. But the very effort to do this may help you to remember things.

CENTRAL PROCESSING OF INFORMATION

If storage and retrieval were the only processes we used to handle information, human beings would be little more than glorified cameras and projectors. But, in fact, we are capable of doing things with information that make the most complex computers seem inept by comparison. These processes—thinking and problem-solving—are most impressive when they show originality or creativity.

Thinking

Thinking may be viewed as changing and reorganizing the information stored in memory in order to create new information. By thinking, humans are able to put together any combination of words from memory and create sentences never devised before—such as this one.

Units of Thought.   The processes of thought depend on several devices or units of thought: images, symbols, concepts, and rules.

The most primitive unit of thought is an *image,* a pictorial representation of a specific event or object. The representation is not usually a photographic copy but rather shows only the highlights of the original. For example, if an adult tries to visualize a grandmother who died when he was seven, he would probably remember only a few details—perhaps the color of her hair or a piece of jewelry that she wore.

A more abstract unit of thought is a *symbol,* a sound or design that represents a thing or quality. The most common symbols in thinking are words: Every word is a symbol that stands for something other than itself. Whereas image represents a specific sight or sound, a symbol may have a number of meanings. The fact that symbols differ from the things they represent enables us to think about things that are not present, to range over the past and future, to imagine things and situations that never were or will be. Numbers, letters, and punctuation marks are all familiar symbols of ideas that have no concrete existence.

When a symbol is used as a label for a whole class of objects or events with certain common attributes, or for the attributes themselves, it is called a *concept.* "Animals," "music," and "liquid" are examples of concepts based on the common attributes of the objects and experiences belonging to each category. Thus the concept "animal" separates mobile organisms from such things as automobiles and carrots. Concepts enable us to chunk large amounts of information. We do not have to treat every new piece of information as unique since we already know something about the class of objects or experiences.

The fourth and most complex unit of thought is a *rule*, a statement or a relation between concepts. Examples of rules are: A person cannot be in two places at the same time; mass remains constant despite changes in appearance. The principles of logic dominate Western thought.

Images, symbols, concepts, and rules are the building blocks of mental activity. They provide an economical and efficient way for people to represent reality, to manipulate and reorganize it, and to devise new ways of acting. A person can think about pursuing several different careers, weigh their pros and cons, and decide which to pursue, without having to try them all.

Kinds of Thinking.   People think in two distinct ways. The first, called *directed thinking,* is a systematic and logical attempt to reach a specific goal, such as the solution of a problem. This kind of thinking depends heavily on symbols, concepts, and rules. The other type, called *nondirected thinking,* consists of a free flow of thoughts through the mind, with no particular goal or plan, and depends more on images.

Nondirected thinking is usually rich with imagery and feelings. Daydreams, fantasies, and reveries are typical examples. People often engage in nondirected thought when they are relaxing or trying to escape tempo-

FIGURE 3.10
This problem was devised by psychologist Edward De Bono. De Bono believes that conventional directed thinking is insufficient for solving new and unusual problems. He refers to traditional thought processes as ''vertical thinking'' and says that to solve problems like this one people need to think ''laterally.'' This approach to problem-solving requires use of nondirected thinking in order to generate new ways of looking at the problem situation. The answer to this problem is provided in Figure 3.15.

An old money-lender offered to cancel a merchant's debt and keep him from going to prison if the merchant would give the money-lender his lovely daughter. Horrified yet desperate, the merchant and his daughter agreed to let Providence decide. The money-lender said he would put a black pebble and a white pebble in a bag and the girl would draw one. The white pebble would cancel the debt and leave her free. The black one would make her the money-lender's, although the debt would be canceled. If she refused to pick, her father would go to prison. From the pebble-strewn path they were standing on, the money-lender picked two pebbles and quickly put them in the bag, but the girl saw he had picked up two black ones. What would you have done if you were the girl?

rarily from boredom or worry. This kind of thinking may provide unexpected insights into one's goals and beliefs. Scientists and artists say that some of their best ideas emerge from drifting thoughts that occur when they have temporarily set aside a problem.

In contrast, directed thinking is deliberate and purposeful. It is through directed thinking that we solve problems, formulate and follow rules, and set, work toward, and achieve goals.

Problem-solving

One of the main functions of directed thinking is to solve problems—to bridge the gap, mentally, between a present situation and a desired goal. The gap may be between hunger and food, a column of figures and a total, lack of money and bills to pay, or cancer and a cure. In all these examples, getting from the problem to the solution requires some directed thinking.

Strategies. Problem-solving depends on the use of strategies, or specific methods for approaching problems. One strategy is to break down a complex problem into a number of smaller, more easily solved problems. For example, a member of your family who lives alone has been confined to bed for a month. You solve the problem of caring for him by breaking it down into small pieces: buying and preparing food; obtaining the necessary medications; arranging for a part-time nurse; providing visitors, books, and other diversions; and so on.

A second strategy for solving problems is working backward from the goal you have set. Mystery writers often use this method: They decide how to end the story ("who did it") and then devise a plot leading to this conclusion.

A third strategy is to examine various ways of reaching a desired goal. Suppose a woman needs to be in Chicago by 11 A.M. on July 7 for a business conference. She checks train departures and arrivals, airline schedules, and car rental companies. The only train to Chicago that morning arrives at 5 A.M. (too early), and the first plane arrives at 11:30 A.M. (too late). So she decides to rent a car and drive.

To determine which strategy to use in a particular situation, most of us analyze the problem to see if it resembles a situation we have experienced in the past. A strategy that worked in the past is likely to work again. The more unusual the problem, the more difficult it is to devise a strategy for dealing with it.

Set. There are times when certain useful strategies become cemented into the problem-solving process. When a particular strategy becomes a habit, it is called a *set*—you are "set" to treat problems in a certain way. For example, a chess player may attempt to always control the four center squares of the chessboard. Consequently, whenever her opponent attacks her, she responds by looking for ways to regain control of those four squares. She has a "set" for this strategy. If this set helps her to win, that is fine. However, sometimes a set *interferes* with problem-solving, and

FIGURE 3.11
Given the materials pictured here, how would you go about mounting the candle vertically on a wooden wall in such a way that it can be lit? This problem was formulated by Carl Duncker to test how well people are able to overcome functional fixedness. The solution is presented in Figure 3.15.

then it is called *rigidity.* You probably know the old riddle, "What is black, white, and read all over? A newspaper." When you say the riddle, the word "read" sounds like "red," which is why some people cannot guess the answer. "Read" is heard as part of the black and white set—it is interpreted as being a color. If you asked, "What is read by people every day and is black and white?" the correct answer would be obvious.

One form of set that can interfere with problem-solving is *functional fixedness*—the inability to imagine new functions for familiar objects. In experiments on functional fixedness, people are asked to solve a problem that requires them to use a familiar object in an unfamiliar way (Duncker, 1945). Because they are set to use the object in the usual way, people tend to pay attention only to the features of the object that relate to its everyday use (see Figure 3.11). They respond in a rigid way.

Another type of rigidity occurs when a person makes a wrong assumption about a problem. In Figure 3.12, for example, the problem is to connect the dots with four straight lines without lifting your pencil. Most people have trouble solving this puzzle because they falsely assume that they must stay within the area of the dots.

People trying to solve the kind of problem shown in Figure 3.13 experience a third kind of rigidity. Most people look for direct methods of solving problems and do not see solutions that require several intermediate steps.

Rigidity can be overcome if the problem solver realizes that his or her strategy is not working and looks for other ways to approach the problem. The more familiar the situation, the more difficult this will be. Rigidity is less likely to occur with unusual problems.

Creativity

Creativity is the ability to use information in such a way that the result is somehow new, original, and meaningful. All problem-solving requires some creativity. However, certain ways of solving problems are simply more brilliant or beautiful or efficient than others. Psychologists do not

FIGURE 3.12
Connect these dots with four straight lines without lifting your pencil. The solution appears in Figure 3.15.

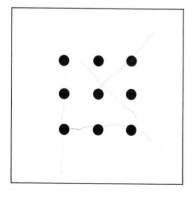

FIGURE 3.13
How would you go about solving this problem: Eight soldiers need to cross a river, but the only way to cross is in a small boat in which two children are playing. The boat can carry at most two children or one soldier. How do the soldiers get across? You'll find the answer in Figure 3.15.

FIGURE 3.14
A test devised to measure flexibility in thinking. The task is to name a single word that all three words on a line have in common. For example, the answer to the first item is "foot." (The other answers are given in Figure 3.15.) The ability to come up with meaningful answers on this test is believed to be related to creativity, in that creativity is thought to involve putting things together in unusual, unexpected ways.

1.	stool	powder	ball
2.	blue	cake	cottage
3.	man	wheel	high
4.	motion	poke	down
5.	line	birthday	surprise
6.	wood	liquor	luck
7.	house	village	golf
8.	card	knee	rope
9.	news	doll	tiger
10.	painting	bowl	nail
11.	weight	wave	house
12.	made	cuff	left
13.	key	wall	precious
14.	bull	tired	hot
15.	knife	up	hi
16.	handle	hole	police
17.	plan	show	walker
18.	hop	side	pet
19.	bell	tender	iron
20.	spelling	line	busy

know precisely why some people are able to think more creatively than others. However, they have identified some of the characteristics of creative thinking—including flexibility and the ability to recombine elements to achieve insight.

Flexibility. Flexibility is, quite simply, the ability to overcome rigidity. Ingenious people have devised a number of tests to measure flexibility. One test is shown in Figure 3.14. The individual is asked to name a word that the three words in each row have in common. To do this, a person must be able to think of many different aspects of each of these words. Another test of flexibility is to ask people how many uses they can imagine for a single object, such as a brick or paper clip. The more uses a person can devise, the more flexible he or she is said to be. Whether such tests actually measure creativity is debatable. Nevertheless, it is obvious that inflexible, rigid thinking leads to unoriginal solutions, if it leads to solutions at all.

Recombination. When the elements of a problem are familiar but the required solution novel, it may be achieved by a new mental re-arrangement of the elements. In football and basketball, for example, there are no new moves—only recombinations of old ones. Such recombination seems to be a vital part of creativity. Many creative people say that no truly great poem, no original invention, has ever been produced by someone who has not spent years studying his or her subject. The creative person is able to take the information that he or she and others have compiled and put it together in a totally new way. For example, the brilliant physicist Isaac Newton, who discovered the laws of motion, once said, "If I have seen further, it is by standing on the shoulders of giants." In other words, he was able to recombine the discoveries of the great scientists who had preceded him to uncover new and more far-reaching truths.

Another famous example of brilliant recombination is Samuel Taylor Coleridge's unusual poem, "Kubla Khan." Scholars have shown that almost every word and phrase came directly from Coleridge's past reading and personal experiences. Coleridge recombined these elements during a period of nondirected thinking—drug-induced sleep. He awoke with the entire poem in his mind, but was only able to commit part of it to paper

hen the girl put her hand into the bag to draw out the fateful pebble, she fumbled and dropped it, where it was immediately lost among the others. "Oh," she said, "well, you can tell which one I picked by looking at the one that's left." The girl's lateral thinking saved her father and herself.

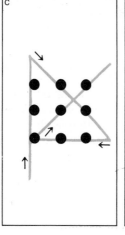

1.	foot	11.	light
2.	cheese	12.	hand
3.	chair	13.	stone
4.	slow	14.	dog
5.	party	15.	jack
6.	hard	16.	man
7.	green	17.	floor
8.	trick	18.	car
9.	paper	19.	bar
10.	finger	20.	bee

FIGURE 3.15
Solutions to the problems presented in the chapter. Note that in each case the solution requires breaking certain habits of thought. (a) In the De Bono money-lender problem, it is difficult to imagine that control of the situation can be taken out of the hands of the powerful money-lender. (b) Solving the Duncker candle problem requires one to look at the matchbox and candle box as more than containers to be discarded. The presence of the useless piece of string usually serves to confuse problem solvers. (c) As the text points out, the solution to this problem is blocked if the person avoids going beyond the boundaries of the dots. (d) The answers to the test of flexibility require that
the individual ignore common associations and look for unusual ones. (e) The first steps in solution of the river problem. Once the solver discovers the first step in the problem's solution, he or she may become further bogged down if he doesn't realize the lengthy cyclical nature of the process required.

before he was interrupted by a knock at his door. When Coleridge returned, the rest of the poem had vanished from his mind.

Insight.   The sudden emergence of a solution by recombination of elements is called *insight*. Insight usually occurs when problems have proved resistant to all problem-solving efforts and strategies. The scientist or artist reaches a point of high frustration and temporarily abandons the task. But the recombination process seems to continue on an unconscious level. When the person is absorbed in some other activity, the answer seems to appear out of nowhere. This sudden insight has appropriately been called the "aha" experience.

Certain animals appear to experience this same cycle of frustration, temporary diversion (during which time the problem "incubates"), and then sudden insight. For example, Wolfgang Köhler (1925) placed a chimpanzee in a cage where a cluster of bananas was hung out of its reach. Also in the cage were a number of wooden boxes. At first the chimpanzee tried various unsuccessful ways of getting at the fruit. Finally it sat down, apparently giving up, and simply stared straight ahead for a while. Then suddenly it jumped up, piled three boxes on top of one another, climbed to the top of the pile, and grabbed the bananas.

Some people have suggested that the period of intense frustration the creative person must go through to achieve insight is somehow linked to the incidence of mental disorders among artists. The inability to solve a problem or to break through a creative "block" may be so frustrating that the person cannot handle it.

SUMMARY

1. Information processing involves three steps: input from the senses, central processing (memory, thought), and output in the form of behavior.

2. Two processes that help narrow down inputs are selective attention and feature extraction. Selective attention is the ability to pick and choose among various incoming channels, focusing on some and ignoring others. Channels are chosen when they help satisfy needs, are unusual, or relate to one's interests. Feature extraction is the ability to respond to specific characteristics of a given input and to ignore others.

3. The shortest form of memory is sensory storage, which lasts less than a second. Next is short-term memory, which retains information for about twenty seconds at most. Items stored in short-term memory are quickly forgotten if they are not rehearsed or transferred to long-term memory.

4. Long-term memory contains information that has some significance. There are at least two theories as to how memories are stored. One theory states that memory is due to changes in the form of protein molecules in the brain. The other theory focuses on chemical-electrical changes in the brain. It is believed that however memories are stored, they are distributed throughout wide areas of the brain.

5. Retrieval is essential if memory is to be useful; consequently, memory must be organized. Retrieval takes two forms: recognition and recall. Recall is an active reconstructive process that may give rise to such errors as con-

fabulation, in which memories are reconstructed incorrectly.

6. Forgetting may possibly be caused by decay, interference, or repression. Decay is the fading away of a memory and, if it occurs at all, is not the main reason for forgetting. Interference occurs when new or old information blocks or erases the memory of a related piece of information. In repression, access to information has been blocked.

7. Information is stored better and is more easily retrieved when (a) it is organized into meaningful chunks; (b) it has many paths, or associations, leading to it; and (c) it has been overlearned.

8. Thinking is the process of reorganizing and rearranging the information in memory to produce new information or ideas. The units of thought are images, symbols, concepts, and rules.

9. Thinking may be directed or nondirected. Directed thinking is deliberate and purposeful, as in problem-solving and decision-making. Nondirected thinking is more loose and passive, as in daydreaming and reverie.

10. Problem-solving is bridging the gap between a present situation and a desired goal by means of specific strategies. When strategies become habitual, they can hamper the problem-solving process. This difficulty is called rigidity.

11. Creativity is the ability to manipulate information to produce something new, original, and meaningful. Flexibility and the ability to recombine elements to achieve insight seem to be important aspects of creativity.

GLOSSARY

central processing: The second stage of information processing—storing (in memory) and sorting (by thought) information in the brain.

chunking: The process of grouping pieces of information for easier handling.

concept: A label for a class of objects or events that share common attributes.

confabulation: The act of filling in memory with statements that make sense but that are, in fact, untrue.

creativity: The capacity to use information and/or abilities in such a way that the results are new, original, and meaningful.

directed thinking: Systematic, logical, goal-directed thought.

eidetic memory: The ability to remember with great accuracy visual information on the basis of short-term exposure; also called "photographic memory."

feature extraction: The identification and analysis of specific features of a sensory input.

image: A rough pictorial representation of specific events or objects (the most primitive unit of thought).

input: The first stage of information processing—receiving information through the senses.

insight: The sudden realization of the solution to a problem.

long-term memory: Information storage that has unlimited capacity and lasts indefinitely.

memory: The compex mental function of storage and retrieval of what has been learned or experienced.

mnemonic devices: Methods for remembering items by relating them to information already held in the brain.

nondirected thinking: The free flow of images and ideas, occurring with no particular goal.

output: The final stage of information processing—sending information out through words or actions.

proactive interference: The hampering of recall of newly learned material by the recall of previously learned material.

recall: The type of memory retrieval in which a person reconstructs previously learned material.

recognition: The type of memory retrieval in which a person is required to identify an object, idea, or situation as one he or she has or has not experienced before.

recombination: Mentally rearranging the elements of a problem in order to arrive at a novel solution.

repression: The unconscious blocking of memories of frightening or disturbing experiences.

retrieval: The process of obtaining information that has been stored in memory.

retroactive interference: The hampering of recall of learned material by the recall of other material learned more recently.

rule: A statement of the relationship between two or more concepts (the most complex unit of thought).

selective attention: Focusing one's awareness on a limited segment of the total amount of sensory input one is receiving.

sensory storage: The momentary storage of sensory information at the level of the sensory receptors.

set: A habitual strategy or pattern of problem-solving.

short-term memory: Memory that is limited in capacity to about seven items and in duration to about twenty seconds.

symbol: An abstract unit of thought that represents an object, event, or quality.

ACTIVITIES

1. Mentally determine where the light switches in your home are located and keep track of them in your head. Do you have to use visual images to count the switches? To keep track of the number? If not, could you do it with images if you wanted to?

2. Present your classmates or other friends with an article or story that presents two perspectives on an issue. Later, test their recall of the article. See if they remember better those facts or arguments that agree with their own.

3. Try this simple learning task on your friends. Give them a list of numbers to memorize: 6, 9, 8, 11, 10, 13, 12, 15, 14, 17, 16, and so on. Tell some of them simply to memorize the material. Tell others that there is an organizational principle behind the number sequence, and to memorize the number with the aid of the principle (which they must discover). In the sequence above, the principle is "plus 3, minus one."

4. Try to remember what you were doing on your last birthday. As you probe your memory, verbalize the mental steps you are going through. What does this exercise tell you about your thought processes?

5. Suppose you wanted to put together a jigsaw puzzle. What are the problem-solving strategies you might use? Which one do you think would work the best?

6. Solve this problem: A sloppy man has twenty blue socks and twenty brown ones in his drawer. If he reaches for a pair of socks in the middle of the night, how many must he pull out to be sure he has a matched pair? How long did it take you to solve the problem? Can you identify what steps you went through in your mind in order to solve it?

7. In the middle of an ordinary activity, like reading a book, stop for a moment and listen for sounds you normally block out. Jot down the sounds you hear and try to identify them. Why don't you usually hear them? Under what circumstances would you notice them?

8. Relax and engage in nondirected thinking—let your thoughts wander. Things may come into your mind that you thought you had forgotten or that you didn't know you knew. Or reflect on a recent dream you had—where might the various images have come from? You may begin to see the vast amount of information you have stored in your brain.

9. You and your friends can test the way your memories are organized by playing a popular game called Categories. Make a grid with five columns and five rows, and put a category, such as fruits or furniture, at the top of each column. Now pick five random letters, and assign one to each row. Give yourself five minutes to think of an item starting with each letter for each category and fill in the boxes in the grid. (Example: If your letters are A, G, P, O, and B, your entries under "fruit" might be apple, grape, peach, orange, and banana.)

10. Try the following game to demonstrate the reconstructive aspects of recall. (You will need at least seven or eight people—the more the better.) Before you gather the group together, write or copy a very short (not more than three or four paragraphs) story containing a fair amount of descriptive detail. Memorize, as best you can, the story, and whisper it to one member of the group, making sure the others are out of earshot. Then instruct your listener to whisper the story to another player, and so on until all the players have heard it. When the last person has been told the story, have him or her repeat it aloud to the entire group. Then read the original story from your written copy. Chances are good that the two versions are quite a bit different. Discuss among yourselves how, when, and why the story changed.

SUGGESTED READINGS

DE BONO, EDWARD. *The Mechanism of Mind.* New York: Simon & Schuster, 1969. A nonscientific book about how to use your mind effectively. It is particularly instructive about the nature of memory and models.

FABUN, DON. *Communication: The Transfer of Meaning.* Rev. ed. Beverly Hills, Calif.: Benziger Bruce & Glencoe, 1968 (paper). A graphic and stimulating analysis of how communication between people is affected by selective attention, use of symbols, different meanings of concepts, and the making of inferences.

GHISELIN, B. (ED.). *The Creative Process.* New York: New American Library, 1952 (paper). An excellent selection of statements by creative people about their own processes of invention.

HALACY, D. S., JR. *Man and Memory.* New York: Harper & Row, 1970. A clearly written, enjoyable presentation of some of the most important research done on memory. Halacy also covers the various theories of memory, the experiments on memory transfer, and the effects of drugs on memory.

HUNTER, I. M. L. *Memory: Facts and Fallacies.* Baltimore: Penguin, 1964 (paper). An interesting introduction to the study of human memory. Hunter surveys a good deal of experimental literature, dating back to the nineteenth century.

HUTCHINSON, ELIOT D. *How to Think Creatively.* New York: Abington Press, 1949 (paper). This book is deceptively titled. Actually, it is a fascinating account of the role insight has played in the work of famous creative thinkers.

LURIA, A. R. *The Mind of a Mnemonist.* New York: Basic Books, 1968. This book is about a man Luria met who could remember anything, any amount, for any length of time. Luria, a Russian psychologist, tried to understand the mnemonist's mind.

WATSON, JAMES D. *The Double Helix.* New York: Atheneum, 1968 (paper). An intensely personal account of the process of the discovery of the DNA structure by a leading contemporary scientist.

BIBLIOGRAPHY

ADAMS, JACK A. *Human Memory.* New York: McGraw-Hill, 1967.

BRUNER, JEROME S., GOODNOW, JACQUELINE J., AND AUSTIN, GEORGE A. *A Study of Thinking.* New York: Wiley, 1956 (paper).

DE BONO, EDWARD. *New Think: The Use of Lateral Thinking in the Generation of New Ideas.* New York: Basic Books, 1968.

DUNCKER, KARL. "On Problem Solving," trans. L. S. Lees. *Psychological Monographs,* 58 no. 270 (1945).

——. *The Mechanism of the Mind.* New York: Simon & Schuster, 1969.

FLEXNER, L. "Dissection of Memory in Mice with Antibiotics." *Proceedings of the American Philosophical Society,* 111 (1967): 343–346.

FLOOD, J. F., BENNETT, E. L., AND ORME, A. E. "Relation of Memory Formation for Controlled Amounts of Brain Protein Synthesis." *Physiology and Behavior,* 15 (1975): 97–102.

GHISELIN, B. (ED.). *The Creative Process.* New York: New American Library, 1952 (paper).

HABER, R. N. "How We Remember What We See." *Scientific American,* 222 (1970): 104–112.

HALACY, D. R., JR. *Man and Memory.* New York: Harper & Row, 1970.

HERNÁNDEZ-PEÓN, R. "Reticular Mechanisms of Sensory Control." In *Sensory Communication,* edited by W. A. Rosenblith. New York: Wiley, 1961, pp. 497–520.

INHELDER, BAERBEL. "Memory and Intelligence in the Child." In *Studies in Cognitive Development,* edited by D. Elkind and J. F. Flavell. New York: Oxford University Press, 1969, pp. 337–364.

KOESTLER, ARTHUR. *The Act of Creation.* New York: Macmillan, 1964.

KOHLER, WOLFGANG. *The Mentality of Apes.* New York: Harcourt Brace Jovanovich, 1925.

LASHLEY, K.S. *Brain Mechanisms and Intelligence.* Chicago: University of Chicago Press, 1929.

LORAYNE, HARRY, AND LUCAS, JERRY. *The Memory Book.* New York: Ballantine, 1974 (paper).

MC CONNELL, J. V. "Cannibalism and Memory in Flatworms." *New Scientist,* 21 (1964): 465–468.

MILLER, GEORGE A. "The Magical Number Seven, Plus or Minus Two: Some Limits on Our Capacity for Processing Information." *Psychological Review,* 63 (1956): 81–97.

MILLER, GEORGE A., GALANTER, EUGENE, AND PRIBRAM, KARL H. *Plans and the Structure of Behavior.* New York: Holt, 1960.

NEISSER, ULRIC. *Cognitive Psychology.* New York: Appleton-Century-Crofts, 1967.

NORMAN, DAVID, AND LINDSAY, PETER. *Human Information Processing.* New York: Academic Press, 1972.

PETERSON, LLOYD R., AND PETERSON, MARGARET. "Short-term Retention of Individual Verbal Items." *Journal of Experimental Psychology,* 58 (1959): 193–198.

SPERLING, G. "The Information Available in Brief Visual Presentations." *Psychological Monographs,* 74 (1960), no. 11.

STROMEYER, C. F. III. "Eidetikers." In *Readings in Psychology Today.* 2nd ed. Del Mar, Calif.: CRM Books, 1972, pp. 357–361.

UNIT II

The Workings of the Mind and Body

Most people think of the mind and body as separate: They imagine the body as something concrete that can be studied in a laboratory and the mind as intangible and beyond the reach of science. Many people assume that we see, hear, and touch with our bodies; plan, dream, decide, and experience moods with our minds. People think that motives and emotions have little in common with vision, hearing, and other bodily phenomena. These cannot, it is thought, be studied in the same way, with the same instruments. Such unusual states of consciousness as hypnotic trances are considered beyond the reach of the scientific method.

This Unit is designed to challenge these common assumptions by showing that the line between mental activities and physiological functions is not as clear-cut as you may have imagined. Chapter 4 explains how the nervous and hormonal systems work and describes the physiological changes that produce feelings of hunger, pain, anger, and fear. Chapter 5 reveals that perception involves a great deal more than "taking in" the sights, sounds, and smells that exist around us. Like movie directors, we select those things we pay attention to and create our own versions of reality. Chapter 6 explores a controversy among psychologists: Which comes first in motivation and emotion, the biological drive or the idea? In Chapter 7 we note that, surprisingly, psychologists have found it easier to define and study dreams and hallucinations than to define and study everyday, waking consciousness.

When you complete this section, you will realize that in studying the workings of the mind and body, psychologists have raised nearly as many questions as they have answered. The years ahead will undoubtedly bring new and startling discoveries in this area of research.

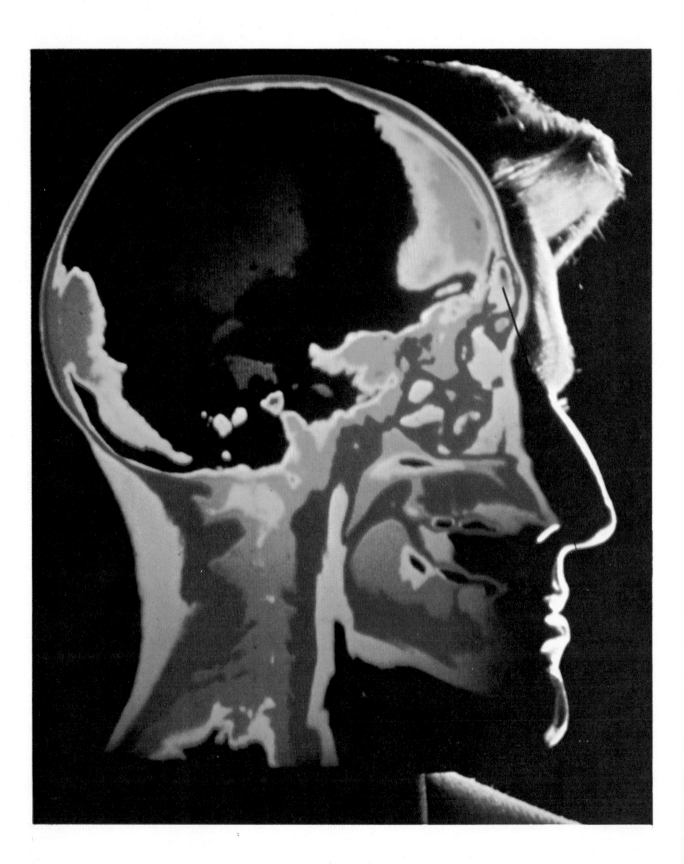

Body and Behavior

There are thirteen billion nerve cells composing your brain. At this moment, some of them are extremely active in handling the information coming in through your eyes. Now, if you take a deep breath and hold it, another set of brain cells will become active, and they will get busier as you read along. Your body will start telling the lower part of your brain, with increasing urgency, that too much carbon dioxide is accumulating and that your body's cells are not getting sufficient oxygen. But as long as you consciously hold your breath, the upper part of brain is telling the lower part not to respond. Nevertheless, the lower part will eventually get its way, and you will be forced to breathe.

This simple experiment effectively demonstrates that you are, among other things, a biological organism built to work in certain ways. By studying the biological nature of man, psychologists have learned a great deal about human behavior that they would not have otherwise discovered.

This chapter will explore those aspects of our biological nature that have the greatest effect on the way we act. It will describe how the nervous system creates and directs behavior, what happens in our bodies when we feel an emotion, and how biological drives influence our life.

THE NERVOUS SYSTEM

FIGURE 4.1
The density scan process, in which the various densities of human tissue are transformed into different colors on photographic film, reveals the layers of protection the body provides for the brain, but tells little of the enormous complexity of what lies within our skulls. In this chapter we will discover some of the biological intricacies and harmonies that underlie our behavior and experience.

In many ways, the nervous system is like the telephone system in a city. Messages are constantly traveling back and forth. As in a telephone system, the messages are basically electrical. They travel along prelaid cables, linked with one another by relays and switchboards. In the body, the cables are *nerve fibers*. The relays are *synapses, the gaps that occur between individual nerve cells.* The switchboards are special cells that are found along the lines of communication (called *interneurons*) and the networks of nerve cells found in the brain and spinal cord. The chief difference is that a telephone system simply conveys messages, while the nervous system actively helps to run the body.

The brain monitors what is happening inside and outside the body by receiving messages from *receptors*—cells whose function is to gather information. The brain sifts through these messages, combines them, and sends out orders to the *effectors*—cells that work the muscles and internal glands and organs. For example, receptors in your eye may send a message

FIGURE 4.2
A representation of a few of the billions of neurons in the human body. These neurons are shown tens of thousands of times bigger than they really are, and just a few of the hundreds of connections between them are shown. One of these neurons (colored blue to distinguish it) has the effect of slowing the firing of the others. The other two have the effect of increasing the firing of any neurons to which they are connected. The connections take place at the synapses, where small amounts of transmitter substances cross the gap from one nerve cell to the other.

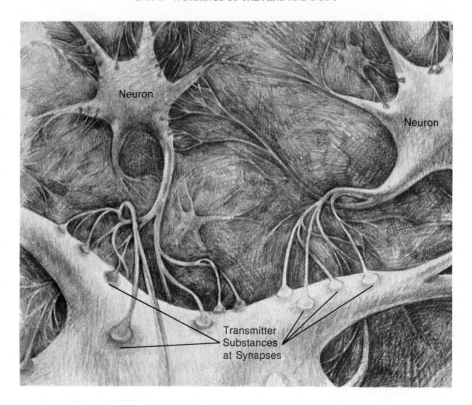

to the brain such as: "Round object. Size increasing. Distance decreasing rapidly." Your brain instantly connects this image with information from memory to identify this object as a baseball. Almost simultaneously your brain orders the effectors in your arms to prepare them for catching the ball.

How the Nervous System Works

Messages to and from the brain travel along the nerves, which are strings of long, thin cells called *neurons* (see Figure 4.2). Chemical-electrical signals travel down the neurons much as flame travels along a firecracker fuse. The main difference is that the neuron can "burn" over and over again, hundreds of times a minute. When a neuron transmits one of these chemical-electrical signals, it is said to be *firing*. When the signal reaches the end or ends of a neuron, it releases chemicals called *transmitter substances* that cross the synapses (gaps) between neurons. These substances make other neurons fire faster or slower. This is how messages travel through the body.

The *central nervous system (CNS)* is a huge mass of neurons clumped together in the brain and spinal cord. You might think of the *spinal cord* as the main cable. It is a bundle of nerves, about as thick as a pencil, running down the length of the back. The spinal cord transmits most of the messages back and forth between the body and the brain.

The spinal cord is well protected by the backbone, just as the brain

FIGURE 4.3
The central nervous system (CNS) and the peripheral nervous system (PNS) in the human body. These systems are made up of billions of nerve cells, or neurons, each of which is capable of transmitting a train of chemical-electrical signals in one direction. In the CNS, these neurons form an immensely complex network that organizes, stores, and redirects vast quantities of information. In the PNS, neurons in every pathway carry information either from receptors (such as the sense organs) toward the CNS or away from the CNS to effectors (in the muscles, for example). There is a close match between information going to the CNS and information coming from it. Every muscle, for example, not only receives from the CNS directions to contract or relax but also sends back information about its present state of contraction or relaxation.

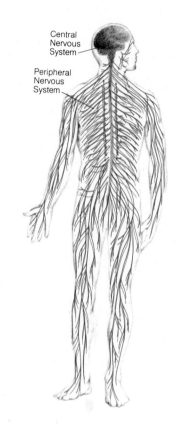

is protected by the skull. This protection prevents interference with the line of communication between the brain and the rest of the body. Without the spinal cord, messages from the brain would never reach any of our muscles except those in the face. We would be paralyzed from the neck down.

Branching out from the spinal cord and, to a lesser extent, from the brain, is a network of nerves called the *peripheral nervous system* (*PNS*) (See Figure 4.3). These nerves conduct information from the bodily organs to the central nervous system and take information back to the organs. The peripheral nervous system is divided into two parts: the autonomic and somatic. The *autonomic nervous system* controls internal biological functions (such as digestion and heart rate); the *somatic nervous system* controls voluntary movement of skeletal muscles (such as lifting your hand to turn a page, which involves a number of coordinated movements).

The Brain

Signals from the receptors in the peripheral nervous system travel up the spinal cord and enter the brain. The first part of the brain the messages reach is the *subcortex*. Together with the spinal cord, the subcortex controls and coordinates such vital functions as sleeping, heart rate, hunger, and digestion. It also controls many reflex actions — blinking, coughing, tearing, and so on.

The subcortex is sometimes called the "old brain" because it is thought to have evolved millions of years ago in our prehuman ancestors; in fact, is resembles the brain found in frogs, fish, and other lower animals. These animals, like humans, need to sleep, eat, digest food, and so on, so it is not surprising that these areas of the brain are similar across many species.

Unlike fish and frogs, people are able to learn to behave in entirely new ways, to think, and to imagine. These powers come from a section of the brain that is miniscule in fish, larger in mammals such as cats and dogs, and huge in humans. This "new brain," the *cerebral cortex*, surrounds the subcortex in humans like a halved peach surrounds the pit. Your subcortex guides your biological needs and "animal instincts." Your cerebral cortex enables you, among other things, to read and to solve problems.

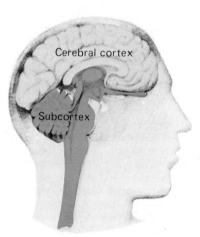

FIGURE 4.4
A cross section of the human brain, showing the subcortex, or lower part of the brain, which humans have in common with most animals, and the cerebral cortex, or upper part of the brain, which humans have in common only with higher animals.

The Subcortex.   The portion of the subcortex that first receives signals is the *reticular formation.* The reticular formation controls an activating network of nerves that runs through the whole brain. This network, the *reticular activating system,* is the brain's waking and attention system. It screens incoming messages, blocking out some signals and letting others pass. During sleep it blocks most inputs, but in response to a loud or unusual sound it sends messages to the rest of the brain, alerting it and raising its activity level to a state of wakefulness.

In the center of the brain is the *thalamus,* the brain's great relaying center. It sorts incoming impulses and directs them to various parts of the brain, and it relays messages from one part of the brain to another.

At the base of the brain, below and to the front of the thalamus, is the *hypothalamus,* a small, closely packed cluster of neurons that is one of the most important parts of the brain. This structure regulates the autonomic nervous system, the system of peripheral nerves that controls internal bodily functioning. The hypothalamus thus regulates such biological functions as digestion, heart rate, and hormone secretion. By sensing the levels of water and sugar in your blood, your hypothalamus can tell when you need food or water and can then cause you to feel hungry or thirsty.

Among its other functions, this portion of the brain regulates body temperature by monitoring the temperature of the blood. If your body

FIGURE 4.5
The structures of the subcortex. (This illustration shows the brain as it would appear if it were sliced exactly in half from front to back.) The structures shown here are the first to receive incoming information, and they regulate all the most fundamental processes of the body. Note that the reticular activating system, which controls the most general responses of the brain to sensory input, is located in the area that connects the brain to the spine and the rest of the nervous system. Also, note that the thalamus has an almost perfectly central location in the brain and that the hypothalamus is very close to the pituitary gland, which controls the activity of the body's other endocrine glands. A few structures of the cerebral cortex are also shown here. Note particularly the corpus callosum, the large band of nerve fibers that connects the two hemispheres of the cerebral cortex.

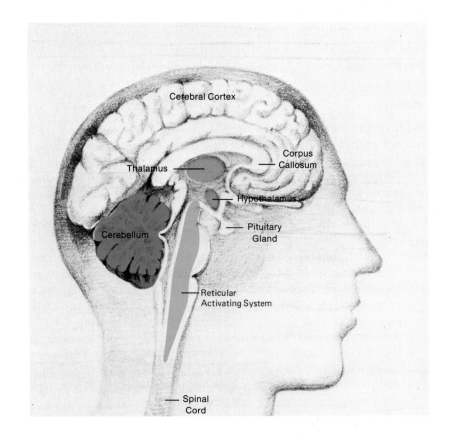

is too cold, the hypothalamus causes tiny vibrations in your muscles (shivering) that bring the temperature up to normal. If your body is too hot, the hypothalamus signals your sweat glands to perspire. As perspiration evaporates, your body is cooled. The hypothalamus also plays an important role in determining emotional responses because it regulates the endocrine system, which will be discussed later in this chapter.

At the very back and bottom of the old brain is the *cerebellum*, the brain's "executive secretary." One of the cerebellum's main functions is to control posture and balance as you move about so that you do not fall over or bump into things. It also helps to regulate the details of major commands from the cerebral cortex. Without your cerebellum, you might hit a friend in the stomach when you reach out to shake hands.

The Cerebral Cortex.   The cerebral cortex, in which most of the higher brain functions take place, is wrapped around the subcortex. It is a great gray mass of ripples and valleys, folded so that its huge surface area can fit inside the skull.

The cerebral cortex is divided into a number of regions, called *lobes* (see Figure 4.6). Some lobes receive specific kinds of information from the senses. Most visual information goes to the *occipital lobes* at the back of the brain. Auditory sensations, or sounds, go primarily to the *temporal lobes* on each side of the brain. The *somatosensory cortex*, located in the

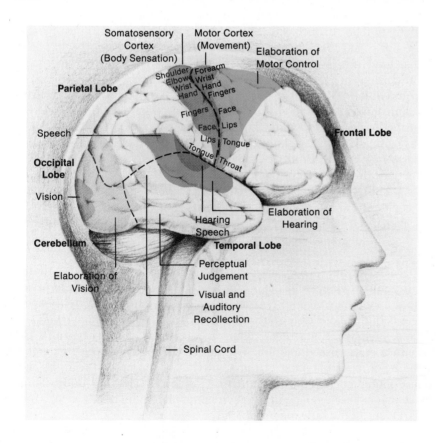

FIGURE 4.6
An external view of the brain from the side. Most of the areas exposed here are parts of the "new" brain. For purposes of reference, the surfaces of each hemisphere of the cortex are divided roughly into the lobes indicated here. The divisions between these lobes are somewhat arbitrary. The functions of the cerebral cortex are not fully understood; areas whose behavioral importance is known are indicated.

FIGURE 4.7
How the body might appear if the parts were proportional to their representation in the sensory and motor areas of the cortex. (*left*) The various regions of the body in the order that they are represented in the area of the brain responsible for bodily sensation. (*right*) A similar orderly arrangement of body regions in the area of the brain that controls muscular movements.

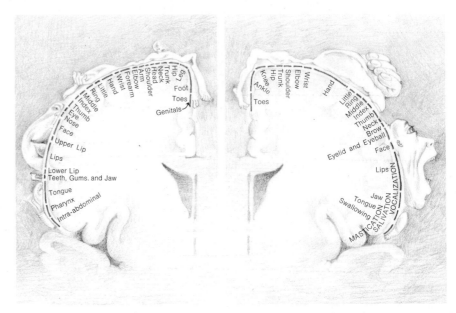

parietal lobes, at the middle of the brain, receives information from the skin senses (such as touch), and from muscles.

The *motor cortex,* which controls body movement, is just in front of the somatosensory cortex, across a deep fold. The motor cortex is part of the *frontal lobes.* It is the area of the brain that controls the parts of the body that perform complex tasks. As you can see from Figure 4.7, areas of the body that receive a great deal of sensory stimulation, such as the hands, send information to both the somatosensory cortex and to the motor cortex.

From what we know, the part of the frontal lobes farthest forward in the skull has nothing to do with bodily functions. This area seems to control creativity and personality: It enables people to be witty, sensitive, or easygoing. How do we know this? Partly by accident. In the mid-1800s, a quarry man named Phineas Gage was injured in an explosion. The force of the blast drove an iron stake through Gage's head, damaging the frontal lobes. Remarkably, Gage survived and was back at work in a few months. The accident did not impair his bodily functions or his memory or skills. However, Gage's personality changed dramatically. This once trustworthy and dependable man became childish, fitful, impatient, and capricious.

The Divided Brain. The cortex is divided into two hemispheres that are roughly mirror images of each other. (Each of the four lobes is present in both hemispheres.) The two hemispheres are connected by a band of nerves called the *corpus callosum,* which carries messages back and forth between the two. Each hemisphere is connected to roughly half of the body in a crisscrossed fashion. The motor cortex of the left hemisphere of the brain controls most of the right side of the body; the right hemisphere motor cortex controls most of the left side of the body. Thus a stroke that causes damage to the right hemisphere will result in numbness or paralysis on the left side of the body.

FIGURE 4.8
This drawing was adapted from one of the sketches made by the doctor who attended Phineas Gage. It shows the path taken by the railroad tamping iron that was propelled through Gage's skull. Gage's intellect did not seem affected by the accident, but aspects of his personality did.

Although the two hemispheres are almost identical, there seem to be major differences in the functions they perform. One piece of evidence for this is handedness. Most people can write with only one hand, usually the right—suggesting that one hemisphere is dominant.

Additional evidence comes from split brain operations, such as that performed on Harriet Lees, who suffered from epilepsy. For most of her life the seizures were mild and could be controlled with drugs. However at age twenty-five they began to get worse, and by thirty Lees was having as many as a dozen violent seizures a day. An epileptic fit usually starts in one hemisphere and spreads to the other. To enable this woman to live a normal life, doctors decided to sever the corpus callosum so that seizures could not spread.

The operation was a success—Lees has not had a seizure since. But something happened to her that has also happened to other people after such surgery. When doctors show the woman a picture while her right eye is covered, she cannot tell them what it is. She sees the picture, and if it is funny or embarrassing she will laugh. If asked to pick the picture out of a series she will select the correct one. But she cannot *say* what it is.

Why is this? Because in most people, the left hemisphere seems to control speech. Remember that the connections between the hemispheres and the left and right sides of the body crisscross. Thus anything seen in the left half of a person's field of vision is transmitted to the right hemisphere. Normally the image is then transferred to the left hemisphere via the corpus callosum. However, when this has been severed, the message is not transferred (Gazzaniga, 1967). Since the left hemisphere controls speech, although Lees sees the image, she cannot speak about it.

Psychologists now believe that this specialization develops over the years. If a child suffers damage to the left hemisphere, the right hemisphere will take over the function of speech. The child may learn more slowly than other children, but he or she will learn to speak. However, almost all adults who suffer damage to the left hemisphere have extreme difficulty speaking—if they can speak at all (Schneider and Tarshis, 1975). Other functions of the brain, such as the ability to discriminate among different sounds or visual patterns, are not so affected by damage to any particular area of the cortex. Although one area may dominate in controlling the function, other parts of the cortex also participate and can take over from the dominant area if necessary (John, 1976). This suggests that learning consists of changes in broad patterns of excitation of the brain cells, not changes in the connections between brain cells. These patterns can occur in many different places in the brain, rather than being confined to one particular set of neurons (John, 1976).

HOW PSYCHOLOGISTS STUDY THE BRAIN

Mapping the brain's mountains, canyons, and inner recesses has supplied scientists with fascinating information about the role of the brain in behavior. Psychologists who do this kind of research are called physiological psychologists. They use three methods for exploring the brain: recording, stimulation, and lesioning.

Recording

By inserting wires called *electrodes* into the brain, it is possible to detect the minute electrical changes that occur when neurons fire. The wires are connected to electronic equipment that amplifies the tiny voltages produced by the firing neurons. Even single neurons can be monitored. For example, two researchers placed tiny electrodes in the sections of cats' and monkeys' brains that receive visual information from the eye. They found that different neurons fired depending on whether a line, an edge, or an angle were placed before the animal's eyes (Hubel and Wiesel, 1962).

The electrical activity of whole areas of the brain can be recorded with an *electroencephalograph* (EEG). Wires from the EEG machine are taped to the scalp so that millions upon millions of neurons can be monitored at the same time. Psychologists have observed that the overall electrical activity of the brain rises and falls rhythmically and that the pattern of the rhythm depends upon whether a person is awake, drowsy, or asleep (as illustrated in Chapter 7). These rhythms, or brain waves, occur because the neurons in the brain tend to increase or decrease their amount of activity in unison.

EEGs can be used to monitor the brain disorder that causes epilepsy. When an epileptic seizure occurs, abnormal electrical activity begins in a small piece of damaged brain tissue. It then spreads to neighboring areas of the brain until much of the brain is showing abnormally large brain waves on the EEG. By monitoring these brain waves, psychologists can locate the site at which the seizure begins and follow its spread through the brain. This helps doctors to determine what kind of surgical procedure (if any) would reduce violent seizures.

Stimulation

Electrodes may be used to set off the firing of neurons as well as to record it. Brain surgeon Wilder Penfield has stimulated the brains of his patients during surgery to determine what functions the various parts of the brain perform. In this way he could localize the malfunctioning part for which surgery was required, for example, for epilepsy. When Penfield applied a tiny electric current to points on the temporal lobe of the brain, he could trigger whole memory sequences. During surgery, one woman heard a familiar song so clearly that she thought a record was being played in the operating room (Penfield and Rasmussen, 1950).

Using the stimulation technique, other researchers have shown that there are "pleasure" and "punishment" centers in the brain. One research team implanted electrodes in certain areas of the "old brain" of a rat, then placed the rat in a box equipped with a lever that the rat could press. Each time the rat pressed the lever, a mild electrical current was delivered to its brain. When the electrode was placed in the rat's "pleasure" center,

FIGURE 4.9
This animal has an electrode implanted in an area of its "old" brain. Each time the rat presses the lever, a tiny pulse is delivered to its brain. The extremely high rates of lever pressing performed by animals with such implants indicate that a "pleasure center" is probably being stimulated by the electricity.

it would push the lever several thousand times per hour (Olds and Olds, 1965).

Scientists have used *chemicals* as well as electricity to stimulate the brain. In this method, a small tube is implanted in an animal's brain so that the end touches the area to be stimulated. Chemicals can then be delivered through the tube to the area of the brain being studied. Such experiments have shown that different chemicals in the hypothalamus can affect hunger and thirst in an animal.

Stimulation techniques have aroused great medical interest. They are now used with terminal cancer patients to relieve them of intolerable pain without using drugs. A current delivered through electrodes implanted in certain areas of the brain seems to provide a sudden temporary relief (Delgado, 1969). Furthermore, some psychiatrists use similar methods to control violent emotional behavior in otherwise uncontrollable patients.

Lesions

Scientists sometimes cut or destroy a part of an animal's brain to see what function that part performs. In a classic lesion study, two researchers

FIGURE 4.10
The technique for stimulating the inside of a rat's brain with chemicals. (a) The rat is prepared for brain surgery. (b) A small funnel at the top of a tiny tube is permanently implanted in the rat's skull. The other end of the tube is deep inside the brain. (c) A small amount of some chemical that affects the nervous system is passed into the tube in a solution of water. The effects of the chemical stimulation of this area of the brain can then be observed.

a

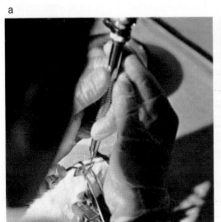

b

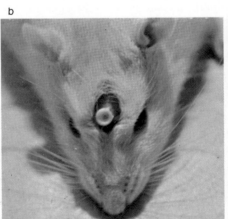

c

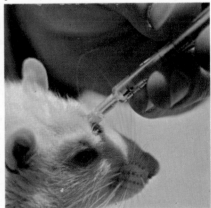

removed a certain area of the subcortex (or "old brain") from rhesus monkeys. Normally, these animals are aggressive and vicious. After the operation they became less fearful and at the same time less violent (Klüver and Bucy, 1937).

We have already discussed the use of lesions in treating violent epileptic seizures (by severing the corpus callosum). Experiments with animals suggest that it might be possible to use similar operations to control violence and other kinds of antisocial behavior in humans who would otherwise have to be isolated from society. However, there is much debate as to whether performing "psychosurgery" is ethical. Encouraged by the positive results of such operations on animals, some neurosurgeons may have overlooked the subtler negative effects on human personality. There is little doubt that this topic will be a source of controversy for some time to come (See Valenstein, 1973).

THE ENDOCRINE SYSTEM

The nervous system is one of two communication systems for sending information to the brain and returning messages to the body's billions of cells. The second is the endocrine, or hormone, system.

The *endocrine system* is a chemical system. Its messages are chemical substances called *hormones,* which are produced by the endocrine glands and distributed by the blood and other body fluids. (The names and locations of these glands are shown in Figure 4.11.) In many ways the endocrine system resembles a postal system. Hormones, or chemical messages, circulate throughout the bloodstream, but are only delivered to a specific address—the particular organs of the body that they influence.

The pituitary and thyroid glands illustrate how hormones work. Together with the brain, the *pituitary gland* is the center of control of the endocrine system—the "master gland." The pituitary gland secretes a large number of hormones, many of which control the output of hormones by other endocrine glands. (The thyroxin-stimulating hormone is but one example.) The brain controls the pituitary gland and so indirectly controls the activity of the others. It also monitors the amount of hormones in the blood and sends out messages to correct imbalances. In return, certain hormones affect the functioning of the brain. For example, recent research indicates that the hormone ACTH improves memory in rats and mice (Rigter *et al.*, 1974). When injected into humans, ACTH reduces anxiety and improves performance on tasks requiring visual attention.

The *thyroid gland* produces the hormone thyroxin. Thyroxin stimulates certain chemical reactions that are important for all tissues of the body. Too little thyroxin makes people feel lazy and lethargic; too much makes them overactive. But the activity of the thyroid gland is itself controlled by a hormone released by the pituitary gland. High levels of thyroxin in the blood reduce the output of the thyroxin-stimulating hormone by the pituitary gland; low levels of thyroxin cause the pituitary gland to produce greater levels of this hormone. The pituitary and thyroid glands thus regulate each other, and the combination regulates general bodily activity.

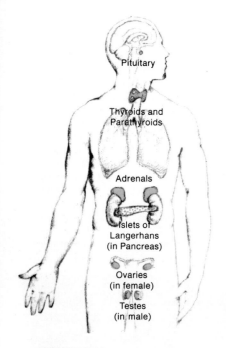

FIGURE 4.11
The endocrine glands. Note how close the pituitary gland is to the brain and refer back to Figure 4.5 to see its association with the hypothalamus. Besides the pituitary, the glands whose activity is most important in the regulation of behavior are the sex glands, the adrenals, and the thyroid.

Through the combined action of the nervous and endocrine systems, the brain monitors and controls most human behavior. In the next section we will see how the endocrine system influences behavior we normally attribute to psychological, not physiological, causes—emotion and motivation.

DRIVES AND FEELINGS: THE PHYSIOLOGY OF MOTIVATION AND EMOTION

Understanding the physiology of motivation and emotion is difficult, because so much of the brain and body is involved. Structures as far removed from each other as the kidneys and the saliva glands play a role in thirst, for example. The sweat glands, the stomach, and the adrenal glands all contribute to the emotion of fear.

A key concept for understanding the relationship between the body and motivation is the biological drive. A *drive* is a physiological state that arises from some kind of physical need, and energizes and directs behavior. The hunger drive, for example, motivates people to look for food.

Emotion is difficult to define, although we all can identify such emotional experiences as joy, grief, anger, and panic. All of these involve a state of physiological arousal combined with specific experiences that enable us to label the emotion. Feelings of joy are usually very different from feelings of anger. In the pages that follow, we will focus on the physiology of motivation and emotion. In the next chapter we will look at the circumstances that shape these processes.

Motivation

All organisms, including humans, have built-in regulating systems which work like thermostats to maintain body temperature, the level of sugar in the blood, the production of hormones, and so on. As we saw earlier, when the level of thyroxin in the bloodstream is low, the pituitary gland secretes a thyroxin-stimulating hormone. When the thyroxin level is high, the pituitary gland stops producing this hormone. Similarly, when your body temperature drops below a certain point, you start to shiver, your blood vessels constrict, and you put on more clothes. All of these activities reduce heat loss and bring body temperature back to the correct level. If your body heat rises above a certain point, you start to sweat, your blood vessels dilate, and you remove clothes. These processes cool you.

The tendency of all organisms to correct imbalances and deviations from their normal state is known as *homeostasis*. Several of the drives that motivate behavior are homeostatic. Hunger is an example.

Hunger.   What motivates people to seek food? Often you eat because the sight and smell of, say, pizza tempts you into a store. Other times you eat out of habit (you always have lunch at 12:30) or to be sociable (a friend invites you out for a snack). But suppose you are working frantically to finish a term paper. You don't have any food in your room, so you ignore the fact that it is dinner time and you keep working. But at some point your body will start to demand food. You'll feel an aching sensation in your stomach. What produces this sensation? What makes you feel hungry?

Your body requires food to function. When you miss a meal, your liver releases stored sugar into your bloodstream to keep you going. After a time, however, this supply runs out and the hypothalamus begins to act.

The hypothalamus, as indicated above, is a structure at the base of the brain that regulates food intake. It not only tells us when we need to eat; it also tells us when to stop eating. How does it work? The hypothalamus is laced with blood vessels that make it extremely sensitive to levels of sugar in the blood. It also has numerous connections to the brain that are capable of raising or lowering the level of certain chemicals in the brain (Ahlskog and Hoebel, 1973). Experiments have shown that this is what makes us crave food or feel too full to eat more.

If the portion of the hypothalamus called the *lateral hypothalamus (LH)* is stimulated with electrodes, a laboratory animal will begin eating, even if it has just finished a large meal. Conversely, if the LH is removed surgically, an animal will stop eating and eventually die of starvation if it is not fed artificially. Thus the LH provides the "go" signals: It tells you to eat.

If a different portion of the hypothalamus, called the *ventromedial hypothalamus (VMH)*, is stimulated, an animal will slow down or stop eating altogether, even if it has been kept from food for a long period. However, if the VMH is removed, the animal will eat everything in sight—until it becomes so obese it can hardly move. This indicates that the VMH provides the "stop" signals: It tells you when you have had enough food.

The level of sugar in the blood is not the only thing that causes the hypothalamus to act. If your stomach is empty, the muscles in the stomach walls contract periodically (producing hunger pangs). These contractions

FIGURE 4.12
(*left*) After the destruction of a small part of its hypothalamus, this rat has overeaten until it is three or four times its normal weight. Interestingly, a rat with this type of lesion will not work for extra food, even though it will eat huge amounts if the food is tasty and easily available. (*right*) A drawing showing the part of the human brain that corresponds to the part lesioned in the rat in (a). This drawing shows a view from the front of the brain, with one of the halves of the brain shown in cross section.

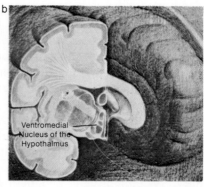

Ventromedial Nucleus of the Hypothalmus

activate the LH, which sends "go" or "eat" signals to your brain. When your stomach is full, the VMH sends "stop" signals to the brain, even though the energy from the food you have just eaten has not yet reached your bloodstream (digestion takes time). In addition, the hypothalamus responds to temperature. The LH, or "go" signal, is more active in cold temperatures; the VMH, or "stop" signal, more active in warm temperatures (presumably because people and other animals need to eat more in cold weather).

In summary, the hypothalamus "interprets" at least three kinds of information: the level of sugar in the blood, the amount of food in the stomach, and body temperature. These determine whether the hypothalamus will tell you (via chemical changes in the brain) to eat or stop eating.

Emotion

We would have a hard time believing that a person who was sitting quietly in a chair was experiencing extreme emotion. We might believe that he or she was remembering, learning, or thinking about something, but not that the person was joyous or furious. We expect people to reveal their stronger emotions through overt behaviors and bodily changes.

Why are emotions tied to behavior and sensations—to changes in the way our bodies feel and the way we look and act? Are there different body states for different emotions? In the pages that follow, we will show how physiological psychologists are attempting to answer these questions. In Chapter 6, we will focus on how people experience and express emotions.

The Role of the Autonomic Nervous System.   Of critical importance in the physiology of emotion is the *autonomic nervous system*, a part of the peripheral nervous system, which, as mentioned earlier, controls the glands, internal organs, and involuntary muscles (such as the heart). The autonomic nervous system itself has two parts: the sympathetic and the parasympathetic systems.

The *sympathetic nervous* system prepares the body for dealing with emergencies or strenuous activities. It speeds up the heart to hasten the supply of oxygen and nutrients to body tissues. It constricts some arteries and relaxes others so that blood flows to the muscles, where it is most needed in emergencies and strenuous activities. It increases the breathing rate and suspends some activities such as digestion.

In contrast, the *parasympathetic nervous system* works to conserve energy and to enhance the body's ability to recover from strenuous activity. It reduces the heart rate, slows breathing, and the like.

Are different autonomic neural patterns associated with different emotions? Researchers have found differences in autonomic activity during fear, anger, hunger, and pain. However, they have not been able to associate subtler emotions such as guilt and jealousy with different patterns of neural activity (Lang, Rice, and Sternbach, 1973).

One interesting fact to emerge from these studies is that autonomic responses vary among individuals. Some people respond with an all-out

FIGURE 4.13

The interactions of neural, endocrine, and other bodily structures in emotion. This diagram is a simplified representation of what is known about the complex systems involved in the physiology of emotion. Orange areas and arrows indicate neural structures and the transmission of information by action potentials in neurons. Broken orange arrows indicate that the transmission is not the sending of specific messages to specific locations but is diffuse and acts to change general levels of activation. Blue areas and arrows indicate endocrine structures and the transmission of information by chemicals in the bloodstream. Note that certain organs—the hypothalamus, the pituitary gland, and part of the adrenal gland—act as transducers between neural and chemical modes of transmission; that is, they receive one kind of transmission and send out the other. Note also that the system is organized in such a way that a structure often receives information from the structures to which it is sending information. This feedback arrangement is important to the control and stability of the system as a whole.

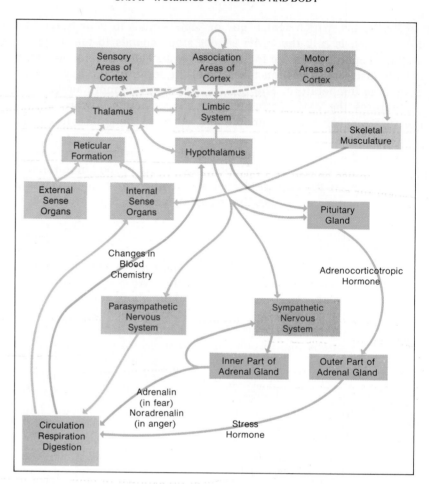

autonomic arousal (a pounding heart, rapid breathing, and so on) to every emotional situation. Others respond only slightly to any emotional situation. Still others respond greatly in some situations and only slightly in others. Thus there is a physiological basis for what people have believed for centuries—there are definite emotional types of individuals.

Stress and Psychosomatic Illnesses

The autonomic changes that occur as an immediate reaction to a threat help a person to mobilize for action—either fight or flight. The perception of a threat thus creates a state of *stress*. Often one can deal with stress on a short-term basis, either by avoiding it or by finding a way to cope with it effectively.

But what happens when a person cannot fight the danger or run away from it? What happens under *chronic stress,* when the strain never stops? In modern society, many threats are not the kind that can be fought or fled. Constant pressure from a tyrannical boss, or the constant threat of competitive pressures in a school are examples of chronic stresses of the sort that were not present when humans first evolved.

One researcher has argued that all types of chronic stress evoke identical physiological responses (Selye, 1956). Whether the stress is the result of prolonged fear or exposure to extreme cold, the body reacts with immediate sympathetic arousal (speeding of the heart and so forth). The endocrine system then acts to sustain this state of arousal. The pituitary gland stimulates the part of the *adrenal glands* that produces hormones that increase blood sugar, for extra energy. At the same time, the brain sends signals to another part of the adrenal glands that secretes *adrenalin*. Adrenalin not only causes rapid heart action and breathing, it enables the body to use energy at a faster rate. All of this is designed to prepare a person for self-defense. However, if stress persists for a long time, the body's resources are used up. The person succumbs to exhaustion and, in extreme cases, death.

Physiological psychologists believe that prolonged stress is probably a major cause of many *psychosomatic diseases*, such as high blood pressure, ulcers, asthma, and spastic colon. Such *diseases* start with a psychological problem, which in turn produces a physical ailment.

"Type A Behavior" and Heart Attacks.   Two researchers have recently suggested that persons who exhibit a behavior pattern they call "Type A" are very likely to have coronary artery disease, often followed by heart attacks, in their thirties and forties. Those who do not have this pattern (Type B people) almost never have heart attacks before the age of seventy (Friedman and Rosenman, 1974).

The Type A person's body is in a chronic state of stress, with an almost constant flow of adrenalin into the bloodstream. This adrenalin apparently interacts with cholesterol or other chemical agents to block the coronary arteries, which lead to the heart. (It may be that high levels of adrenalin prevent the normal chemical breakdown of cholesterol in the blood.)

Type A people are always prepared for fight or flight. They have a great deal of "free-floating" hostility—that is, anger that has no real object or focus. They are extremely irritable, and one of the things that irritates Type A people most is delay of any kind. They become impatient waiting in line, always move and eat rapidly, often try to do two or three things at once (such as reading while eating), and feel guilty when they aren't doing *something*. They are also extremely competitive. In short, Type A people are always struggling—with time, other people, or both. Note that we have been describing an extreme version of the Type A personality. Most people respond to the world with Type A behavior at some times, but are not in a constant state of stress. According to Friedman and Rosenman, about half of the American white male population exhibits enough Type A behavior to bring on the high adrenalin and cholesterol levels that precede coronary disease.

Interestingly, very few American white women have Type A personalities and very few develop coronary diseases. However, those who are Type A have even more heart attacks than do Type A men.

Ulcers and Executives.   In a classic experiment on stress, Joseph Brady

(1958) linked two monkeys together so that they received an equal number of shocks. The only difference between them was that one of the monkeys could prevent the shocks by pushing a lever. The other monkey could not. One of the monkeys developed ulcers. Which was it? The one that was powerless to protect itself? No. It was the other monkey—later named the "executive monkey." Brady concluded that constantly worrying about when to press the lever made this monkey sick.

More recent research suggests that people develop ulcers when they have to make a great many responses, but receive no feedback about whether their responses were correct or not (Weiss, 1971). Lack of feedback produces uncertainty, and uncertainty is stressful. According to this view the "executive monkeys" developed ulcers because they were never sure whether pressing the lever would prevent the shock.

One might extend this reasoning to a group of people known for developing ulcers: human executives. Those who get ulcers are probably men and women who never quite know where they stand with their superiors and those who have to wait years to see if the work they are doing is successful.

Stress is an unavoidable part of life. Physiological responses to stress can assist a person in coping with stress. But the same responses can ultimately cause bodily harm if the stress continues for too long.

THE RELATIONSHIP BETWEEN HUMANS AND ANIMALS

Much of the research described in this chapter has been done primarily with animals. The reason for this recourse to animals is simply that researchers cannot perform a risky operation on a human being without a better reason than scientific inquiry. The research that has been done on humans has either occurred as a part of some necessary medical operation or it has involved observing people who have suffered some injury by accident.

It is now commonly accepted that the study of animals can help in the study of human beings, even though direct experiments on humans would be even more useful if they could be done. Animal studies are especially valuable in medicine and physiology. Drugs, vaccines, and new forms of surgery are regularly tested on animal subjects. The reason that such research is considered useful is that human beings are believed to have evolved from more primitive animal origins and that their bodies are therefore similar to the bodies of other animals.

The Evolution of Behavior

What many people do not often realize is that *evolution* applies not only to anatomy and physiology but also to behavior. Charles Darwin, the biologist who in 1859 published his theory of evolution, believed that all animal species are related to one another. Consequently, the configurations of their bodies and the patterns of their behavior can be distinguished and compared just as one may compare a child's nose or his temper to that of his father. Just as the bones in a bird's wing are different but comparable to the bones in a human arm, so the way birds flock together can be compared to the way humans gather in groups. And just as the parts of a chimpanzee's brain can be compared to a human's, so can a chimpanzee's ability to solve problems be compared to human thinking ability.

Darwin's theory does not mean that humans do not possess unique qualities, but it does make it possible to think of humans as members of a particularly complex, interesting species instead of as totally different from other animals.

Ethology: The Biology of Behavior

One of the major outgrowths of Darwin's theory of evolution is *ethology,* the study of human and animal behavior from a biological point of view. Ethologists are interested in studying the natural behavior patterns of all species of animals. They attempt to understand how these patterns have evolved and changed, and how they are expressed in humans. Ethologists call these natural behavior patterns *species-specific behaviors:* behaviors that are characteristic of a particular animal species. By observing animals in their natural environment, ethologists hope to discover the links between a species' surroundings and its behaviors.

Ethologists have found that the behavior and experience of more primitive animals (such as insects or fish) are less flexible, or more stereotyped, than the behavior of higher animals, such as apes or humans. Stereotyped behaviors consist of patterns of responses that cannot change readily in response to changes in the environment. They work well only if the environment stays as it was when the behavior pattern evolved.

For example, when a horse is confronted with danger and requires a quiet escape, it is impossible for it to tiptoe away. Its escape behavior consists of only three patterns: walking, trotting, and galloping. Each pattern is a distinct series of movements that vary little from one horse to another, and all normal horses display these patterns. Such patterns are called *fixed action patterns* because they are inflexible—an animal can react to certain situations only in these ways.

Fixed action patterns are one kind of *instinct*—a behavior pattern that is inborn rather than learned. People often misuse the word "instinct" to refer to behaviors that become automatic after long practice. A professional baseball player may be described as "instinctively" making the right play, for example. But ethologists use the term "instinct" to refer only to those abilities that seem to be present from birth.

Ethologists have found that animals are born with special sensitivities to certain cues in the environment (as well as with special ways of behaving). These cues are called *sign stimuli.* For example, Niko Tinbergen showed that the male stickleback, a small fish, will attack a model of another stickleback if it has a red belly. Even if the model is distorted, as in Figure 4.14, the male will still attack. Yet if it sees a very lifelike

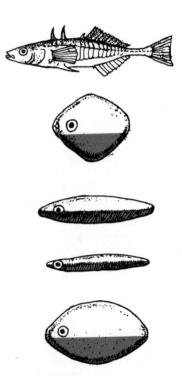

FIGURE 4.14
In the spring the male stickleback develops a bright red belly. This coloration is a sign stimulus for attack from other sticklebacks. They will attack red-bellied models like the ones above before they will respond to a realistic model of a stickleback that does not have a red belly.

FIGURE 4.15
The oystercatcher, a European coastal bird, responds to the sight of its eggs with a pattern of nesting and brooding behavior. The significant aspect of the stimulus seems to be size: If the bird is offered a huge dummy egg, a ''supernormal'' sign stimulus, it will try to brood it rather than its real, regular-sized eggs.

model of a stickleback without a red belly, the male will leave it alone. In this case, the sign stimulus that triggers attack is the color red. In other species other sign stimuli can trigger certain behaviors, as shown in Figure 4.15.

Do sign stimuli occur in humans? Although instincts are less common and less powerful in human behavior, there is evidence that some stereotyped behaviors exist. For example, Konrad Lorenz found that a "parental

FIGURE 4.16
Certain stimulus patterns seem to trigger predictable sets of responses even in human beings. The profiles on the right of each pair all share certain features that trigger the kind of feeling in humans that makes people smile and say, ''Isn't he cute?'' The adult profiles elicit no such response. In this sense, then, humans can be said to have certain instinctive reactions in common with animals.

instinct" seems to be aroused by the appearance of the human baby. When he compared human infants to other young animals, he noticed that they all seem to display a similar set of sign stimuli which appear to stir up parental feelings. Short faces, prominent foreheads, round eyes, and plump cheeks all seem to arouse the parental response (see Figure 4.16). Generally, though, automatic inborn reactions seem to play a fairly minor role in human behavior.

HEREDITY AND ENVIRONMENT

People often argue about whether human behavior is instinctive (due to heredity) or learned (due to environment). Do people learn to be good athletes, or are they born that way? Do people learn to do well in school, or are they born good at it? Do people learn to be homosexual, or are they born that way? The reason for the intensity of the argument is that something learned can probably be changed, whereas something inborn will be difficult or impossible to change. But whenever psychologists investigate a particular case they find that the issue is not that simple. In every case inherited factors and environmental conditions act together in complicated ways. Asking whether heredity or environment is responsible for something always turns out to be like asking, "What makes a cake rise, baking powder or heat?" Obviously, an interaction of the two is responsible.

In some cases, the relationship between heredity and environment is obvious. If a boy inherits his tallness from his parents, there is a greater likelihood that he can become an outstanding basketball star—but he has to learn to play basketball first. Other cases are much more complex.

Ethologists have studied the dynamic relationship between heredity and environment by asking questions like, "What makes a bird able to sing its own song?" A chaffinch is born able to produce all the parts of the chaffinch song even if it has never heard another chaffinch. The ability of the bird to sing is inherited. However, the isolated bird does not put the parts together properly unless it hears other chaffinches. If it listens to tape recordings of backward songs, it begins to sing its own song backward. In this case, the bird couples instinct with learning to produce unusual songs.

These findings are readily applicable to the human situation, keeping in mind that human beings are more flexible and capable of learning than any other species. Environmental influences play such a large part in human life that the hereditary influences may be hard to see. Significantly more than chaffinches, humans may develop differently depending on the experiences they have. There has been particularly intense discussion of this matter with regard to sex roles (see Chapters 8 and 9) and intelligence (see Chapter 17).

But it should not be concluded that human beings are infinitely flexible. This chapter has shown that the human body, like the bodies of other animals, is built to work in certain ways. The huge cortex of the human brain enables us to change ourselves and our environment more than any other animal can, but we remain animals. We must live with hunger and thirst, fear and desire, anger and pain. We cannot escape these natural processes even if we want to.

FIGURE 4.17

The interaction of heredity and environment can be seen in the behaviors of this domesticated wolf. Although this wolf has never heard or seen another of its species since birth, it does not have to be taught to howl. Certain stimuli, in this case the sound of a clarinet, will bring out this inherited behavior. An innate ability might be best thought of as something that is very easily learned. Other abilities may be less easily learned depending on the inheritance of the organism. Wolves, for example, find it fairly easy to learn to shake hands because they have some innate tendencies to use their paws in this way. It is much more difficult to teach a wolf to sit because sitting is not something wolves naturally do.

SUMMARY

1. Messages are constantly traveling back and forth in the body, through the nervous system, to the brain. The spinal cord, located in the nervous system, transmits most of the messages back and forth between the body and the brain. The messages to and from the brain are communicated by chemical-electrical signals traveling down long, thin cells called neurons.

2. The brain monitors what is happening inside and outside of the body through the use of receptors and effectors. The brain is composed of the cerebral cortex and the subcortex. The subcortex guides a person's biological needs and animal instincts. The cerebral cortex enables a person to read and solve problems.

3. The cortex is divided into two hemispheres,

each containing four lobes. The left hemisphere controls the right side of the body, while the right hemisphere controls the left.

4. The endocrine or hormone system is a chemical system of communication between the body and the brain. Through the combined action of the nervous and endocrine systems, the brain monitors and controls most of human behavior.

5. The physiology of motivation and emotions involves the brain and many parts of the body. The concept of "drive" is central to understanding the relationship between the body and motivation.

6. Several of the drives that motivate human behavior are homeostatic, that is, they represent

a need to correct deviations from the normal state.

7. The autonomic nervous system plays a key role in the physiology of emotion. One of its components, the sympathetic nervous system, prepares the body for dealing with emergencies or strenuous activities. The parasympathetic nervous system, the other part of the autonomic nervous system, works to conserve energy and to enhance the body's ability to recover from strenuous activity.

8. Physiological psychologists believe that chronic stress is probably a major cause of many psychosomatic illnesses. Both heart disease and ulcers may result from chronic stress.

9. Studies of animal behavior have revealed that many species respond to their environments in terms of fixed action patterns, that is, they can react to certain situations only in set ways—such automatic responses play a minor role in human behavior.

10. Inherited factors and environmental conditions work together in complicated ways in all human beings, but often environmental influences play such a large part in human life that the hereditary influences may be hard to see.

GLOSSARY

adrenal glands: The glands that produce adrenalin and other hormones that increase energy.

adrenalin: The substance produced by the adrenal glands which enables the body to use energy at a faster rate, thus preparing a person to defend him- or herself.

autonomic nervous system: The half of the peripheral nervous system that controls internal biological functions.

central nervous system (CNS): A huge mass of neurons clumped together in the brain and spinal cord.

cerebellum: The lower bottom portion of the brain, which controls posture and balance and regulates the details of major commands from the cerebral cortex.

cerebral cortex: The gray mass surrounding the subcortex, which controls most of the higher brain functions, such as reading and problem solving.

corpus callosum: A band of nerves which connects the two hemispheres of the cortex and carries messages back and forth between them.

drive: A physiological state which arises from some kind of physical need and energizes and directs behavior.

effectors: The cells that work the muscles, internal glands, and organs.

electrode: A type of wire used by scientists to detect the minute electrical changes that occur when neurons fire.

electroencephalograph (EEG): A machine used to record the electrical activity of whole areas of the brain.

endocrine system: A chemical communication system, using hormones, by which messages are sent through the bloodstream to particular organs of the body.

ethology: The study of human and animal behavior from a biological point of view.

firing: The transmitting, by a neuron, of a chemical-electrical signal across the synapse to another neuron.

fixed action patterns: Patterns of behavior that are inflexible. Such responses are common to many animal species, but not to humans.

frontal lobes: The lobes located in the front of the brain, which control intellect and personality.

homeostasis: The tendency of all organisms to correct imbalances and deviations from their normal state.

hormones: The chemical substances produced by the blood and body fluids that carry messages to certain parts of the body.

hypothalamus: A small cluster of neurons in the brain which regulate the autonomic nervous system.

instinct: A behavior pattern that is inborn rather than learned.

interneurons: The special cells which link together nerve fibers.

lateral hypothalamus (LH): The part of the hypothalamus that produces hunger signals.

lobes: The different regions into which the cerebral cortex is divided.

motor cortex: The portion of the brain located in the front of the somatosensory cortex, which controls body movement.

nerve fibers: The slender threadlike pieces of nerve cells through which messages are sent to the brain.

neurons: The long thin cells that constitute the structural and functional unit of nerve tissue, along which messages travel to and from the brain.

new brain: Another name for the cerebral cortex.

occipital lobes: The lobes located at the back of the brain, which receive visual information for the body.

old brain: Another name for the *subcortex*.

parasympathetic nervous system: The system which works to conserve energy and enhance the body's ability to recuperate after strenuous activity.

parietal lobes: The lobes located in the middle of the brain, which contain the somatosensory cortex.

peripheral nervous system (PNS): A network of nerves branching out from the spinal cord which conduct information from the bodily organs to the central nervous system and take information back to the organs.

pituitary gland: The center of control of the endocrine system which secretes a large number of hormones.

psychosomatic disease: A disease that originates with a psychological problem and develops into a physical ailment.

receptors: Cells whose function it is to gather information and send messages to the brain.

reticular activating system: The system in the brain that screens oncoming messages, blocking out some signals and letting others pass.

reticular formation: The portion of the subcortex that first receives signals and controls an activating network of nerves that run through the whole brain.

somatic nervous system: The half of the peripheral nervous system that controls voluntary movement of skeletal muscles.

somatosensory cortex: An area of the brain, within the cerebral cortex, that receives information from the skin and muscles.

species-specific behavior: Behavior that is characteristic of a particular animal species.

spinal cord: The bundle of nerves that run down the length of the back and transmit most messages back and forth between the body and the brain.

stress: An emotional state, characterized by physical strain, which arises from the perception of a threat.

subcortex: The part of the brain where all messages are first received and which, together with the spinal cord, controls and coordinates vital functions and reflex actions. It is sometimes called the "old brain."

sympathetic nervous system: The system that prepares the body for dealing with emergencies or strenuous activities.

synapses: The gaps that occur between individual nerve cells.

temporal lobes: The lobes on each side of the brain, which receive auditory information.

thalamus: The portion of the brain that sorts incoming impulses and directs them to various parts of the brain. It also relays messages from one part of the brain to another.

thyroid gland: The gland in the endocrine system that produces several hormones, including thyroxin.

thyroxin: A hormone that stimulates chemical reactions important for all tissues of the body

and regulates the rate of an individual's activity.

transmitter substances: The chemicals released by neurons which determine the rate at which other neurons fire.

ventromedial hypothalamus (VMH): The part of the hypothalamus that produces feelings of fullness as opposed to hunger, and causes one to stop eating.

ACTIVITIES

1. Try eliminating salts or sweets from your diet for a few days, and observe the changes in your desire for those substances. Describe the changes in their taste and smell as a result of deprivation.

2. Can you observe species-specific behaviors in cats, dogs, or any other animals you see regularly? If you have an animal that you can observe carefully, try to identify fixed action patterns that are common to the animal's species. Do they exist in any form in yourself?

3. What aspects of your personality, your way of acting, and your appearance are most obviously the result of heredity? Which seem to be more related to your environmental upbringing? What factors make it difficult to decide whether hereditary or environmental factors are of greatest influence?

4. To gain a clearer understanding of the range

of emotional reactions you experience, keep an "emotion diary" for one day. Try to jot down what you felt, how you interpreted your feelings, and what brought on your reaction. At the end of the day, analyze your diary to determine the differences in physiological reactions that you experienced in response to each situation. What conclusions can you draw about your emotional responses on that day?

5. Ask several of your friends (individually) to perform some mental task, such as multiplying 31 by 24 in their heads, or counting the number of letters in a simple phrase (such as "early to bed"). Observe which way their eyes shift as they begin to think about the problem. If their eyes shift to the right, they are doing the counting in the left hemisphere of the cortex, and vice versa. For more information about the significance of this simple observation, see the Bakan article mentioned in the Suggested Readings.

SUGGESTED READINGS

BAKAN, P. "The Eyes Have It." *Psychology Today* (April 1971): 64–67, 96. Here Bakan describes his observation that the direction people look in when they think is related to the part of their cortex involved with thinking. He relates this to split-brain research.

CRICHTON, MICHAEL. *The Terminal Man.* New York: Knopf, 1972. An engrossing novel about

a man who is turned into a machine, with forty microscopic wires buried in his head. At the end of the novel is a five-page annotated scientific appendix on mind control.

FRENCH, GILBERT M. *Cortical Functioning in Behavior: Research and Commentary.* Glenview, Ill.: Scott, Foresman, 1973. Up-to-date readings and commentary dealing with current views on localization of function within the cortex.

KIMBLE, DANIEL P. *Psychology as a Biological Science.* Pacific Palisades, Calif.: Goodyear, 1973. A readable elementary introduction to physiological psychology.

LAWICK-GOODALL, JANE VAN. *In the Shadow of Man.* Boston: Houghton Mifflin, 1971. For ten years Jane Goodall lived in the midst of wild chimpanzees, and in this book she writes about their social structure, their behavior, and their personalities somewhat as if they comprised an interesting and intimate circle of friends. The narrative style of the book reads much like a good novel—it is difficult to put down.

LORENZ, KONRAD Z. *King Solomon's Ring.* New York: Crowell, 1952. A classic study of nature by one of the world's outstanding scientists. An absorbing and beautiful book of essays; light and easy to read.

LUCE, GAY G. *Body Time: Physiological Rhythms and Social Stress.* New York: Pantheon, 1971. Survey of data and theories on how biological rhythms affect behavior and mental life.

MC GAUGH, J., WEINBERGER, N. M., AND WHALEN, R. L., (EDS.). *Psychobiology.* San Francisco: Freeman, 1967. A volume of readings from *Scientific American* on the biological basis of behavior. Research in numerous disciplines is included in this comprehensive book.

OLDS, J. "Ten Milliseconds into the Brain." *Psychology Today* (May 1975): 45–48. The author discusses the way he has tracked the changes in the brain caused by learning.

TAYLOR, J. G. *The Shape of Minds to Come: A Startling Report on the Mind-Mechanics of the Future.* Baltimore: Penguin, 1975. A popular discussion of the possible applications of current research on brain stimulation and recording from brain cells.

THOMAS, D. W., AND MAYER, J. "The Search for the Secret of Fat." *Psychology Today* (September 1973): 74–76, 79. The authors relate research on the hypothalamus to weight control in both rats and humans. They also discuss the interaction of the physiological factors with environmental cues for eating.

BIBLIOGRAPHY

AHLSKOG, J. ERIC, AND HOEBEL, BARTLEY G. "Overeating and Obesity from Damage to a Noradrenergic System in the Brain." *Science,* 182 (1973): 166–169.

BRADY, JOSEPH V. "Ulcers in 'Executive' Monkeys." *Scientific American,* 199 (October 1958): 95–100.

DELGADO, J. M. R. *Physical Control of the Mind.* New York: Harper & Row, 1969.

FRIEDMAN, M., AND ROSENMAN, R. H. *Type A Behavior and Your Heart.* New York: Knopf, 1974.

GAZZANIGA, MICHAEL S. "The Split Brain in Man." *Scientific American,* 217 (August 1967): 24–29.

HILDEGARD, E. R., ATKINSON, R. C., AND ATKINSON, R. L. *Introduction to Psychology.* 6th ed. New York: Harcourt Brace Jovanovich, 1975.

HUBEL, DAVID H., AND WIESEL, TORSLEN N. "Receptive Fields, Binocular Interaction, and Functional Architecture in the Cat's Visual Cortex." *Journal of Physiology,* 160 (1962): 106–154.

JOHN, E. R. "How the Brain Works: A New Theory." *Psychology Today,* 9 (May 1976): 48–52.

KLÜVER, H., AND BUCY, P. C., "Psychic Blindness and Other Symptoms Following Bilateral Temporal Lobectomy in Rhesus Monkeys." *American Journal of Physiology,* 119 (1937): 532–535.

LANG, PETER J., RICE, DAVID G., AND STERNBACH,

RICHARD A. "The Psychophysiology of Emotion."
In N. S. Greenfield and R. A. Sternbach (eds.),
Handbook of Psychophysiology. New York:
Holt, Rinehart and Winston, 1973.

OLDS, J., AND OLDS, M. E. "Drives, Rewards and
the Brain." In F. Barron, *et al., New Directions
in Psychology II.* New York: Holt, Rinehart and
Winston, 1965.

PENFIELD, WILDER, AND RASMUSSEN, THEODORE.
The Cerebral Cortex of Man. New York: Macmillan, 1950.

RIGTER, H., VAN RIEZE, H., AND WIED, D. D.
"The Effects of ACTH and Vasopressin Ana-
logues on CO_2-induced Retrograde Amnesia

in Rats." *Physiology and Behavior,* 13 (1974):
381–388.

SCHNEIDER, A. M., AND TARSHIS, B. *An Introduction to Physiological Psychology.* New York:
Random House, 1975.

SELYE, HANS. *The Stress of Life.* New York: Mc-
Graw-Hill, 1956.

VALENSTEIN, E. *Brain Control: A Critical Examination of Brain Stimulation and Psychosurgery.*
New York: Wiley, 1973.

WEISS, JAY M. "Effects of Coping Behavior in
Different Warning-Signal Conditions on Stress
Pathology in Rats." *Journal of Comparative and
Physiological Psychology,* 77 (1971): 1-13.

5 Awareness of the World

FIGURE 5.1
The play of light on our surroundings allows us to comprehend their nature, normally without a second thought. It is only when we must stop to puzzle out "what must be happening here" that we become aware of the complex processes normally occurring in the act of perception.

In the next few seconds, something peculiar will start hap pening to the material youa rereading. Iti soft ennotre alized howcom plext heproces sofrea ding is. Afe w sim plerear range mentscan ha vey oucomp lete lycon fused!

As you can see, your success in gathering information from your environment, interpreting this information, and acting on it depends considerably on its being organized in ways you already expect. By the end of this chapter, you will have begun to understand why this is so.

Your knowledge of the external world—and of your internal state as well—comes entirely from chemical and electrical processes occurring in the nervous system, particularly in the brain (as indicated in the preceding chapter). Basically what happens is this. Physical change in the external or internal environment triggers chemical-electrical activity in sense receptors. After a complex series of sequential processing in the nervous system, a pattern of activity is produced in certain areas of the brain. You experience this electrical activity as a *sensation*—awareness of colors, forms, sounds, smells, tastes, and so on. Usually you experience some meaningful whole—you see a person, hear a voice, smell perfume—rather than a collection of sensations. The organization of sensory information into meaningful wholes is known as *perception*.

This entire process can be seen in the simple act of eating. Food stimulates receptors in your eyes to send messages to the brain about the size, shape, and color of the food. Receptors in your nose and mouth inform the brain of the food's taste and odor. Receptors in your hands provide additional input as to the texture and heat of the food. The brain combines ball these inputs into the perception of the particular food, whether an apple, a hamburger, or blue cheese.

In this chapter we will look at each of these steps more closely, focusing on how each organ converts physical changes into chemical-electrical signals to the brain and how perceptions are built from this information. In the last section we will discuss the possibility of gaining information without the known senses—through the process of extrasensory perception.

SENSATION

The world is filled with physical changes—an alarm clock sounds; a flip of a switch fills the room with light; you stumble against a door; steam

101

from a hot tub billows out into the bathroom, changing the temperature and clouding the mirror. All these changes result in sensations—of loudness, brightness, pain in the elbow you bump, heat, tastes, smells, and so on. Any change in the environment to which an organism responds is called a *stimulus.* An alarm, an electric light, and an aching muscle are all stimuli for human beings.

A stimulus can be measured in some way—by its size, its duration, its intensity, its wavelength, and so on. A sensory experience can also be measured (at least, indirectly). But a sensory experience and a stimulus are not the same. For example, the same English muffin (stimulus) might taste (sensory experience) one way if you had just eaten thirty other muffins and quite a different way if you hadn't eaten anything for a week. On the other hand, the same sensory experience (flashing lights, for example) might be produced by different stimuli (a blow to the head or a fireworks display).

Psychologists are interested in the relationship between stimuli and sensory experiences. In vision, for example, the chief stimulus is light. People exposed to this stimulus experience the sensations of color and brightness. The sensation of color corresponds to the *wavelength* of the light, whereas brightness corresponds to the *intensity* of this stimulus.

What is the relationship between color and wavelength? How does changing a light's intensity affect one's sensation of its brightness? The psychological study of such questions is called *psychophysics.* The goal of psychophysics is to develop a quantified relationship between stimuli from the world (such as frequency and intensity) and the sensory experiences (such as pitch and loudness) produced by them.

FIGURE 5.2
This sequence of colored circles gradually decreases in brightness until the last circle cannot be distinguished from the surrounding blackness. In the next-to-last frame, there is a just-noticeable difference between the brightness of the circle and its surroundings, and you can just barely tell that the circle is there. In the final frame the circle is said to have gone below the threshold. Its brightness is no longer sufficient for you to distinguish it.

Threshold

In order to establish laws about how people sense the external world, psychologists first try to determine how much of a stimulus is necessary for a person to sense it at all. How much energy is required for someone to hear a sound or to see a light? How much of a scent must be in the room before one can smell it? How much pressure must be applied to the skin before a person will feel it?

To answer such questions, a psychologist might set up the following experiment. First, a person (the subject) is placed in a dark room and is instructed to look at the wall. He is asked to say, "I see it," when he is able to detect a light. The psychologist then uses an extremely precise machine that can project a low-intensity beam of light against the wall. The experimenter turns on the machine to its lowest light projection. The subject says nothing. The experimenter increases the light until finally the subject responds, "I see it." At this point, the experimenter has determined the subject's *absolute threshold*—the smallest amount of energy that will produce a sensation. The absolute threshold is the amount of energy that makes the subject say, "Yes, I experience the sensation," about half the time it is presented.

After reaching the threshold, the experimenter continues to slowly increase the light. At first the subject detects no change, but as the light is increased, he finally responds, "I see a difference." The experimenter can now establish how much increase in light energy is necessary for the subject to experience a change in sensation. The smallest change in the light that produces a change in sensation ("I see a difference") about half the time is called the *difference threshold*.

Sensory Ratios

By conducting such experiments, psychologists have found that a particular sensory experience depends more on *changes* in the stimulus than on the absolute size or amount of the stimulus. For example, if you put a three-pound package of food into an empty backpack, the sensation of weight will be greatly increased. But if you add the same amount to a hundred-pound backpack, the sensation will hardly increase at all. This is because sensation of weight reflects the proportional change in weight—and three pounds is not much change at all in a one-hundred-pound load.

In psychophysics, this idea is known as *Weber's law:* The larger or stronger a stimulus, the larger the change required for an observer to notice that anything has happened to it (to experience a just-noticeable difference) (Weber, 1834).

The amount of stimulus change necessary to produce some increase in sensory experience is different for different senses, but it is always proportional. Suppose, for example, that you have a glass of unsweetened lemonade. In order to make it sweet, you add two spoonfuls of sugar. Now to make the lemonade taste "twice as sweet," you must add six spoonfuls—three times the original amount of sugar. Then you discover that in order to make the lemonade "four times as sweet," you must add a total of eighteen spoonfuls. Each time the sweetness doubles, the amount of sugar triples (see Stevens, 1962).

By experimenting in this way with variations in sounds, temperatures, pressures, colors, tastes, and smells, psychologists are learning more about how each sense responds to stimulation. Some senses produce huge increases in sensation in response to small increases in energy. For example, the pain of an electric shock can be increased more than eight times by doubling the voltage.

FIGURE 5.3
These lines help to demonstrate Weber's law. Most people can detect the difference between the two short lines more readily than they can between the two long lines. Yet the difference between the two long lines is actually greater. If you have a three-way light bulb, you can try another demonstration. Compare the difference in sensory experience between 50 and 100 watts to the difference between 100 and 150 watts. The wattage difference is the same in both cases, but is your judgment of the brightness difference also the same? According to Weber's law, which difference should appear to be greater?

Sensory Adaptation

Psychologists have focused on people's responses to changes in stimuli because they have found that the senses are tuned to change: They are most responsive to increases and decreases, to new events rather than to ongoing, unchanging stimulation. This is because our senses have a general ability to *adapt,* or adjust themselves, to a constant level of stimulation. They get used to a new level and respond only to changes away from it.

A good example of this process of adaptation is the increase in visual sensitivity that you experience after a short time in a darkened movie theater. At first you see only blackness, but after a while your eyes adapt to the new level, and you can see seats, faces, and so on. Adaptation occurs for the other senses as well: Receptors in your skin adapt to the cold water when you go for a swim; disagreeable odors in a lab seem to disappear after a while; street noises cease to bother you after you've lived in a city for a time. Without sensory adaptation, you would feel the constant pressure of the clothes on your body, and other stimuli would seem to be bombarding all your senses at the same time.

Effects of Motivation

Sensory experience does not depend on stimulus alone, however. A person's ability to detect a stimulus also depends on motivation. The individual does not simply receive a signal passively—rather, one's perceptual system makes a decision as to its presence, though the decision process is usually entirely unconscious.

For example, if you are anxious for a class to end, you may think you hear the bell ring even when it has not. On the other hand, you may be so involved in a classroom discussion that you don't notice that the bell has rung until you see other people collecting their books. Thus feelings and motivations influence whether or not you experience a sensation, regardless of the presence or level of the stimulus.

THE SENSES

Although traditionally people are thought to have five senses, there are actually many more. In addition to vision, hearing, taste, and smell, there are several skin senses and two "internal" senses: vestibular and kinesthetic.

Each type of sensory receptor takes some sort of external stimulus—light, chemical molecules, sound waves, pressure—and converts it into a chemical-electrical message that can be understood by the brain. So far we know most about these processes in vision and hearing; the other senses have received less attention and are a bit more mysterious in their functioning.

Vision

Vision is the most studied of all the senses, reflecting the high importance we place on our sense of sight. Vision provides a great deal of information about one's environment and the objects in it—the sizes, shapes, and locations of things, and their textures, colors, and distances.

How does vision occur? Light enters the eye through the *pupil* (see Figure 5.4a) and reaches the *lens,* a flexible structure that focuses light on the *retina,* which contains the light-sensitive receptor cells. The retina contains two types of light-sensitive receptors: the *rods* and the *cones* (see Figure 5.4b). These are the cells responsible for changing the light energy into chemical impulses, which then travel over the *optic nerve* to the brain.

The cones require more light than the rods before they begin to respond; they work best in daylight. The rods are sensitive to much lower levels of light than the cones and are particularly useful in night vision. There are many more rods (75 to 150 million) than there are cones (6 to 7 million), but only the cones are sensitive to color. The rods and cones can be compared to black-and-white and color film: Color film takes more light and thus works best in daylight; sensitive black-and-white film works not only in bright light but in shadows, dim light, and other poor lighting conditions.

Color Blindness.   When some or all of a person's cones do not function properly, he or she is said to be color-blind. There are several kinds of color blindness; most color-blind people do see *some colors.* For example, some people have trouble distinguishing between red and green. Other people are able to see red and green but cannot distinguish between yellow and blue. A very few people are totally color-blind. They depend on their rods, so to them the world looks something like black-and-white television programs—nothing but blacks and whites and shades of gray.

Color blindness affects about 8 percent of American men and less than 1 percent of American women. It is believed to result from a hereditary

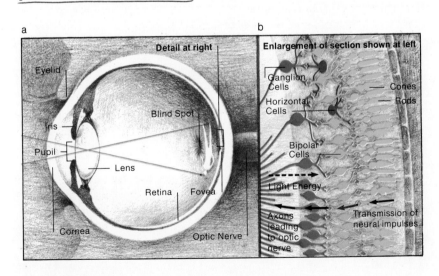

FIGURE 5.4
The process of vision. (a) A cross-section of the human eye, showing the passage of light. Note that the eye receives an inverted image of the external world, although people are never aware of this inversion. The place where the optic nerve leaves the eye is called the blind spot because it is the only spot on the retina where no sensation takes place. (b) The cell structure of the retina. Note that the light-sensitive cells (the rods and cones) are those furthest from the light, not the closest as one might expect. Light arriving at the retina must pass through various other cells before striking the rods and cones, which convert it into nervous impulses. The impulses then pass through these other cells to be coded and organized before traveling over the optic nerve to the brain.

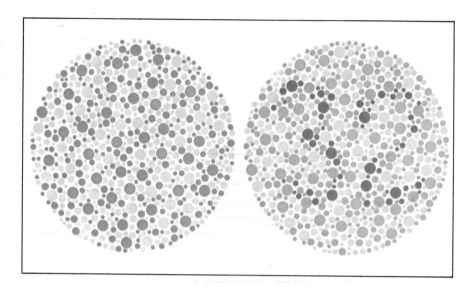

FIGURE 5.5
A test for color blindness. You should be able to see numerals in the dot patterns that make up these two figures. If you cannot distinguish the numerals in the circle on the left, you may be yellow-blue color-blind. If you cannot see those on the right, you may be red-green color-blind. Color-blind people use brightness differences to distinguish objects that most other people distinguish by color. In this test the dots are carefully equated for brightness, so the only way to see the numerals is to see the color differences. Due to the limitations of color printing, the illustration here may not pick up all cases of color blindness.
(The Dvorine Pseudo-Isochromatic Plates.)

FIGURE 5.6
To experience stereoscopic depth perception, take a tall, thin piece of cardboard and place it perpendicular to the page on the line that marks the separation of the two pictures. Then, with the edge of the cardboard resting between your eyes (as shown in the drawing), look at the left photo with your left eye and the right photo with your right eye and try to let the two images come together as one. (It helps to concentrate on the white dot.) If you are successful in fusing the images, the scene will suddenly jump out in depth. Children's Viewmaster slides work on the same principle: Two slightly different images of the same scene fuse to produce a single, three-dimensional image. This process of binocular fusion contributes continuously to your ability to perceive depth.

defect in the cones. This defect is carried in the genes of women whose vision is usually normal; these women pass the color blindness genes on to their sons, who are born color-blind (see Wald, 1964).

Binocular Fusion and Stereopsis.   Because we have two eyes, located 2.5 inches apart, the visual system receives two images. But instead of seeing double, we see a single image, probably a composite of the views of two eyes. The combination of the two images into one is called *binocular vision*.

Not only does the visual system receive two images, but there is a difference between the images on the retinas. This difference is called *retinal disparity*. You can easily observe retinal disparity by bringing an object such as an eraser close to your eyes. Without moving it, look at the eraser first with one eye, then with the other. You will see a difference

in the two images because of the different viewpoint each eye has. When you open both eyes you will no longer see the difference, but will instead see the object as solid and three-dimensional, if you have good binocular vision. The derivation of depth from retinal disparity is called *stereopsis*.

Hearing

Hearing depends on vibrations of the air, called sound waves. Sound waves from the air pass through various bones and fluids (shown in Figure 5.7) until they reach the inner ear, which contains tiny hairlike cells that move back and forth (much like a field of wheat waving in the wind). These hair cells change sound vibrations into chemical-electrical signals that travel through the *auditory nerve* to the brain.

The main functions of hearing are to detect, identify, and locate sounds. We detect the source and distance of a sound largely on the basis of *loudness*. The sensation of loudness depends on the strength of the vibrations in the air. This strength, or energy, is measured in *decibels*. The sounds we hear range upward from zero decibels, the softest sound the human ear can detect, to about 140 decibels, which is roughly as loud as a jet plane taking off. Any sound over 110 decibels can damage hearing, and any sound that is painful when you first hear it *will* damage your hearing if you hear it often enough. Figure 5.8 lists the decibel levels of some common sounds.

We identify sounds—that is, we determine what we are hearing—chiefly through pitch. *Pitch depends on sound frequency, or the rate of the vibration of the medium through which the sound is transmitted.* Frequencies range from low to high: Low frequencies produce deep bass sounds; high frequencies produce shrill squeaks. If you hear a sound composed of a combination of different frequencies, you can hear the separate pitches

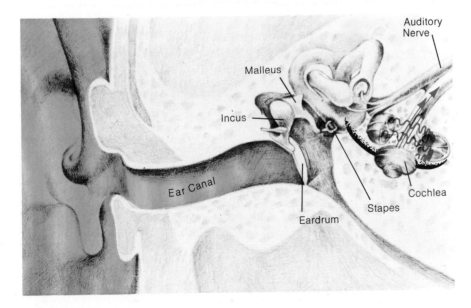

FIGURE 5.7
The hearing process. Sound vibrations in the air strike the eardrum and set a chain of three tiny bones into motion. These bones are attached to another drum, the oval window, which sets up vibrations in the fluid of the inner ear. The vibrations travel through the cochlea, a long coiled tube with a skinlike membrane running down the center of it. (The dotted line in the diagram represents the end of the cochlea that attaches to the oval window.) Stimulation of the hair cells on this membrane causes them to convert the vibrations into electrical impulses, which are relayed by the auditory nerve to the brain.

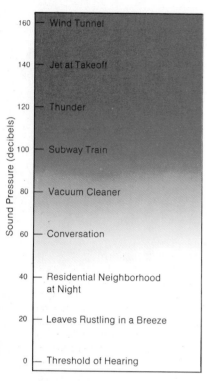

FIGURE 5.8
The decibel ratings for various common sounds. Sound actually becomes painful at about 130 decibels. Decibels represent ratios: A 20-decibel difference between two sounds indicates that one sound is ten times more intense than the other. Thus a vacuum cleaner puts ten times as much pressure on your eardrums as conversation does, and a subway train puts ten times as much pressure on them as a vacuum cleaner.

even though they occur simultaneously. For example, if you strike two keys of a piano at the same time, your ear can detect two distinct pitches.

Sounds are located through the interaction of the two ears. When a noise occurs on your right, for example, the sound comes to both ears, but it reaches your right ear a fraction of a second before it reaches the left. It is also slightly louder in the right ear. These differences tell you which direction it is coming from.

Smell and Taste

Smell and taste are known as the chemical senses because their receptors are sensitive to chemical molecules rather than to light energy or sound waves. For you to smell something, the smell receptors in your nose must come into contact with the appropriate molecules. These molecules enter your nose in vapors, which reach a special membrane in the nasal passages on which the smell receptors are located. These receptors send messages about smells over the *olfactory* nerve to the brain.

For you to taste something, appropriate chemicals must stimulate receptors in the taste buds on your tongue. Taste information is relayed to the brain along with data about the texture and temperature of the substance you have put in your mouth.

Some scientists have proposed that all smells are made up of the six qualities shown in Figure 5.9: flowery, fruity, spicy, resinous, putrid, and burned (Henning, 1916). Other scientists have come up with a similar scheme for taste, which they say is composed of four primary qualities, shown in Figure 5.10: sour, salty, bitter, and sweet (Beebe-Center, 1949).

Much of what is referred to as taste is actually produced by the sense of smell, however. In fact smell receptors may be as much as 10,000 times more sensitive than taste buds. You have undoubtedly noticed that when your nose is blocked by a cold, foods usually taste bland.

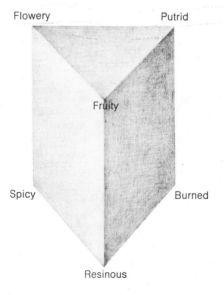

FIGURE 5.9
Henning's smell prism. This three-dimensional map was designed to encompass every possible smell. Supposedly, each smell can be located on one of the surfaces of this prism shape. For example, it should be possible for something to smell somewhat putrid, flowery, burnt, and spicy, but it should be impossible to have a smell that is spicy, resinous, and putrid. Where on Henning's smell prism would you place the smell of fresh cantaloupe?

Sensations of warmth, cold, and pressure also affect taste. Try to imagine eating cold chicken soup or drinking a hot soft drink, and you will realize how important temperature is to the sense of taste. Now imagine the textural differences between a spoonful of pudding and a crunchy chocolate bar, and you will see how the pressure of food also influences taste.

The chemical senses play a relatively unimportant role in human life when compared to their functions in lower animals. Insects, for example, often depend on smell to communicate with one another, especially in mating. In humans, smell and taste have become more a matter of aesthetics than of survival.

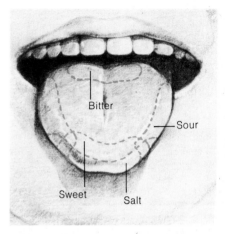

FIGURE 5.10
A map of the human tongue, indicating the areas that seem more sensitive to one kind of stimulation than to others. Interestingly, it is possible to be taste-blind as well as color-blind. There is a chemical called phenylthiocarbamide (PTC) that tastes extremely bitter to some people and is quite tasteless to others.

The Skin Senses

Receptors in the skin are responsible for providing the brain with at least four kinds of information about the environment: (1) pressure, (2) warmth, (3) cold, and (4) pain.

Sensitivity to pressure varies from place to place in the skin. Some spots, such as your fingertips, are densely populated with receptors and are therefore highly sensitive. Other spots, such as the middle of your back, contain relatively few receptors. Pressure sensations can serve as protection. For example, feeling the light pressure of an insect landing on your arm warns you of the danger of being stung.

Some skin receptors are particularly sensitive to hot or cold stimuli. In order to create a hot or cold sensation, a stimulus must have a temperature greater or less than the temperature of the skin. If you plunge your arm into a sink of warm water on a hot day, you will experience little or no sensation of its heat. If you put your arm in the same water on a cold day, however, the water will feel quite warm.

About three million skin receptors are particularly sensitive to pain. Many kinds of stimuli—scratches, punctures, severe pressure, heat, and cold—can produce pain. Their common property is real or potential injury to bodily tissues. Pain makes it possible for you to prevent damage to your body—it is an emergency system that demands immediate action.

Because pain acts as a warning system for your body, it does not easily adapt to stimulation—you rarely get "used to" pain. Pain tells you to avoid a stimulation that is harmful to you. Without this mechanism, you might "adapt" to a fire when you stand next to it. After a few minutes you would literally begin to cook, and your tissues would die.

Although pain is primarily a protective sense, the other skin senses serve many nonprotective functions. Touch is particularly important in interpersonal relations, for example.

Balance

The body's sense of balance is regulated by the *vestibular system* inside the inner ear. Its prominent feature is the three *semicircular canals*, as shown in Figure 5.11. When your head starts turning, the movement causes the liquid in the canals to move, bending the endings of receptor hair

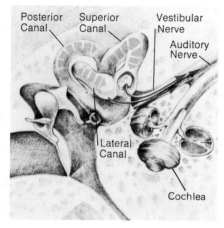

FIGURE 5.11
The vestibular system. The organs of balance consist of three semicircular canals arrayed at right angles to one another and filled with a freely moving fluid. Continuous motion in a straight line produces no response in this system, but starting, stopping, turning, speeding up, or slowing down makes the fluid in at least one of the canals move, stimulating the hair cells attached to the canal walls. These hair cells convert the movement into electrical impulses that are sent to the brain via the auditory nerve.

cells. The cells connect with the *vestibular nerve*, which joins the auditory nerve with the brain.

The stimuli for vestibular responses include movements such as spinning, falling, and tilting the body or head. Overstimulation of the vestibular sense by such movements can result in dizziness and "motion sickness," as you probably have experienced by going on amusement park rides or by spinning around on a swivel stool. Although you are seldom directly aware of your sense of balance, without it you would be unable to stand or walk without falling or stumbling.

Body Sensations

Kinesthesis is the sense of movement and body position. It cooperates with the vestibular and visual senses to maintain posture and balance. The sensation of kinesthesis comes from receptors in and near the muscles, tendons, and joints. When any movement occurs, these receptors immediately send messages to the brain.

Without kinesthetic sensations, your movements would be jerky and uncoordinated. You would not know what your hand was doing if it was behind your back, and you could not walk without looking at your feet. Furthermore, complex physical activities, such as surgery, piano playing, and acrobatics, would be impossible.

Another type of bodily sensation comes from receptors that monitor internal body conditions. These receptors are sensitive to pressure, temperature, pain, and chemicals inside the body. For example, a full stomach stretching these internal receptors informs the brain that the stomach has ingested too much.

Little is known about pain from the interior of the body except that it seems to be deep, dull, and much more unpleasant than the sharply localized pain from the skin. In some cases internal pain receptors may send inaccurate messages. They may indicate, for example, that a pain is located in the shoulder when in reality the source of irritation is in the lower stomach. Such sensation of pain in an area away from the actual source is called *referred pain.*

PERCEPTION

People do not usually experience a mass of colors, noises, warmths, and pressures. Rather we see cars and buildings, hear voices and music, and feel pencils and desks. We do not merely have sensory experiences; we perceive objects. The brain receives information from the senses and organizes and interprets it into meaningful experiences—unconsciously. This process is called *perception.*

Principles of Perceptual Organization

Through the process of perception, the brain is always trying to build "wholes" out of the confusion of stimuli that bombard the senses. The

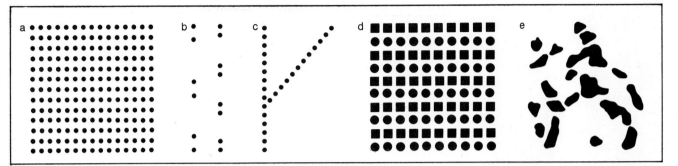

FIGURE 5.12
Principles of perceptual organization. A group of psychologists in the 1920s, 1930s, and 1940s became interested in the fact that human beings see patterns and groupings in their environments rather than disorganized arrays of bits and pieces. These Gestalt psychologists noted, for example, that it is impossible to look at the array of dots in (a) without seeing shifting patterns of squares and lines. They tried to identify the rules whereby disordered elements are organized into stable patterns. Proximity, or closeness of elements, as shown in (b), is one obvious factor. Elements that are close to one another seem to belong together. However, as (c) shows, continuity can be more important than proximity: Although the bottom dot in the inclined series of dots is closer to the vertical series of dots, it is not seen as belonging to the vertical row. It is seen as a continuation of the inclined row and therefore as part of it. (d) Similarity also organizes elements. The similar elements seem to belong to one another and therefore one sees the array as a set of horizontal rows rather than vertical columns as one might if all the elements were the same. Finally, in (e) a principle known as closure is demonstrated. The human brain has a tendency to fill in the gaps once an organization has emerged. The breaks are ignored; what is seen is a "whole."

"whole" experience that comes from organizing bits and pieces of information into meaningful objects and patterns is called a *Gestalt*. (This is a German word meaning pattern or configuration.)

Gestalt psychologists have tried to identify the principles the brain uses in constructing perceptions (Koffka, 1963). Some of the principles they have discovered are demonstrated in Figure 5.12. For example, they have found that people tend to see dots in patterns and groups. Thus when you look at Figure 5.12a you see shifting patterns of lines and rectangles, not just as an array of dots.

Two principles that people use in organizing such patterns are *proximity* and *similarity*. If the elements of the pattern are close to one another or are similar in appearance, they tend to be perceived as belonging to one another. These principles are demonstrated in Figures 5.12b, 5.12c, and 5.12d.

The Gestalt principles of organization help to explain how people group their sensations and fill in gaps in order to make sense of the world. In music, for instance, you tend to group notes on the basis of their closeness to one another in time—you hear melodies, not single notes. Similarity and continuity are also important. They allow you to follow the sound of a particular voice or instrument even when many other sounds are occurring. For example, you can follow the sound of a bass guitar through a song.

Figure and Ground

The simplest form of perceptual organization is the division of experience into *figure* and *ground*. Look at Figure 5.13. What do you see? Sometimes the figure looks like a white vase against a black background. At other times it appears to be two black faces against a white background.

When you look at a three-dimensional object against the sky or some other unstructured background, you have no trouble deciding which areas represent objects and which represent spaces between objects. It is when something is two-dimensional, as in Figure 5.13, that you may have trouble telling the figure from the ground. Nevertheless, such figure-ground problems give clues as to the active nature of perception. The fact that a single pattern can be perceived in more than one way demonstrates that we are not passive receivers of stimuli.

FIGURE 5.13
What did you see the first time you looked at this famous illustration? Whatever you saw, you saw because of your past experiences and current expectations. People invariably organize their experience into figure and ground. Whatever appears as figure receives the attention, is likely to be remembered, and has a distinctness of form that is lacking in the vague, formless ground. But, as this figure shows, what is meaningless ground one minute may become the all-important figure the next.

Figure and ground are important in hearing as well as in vision. When you follow one person's voice at a noisy meeting, that voice is a figure and all other sounds become ground. Similarly, when you listen to a piece of music a familiar theme may "leap out" at you: The melody becomes the figure, and the rest of the music, merely background.

Perceptual Inference

Often we have perceptions that are not based entirely on current sensory information. When you hear barking as you approach your house, you assume it is your dog—not a cat or a rhinoceros or even another dog. When you take a seat in a dark theater, you assume it is solid and will hold your weight, even though you cannot see what supports the seat. When you are driving in a car and see in the distance that the road climbs up a steep hill, then disappears over the top, you assume the road will continue over and down the hill—not come to an abrupt halt.

This phenomenon of filling in the gaps in what our senses tell us is known as *perceptual inference* (Gregory, 1970). Perceptual inference is largely automatic and unconscious. We need only a few cues to inform us that a noise is our dog barking or that a seat is solid. Why? Because we have encountered these stimuli and objects in the past and know what to expect from them in the present. Perceptual inference thus sometimes depends on experience. On the other hand, we are probably born with some of our ability to make perceptual inferences. For example, experimenters have shown that infants just barely able to crawl will avoid falling over what appears to be a steep cliff (Gibson and Walk, 1960). (See Figure 5.16.)

Learning to Perceive

In large part, perceiving is something that people *learn* to do. For example, infants do not see the human face as a perceptual whole, as something particularly significant. Infants under one month will smile at a nodding object the size of a human face, whether or not it has eyes, a nose, or other human features. At about twenty weeks, however, a blank oval will not make most babies smile, but a drawing of a face or a mask will. The baby has learned to distinguish something that looks like a person from other objects. Babies twenty-eight weeks and older are more likely to smile at a female than a male face (suggesting they can discriminate which type of face is most likely to care for them). By thirty weeks most smile more readily when they see a familiar face than when they see someone they do not know. But it takes seven or eight months for babies to learn to recognize different people (Ahrens, 1954).

Experiments show that people and animals must be actively involved in their environments to develop perception. An experiment with newborn kittens demonstrates this. A number of kittens were raised in the dark until they were ten weeks old. Then they were divided into two groups: actives and passives.

For three hours a day an active kitten and a passive kitten were linked

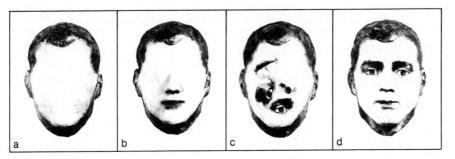

FIGURE 5.14
Clay masks used in an experiment on the perceptual abilities of infants. Psychologists learned that babies show a preference for complex patterns and human features almost from birth. Four-month-old babies pay much more attention to the masks in (c) and (d) than to those in (a) and (b) and seem to slightly prefer the face with the regular features. By the age of two years, however, babies spend more time looking at the face with the mixed-up features. By this time they have a good conception of what a human face looks like and find exceptions to the rule interesting.

together, as shown in Figure 5.15. The kittens were harnessed in such a way that every action of the active kitten moved the passive kitten an equal distance, forward, backward, up, down, and from side to side. The visual stimulation for the two kittens was approximately the same, but the active animal produced its *own* changes in stimulation (by walking, for example). The other kitten was merely a passive receiver of stimulation. When the kittens were tested later, the passive one was not able to discriminate depth—to judge how close or far away various objects were. But the active kitten, developed this ability normally. Not until the passive kitten had been allowed to live normally for two days—to move around in a visual environment of its own—did it develop normal depth perception (Held and Hein, 1963).

Experiments with human beings have also shown that active involvement in one's environment is important for accurate perception. People who have been blind from birth and who have had their sight restored by an operation (which is possible in only a few cases) have visual sensations, but initially they cannot tell the difference between a square and

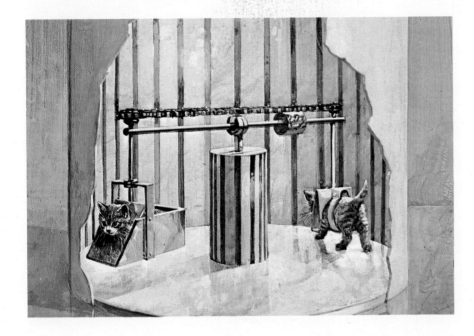

FIGURE 5.15
A cut-away view of the apparatus used to show that active involvement is necessary for perceptual learning. Both of these kittens are receiving roughly the same visual input as they move in relation to the vertical stripes painted on the walls of the cylinder, but one kitten is producing the changes in what it sees by its own muscular movements. The other kitten sees similar changes because of the way it is harnessed to the first kitten, but what it sees has nothing to do with its own movements. This second kitten was found not to have developed the ability to see depth in this situation, while the active kitten developed depth perception normally.

a circle or see that a red cube is like a blue cube (Valvo, 1971). In fact some had difficulty making such simple distinctions six months after their vision was restored.

Depth Perception

Depth perception—the ability to recognize distances and three-dimensionality—is one of the first types of perception humans develop. If you place a baby on a large table, he or she will not crawl over the edge. He or she is able to perceive that it is a long distance to the floor. Psychologists test depth perception in infants with a device called the visual cliff, shown in Figure 5.16 (Gibson and Walk, 1960).

People use many cues to perceive depth. One is the information provided by retinal disparity, as discussed earlier in the chapter. Another is *motion parallax*—the apparent movement of objects that occurs when you move your head from side to side or when you walk around. You

FIGURE 5.16
The visual cliff apparatus. A human infant of crawling age (about six months) will refuse to cross the glass surface over the "deep" side even if his mother is on the other side and is urging the child to join her. The infant is perfectly willing to cross the "shallow" side to reach his mother, however. Even though the child can feel the hard solid glass surface beneath him, he refuses to venture out over an edge that appears to be a sudden drop. A variety of animals such as chicks, lambs, and kittens respond in the same way. These animals can walk almost as soon as they are born. It seems, then, that animals are born with enough depth perception to avoid such hazards as walking off cliffs.

can demonstrate motion parallax by looking toward two objects in the same line of vision, one near you and the other some distance away. If you move your head back and forth, the near object will seem to move more than the far object. In this way, motion parallax gives you clues as to which objects are closer than others.

You are probably familiar with many other cues to distance. Nearby objects sometimes obscure parts of objects that are farther away. The more distant an object is, the smaller its image. Continuous objects such as railroad tracks, roads, rows of trees, and the walls of a room form converging lines, another cue to distance.

Constancy

When we have learned to perceive certain objects in our environment, we tend to see them in the same way, regardless of changing conditions. You probably judge the whiteness of the various portions of these pages to be fairly constant, even though you may have read the book under a wide range of lighting conditions. The light, angle of vision, distance, and therefore the image on the retina all change, but your perception of the object does not. Thus despite changing physical conditions people are able to perceive objects as the same by the processes of size, shape, and brightness *constancy.*

An example of *size constancy* will illustrate how we have an automatic system for perceiving an object as being the same size whether it is far or near. A friend walking toward you does not seem to change into a giant even though the images inside your eyes become larger and larger as she approaches. To you, her appearance stays the same size because even though the size of your visual image is increasing, you are perceiving an additional piece of information: distance is decreasing. The enlarging eye image and the distance information combine to produce a perception of an approaching object that stays the same size.

Distance information compensates for the enlarging eye image to produce size constancy. If information about distance is eliminated, your perception of the size of the object begins to correspond to the actual size of the eye image. For example, it is difficult for most people to estimate the size of an airplane in the sky because they have little experience judging such huge sizes and distances. Pilots, however, can determine whether a flying plane is large and far away or small and close because they are experienced in estimating the sizes and distances of planes.

Illusions

Illusions are perceptions that are misrepresentations of reality. For example, look at the lines in Figure 5.18a. Which lines are longer? Measure the lengths of the pairs of lines with a ruler, then look again. Do the lines *look* as long now that you *know* they are the same? For most people, the answer is no.

A possible explanation of this type of illusion is that even though the patterns are two-dimensional, your brain treats them as three-dimen-

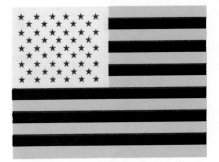

FIGURE 5.17
This figure can be used to demonstrate two striking features of vision. Stare steadily at the lowest right-hand star for about forty-five seconds, or until the colors start to shimmer. Then stare at a blank piece of paper. After a second or two you should see a *negative afterimage* of this figure in which the flag shows the normal colors. This occurs because the receptors for green, black, and yellow become fatigued, allowing the complementary colors of each to predominate when you stare at the white paper. Since these complements are, respectively, red, white, and blue, you see a normal American flag. Now shift your glance to a blank wall some distance away. Suddenly the flag will appear huge. This happens because of the principle of constancy—the brain interprets the same image as large when it is far away (apparently on the wall) and small when it is close (apparently on a piece of paper in your hand).

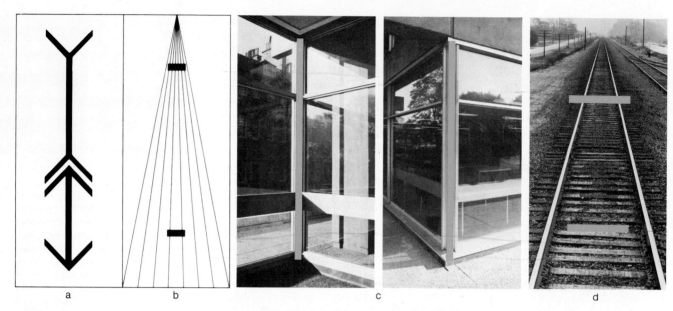

FIGURE 5.18
The Muller-Lyer illusion (a) and the Ponzo illusion (b) are two of the most famous illusions in psychology. The lines between the arrow heads in (a) are exactly the same length, as are the heavy black lines in (b). Some psychologists believe that the reason these lines appear to be different in length is that the brain interprets the diagrams in (a) and (b) as though they are scenes such as those in (c) and (d).

sional. These illusions have features that usually indicate distance in three-dimensional space. The top line in Figure 5.18a, for example, can be thought of as the far corner of a room; the bottom line is like the near corner of the building. In Figure 5.18b the converging lines create the illusion of distance so that the lower bar looks nearer and shorter than the upper bar. This "perceptual compensation" seems to be unconscious and automatic (Gregory, 1966).

Figure 5.19a shows two women in a room. The sizes of the women look dramatically different because you perceive the room as rectangular. In fact the ceiling and walls are slanted so that the back wall is both shorter and closer on the right than on the left (as shown in Figure 5.19b). But even when you know how this illusion was achieved, you still accept the peculiar difference in the women's sizes because the windows, walls, and ceiling appear rectangular.

Person Perception

The principles of perception apply to all possible objects and stimuli in one's environment—even to other people. People build Gestalts of one another—they base their perceptions on a few of a person's characteristics and then fill in the gaps in the person's personality.

Relying on perceptual inference in interpersonal relations can be helpful. For instance, it is useful to be able to assume that a pilot will be reliable or that a bank teller will be honest. But problems arise when people perceive and categorize others on the basis of skin color, ethnic characteristics, or other such broad criteria without regard to individuality. (Such aspects of interpersonal relations are more fully discussed in Chapter 10.)

Person perception then, like all types of perception, is an active process

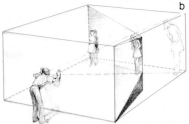

FIGURE 5.19
These two women appear to be a giant and a midget in an ordinary room. In fact, they are ordinary-sized women in a very peculiar room. This room, the true design of which is shown in the accompanying diagram, was constructed by psychologist Adelbert Ames. Again, the illusion is produced by tricking the brain into accepting an unusual situation as usual.

that involves interpreting input from the senses in light of one's past experiences and current expectations in order to arrive at a whole picture of a person.

EXTRASENSORY PERCEPTION

Is our awareness of the world limited to the information we receive through the senses described in the preceding pages? Are the people who claim to be able to predict the future or read other people's minds mere tricksters? Is it mere coincidence when we foresee the future?

Extrasensory perception (ESP)—receiving information about the world through channels other than the normal senses—is still a hotly debated topic. Parapsychologists, who study supernatural phenomena, focus on three distinct forms of ESP: telepathy or mind reading, the transference of thoughts from one person to another (without words, gestures, or glances); precognition, the ability to foresee the future; and clairvoyance, knowledge of events that could not have been acquired through the normal senses. (An example of clairvoyance would be "knowing" that a friend was in a car accident hundreds of miles away before you heard the news.) Parapsychologists also study psychokinesis, the ability to move objects without touching them.

Scientists have been investigating ESP since the early 1900s. One of the most famous researchers to put ESP to the scientific test is J. B. Rhine (1964). In tests of telepathy, for example, a "sender" focuses one at a time on each of twenty-five cards in a special deck. (The deck includes five cards for each of five different symbols.) A "receiver" locked in a distant room states which card he thinks the sender is focusing on. With luck alone, the receiver will guess about five cards correctly, sometimes a few more, sometimes a few less. Yet thousands of tests have shown that some people consistently respond above the average. Scientists have calculated that this would happen by chance only once in a thousand years. The conclusion? That these people are receiving information through senses or other channels we do not know about.

A similar experiment was carried out during one of the Apollo 14 flights. On four occasions astronaut Edgar Mitchell concentrated on twenty-five symbols arranged in different sequences. Some of the "receivers" back on earth tried to foresee the sequence Mitchell would select (precognition). Some tried to detect the sequence while he was concentrating on the symbols (telepathy). The results were mixed, with only one trial suggesting that telepathy had occurred (Mitchell, 1971).

Other parapsychologists work with animals in order to eliminate the possibility that interpersonal factors, that is, individual personalities, interfere with ESP. For example, Adrian Parker (1974) studied precognition with gerbils. An aminal was put into a cage with two keys. Pressing one of the keys would bring a reward of sunflower seeds. The gerbil's "problem" was to decide which was the right one, for the keys were linked to a computer that shifted the seeds from one key to the other at random. Parker assumed that if a gerbil moved from one key to the other, it did so because it had a "hunch"—a precognition—that the other key would release the seeds. The gerbils were correct 55 percent of the time.

As you might guess, research into ESP is highly controversial. The results vary from experiment to experiment, person to person, and even from day to day with the same person. This fact alone arouses skepticism in many scientists. Others reject the very notion of ESP because it contradicts established scientific laws. Precognition, for example, violates everything we know about time. How could a person jump ahead to see the future, then jump back again to tell about it? Not all critics of parapsychology dismiss the possibility that ESP exists. They are simply waiting for solid proof.

A minority of scientists believes that ESP can—and will—be explained on the basis of natural laws we have yet to discover. Some argue that the results of experiments are uneven because the laboratory stifles ESP. According to these scientists, ESP "turns on" in highly emotional situations (such as a friend being in an accident) and in very personal settings, but functions poorly in something as meaningless as a card-guessing game. It is up to these scientists to prove this to an interested but cautious scientific community.

SUMMARY

1. Our information about the outside world comes in through our senses. The sense organs convert stimuli in the environment into chemical-electrical activity that travels to the brain. This process results in sensation.

2. Psychophysics is the study of the relationship between physical stimuli and the sensory experiences they produce. The smallest amount of energy that will produce a sensation is called an absolute threshold. The smallest change in a stimulus that produces a change in sensation is called the difference threshold.

3. The experiencing of a sensation depends more on changes in the stimulus than on the absolute size or amount of the stimulus. Sensory adaptation occurs when a stimulus continues without changing. Motivation can influence whether or not certain stimuli will be detected.

4. The chief stimulus in vision is light. The rods and cones in the retina of the eye convert light energy to chemical impulses that travel over the optic nerve to the brain. The cones respond to color and work best in daylight. The rods are more sensitive but do not detect color. Color blindness results when cones are absent or malfunctioning. Binocular fusion, the combination of images from both eyes, is accompanied by stereopsis—the three-dimensional interpretation of the world. This is made possible by retinal disparity, which is the difference between the images in the two eyes.

5. The stimuli for hearing are sound waves, which are converted to chemical-electrical impulses by hair cells in the inner ear. These messages reach the brain via the auditory nerve. The main functions of hearing are detection, identification, and location of sounds.

6. Smell and taste are chemical senses. Receptors in the nose and on the tongue respond to contact with molecules. Most taste sensations involve the sense of smell to some extent.

7. Skin receptors respond to pressure, warmth, cold, and pain. These sensations play an important role in warning the brain of possible external dangers.

8. Internal bodily sensations include balance, kinesthesis, and internal sensitivity to pressure, temperature, pain, and chemicals.

9. Perception is the process of creating meaningful wholes out of information from the senses. Perceptual wholes are called Gestalts. Psychologists study such phenomena as figure-ground relationships, perceptual inference, perceptual development, depth perception, constancy, illusions, and interpersonal relationships to determine how perception works.

10. Telepathy, precognition, clairvoyance, and psychokinesis—all forms of extrasensory perception—are the subjects of ongoing and controversial research.

GLOSSARY

absolute threshold: The lowest level of physical energy that will produce a sensation in half the trials.

adaptation: In sensation, an adjustment of the sensitivity of sensory receptors in response to prolonged stimulation.

auditory nerve: The nerve that carries impulses from the inner ear to the brain, resulting in the sensation of sound.

binocular fusion: The process of combining the images received from the two eyes into a single, fused image.

clairvoyance: A form of extrasensory perception in which the perceiver gains awareness of events not detectable by the normal senses.

color blindness: Complete or partial inability to distinguish colors, resulting from malfunction in the cones.

cones: Receptor cells in the retina that are sensitive to color. Because they require more light than rods to function, they are most useful in daytime vision.

constancy: The tendency to perceive certain objects in the same way, regardless of changing angle, distance, or lighting.

decibel: A measure of the intensity, or "loudness," of sound.

difference threshold: The smallest change in a physical stimulus that produces a change in one's response to that stimulus in half the trials.

extrasensory perception: An ability to gain information by some means other than the ordinary senses (such as taste, hearing, vision, and so on).

figure-ground: The division of the visual field into two distinct parts, one being the object or objects, the other the background or space between objects.

Gestalt: In perception, the experience that comes from organizing bits and pieces of information into meaningful wholes.

illusions: Perceptions that are misrepresentations of reality.

kinesthesis: The sense of movement and body position, acquired through receptors located in and near the muscles, tendons, and joints.

lens: A flexible, transparent structure in the eye that, by changing its shape, focuses light on the retina.

motion parallax: The apparent movement of stationary objects relative to one another that occurs when the observer changes position. Near objects seem to move greater distances than far objects.

olfactory nerve: The nerve that carries impulses from the nose to the brain.

optic nerve: The nerve that carries impulses from the retina to the brain.

perception: The organization of sensory information into meaningful experiences.

perceptual inference: The process of assuming, from past experience, that certain objects remain the same and will behave as they have in the past.

pitch: The sensation associated with a sound's frequency: the "highness" or "lowness" of a sound.

precognition: A form of extrasensory perception in which the perceiver claims the ability to predict future events.

psychokinesis: The ability to move objects without touching them.

psychophysics: The study of the relationships between sensory experiences and the physical stimuli that cause them.

pupil: The opening in the iris that regulates the amount of light entering the eye.

referred pain: The sensation of pain in an area away from the actual source; most commonly experienced with internal pain.

retina: The innermost coating of the back of the eye, containing the light-sensitive receptor cells.

retinal disparity: The differences between the images on the two retinas.

rods: Receptor cells in the retina that are sensitive to low-intensity light, but not to color. Rods are particularly useful in night vision.

sensation: The result of converting physical stimulation of the sense organs into sensory experience.

stereopsis: The use by the visual system of retinal disparity to give depth information — providing a three-dimensional appearance to the world.

stimulus: Any change in the environment to which an organism responds.

telepathy: A form of extrasensory perception in which the perceiver can supposedly "read" the thoughts of others.

vestibular system: Three semicircular canals located in the inner ear and connected to the brain by the vestibular nerve. They regulate the sense of balance.

Weber's law: The principle that the larger or stronger a stimulus, the larger the change required for an observer to notice a difference.

ACTIVITIES

1. Hold a pencil about twelve inches in front of your face. Look at it with your left eye closed, then with your right eye closed. Notice how the pencil seems to jump around. What happens when you look at the pencil with both eyes? What principle does this experiment demonstrate?

2. Fill three bowls with water—hot water in one, cold in another, and lukewarm in the third. Put one hand in the cold water and the other in the hot water and leave them there for thirty seconds. Now put both hands in the lukewarm water at the same time. What do you feel? How does this demonstrate the principle of sensory adaptation?

3. Get a fresh potato and peel it. Do the same with an apple. Now have a friend close his eyes and smell a fresh onion while he takes a bite of each one. Can he tell which food is which without his sense of smell? Try this experiment with various people, using different foods that have similar textures.

4. If sensation consists entirely of electrical signals in the brain that are subject to interpretation by perception, does everyone experience the world differently? Animals have different sensory apparatus than humans—do they live in a different perceptual world?

5. Have a friend stand with her back to you. Touch various parts of her back with one pencil or with two pencils held close together. Each time you touch her back, ask her how many points she felt. Now touch the points to her hand and arm, again asking how many points she feels. What are your results? What accounts for these results?

6. To demonstrate the information shown in Figure 5.10, prepare solutions of salt water (salt), lemon juice (sour), baking soda (bitter), and sugar water (sweet). Dab each solution on various points on your tongue, and see if you can verify which area of the tongue is predominately sensitive to each of these major tastes.

7. Perform the following experiment to test one kind of sensory adaptation. Write a sentence while looking at your writing in a mirror. Do this until it begins to feel natural. Then write the sentence normally. Does normal writing now feel strange?

8. Try the following experiment to demonstrate an illusion of the sense of touch. Stretch a foot-square piece of chicken wire tautly over a frame. Blindfold your subject(s) and ask him or her to hold the thumb and forefinger of his or her hand to lightly touch each side of the chicken wire. Slide the wire rapidly back and forth between his or her fingers. Ask your subject to report the sensation he or she feels. Most people report feeling a continuous slippery or oily surface. This illusion will probably be stronger if the subject does not know in advance the actual nature of the material he or she is feeling.

9. Station yourself behind a window or glass door (to eliminate sounds and smells that you might give off) and stare intently at someone who has his or her back toward you. Pick someone who is within a ten-yard range and who is not engaged in any particular activity at the moment. Does the person turn around and look at you? If so, how long does it take him or her to "sense" your presence? How can you explain this phenomenon?

SUGGESTED READINGS

ARNHEIM, RUDOLF. *Art and Visual Perception: A Psychology of the Creative Eye.* Berkeley: University of California Press, 1974. A revision of a classic book by a prolific writer on visual perception. Arnheim relates the Gestalt laws of organization to visual perception in general and to the perception and structure of artistic works in particular.

CHANCE, PAUL. "Telepathy Could Be Real." *Psychology Today,* 9 (February 1976): 40–44, 65. A review of several large-scale experiments that lend support to the theory that some form of ESP or telepathic communication does indeed exist.

GREGORY, R. L. *The Intelligent Eye.* New York: McGraw-Hill, 1970 (paper). Gregory stresses his view that perception is a set of simple hypotheses about reality that depend upon sensory experiences. The book is particularly strong on visual illusions.

HELD, RICHARD, AND RICHARDS, WHITMAN (EDS.). *Perception: Mechanisms and Models.* San Francisco: Freeman, 1972. This book of readings from *Scientific American* provides accounts of some of the most famous research on perceptual processes in animals, including the visual cliff and the active and passive kittens.

KAUFMAN, LLOYD. *Sight and Mind: An Introduction to Visual Perception.* New York: Oxford University Press, 1974. Besides covering such topics as depth perception, attention, and color perception, Kaufman reviews and critiques many of the perceptual principles discussed in this chapter. This book provides a challenging, comprehensive, and well-written text on the nature of visual perception.

KOESTLER, ARTHUR. *The Roots of Coincidence.* New York: Random House, 1972. Koestler writes eloquently and interestingly, asking only that the reader keep an open mind with regard to the possible existence of ESP. He describes ESP research and delves into modern physics for an explanation of ESP phenomena.

MUELLER, C. G., AND RUDOLPH, M. *Light and Vision.* New York: Time-Life Books, 1966. This beautifully illustrated book is an excellent introduction to eye function as well as to the nature of light.

STEVENS, S. S., AND WARSHOVSKY, F. *Sound and Hearing.* New York: Time-Life Books, 1967. A highly readable and well-illustrated exploration of the nature of sound, the structure of the ear, and the phenomenon of hearing.

BIBLIOGRAPHY

AHRENS, R. "Beitrag zur Entwicklung des Physiognomie-und Mimikerkennens." *Z. exp. angew. Psychol.,* 2 (1954): 412–454.

ARNHEIM, RUDOLPH. *Art and Visual Perception: A Psychology of the Creative Eye.* Berkeley: University of California Press, 1974.

BEEBE-CENTER, J. G. "Standards for the Use of Gust Scale." *Journal of Psychology,* 28 (1949): 411–419.

GELDARD, FRANK A. *The Human Senses.* New York: Wiley, 1953.

GIBSON, E. J., AND WALK, R. D. "The Visual Cliff." *Scientific American,* 202 (1960): 64–71.

GREGORY, R. L. *Eye and Brain.* New York: McGraw-Hill, 1966 (paper).

——. *The Intelligent Eye.* New York: McGraw-Hill, 1970 (paper).

HANSEL, C. E. M. *ESP: A Scientific Evaluation.* New York: Scribner's, 1966.

HELD, R., AND HEIN, A. "A Movement-produced Stimulation in the Development of Visually Guided Behavior." *Journal of Comparative*

Physiology and Psychology, 56 (1963): 606–613.

HENNING, HANS. "Die Qualitatenreihe des Geschmacks." *Zeitschrift fur Psychologie,* 74 (1916): 203–219.

HOCHBERG, JULIAN. *Perception.* Englewood Cliffs, N.J.: Prentice-Hall, 1964 (paper).

KOFFKA, K. *Principles of Gestalt Psychology.* New York: Harcourt Brace Jovanovich, 1963.

MITCHELL, EDGAR T. "An ESP Test from Apollo 14." *Journal of Parapsychology,* 38 (1971): 89–107.

OSTRANDER, SHEILA, AND SCHROEDER, LYNN. *Psychic Discoveries Behind the Iron Curtain.* Englewood Cliffs, N.J.: Prentice-Hall, 1970.

PARKER, ADRIAN. "ESP in Gerbils Using Positive Reinforcement." *Journal of Parapsychology,* 38 (1974): 301–311.

RHINE, JOSEPH B. *Extra-sensory Perception.* Boston: Branden, 1964.

RHINE, LOUISA E. *Hidden Channels of the Mind.* New York: Apollo, 1961 (paper).

SENDEN, M. VON. *Space and Sight: The Perception of Space and Sight in the Congenitally Blind Before and After Operation.* Translated by P. Heath. London: Methuen, 1960.

STEVENS, S. S. "The Surprising Simplicity of Sensory Metrics." *American Psychologist,* 17 (1962): 29–39.

VALVO, ALBERTO. *Sight Restoration after Long-term Blindness: The Problems and Behavior Patterns of Visual Rehabilitation.* New York: American Foundation for the Blind, 1971.

WALD, G. "The Receptors of Color Vision." *Science,* 145 (1964): 1007–1016.

WEBER, ERNST H. *De Pulse, Resorptione, Audito et Tactu.* Leipzig: Kohler, 1834.

WORRALL, AMBROSE, AND WORRALL, OLGA. *Explore Our Psychic World.* New York: Harper & Row, 1970.

6 Motivation and Emotion

Motivation
Drive Reduction Theory/Drive Reduction Theory Reconsidered / Social Motives / Abraham Maslow's Hierarchy of Needs
Emotion
The Inside and Outside of Emotion / Physiological Theories / Cognitive Theories

All people are born with the same biological needs for food, water, and shelter, and with essentially the same kinds of nerves and hormones. But the biology we discussed in Chapter 4 cannot explain all the mysteries of human behavior. For example, it cannot explain why a sports event or an operatic aria causes one person's heart to beat faster in excitement but puts another person to sleep. Nor can it explain what drives some people to practice the piano for six hours each day or to endure the struggle of climbing a steep, barren mountain.
To answer such questions we have to examine human motives and emotions. That is our plan in this chapter.

MOTIVATION

What do we refer to when we say someone is motivated? In a broad sense we mean, what is the cause of the person's behavior? Considered in this way, the study of motivation would seem to include most of psychology. Therefore, many psychologists prefer a more specific definition: *motivation* energizes behavior and gives it direction. A person motivated by hunger will probably be energized to get up and go in some particular direction—probably toward the kitchen. Similarly, a geology student whose energies always seem to be directed toward studying rocks, going on field trips, and so on, is described as highly motivated to learn geology.

Still, not all psychologists would agree about the kinds of things motivation refers to. Some feel we need such a term only to describe the energizing factors in behavior; they believe that learning can account for the direction of behavior (Cofer, 1972). One theory of this type is drive reduction theory.

FIGURE 6.1
What motivates these mountaineers to endure the discomfort and danger of a steep climb? Early psychological theories, which tried to account for human activity in terms of the reduction of biological drives, do not sufficiently explain motives like the mountaineers'. Later theories offer explanations that depend more on social motives, learned from interacting with other people.

Drive Reduction Theory

Drive reduction theory, which dominated psychological thinking in the 1940's and early 1950's, emerged from the work of experimental psychologist Clark Hull and his associates (1943). Hull traced motivation back to the basic physiological needs we described in Chapter 4. According to Hull, when an organism is deprived of something it needs (such as food, water, or sex) it becomes tense and agitated. To relieve this tension

FIGURE 6.2
Drive reduction theory suggested
that all motives stem from biological needs. Hard workers, it was
thought, work for social approval,
because as infants they were fed
by a smiling mother. Eventually,
the need for approval became an
end in itself.

it engages in more-or-less random activity. Thus biological needs *drive* an organism to act.

If one of these random behaviors reduces the drive, the organism will begin to acquire a habit; that is, when the drive is again felt, the organism will first try the same response again. Habits channel drives in certain directions. In short, *drive reduction theory* states that *physiological needs drive an organism to act in either random or habitual ways until its needs are satisfied.*

Hull and his colleagues suggested that all human motives—from the desire to acquire property to striving for excellence and seeking affection or amusement—are extensions of basic biological needs. For example, people develop the need for social approval because as infants they were fed and cared for by a smiling mother or father. Gradually, through generalization and conditioning, the need for approval becomes important in itself. Approval becomes a learned drive.

Drive Reduction Theory Reconsidered

Drive reduction theory dominated psychologists' thinking for over a decade. However, the results of experiments conducted in the late 1950s suggested that Hull and his colleagues had overlooked some of the more important factors in human—and animal—motivation.

According to drive reduction theory, infants become attached to their mothers because mothers usually relieve such drives as hunger and thirst. Harry Harlow (among others) doubted that this was the only or even the main source of an infant's love for its mother. Harlow decided to challenge drive reduction theory with an experiment. He took infant monkeys away from their mothers and put them alone in cages with two surrogate "mothers" made of wire. One of the wire mothers was equipped with a bottle. If drive reduction theory were correct, the monkeys would become attached to this figure, because it was their only source of food. The other wire mother was covered with soft cloth but could not provide food and relief from hunger.

In test after test, the small monkeys preferred the cloth mother, particularly when strange, frightening objects were put into their cages. They valued physical contact more than they did food or reduction in hunger.

Thus one of the factors that many drive theorists overlooked is that some experiences (such as hugging something or someone soft) are inherently pleasurable. Although they do not seem to reduce biological drives, these experiences serve as incentives or goals for behavior. In emphasizing the "push" or inner drives, drive reduction theory could not account for the "pull" of incentives.

Another factor drive theorists overlooked was the pleasure humans and related animals derive from stimulation or arousal. Just think for a moment about how dogs love to be petted, or how children love horror movies and rides at amusement parks that are designed to terrify them. In the end, then, a drive *for* stimulation looked as plausible as a drive to *reduce* stimulation.

Many psychologists concluded that there could be no general theory

FIGURE 6.3
In Harlow's classic experiment on the determinants of mother love, infant monkeys chose between two surrogate mothers. One was made of wire and was equipped with a feeding nipple; the other was made of soft terrycloth. The monkeys spent most of their time with the terrycloth mother even though they fed from the wire mother, and they used the terrycloth mother as a security base when frightened by strange objects introduced by the experimenter. A drive-reduction explanation of their behavior is inadequate because the monkeys chose the mother that did not provide food—the one that was least obviously associated with the termination of an unpleasant state (hunger). The effective reward seemed to be a positive event rather than escape from a negative one.

of motivation of the type Hull suggested. Instead of a drive reduction theory, we are left with a list of unlearned, innate drives that include hunger and thirst, but also curiosity, contact with soft things, and many others. As we saw in Chapter 4, we know a few things about the physiological basis of hunger and thirst, but we do not yet know much about the physiological basis of the various drives for stimulation.

Social Motives

Many psychologists have concentrated their research on social motives, rather than on the unlearned, biological motives we have been discussing. Social motives are learned from our interactions with other people.

In Chapter 13, we will discuss the theories of several psychologists who sought to explain the development of personality. One such psychologist was Henry Murray, whose theory of personality identifies sixteen basic needs (see Figure 6.4). Note that most of these are social motives, rather than biological needs. Lists such as these are sometimes forgotten shortly after they appear in print, because in itself such a list is not very useful. Murray's list has not been forgotten, however. In fact, hundreds of studies have been performed on just one of these needs, the need for achievement.

McClelland and the Need for Achievement.   One reason the achievement motive has been so well researched is that a man named David McClelland became very interested in finding some quantitative way of measuring social motives (McClelland *et al.*, 1953). Once he did this, he believed

FIGURE 6.4
Needs identified by Henry Murray in his formulation of a theory of human personality. Note that Murray distinguishes between a class of primarily physical needs and a—much larger—class of psychological needs.

n Acquisition
    (to gain possessions and property)

n Conservance
    (to collect, repair, clean, and pre-
    serve things)

n Order
    (to arrange, organize, put away
    objects)

n Construction
    (to organize and build)

n Achievement
    (to overcome obstacles, to exercise
    power, to strive to do something
    difficult as well and as quickly as
    possible)

n Recognition
    (to excite praise and commenda-
    tion)

n Defendance
    (to defend oneself against blame
    or belittlement)

n Dominance
    (to influence or control others)

n Autonomy
    (to resist influence or coercion)

n Aggression
    (to assault or injure)

n Affiliation
    (to form friendships and associa-
    tions)

n Rejection
    (to snub, ignore, or exclude)

n Nurturance
    (to nourish, aid, or protect)

n Succorance
    (to seek aid, protection, or sympa-
    thy)

n Play
    (to relax, amuse oneself, seek di-
    version and entertainment)

n Cognizance
    (to explore)

he could search for a technique of changing motivation, because he could then have a method for measuring whether a change had occurred. Mc-Clelland concentrated his research on the need for achievement because he felt that techniques for increasing this motive might be very useful in improving the lives of millions of people. Many minority children, for example, get little encouragement for achievement from their environments. The same is true of most girls, and of children in some other cultures.

McClelland's main tool for measuring achievement motivation was the Thematic Apperception Test (TAT). This test consists of a series of pictures. Subjects are told to make up a story which explains each picture. Then each story is "coded" by looking for certain kinds of themes, and scoring these themes according to their relevance to various types of needs, such as achievement. This coding has by now been refined to the point where trained coders agree about 90 percent of the time.

McClelland noted first that hungry subjects tended to include more food-related themes in their TAT stories than satiated subjects. Next he performed an analogous test for the need for achievement: he created a group of subjects who were "deprived" of achievement. He did this by giving them a series of tests designed so that they did poorly and knew it. They were allowed to try again and still did poorly. Then he administered the TAT, saying that it was being used to look for creative, intelligent group leaders. As a control, he gave the TAT to another group with a "relaxed" set of instructions, encouraging them to write stories that pleased them. Then he analyzed the stories to see how they differed. In addition, the TAT stories of all kinds of known successful achievers were studied and compared to control groups.

The most important themes related to achievement include these:

1. High achievers preferred to write stories in which the hero has personal responsibility for the outcome of the story, rather than stories in which the outcome happens by chance, as in gambling. If the results are due to chance or to outside factors, then the person who needs achievement will not feel he or she can exercise any control, and therefore cannot even try to achieve.

2. High achievers tended to include themes in which challenging goals were chosen. They were not so high that they could never be met, but they were not so low as to deprive a person of a sense of achievement.

3. High achievers preferred to describe situations in which they (or the hero of the story, if not themselves) could find out the results of their actions quickly. That way they would know how well they were doing.

High achievers, then, tend to be people who take "personal responsibility to solve problems and achieve moderate goals at calculated risks—in situations that provide real feedback." (McClelland and Winter, 1969).

To test these ideas, those who scored high on achievement themes were compared with others in performing various tasks. For example, it was found that high achievers were able to solve anagrams (unscrambling and rearranging letters into meaningful words) faster than those less interested

FIGURE 6.5
A picture of the sort that might be used in the measurement of the Need for Achievement (n Ach). Examples of stories that would be scored from fairly high to low are shown beside the picture. The portions of the stories printed in italics are the kinds of themes considered to reflect n Ach.

This guy is just getting off work. These are all working guys and they don't like their work too much either. The younger guy over on the right knows the guy with the jacket.

Something bad happened today at work—a nasty *accident that shouldn't have happened*. These two guys don't trust each other *but they are going to talk* about it. *They mean to put things to rights*. No one else much cares, it seems.

The guy with the jacket is *worried*. He feels that *something has to be done*. *He wouldn't ordinarily talk to* the younger man *but now he feels he must*. The young guy is ready. He's *concerned* too but doesn't know what to expect.

They'll both realize after talking that you never know where your friends are. *They'll both feel better* afterward because they'll feel they have someone they can rely on next time there's trouble.

Harry O'Silverfish has been working on the Ford assembly line for thirteen years. Every morning he gets up, eats a doughnut and cup of coffee, takes his lunch pail, gets in the car, and drives to the plant. It is during this morning drive that his mind gets filled with *fantasies of what he'd like to be doing* with his life. Then, about the same time that he parks his car and turns off his ignition, he also *turns off his mind*—and it remains turned off during the whole working day. In the evenings, he is *too tired and discouraged to do much* more than drink a few beers and watch TV.

But this morning Harry's mind didn't turn off with the car. He had witnessed a car accident on the road—in which two people were killed—soon after leaving home. Just as he reaches the plant gate, Harry suddenly turns. Surprised, he discovers that he has made *a firm decision* never to enter that plant again. He knows that *he must try another way* to live before he dies.

These are hard-hats. It's the end of the shift. There is a demonstration outside the plant and the men coming out are looking at it. Everyone is just walking by. They are not much interested. One person is *angry and wants to go on strike*, but this does not make sense to anyone else. He is out of place. Actually he is not really angry, he is just bored. He looks as though he might do a little dance to amuse himself, which is more than the rest of them do. *Nothing will happen* at this time *till more people join* this one man in his needs.

in achievement (Kolb, 1973). More significantly, McClelland followed up the careers of some students at Wesleyan University who had been tested with the TAT in 1947. He wanted to see which students had chosen entrepreneurial work—that is, work in which they had to initiate projects on their own. He found that eleven years after graduation, 83 percent of the entrepreneurs (business managers, insurance salesmen, real estate investors, consultants, and so on) had scored high in achievement, but only 21 percent of the nonentrepreneurs had scored that high (McClelland, 1965).

Next, McClelland checked to see whether the achievement motive had any real effects on society (1961). He and his associates studied the children's literature of England, Spain, and ancient Athens, scoring it for achievement in the same manner as he would a TAT story. They found that in general, high levels of achievement motivation appeared 50 to 100 years before improvements in the economic situation of each country.

Encouraged by this finding, McClelland and others then set about devising a training course in achievement motivation. Briefly, the trainees in this course learned to score their own TAT stories and to recognize achievement themes in them. They also rewrote their stories again and again, attempting to include more achievement themes in them. Then they discussed everyday life situations and case histories with other members of the group, focusing on achievement themes. Group members also played a business game designed to give them quick feedback for good decisions and problem solving.

Success with this program has been reported after applying it in such diverse places as Spain, Mexico, Italy, India, and poverty areas of Kentucky (McClelland and Winter, 1969). For example, a group of seventy-six men running small businesses in Indian villages was given the training and was later compared to a similar group not given the training. The trained groups showed significant and large increases in entrepreneurial activity (such as starting new businesses or gaining large increases in salary), while the untrained group did not change.

McClelland does not believe that we should all train ourselves as high achievers. In fact he has said that such persons are not always the most interesting, and they are usually not artistically sensitive (McClelland and Harris, 1971). They would also be less likely to value intimacy in a relationship. Studies have shown that high achievers prefer to be associated with experts who will help them achieve, instead of with more friendly people.

There are many other motives besides achievement, all of which may be equally important to having a highly developed culture. But in a competitive world where some nations are affluent and some extremely deprived, a nation or culture that lacks a sufficient number of high achievers may find it quite difficult to prosper economically.

Fear of Success. McClelland's work has inspired a wide variety of research on other aspects of motivation. One of his most important findings was that women typically scored lower than men on achievement motivation. It was not until the 1960s that someone decided to investigate this fact.

Matina Horner (1970, 1972) asked eighty-nine men to write a story beginning with the line, "After first term finals, John finds himself at the top of his medical school class." She also asked ninety women to write a story, substituting the name Anne for John in the opening line. Ninety percent of the men wrote success stories. However, over sixty-five percent of the women predicted doom for Anne.

Some of the women feared for Anne's social life. They described her as undatable or unmarriageable, and suggested that she would be socially isolated if she excelled in her studies and career. Some wrote about the guilt and despair she would experience if she continued to succeed. And some refused to believe the opening line. It was impossible for Anne to be first in her class; there must be some mistake.

On the basis of this study Horner identified another dimension of achievement motivation, the *motive to avoid success*. Females in our society are (or were) raised with the idea that being successful in all but a few careers is odd and unfeminine. Thus a woman who is a success in medicine, law, and other traditionally male occupations must be a failure as a woman. It might have been all right for Anne to pass her e ,ams, but the fact that she did better than all the men in her class made the female subjects anxious.

Horner discovered that bright women, who had a very real chance of achieving in their chosen fields, exhibited a stronger fear of success than did women who were average or slightly above average. (The expectancy of success strengthened the motive to avoid success, overshadowing the incentive of a rewarding career.) This seemed to confirm Horner's belief that success involves deep conflicts for women.

Relatively little research has been done with men who are low in achievement motivation. The gap between women and men may not be as great as this study implies; perhaps many men as well as women are motivated to avoid success (see Tresemer, 1974).

Abraham Maslow's Hierarchy of Needs

Abraham Maslow believes that *all* human beings need to feel competent, to win approval and recognition, and to sense that they have achieved something. He places achievement motivation in the context of a hierarchy of needs all people share.

Maslow's scheme, shown in Figure 6.6, incorporates all of the factors we have discussed so far in this chapter, and goes a step further. He begins with biological drives, including the need for physical safety and security. In order to live, people have to satisfy these *fundamental needs*. If a person is hungry, most of his activities will be motivated by the drive to acquire food, and he will not be able to function on a higher level.

The second level in Maslow's hierarchy consists of *psychological needs*: the need to belong and to give and receive love, and the need to acquire esteem through competence and achievement. Maslow suggests that these needs function in much the same way that biological needs do, and that they can be filled only by an outside source. A lack of love or esteem makes people anxious and tense. There is a driven quality to their behavior. They may engage in random, desperate, and sometimes neurotic or maladaptive activities to ease their tensions. Unless these needs are satisfied, a person will be unable to move on. Most of their behavior will be motivated by unfulfilled psychological needs. Thus an unusually intelligent woman who does not feel loved may avoid success in the hope of being accepted as one of the crowd.

Self-actualization needs occupy the top of Maslow's hierarchy. These may include the pursuit of knowledge and beauty, or whatever else is required for the realization of one's unique potential. Maslow believes that although relatively few people reach this level, the needs lie dormant in all of us. To be creative in the way we conduct our lives and use our talents, we must first satisfy our fundamental and psychological needs. The satisfaction of these needs motivates people to seek self-actualization.

Maslow thus adds to motivation theory the idea that some needs take precedence over others and the suggestion that achieving one level of

FIGURE 6.6
This pyramid graphically represents Maslow's hierarchy of needs.
According to Maslow, it is only
after satisfying the lower levels of
needs that a person is free to
progress to the ultimate need of
self-actualization.

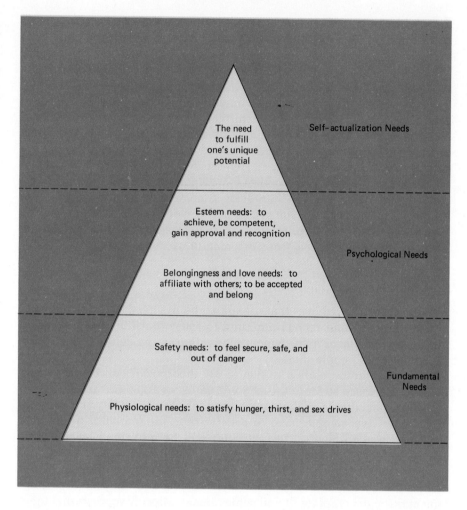

satisfaction releases new needs and motivations. (We will return to
Maslow in Chapter 13, where we discuss theories of personality.)

EMOTION

It is difficult to draw a clear line between motives and emotions. We saw
in Chapter 4 that when a person needs food, his stomach contracts, the
level of sugar in his blood drops, his neural and endocrine systems are
thrown slightly off balance, and his taste buds become more sensitive.
We saw that when a person is frightened, his heart and breathing rates
quicken, his energy level rises, his senses mobilize, and blood rushes away
from his stomach, into his brain, heart, and other muscles. Of course a
poet might diagnose a pounding heart, loss of appetite, and heightened
awareness of the moonlight and scented breezes as love. Why, if all three
involve identifiable physiological changes, do we call hunger a biological
drive, fear and love emotions?

It depends on whether we are describing the source of our behavior or the feelings associated with our behavior. When we want to emphasize the needs, desires, and mental calculations that lead to goal-directed behavior, we use the words "drive" or "motivation." When we want to stress the feelings associated with these decisions and activities, we use the words "emotion" or "affect."

Clearly, the two are intertwined. Indeed we frequently explain our motives in terms of emotions. Why did you walk out of the meeting? You were angry. Why do you go to so many parties? You enjoy meeting new people and love to dance. Why did you lend someone you don't particularly like your notes? You felt guilty about talking behind her back. Why did you apply for a summer job overseas? Traveling excites you—and so on.

As these examples demonstrate, emotions push and pull us in different directions. Sometimes emotions function like biological drives: our feelings energize us and make us pursue a goal. Which goal we pursue may be determined by our social learning experiences. Other times we do things because we think they will make us feel good: Anticipated emotions are the incentive for our actions. The consequences of striving for one goal or another also evoke emotions.

The Inside and Outside of Emotion

In addition to the physiological measures described in Chapter 4, there are essentially two ways to study emotion. The first is to observe the ways in which people express different emotions. The second is to analyze subjective reports of what it feels like to be joyful, angry, afraid, and so on.

Expressing Emotions: Innate and Learned Behavior.   In *The Expression of the Emotions in Man and Animals* (1872), Charles Darwin argued that people the world over express certain basic feelings in the same ways. Without knowing a person's language, you can tell whether he or she is amused or infuriated just by looking at his or her face.

Recent studies indicate that Darwin was right. One group of researchers selected a group of photographs which they thought depicted surprise, anger, sadness, and happiness. Then they showed the photographs to people from five different cultures and asked them to say what the person in each photograph was feeling. The results of this experiment are shown in Figure 6.7. The overwhelming majority of the subjects identified the emotions as the researchers expected they would. Was this simply because they had met Americans, or at least seen American television shows and movies, and so learned how to "read" our facial expressions? Apparently not, for a second study was conducted in a remote part of New Guinea, with people who had had relatively little contact with outsiders and virtually no exposure to mass media. They, too, were able to identify the emotions being expressed (Ekman, Friesen, and Ellsworth, 1972).

These studies imply that certain basic facial expressions are *innate*— that is, part of our biological inheritance. Observations of children who

Photograph Judged						
Judgment	Happiness	Disgust	Surprise	Sadness	Anger	Fear
Culture			**Percent Who Agreed with Judgment**			
99 Americans	97	92	95	84	67	85
40 Brazilians	95	97	87	59	90	67
119 Chileans	95	92	93	88	94	68
168 Argentinians	98	92	95	78	90	54
29 Japanese	100	90	100	62	90	66

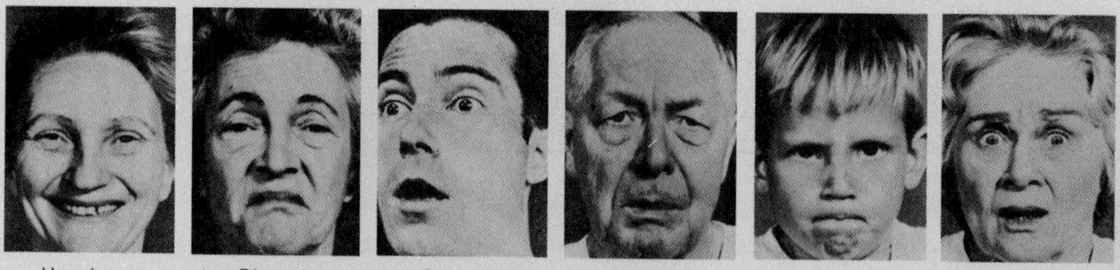

FIGURE 6.7
The data in this table show that there is substantial agreement among the members of different cultures about the meaning of various facial expressions. The muscular movements that produce these expressions are probably innate human responses. (After Ekman, Friesen, and Ellsworth, 1972.)

were born blind and deaf lend support to this view. These youngsters could not have learned how to communicate feelings by observing other people. Still they laugh like other children when they're happy; pout and frown to express resentment; clench their fists and teeth in anger (See Goodenough, 1932).

Even the most basic emotions can be changed by learning, however. We saw in Chapter 2 how Watson used classical conditioning to teach a young child to fear white, furry objects. And we will see in Chapter 16 how psychotherapists use the same techniques in reverse to help people "unlearn" or rid themselves of irrational fears. Although parents may not consciously apply classical conditioning, they (and others) modify their children's emotions by responding angrily to some outbursts, sympathetically to others, and on occasion ignoring their youngsters. In this way, children are taught which emotions are considered appropriate in different situations, and which emotions they are expected to control. For example, in our society, girls are allowed—even expected—to cry, but boys beyond a certain age are not.

Learning explains the differences we find among cultures once we go beyond such basic expressions as laughing or crying. For example, in Victorian English novels, women closed their eyes, opened their mouths with a gasp, and fainted when they were frightened or shocked. In Chinese novels, men fainted when they became enraged. Medical records from the period indicate that Chinese men did indeed faint from anger (Klineberg, 1938). What these findings suggest is that all of us are born with the capacity for emotion and with certain basic forms of expression, but that when and where we express different feelings depends in large part on learning.

Subjective Reports.   The English language contains literally hundreds of words to describe subtle variations in emotions. What do people mean when they apply these words to themselves? What are they actually feeling?

Joel Davitz (1969) asked forty people to read through a list of four hundred words, marking the ones they might use to describe their feelings. This enabled him to reduce the list to fifty common words that he believed represented the range and variety of emotional states. The list included terms such as amusement, disgust, gratitude, impatience, reverence, and jealousy.

Then Davitz asked a second group of people to match these words to phrases that describe emotional experiences or behavior—for example: my hands are shaky; I'm jumpy, jittery; I feel dirty and ugly; I want to scream and yell; tears well up. Analysis of their choices revealed a good deal of common ground. Many subjects matched the word "anger" to the phrases "Fists are clenched" and "I want to say something nasty," for example.

The next step was to eliminate repetition. When Davitz had done this he found that the subjects had described essentially twelve different types or clusters of emotions. Some were related to levels of energy or activation; some, to feelings for other people or relatedness. A third category involved sensations; a fourth, feelings of self-worth or competence. Within these categories, emotions ranged from positive to extremely negative. An adaptation of Davitz's results is shown in Table 6.1.

Analyzing facial expressions and kinds of feelings helps us to describe emotions. But it does not tell us where emotions come from. Over the years, psychologists have proposed several answers to these questions. Some believe emotions derive from physical changes; others, that emotions result from mental processes.

Physiological Theories

In *Principles of Psychology*, a classic work published in 1890, William James attempted to summarize the best available literature on human behavior, motivations, and feelings. But when it came to drawing up a catalogue of human emotions, James gave up. He felt that there were too many subtle variations, too many personal differences.

But James was struck by the fact that nearly every description of emotions he read emphasized bodily changes. James's observations of his own and other people's emotions confirmed this point. We associate feelings with sudden increases or decreases in energy, muscle tension and relaxation, and sensations in the pits of our stomachs.

Table 6.1 Experiencing Emotions

	POSITIVE	NEGATIVE	EXTREMELY NEGATIVE
ACTIVATION	CLUSTER 1: ACTIVATION A special lift in everything I do and say; I feel bouncy, springy A sense of lightness, buoyancy, and upsurge of the body A strong sense of interest and involvement in things around me	CLUSTER 2: INACTIVE I feel empty, drained, hollow I feel tired, sleepy I feel mentally dull	CLUSTER 3: OVERACTIVE My blood pressure goes up; blood seems to rush through my body There's an excitement, a sense of being keyed up, overstimulated, supercharged My heart pounds
RELATEDNESS	CLUSTER 4: MOVING TOWARD I want to help, protect, please another person Realization that someone else is more important to me than I am to myself A sense of being wanted, needed	CLUSTER 5: MOVING AWAY I want to withdraw, disappear, draw back, be alone, away from others, crawl into myself A feeling of a certain distance from others; everyone seems far away A sense of wandering, lost in space with nothing solid to grab onto	CLUSTER 6: MOVING AGAINST There is an impulse to strike out, to pound or smash or kick or bite; to do something that will hurt Fists are clenched I keep thinking of getting even, of revenge
SENSATIONS	CLUSTER 7: COMFORT A feeling of warmth all over A sense of being very integrated and at ease with myself, in harmony with myself A sense of smiling at myself	CLUSTER 8: DISCOMFORT An inner ache you can't locate There is a sense of loss, of deprivation I feel as if I'm under a heavy burden	CLUSTER 9: TENSION My whole body is tense A tight knotted feeling in my stomach I'm easily irritated, ready to snap
COMPETENCE	CLUSTER 10: ENHANCEMENT I feel taller, stronger, bigger A sense of more confidence in myself; a feeling that I can do anything There is a sense of accomplishment, fulfillment	CLUSTER 11: INCOMPETENCE: DISSATISFACTION Seems that nothing I do is right I get mad at myself for my feelings or thoughts or for what I've done I keep blaming myself for the situation	CLUSTER 12: INADEQUACY A sense of being totally unable to cope with the situation I feel vulnerable and totally helpless I want to be comforted, helped by someone

SOURCE: Joel R. Davitz, *The Language of Emotion* (New York: Academic Press, 1969).

The James-Lange Theory.   After much thought, James concluded that we use the word "emotion" to describe our visceral or "gut" reactions to the things that take place around us. In other words, James believed that emotions *are* the perception of certain internal bodily changes (1890).

> My theory . . . is that *the bodily changes follow directly the perception of the exciting fact, and that our feeling of the same changes as they occur IS the emotion.* Commonsense says, we lose our fortune, are sorry and weep; we meet a bear, are frightened and run; we are insulted by a rival, are angry and strike. . . . [T]he more rational statement is that we feel sorry because we cry, angry because we strike, afraid because we tremble. . . . Without the bodily states following on the perception, the latter would be . . . pale, colorless, destitute of emotional warmth.

In a sense, James was putting the cart before the horse. Other psychologists had assumed that emotions trigger bodily changes; James argued that the reverse is true. Because Carl Lange came to the same conclusion about the same time, this position is known as the *James-Lange Theory* (Lange and James, 1922).

The Cannon-Bard Theory.   Techniques for studying bodily changes improved over the next three decades, and evidence that contradicted the James-Lange Theory began to grow. For example, the physiological changes that occur during emotional states also occur when people are not feeling angry or sad—or anything. In fact, injecting a drug that produces physiological arousal of the body does not produce changes in emotions. (If James and Lange had been correct, such physiological changes would always produce emotions.)

Also the internal state of the body changes only slowly. "Gut" reactions could not produce the rushes of emotion we all experience from time to time. Indeed, if bodily changes were the seat of emotion, we would all be rather sluggish and dull.

In 1929, Walter B. Cannon published a summary of the evidence against the James-Lange Theory. Cannon argued that the thalamus (part of the lower brain), and not our visceral organs, is the seat of emotion—an idea Philip Bard (1934) expanded and refined. According to the *Cannon-Bard Theory,* certain experiences activate the thalamus, and the thalamus sends messages to the cortex (or higher brain) and to the body organs. Thus when we use the word "emotion," we are referring to the *simultaneous* burst of activity in the brain and "gut" reactions. In Cannon's words, "The peculiar quality of emotion is added to simple sensation when the thalamic processes are aroused" (1929).

Like the James-Lange Theory, the Cannon-Bard Theory has since been improved. More sophisticated experiments showed that the thalamus is not involved in emotional experience, but the hypothalamus is. Investigation of the links between physical changes and emotions continues. In recent years, however, some psychologists have begun to view emotions as strongly related to the way we perceive our bodies and our social surroundings.

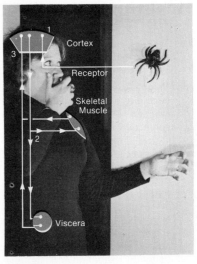

FIGURE 6.8
A schematic representation of the sequence of events that occur in the experience of an emotion according to the James-Lange Theory. An emotion-eliciting event is sensed by a receptor (1) and is perceived in the cerebral cortex, but the event is not yet experienced emotionally. The cortex responds by activating the viscera and the skeletal muscles (2). These changes are, in turn, perceived in the cortex (3), and the original event is then experienced emotionally. As James put it: "The feeling of bodily changes as they occur *is* the emotion."

Cognitive Theories

Cognitive theorists believe that bodily changes and thinking *work together* to produce emotions. Physiological arousal is only half of the story. What you feel (excitement, anger, etc.) depends on how you interpret your symptoms. And this in turn depends on what is going on in your mind and in your environment.

The Schachter-Singer Experiment.   Stanley Schachter and Jerome Singer designed an experiment to explore this. They told all of the subjects that they were testing the effects of vitamin C on eyesight. In reality, most received an adrenalin injection. One group was told that the "vitamin" injection would make their hearts race and their bodies tremble (which was true). Another group was deliberately misinformed: The injection would make them numb. A third group was not told anything about how their bodies would react to the shot. And a fourth group was not given adrenalin, but received a neutral injection that did not produce any symptoms. Like the third group, they were not given any information about possible side effects.

After the injection, each subject was taken to a reception room to wait for the "vision test." There they found another person who was actually part of the experiment—a stooge. But the subjects thought he'd had the same injection they'd had. With some subjects, the stooge acted happy and a bit wild—dancing around, laughing, making paper airplanes with the questionnaire they'd been asked to fill out. With other subjects, the stooge began complaining about the questionnaire right away and eventually became quite angry.

Subjects from the first group, who had been told how the injection would affect them, watched the stooge with mild amusement. So did subjects who had received the neutral injection. However, those from the second and third groups, who either had no idea or an incorrect idea about

FIGURE 6.9

Magda Arnold's theory of emotion describes a continuous process of reaction and appraisal. Both the subjective state and the physiological changes that accompany emotion are seen as effects of appraisal rather than as causally related to each other. Arnold's theory accounts for a wide variety of possible outcomes in emotion-provoking situations. This figure shows how a man may respond immediately and effectively in a dangerous situation and later misinterpret the aftereffects. The sequence could have taken other courses: Suppose the pilot *had* attended to his fear and the accompanying physiological changes. His awareness (Stage 5) would have been immediate and his secondary estimate might have been, ''I am afraid and unable to handle the situation.'' Stages 7 and 8 would then have been panic and its physiological correlates. Alternatively, his secondary estimate might have been, ''Not surprisingly, I am afraid. I must act anyway.'' No misinterpretation of his later tremor and fatigue would then have followed.

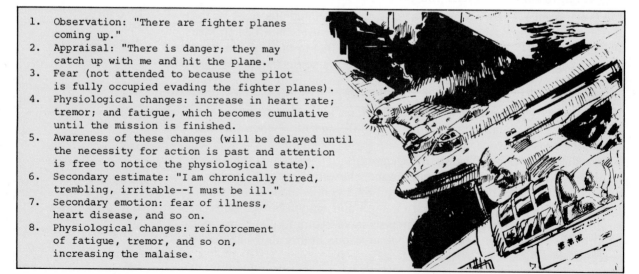

1. Observation: "There are fighter planes coming up."
2. Appraisal: "There is danger; they may catch up with me and hit the plane."
3. Fear (not attended to because the pilot is fully occupied evading the fighter planes).
4. Physiological changes: increase in heart rate; tremor; and fatigue, which becomes cumulative until the mission is finished.
5. Awareness of these changes (will be delayed until the necessity for action is past and attention is free to notice the physiological state).
6. Secondary estimate: "I am chronically tired, trembling, irritable--I must be ill."
7. Secondary emotion: fear of illness, heart disease, and so on.
8. Physiological changes: reinforcement of fatigue, tremor, and so on, increasing the malaise.

the side effects, joined in with the stooge. If the stooge was euphoric, so were they; if he was angry, they became angry.

What does this experiment demonstrate? That internal components of emotion (such as those adrenalin produces) affect a person differently, depending on his or her interpretation or perception of the social situation. When people cannot explain their physical reactions, they take cues from their environment. The stooge provided cues. The experiment also shows that internal changes are important—otherwise the subjects from the neutral group would have acted in the same way as those from the misinformed groups. Thus perception and arousal *interact* to create emotions.

Emotions Outside the Laboratory. Of course, Schachter and Singer's subjects had received an injection of adrenalin before they became angry or silly. How do emotions develop in real life? You *perceive a person,* object, or event. This is the first stage. It may take place in your imagination, as when you think about something you expect to happen in the future or replay a scene from your past.

The next stage is *appraisal.* You decide whether what is happening will help you, hurt you, or have no effect on you. Suppose you see one of your instructors walking toward you. If you have nothing special to gain and nothing to fear from her, you do not react emotionally. You say hello, chat for a moment, and walk on.

However, if you have been cutting class and suspect that the instructor is going to ask for an explanation, or if you know that she was impressed with a term paper you wrote and will probably compliment you, you will react—physiologically and emotionally. Your heart begins to beat a little faster, and you feel nervous or excited (depending on whether you cut classes or wrote an excellent paper). These are the third and fourth stages: *bodily change* and *emotion.*

In most cases, emotion and bodily change occur at the same time. However, in some situations you skip from stage three (bodily changes) to stage five, which is *action.* You see a car rushing toward you, adrenalin pours into your system, and you jump back without stopping to think. Only after you've leaped to safety do you sense your heart pounding and experience the emotion of fright (Arnold, 1960, 1970).

Emotions and physical changes are intertwined. In recent years many people have experimented with this connection by studying the effects of yoga and transcendental meditation, for example. The result of these investigations should be clear in the next ten or twenty years.

SUMMARY

1. Motivation is what energizes behavior and gives it direction.

2. Drive reduction theory states that physiological needs drive an organism to act in either random or habitual ways until its needs are satisfied. But drive reduction theory overlooks the fact that some experiences are inherently

pleasurable, and even though they do not reduce biological drives, they still provide incentives or goals for behavior.

3. Social needs also motivate behavior. One of these, the need for achievement, has been intensively studied by David McClelland. He and his associates devised a method for measuring achievement motivation. They have also developed achievement training programs which have been successful cross-culturally.

4. McClelland's work inspired a wide variety of research on other aspects of motivation. One researcher, Matina Horner, discovered another dimension of achievement motivation: the motive to avoid success. Horner discovered that bright women, who had a very real chance of achieving in their chosen fields, exhibited a stronger fear of success than did women who were average or slightly above average.

5. Abraham Maslow believed that all people want to feel competent, to win approval and recognition, and to sense they have achieved something. According to his theory, there is a hierarchy of needs: fundamental needs, psychological needs, and self-actualization needs.

Some needs take precedence over others and the achievement of one level of satisfaction releases new needs and motivations.

6. Emotions and motivations are intertwined.

7. There are two ways to study emotion. The first is to observe the ways in which people express different emotions. The second is to analyze subjective reports of what it feels like to experience these emotions.

8. All of us are born with the same basic capacity for emotion. When and where we express different feelings depends in large part on learning.

9. Investigation of where emotions come from brought cognitive theorists to the conclusion that bodily changes and thinking *work together* to produce emotions.

10. Internal sensations affect each person differently, depending on mental interpretation and the social situation.

11. There are four stages in the development of emotion: perception, appraisal, bodily change, and emotion. The stage following this is action.

GLOSSARY

Cannon-Bard Theory: A theory introduced by psychologists Cannon and Bard, which attributed emotion to the simultaneous activity of the brain and "gut" reactions.

drive reduction theory: A theory formulated by psychologist Clark Hull, which states that physiological needs drive an organism to act in random or habitual ways until its needs are satisfied.

fundamental needs: In Maslow's hierarchy of needs theory, these are the biological drives that must be satisfied in order to maintain life.

innate behavior: Behavior that is part of one's biological inheritance.

James-Lange Theory: A theory formulated by psychologists James and Lange which suggests that emotions are the perception of bodily changes.

motivation: Inducement to direct one's energies toward achieving a goal that has acquired meaning.

psychological needs: In Maslow's hierarchy of needs theory, these include the need to belong and to give and receive love, and the need to acquire esteem through competence and achievement. If these needs are frustrated, it will be difficult for the person to strive for fulfillment of the next level in the hierarchy—*self-actualization needs.*

self-actualization needs: The top of Maslow's hierarchy of needs. These include the pursuit of knowledge and beauty, or whatever else is required for the realization of one's unique po-tential. Before these needs can be satisfied, people must first meet their *fundamental* and *psychological needs.*

ACTIVITIES

1. Try going without bread in your meals for several days a week. Do you find that you are beginning to think about bread more often, even dream about it? Are you becoming more aware of advertisements for bread? Compare your experience with the description of drive reduction behavior in this chapter.

2. Write down several activities or behaviors you do when your time is your own. In which level of Maslow's hierarchy of needs would you place each of these activities or behaviors; that is, what really motivates you to engage in each of them? Perhaps you will discover a different kind of motive, one that doesn't seem to fit in with Maslow's set. Check the chapter on personality and the Maslow readings to see whether or not it might fit. If none of the activities on your list seems to be motivated by self-actualization, can you imagine activities which would be, and which you might enjoy doing?

3. With a partner or as a group, select ten emotions to express. Then play a variation of charades, with one person attempting to convey each of these emotions by facial expression alone. Are some emotions harder to convey than others? Are there consistent differences in interpretation between individuals? How important do you think context (the social situation in which the facial expression occurs) is in perceiving other people's emotions?

4. Recall the four stages of development of an emotion, described in this chapter. Then observe them in yourself, at a time when you are entering an emotional state. If possible you should take notes, at least "mental notes," to enable you to view yourself with some objectivity even while you are having the emotion. To induce the emotion you might go to a movie that you know will be scary or sad. Or you might attend a religious service or mystical ritual of some sort if that affects you.

5. If you are interested in the achievement motive, you might try the story-writing techniques described in this chapter. Try writing stories with and without achievement themes. Supposedly, those who deliberately attempt to include themes related to the three aspects of achievement motivation will increase their own ability to achieve; at least, such an exercise makes a person more aware of achievement.

6. Collect the fantasies of people in your class. Each person should write several stories or fantasies, possibly around a set of ambiguous pictures. Names should not be placed on fantasies (so as to insure privacy), but each person should mark male or female on the fantasy. Then compare the fantasies of men and women for the achievement motive. Are there differences? Do you think there have been changes in this factor in the last few years?

SUGGESTED READINGS

ARNOLD, MAGDA (ED). *Feelings and Emotions.* New York: Academic Press, 1970. A collection of recent symposium papers by many of the theorists mentioned in this chapter and by several others who could not be mentioned because of limited space. An excellent cross-section of the field as it exists today.

COFER, CHARLES N. *Motivation and Emotion.* Glenview, Ill.: Scott, Foresman, 1972. A short, comprehensive paperback textbook covering drive and incentive theories, biological aspects of motivation, the need for stimulation, and cognitive consistency theories.

EKMAN, PAUL. "Face Muscles Talk Every Language." *Psychology Today* (September, 1975): 35–39. Does evolution or culture determine the way in which our faces express emotion? This author discusses his research showing that at least some emotions produce the same facial expressions in fifteen different cultures.

GREENE, D., AND LEPPER, M.R. "Intrinsic Motivation: How to Turn Play into Work." *Psychology Today* (September, 1974): 49–54. Suggests that rewarding children (or anyone) for something they like to do may turn enjoyment into drudgery. In the words of the authors, "a person's intrinsic interest in an activity may be decreased by inducing him to engage in that activity as a means to some . . . goal."

HORNER, MATINA S. "Toward an Understanding of Achievement-Related Conflicts in Women." *Journal of Social Issues,* 28 (1972): 157–175. One of several article-length statements of Horner's theory and findings. Contains a useful bibliography of related works, including papers by Horner in which her scoring system is described.

LEVENTHAL, HOWARD. "Emotions: A Basic Problem for Social Psychology." In C. Nemeth (ed.), *Social Psychology: Classic and Contemporary Integrations.* Chicago: Rand McNally, 1974. An excellent review article. Includes criticisms and proposed modifications of Schachter's theory

that deserve the attention of advanced students and researchers.

MASLOW, A.H. *The Farther Reaches of Human Nature.* New York: Viking Press, 1971. Maslow here elaborates his concept of self-actualization and other aspects of human potential.

MC CLELLAND, DAVID. *The Achieving Society.* New York: Van Nostrand Reinhold, 1961. This book addresses the question of the social origins and consequences for society of achievement motivation.

———, AND HARRIS, T. G. "To Know Why Men Do What They Do: A Conversation with David C. McClelland." *Psychology Today,* 4 (January 1971): 35–39. Here McClelland talks about how he began studying achievement and other motives, and about some of the ways his research could be used to improve our lives.

WEINER, BERNARD. *Theories of Motivation: From Mechanism to Cognition.* Chicago: Markham, 1973. A textbook covering, among other topics, drive theory, achievement theory, and—most important—the author's attribution-theory approach to achievement motivation. Presents clearly the differences between mechanistic (for example, drive) and cognitive (for example, attribution) theories.

WINTER, D. G. *The Power Motive.* New York: Free Press, 1973. Winter discusses research on this motive, which can be analyzed by means of the TAT in the same manner as McClelland did for the achievement motive. As Winter makes clear, the two kinds of motives are quite different.

BIBLIOGRAPHY

ARNOLD, MAGDA B. *Emotion and Personality.* New York: Columbia University Press, 1960.

———. *Feelings and Emotions: The Loyola Symposium.* New York: Academic Press, 1970.

ATKINSON, JOHN W. (ED.). *Motives in Fantasy, Action, and Society.* New York: Van Nostrand Reinhold, 1958.

———, AND NORMAN T. FEATHER. *A Theory of Achievement Motivation.* New York: Wiley, 1966.

BARD, PHILIP. "On Emotional Expression After Decortication with Some Remarks of Certain Theoretical Views: Part I." *Psychological Review,* 41 (1934), 309–329; "Part II," 41 (1934), 424–449.

CANNON, WALTER B. *Bodily Changes in Pain, Hunger, Fear and Rage.* New York: Appleton-Century-Crofts, 1929.

COFER, C. N. *Motivation and Emotions.* Glenview, Ill.: Scott, Foresman, 1972.

DARWIN, CHARLES. *The Expression of Emotions in Man and Animals.* University of Chicago Press, 1967 (orig. pub. 1872).

DAVITZ, JOEL R. *The Language of Emotion.* New York: Academic Press, 1969.

EKMAN, PAUL, FRIESEN, WALLACE V., AND ELLSWORTH, PHOEBE. *Emotion in the Human Face: Guidelines for Research and an Integration of Findings.* Elmsworth, N.Y.: Pergamon, 1972.

GOODENOUGH, FLORENCE L. "Expression of the Emotions in a Blind-Deaf Child." *Journal of Abnormal and Social Psychology,* 27 (1932): 328–333.

HARLOW, HARRY F., AND ZIMMERMAN, ROBERT F. "Affectual Responses in the Infant Monkey." *Science,* 120 (1959): 421–432.

HORNER, MATINA S. "Femininity and Successful Achievement: A Basic Inconsistency." In J. Bardwick, E. M. Douvan, M. S. Horner, and D. Gutman (eds.), *Feminine Personality and Conflict.* Belmont, Calif.: Brooks/Cole, 1970.

——. "Toward an Understanding of Achievement-Related Conflicts in Women." *Journal of Social Issues,* 28 (1972): 157–175.

HULL, CLARK. *Principles of Behavior: An Introduction to Behavior Theory.* New York: Appleton-Century-Crofts, 1943.

JAMES, WILLIAM. *The Principles of Psychology.* Vol. 2. New York: Holt, 1890.

KLINEBERG, OTTO. "Emotional Expression in Chinese Literature." *Journal of Abnormal and Social Psychology,* 33 (1938): 517–520.

KOLB, D. A. "Changing Achievement Motivation." In R. Schwitzgabel, and D. A. Kolb (eds.), *Behavior Change.* McGraw-Hill, 1973.

KRETCH, D. AND CRUTCHFIELD, R. S., *Elements of Psychology.* New York: Knopf, 1961.

LANGE, CARL G. AND JAMES, WILLIAM, *The Emotions.* Knight Dunlap (ed.), I. A. Haupt (tr.). Baltimore, Md.: Wilkins & Wilkins, 1922.

MC CLELLAND, D. C. *The Achieving Society.* Princeton: Van Nostrand, 1961.

——. "Need Achievement and Entrepreneurship: A Longitudinal Study." *Journal of Personality and Social Psychology,* 1 (1965): 389–392.

——, ET AL. *The Achievement Motive.* New York: Appleton-Century-Crofts, 1953.

MC CLELLAND, D. C., AND HARRIS, T. G. "To Know Why Men Do What They Do: A Conversation with David C. McClelland." *Psychology Today,* 4 (January 1971): 35–39.

MC CLELLAND, D. C., AND WINTER, D. G. *Motivating Economic Achievement.* New York: Free Press, 1969.

MARANON, GREGORIO. "Contribution à l'Etude de l'Action Emotive de l'Adrenaline." *Revue Français d'Endocrinologie,* 2 (1952): 141–147.

MURRAY, HENRY A., ET AL. *Exploration in Personality.* New York: Oxford University Press, 1934.

SCHACHTER, STANLEY, AND SINGER, JEROME. "Cognitive, Social, and Physiological Determinants of Emotional State." *Psychological Review,* 69 (1962): 379–399.

TRESEMER, DAVID. "Fear of Success: Popular but Unproven." *Psychology Today,* 7 (March 1974): 82–85.

WHITE, ROBERT W. "Motivation Reconsidered: The Concept of Competence." *Psychological Review,* 66 (1959): 297–333.

7 States of Consciousness

Consciousness Is Limited
Consciousness Is an Active Process
Altered States of Consciousness
- Sleep/Hypnosis/Hallucinations/Drug States/Meditation

Philosophers have pondered the meaning of consciousness for centuries. Consciousness includes all the mental sensations that are roaming through your mind at a given moment—ideas, emotions, perceptions, and so on. This is essentially the definition philosopher John Locke gave in the seventeenth century: "Consciousness is the perception of what passes in a [person's] own mind." It is being aware of yourself. More specifically, it is an awareness of an awareness.

To date, no one has produced a wholly satisfactory definition or explanation of consciousness, although countless philosophers and psychologists have tried. Perhaps the only points on which all would agree are, first, that consciousness is limited; second, that it actively constructs experiences; and third, that it can take many forms.

CONSCIOUSNESS IS LIMITED

Consciousness is limited in the sense that we are not aware of much that is going on, inside and outside of our bodies. If we tried to pay attention to all the sights, sounds, smells, and feelings that are available to our senses at any given moment, we would be overwhelmed (as suggested in Chapter 5). This also applies to internal processes and events. Parts of the nervous system constantly monitor and control our heartbeats, our breathing, our level of fatigue, our walking, our speech—and much, much more. Only occasionally do we become aware, or conscious, of these activities.

FIGURE 7.1
The Sleeping Gypsy, Henri Rousseau. The poet Jean Cocteau first pointed out that the lion and the river in this painting may be the dream of the sleeper, since there are no footprints in the sands around the gypsy woman. This kind of deliberate inclusion or omission of detail is one of the characteristics of dreaming that sets it apart from our normal, waking state of consciousness.

The next time you are engaged in conversation, try to follow everything that is happening in your mind. Thoughts bubble in and out of consciousness, but probably not in the form of finished sentences. When you decide to speak, sentences seem to take shape automatically. The words flow spontaneously, particularly if you have a lot to say. Even when you try to formulate a sentence *before* you speak, you do not think consciously about the grammatical rules for putting words together.

These automatic processes are very useful. It would be virtually impossible to live if you had to think about each breath you take, each word you speak, each movement you make when walking or running, tying a

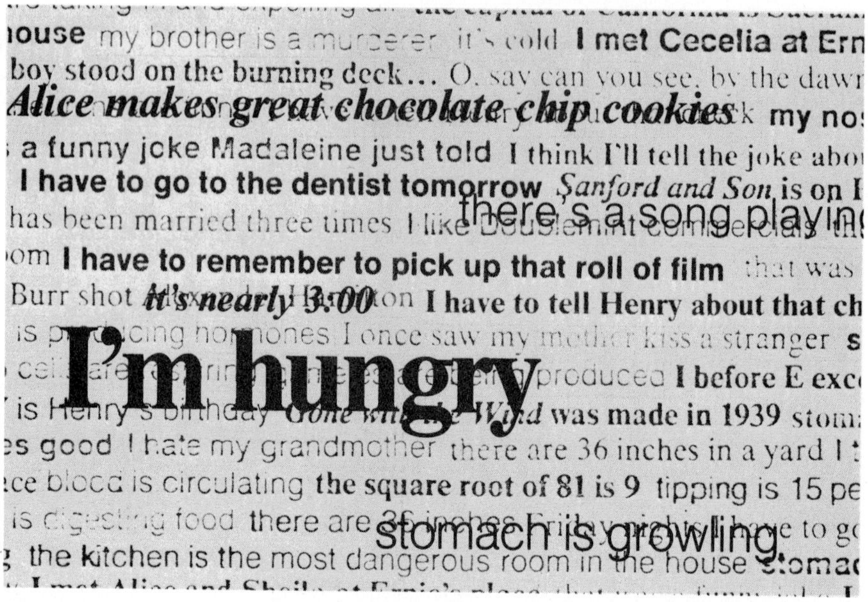

FIGURE 7.2

Consciousness is not infinite in its range. Some things can never be made conscious. And of the items that are available to consciousness, only a few can be focused on at once. Consciousness has therefore been compared to a searchlight: It illuminates powerfully, but only a small area at a time.

house my brother is a murderer it's cold I met Cecelia at Ern
boy stood on the burning deck... O, say can you see, by the dawn
Alice makes great chocolate chip cookies k my nos
a funny joke Madaleine just told I think I'll tell the joke abou
I have to go to the dentist tomorrow *Sanford and Son* is on
has been married three times I like Doublemint commercials th
om **I have to remember to pick up that roll of film** that was
Burr shot *It's nearly 3:00* on I have to tell Henry about that ch
is producing hormones I once saw my mother kiss a stranger s

I'm hungry

there's a song playing

is Henry's birthday *Gone with the Wind* was made in 1939 stom
s good I hate my grandmother there are 36 inches in a yard I
ce blood is circulating the square root of 81 is 9 tipping is 15 pe
is digesting food there are 36 inches to go
g the kitchen is the most dangerous room in the house stomac

stomach is growling

shoelace, or taking a shower. Even complex behavior can become automatic or unconscious. A person may be able to read music, play a guitar, and sing simultaneously, even though all three of these behaviors involve complex skills that must be learned separately.

Many automatic behaviors are readily accessible to consciousness: You can notice them if you try. For example, you are able to regulate your breathing when you exercise, practice yoga, or dive underwater. If you study acting, you will learn to be acutely aware of such routine movements as picking up a book from a table or turning to face someone who has just entered the room.

However, other automatic processes are not accessible to consciousness. For example, you cannot focus on the functioning of your liver. More importantly, many thoughts and feelings occur outside of awareness, yet we may act on these unconscious feelings and be unable to understand or explain our behavior. Everyone has had the experience of calling someone they know well by the wrong name, or saying the exact opposite of what they intended to say (finding yourself saying "I hate Jim" when you meant to say "I like Jim"). Sigmund Freud considered such slips of the tongue clues to the unconscious desires, feelings, impulses, and needs that motivate much of our behavior. (This is where we get the term "Freudian slip.") Freud believed it could take years of psychoanalysis to uncover the roots of unconscious motivations and bring them into awareness.

Thus consciousness is limited in two ways: by the number of internal and external events a person can pay attention to at one time, and by the accessibility or inaccessibility of internal processes and emotions, or automatic routines.

CONSCIOUSNESS IS AN ACTIVE PROCESS

We tend to think of consciousness as simple awareness of what is happening inside and outside ourselves—as passive acceptance of information sent to the brain by the sense organs. Scientists have shown, however, that consciousness is more than a mirror reflection of events. Rather, it is an active process of constructing reality from bits and pieces of information provided by the senses.

Sensation (the gathering of information by the eyes, ears, and other sense organs) is only part of consciousness. Being aware also involves perception (the organization of information received through the senses into meaningful wholes) and thought (the reorganization of information in the brain).

We described the processes of thought, sensation, and perception in some detail in Chapters 3 and 5. To review: When you see a table, your senses collect information about the size, shape, color, and texture of the object in front of you and send it to your brain. Perceptual processes take this information and create a whole, meaningful picture in your mind. It is something you know—a table. You have automatically sifted through memories and quickly identified the object. Even though you have never seen this particular table before, you know what it is because you have built up a concept of tables in your mind.

Cognitive processes enable you not only to construct concepts of objects but also to build concepts of concepts. You group tables with other objects that fit the concept "furniture." In turn, "furniture" is grouped with other objects that are manufactured. In this way you are able to contemplate simple objects and to think abstractly about their relationships with other objects. Contemplation can extend infinitely—from "tables" to "furniture" to "manufactured objects" to "industry," "society," and "the universe"—there are no limits.

Consciousness involves all three processes: sensation, perception, and cognition. You create an awareness of yourself and the things around you by focusing your attention, and integrating the information picked up during this attention with the structure of your mind.

ALTERED STATES OF CONSCIOUSNESS

Most people believe that they spend most of their lives in a normal state of consciousness—that is, their sensations, perceptions, and thoughts seem

FIGURE 7.3
A demonstration of the constructive nature of consciousness. Hold the book out at arm's length, close your left eye, and focus your right eye on the center of the X. As you slowly pull the book toward you, you should find a position at which the red spot disappears. The image of the red spot is now falling on an area at the back of your eye called, for obvious reasons, the blind spot. The image disappears because there are no light-sensitive cells in this area; the blind spot is the place where nerve fibers from the eye exit to the brain. The fact that no one is normally aware of this "hole" in his or her vision shows why consciousness can be said to be an active, constructive process.

natural and real. Whether everyone constructs reality in the same way is debatable. Perhaps we all experience our environments differently. There is no way to know.

What we do know is that everyone also experiences altered states of consciousness from time to time. An *altered state of consciousness* involves a change in mental processes, not just a quantitative shift (such as feeling more or less alert). Sensations, perceptions, and thought patterns actually change. The most obvious and familiar example is sleep. People spend about a third of their lives in this altered state of consciousness. Other examples include daydreams, hallucinations, delirium, hypnotic states, being drunk or "high" on drugs, and the heightened awareness people experience during various forms of meditation (Tart, 1972).

In the past twenty years, psychologists have begun to examine altered states of consciousness by having people sleep, undergo hypnosis, or take drugs during laboratory experiments. In the laboratory, researchers can observe changes in behavior and measure changes in breathing, pulse rate, body temperature, and brain activity. (Brain activity or "waves" can be recorded with a device known as an electroencephalograph, or EEG.) The subjects' own reports of how they feel or what they remember supplement these data. What have psychologists learned about these phenomena? We begin with sleep.

Sleep

Most people think of sleep as a state of unconsciousness, punctuated by brief periods of dreaming. This is only partially correct. Sleep is a state of *altered* consciousness, not unconsciousness. (The brain is active the entire time.)

As you begin to fall asleep, your body temperature declines, your pulse rate drops, and your breathing grows slow and even. Gradually your eyes close and your brain briefly emits alpha waves, as observed on the EEG, which are associated with the absence of concentrated thought and with relaxation. Your body may twitch, your eyes roll, and brief visual images flash across your mind (although your eyelids are shut) as you enter Stage I sleep.

In Stage I sleep your muscles relax and your pulse slows a bit more, but your breathing becomes uneven and your brain waves grow irregular. This lasts for about ten minutes. At this point your brain waves begin to fluctuate between high and low voltages—a pattern that indicates you have entered Stage II sleep. Your eyes roll slowly from side to side. Some thirty minutes later you drift down into Stage III sleep and low-voltage waves begin to sweep your brain every second or so.

Stage IV is deep sleep. Large, regular delta waves indicate you are in a state of oblivion. If you are awakened by a loud noise or sudden movement, you will not remember anything and may feel disoriented. Talking out loud, sleepwalking, and bed wetting—all of which may occur in this stage—leave no trace on memory. Deep sleep is important to your physical and psychological well-being. Perhaps this is why people who, for one

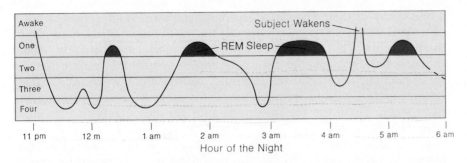

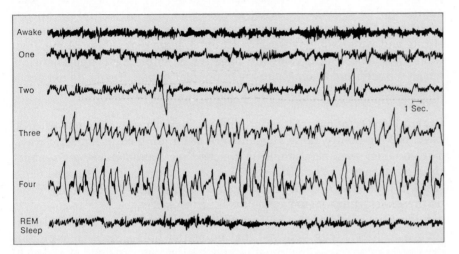

FIGURE 7.4

(top) A diagram showing the passage of a sleeper through the various stages of sleep over a seven-hour period. Note that after first falling asleep and after each REM period, the sleeper rapidly descends into the deepest stage of sleep and then gradually rises out of it. *(bottom)* The patterns of electrical activity (EEGs) in the brain that correspond to the various stages of sleep. The EEG pattern shown for being awake is one that occurs when the person is resting quietly with eyes closed. It is referred to as the ''alpha'' pattern.

reason or another, are only able to sleep a few hours at a time descend rapidly into Stage IV and remain there for most of their nap.

However, on an average night, Stage IV sleep lasts only for an hour or an hour and a half. You then climb back through Stages III and II to Stage I. At this point, something curious happens. Although your muscles are even more relaxed than before, your eyes begin to move rapidly. You have entered rapid-eye-movement or *REM sleep*. Your pulse rate and breathing become irregular and the levels of adrenal and sexual hormones in your blood rise—as if you were in the midst of an intensely emotional or physically demanding activity. Your brain sends out waves that closely resemble those of a person who is fully awake. It is during this stage that almost all dreaming takes place, although sleepwalking and sleeptalking rarely occur during this phase.

REM sleep lasts for about ten minutes, after which you retrace the descent to Stage IV. You go through this cycle every ninety minutes or so. Each time the period of Stage IV sleep decreases and the length of REM sleep increases—until you eventually wake up (Leichtling, 1973). But at no point does your brain become inactive.

Dreams.   We call the mental activity that takes place during sleep *dreaming.* Everybody dreams, although most people are only able to recall a few if any of their dreams. Sleep researchers sometimes make a point of waking subjects at regular intervals during the night to ask them about their dreams. The first few dreams are usually composed of vague thoughts left over from the day's activities. A subject may report that she was watching television, for example. As the night wears on, dreams become more vivid and dramatic, especially dreams that take place during REM sleep. These are the dreams people are most likely to remember when they wake up.

Researchers who have recorded the contents of thousands of dreams have found that most—even the late-night REM adventures—occur in such commonplace settings as living rooms, cars, and streets. Most dreams involve either strenuous recreational activities or passive events such as sitting and watching, not work or study. A large percentage of the emotions experienced in dreams are negative or unpleasant—apprehension, anger, sadness, and so on. Contrary to popular belief, dreams do not occur in a "split second" but rather correspond to a realistic time scale.

Dream Interpretation.   Although dreams may contain elements of ordinary, waking reality, these elements are often jumbled in fantastic ways. The dreamer may see people in places they would never go, wander through strange houses with endless doors, find himself transported backward in time. The dreamer may be unable to speak—or able to fly. What do these distortions mean?

It was Sigmund Freud who first pointed out the importance of dreams for psychology. Freud believed that no matter how simple or mundane, dreams contain clues to thoughts and desires the dreamer is afraid to acknowledge or express in his or her waking hours. Indeed, he maintained that dreams themselves are full of hidden meanings and disguises.

Freud believed that the symbolism of dreams is a private language that each individual has invented for himself or herself. These symbols vary greatly from person to person. Suppose that a dreamer sees herself standing naked among fully clothed strangers. For one person, this dream may symbolize a desire to show her true self to people, without pretense. For another person, the dream may symbolize a fear of having her inadequacies exposed in public. In his work with patients, Freud tried to break through the disguise of dream imagery and discover the true desires and wishes of the dreamer.

Not all psychologists agree with Freud's analysis of dreams or with the emphasis on sexual imagery. For example, Ann Faraday (1974) believes that dreams are always relevant to the dreamer's personal life, and can be of great aid in analyzing one's hidden self. However, before looking for a symbolic or metaphorical meaning in the dream, one should first look for a more literal interpretation. Many dreams can be taken at face value. If you find yourself fighting with a friend in a dream, the meaning is obvious, not hidden. You are angry at that friend. Other dreams express what you hope might happen; still others what you are afraid might happen.

Whether or not the dreamer makes conscious use of the content of his

FIGURE 7.5

The paintings of Marc Chagall—this one is titled "I and the Village"—often have a dreamlike quality. Images are intermingled, and space, time, and color are rearranged in ways that are rarely experienced in a waking state but that seem natural in the dream state.

(Marc Chagall, *I and the Village,* 1911. Oil on canvas, 75 5/8" x 59 5/8". Collection, The Museum of Modern Art, New York. Mrs. Simon Guggenheim Fund.)

or her dreams in self-analysis, dreaming is apparently essential to psychological well-being. Numerous experiments have shown that when people are deprived of the opportunity to dream they become anxious and irritable, have difficulty concentrating, and may experience hallucinations (see Jouvet, 1967).

Hypnosis

Hypnosis is a form of altered consciousness in which a person becomes highly suggestible and does not use his critical thinking ability. By allowing the hypnotist to guide and direct him, a person can be made conscious of things he is usually unaware of and unconscious of things he usually notices. (The subject may recall in vivid detail an incident he had forgotten; or feel no pain when his hand is pricked with a needle.)

Hypnosis does not put the subject to sleep, as many people believe. A hypnotic trance is quite different from sleep. In fact, the subject becomes highly receptive and responsive to certain internal and external stimuli. He is able to focus his attention on one tiny aspect of reality and totally ignore all other inputs. The hypnotist induces a trance by slowly persuading the subject to relax and to lose interest in external distractions. Whether this takes a few minutes or months of interaction depends on the purpose of the hypnosis and the method of induction.

Psychologists who use hypnosis stress that the relationship between the hypnotist and subject involves cooperation, not domination. The subject is not under the hypnotist's "power" and cannot be forced to do things against his or her will. Rather, the person is simply cooperating with the hypnotist by becoming particularly responsive to the hypnotist's suggestions. *Together* they try to solve a problem or to learn more about how the subject's mind works. Anyone can resist hypnosis by simply refusing to open his or her consciousness to the hypnotist, and people under hypnosis cannot be induced to do things they would not do when "awake" unless they want to.

Many people—including many psychologists—are skeptical about hypnosis. Critics tend to regard it as a sophisticated form of trickery. However, one study provided convincing evidence that hypnosis is a real phenomenon.

A hypnotist was asked to put several people into a trance. What the hypnotist did not know was that some of these people had been instructed to fake the trance. The hypnotist told each subject that he would see a third person sitting in a chair. In fact, this person was standing behind the subject and the chair was empty. The researchers found that the subjects who were faking acted quite differently from the others. They said they saw the person sitting in the chair, as the hypnotist suggested. When they turned around and saw the person standing behind them they either said they did not see see him or that he was a different person. The hypnotized subjects, in contrast, acted surprised when they saw the third person standing behind them and reported seeing two images of the same person. This is known as *trance logic*. With trance logic, a person readily perceives hallucinations suggested by the hypnotist and mixes them freely with perceptions based on real objects and events, without attempting to be logical. The fakers were exposed by their effort to respond in a conventionally logical way (Orne, 1959).

Hypnotists can also suggest things for their subjects to remember when the trance is over, a phenomenon known as *post-hypnotic suggestion*. For example, the hypnotist might suggest that after the person is awakened she will be unable to hear the word "psychology." When she comes out of the trance, the subject may report that some people around her are speaking strangely. They seem to leave out some words occasionally, especially when they are talking about topics involving the taboo word

FIGURE 7.6
Hypnosis, as depicted in an engraving and a woodcut from the
late eighteenth and early nineteenth centuries. Hypnosis was
originally called Mesmerism after
Anton Mesmer, its first proponent.
Mesmer believed hypnosis to be
some kind of psychic magnetic
force. Later, it was thought of as
artificially controlled sleepwalking.
This form of consciousness is still
not fully understood; in fact, some
psychologists consider it to be
nothing more than deliberate self-
deception.

"psychology." The subject is not aware that part of her consciousness has
been instructed to block out that word. Post-hypnotic suggestion has been
found to be particularly helpful in changing unwanted behaviors, such
as smoking or overeating.

A form of hypnosis may occur in everyday life when one becomes so
entranced by another person—an orator, for example—that the rest of

reality seems to slip away and all that exists is the speaker's words. At the other extreme, particularly boring stimuli can cause a trancelike state, as any long-distance truck driver knows.

Hallucinations

Hallucinations are sensations or perceptions that have no direct external cause—seeing, hearing, smelling, tasting, or feeling things that do not exist.

Hypnosis, meditation, certain drugs, withdrawal from a drug to which one has become addicted, and psychological breakdown may produce hallucinations. (We discuss the hallucinations associated with drug withdrawal and mental breakdowns in Chapter 15.) But they also occur under "normal" conditions. People hallucinate when they are dreaming and when they are deprived of the opportunity to dream, as indicated in the section on sleep. Periods of high emotion, concentration, or fatigue may also produce false sensations and perceptions. For example, truck drivers on long hauls have been known to swerve suddenly to avoid stalled cars that do not exist. Even daydreams involve mild hallucinations.

One of the most interesting facts that psychologists studying altered states of consciousness have discovered is that people who are not permitted to see, hear, or touch begin to hallucinate (see Figure 7.7). It is as if we cannot tolerate the absence of sensory stimulation. The mind keeps working even when it has nothing to work with: the "stream of consciousness" flows on.

Drug States

Hallucinogenic (hallucination-producing) drugs were not invented in the 1960s. People have been using these drugs to cure illness, relieve pain,

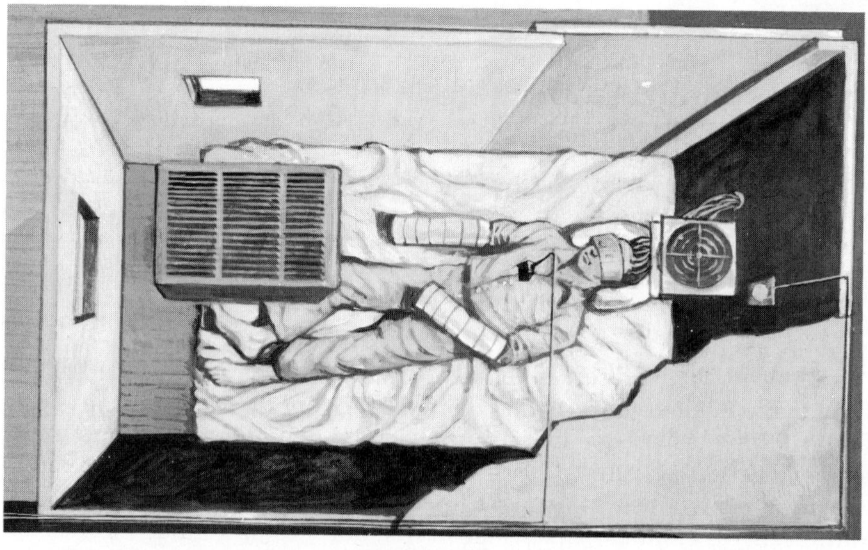

FIGURE 7.7
A classic series of experiments on boredom was conducted at McGill University in the 1950s. Subjects were paid $20.00 a day to live with as little sensory input as the experimenters could arrange. Gloves and cotton cuffs prevented input to the hands and fingers; a plastic visor diffused the light coming into the eyes; a foam pillow and the continuous hum of the air conditioner and fan made input to the ears low and monotonous. Except for eating and using the bathroom, the subjects did nothing but lie on the bed. After a day or so of this routine, subjects began to report hallucinations: geometrical shapes, abstract patterns repeated like a wallpaper design, feelings that another body overlapping with their own was lying beside them, cartoon sequences, or sometimes voices or music. Similar experiences are common in certain drug states.

(After "The Pathology of Boredom," by Woodburn Heron © 1957 by Scientific American, Inc. All rights reserved.)

induce sleep, and to produce altered states of consciousness for centuries. In many non-Western societies they are an accepted part of religious and social life. People in such societies take drugs to heighten mystical experiences, bolster their courage in battle, and the like.

We will discuss two widely abused drugs—heroin and alcohol—in some detail in Chapter 15. Here we are concerned with two drugs people use for the express purpose of producing altered states of consciousness: marijuana and LSD.

Marijuana is a mild hallucinogen that has been used as an intoxicant among Eastern cultures for many centuries. Marijuana smokers often report that when they get "high" most of their perceptions are greatly enhanced—colors are brighter, smells are richer, foods taste better. Users often experience feelings of serenity, may become happy and talk or laugh a great deal, and may discover that even the most ordinary events and objects are suddenly more meaningful.

Marijuana can intensify unpleasant as well as pleasant experiences. If a person is frightened or unhappy when he takes the drug, these feelings may be increased enough to make his world, temporarily at least, very upsetting. Nervousness and irrational fears are commonly experienced.

In one study of marijuana's effects, seventeen college students were given marijuana for the first time. Only one student said he actually got high, but all performed less well than usual on tests of both intellectual ability and physical skills. Experienced users, on the other hand, showed no impairment of either intellectual abilities or of physical skills when they smoked marijuana.

LSD is the most potent of the hallucinogens. Its effects, although far more profound than those of marijuana, also seem to depend heavily on the people around the user, on where and when he or she takes the drug, on his or her previous experience, and on what he or she expects to happen. LSD usually produces a pronounced alteration in awareness, called a *trip,* which lasts for several hours. A trip often includes intense hallucinations and emotions that can range anywhere from intense happiness to extreme panic. Thoughts become vivid and generally seem to be beyond the individual's control—somewhat as in a dream.

While "tripping," a person may focus on a single object for hours as if seeing it and understanding it for the first time. For example, one person reported that he finally understood the meaning of an empty cola bottle and its relationship to the universe. These discoveries often lose their importance once the user "comes down" from his or her trip, but sometimes people find that their religious feelings have been increased or that their understanding of themselves has changed.

Why do people take hallucinogens? Research conducted in the 1960s, when concern over these drugs reached the crisis level, suggests several reasons. The first and most obvious reason for experimenting with marijuana or LSD is curiosity. People try psychedelics because they want to know what it feels like to get high. The risk involved in using illegal drugs (as opposed to a legal drug such as alcohol) may add to their allure. A second reason is that "everybody is doing it." If you are at a party and

Marijuana

FIGURE 7.8
The active chemical in marijuana and hashish is tetrahydrocannabinol (THC); in various forms it may exert an effect for up to four hours. Marijuana produces relaxation, euphoria, and increased appetite, and may cause some general impairment of judgment and perception (although its effects on experienced users are unclear).

drugs are being passed around, you may feel uncomfortable refusing a joint or pill. The social risks of abstaining may seem greater than the risks associated with the drug. Who wants to be considered square or uptight? In addition, people take these drugs in the hope of solving problems or improving their performance—in other words, as a form of self-medica-tion. Truck drivers use drugs to relieve the boredom of long hours of driving; athletes, to heighten their senses during an important game. Others hope that drugs will relieve anxiety or provide insight into per-sonal problems (National Commission on Marijuana and Drug Abuse, 1973: 92–98).

Are marijuana and LSD harmful or dangerous? There is evidence that people who smoke large amounts of marijuana regularly over extended periods develop bronchitis, asthma, and other respiratory diseases. Some heavy users have problems with their skin and develop stomach ailments as well (Tennant et al., 1971). Although it appears to be safe for emo-tionally stable people to take LSD in comfortable and secure settings, its effects on any individual cannot be predicted. The possible chemical and physiological effects of LSD are not fully known. Illegal LSD, sold on the street, is almost always contaminated with chemicals other than LSD, some of which are extemely dangerous, such as strychnine.

Neither marijuana nor LSD is physically addictive. Indeed, two re-searchers found the opposite is true for LSD. A ten-year study revealed that the longer people take LSD, the less attractive it becomes. Why? Because a major reason people try psychedelics is to experience new sensations and perceptions. After a time, the novelty of "tripping" wears off. Moreover, LSD is unpredictable: "Bad trips" (in which one is con-fronted with the worst of one's self) are as common as exhilarating revela-tions. A person who takes drugs because he or she wants to escape prob-lems and tension is not likely to use LSD regularly (McGlothlin and Arnold, 1971). Individuals may acquire the social habit of smoking mari-juana more or less regularly, just as other people develop the social habit of drinking alcohol regularly. There is no evidence that using marijuana

FIGURE 7.9
Drawings done by a man on an LSD trip. (a) Twenty minutes after taking the drug: no effect yet. (b) Eighty-five minutes after first tak-ing the drug and twenty minutes after taking a second dose: The subject sees the model clearly but has some difficulty controlling the wide sweeping movements of his hand. (c) One hour later: The sub-ject sees the model very vividly, with changed colors. He says, "I feel as if my consciousness is situ-ated in the part of my body that is now active." (d) A few minutes later: "The outlines of the model are normal but those of my draw-ing are not. I pull myself together and try again: it's no good. I give up trying and let myself go at the third attempt." (e) Shortly after the fourth drawing: "I try again and produce this drawing with one flourish." (f) Two and three-quarter hours after first taking the drug: "The perspective of the room has changed, everything is moving . . . everything is inter-woven in a network of color. . . . The model's face is distorted to a diabolic mask." (g) Four and one-quarter hours: The subject is in a very happy state. As he attempts yet another portrait he says, "If I am not careful, I lose control of my movements." (h) Five and three-quarter hours: "It is probably because my movements are still too unsteady that I am unable to draw as I normally do. . . . The intoxication is wearing off, but I can both feel and see it ebbing and flowing about me (now it only reaches to my knees); finally, only an eddying motion remains." (i) Eight hours: The effects of the drug have now worn off except for a few small waves (for example, sudden distortions of faces from time to time). The subject feels bewildered and tired. "I have nothing to say about the last draw-ing, it is bad and uninteresting."

in this way is the first step in a descent into heroin addiction, as many people once believed.

However, a person may become psychologically dependent on either marijuana or LSD—*if* that person believes the drug magically changes him or her into another, more attractive kind of person and that he or she cannot function well without it. This attitude is based on a misconception. The sensations, perceptions, and thoughts an individual experiences while high are not *contained* in the marijuana or LSD. They come from the person who takes them. All the drugs do is to release or trigger elements of human consciousness that were inaccessible or new and un-imagined (Weil, 1972). There are other, drug-*free* ways of relieving tension and getting high.

Meditation

When you hear the word "meditation," you probably think of religion. It is true that the followers of certain Eastern religions practice meditation as a way of achieving a "higher consciousness." Many meditators report that they can separate their minds from their senses at will and that meditation can produce states of consciousness that are free from worry. They say they can experience something for the thousandth time as freshly as they did the first time. In recent years this method for creating an altered state of consciousness has spread to the Western world, where it may or may not be associated with religion.

What is meditation? The basic goal is to combine heightened awareness with deep passivity. The meditator assumes a comfortable position that enables him or her to relax without becoming drowsy, usually sitting on the floor or on a pillow. He or she may sway slowly back and forth, concentrate on breathing slowly and regularly, or focus on relaxing the muscles in each part of the body. He or she attempts to suspend all purposeful, directed thinking—all striving, all mental "busyness." Concentrating on an object or a spot on the wall, or repeating a soothing sound such as "Om," helps to induce the desired state of restful contemplation. In the words of one meditator:

> It is extremely misleading to strive toward any particular state of mind, but all of these exercises will sometimes make possible a state of clear, relaxed awareness in which the flow of thought is reduced and an attitude of detached observation is maintained. In contrast with the usual thinking activity, which carries one off into abstractions or fantasies, this observing attitude keeps close contact with the here-and-now of experience. Thoughts are not prevented, but are allowed to pass without elaboration. It is not a blank state or trance, and it is different from sleep. It involves letting go. . . . (Maupin, 1969: 181).

In studies of meditative concentration, people who have not meditated before have learned to meditate on a certain object. In one case subjects were taught to meditate on a blue vase. The participants soon reported that the color of the vase became very vivid and that time passed quickly. The people could not be distracted as easily as they normally might. Some

FIGURE 7.10

The goal of meditation is to concentrate one's attention and consciousness completely upon some single object. A mandala like this one aids meditation because its visual forms continually return one's eye to the center of the figure.

people felt themselves merging with the vase. Others reported that their surroundings became unusually beautiful, filled with light and movement. All the meditators found the experience pleasant. After twelve sessions they all felt a strong attachment to the vase and missed it when it was not present during the next session (Deikman, 1963).

Evidence that meditation is a different state than ordinary consciousness has come from studies on the bodily functions of yogis and Zen monks. Researchers found that during meditation distinct EEG patterns appeared and that the meditators were highly relaxed but awake. There were also indications that meditation reduced anxiety and other signs of stress (Wallace and Benson, 1972).

Some psychologists have suggested meditation as a way of releasing anxiety and thus increasing alertness, as a substitute for drugs (including such legal drugs as tranquilizers), and as a help for such problems as insomnia and alcoholism.

SUMMARY

1. Consciousness is difficult to define, but in general, it is the ability of the mind to be aware of itself and of external events.

2. Consciousness is limited in that people are not conscious of much that goes on, inside and outside their bodies. It is, however, an active process, in which one's experience of reality is constructed rather than passively received.

3. The most common altered state of consciousness is dreaming. People are mentally active throughout the night, although the degree of activity varies with each stage in the dream cycle.

4. The stage of sleep in which vivid dreams occur is called REM sleep. Dreams often symbolically depict significant emotional problems and disturbances that are part of a person's daily experiences.

5. Hypnosis is an altered state of consciousness

in which a subject becomes highly receptive to the suggestions of another person and exhibits trance logic. He or she does so willingly and cannot be made to do anything he or she would not normally do while awake.

6. Hallucinations—sensations or perceptions that have no direct external cause—may occur during sleep, drug states, or under sensory deprivation.

7. Among the drugs that alter awareness are hallucinogens, or psychedelics. Marijuana and LSD are the two most common of these drugs. Although both may have side effects, neither is physically addictive.

8. Meditation is a state of consciousness involving high levels of concentration—a drug-free "high" for many people. Experienced meditators are able to achieve a high state of relaxation with greatly reduced anxiety.

GLOSSARY

consciousness: That part of the self that is aware of its own sensations, ideas, and actions.

The activity of the brain that actively constructs experiences.

hallucination: A sensation or perception that has no direct external cause.

hallucinogens: Drugs that are used primarily to produce hallucinations (also called psychedelics).

hypnosis: An altered state of consciousness resulting from a narrowed focus of attention and characterized by heightened suggestibility.

LSD: An extremely potent psychedelic drug that produces hallucinations and distortions of perception and thought.

marijuana: The dried leaves and flowers of Indian hemp (*Cannabis sativa*) that produce an altered state of consciousness when smoked or ingested.

meditation: Prolonged reflective thought or contemplation, usually achieved by clearing one's mind of all conscious thoughts and concentrating on a particular image or sound.

post-hypnotic suggestion: A suggestion made during a hypnotic trance that influences the subject's behavior after the trance is ended.

REM sleep: The period of sleep during which the most active and vivid dreaming occurs (also called rapid-eye-movement sleep).

trance logic: A hypnotic phenomena, in which the subject readily perceives hallucinations suggested to him or her and mixes them freely with the perception of real objects and events.

ACTIVITIES

1. What behaviors do you perform automatically? This chapter mentions breathing, walking, running, tying shoelaces, taking a shower, and using speech mannerisms. What are some others? Pick one of your automatic behaviors and pay close attention to how you perform it. What are the individual parts that make up the behavior? How does consciously thinking about the behavior affect your performance of it?

2. Keep track of your dreams for at least a week. Dreams are difficult to remember, so keep a paper and pencil by your bed. When you wake up after a dream, keep your eyes closed and try to remember it in your mind. Then write it down, including as much detail as you can. Also write down any ideas you may have about what the dream means and any feelings you may have about the dream. After you have kept track of your dreams for several days, ask yourself: Am I able to consciously control my dreams in any way? Am I better able to understand myself by examining my dreams?

3. One way of becoming aware of your consciousness is through meditation. Meditation is not concentration in the normal sense of the word. It is opening up one's awareness to the world at the present. Try the following for ten to fifteen minutes a day. Find a quiet spot without distractions. Listen quietly without making any generalizations on what you hear. Listen for the sounds without naming them. After each period, write down your observations. Which sounds did you "hear" for the first time? In this simple form of meditation, do not be surprised if you actually hear yourself talk to yourself.

4. Hypnosis is a form of suggestibility. You may discover which of your friends is susceptible to hypnosis by doing the following test in hypnosis. Have your subjects place a coin in their open palm. Repeatedly suggest to them that they feel the palm slowly turning over, until the coin falls out of the palm. You may be surprised at the results.

5. Pick any word and say it one hundred times. What happens?

6. Have you ever hallucinated a sight or sound —perhaps when you were very tired or upset? What did you experience? Why do you suppose you created this particular hallucination?

7. Make a list of as many fairly common dream symbols as you can think of. Next to each symbol give an interpretation of what you think that symbol represents. Compare your interpretations with those of other students in the class. Do you find any patterns of interpretations? Are interpretations by females different from interpretations by males?

8. Here is another simple experiment you can try to test suggestibility. Think of a lemon. Picture its shape and its yellowness. Smell the aroma. Now imagine a person starting to slice it in half. Visualize the knife slicing the skin and separating the two halves. Smell the increased aroma. How do the insides of your cheeks feel? Repeat the above sentences to a friend and see what kind of reaction you get. What is the difference between reading this description and hearing it? How willing were you to accept these suggestions? How willing were your subject(s)?

9. Many people argue in favor of repealing all drug laws. They maintain that adult individuals should have the right to decide for themselves, without fear or punishment, what to do with, and to, their own bodies. Do you feel that most people would behave responsibly if all drugs, including narcotics, were available for sale? What does it mean to "behave responsibly"? Debate this issue with a friend, then reverse positions and continue the debate. How does this argument apply to such other issues as suicide and abortion?

SUGGESTED READINGS

BORING, E. G. *The Physical Dimensions of Consciousness*. New York: Dover, 1963. In describing and analyzing the diverse aspects of our conscious experience, Professor Boring, who was one of the wisest men in psychology, changed the whole philosophical basis of psychology in 1933, when this book first appeared. His observations are just as fresh and relevant today, especially in relation to the so-called altered states of consciousness.

CASTANEDA, CARLOS. *A Separate Reality*. New York: Simon & Schuster, 1971 (paper). In this sequel to his first book, *The Teachings of Don Juan: A Yaqui Way of Knowledge,* Castaneda describes his continuing efforts to learn to think in a new way, to move outside old patterns of thought learned in his own culture.

DEMENT, W. C. *Some Must Watch While Some Must Sleep.* Stanford, Calif.: Stanford Alumni Association, 1972. The psychologist who is probably the best-known researcher on dreams and sleep sums up his research here.

FARADAY, ANN. *Dream Power.* New York: Coward, McCann & Geoghegan, 1972. As an alternative to classical Freudian dream analysis, Faraday explains the kinds of messages that dreams convey and gives the best procedures for decoding them into useful self-knowledge.

LUCE, GAY GAER, AND SEGAL, JULIUS. *Sleep.* New York: Coward, McCann & Geoghegan, 1966 (Lancer paperback). An enlightening sojourn into existing knowledge on the nature of sleep and dreams.

NARAJANO, C., AND ORNSTEIN, R. *On the Psychology of Meditation.* New York: Viking, 1971. A comparative discussion on the wide range of meditative techniques and their relations to the control of internal body and brain states.

ORNSTEIN, ROBERT. *The Psychology of Consciousness.* New York: Viking, 1972. Ornstein explores the idea that humans have two modes of consciousness, one in each brain hemisphere. Among the phenomena he discusses are meditation and biofeedback.

SMITH, A. *"Sport Is a Western Yoga."* *Psychology Today,* 9 (October 1975): 48–51. (This is an excerpt from Smith's new book, *Powers of Mind,* Random House, 1975.) An attempt to integrate Western psychological research with Eastern mysticism. Smith discusses concentration, energy, and altered states of consciousness.

——. "Sensory Deprivation: The Benefits of Boredom." *Psychology Today*, 9 (April 1976): 46–51. In this article, the author describes how sensory deprivation can be of great benefit as a mild form of therapy that cures smoking and obesity.

TART, C. T. (ED.). *Altered States of Consciousness.* New York: Wiley, 1969. A collection of fascinat-ing readings on a wide range of topics, including dreaming, hypnosis, drugs, and meditation. Also included is a "fact sheet" on marijuana and many useful papers that are difficult to obtain elsewhere.

WEIL, ANDREW. *The Natural Mind.* Boston: Houghton Mifflin, 1972. Weil examines alterna-tives to ordinary consciousness. He is particu-larly interested in what he calls "stoned think-ing," a non-drug-induced state.

BIBLIOGRAPHY

AARONSON, BERNARD, AND OSMOND, H. *Psychedel-ics: The Uses and Implications of Hallucino-genic Drugs.* Garden City, N.Y.: Doubleday, 1970.

BEERS, C. W. *A Mind That Found Itself.* Garden City, N.Y.: Doubleday, 1948.

BUCKE, RICHARD. *Cosmic Consciousness.* Rev. ed. New York: Citadel Press, 1970.

CHAUDHURI, H. *Philosophy of Meditation.* New York: Philosophical Library, 1965.

CUSTANCE, J. *Wisdom, Madness and Folly.* New York: Farrar, Straus & Giroux, 1952.

DEIKMAN, ARTHUR J. "Experimental Meditation." *Journal of Nervous and Mental Disease,* 136 (1963): 329–373.

ESTABROOKS, G. (ED.). *Hypnosis: Current Prob-lems.* New York: Harper & Row, 1962.

FARADAY, ANN. *The Dream Game.* New York: Harper & Row, 1974.

FOULKES, DAVID. *The Psychology of Sleep.* New York: Scribner's, 1966.

GAZZANIGA, M. S. "The Split Brain in Man." *Scientific American,* 217 (1967): 24–29.

GRINSPOON, LESTER. *Marijuana Reconsidered.* Cambridge, Mass.: Harvard University Press, 970.

HILGARD, E. R. *Hypnotic Susceptibility.* New York: Harcourt Brace Jovanovich, 1965.

HUXLEY, ALDOUS. *Brave New World.* New York: Harper & Row, 1932 (paper).

——. *Doors of Perception.* New York: Harper & Row, 1970; originally published, 1956.

JOUVET, MICHEL. "The Stages of Sleep." *Scientific American,* 216 (1967): 62–72.

KLEITMAN, N. *Sleep and Wakefulness.* Rev. ed. Chicago: University of Chicago Press, 1963.

LEICHTLING, B. "Sleep and Dreaming." In *Psy-chosources,* edited by Evelyn Shapiro. New York: Bantam, 1973 (paper).

LUCE, GAY GAER, and SEGAL, JULIUS. *Sleep.* New York: Coward, McCann & Geoghegan, 1966 (Lancer paperback).

MAUPIN, E. W. "On Meditation." In *Altered States of Consciousness,* edited by C. T. Tart. New York: Wiley, 1969, pp. 177–186.

MCGLOTHIN, WILLIAM H., and ARNOLD, DAVID O. "LSD Revisited." *Archives of General Psychia-try,* 24 (1971): 35–49.

NARAJANO, C., and ORNSTEIN, R. *On the Psycho-logy of Meditation.* New York: Viking, 1971.

NATIONAL COMMISSION ON MARIJUANA AND DRUG ABUSE. Washington, D.C.: U.S. Government Printing Office, 1973.

ORNE, MARTIN T. "The Nature of Hypnosis: Artifact and Essence." *Journal of Abnormal and Social Psychology,* 58 (1959): 277–299.

ORNSTEIN, ROBERT, *The Psychology of Consciousness.* New York: Viking, 1972.

SHOR, R. E., AND ORNE, M. T. (EDS.). *The Nature of Hypnosis.* New York: Holt, Rinehart & Winston, 1965.

TART, C. T. (ED.). *Altered States of Consciousness.* 2nd ed. New York: Wiley, 1972.

TENNANT, FOREST S., JR. et al. "Medical Manifestations Associated with Hashish." *Journal of the* American Medical Association, 216 (June 21, 1971): 1965–1971.

THOMPSON, RICHARD F. (ED.). *Physiological Psychology.* San Francisco: Freeman, 1971.

WALLACE, ROBERT K., and BENSON, HERBERT. "The Physiology of Meditation." *Scientific American,* 226 (February 1972): 84–90.

WEIL, ANDREW. *The Natural Mind.* Boston: Houghton Mifflin, 1972.

WEIL, ANDREW, et al. "Clinical and Psychological Effects of Marijuana in Man." *Science,* 162 (1968): 1234–1242.

UNIT III

Human Development

Human beings have an extended childhood. We are physically immature and dependent on others for much longer than any other animal. During this period, we learn to use our bodies and our minds. We develop a distinctive personality and an understanding of the social rules that govern the people among whom we live, and acquire language and the ability to think in more complex ways than any other creatures on earth.

Development does not stop with full physical and mental growth, however. Our bodies continue to change. As we grow older, society makes new demands on us, and we demand new kinds of satisfaction from society. We learn to adjust to—and perhaps enjoy—young adulthood, middle age, and old age.

This Unit surveys the entire life cycle, from birth to death. Chapter 8 details the intellectual, social, and psychological developments of childhood, with special emphasis on how a child develops into a unique individual and member of society. Chapter 9 examines the different ways people respond to the opportunities and problems of adolescence, adulthood, and old age.

There was a time when Western peoples considered children miniature adults. Maturing was thought to be a simple matter of growing bigger and learning more. However, psychologists have shown that human development involves qualitative as well as quantitative changes—transformations in the way we think and feel as well as in growth.

Infancy and Childhood

8

FIGURE 8.1
Childhood is a time of exploration, growth, and learning. Children not only have fun when they play, but they discover things about themselves and develop skills and abilities that will enhance their feelings of self-esteem.

Can you recall your first toy or the first time you stood on two legs? Do you remember the first time your father lifted you in his arms or the moment you realized what the word "no" meant? You have probably forgotten all of these events, yet you changed faster and learned more in your early years than you ever will again.

You were an explorer—charting paths in the strange new world beyond your crib, conquering the living room floor, your backyard, and your first classroom. You experimented to find out how your own body and the things in your environment worked. You tested your power to get what you wanted by staging a tantrum or acting cute. You played house, doctor, or cowboys-and-Indians with the conviction of a professional actor. You learned that games have rules—and so do people, young and old. All this time you were growing, physically and mentally.

Developmental psychology is the study of the changes that occur as people grow up and grow old. It covers the entire life cycle, from conception to death. What are people born with? How do we learn to walk and talk, to think, to love and hate? What makes each human being become a unique individual? How do people change over the years? These are the questions developmental psychologists attempt to answer.

In this chapter we describe the many different psychological processes we experience from infancy through childhood. In the next chapter we will look at adolescence, adulthood, and old age.

THE BEGINNING OF LIFE

Life begins long before an infant is born. Expectant mothers can feel strong kicking and sometimes hiccupping inside them during the later stages of pregnancy, and it is common for a fetus (an unborn child) to suck its thumb, even though it has never tasted its mother's breast or a bottle.

Birth puts staggering new demands on a baby's capacity to adapt and survive. He goes from an environment in which he is totally protected from the world to one in which he is assaulted by lights, sounds, touches, and extremes of temperature. The newborn is capable of certain coordinated movement patterns that can be triggered by the right stimulus. The grasping reflex, for example, is a response to a touch on the palm of the hand. Infants can grasp an object, such as a finger, so strongly that they can be lifted into the air. We suspect this reflex is left over from an earlier stage in human evolution, when babies had to cling to their apelike mothers' coats while their mothers were climbing or searching for food.

Also vital is the *rooting reflex*. If an alert newborn is touched anywhere around the mouth, he will move his head and mouth toward the source of the touch. In this way the touch of his mother's breast on his cheek guides the baby's mouth toward her nipple. The sucking that follows contact with the nipple is one of the baby's most complex reflexes. The baby is able to suck, breathe air, and swallow milk twice a second without getting confused.

Besides grasping and sucking, the newborn spends a lot of time just looking. From birth, unless he is sleeping, feeding, or crying, the baby is watching with curiosity, directing his gaze toward bright patterns and tracing the outlines of those patterns with his eyes.

HOW DO BABIES GROW?

In the space of two years this grasping, rooting, searching infant will develop into a child who can walk, talk, and feed himself. This transformation is the result of both maturation and learning.

Maturation

To some extent a baby is like a plant that shoots up and unfolds according to a built-in plan. Unless something is wrong with an infant, she will begin to lift her head at about three months, smile at four months, and grasp objects at five to six months. Crawling appears at eight to ten months. By this time the baby may be able to pull herself into a standing position, although she will fall if she lets go. Three or four months later she will begin to walk, tentatively at first, but gradually acquiring a sense of balance.

Psychologists call internally programmed growth *maturation*. Maturation is as important as learning or experience, especially in the first years. Unless a child is persistently underfed, severely restricted in her movements, or deprived of human contact and things to look at, she will develop more or less according to this schedule. Conversely, no amount of coaching will push a child to walk or speak before she is physiologically ready.

This was demonstrated in an experiment with identical twins (Gesell and Thompson, 1929). One twin, but not the other, was given special training in climbing stairs, building with blocks, and the like. This child did acquire some skill in these areas. But in a short time the second child learned to climb and build just as well as his twin—and with much less practice. Why? Because he had matured to the point where he could coordinate his legs and hands more easily.

The process of maturation becomes obvious when you think about walking. An infant lacks the physical control walking requires. However,

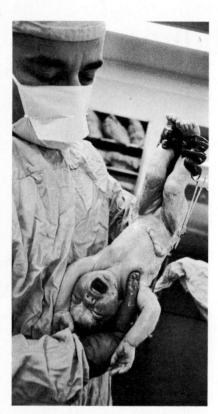

FIGURE 8.2
Birth must be an overwhelming experience for the baby as well as for the mother. Unfortunately, no one really knows what the newborn infant feels.

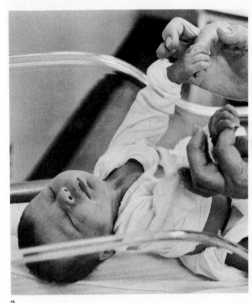
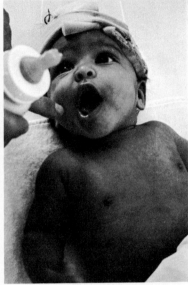

a   b

FIGURE 8.3
Reflexes in infants: (a) The strength of the grasping reflex is demonstrated in a baby who is only a few days old. (b) This infant is responding to a touch on the cheek by opening his mouth and turning his head. This response is called the rooting reflex. The baby has been placed in the apparatus by an experimenter so that his head movements can be recorded.

by the end of the first year the nerves connected to the child's muscles have grown. He or she is ready to walk.

By recording the ages at which thousands of infants first began to smile, to sit upright, to crawl, and to try a few steps, psychologists have been able to draw up an approximate timetable for maturation. This schedule helps doctors and other professionals to spot problems and abnormalities. If a child has not begun to talk by the age of two and a half, a doctor will recommend tests to determine if something is wrong.

However, one of the facts to emerge from this effort is that the maturational plan inside each child is unique. On the average, babies start walking at twelve to thirteen months. However, some are ready at nine months, and others delay walking until eighteen months. And each baby has his own *temperament*. Some infants are extremely active from birth and some quiet. Some are cuddly and some stiff. Some cry a great deal while others hardly ever whimper. No two babies are exactly alike, and no two mature according to the same timetable.

Learning

Maturation is only part of the process of growing up. Infants and small children are exceptionally responsive. Each experience changes the child, teaches him something, pushes him in some direction. The child learns to make associations, to expect certain events—such as mother and food—to come together. Children learn to do things that produce rewards and to avoid doing things that produce punishments. They also learn by imitating other people.

Recent experiments indicate that infants too are able to learn new behaviors. Even newborn babies change their behavior in response to the

FIGURE 8.4

Maturation is the principal factor that determines when a child begins to walk. As the child's nerves and muscles develop, he or she is able first to lift his or her head (at about twelve weeks), then to sit (at about six months), then to crawl (at ten months), then to walk with one hand held (at about one year). Running and climbing stairs are not mastered until about the age of two. Although maturation controls this development, learning is very much involved. The mastery of every new ability is an exciting adventure full of risks, mistakes, and triumphs.

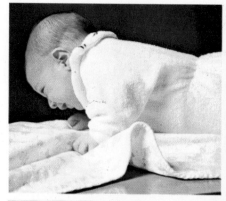
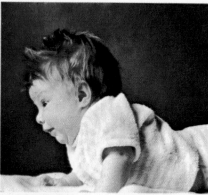

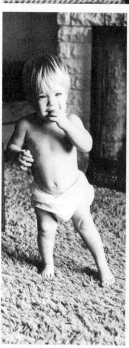

environment—which, as you will recall from Chapter 2, is the basic definition of learning. One team of psychologists taught two- and three-day-
old infants to turn their heads at the sound of a buzzer by rewarding them
with a bottle each time they did so.

Another researcher built a small theater for four- to five-week-old
babies. The infants were placed in a well-padded seat opposite a blank
wall that served as a movie screen, and given pacifiers. The pacifiers were
connected to the projector. To focus the picture, the infants had to suck
on the pacifiers. Soon the babies had learned the trick and sucked hard,
pausing for only a few seconds to catch their breath. When the researcher
reversed the procedure, so that sucking blurred the picture, they quickly
learned to lengthen the pause to eight seconds (Pines, 1970). We can
assume that infants are just as responsive to everyday events as they are
to experiments.

Clearly, then, learning is an important part of the process of growing
up. In the pages that follow we will show how inner plans and outside
influences—maturation and learning—work together in the development
of intellect, language, love, and morality.

INTELLECTUAL DEVELOPMENT

If you have a younger brother or sister, you may remember times when
your parents insisted that you let the little one play with you and your
friends. No matter how often you explained hide-and-seek to your four-
year-old brother, he spoiled the game. Why couldn't he understand that
he had to keep quiet or he'd be found right away?

This is a question Swiss psychologist Jean Piaget set out to answer more
than fifty years ago. Of the several theories of intellectual development,
Piaget's is the most comprehensive and influential. Common sense told
him that intelligence, or the ability to understand, develops gradually, as
the child grows. The sharpest, most inquisitive four-year-old simply
cannot understand things a seven-year-old grasps easily. What accounts
for the dramatic changes between the ages of four and seven?

Piaget spent years observing, questioning, and playing games with
babies and young children—including his own. He concluded that younger
children aren't "dumb," in the sense of lacking a given *amount of information.* Rather they think in a different *way* than older children and
adults; they use a different kind of logic. A seven-year-old would never
ask, "Mommy, who was born first, you or I?" (Chukovsky, 1963). But four-
year-olds, who think they are the center of the universe, often do. Intellectual development involves quantitative changes (growth in the *amount*
of information) as well as qualitative changes (differences in the *manner*
of thinking).

In time Piaget was able to detail the ways in which a child's thinking
changes, month by month, year by year. Although the rate at which different children develop varies, every child passes through the same
predictable *stages.* Each stage builds on the last, increasing the child's
ability to solve more complex problems.

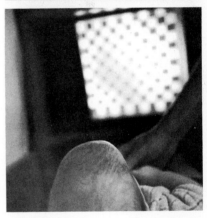

FIGURE 8.5
Psychologists have tried to devise
experiments to determine how
infants think and learn. In this
experiment, a four-month-old
infant is shown a pattern on a
screen. He can keep the pattern
in focus by sucking on a pacifier
hooked up to the projector. For
a while the infant will suck with
great energy and interest to obtain
the reward of the picture. He eventually gets somewhat bored,
however, so he does not suck as
hard, and the picture fades. When
a different picture is made available, the energy he puts into sucking once again increases.

FIGURE 8.6
(*reading from left to right and top to bottom*) This child possesses a scheme for grasping objects and pulling them to her that does not adequately match the features of the environment that she is now trying to assimilate. Her scheme will not get the toy through the bars of the playpen. An accommodation to her scheme—the addition of turning to grasping and pulling—achieves a state of equilibrium.

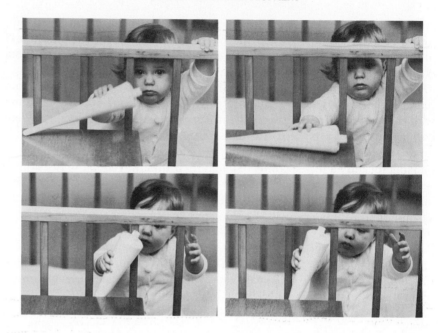

The Process of Knowing

Understanding the world involves the construction of schemes, or plans for knowing. Each of us is an architect and engineer in this respect, constructing schemes, applying them, and changing them as necessary. When we put a scheme into action, we are trying to understand something. In this process, we *assimilate*—we try to fit the world into our scheme. We also *accommodate*—we change our scheme to fit the characteristics of the world.

According to Piaget, a baby begins with two schemes, grasping and sucking. In other words, the baby understands things by grasping or sucking them—whether they be breasts, bottles, fingers, rattles, or wooden blocks. Consider what happens when a baby grasps a block. He assimilates the block to his grasping scheme. But he cannot do so without also accommodating—fitting his grasp to the particular block. Similarly, a seventh-grader uses her knowledge of arithmetic in an algebra class (assimilation). But she also has to modify her way of thinking to understand the new concepts (accommodation).

How Knowing Changes

Assimilation and accommodation work together to produce intellectual growth. When events do not fit into existing schemes, new and grander schemes have to be created. The child begins to see and understand things in a new light. Progressive changes in the way a baby conceives objects illustrate this.

Object Permanence. A baby's understanding of things lies totally in the here and now. The sight of a toy, the way it feels in her hands, the sensa-

a

b

FIGURE 8.7
This infant of about six months cannot yet understand that objects have an existence of their own, away from her presence. (a) The infant gazes intently at a toy elephant. (b) When the elephant is blocked from view, she gives no indication that she understands the toy still exists—she does not look for it. This thinking pattern changes by age two, as shown in Figure 8.8.

tions it produces in her mouth are all she knows. She does not imagine it, picture it, think of it, remember or even forget it. How do we know this?

When an infant's toy is hidden from her, she acts as if it had ceased to exist. She doesn't look for it; she grabs whatever else she can find and plays with that. Or she may simply start crying. At ten to twelve months, however, this pattern begins to change. When you take the baby's toy and hide it under a blanket—while she is watching—she will search for it under the blanket. However, if you change tactics and put her toy behind your back, she will continue to look for it under the blanket—even if she was watching you the whole time.

You can't fool a twelve- to eighteen-month-old baby quite so easily. A

FIGURE 8.8
By the age of two, a child realizes that the disappearance of an object does not mean that it no longer exists. In fact, if an object is concealed, a child will search for it because he or she knows that it still exists somewhere. This kind of understanding is called object permanence.

child this age watches closely and searches for the toy in the last place she saw you put it. But suppose you take the toy, put it under the blanket, conceal it in your hands, and then put it behind your back. A twelve-month-old will act surprised when she doesn't find the toy under the blanket—and keep searching there. An eighteen- or twenty-four-month-old will guess what you've done and walk behind you to look. She knows the toy must be somewhere (Ginsburg and Opper, 1969, pp. 50–56).

This is a giant step in intellectual development. The child has progressed from a stage where she apparently believed that her own actions created the world, to a stage where she realizes that people and objects are independent of her actions. This new scheme, *object permanence,* might be expressed: "Things continue to exist even though I cannot see or touch them." The child now conceives of a world of which she is only a part.

Representational Thought.   The achievement of object permanence suggests that a child has begun to engage in what Piaget calls *representational thought.* The child's intelligence is no longer one of action only. Now, children can picture (or represent) things in their minds. They can imagine and remember. At fourteen months of age, Piaget's daughter demonstrated this. When she was out visiting another family, she happened to witness a child throwing a temper tantrum. She had never had a tantrum herself, but the next day she did—screaming, shaking her playpen, and stamping her feet as the other child had. She had formed so clear an image of the tantrum in her mind that she was able to create an excellent imitation a day later (Ginsburg and Opper, 1969, p. 65). To Piaget, this meant that his daughter was using *symbols* to represent something. Soon she would be learning to use a much more complex system of symbols—spoken language. Where the infant is limited to solving problems with his or her actions, the older child can mentally represent the problem and use language to think it through. Thinking with actions, in other words, comes before thinking with language.

The Principle of Conservation.   More complex intellectual abilities emerge as the infant grows into childhood. At about the ages of five and seven, most children begin to understand what Piaget calls *conservation,* the principle that a given quality does not change if the shape of its container is changed. For example, if you have two identical short, wide jars filled with water and you pour the contents of one of these jars into a tall, thin jar, a child under five will say that the tall jar contains more water than the short one. If you pour the water back into the short jar to show the amount has not changed, the child will still maintain that there was more water in the tall container. Children under five do not seem to be able to think about two dimensions (height and width) at the same time. That is, they do not understand that a change in width is made up for by a change in the height of the tall glass.

Within two years, the same child will tell you that the second jar contains the same amount of water as the first. If you ask why, he may say because the short jar is fatter than the tall jar—indicating that he is able

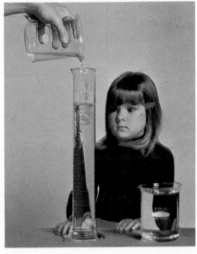

to coordinate his perceptions of height and width. Or he may point out that if you poured the water back into the short jar, it would be the same—indicating that he is able to think in reverse, to retrace the steps of the experiment. Younger children generally cannot do this.

FIGURE 8.9
The girl taking part in this demonstration has not yet acquired what Piaget calls conservation of quantity of liquid. Although she has seen the liquid poured from one beaker to another, she reacts only to the apparent increase of quantity in the tall beaker.

Table 8.1: Piaget's Stages of Cognitive Development

SENSORIMOTOR STAGE (birth to two years)	PREOPERATIONAL STAGE (two to six years)	CONCRETE OPERATIONAL STAGE (six to twelve years)	FORMAL OPERATIONAL STAGE (twelve years to adulthood)
Thinking is displayed in action, such as the grasping, sucking, and looking schemes. Child gradually learns to discover the location of hidden objects at about eighteen months, when the concept of object permanence is fully understood.	Beginning of symbolic representation. Child can now remember past events; language first appears; child begins to draw pictures that represent things. Child cannot represent a series of actions in his head in order to solve problems.	Ability to understand conservation problems. Ability to think of both height and width of an object at same time. Child can now do elementary arithmetic problems, such as judging the quantity of liquid containers and checking addition of numbers by subtraction. But thinking is still limited to solving problems with concrete objects that the child can manipulate.	Thinking becomes more abstract. The individual can consider many alternative solutions to a problem, make deductions, contemplate the future, and formulate personal ideals and values.

Many such cognitive advances take place between the years of five and twelve. This is the stage when children develop a working knowledge of the world. They develop skills in the trial-and-error approach to problem solving. But in general, their thinking is extremely concrete in this stage. They need to try solutions out; they cannot work through problems in their heads, and have difficulty thinking about hypothetical situations or abstract concepts.

Some Implications of Intellectual Development

Piaget's theory of cognitive development sheds light on some of the other areas of child behavior. For example, at about ten or twelve months, many children go through a period of *separation anxiety*. They become extremely upset when their mothers take them to a friend or relative's house and leave without them. A five-month-old baby does not react this way. Why does a one-year-old? Because the older child has learned to distinguish his mother from other people and realizes that she is a unique person. He knows she is going away. A young infant, who has not developed the scheme of object permanence, thinks of his mother as always there to feed and comfort him when he cries. He cannot imagine her being somewhere else or leaving him. The year-old child knows that he is away from home. All the infant knows is that the scene and the faces around him have changed. Thus the development of object permanence explains the rather sudden appearance of separation anxiety.

Piaget's theory also explains why seven- and eight-year-olds are more conscious of *sexual identity* than younger children are. If you've worked with children, you will know that four- or five-year-old boys object loudly to playing baseball with girls—and vice versa. Why?

Four-year-old children can tell you whether they are boys or girls, and many are fully informed about anatomical differences. Yet if you question children this age, you'll find that they believe people can change their sex by wearing clothes designed for the opposite sex, changing their haircut, playing games associated with the opposite sex, and the like. In other words, if you "pour" a boy into a female "container" he'll change. Only when they understand conservation do they realize that one's sex is permanent. It is at this point that children become concerned about their own sexual identity.

MENTAL RETARDATION

The term "mentally retarded" is applied to people who have since childhood been less able to learn and understand things than most people of the same age. Retarded children have difficulty learning to tie their shoes, find it impossible to keep up in school, and cannot join in the games that other children their age enjoy.

Mental retardation is an intellectual disability rather than an emotional one. But it is possible for retarded people to find the world so unpleasant that they withdraw from it in a neurotic or psychotic manner. Retarded people are often made worse by the way other people treat them. Most retarded people are capable of living normal lives if given the chance. They must, however, be given special attention, affection, and understanding if they are to reach their full potential as human beings.

Unfortunately, retardates are often treated as if they were unseeing, unhearing, uncomprehending "objects" devoid of human responses. The presence of a retarded child in a household may cause a great deal of friction and resentment among members of the family. This situation does not go unnoticed by the retarded child. Despite his intellectual handicaps, the child is a sensitive human being who understands the meaning of anger and resentment, as well as of love and acceptance. Conflict and rejection can rob the child of the supportive environment necessary for his maximum development.

Only about one-fourth of the six million people who are called retarded in the United States actually have something physically wrong with their brains. Their retardation is due to diseases contracted before birth or during early infancy, to brain injuries, to poor nutrition in childhood, or to some other physical factor.

The majority of people who are called retarded are people who seem never to have learned to use their minds. They may have been brought up in lonely, dull, or frightening environments in which there was no opportunity or reward for thinking. This situation occurs most often with children born into poor or unstable families and reared in slums or orphanages. If such children are given the opportunity and the encouragement to use their minds early enough, they are almost always able to live normal lives.

THE DEVELOPMENT OF LANGUAGE

Language and thought are closely intertwined. Both of these abilities involve using symbols, as we saw in Chapter 3. We are able to think and talk about objects that are not present and about ideas that are not necessarily true. A child begins to think, to represent things to himself, before he is able to speak. But the acquisition of language propels the child into further intellectual development (see Piaget, 1926). We have been able to learn a good deal about the acquisition of language from our nearest relative in the animal kingdom, the chimpanzee.

Can Animals Use Language?

Psychologists believe that chimpanzees must develop at least as far as two-year-old humans because, like two-year-olds, they will look for a toy or a bit of food that has disappeared. They can represent the existence of that toy or bit of food in their minds. Can they be taught to "talk" about it?

Many psychologists have tried to teach chimpanzees to use language, but only recently have such efforts been successful. One husband-and-wife team, the Gardners, raised a baby chimp named Washoe in their

FIGURE 8.10
Washoe at about five years of age. She is shown here using the American Sign Language sign for "hat."

home and taught her to use the American Sign Language for deaf people. At three and one-half years of age, Washoe knew eighty-seven signs for words like "food," "dog," "toothbrush," "gimmee," "sweet," "more," and "hurry."

Making these signs at the appropriate times would not be enough to be called language, though. A dog or a parrot might make signs that its owner could interpret as demands for a walk or for food. Washoe's remarkable achievement was that some of her signs had abstract meanings and that she could put signs together in new ways to produce new meanings. For example, she learned the sign for "more" (putting her fingertips together over her head) because she loved to be tickled and wanted more. But she was not simply doing something like what a dog does when he rolls over to be tickled; she was able to use the same sign later in entirely new circumstances—asking for more food, or more hair brushing.

The ability to arrange symbols in new combinations to produce new meanings is especially well developed in the human brain. The rules for such organization of symbols are called *grammar.* Grammatical rules are what make the sentence "the rhinoceros roared at the boy" mean the same thing as "the boy was roared at by the rhinoceros." On the surface, these sentences appear different because the word position is changed. But on a deeper level, we know that the first is an active sentence and the second a passive transformation of it. It may be in our ability to use such grammatical rules that we surpass the simpler language of the chimpanzee.

How Children Acquire Language

The example of Washoe shows that there are several steps in learning language. First, one must learn to make the signs; then, one must give them meaning; and finally, one must learn grammar. Each child makes these steps at his or her own rate. During the first year of life, the "average child" makes many sounds. Crying lessens, and the child starts making mostly cooing sounds, which develop into a *babble* that includes every sound humans can make—Chinese vowels, African clicks, German rolled r's, and English o's.

Late in the first year, the strings of babbles begin to sound more like the language that the child hears. Children imitate the speech of their parents and their older brothers and sisters, and are greeted with approval whenever they say something that sounds like a word. In this way children learn to speak their own language, even though they could just as easily learn any other.

The leap to using sounds as symbols occurs some time in the second year. The first attempts at saying words are primitive, and the sounds are incomplete: "Ball" usually sounds like "ba," and "cookie" may even sound like "doo-da." The first real words usually refer to things the infant can see or touch. Often they are labels or commands ("dog!" "cookie!").

By the time children are two years old, they have a vocabulary of at least fifty words. Toward the end of the second year, children begin to express themselves more clearly by joining words into two-word phrases.

But at age two, a child's grammar is still unlike that of an adult. Children use what psychologists call *telegraphic speech*—for example, "Where my apple?" "Daddy fall down." They leave out words but still get their messages across. As psychologists have discovered, two-year-olds already understand certain rules (Brown, 1973). They keep their words in the same order adults do. Indeed, at one point they overdo this, applying grammatical rules too consistently. For example, the usual rule for forming the past tense of English verbs is to add "ed." But many verbs are irregular: go/went, come/came, swim/swam, fall/fell. At first children learn the correct form of the verb: "Daddy went yesterday." But once children discover the rule for forming past tenses, they replace the correct form with sentences like "Daddy *goed* yesterday." Although they have never heard adults use this word, they construct it in accordance with the regularities of grammar that they have extracted from the speech they hear.

By the age of four or five children have mastered the basics of the language. Their ability to use words will continue to grow with their ability to think about and understand things.

EMOTIONAL DEVELOPMENT

While the child is developing his ability to use his body, to think and to express himself, he is also developing emotionally. He begins to become attached to specific people and to care what they think and feel. In most cases, the child's first relationship is with his mother.

Experiments with Animals

The early attachment of a child to his mother and the far-reaching effects of this attachment provide a good example of the way in which maturation and learning work together in development. Experiments with baby birds and monkeys have shown that there is a maturationally determined time of readiness for attachment early in life. If the infant is too young or too old, the attachment cannot be formed. But the attachment itself is a kind of learning. If the attachment is not made, or if an unusual attachment is made, the infant will develop in an unusual way as a result of this experience.

Imprinting.   Konrad Lorenz, a student of animal behavior, was a pioneer in this field. Lorenz discovered that infant geese become attached to their mothers in a sudden, virtually permanent learning process called *imprinting*. A few hours after they struggle out of their shells, goslings are ready to start waddling after the first thing they see. Whatever it is, they stay with it and treat it as though it were their mother from that time on. Usually, of course, the first thing they see is the mother goose, but Lorenz found that if he substituted himself or some moving object like a green box being dragged along the ground, the goslings would follow that. Goslings are especially sensitive just after birth, and whatever they learn then makes a deep impression that resists change. From this early experience with their mother—or mother substitute—the goslings form their idea of what a goose is. If they have been imprinted with a human being instead of a goose, they will prefer the company of human beings to other geese and may even try to mate with humans later in life.

Surrogate Mothers.   Lorenz's experiments showed how experience with a mother—whether real or a substitute—can determine an infant bird's entire view of himself and others. An American psychologist, Harry Harlow, went on to study the relationship between mother and child in a species closer to humans, the rhesus monkey. His first question was what makes the mother so important. He tried to answer this question by taking baby monkeys away from their natural mothers as soon as they were born, as described in Chapter 6. To review: Harlow raised the monkeys with two surrogate, or substitute, mothers. Each monkey could choose between a mother constructed of wood and wire and a mother constructed in the

FIGURE 8.11
Imprinting. A few hours after they were hatched, these baby geese saw Dr. Konrad Lorenz instead of a mother goose. Because goslings have an inborn readiness to attach themselves to their mother within the first few hours of life, these goslings attached themselves to Dr. Lorenz. Thereafter, they followed him around as though he were their mother.

FIGURE 8.12
An infant rhesus monkey in one of Harry Harlow's experiments. The infant monkey got its food from the wire surrogate mother but maintained contact with the soft, terrycloth mother. Before these experiments were done psychologists believed that children loved their mothers because mother fed them. These experiments showed that, to monkeys at least, feeding is less important than touching. A rhesus monkey loves the mother who is soft and comfortable.

same way but covered with soft, cuddly terrycloth. In some cages, the cloth mother was equipped with a bottle; in others, the wire mother was.

The purpose of the experiment was to see which surrogate made the better mother. The results were dramatic: The young monkeys became strongly attached to the cloth mother, whether she gave food or not, and for the most part ignored the wire mother. If a frightening object was placed in the monkey's cage, he would run to the terrycloth mother for security, not to the wire mother. It was the touching that mattered, not the feeding.

Effects Later in Life.   In another set of experiments, Harlow discovered that monkeys raised without real mothers grew up with serious emotional problems. As adults they did not seem to know how to play or defend themselves, or even mate, although they tried. In fact, when frightened by a strange human they often attacked their own bodies instead of making threatening signs of aggression as normal monkeys do.

The monkeys who had cloth mothers with bottles grew up more normally than the others, but even they were not well adjusted to normal monkey life. A partially adequate substitute for a mother turned out to be peers—other baby monkeys. Infant monkeys who played with other monkeys like themselves grew up fairly normally even if they never saw their mothers. To grow up completely normally, however, both mother and peers were necessary. Why were real mothers and other infant monkeys so essential in raising normal monkeys?

One possible answer is that no matter how much contact comfort the cloth mother could provide, "she" could not encourage independence. A normal mother, brother, or sister often becomes annoyed at an infant's clinging as he gets older, forcing him to stand on his own two feet. The cloth mother, however, is always available. The encouragement of independence is, of course, only one factor. Interactions with mother and peers also allow the baby to see and learn from the behavior of other monkeys. The motionless surrogate provided no such opportunities.

Human Babies

Can these findings be applied to human babies? Is there a critical period when infants need to become attached to a mothering person, as Lorenz's experiments suggest? Do children who are temporarily or permanently separated from their mothers or raised in institutions without the benefit of a single mothering person develop abnormally, as Harlow's monkeys did?

Some psychologists would answer these questions with a firm "yes." Babies begin to form an attachment to their mothers (or to a surrogate mother) at about six months, when they are able to distinguish one person from another and are beginning to develop object permanence. This attachment seems to be especially strong between the ages of six months and three years. By three years, the child has developed to the stage where he is able to remember and imagine his mother, and maintain a relationship with her (in fantasy) even if she is absent.

FIGURE 8.13
Harry Harlow performed one set of experiments with rhesus monkeys that showed the importance of early peer contact for normal development. Such contact can make up, at least in part, for lack of a mother, and these results seem to be true for human children as well.

According to one psychologist, children who are separated from their mothers during this period may never be able to form attachments to other people. Suppose a child is hospitalized for an extended period. At first she will show signs of intense distress, crying and fussing as if she were trying to bring her mother back. When this fails, she will lapse into a state of apathy, which may last for several days. If the separation continues, she will begin to respond to attention and to act cheerfully, but her relations with others take on a superficial quality. She does not become attached to any one person (Bowlby, 1960).

Some psychologists believe that institutionalization causes intellectual as well as psychological damage. Their studies indicate that children who are deprived of a stable mothering person at an early age are retarded in their ability to use words and solve problems. Restless and unable to concentrate, they do poorly in school. Their aggressiveness makes them unpopular with their schoolmates (Spitz, 1946).

However, new research suggests that inadequate care and lack of learning opportunities, not mother deprivation, cause these problems. Orphanages and other institutions vary considerably in the care they give children, and so do the children who enter them. One team of psychologists found that although infants in an orphanage were slow to develop, they caught up with children raised at home by the age of four or five. Other researchers were unable to detect any difference in intelligence or emotional development between institutionalized and noninstitutionalized children. Indeed, a few psychologists believe that children raised in well-run orphanages are friendlier, more inquisitive, and in general develop faster than children raised in the average home. It depends on the child and the institution. (See Thompson and Grusec, 1970, pp. 606–607.)

The debate over this issue is likely to continue for some time. What we do know is that up to six or seven months, most infants are indiscriminate. They respond to strangers as readily as they respond to their mothers and other familiar people; they will coo or whine at just about anyone. At six months, however, they begin to develop a strong attachment to their mother (or whoever is caring for them). In fact, at about eight months many babies rather suddenly develop an intense fear of strangers—crying, hiding against their mothers, and showing other signs of distress when someone they do not know or remember approaches them. Separation anxiety, which appears at ten to twelve months (as indicated earlier), is further proof of attachment. Children do not remain exclusive for long, however. By eighteen months nearly all babies have developed attachments to their fathers, siblings, grandparents, or other people who play an active role in their lives (Maccoby and Masters, 1970).

SOCIALIZATION: SEX ROLES AND MORAL DEVELOPMENT

Learning the rules of behavior of the culture in which you are born and grow up is called *socialization.* To live with other people, a child has to learn what is considered acceptable and unacceptable behavior. This is not as easy as it sounds. Some social rules are clear and inflexible. For example, you are not permitted to have sexual relations with members of your immediate family. But such fixed rules are exceptions.

Most social rules leave room for individual decisions, so that the "gray area" between right and wrong is vast. Some rules change from situation to situation. Some apply to certain categories of people but not others. For example, the rules for boys in our society are different from the rules for girls. We tend to encourage boys to express aggression but not fear; traditionally, girls have been raised to express emotions but not ambitions. Of course the rules for feminine behavior change over the years. We do not expect adolescent girls to act like little girls, or middle-aged women to act like adolescents. To complicate matters, we require different behavior from single and married women, housewives and career women, female executives and female secretaries.

Learning what the rules are, when to apply and when to bend them, is only part of socialization. Every society has ideas about what is meaningful, valuable, beautiful, and worth striving for. Every society classifies people according to their family, sex, age, skills, personality characteristics, and other criteria. Every culture has notions about what makes individuals behave as they do. In absorbing these notions, a child acquires an identity as a member of a particular society, a member of different social categories (such as male or female), a member of a family—and an identity as an individual. This is a second dimension of socialization.

Finally, socialization involves learning to live with other people and with yourself. Anyone who has seen the shock on a two-year-old's face when another child his age takes a toy he wants, or the frustration and humiliation a four-year-old experiences when she discovers she can't hit a baseball on the first try, knows how painful it can be to discover that other people have rights and that you have limitations.

In the pages that follow we examine several theories about how the child becomes socialized. We begin with Freud's theory of psychosexual development, which has been a major influence on our understanding of socialization.

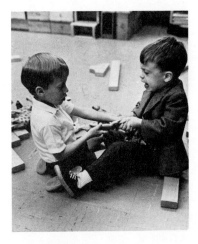

FIGURE 8.14
Knowing when to defer to another's wishes does not come easily. Gradually, children learn that they cannot always have their own way.

Freud's Theory of Psychosexual Development

Freud believed that all children are born with powerful sexual and aggressive urges that must be tamed. In learning to control these impulses, children acquire a sense of right and wrong. They become "civilized." The process—and the results—are rather different for boys and girls.

In the first few years of life boys and girls have similar experiences. Their erotic pleasures are obtained through the mouth, sucking at their mother's breast. Weaning is a period of frustration and conflict—it is the child's first experience with not getting what he wants. Freud called this the *oral* stage of development. Later the anus becomes the source of erotic pleasure, giving rise to what Freud called the *anal* stage. The child enjoys holding in or pushing out his feces until he is required, through toilet training, to curb this freedom.

The major conflict comes between the ages of three and five, when children discover the pleasure they can obtain from their genitals. As a consequence, they become extremely aware of the differences between themselves and members of the opposite sex. In this *phallic* stage, according to Freud, the child becomes a rival for the affections of the parent of the opposite sex. The boy wants to win his mother for himself and finds himself in hostile conflict with his father. The girl wants her father for herself and tries to shut out her mother. These struggles take place on an unconscious level; generally the child and the parents do not have any clear awareness that it is going on.

Freud called this crisis the *Oedipal conflict,* after Oedipus, the king in Greek tragedy who unknowingly killed his father and married his mother. Freud believed that the boy's feelings for his mother create intense conflicts. The boy finds that he hates his father and wishes him gone or dead. But his father is far stronger than he is. The boy fears that his father will see how he feels and punish him, perhaps by castrating him. (A parent telling the child that masturbation is nasty, or perhaps that it will make him sick, merely confirms his fears.) To prevent this horrible punishment, the boy buries his sexual feelings and tries to make himself "good." He tries to become as much like his father as possible so that his father will not want to hurt him. He satisfies himself with becoming *like* the person who possesses mother, instead of trying to possess her himself. In this process, which is called *identification* with the aggressor, the boy takes on all his father's values and moral principles. Thus, at the same time that he learns to behave like a man, he *internalizes* his father's morality. His father's voice becomes a voice inside him, the voice of conscience.

Freud believed that in girls the Oedipal conflict takes a different form. The girl finds herself in the similarly dangerous position of wanting to possess her father and to exclude her mother. To escape punishment and to possess the father vicariously, she begins to identify with her mother. She feels her mother's triumphs and failures as if they were her own, and she internalizes her mother's moral code. At the same time, the girl experiences what Freud called *penis envy.* Whereas the boy is afraid of being castrated, the girl suspects that her mother has removed the penis she once had. To make up for this "deficiency," she sets her sights on marrying a man who is like her father and develops the wish to have babies.

Freud believed that at about age five children enter a *latency* stage. Sexual desires are pushed into the background and children busy themselves with exploring the world and learning new skills. This process of redirecting sexual impulses into learning tasks is called *sublimation.* Although children this age often avoid members of the opposite sex, sexual interest reappears in adolescence. The way in which a person resolves the Oedipal conflict in childhood influences the kind of relationships he or she will form with members of the opposite sex in adolescence and beyond. Ideally, when one reaches the *genital* stage, one derives as much satisfaction from giving pleasure as from receiving it.

Today relatively few psychologists believe that sexual feelings disappear in childhood, that all young girls experience penis envy or that all young boys fear castration. Freud was attempting to set off a revolution in our thinking about childhood. Like many revolutionaries, he probably overstated the case. Yet the idea that children have to learn to control powerful sexual and aggressive desires, and the belief that such early childhood experiences have a long-term effect on adult personality and behavior, would be difficult to deny. (We shall return to Freud in the chapter on personality theories.)

Erikson's Theory of Psychosocial Development

To Erik Erikson, socialization is neither so sudden nor so emotionally violent. Erikson takes a broader view of human development than Freud in terms of both time and scope. Although he recognizes the child's sexual and aggressive urges, he believes that the need for social approval is just as important (hence the term *psychosocial development*). And although he believes that childhood experiences have a lasting impact on the individual, he sees development as a lifelong process.

We all face many "crises" as we grow from infancy to old age, as we mature and people expect more from us. Each of these crises represents an issue that everyone faces. The child—or adolescent or adult—may develop more strongly in one way or another depending on how other people respond to his or her efforts.

For example, the two-year-old is delighted with his new-found ability to walk, to get into things, to use words, and to ask questions. The very fact that he has acquired these abilities adds to his self-esteem. He's eager

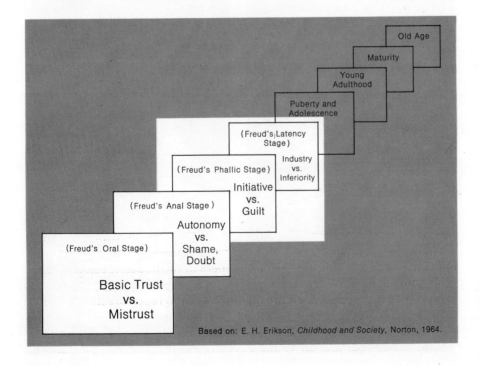

Based on: E. H. Erikson, *Childhood and Society*, Norton, 1964.

FIGURE 8.15
Erik Erikson's eight psychosocial stages, each of which contains a specific task to be accomplished. These stages are extensions of Freud's psychosexual stages. Erikson has elaborated on Freud's approach by adding the dimension of interpersonal relations to it.

to use them. If the adults around him applaud his efforts and acknowledge his achievements, he begins to develop a sense of autonomy, or independence. However, if they ignore him except to punish him for going too far or being a nuisance, the child may begin to doubt the value of his achievements. He may also feel shame because the people around him act as if his new desire for independence is bad.

This is the second of eight stages in Erikson's theory (see Figure 8.16). Each stage builds on the last. A child who has learned to trust the world is better equipped to seek autonomy than one who is mistrustful; a child who has achieved autonomy takes initiative more readily than one who doubts himself—and so on. The basic question in each stage is whether the individual will find ways to direct his needs, desires, and talents into socially acceptable channels and learn to think well of himself.

FIGURE 8.16

Erikson's first four stages.

(*top left*) Freud called the first stage the oral stage because the most important aspect of an infant's life is sucking. For Erikson, the crisis at this stage is basic trust versus mistrust. The infant needs to know that he will be looked after and that the world is an orderly place. If he experiences too much uncertainty to establish this confidence, he will thereafter tend to look at the world with fear and suspicion.

(*top right*) Freud's anal stage (the time of toilet training) is thought by Erikson to involve a crisis of autonomy versus shame and doubt. The child is learning self-control and self-assertion. But if he receives too much criticism, he will be ashamed of himself and doubt his right to be independent.

(*bottom left*) At about age three or four the child enters what Freud calls the phallic stage, a stage of sexual awareness. Erikson sees the issue here as initiative versus guilt. The child learns to make decisions with little worry about other people. If he is constantly discouraged or punished for going too far, he will feel guilty and mistakenly believe that his impulses are bad.

(*bottom right*) Freud believed that sexuality is temporarily forgotten, or latent, during the years from six to twelve. According to Erikson, at this stage the child struggles with industry versus inferiority. She gains mastery of skills that interest her, and she finds pride in her competence. But if people around her criticize her work as silly or useless, she will feel that she is somehow inferior.

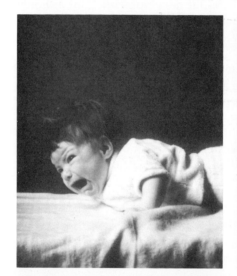

Learning Theories of Development

Both Freud and Erikson stress the emotional dynamics of social development. Their theories suggest that learning social rules is altogether different from learning to ride a bicycle or to speak a foreign language. Many psychologists disagree with this, however.

These psychologists believe children learn the ways of their social world because they are rewarded for conforming and because they copy older children and adults in anticipation of future rewards. In other words, social development is simply a matter of conditioning and imitation.

Conditioning.   Adults—especially parents and teachers—have the power to reward and punish. Consciously and unconsciously they use praise, smiles, and hugs to reward a child for behaving in ways they consider good and for expressing attitudes that support their own. They tend to ignore or to be hostile toward the expression of opinions that are contrary to their own and toward behavior of which they disapprove.

Sex-role training provides obvious examples of this. At home and in school, boys are encouraged to engage in athletics and to be assertive. Girls are discouraged from doing these things, but are rewarded for being helpful and nice, looking neat, and acting cute. Even the rewards children receive are usually sex-typed. How many girls receive footballs or tool kits as presents? How many boys get dolls or watercolor sets?

These are some of the ways in which adults use conditioning to shape a child's development. Children gradually learn to behave in the way that leads to the greatest satisfaction, even when no one is watching. To avoid punishment and gain rewards from those around them, they learn to reward and punish themselves. A child may criticize herself for making a mistake that has led to punishment in the past. The mistake may be a moral one—lying for example. A boy may learn to be hard on himself for showing sensitivity, because in the past his tears and blushes met with humiliating laughter.

This is not to say that children always do as they are told. Unwittingly perhaps, adults also teach youngsters how to get away with misbehavior—for example, by apologizing or by giving a present to someone they have wronged. In this way, some children learn that they may receive praise instead of punishment for bad conduct.

Imitation.   A second way in which children learn social rules is by observing other people. When youngsters see another child or an adult being congratulated for behaving in certain ways or expressing certain attitudes, they are likely to imitate that person in the hope of obtaining rewards themselves.

Albert Bandura's experiments indicate that children are very quick indeed to imitate other people's behavior (Bandura and Walters, 1963). Bandura's basic technique is to show children movies of a person reacting to a situation. He then puts the children in the same situation to see how they behave.

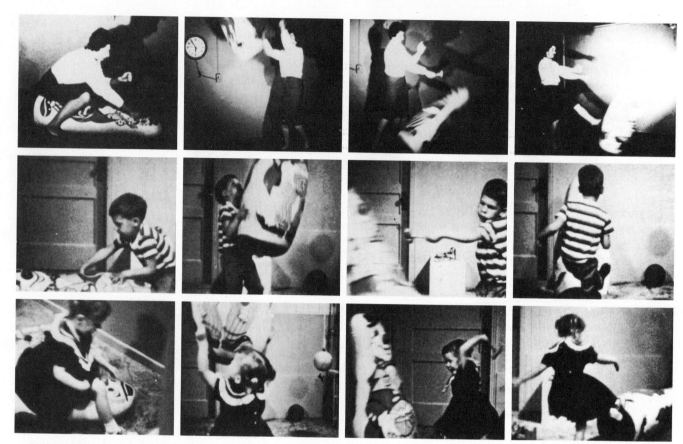

FIGURE 8.17
Imitation of aggression in children. (*top row*) Frames from one of the films that psychologist Albert Bandura showed to children. (*bottom two rows*) Behavior of children who watched the film and were given a chance to play with similar objects. As you can see, these children seem to be imitating the behavior they had watched. Such imitation was particularly likely if the adult in the film was rewarded for her aggressive actions.

In one experiment Bandura showed a film of a frustrated adult taking out her anger on a "Bobo" doll. The woman literally assaulted the doll—yelling, kicking, and pummeling it with all her might. After the film, children who had been deliberately frustrated with broken promises and delays were led to a room that contained an identical doll. Taking their cue from the film, they launched furious attacks—imitating the actress's behavior down to the last kick.

Later Bandura added two different endings to the film. In one the actress was praised and given candy and soft drinks after she had attacked the doll. In the other she was severely scolded for her behavior. Most of the children who saw the second version learned from the actress's experience and held their anger in, to avoid punishment. What this suggests is that conditioning and modeling work together. Children do not imitate everything they see, only the behavior that seems to bring rewards.

The Cognitive–developmental Approach

The theorists who emphasize the role of cognition or thinking in development view the growing child quite differently. Learning theory implies that the child is essentially passive—a piece of clay to be shaped. The people who administer rewards and punishments and serve as models do the shaping. Cognitive theorists see the *child* as the shaper. Taking their cue from Piaget, they argue that social development is the result of the child's acting on the environment and trying to make sense out of his experiences. The games children play illustrate this.

Play.   Children's games are serious business. When left to their own devices, youngsters spend a great deal of time making up rules. This enables them to learn for themselves the importance of agreeing upon a structure for group activities. A child can relax and enjoy himself, without fear of rejection—as long as he does not violate the established code. The world of play thus becomes a miniature society, with its own rules and codes.

Another function of most games is to teach children about aspects of adult life in a nonthreatening way. In young children's games, it is the

FIGURE 8.18
As a valuable component of socialization, play provides young children with opportunities for testing and further developing a wide variety of physical, social, and cognitive skills.

experience of playing, not winning, that counts. Children can learn the dimensions of competition of various kinds, including testing themselves against their outer limits, but they will not be hurt by comparison as they may be in win-or-lose situations.

Much of children's play involves *role taking*. Youngsters try on such adult roles as mother, father, teacher, storekeeper, explorer, and rock star. Role taking allows them to learn about different points of view firsthand. Suppose a child plays a mother opposite another child who plays a whiny, disobedient baby. When she finds herself totally frustrated by the other child's nagging she begins to understand why her mother gets mad. You can't cook even a pretend meal when the baby keeps knocking over the pots and pans.

Stages of Moral Development. Lawrence Kohlberg's studies show just how important being able to see other people's points of view is to social development in general and to moral development in particular. Kohlberg (1968) studied the development of moral reasoning by presenting children of different ages with a series of moral dilemmas. For example,

> In Europe, a woman was near death from cancer. One drug might save her, a form of radium that a druggist in the same town had recently discovered. The druggist was charging $2,000, ten times what the drug cost him to make. The sick woman's husband, Heinz, went to everyone he knew to borrow the money, but he could only get together about half of what it cost. He told the druggist that his wife was dying and asked him to sell it cheaper or let him pay later. But the druggist said "No." The husband got desperate and broke into the man's store to steal the drug for his wife. Should the husband have done that? Why?

At every age, some of the children said that the man should steal, some that he should not. What interested Kohlberg, however, was how the children arrived at a conclusion. He wanted to know what sort of reasoning they used. After questioning about one hundred children, Kohlberg identified six stages of moral development. He then replicated his findings in several different cultures. In Kohlberg's model, each stage represents an advance in the child's ability to take the roles of other people.

In stage one, children are totally egocentric. They do not consider other people's points of view and have no sense of right and wrong. Their main concern is avoiding punishment. A child in this stage will say that the man should steal because people will blame him for his wife's death if he does not, or that he should not steal because he might get caught and go to prison.

Children in stage two have a better idea of how to "work the system" to receive rewards as well as to avoid punishment. Kohlberg calls this the "marketplace orientation." Youngsters at this level interpret the Golden Rule as "help someone if he helps you, and hurt him if he hurts you." They are still egocentric and premoral, evaluating acts in terms of the consequences, not in terms of right and wrong.

In stage three, children become acutely sensitive to what other people want and think. A child in this stage will say that the man in the story should steal because people will think he is cruel if he lets his wife die, or that he should not steal because people will think he is a criminal. In other words, children become conformists in stage three: They apply the rules other people have decreed literally and rigidly.

It is only in stage four that youngsters begin to see other sides of the story. They examine the dilemma from both the wife's and the pharmacist's points of view. They base their judgments on how stealing or not stealing will affect other people, not so much on the consequences for the husband. This ability to see things through other people's eyes is the beginning of morality, in Kohlberg's view. But the sense of morality is still in terms of maintaining the authority of society. They adopt a "law and order" kind of thinking.

In stages five and six children begin to broaden their perspective. They see society's point of view (What would happen if everybody stole?); grasp the notion of the social contract (that members of a society must agree upon rules in order to live together and settle disputes over competing rights); and finally develop universal ethical principles based on the ideals of reciprocity and human equality.

To reach this stage, a child must first be able to see other people's points of view and to consider several different views simultaneously. In short, moral development depends on cognitive development, which in turn depends on the child actively trying to understand his experiences.

IMPLICATIONS FOR CHILD REARING

All of the theories we have discussed are best treated as different perspectives on the same process. The most complete picture of child development would contain all of these points of view, which all have practical implications for child rearing.

First, each child is unique. As suggested earlier, infants exhibit temperamental differences from birth. Some babies are active and responsive; some fussy; some passive and withdrawn. Some quickly develop regular schedules for eating and sleeping; some are erratic and resist schedules. Individual differences become more apparent as the months and years go by. Each baby, each growing child, requires a different style of parenting. Each of the theories we presented stresses this view. Psychoanalysts trace the unique way each child experiences various conflicts; cognitive–developmentalists recognize that while each child goes through the stages in the same order, children move at different paces, and teaching should respect the child's current developmental stage; and behaviorists believe that good instruction is individualized.

Second, from Piaget's theory we learn how important it is that the child is trying to understand the world for himself. A child who is given the freedom to figure out certain things on his own will begin to structure the world according to his individual needs. Many parents do not realize how important it is that the child develop skills on his own. A mother who tells her young child to color the sky blue instead of orange may not realize that she is inhibiting the child's natural tendency to experiment. Or a mother who finds it more convenient to tie her five-year-old's shoelaces, instead of teaching him to do it himself, may not realize that she is depriving her child of the satisfaction and sense of accomplishment he could be deriving.

Third, behaviorists teach us the value of having rules for reward and punishment that are appropriate, clear, and consistent. A child who grows up with no boundaries has no framework within which to operate. He does not know what is possible and what is not possible. He may also feel that his parents do not really care about him, because they do not seem sufficiently interested to direct his behavior.

Rules must not require more of a child than he is capable of giving. If a two-year-old is punished for spilling her milk, she will begin to feel responsible for things she cannot control. If parents consistently punish clumsy two-year-old behaviors, the child may eventually come to view herself as worthless—everything she does is bad.

Consistent rules are important because they allow the child to generalize from one situation to the next. If he is punished for hitting his younger brother one day but not punished the next, he cannot know whether the behavior is permissible. He may experience the punishment as cruelty rather than as a consequence of hitting the smaller child. One way to establish consistency is to keep charts and records of misbehavior and the consequences. What times of day do the children fight? Are they quarreling because they have nothing better to do, or to get a parent's attention? How do older members of the family react to their misbehavior? Keeping records enables a parent to see patterns in the children's behavior, gain insight into the children's motives, and to see the effects of his or her reaction. A chart recording good behavior—for example, with the stars teachers often use—will give a child concrete evidence of his progress.

Parents and older brothers and sisters should remember that small children use them as *models*. A child learns to behave as he observes others behaving, whether they want him to or not.

Finally, from the psychoanalysts we learn that one of the most important things that parents can teach their child is how to express his or her feelings. In this sense, it is more to the child's advantage to grow up in a home where there is screaming and yelling when something goes wrong than in a home where there is nothing but bitter silence. People who are able to express anger not only release feelings that can become destructive if repressed, but are also able to express their positive feelings of joy and love. Parents should encourage their children to show their anger, their hurt, and their resentment, as well as their happy and positive feelings. Children need to know that their feelings are valid and important. Parents can give this confidence to their children simply by listening to them and responding with understanding. Children need to learn that they are responsible for controlling their actions but not their feelings.

SUMMARY

1. Developmental psychology is the study of the changes that occur as people mature.

2. At birth an infant is capable of certain coordinated movement patterns that can be triggered by the right stimulus. One of these, the grasping reflex, is a response to a touch on the palm. Another, the rooting reflex, involves the movement of the infant's head toward the source of any touch near his or her mouth.

3. As a result of maturation (internally programed growth) and learning, infants are able to walk, talk, and feed themselves in about two years' time. Learning and maturation work together in the development of intellect, language, love, and morality.

4. Swiss psychologist Jean Piaget has formulated a comprehensive theory of intellectual development. Intellectual growth involves changes in the amount of information we have as well as in the way we think.

5. The child's grasp of object permanence at about eighteen months marks a giant step in his or her intellectual development. Understanding that objects still exist when out of sight means the child can now engage in representational thinking. He or she can picture an object in his or her mind without seeing or touching the object.

6. Mental retardation is an intellectual disability rather than an emotional one. It means that the person afflicted is less able to learn and understand things than most people of the same age.

7. In order to acquire language the child spends the first year of life practicing sounds, then imitating the speech he hears around him. In the second year he uses sounds as symbols, and his first real words usually refer to something he can see or touch. By four or five years of age, the child has usually mastered the basics of his native language.

8. While the child learns to use his body, to think, and to express himself, he also develops emotionally. He begins to form attachments to people; his first relationship is usually with his mother. By eighteen months nearly all babies have developed attachments to their fathers, siblings, grandparents, or anyone else playing an active role in their lives.

9. Socialization involves learning the rules of behavior of the culture in which a child is born and will grow up.

10. The theories of Freud and Erik Erikson stress the emotional dynamics of social development. They both believe that the child must learn to control the sexual and aggressive urges he is born with, but Erikson would add that the child's need for social approval is just as important to his social development.

11. Learning theorists give much less emphasis to the emotional dynamics of social development. They argue that children learn appropriate social behavior.

12. Cognitive theorists argue that social development is more than just the result of the child being shaped by rewards and punishments. These psychologists see the *child* as the shaper. They argue that social development results from the child acting on the environment, trying to make sense out of his or her experience.

13. Lawrence Kohlberg has observed that the moral development of a child progresses in six stages. Essentially, each stage represents an advance in the child's ability to take the roles of other people. At stage one, the child is egocentric and has no sense of right or wrong. At each successive stage, the child's awareness of other people and society increases, until at stages five and six he is finally able to develop universal ethical principles based on ideals of reciprocity and human equality.

14. The implications for child rearing of the various theories of child development (emo-

tional, behavioral, and cognitive) are numerous. Each child is unique and should be given the freedom to understand the world for himself. A child should have rules for punishment and rewards that are appropriate, clear, and consist- ent. Parents and older siblings should re- member that small children use them as models. And it is most important that children should be allowed to express their feelings.

GLOSSARY

accommodation: In Piaget's theory of cognitive development, the adjustment of one's scheme for understanding the world to fit newly ob- served objects.

anal stage: According to Freud, the stage at which children associate erotic pleasure with the elimination process.

assimilation: In Piaget's theory of cognitive development, the process of fitting objects and experiences into one's scheme for understand- ing the environment.

conservation: The principle that a given quality is not altered if the shape of its container is changed. The discovery of this principle between the ages of five and seven is important to the intellectual development of the child.

developmental psychology: The study of changes that occur as individuals mature.

genital stage: According to Freud, the stage during which an individual's sexual satisfaction depends as much on giving sexual pleasure as on receiving it.

grasping reflex: An infant's clinging response to a touch on the palm of his or her hand.

identification: The process by which a child adopts the values and principles of the same- sex parent.

imprinting: A social learning capacity in some species by which attachments are formed to other organisms or to objects very early in life.

internalization: The process of incorporating the values, ideas, and standards of others as a part of oneself.

latency stage: According to Freud, the stage at which sexual desires are pushed into the back- ground and the child becomes involved in ex- ploring the world and learning new skills.

maturation: The internally programed growth of a child.

object permanence: A child's realization, de- veloped between the ages of one and two, that an object exists even when he or she cannot see or touch it.

Oedipal conflict: According to Freud, a boy's wish to possess his mother sexually, coupled with hostility toward his father. Correspond- ingly, girls desire their fathers sexually and feel hostile toward their mothers. In order to reduce his or her fear of punishment from the same-sex parent, the child begins to identify with the parent of the same sex.

oral stage: According to Freud, the stage at which infants associate erotic pleasure with the mouth.

phallic stage: According to Freud, the stage at which children associate sexual pleasure with their genitals.

representational thought: The intellectual abil- ity of a child to picture something in his or her mind.

role taking: An important aspect of children's play that involves assuming adult roles, thus enabling the child to experience different points of view first hand.

rooting reflex: An infant's response toward the

source of touching that occurs anywhere around his or her mouth.

separation anxiety: A phase many children experience after twelve months, characterized by fear and anxiety at any prolonged absence of the mother.

socialization: The process of learning the rules

of behavior of the culture within which an individual is born and will live.

sublimation: The process of redirecting sexual impulses into learning tasks that begins at about the age of five.

telegraphic speech: The kind of speech used by young children. Words are left out, but the meaning is still clear.

ACTIVITIES

1. Observe an infant under eighteen months of age, keeping a log of the baby's activities. Compare your notes with the developmental descriptions in this chapter. How closely does the baby follow the norm? What differences did you note?

2. Talk with children who are under five years old, paying particular attention to their grammar. What kinds of errors do they make? What kinds of grammatical rules do they already seem to know?

3. Do you and your parents share the same religious beliefs? Political orientation? Feelings about violence? Attitudes toward sex? Goals for living? Opinions about money? Views on drugs? Do you have similar tastes in clothing colors and styles? Music? Pets? Housing? Furniture? Foods? Cars? Entertainment? After asking yourself these questions, determine how well your beliefs, opinions, and tastes agree with those of your parents. How important do you think your early social training was for what you believe, think, and like?

4. What happens when a boy plays with G.I. Joe dolls? How does this behavior fit into the concept of modeling? Is this behavior liberating to boys, or does it feminize their behavior? Explain your answer. What would be the effect of girls playing football? Explain the difference(s) between your answers about boys and girls.

5. How are sex roles communicated to people in American society? Look carefully through magazines and newspapers, watch television commercials, and listen to the radio. What activities, interests, worries, virtues, weaknesses, physical characteristics, and mannerisms are presented as attributes of typical men and women? Are sex roles portrayed differently in different media? Are there various stereotypes within each sex?

6. Write a brief autobiography. What are the events that you feel have been the most significant in your life? What have been the main influences on your social and emotional development?

7. If you have an infant brother or sister, or a pet dog or cat, perform a simple experiment to test for object permanence. Be sure to use several different objects for your test, and be certain that the baby or animal is not afraid of, or uninterested in, the object. Most dogs or cats will probably search for vanished objects.

8. Ask children of different ages the following questions: Where does the sun go at night? Could you become a girl (a boy) if you wanted to? Does your brother (sister) have any brothers (sisters)? What makes leaves fall off trees? If you find some of their theories interesting, it is easy to think of many other questions.

SUGGESTED READINGS

FLEMING, J. D. "Field Report on the State of the Apes." *Psychology Today*, 7 (January 1974): 31. A current review of all the work across the country in teaching language to chimpanzees.

GINOTT, HAIM. *Between Parent and Child*. New York: Macmillan, 1965 (paper). Ginott sees a child's behavior as a special way of communicating ideas he or she may not be able to verbalize. Based on psychoanalytic principles, the author provides practical advice toward better relationships between parents and their children.

GINSBURG, HERBERT, AND OPPER, SYLVIA. *Piaget's Theory of Intellectual Development: An Introduction*. Englewood Cliffs, N. J.: Prentice-Hall, 1969 (paper). The clearest, most popular introduction to Piaget's work available.

KAGAN, JEROME. *Personality Development*. New York: Harcourt Brace Jovanovich, 1969 (paper). A lively little book that presents a clear and well-illustrated introduction to the development of personality.

KOHLBERG, LAWRENCE. "Stage and Sequence: The Cognitive–Developmental Approach to Socialization." In D. Goslin (ed.), *Handbook of Socialization*. Chicago: Rand McNally, 1969, pp. 347–480. An inspired summary of Kohlberg's work on moral development that shows how he developed his six-stage theory.

LIEBERT, R. M., NEALE, J. M., AND DAVIDSON, E. S. *The Early Window: Effects of Television on Children and Youth*. New York: Pergamon Press, 1973 (paper). A balanced discussion of the effects of television on children. The book also provides a good introduction to social learning, since most of the research on television's impact has been done from this perspective.

PINES, MAYA. *Revolution in Learning: The Years from Birth to Six*. New York: Harper and Row, 1966 (paper). An exciting, easy-to-read account of the new work that is being done on what children learn before they start elementary school.

RUGH, R., AND SHETTLES, L. *From Conception to Birth: The Drama of Life's Beginnings*. New York: Harper and Row, 1971. Extraordinary pictures of life as it actually begins and develops in the uterus. Color photographs of the fetus, showing close-ups of its hands, face, and actions.

SPOCK, BENJAMIN. *Baby and Child Care*. New York: Pocket Books, 1971 (paper); originally published, 1946. For decades this book has served as a handy and practical guide for parents on almost every conceivable issue of child rearing. In recent editions, Dr. Spock has recommended a less rigid approach to child rearing than he used to advocate.

SUTTON-SMITH, BRIAN, AND SUTTON-SMITH, SHIRLEY. *How to Play with Your Children (and When Not To)*. New York: Hawthorn Books, 1974 (paper). What children play at different ages is presented along with a host of good ideas about how adults can join in and help children develop further. The first author is the leading authority on the psychology of play, the second has taught elementary school for many years, and both are quite playful themselves. The result is a fascinating and very funny book.

BIBLIOGRAPHY

BALDWIN, ALFRED A. *Theories of Child Development*. New York, Wiley, 1967.

BANDURA, A., AND WALTERS, R. H. *Social Learning and Personality Development*. New York: Holt, Rinehart and Winston, 1963.

BELLUGI, U., AND BROWN, R. (EDS.). *The Acquisition of Language*. University of Chicago Press, 1970.

BOWLBY, J. "Separation Anxiety: A Critical Review of the Literature." *Journal of Child Psychology and Psychiatry*, 1 (1960–61): 251–269.

——. *Child Care and Growth of Love.* 2nd ed. Baltimore: Penguin, 1965.

BROWN, ROGER. *A First Language: The Early Stages.* Cambridge, Mass.: Harvard University Press, 1973.

CHUKOVSKY, K. *From Two to Five.* Berkeley: University of California Press, 1963.

FISCHER, KURT W. *Piaget's Theory of Learning and Cognitive Development.* Chicago: Markham, 1973.

FLAVELL, JOHN H. *The Developmental Theory of Jean Piaget.* New York: Van Nostrand, 1963.

FURTH, HANS. *Piaget and Knowledge.* Englewood Cliffs, N.J.: Prentice-Hall, 1969.

GARDNER, R. A., AND GARDNER, B. T. "Teaching Sign Language to a Chimpanzee." *Science*, 1965 (1969): 644–672.

GESELL, A., AND THOMPSON, HELEN. "Learning and Growth in Identical Twin Infants." *Genetic Psychological Monograph*, 6 (1929): 1–124.

GINSBURG, HERBERT, AND OPPER, SYLVIA. *Piaget's Theory of Intellectual Development: An Introduction.* Englewood Cliffs, N.J.: Prentice-Hall, 1969.

HARLOW, HARRY F. "The Development of Affectional Patterns in Infant Monkeys." In B. M. Foss (ed.), *Determinants of Infant Behavior.* New York: Wiley, 1961, 75–100.

HARLOW, HARRY F., AND ZIMMERMAN, R. R. "Affectional Responses in the Infant Monkey." *Science*, 140 (1959): 421-432.

KOHLBERG, LAWRENCE. "The Child as Moral Philosopher." *Psychology Today*, 2 (September 1968): 25–30.

KOHLBERG, LAWRENCE, AND TUNEL, E. *Research in Moral Development: The Cognitive-Developmental Approach.* New York: Holt, Rinehart and Winston, 1971.

LORENZ, KONRAD Z. *Studies in Animal and Human Behavior.* Robert Matrin, trans. 2 vols. Cambridge, Mass.: Harvard University Press, 1972.

MACCOBY, ELEANOR, AND MASTERS, JOHN C. "Attachment and Dependency." In Paul H. Mussen (ed.), *Manual of Child Psychology*, Vol. 2: 159–260. New York: Wiley, 1970.

PIAGET, JEAN. *The Language and Thought of the Child.* London: Routledge and Kegan Paul, 1926.

PINES, MAYA. "Infants Are Smarter than Anybody Thinks." *The New York Times Magazine* (November 29, 1970).

SEARS, ROBERT, MACCOBY, ELEANOR, AND LEVIN, HARRY. *Patterns of Child Rearing.* New York: Harper & Row, 1957.

SPITZ, RENÉ, AND WOLFF, K. M. "Analclitic Depression: An Inquiry into the Genesis of Psychiatric Conditions in Early Childhood," II. In A. Freud *et al.* (eds.), *The Psychoanalytic Study of the Child*, Vol. II: 313–342. New York: International Universities Press, 1946.

THOMPSON, WILLIAM R., AND GRUSEC, JOAN. "Studies of Early Experience." In Paul H. Mussen (ed.), *Manual of Child Psychology*, Vol. 2: 565–656. New York: Wiley, 1970.

9

Adolescence, Adulthood, and Old Age

FIGURE 9.1
Psychological growth does not stop with the onset of adolescence. Each of the three generations in this picture faces different social demands and challenges to psychological adjustment. This chapter discusses the problems and opportunities unique to adolescence, adulthood, and old age.

Thousands of thirteen-year-olds are looking in their mirrors to see if they measure up. Dreams of being a superstar and falling madly in love dance in their heads. Young couples are discovering, with the birth of their first child, that being a parent is not quite what they expected. Their love nest has become a threesome. Parents whose last child has just left home are finding the prospect of spending their evenings alone together somewhat depressing. Divorced people in their mid-twenties or early sixties are realizing that being single again is liberating or lonely or both. Some adults are trying to recapture their youth with a new wardrobe or a love affair. Others are watching their grandchildren play with a sense of pride and completeness. Any number of old people are facing the fact that they cannot manage by themselves any more, that their minds are wandering, that they are going to die. Some are afraid, some are bitter, and some are at peace.

A list of the variations in adult lifestyles and adjustments to changing circumstances would fill volumes. But until recently, developmental psychologists paid relatively little attention to the changes that take place after people are grown. As indicated in the preceding chapter, Freud believed that human beings reach the final stage of psychosexual development—the genital stage—in adolescence. Piaget's study of intellectual development led him to a similar conclusion: The adolescent is fully equipped mentally. Indeed, most psychologists have looked at adulthood as variations on themes written in childhood.

Erik Erikson (1950) was one of the first to consider the psychosocial tasks that confront human beings as they grow older. Following his lead, increasing numbers of psychologists have begun to study the physiological, social, psychological, and intellectual changes that occur from adolescence through old age. In this chapter we shall attempt to summarize their findings, completing the story we began in the preceding chapter.

ADOLESCENCE

In most preliterate societies, the village or tribe holds elaborate ceremonies to mark the transition from childhood to adulthood. Once a young person has been initiated, he or she is considered ready for courtship and marriage, and is expected to assume adult responsibilities. Choices

FIGURE 9.2
Many preliterate societies hold elaborate initiation ceremonies to mark the abrupt transition of their young people from childhood to adulthood. In these societies, adolescence, the developmental stage between childhood and adulthood, is not recognized.

in lifestyle are limited: the economic, social, and sexual roles of adulthood are clearly defined. As a result, there are few questions about "how far to go" sexually or what to do with one's life—and hence few conflicts (see Mead, 1961). The no-man's-land between childhood and adulthood that we call "adolescence" simply does not exist.

In 1904, G. Stanley Hall published a book that made "adolescence" a household word in America. Hall pointed out that through most of the nineteenth century, the family was an economic unit in this country. All hands were needed. Youngsters worked alongside their parents in fields and shops and small factories, gradually assuming more and more responsibility. The line between children and adults was not as clearly drawn as it is today.

Industrialization changed this. First, machines made it possible for one person to do the work of many. The economy no longer needed child and teenage labor. Second, the demand for specialized skills increased, and parents could not teach children these new skills. Moreover, with the decline of family businesses and the rise of wage labor, young people could not know for sure what they would be doing with their lives. The solution to all of these problems was school. School kept unemployed young people off the streets, gave them training, and provided some with career options their parents had not enjoyed.

This combination of events created what we call adolescence—a developmental stage between childhood and adulthood. Young people who were physically mature began to remain in training, doing economically nonproductive work, depending on their families for support, and delaying decisions about their future for longer and longer periods. Today, a large number of young Americans remain in school well into their twenties.

Hall believed adolescence to be a period of great "storm and stress"—perhaps the most difficult stage of human development. Being an adolescent is something like being a fully grown animal in a cage, an animal who sees freedom but doesn't know quite when he will be freed or how he will handle it. Society treats the adolescent as a child one minute, as an adult the next. Adolescents are expected to act maturely, but also to do as they are told. They are denied the chance to earn a living (unemployment rates among teenagers are higher than among any other group), but often reminded that their parents had to work at their age. They are envied for their youth, but resented for their lack of responsibility.

Because adolescence is inevitably painful and distressing in technological societies, Erik Erikson, for one, believes that many young people need a *psychological moratorium*. By this he means a period during which they can explore and experiment without having to commit themselves to a lifestyle, career, or mate, or to suffer the consequences of mistakes (Erikson, 1968, pp. 125–138). But let us begin our discussion where adolescence begins.

Physical Changes

Puberty, or sexual maturation, is the biological event that marks the end of childhood. Hormones trigger a series of internal and external changes. At about ten, girls rather suddenly begin to grow—sometimes as much as two or three inches a year. During this growth spurt, a girl's breasts and hips begin to fill out, and she develops pubic hair. Between ten and seventeen she has her first menstrual period, or *menarche*. Another year or so will pass before her periods become regular and she is capable of conceiving a child. Yet girls in most societies consider menarche the beginning of womanhood.

At about twelve, boys begin to develop pubic hair and larger genitals. Within a year or two they become capable of ejaculation. They too begin to grow rapidly and to fill out, developing the broad shoulders and thicker trunk of an adult man. Their voices gradually deepen. Hair begins to grow on their faces and later on their chests.

Variations in the rate of sexual maturation make it difficult to apply norms or standards to puberty. In general, girls begin to develop earlier than boys, and for a year or two may tower over male age-mates.

Reactions to Growth.   In general young people today are better informed about sex than they were two or three generations ago. Most do not find menarche or nighttime ejaculations upsetting. Nevertheless the rather sudden bodily changes that occur during puberty make all adolescents somewhat self-conscious. This is particularly true if they are early or late to develop. Adolescents desperately want to be accepted by their peers, to conform to ideals of how a male or female their age should act, dress, and look. In one study, over half of the adolescent girls and a third of the boys spontaneously expressed concern about their appearance (Dwyer and Mayer, 1968–1969).

FIGURE 9.3
A child begins the long transition to adulthood when he or she first experiences the physiological changes of puberty. These changes bring a new kind of self-awareness that did not exist in childhood.

Research indicates that boys who mature early have an advantage. They become heroes in sports, leaders in formal and informal social activities. Other boys look up to them; girls have crushes on them; adults tend to treat them as more mature. As a result they are generally more self-confident and independent than other boys. Late-maturing boys, whose high-pitched voices and less-than-ideal physiques may make them feel inadequate, tend to be withdrawn or rebellious. However, the early advantage soon fades. Indeed, in their mid-thirties, men who were late to mature tend to be more flexible and expressive than early-maturers.

With girls the pattern is somewhat different. Girls who mature early may feel embarrassed rather than proud of their height and figures at first. Some begin dating older boys and become bossy with people their own age. Late-maturing girls tend to be less quarrelsome and to get along with their peers more easily. In their late teens, girls who matured early may be more popular and have a more favorable image of themselves than girls who matured slowly. However, the differences between early- and late-maturers do not seem to be as pronounced among girls as they are among boys (Dwyer and Mayer, 1968–1969).

Sexual Attitudes and Behavior.   Most adolescent girls are less conscious of sexual urges than boys. They are less likely to be aroused by sexual symbols, to have explicitly sexual fantasies, or to reach sexual climax in dreams than are boys their age. They are less concerned about finding sexual release than boys are, and more concerned about affection, trust, sharing, and love. In a word, girls are more romantic. Yet most adolescent girls (more than two-thirds in one survey) believe that women enjoy sex as much as men (Mussen, Conger, and Kagan, 1974, p. 565).

Recent data indicate that 95 percent of boys have experienced orgasm by the age of fifteen. Although 90 percent of women age thirty-five have had orgasms, only 23 percent report orgasms by age fifteen, 53 percent by age twenty. About 65 percent of men reach their first climax through masturbation, whereas 50 percent of women discover orgasm through petting or sexual intercourse. On the average, sixteen- or seventeen-year-old boys masturbate about three times a week. There is no average for girls: some never masturbate, some very occasionally (about twice a year), some as often as ten or twelve times a week. By age nineteen, over 70 percent of males and nearly 60 percent of females have had sexual intercourse—usually with one person with whom they are emotionally involved.

Do these statistics represent a dramatic change over behavior in past generations—a "sexual revolution?" The answer is a qualified no. Middle- and upper-class girls who attend college seem to be more sexually active than college girls were twenty years ago. But sexual behavior in other social categories is about the same today as it was when Kinsey made his famous studies in the late 1940s.

The main change in recent years seems to be in attitudes. The majority of young people believe it is morally acceptable for an engaged couple to have sexual intercourse; the majority of adults do not. This is not to say that the younger generation approves of promiscuity. To the contrary. According to one survey, young people place more emphasis on affection and meaningful relationships than adults do. They consider premarital intercourse between two people who love each other more acceptable than casual petting between two people who are not attached to each other (something adults accept more readily). Perhaps the most significant change is that most adolescents today believe in being open and honest about sex (Simon and Gagnon, 1970; Yankelovich, 1969).

Social Development: Family and Friends

One of the principal developmental tasks for adolescents is becoming independent of their families. Unfortunately the means of achieving this status are not always clear, either to the adolescents or to their parents. First, there is ambivalence on both sides. Some parents have built their lifestyles around the family and are reluctant to let the child go. Such parents know they will soon have to find someone else on whom to shift their emotional dependence. Also, parents whose children are old enough to leave home sometimes have to wrestle with their own fears of advancing age. Many parents worry whether their children are really ready to cope with the harsh realities of life—and so do adolescents. At the same time that young people long to get out on their own and try themselves against the world, they worry a lot about failing there. This internal struggle is often mirrored in the adolescent's unpredictable behavior, which parents may interpret as "adolescent rebellion." Against this background of ambivalence, which is almost universal, there are various family styles of working toward autonomy.

Family Styles.   The way in which adolescents seek independence and the ease with which they resolve conflicts about becoming adults depends in large part on the parent–child relationship.

In *authoritarian* families parents are the "bosses." They do not feel that they have to explain their actions or demands. In fact such parents may feel the child has no right to question parental decisions. (In many families the father is more authoritarian than the mother, but in some the mother or both parents rule in this autocratic style.)

In *democratic* families adolescents participate in decisions affecting their lives. There is a great deal of discussion and negotiation in such families. Parents listen to their children's reasons for wanting to go somewhere or do something, and make an effort to explain their rules and

FIGURE 9.4
In democratic families, young people and their parents discuss plans and problems together. Adolescents are encouraged to reach their own decisions, but parents will intervene when they strongly disapprove.

expectations. The adolescents make many decisions for themselves, but the parents retain the right to veto plans of which they disapprove.

In *permissive* or *laissez-faire* families children have the final say. The parents may attempt to guide the adolescents, but give in when they insist on having their own way. Or they may simply give up their child-rearing responsibilities—setting no rules about behavior, making no demands, voicing no expectations, virtually ignoring the young people in their house.

Numerous studies suggest that adolescents who have grown up in democratic families are more autonomous, in the sense of having more confidence in their own values and goals than other young people do. They are also more independent, in the sense of wanting to make their own decisions (with or without advice). There are several reasons for this.

First, the child is able to assume responsibility gradually. He is not denied the opportunity to exercise his own judgment (as in authoritarian families) or given too much responsibility too soon (as in permissive families). Second, a child is more likely to identify with parents who love and respect him than with parents who treat him as incompetent or who seem indifferent to him. Finally, through their behavior toward the child, democratic parents present a model of responsible, cooperative independence for the growing person to imitate.

Children raised in authoritarian families lack practice in negotiating for their desires and exercising responsibility. They tend to resent all authority, to rebel without cause. Children raised in permissive families tend to feel unwanted and to doubt their own self-worth. They often do not trust themselves or others (Conger, 1973, pp. 208–215).

Friends.   The people all adolescents can trust not to treat them like children are their peers. Teenagers spend much of their time with friends—they need and use each other to define themselves. The patterns of social interaction have changed somewhat over the past decade or so. There is not the same emphasis on dating. There seems to be more group and communal activity. And although the meaning of "being popular" has changed somewhat since the dating era, popularity is still extremely important.

High schools are important as places for adolescents to get together. And they do get together in fairly predictable ways. Most schools contain easily recognizable and well-defined sets, or crowds. And these sets are arranged in a fairly rigid social hierarchy—everyone knows who belongs to what set and what people in that set do with their time. Early in adolescence the sets are usually divided by sex, but later the sexes mix. Sets usually form along class lines. Some school activities bring teenagers of different social classes together, but it is the exception rather than the rule that middle-class and lower-class adolescents are close friends. Belonging to a *clique* (a group within a set) gives the adolescent status and a means of defining himself; it is a handle the adolescent can hold onto while shaping an identity.

Of course, there are drawbacks to this kind of social organization. One of the greatest is that the fear of being disliked leads to *conformity*. A

FIGURE 9.5
Social acceptance, so important to adolescents, often leads to conformity. Teenagers tend to dress alike and to succumb to group pressure.

teenager's fear of wearing clothes that might set him apart from others is well known. But group pressures to conform often lead young people to do things that run contrary to their better judgment—or to do things they fear. One of the factors that undoubtedly made it possible for the use of drugs to spread so rapidly in many American schools is the social pressure for adolescents to conform to the group (We will discuss social pressures and conformity again in Chapter 11.)

The Transition to Adult Thinking

During adolescence, the thinking patterns characteristic of adults emerge. From about age eleven or twelve, people are capable of systematic experimentation; that is, given a problem—in school, under the hood of a car, or in an art studio—the adolescent can consider all possible combinations of events and eliminate all the combinations that are irrelevant to the task until he or she discovers the correct one. One important side effect of this new intellectual skill is the ability to consider hypothetical propositions and to reason from them. Adolescents can, for example, consider what would happen if there were another Civil War or imagine what the world would be like without cars. Such situations would seem absurd to eight-year-olds because they are so contrary to their experience (Inhelder and Piaget, 1958).

The new intellectual capacities also enable the adolescent to deal with overpowering emotional feelings through *rationalization*. After failing a test, for example, an individual may rationalize that it happened "because I was worried about the date I might be going on next week." An eight-year-old is too tied to concrete reality to be worrying about future events.

With comprehension of the hypothetical comes the ability to understand abstract principles. Not only is this capacity important for studying higher-level science and mathematics, it leads the adolescent to deal with such abstractions in his or her own life as ethics, conformity, and phoniness. It allows for introspection—examining one's own motives and thoughts. One adolescent is quoted as saying, "I found myself thinking about my future, and then I began to think about why I was thinking about my future, and then I began to think about why I was thinking about why I was thinking about my future."

Perhaps the main difference between the way adolescents and adults think is that young people are highly idealistic. They often become impatient with what they see as the adult generation's failure to implement ideals of social justice. They don't understand why, for example, a person who feels a job compromises his or her principles doesn't just quit. In other words, adolescents tend to be somewhat unrealistic about the complexities of life.

The Generation Gap

A great deal has been written in the press about a generation gap. The implication is that adolescents and their parents are engaged in some sort of cold war; that their standards are so different that they are unable to communicate. Differences do exist—in attitudes towards sex (as we have seen), education, politics, religion, social customs, dress and—of course—music. According to recent surveys, two out of three young people and seven out of ten adults believe that a gap exists.

However, all available evidence suggests that the generation gap has been greatly exaggerated. A majority of young people (57 percent) stated that they got along well with their parents and enjoyed being with them. Most of the adolescents (74 percent) who reported that they had trouble communicating with their parents said it was "both our faults." Although young people often quarrel with their parents over the friends they choose, the way they dress, or the language they use, they generally agree with their parents about such things as career aspirations and life goals. Most adolescents (75 percent) said that they accepted their parents' ideals and values, and most parents (91 percent) reported only slight to moderate differences between themselves and their children. Indeed a large number of young people hold such traditional values as respect for hard work, self-reliance, and competition (Yankelovich, 1969).

Why, then, do we hear so much about the generation gap? One reason is that adolescents and their parents occupy different stages in the life cycle.

> The adolescent who is just becoming aware of the insistent stirrings of sexual impulses will inevitably differ from the middle-aged adult who perceives their urgency waning. Adolescents need ways to consume their energy; adults look for ways to conserve it. Young people are concerned about where they are going; adults are concerned about where they have been. Adults, having personally experienced the many partial victories and defeats and the inevitable compromises of living, tend to be tempered in their enthusiasms, and cautious in their moral judgments. Young people, in contrast, tend to be impatient, impulsive, and given at times to imperious moral judgments that allow little room for shades of gray. They are more likely to move from profound joy to despair. Adults must worry more about their children; adolescents must worry more about themselves (Conger, 1973, p. 188).

IDENTITY: SELF AND SOCIETY

A major developmental task in adolescence is building an identity. Children are aware of what other people (adults and peers) think of them. They know the labels others apply to them (good, naughty, silly, talented, brave, pretty, and the like). They are also aware of their biological drives and of their growing physical and cognitive abilities. Children may dream of being this or that person and act these roles out in their play. But they do not brood about who they are or where they are going in life. Children live in the present; adolescents begin to think about the future.

Several factors contribute to what Erik Erikson (1968) has called the adolescent *identity crisis*—worrying about who you are. These include the physiological changes we have described, awakening sexual drives and the possibility of a new kind of intimacy with the opposite sex, and cognitive developments. Adolescents begin to see the future as a reality, not just a game. They know they have to confront the almost infinite and often conflicting possibilities and choices that lie ahead. In the process of reviewing their past and anticipating their future, they begin to think about themselves.

Building an identity involves looking both inward and outward. Looking inward, adolescents seek the feeling of self-sameness: that they know how they feel about different issues, situations, and people, and that their thoughts and behavior make sense. Looking outward, they seek confirmation of this self. Do other people see them as they see themselves? The feeling that nobody really knows or understands you is quite common in adolescence. Another dimension to the problem of identity is developing a sense of continuity—a feeling that in an important way you are the same person you were when you were younger and that you will be in the future. Although you have changed in many ways, your basic identity remains the same.

Erikson suggests that the identity crisis stems from the adolescent's desire to feel unique and distinctive on the one hand, and to "fit in" on the other. Some young people have great difficulty satisfying these contradictory desires. This may be one reason why so many adolescents are drawn to radical political or religious movements, fraternities and sororities, or gangs. These groups provide a ready-made identity. Strict codes of dress and behavior relieve the young person of the burden of making choices. The adolescent rebels against adult rules by rigidly conforming to peer-group standards. Erikson calls such complete immersion in a group *totalism*.

Adolescents who are comfortable with their maturing bodies, who have a realistic sense of where they want to go in life, and who feel sure of acceptance by the people who matter to them will not experience as severe an identity crisis. But to some degree all adolescents become conformists for a period. Peer groups provide structure when adolescents are ready to be less dependent on their families, but not quite ready to be independent.

Sexual Identity

A significant part of a person's self-definition and self-knowledge is his or her sexual identity. Sexual identity is related not only to one's personal relationships but also to the work one does, the opinions one holds, and the responsibilities one feels. American society appears to be undergoing major changes in its definition of the roles the sexes should play and in the attitudes it holds toward sexual behavior itself.

In a classic work on adolescents, James Coleman (1961) showed how stereotypes about the way males and females should behave operate in high school. Typically, boys considered having a car one of the most important things in life; girls, having nice clothes. When asked if they wanted to be remembered as the "best scholars," more freshman boys than girls answered yes. The gap increased as students moved toward their senior years. Girls' grades were more consistent over the years, but few

What Men Would Like to Be

creative
happy
honest
independent
intelligent
sensitive to others
understanding

What Women Would Like to Be

attractive
friendly
independent
intelligent
loving

Men's Ideal Woman

creative
friendly
sensitive

Women's Ideal Man

good-looking
intelligent
loving
understanding

What Men Think Women Would Like to Be

honest
independent
intelligent
sensitive to others

What Women Think Men Would Like to Be

brave
dominant
rich

What Men Think Women Would Like Them to Be

friendly
good-looking
honest
intelligent
sensitive to others

What Women Think Men Would Like Them to Be

beautiful
dependent
physically well-proportioned

FIGURE 9.6
Chart showing the characteristics that young men and women list as ideal for themselves and for a person of the opposite sex, and the characteristics that they think the opposite sex considers ideal for both men and women.

excelled. Apparently they operated on the principle "Girls should get good grades—but not too good."

Matina Horner's studies of college women (1969), described in Chapter 6, tend to support this. Many women apparently believe that competing with, and especially doing better than, their male peers will make them unpopular. Success is not feminine; girls and women look for other sources of self-esteem.

A recent study of the characteristics young men and women consider ideal for members of their own and the opposite sex leads to similar conclusions (Rosenau, 1974). Sex-role stereotypes seem to have more influence on women than they do on men, although there are many areas where the sexes agree (see Figure 9.6).

Whether these stereotypes will persist in the next generation is difficult to say. We have seen that attitudes toward sex itself have changed. Both male and female adolescents today are looking for more egalitarian relationships that involve more than sex. There is every reason to believe that this will affect the way young people of both sexes look at success and the ideals they hold for themselves and members of the opposite sex.

Homosexuality. Identification of oneself as a male or female takes place very early. After that primary understanding, one goes on to learn—by trial and error, by watching and listening—what it is that men do and what it is that women do. One thing that becomes clear is that men desire sexual relations with women, and women with men. However, some men and women end up preferring the company of their own sex. How does this happen?

No one really knows yet. Biologists have not been able to find any hormonal differences between heterosexual men and women and homosexuals. There is no evidence of genetic differences. Because no biological differences have been discovered, many psychologists have come up with explanations based on early childhood experiences. Some theorize that male homosexuals, by loving men, are trying to cover up intense hatred for their fathers or, by avoiding women, are reacting to a mother who tried to make them a "mama's boy." Other psychologists believe that homosexuality develops because of certain adolescent experiences. If a boy is rejected by most of his male peers—because he dislikes sports, for example—and is not attractive to girls, he may come to have serious doubts about his masculinity and prefer the companionship of men whom he sees as being like himself and who accept him more readily.

The factors that make a person prefer homosexual relations to heterosexual ones are not yet known. But certain things are known about homosexuality and sexuality in general that should be made clear: (1) The influence of cultural conditioning on an individual's sexual behavior, though strong, is not absolute and invariable. Consequently everyone possesses some capacity for homosexual feelings, and most people have had at least some sexual experience with someone of the same sex at some time in their lives. (2) A person's sexual preferences cannot be identified just by looking at him or her. Homosexual men are not necessarily effeminate and lesbians are not necessarily mannish. Nor are effeminate men and mannish women necessarily homosexuals. (3) There is no one "homosexual" personality, just as there is no one "heterosexual" personality. Indeed, the only thing all homosexuals seem to have in common is their sexual preference. (4) A large proportion of a homosexual's difficulties in life is due to the fact that American society has treated homosexuals as outcasts and criminals. It is a myth that homosexuals are more likely than others to commit sex crimes against unwilling victims.

Identity Resolution

Resolution of the identity problem is necessary to form further commitments to adult life. Without a clear sense of who one is, it is impossible to make a mature commitment in love. And without a clear sense of what one's goals are, it is difficult to choose work that will be fulfilling. It may be, with the prolongation of adolescence, that the resolution of the identity crisis does not take place until after the adolescent years. No one wakes up one morning before his or her twentieth birthday and bounds out of bed saying, "Eureka! I know who I am!" A few people do have a good sense of self early in life. For others, it may not come until much later. But of all human psychological processes, the knowledge of who one is—and a commitment to that self—is probably the most important.

ADULTHOOD

Until quite recently psychologists tended to treat the changes that occur as a person moves from adolescence to adulthood to old age as responses to changing circumstances. One reason is that it is difficult to study the entire life cycle. A cross-sectional study (which compares individuals of different ages at the same point in time) may reflect changes in the way different generations were raised and the challenges they face, not changes that occur as a result of aging. A longitudinal study (which compares the way the same individuals think and act at different points in time) would take years to complete. However, by combining these techniques psychologists have begun to shed new light on the process of growing older. The opportunities and problems individuals face and the nature of their interests do change significantly over the adult years. In the pages that follow we will look at the developmental tasks of young adulthood, middle age, and old age, and at different ways of handling these tasks.

Physical Changes

In general, human beings are at their physical peak between the ages of eighteen and twenty-five. This is the period when we are strongest, healthiest, and have the quickest reflexes. One has only to think of the average age of professional athletes or dancers to verify this.

For most adults, the process of physical decline is slow and gradual. Strength and stamina begin to decline in the late twenties. A twenty-year-old manages to carry four heavy bags of groceries; a forty-year-old finds it easier to make two trips. In middle age appearance changes. The hair starts to turn gray and perhaps to thin out. The skin becomes somewhat dry and inelastic; wrinkles appear. People may become overweight, or develop hypertension or arthritis, which accelerate the aging process. In old age, muscles and fat built up over the years break down, so that people often lose weight, become shorter, and develop more wrinkles, creases, and loose skin.

With time the senses require more and more stimulation. During their forties most people begin having difficulty seeing distant objects, adjusting to the dark, and focusing on printed pages, even if their eyesight has always been good. Many experience a gradual or sudden loss of hearing in their later years. In addition, reaction time slows. If an experimenter asks a young person and an older person to push a button when they see a light flash on, the older person will take longer to do so. People over sixty-five have a higher rate of accidents on the road and in jobs requiring coordination than middle-aged people—although not as high as the rate for late adolescents (Kimmel, 1974).

Some of the changes we associate with growing older are the result of the natural processes of aging. Others result from diseases and from simple disuse. A person who eats sensibly, exercises, avoids cigarettes, drugs, and alcohol, and is not subjected to severe emotional stress will look and feel younger than someone who neglects his or her health.

Reactions to Aging. Most people learn to compensate for declining strength and reaction time by adopting a less vigorous lifestyle. They turn to recreational activities that require skill rather than stamina (for example, golf or cards); they take breaks when they do engage in strenuous activities (such as tennis or shoveling snow). By middle age, many have worked their way into jobs that depend on experience, skill in dealing with people, and contacts, rather than on speed and coordination.

Adjusting to changes in appearance may be more difficult. Judging by the amount of hair dyes, face creams, and "miracle vitamins" purchased in this country and the number of men as well as women who undergo cosmetic surgery, Americans do not like to look their age. However, according to one survey people over forty-five are as happy with their

FIGURE 9.7
Skin creams and cosmetics appeal to many middle-aged women and men who wish to look younger than their years.

overall physical appearance as people under forty-five (Berscheid, Walster, and Bohrnstedt, 1973).

Sexual Attitudes and Behavior.   Many children find it difficult to imagine their parents having sexual relations. And most of us wonder if our sexual appetite won't decline with the years. There is a good deal of evidence that wondering and worrying have more effect on sexual activity in middle and old age than physiological changes do.

Between the ages of forty-five and fifty, a woman's production of sex hormones is sharply reduced. This biological event is called *menopause*. The woman stops ovulating (producing eggs) and menstruating, and therefore cannot have any more children. However, menopause does not cause any reduction in a woman's sexual drive or sexual enjoyment.

Many women experience hot flashes and some degree of discomfort during menopause. However, the headaches, dizzy spells, anxiety attacks, irritability, and severe depression some women experience with "the change of life" appear to have an emotional rather than physical origin. Menopause may occur at a time when a woman is worrying about her children leaving home (and what she will do if she has been a full-time homemaker), concerned about her own and her husband's health, and for the first time facing the fact that she is growing old. In addition, some women have heard that menopause is painful and that they will never feel the same again. This combination of worries may produce the symptoms listed above.

A recent study shows that these negative effects are greatly exaggerated. Half of the women interviewed said they felt better, more confident, calmer, and freer after menopause than they had before. They no longer had to think about their periods or getting pregnant. Their relations with their husbands improved; they enjoyed sex as much as or more than they had before. Many said the worst part of menopause was not knowing what to expect (Neugarten *et al.*, 1963).

Men do not go through any biological change equivalent to menopause. The number of sperm a man's body produces declines gradually over the years, but men have fathered children at an advanced age. Some men do experience a loss of sexual responsiveness after fifty, but the causes are psychological, not physical. Monotony, preoccupation with economic pursuits, physical or mental fatigue, and "fear of failure" may all affect sexual behavior. If a man expects his sexual drive and sexual prowess to decline in middle age, they may—*because* he expects them to. It is a self-fulfilling prophecy.

Masters and Johnson (1966, 1968) found that men who are sexually active in their younger years continue to be so in middle and old age—if they have an interesting and willing partner, if they are in reasonably good health, and if they do not fear aging and its effects. The same may be said about women. Sexual activity does decline somewhat in old age. Women experience a decrease in vaginal flexibility and lubrication. Men take longer to achieve an erection and may find orgasms less intense. But sex continues to interest older people and to play an important role in their lives.

Intellectual Changes

People are better at learning new skills and information, solving problems that require speed and coordination, and shifting from one problem-solving strategy to another in their mid-twenties than they were in adolescence (Baltes and Schaie, 1974). These abilities are considered signs of intelligence; they are the skills intelligence tests measure.

At one time many psychologists thought that intellectual development reached a peak in the mid-twenties and declined thereafter. The reason was that people do not score as high on intelligence tests in middle age as they did when they were younger. However, further investigation revealed that some parts of the tests in common use measure speed, not intelligence (Bischof, 1969). As indicated above, a person's reaction time begins to slow in the early thirties. Intelligence tests "penalized" adults for this fact.

Allowing for the decline in speed, we find that people continue to acquire information and to expand their vocabularies as they grow older. The ability to comprehend new material and to think flexibly improves with the years. This is particularly true if a person has had higher education, lives in a stimulating environment, and works in an intellectually demanding career. One researcher studied over seven hundred individuals who were engaged in scholarship, science, or the arts. Although the patterns varied from profession to profession, most of the subjects reached their peaks of creativity and productivity in their forties (Dennis, 1966).

In old age most people slow down dramatically. In addition, many older people tend to be somewhat rigid or conservative in their thinking. They are more likely to agree with clichés; they are reluctant to guess when they do not know the answer to a question. However, memory loss and senility are not part of the natural process of aging. They result from hardening of the arteries and other diseases. Many elderly people continue to be alert, productive, and inventive throughout their lives. Leo Tolstoy, Pablo Picasso, Arthur Rubinstein, Eleanor Roosevelt, and Grandma Moses are some of the obvious examples.

Social and Personality Development During Young Adulthood

Moving away from one's parents, taking a full-time job, and having a family to support and care for may bring out qualities that were not visible in adolescence. In one study, young adults who had not gotten along well in school or at home were managing their own families quite well (Kuhlen and Thompson, 1970, p. 535). Whether this was the result of maturation or of changed circumstances is difficult to say.

All available evidence suggests that an individual's basic character—his or her style of adapting to situations—is relatively stable over the adult years. A number of researchers have given the same attitude and personality tests to individuals in late adolescence and again ten or fifteen years later. Many of the subjects believed that they had changed dramatically. But the tests indicated they had not. The degree of satisfaction they expressed about themselves and about life in general in their middle years

CHAPTER 9 ADOLESCENCE, ADULTHOOD, AND OLD AGE

was consistent with their earlier views. Confident young people remained confident; self-haters, self-hating; passive individuals, passive—unless something upsetting had happened to them, such as a sudden change in economic status (see Kimmel, 1974).

Social Roles.   As Robert White (1966) has suggested, committing oneself to a *social role* is a step toward consolidating one's personal identity. Suppose a young woman decides to become a psychologist. The longer she persists in this study, the more she and her friends and colleagues will see her *as a psychologist*. This social identity is reinforced (assuming she is successful and happy with her choice). In time she will begin to resolve questions about how she will perform the role of psychologist and how she will integrate this with other social roles. (She is also a grown daughter, a friend, and perhaps a wife and mother.) The choice of career provides a focus.

The same would be true if she decided to go on the stage, to marry and become a full-time homemaker, or to marry and work until her husband finished school or achieved the financial security they wanted before they had children.

There is a *deepening of interests in young adulthood*. In their late twenties and early thirties, people generally devote much of their time to increasing their command and effectiveness in their field of interest—whether it be a career or motherhood. Many young adults also develop serious outside interests. Adolescents tend to devote themselves

FIGURE 9.8
During young adulthood interests deepen. The sports or interests that were attended to during adolescence, because they made one belong to a crowd or stand out in it, are now pursued for their own rewards.
(©Henri Cartier-Bresson.)

to sports or hobbies either because it makes them stand out from the crowd or because it makes them one of the crowd. For young adults, hiking, politics, collecting, or other interests become ends in themselves, pursued for their own rewards (White, 1966).

Personal Relationships.   As young adults become more stable in their identities, they become more responsive to other people. In general adolescents are too concerned about the impression they are making to think much about how other people feel. They tend to see others in terms of their own needs and fantasies, not as they really are. Young adults are less anxious: They listen to what other people are saying about themselves, directly and indirectly. Their concern for others grows. They begin to empathize—to feel other people's joys and sorrows as their own—and to care.

Perhaps the most obvious illustration of this is the young adult's relationship with his or her parents. In his late twenties, a man may suddenly realize that he is talking to his parents as friends—listening calmly to their views, offering advice, speaking frankly. The desire to see his parents as invulnerable and the need to demonstrate his independence by being contrary have all but disappeared (White, 1966).

The ability to create intimate relationships depends in large part on whether a person has established a sense of identity, as Erik Erikson (1968) has stressed. Someone who is insecure is likely to avoid closeness —because he fears the other person will see through him, or because he feels uncomfortably dependent on people he is close to. Erikson believes that the failure to achieve intimacy leads to isolation, perhaps disguised by a series of intense but brief affairs or a stable but distant relationship. In his view this is the major risk or crisis of early adulthood: *intimacy vs. isolation.*

Marriage and Parenthood.   Nearly everyone in America (between 95 and 98 percent of the population) gets married, usually in early adulthood (Carter and Glick, 1970). Whether a couple has lived together before making this legal commitment or not, staying happily married requires adaptability. As we have suggested, young adults are in the process of consolidating their identities. This means they need some degree of freedom. Psychotherapist Carl Rogers (1972) believes the quality of a marriage depends on the partners' capacity for intimacy, willingness to let each other grow, patience, and open communication.

Over 90 percent of American women have at least one child during their life, usually in early adulthood (Lasswell and Lasswell, 1973). In contrast to marriage, parenthood is irreversible. Becoming a parent can be something of a shock. One day the couple is free to come and go as they please. The next, they have a tiny baby who is totally dependent upon them and will remain so for years to come.

Recent social changes may be making the transition to parenthood easier. Birth-control devices are readily available to those who want them, enabling a couple to decide when to become parents. There is also less social pressure on a woman to have children today than there was a

FIGURE 9.9
It is no longer uncommon for a father to participate actively in the care of his children. Egalitarian relationships in which both partners contribute to the family's income and both share the responsibilities of child care are much more common today than they were a generation ago.

generation ago. As a result parenthood is largely voluntary. In addition, many couples wait a year or more after marriage to conceive a child. In most cases the wife works during this period. Couples are more likely to develop an egalitarian relationship when both partners work than when only one does and to share the responsibilities of parenthood when they do have a child. This gives both more freedom. A mother does not bear total responsibility for child care, a father total responsibility for support; a mother need not be divorced from the world of work, a father need not be a stranger to his children (see Rossi, 1968).

Middle Age

The point at which a person begins to feel middle-aged varies with social class, occupation, sex, and personality. In general, working-class people sense that they have passed their prime in their early forties; middle-class and particularly professional people often consider this a time of maximum productivity. Women tend to mark time in terms of the family life cycle. A married woman and mother begins to feel middle-aged when her children leave home for college or a job. A single woman feels middle-aged when she begins to think that she will never have a family. Men tend to use occupational markers. A man who realizes that the chances of reaching occupational goals he set for himself are lost senses his age.

The Tasks of Middle Age.   Young adults are busy establishing themselves in their careers, raising families, and creating a lifestyle. The tasks middle-aged people face are rather different. However ambivalent they may feel about it, parents must now encourage their children to seek independence. Parents have to learn to be a couple—a two-person household—all over again. And many begin caring for aging parents in this stage.

Single people often seek a special companion with whom they can travel, entertain, and spend their leisure hours in middle age. They may take a more active role in guiding grown nieces, nephews, and friends' children than they did before. They too care for aging parents.

Other tasks include maintaining one's position at work (perhaps through additional schooling); establishing an economic standard that satisfies current needs, and planning for retirement; keeping one's marriage and friendships alive and rewarding; and perhaps finding new, less strenuous leisure-time activities.

Generativity vs. Stagnation.   In his description of the "Eight Ages of Man," Erik Erikson (1950) suggests that middle age may trigger either a new sense of generativity or a slide into stagnation. By generativity, Erikson means the desire to use one's accumulated wisdom to guide future generations—directly, as a parent, or indirectly. Stagnation occurs when a person wants to hang onto the past. The most graphic examples of this are women who try to recapture youth with face-lifts, and men who attempt to recapture it by having affairs with young women. Stagnation may take the form of childish self-absorption, preoccupation with one's health, and bitterness about the direction one's life has taken.

FIGURE 9.10
Many women approaching middle age find they now have the time to pursue professional or academic interests. Such involvement enables these women to develop and express abilities that full-time motherhood may have blocked.

Ideally, a middle-aged person feels that the way he sees himself, what he would like to be, and the way others perceive him fit together. He has developed a number of effective strategies for dealing with stress and the complexities of life. He has a new self-assurance born of the feeling that he knows he can handle things. And he wants to share this experience with others.

In middle age, people begin to devote more time and energy to the outside world. Although their interest in family and friends continues, they become more deeply involved in organizations—professional associations, unions, political campaigns, civic committees, and the like. This new outward orientation may be most obvious in housewives who now have the time to go back to school or to full-time work, to chair committees or run for political office. But it is also true of working people whose experience and heightened productivity command new respect. Involvement in outside affairs is an extension of generativity beyond the family.

Time Orientation. Middle age is also a period of self-examination. Although some people do make dramatic changes in lifestyle in their forties or fifties, most feel it is too late to start over. Whereas young people tend to think in terms of time-since-birth, middle-aged people tend to think in terms of time-left-to-live. Some relax, feeling they have done well. They are glad to be free of the driven feelings of youth. Some forge ahead, intent on finishing the work they have begun. Others feel a quiet desperation. They become bitter about lost opportunities and goals that may never be accomplished, and may try to lose themselves in dreams of what might have been.

OLD AGE

According to Erikson, old age and the imminent prospect of dying lead some people either to a heightened sense of ego integrity or to despair. By ego integrity, Erikson means greater self-acceptance. Looking back, the elderly person concludes that if he had his life to live over, he'd like it as it was—with all the bumps, false starts, and disappointments as well as the joys and triumphs. By despair, Erikson means regret—the inability to accept oneself and one's life. Looking back, the old person may see little but lost chances, bad decisions, people who spoiled his plans.

American culture makes it difficult for an old person to maintain a sense of integrity. In other societies (most notably in the East), old age is considered an achievement and old people are revered. In contrast, we tend to fear growing old and to be somewhat patronizing toward the elderly.

A number of stereotypes support these attitudes. We assume—wrongly—that a person's mind deteriorates as he or she grows old. Loss of memory and senility are not inevitable side-effects of aging; they are symptoms of disorders. Second, we tend to believe that old people resist change. In fact, people who have always enjoyed challenges may become increasingly imaginative and flexible in their old age. The people who fight change in their seventies usually fought change in their thirties and forties. Finally, we tend to regard old people as useless. In truth, one-third of this country's senior citizens work at least part time and take an active role in civic affairs (Butler and Lewis, 1973).

Adjusting to Old Age

The elderly face a number of special problems that may be difficult for younger people to understand. The first is often retirement. Whether they

FIGURE 9.11
Many of our society's stereotyped attitudes about the elderly are not valid. Old people do not inevitably become senile; they are not, by virtue of their age, resistant to change; and they are not useless. Though they do face special age-related problems, they are capable of making continuing and valuable contributions to their families and to society.

want to or not, many workers are forced to retire at age sixty-five. This means loss of an occupational identity, perhaps too much time on one's hands, and often feelings of uselessness. Second is the loss of loved ones. The older a person gets, the more of his friends and relatives die. This happens at a time when it is becoming increasingly difficult to get around, visit distant friends, and meet new people. Losing one's life-long spouse may be devastating, particularly for old people who do not live near other members of their family. Finally, there is the fear of becoming sick, disabled, and physically and financially dependent on others. Maintaining a sense of pride and dignity when one can no longer care for oneself requires a good deal of inner strength.

What are the solutions to these problems? Some psychologists believe that aging is easier if a person gradually and voluntarily disengages himself from such social roles as worker or head of household. Forced disengagement (being told you can no longer participate) or forced engagement (being expected to do things you do not feel capable of performing) can be damaging. According to this view, elderly people want to slow down, withdraw, spend time thinking about themselves and reminiscing. Other psychologists believe that aging is easier if a person remains active, gets out, finds substitutes for social roles they have given up and loved ones they have lost (see Havighurst, 1972).

Which course a person chooses reflects his or her earlier life. People who always led active lives adapt more easily to old age if they remain as active as they can. People who were always somewhat withdrawn and introspective adapt best to aging through disengagement.

Dying

Elisabeth Kübler-Ross's work (1969) has become a classic in the relatively new field of *thanatology*—the study of death and dying. Kübler-Ross has

FIGURE 9.12
These patients at St. Christopher's Hospice in England are spending their last days surrounded by ongoing life. Rather than prolonging life with machines, doctors at hospices seek to provide a warm, human atmosphere for the terminally ill. This approach to treating the dying is beginning to influence American medical personnel. Hospices are being planned in New Haven, Connecticut and Santa Barbara, California.

identified five stages of psychological adjustment to terminal illness, based on interviews with over two hundred patients. The first stage is *denial*. The most common response is, "It can't happen to me; there must be a mistake." The second stage is *anger*: "Why me?" The dying person may resent and become hostile toward the people he will leave behind and toward all healthy people. He attempts to *bargain* (perhaps with God) for more time. The next stage is a growing sense of loss, or *depression*. Kübler-Ross suggests that it helps a dying person if loved ones allow him to express his sadness and do not attempt to cover the situation up or force him (by their own denial) to act cheerful. Near the end, when the person is tired and weak, he *accepts the inevitable.* It is almost as if the dying person had said his goodbyes, made his peace with himself, and is resting before the final journey. *how quaint*

SUMMARY

1. Adolescence is the transition period between childhood and adulthood during which people reach the final stage of psychosexual development.

2. Adolescents have a strong need to be accepted by their peers and tend to conform to ideals of how males and females their age should look, act, and dress.

3. One of the principal developmental tasks for adolescents is becoming independent of their families. The way in which an adolescent seeks independence and the ease with which he or she resolves conflicts about becoming a full-fledged adult depend in large part on the parent–child relationship.

4. In adolescence the thinking patterns of adulthood emerge. The main difference between the way adolescents and adults think is that young people are highly idealistic and tend to be unrealistic about the complexities of life.

5. A major developmental task in adolescence is building an identity. This involves looking both inward and outward to discover who one truly is. A significant part of a person's self-identification and self-knowledge is his or her sexual identity. Society is undergoing major changes in its definition of the roles the sexes should play and in the attitudes it holds toward sexual behavior itself. Both male and female adolescents today are looking for more egali-

tarian relationships that involve more than sex.

6. All evidence suggests that an individual's basic character is relatively stable over the adult years. However, the opportunities and problems individuals face and the nature of their interests do change significantly. Early adulthood is the period during which an individual makes choices that give him or her a social identity. The point at which a person begins to feel middle-aged varies with social class, occupation, sex, and the individual.

7. Middle-aged tasks include encouraging children to seek independence, maintaining one's position at work, establishing an economic standard that satisfies current needs, planning for retirement, keeping marriage and friendships rewarding, and perhaps finding new, less strenuous leisure-time activities. It is also a period of self-examination.

8. Old age and the imminent prospect of dying lead some people to a heightened sense of integrity, others to despair. American culture makes it difficult for an old person to maintain a sense of integrity.

9. Some psychologists believe that aging is easier if people gradually and voluntarily disengage themselves from social roles as worker or head of household. Forced disengagement or forced engagement can be damaging.

GLOSSARY

adolescence: The developmental stage between childhood and adulthood during which sexual maturation begins, identity is shaped, and life goals are considered.

authoritarian family: A family in which parents are the "bosses" and do not feel they have to explain their actions or demands to their children.

clique: A group within a set or crowd.

conformity: Compliance to group standards.

continuity: A person's sense of the constancy of his or her identity throughout life.

democratic family: A family in which the adolescent participates in decisions affecting his or her life. Parents maintain the ultimate right to veto plans of which they disapprove.

generativity: The desire, in middle age, to use one's accumulated wisdom to guide future generations.

identity crisis: The period in a person's life during which he or she seeks confirmation of self by selecting, among many and often conflicting possibilities, the direction and goals of his or her life.

laissez-faire family: A permissive family in which the children have the final say in decisions concerning themselves.

menarche: The onset of menstruation, considered in most societies to be the beginning of womanhood.

menopause: The period, occurring at approxi-mately forty to fifty years of age, when a woman ceases to ovulate, menstruate, and produce sex hormones.

permissive family: A family in which the children have the final say in decisions concerning themselves; sometimes termed *laissez-faire*.

psychological moratorium: A period during which young people can explore and experiment without having to commit themselves to a lifestyle, career, or mate, or suffer the consequences of mistakes.

puberty: Sexual maturation; the biological event that marks the end of childhood.

rationalization: A process whereby an individual seeks to explain an often unpleasant emotion or behavior in a way that will preserve his or her self-esteem.

self-sameness: An individual's sense of knowing how he or she feels about different issues, situations, and people, and that these opinions make sense.

social role: A career or lifestyle to which one makes a commitment and which acts as a step toward consolidating one's personal identity.

stagnation: A discontinuation of development and desire to recapture the past, characteristic of some middle-aged people.

thanatology: The study of death and dying.

totalism: Complete immersion in a group or movement.

ACTIVITIES

1. The notion of establishing an identity, though discussed at length in the popular press as well as in psychological literature, remains difficult to pin down in concrete terms. Try to write one or two paragraphs describing your own identity. From these descriptions compare the dimensions which you and your classmates focused on in your written descriptions.

2. Ask your parents how they think they've changed since their youth. Do they perceive their basic personalities as remaining relatively

stable or going through marked changes? What are the major factors they think had the most significant effects on their personality development?

3. What provisions does your community provide for its retired and elderly adults? How do you think these services could be improved to make the experience of old age a more fruitful and happier time?

4. Do some reading on how the transition from childhood to adulthood was made in a past period of history and in other cultures. Compare the concerns of today's youth with those of yesteryear and in other cultures.

5. Death and dying have only recently become topics that are discussed openly. Given this growing openness, what changes do you see

being made to make the adjustment to the prospect of dying less severe? How do you think hospitals and homes for the aged might change in the future along these lines?

6. Look at some magazine articles about alternative life styles. How do the phases of adult development of persons choosing these alternative styles differ from the traditional developmental phases of the typical American adult?

7. List several controversial questions, such as, "Do you believe in fighting for your country no matter what the circumstances?" Ask people of different age groups to respond to your questions. Do you notice differences in the levels of reasoning? Use the explanations contained in this chapter to account for the differences.

SUGGESTED READINGS

BEM, SANDRA L. "Androgyny vs. the Little Lives of Fluffy Women and Chesty Men." *Psychology Today* (September 1975): 59–62. Bem argues, with supporting data, that the most flexible and adaptable male or female is one who possesses both the qualities traditionally associated with men and the qualities traditionally associated with women.

CHOWN, SHEILA M. *Human Aging*. Baltimore, Md.: Penguin Books, 1972. A comprehensive collection of readings on various aspects of aging, including intellectual performance, learning and memory, adaptation to stress, and general personality development during old age.

CONGER, JOHN J. *Adolescence and Youth*. New York: Harper & Row, 1973. An excellent overview of physical, personality, and intellectual development during adolescence. Also includes such topics as alienation and commitment, dropping out and delinquency, sexual attitudes and drug use.

EVANS, R. I. *Dialogue with Erik Erikson*. New York: Dutton, 1967 (paper). A long interview with Erikson, in which he discusses his eight stages of psychosocial development and problems young people have in finding their identity, a satisfying life career, and an intimate relationship with another person.

FRANK, ANNE. *The Diary of a Young Girl*. New York: The Modern Library, 1952 (paper). This tender and tragic tale is made even more remarkable by the fact that it is a true account—the personal diary of a fourteen-year-old Dutch girl while she was in hiding from the Nazis.

FRIEDENBERG, EDGAR Z. *The Vanishing Adolescent*. Boston: Beacon, 1959. One of the best-known authorities on adolescence presents his views in an exciting and highly readable fashion. Friedenberg stresses the importance of adolescent conflict as a means of establishing a relationship between the individual and the society.

GORDON, SOL. *Facts About Sex—A Basic Guide*. New York: John Day, 1970. The author describes this book as "simple and brief—especially useful if you don't like to read too much and welcome lots of pictures."

224

UNIT III HUMAN RELATIONS

KIMMEL, DOUGLAS C. *Adulthood and Aging.* New York: John Wiley, 1974. Provides an excellent and highly readable summary of psychological and sociological research and theory on the developmental changes and tasks during adulthood and old age. Includes such topics as identity and intimacy, families and singles, work and retirement, and the physical changes that occur during these years.

KÜBLER-ROSS, ELISABETH. *On Death and Dying.* New York: Macmillan, 1969 (paper). As we read a number of very moving interviews with pa-

tients who are terminally ill, the author allows us to share their private pain and final dignity. We see the stages they pass through: from denial, anger, bargaining, and depression to eventual acceptance.

SALINGER, J. D. *Catcher in the Rye.* New York: Bantam, 1951 (paper). A funny and poignant novel about a boy's search for meaning in the confusion and chaos of adolescence. This book has been a favorite on reading lists for more than twenty years.

BIBLIOGRAPHY

BALTES, P. B., AND SCHAIE, K. W. "Aging and IQ: The Myth of the Twilight Years." *Psychology Today,* 7 (March 1974): 35–40.

BERSCHEID, E., WALSTER, E., AND BOHRNSTEDT, G. "Body Image." *Psychology Today,* 7 (November 1973): 119-131.

BISCHOF, L. *Adult Psychology.* New York: Harper & Row, 1969.

BUTLER, R. N., AND LEWIS, M. I. *Aging and Mental Health.* St. Louis: Mosby, 1973.

CARTER, H., AND GLICK, P., *Marriage and Divorce: A Social and Economic Study.* Cambridge, Mass.: Harvard University Press, 1970.

COLEMAN, J. S. *The Adolescent Society.* New York: Free Press, 1961.

CONGER, J. J. *Adolescence and Youth: Psychological Development in a Changing World.* New York: Harper & Row, 1973.

DENNIS, W. "Creative Productivity Between the Ages of Twenty and Eighty Years." *Journal of Gerontology,* 21 (1966): 1–8.

DWYER, JOHANNA, AND MAYER, JEAN. "Psychological Effects of Variations in Physical Appearance During Adolescence." *Adolescence* (1968–1969): 353–368.

ERIKSON, ERIK. *Childhood and Society.* New York: Norton, 1950.

——. *Identity: Youth and Crisis.* New York: Norton, 1968.

HALL, G. STANLEY. "The Moral and Religious Training of Children." *Princeton Review* (January 1882): 26–48.

HAVIGHURST, R. J. *Developmental Tasks and Education.* 3rd ed. New York: McKay, 1972.

HORNER, M. "Fail: Bright Women." *Psychology Today,* 3 (November 1969): 36—38ff.

INHELDER, B., AND PIAGET, J. *The Early Growth of Logic in the Child.* New York: Harper & Row, 1964.

KIMMEL, DOUGLAS C. *Adulthood and Aging.* New York: Wiley, 1974.

KÜBLER-ROSS, ELISABETH. *On Death and Dying.* New York: Macmillan, 1969.

KUHLEN, RAYMOND G., AND THOMPSON, GEORGE C. *Psychological Studies of Human Development.* New York: Appleton-Century-Crofts, 1970.

LASSWELL, M. E., AND LASSWELL, T. E. (EDS.) *Love, Marriage, Family: A Developmental Approach.* Glencoe, Ill.: Scott Foresman, 1973.

MASTERS, W. H., AND JOHNSON, V. E. *Human Sexual Response.* Boston: Little, Brown, 1966.

——. "Human Sexual Response: The Aging Female and the Aging Male." In B. L. Neugarten (ed.), *Middle Age and Aging*: 269–279, University of Chicago Press, 1968.

MEAD, MARGARET. *Coming of Age in Samoa.* New York: Morrow, 1961.

MUSSEN, PAUL H., CONGER, JOHN J., AND KAGAN, JEROME. *Child Development and Personality.* 4th ed. New York: Harper & Row, 1974.

NEUGARTEN, BERNICE, WOOD, V., ET AL. "Women's Attitudes Towards the Menopause." *Vita Humana*, 6 (1963): 140-151.

ROGERS, CARL C. *Becoming Partners: Marriage and Its Alternatives.* New York: Delacorte, 1972.

ROSENAU, N. "Sex Differences in Ideal Self-Concepts." Unpublished manuscript, Anders Gerontology Center, Los Angeles, 1974.

ROSSI, A. "Transition to Parenthood." *Journal of Marriage and Family*, 30 (1968): 26–39.

SIMON, W., AND GAGNON, J. H. (EDS.) *The Sexual Scene.* Chicago: Transaction Books, 1970.

WHITE, ROBERT. *Lives in Progress: A Study of the Natural Growth of Personality.* 2nd ed. New York: Holt, Rinehart and Winston, 1966.

YANKELOVICH, D. *Generations Apart.* New York: CBS News, 1969.

UNIT IV

Human Relations

Although we may deny it, all of us are concerned with the impression we make on other people and attempt to "read" their reactions to what we say and do. The way we interact with friends and strangers is governed by a variety of social rules. We may not think about these rules very often, but we become embarrassed when we break them. We relate to other people in terms of the social groups to which they belong (their sex, age, occupation, and the like), as well as in terms of individual characteristics. And we all try to influence other people's attitudes and behavior. These familiar, everyday occurrences are what social psychologists, who specialize in human relations, study.

In this Unit we look at three different dimensions of human relations. Chapter 10 deals with interpersonal relationships—the kinds of interactions that occur between two people, whether they are strangers meeting for the first time, friends, or lovers. Chapter 11 focuses on the kinds of interactions that occur within and between groups, from families to communities to corporations. Chapter 12 explores the roles that people play in influencing one another. Your friends and relatives, television producers, advertising executives, textbook publishers, and lawmakers all affect your thoughts, your feelings, and your actions. This chapter explains how and why they do.

Many people take these social processes for granted. Because they are familiar, we assume we understand them. But the scientific study of human relations has revealed that common-sense ideas about "how things are" are often wrong. The main goal of this Unit is to help you achieve a deeper understanding of social interaction. Along the way, you may discover many things that surprise you.

10 Person to Person

People vary considerably in their need for social contact and in their desire and ability to be alone. You have probably read or heard about hermits and recluses who voluntarily isolate themselves, but most people would not welcome a solitary life.

Michel Siffre, a geologist, volunteered to spend six months alone in a cave one hundred feet underground so that scientists could study the effects of prolonged isolation. Siffre was wired to machines that measured his bodily functions, and each day performed a number of tests that measured his mental abilities, memory, and coordination.

The first months of the experiment went smoothly. The experimental tasks, household chores, a journal, and abundant reading material kept Siffre busy. However, by the 156th day he had sunk into despair.

In my journal I scrawl this disorganized—but true—sentence: "When you find yourself alone, isolated in a world totally without time, face-to-face with yourself, all the masks that you hide behind—those to preserve your own illusions, those that project them before others—finally fall, sometimes brutally" (1975: 432).

Reflecting on his experience after he had returned to the surface and rejoined human company, Siffre wrote:

Whether because of confinement, solitude, or both, my mental processes and manual dexterity deteriorated gravely and inexorably toward the end of my stay in Midnight Cave.
   Now, after my long months in Midnight Cave, I still suffer severe lapses in memory. . . . I suffer psychological wounds that I do not understand (p. 435).

For Michel Siffre, as for prisoners in solitary confinement, prolonged isolation is torture. The question psychologists ask is, why?

THE NECESSITY FOR HUMAN INTERACTION

A number of psychologists have suggested that human beings are born with an *instinctive* need to associate with others of their species—just as some animals and birds are born with an instinctive drive to gather in herds and flocks. This is difficult to prove or disprove, but we do know

FIGURE 10.1
Being in love or sharing a deep friendship are the most intimate kinds of relationships people can have. Over the years, psychologists have learned a great deal about the need for human contact, from the infant's need for comfort and affection to the adult's need for love.

229

FIGURE 10.2
This famous passage, by English poet and essayist John Donne, eloquently states that human beings cannot exist in isolation from one another.

(From "Meditation XVII of Devotions upon Emergent Occasions," *The Norton Anthology of English Literature*, Vol. 1. New York: W. W. Norton & Company, 1968, p. 917.)

what can happen to children who are deprived of human contact during their early years.

One famous example is the case of Anna. A disgrace to her unmarried mother, Anna was hidden alone in an attic. Her mother fed her enough to keep the child alive, but otherwise ignored her. At the age of six, Anna was discovered by social workers, who found her unable to sit up, walk, or talk.

Given proper care, Anna did learn to walk and talk, but she died four years later. Psychologists learned an important lesson from Anna's terrible experience. From birth, people need attention to develop normally (Davis, 1948).

From infancy we depend on others, usually our mother, to satisfy our basic needs. In this relationship we learn to associate close personal contact with the satisfaction of basic needs. In later life we seek personal contact for the same reason, even though we can now care for ourselves.

Being around other human beings, interacting with others, has become a habit that would be difficult to break. Moreover, we have developed needs for praise, respect, love and affection, the sense of achievement, and other rewarding experiences. And these needs, acquired through social learning, can only be satisfied by other human beings (Freedman, Carlsmith, and Sears, 1970). Furthermore, while a mother is caring for a small child, she often depends on others for protection and to some extent for the satisfaction of her needs. Thus one reason why humans congregate in groups is for survival.

Anxiety and the Need for Contact

Social psychologists are interested in discovering what circumstances intensify our desire for human contact. It seems that we need company most when we are afraid or anxious, and when we are unsure of ourselves and want to compare our feelings with other people's.

Psychologist Stanley Schachter (1959) sought to test the old saying, "Misery loves company." His experiment showed that people suffering from a high level of anxiety are more likely to seek out company than those who feel less anxious. He arranged for a number of college women to come to his laboratory. One group of women was greeted by a frightening-looking man in a white coat who identified himself as Dr. Gregor Zilstein of the medical school. Dr. Zilstein told each woman that she would be given electric shocks in order to study the effect of electricity on the body. He told the women, in an ominous tone, that the shocks would be extremely painful. With a devilish smile, he added that the shocks would cause no permanent skin damage. For obvious reasons, this group of women was referred to as the *high-anxiety* group.

The doctor was friendly to the other group of women, and told them that the shocks would produce only ticklish, tingling sensations, which they might even find pleasant. These women formed the *low-anxiety* group.

Zilstein told each subject that she would have to leave the laboratory while he set up the equipment. He then asked each woman to indicate on a questionnaire whether she wished to wait alone in a private room or with other subjects in a larger room. Most women in the low-anxiety group were satisfied to wait alone. However, the overwhelming majority of high-anxiety women preferred to wait with others. Thus the experiment demonstrated that high anxiety produces a need for human contact.

Comparing Experiences and Reducing Uncertainty

People also like to get together with one another to reduce their uncertainties about themselves. For example, when you get exams back, you probably ask your friends how they did. You try to understand your own situation by comparing it to other people's. You learn your strengths and weaknesses by asking: Can other people do it, too? Do they do it better or worse? Many individuals use the performance of others as a basis for self-evaluation. According to this theory, one of the reasons why the women in the shock experiment sought company was to find out how they should respond to Dr. Zilstein. Should they feel fear or anger, or should they take the whole thing in stride? One way to get this information was to talk to others.

Schachter conducted another experiment to test this idea. It was essentially the same as the Dr. Zilstein experiment, but this time *all* the women were made anxious. Half of them were then given the choice between waiting alone and waiting with other women about to take part in the same experiment. The other half were given the choice between waiting alone and passing the time in a room where students were waiting to see their academic advisers.

As you might expect, the women who had a chance to be with other women in the same predicament seized the opportunity. These women wanted to compare their dilemma with others. But most of the women in the second group chose to spend the time alone rather than with the unconcerned students. As the experimenter put it, "Misery doesn't love just any kind of company, it loves only miserable company."

Other researchers have shown that the more uncertain a person is, the more likely he or she is to seek out other people. Like Schachter, Harold Gerard and his colleagues recruited volunteers for an experiment. Again, the real experiment took place in the waiting rooms. When they arrived, some of the subjects were escorted to a booth and wired to a machine that was supposed to measure emotionality. The machine was turned on, and the subjects were able to see not only their own ratings but the ratings of three other participants as well. In each case the dial for the subject registered 82 on a scale of 100; the dials for the other participants, 79, 80, and 81. (As you've undoubtedly guessed, the machine was rigged.) A second group of subjects was wired to a similar machine and shown their own ratings but not those of other participants. A third group was not given any information about themselves or other participants in the experiment. When asked whether they wanted to wait alone or with other subjects, most of the people in the first group chose to wait alone. They had seen how they compared to others and felt they were reacting appropriately. However, most of the subjects in the other two groups, who had no basis for evaluating themselves, chose to wait with other people (Gerard and Rabbie, 1961).

Seeking company when you are frightened or uncertain about your feelings seems to work. People who choose to be in a group when they are afraid of an experimental procedure or lack information about how they compare to others are less anxious than those who "tough it out" and wait alone (Wrightsman, 1960).

INTERACTION AND COMMUNICATION: THE INFLUENCE OF SOCIAL NORMS

When one person comes in contact with another, he or she may be lonely and looking for a friend, boastful and searching for an audience, or hungry and seeking something to eat. Whatever the reason, he or she will have to establish some relationship with the other person. This process of establishing relationships is made easier by social rules. A *social rule* or *norm* is any agreement among members of a society about how people should act in particular situations.

The rules governing laughter are an example. Laughter is not acceptable during religious ceremonies. If you do laugh on these occasions, you will undoubtedly draw hostile stares. Laughing when Charlie Chaplin stumbles and crashes to the ground is fine. But laughing when a blind person walks into a telephone pole or an older person falls down is not. On the other hand, you are obliged to laugh or at least to emit a polite chuckle when someone you do not know well tells a joke, or you will be considered rude.

Attitudes toward public nudity show how powerful social rules can be. It is all right for a small child to wander nude into a party his parents

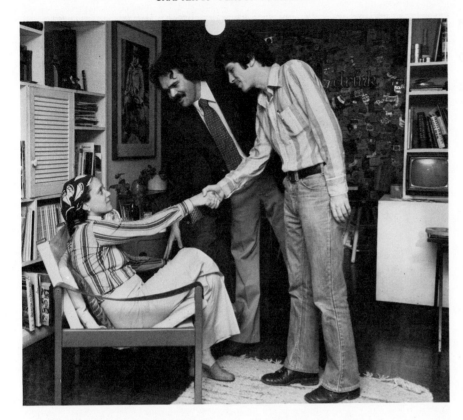

FIGURE 10.3
When people in American society are introduced, they often shake hands. This social norm helps to ease the strain that people feel when meeting for the first time.

are giving, but it is not all right for an adolescent or adult to do so. Even people who deliberately violate the rule that adults should wear clothes set limits on themselves, following the rule at the same time they are breaking it. Thus people at a nudist camp stare intently into one another's faces, carefully avoiding looking at other parts of their bodies, and patrons of topless bars will avert their eyes when a waitress comes to the table (see Goffman, 1971).

Nonverbal Communication

Underlying all the things you say to other people and do in company are subtle, indirect communications about yourself and your relationships to others. The nudists and patrons of topless bars are "saying," through their behavior, that they are basically decent, respectful people. When you laugh at a dull joke you may be saying that you do not want to break the circle of politeness and become more intimate with the other person. If a close friend cracks a bad joke, you tell him or her so. Laughing politely is a way of maintaining distance. Communication that takes place without words is known as *nonverbal communication.*

All of us are conscious of nonverbal communications from time to time. You have probably heard someone say, "It doesn't matter" but show, by speaking in a low voice and looking away, that he or she really means "My feelings are hurt." You don't need to be told in so many words that

FIGURE 10.4
Nonverbal communication has been made a high art by the famous mime Marcel Marceau. Relying solely on facial expression, gesture, and posture, Marceau is able to communicate any impression he wishes.

a friend is elated or depressed, angry or pleased, nervous or contented. You sense these things. How do people communicate nonverbally? Through their use of space, body language (their posture and gestures), and, of course, facial expressions.

Social Space.   Anthropologist Edward T. Hall became acutely aware of the importance people attach to space when he found himself backing away from a colleague he particularly liked and respected. The associate was not an American, which led Hall to wonder if people from different cultures have different ideas about the proper distance at which to hold an informal conversation. He decided to pursue the question.

   After much observation, Hall concluded that Americans carry a two-foot "bubble" of privacy around them. If another person invades this bubble, we feel slightly threatened, imposed upon, and generally uncomfortable. For Germans, the bubble of privacy is much larger; for Arabs, much smaller. Thus when an Arab is talking to a German he will try to establish his accustomed talking distance. He moves closer. The discomforted German concludes that the Arab is "pushy." When the German moves back to what he feels is normal distance, the Arab interprets this as a sign of coldness and concludes that the man is aloof (Hall, 1959).

   Hall observed Americans to see how we use space to communicate our feelings about other people and to define relationships. He found that Americans allow only intimates (lovers, close friends, and family members) closer than two feet, a point at which touching is almost inevitable and voices are lowered. When we are forced to stand very close to nonintimates, as in a crowded elevator, we try to hold our bodies immobile and avoid eye contact.

When we maintain a distance of four feet or so, we are essentially holding the other person "at arm's length." People who work together generally observe this boundary. When we want to hold people off we create a four- to seven-foot bubble between us and them. Sometimes we use social distance to show status. An executive of a large corporation may put visitors' chairs nine feet from her desk to create this impression of status, but many executives are aware of this form of communication and will try to counter this impression by placing the chairs closer than four feet.

If you go to an uncrowded beach you will probably settle down between twelve and twenty-five feet from other people. If you arrange a room for a speaker, you will probably leave a similar amount of space between the podium and the first row of seats. Hall calls this "public distance" and suggests it provides a sense of safety. At twelve feet an alert person can take defensive action if threatened. At the same time, twelve feet or more does not invite personal communication. To talk, two people would move closer (Hall, 1966: 199–122).

The ways in which people use space to communicate will become clear if you keep this scheme in mind. When you put your beach towel five feet from another person's when there is plenty of empty space, you are issuing an invitation. If you step back when someone at a party comes within two feet you are discouraging further intimacy.

Body Language.   The way you carry your body also communicates information about you. If you stand tall and erect, you convey the impression of self-assurance. If you sit and talk with your arms folded and legs crossed, you communicate that you are protecting yourself. But when you

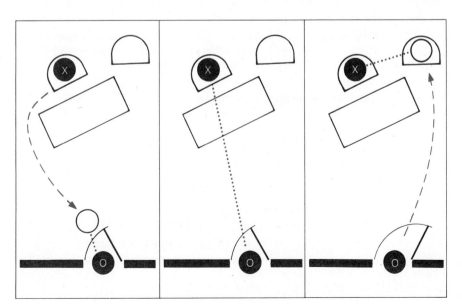

FIGURE 10.5
These diagrams illustrate how unwritten rules about occupational status are subtly communicated by physical position. A desk and two chairs are shown situated a short distance from the office door. O comes to visit X. The broken lines indicate movement; the dotted lines indicate conversation. See whether you can tell, before reading further, who has the superior status in each of these three cases. (*left*) X rises from his desk and moves to greet O. X's deference indicates that O is senior in rank. (*center*) O speaks from the doorway while X remains seated. O is deferring this time, suggesting that X is the superior. (*right*) O walks in, sits down beside X, and they start talking. This interaction indicates that X and O have roughly equal status.

FIGURE 10.6
People tend to like and trust someone who sits in an open position.
In one experiment, students who
saw a slide of a woman in an open
position reported liking her, and
even changed some of their opinions to agree with hers. Subjects
who viewed the same woman in
a closed position did not respond
to her as favorably.

unfold your arms and stretch out, you are saying that you are open to
people.

One group of researchers found that people who adopt an open body
position are better liked and are listened to more closely than are people
who assume a closed position. A number of students were given a questionnaire that measured their opinions on everything from the legalization
of marijuana to the custom of tipping. A few weeks later they were invited
back and asked to evaluate one student's responses. Some were shown
a slide of this student sitting in a closed position; others saw a slide of
her sitting in a neutral or open position. A high percentage of those who
saw the open-looking student indicated they liked her and changed many
of their opinions to agree with hers when they filled out a second questionnaire (McGinley, LeFevre, and McGinley, 1975).

Although the use of body language is often unconscious, many of the
postures we adopt and gestures we make are governed by social rules.
These rules are very subtle. For example, most American boys will wait
for a girl to acknowledge that he is holding her hand by squeezing his
hand back before intertwining fingers, will engage in a good deal of kissing before crossing the line to petting, and so on. (One researcher actually
counted twenty-four steps in the American "courtship dance," in Knapp,
1972: 18.)

There are cultural differences in body language, just as there are in
the use of space. For example, the English indicate that they are paying
attention to a person by focusing on his or her eyes. Americans nod their
heads and make sounds ("uhuh") to show they are listening, but consider
it rude to stare. Americans move their heads up and down to show agreement and shake them back and forth to show disagreement. The Semang

of Malaya thrust their heads sharply forward to agree and lower their eyes to disagree, while the Dayak of Borneo agree by raising their eyebrows and disagree by bringing them together.

PRESENTING AND SEEING OURSELVES

In book after book, sociologist Erving Goffman has argued that the world of social behavior is a stage and all of us, actors. Nearly everything we say and do in public is part of a performance, tailored for the audience at hand. Like actors, we use our faces, movements, and words to create an effect. Only in the privacy of our own rooms do we drop our social masks (Goffman, 1959, 1971).

Creating Impressions

Goffman's view may sound extreme, but if you think about the different ways you act with different people and in different situations, you will begin to see the truth in what Goffman says.

Like professional actors, people in everyday life play a number of *roles* —they behave in different ways in different situations. You undoubtedly behave one way with your family, another way with friends, and still another way with teachers. In your life you may play many other roles, such as "worker," "parent," "customer," "athlete," "lover," and so on, and you will undoubtedly create a different impression in each one.

Why do people play different roles? One reason is that other people treat us as *they* see us and cast us into different roles. To a degree, your parents will always see you as a child, even when you approach middle age. One friend may look to you as an older brother or sister and come to you for advice; another may consider you scatter-brained, impractical, and amusing. Each of us has a little bit of the older brother or sister as well as the child in us; each of us, a touch of the clown. So we go along with the roles other people write for us. In time, the friend seeking comfort begins to elicit serious behavior from you, while the other friend makes you feel and act frivolous. You learn to associate different parts of yourself with different people.

A second reason why people perform is to get what they want out of a social interaction. All of us seek praise and other rewards and try to avoid blame and punishment. As a result, all of us are somewhat manipulative. Suppose you are given a promotion and put in charge of a number of workers who are older and more experienced in some ways than you are. You would probably make a big show of feeling self-confident, even when you were confused and afraid, to earn their respect. Otherwise, you might not be able to carry out your new responsibilities. Thus in many cases we try to create false impressions to achieve our goals—whether that goal be inspiring confidence in subordinates or reassuring patients, getting a job or obtaining sexual satisfaction.

The situation in which you find yourself may call for a specific kind of behavior or role. You wouldn't act the same way at a football game as you would at a formal tea with the dean, for example—unless you wanted to outrage your "audience."

Perhaps the most interesting thing about role playing is that people do not seem to go through life consciously and deliberately faking. Psychologists who studied people as they went from role to role found that most subjects felt that they were presenting true and accurate pictures of themselves from moment to moment (Gergen, 1971: 86). Apparently, individuals are capable of wide ranges of behavior depending on the context—they may appear dominant and powerful in one setting and weak and submissive in another. Yet, in all settings, people usually *feel* that they are honest and authentic. The implication is that people have many potential ways of being that are often inconsistent and unrelated to one another. At any particular moment they are aware of only a small number of these ways and are thereby able to feel true to themselves. People are convinced by their momentary thoughts and actions that they truly are what they seem to be. In other words, we tend to believe our own performances.

Self-concept

Psychologists have found that the way we view ourselves—our *self-concept* —is influenced by the way other people react to us. The following study suggests the truth of this theory. A researcher asked thirty students in a speech class to evaluate their ability to communicate orally. He then had each student read a number of poems before a "visiting expert," who was aware of the experiment. The "expert" praised fifteen students who were chosen at random, regardless of their performance. The other fifteen were criticized for not controlling their voices well or for not conveying the meaning of the poems, regardless of their performances. When asked to evaluate themselves for a second time, the students who had been praised for their speaking abilities gave themselves "higher marks" than they had before. The students who had been criticized now thought less of their abilities (Videbeck, 1960). This study confirms that our self-concept is strongly affected by the way we think others view us.

The degree of influence others have on a person's self-concept depends on several factors. People are most likely to be influenced by those who

FIGURE 10.7
An individual's self-concept contains a number of components. This woman's "me" is probably a composite of all the aspects shown here. The reactions of others, the reactions she would like from others, the way she wishes to see herself, and the objective facts all enter into the overall "self."

As she sees herself: ten years younger than her age. Competent desirable.

As her husband sees her: older than she actually is.

As the camera sees her: she is thirty-seven and chic but looks inhibited.

As she thinks others see her: sophisticated and sexy, a focus of masculine approval.

know them personally, by individuals who are experts (as the visitor to
the speech class was described), or by people who seem to be good judges
of character. When a number of people appraise an individual in the same
way, he is likely to begin reevaluating himself, even if their appraisal does
not match his self-image. For example, if you've always thought of yourself as shy and retiring and you hear people describing you as charming,
you may begin to wonder about your self-concept.

In short, each of us does have a self-concept, or "true self." Other people
may influence it and sometimes help us to change it significantly, but
it will not be totally replaced. Perhaps George Herbert Mead expressed
this best when he divided the self into two parts (1934). The "me" is the
aspect of the self that is defined by self-concept; it is formed by looking
at oneself through the eyes of others. The "I" is the self as experienced
from the inside. The "I" is a process, the self in action—feeling, thinking,
imagining, planning, listening, watching. For example, if you are riding
a roller coaster, you may lose all sense of "me." Your entire consciousness
is filled with the sensation of speed and flight, and you may scream with
exhilaration or terror. But when the ride slows down you may become
self-conscious. You think about the fact that you were screaming and
wonder how you looked to other people. You regain your sense of "me."

HOW PEOPLE PERCEIVE ONE ANOTHER

How do the processes we have been discussing work in reverse? How
do we perceive others? It takes people very little time to make judgments
about one another. From one brief conversation, or even by watching a
person across a room, you may form an impression of what someone is
like. And first impressions influence the future of a relationship. If a
person *seems* interesting, he or she becomes a candidate for future interaction. A person who seems to have nothing interesting to say—or much
too much to say—does not. We tend to be sympathetic toward someone
who seems shy; to expect a lot from someone who impresses us as intelligent; to be wary of a person who strikes us as aggressive.

However, forming an impression of a person is not a passive process
in which certain characteristics of the individual are the input and a
certain impression is the automatic outcome. If impressions varied only
when input varied, then everyone meeting a particular stranger would
form the same impression of him or her, which, of course, is not what
happens. One individual may judge a newcomer to be "quiet," another
might judge the same person to be "dull," and still another person might
think the newcomer "mysterious." These various impressions lead to different expectations of the newcomer and to different patterns of interaction with him or her as well.

Implicit Personality Theory

One reason that different people tend to develop different impressions
of the same stranger is that we each have our own *implicit personality*

FIGURE 10.8
What is your impression of this character? Do you think you would like him? What do you think of the way he is dressed? What sort of expression does he have on his face? When you have given your first impressions, turn to the drawing in Figure 10.9 and do the same.

Intelligent
Warm
Confident
Practical

theory—our own set of assumptions about how people behave and what traits or characteristics go together. When you meet someone who seems unusually intelligent, you may assume she is also active, highly motivated, conscientious, and so on. Another person in the group may have an altogether different "theory" about highly intelligent people—that they are unrealistic, boastful, insensitive, and the like. Whatever the person does provides "evidence" for both theories. You are impressed by how animated she becomes when talking about her work; the other person is impressed by how little attention she pays to other people. Both of you are filling in gaps in what you know about the person; fitting her into a type you carry around in your head.

Experiments indicate that our impressions are strongly influenced by a few traits. For example, one researcher invited a guest lecturer to a psychology class. Beforehand all the students were given a brief description of the visitor. The descriptions were identical in all traits but one. Half the students were told that the speaker was cold, the other half that he was warm. After the lecture the researcher asked all the students to evaluate the lecturer. Reading their impressions, you would hardly know that the two groups of students were describing the same person. The students who had been told he was cold saw a humorless, ruthless, self-centered person. The other students saw a relaxed, friendly, concerned person. Changing one word—substituting "warm" for "cold"—had a dramatic impact on the audience's perception of the lecturer. It also affected their behavior. Students in the "warm group" were warm themselves, initiating more conversations with the speaker than did the students in the other group (Kelley, 1950).

Stereotypes.   The line between applying implicit personality theories to people (as the students did) and thinking in stereotypes is a very thin one. A *stereotype* is a set of assumptions about people in a given category. The belief that Jews are clannish or that students with beards are radicals are examples. Stereotypes are based on half-truths and nontruths, and tend to blind us to differences among people and to the way individuals actually behave.

Implicit personality theories are useful in that they help us to predict with *some degree* of accuracy how people will behave. Without them, we would spend considerable energy observing and testing people to find out what they are like, whether we want to pursue a relationship with them, and so on. Like stereotypes, the assumptions we make about people from our first impressions tend to weaken as we get to know them better.

Personality vs. Circumstance

First impressions and the decision to pursue or abandon a relationship depend in large part on the situations in which we observe people. Suppose you walk into a library and find a man pacing back and forth. You sit down. He continues to pace for what seems like hours. The chances are you would want to avoid this man. He seems like an extremely unhappy and nervous person. But suppose the setting is the waiting room for a maternity ward. Your feelings about him would be entirely different (Rubin, 1973: 100–101).

The conclusions we draw about people thus vary according to whether we attribute their actions to personal qualities (such as general nervousness) or to the situation or role in which they find themselves (such as an expectant father). Psychologists have conducted a number of experiments to determine when and why people attribute behavior to personal qualities or to external pressures.

In one experiment, a researcher asked teachers to suggest why a particular student did well in some classes but poorly in others. Most blamed the student's low grades on lack of ability or lack of motivation (personal qualities), but attributed the same student's high grades to good teaching (external causes) (Johnson, Feigenbaum, and Weiby, 1964). Why were the teachers inconsistent? To protect their self-esteem. It would have made them uncomfortable to think that the student's low grades were the result of poor teaching.

Another group of researchers found a similar pattern. They asked subjects to watch three individuals take a test, and to evaluate their intelligence at various points during the test and after it was finished. *All* three individuals answered fifteen of thirty questions correctly. However, one started out well but then did poorly; the second did poorly at first but then improved; the third alternated between right and wrong answers, showing no pattern. Most subjects indicated that they thought the first individual was more intelligent than the others, although they all received the same score (Jones *et al.*, 1968). Why? Because once you have committed yourself to a judgment about a person (as subjects were required to do), changing your evaluation means admitting you made a mistake. Most of

FIGURE 10.9
If your impressions of this character are different from your impressions of the fellow in Figure 10.8, the difference must be due to the change in a single word—the illustrations are otherwise identical. It seems to be impossible to see a person believed to be warm in the same way one sees a person believed to be cold. Such significant character traits are called central organizing traits.

Intelligent
Cold
Confident
Practical

us find this somewhat hard to do. The subjects in this experiment clung to their original evaluation rather than admit a mistake.

These experiments bring us back to points made at the beginning of this section: (1) first impressions do make a difference, even though they are based on imagination (implicit personality theories) rather than on observation; and (2) your impressions of other people come at least partially from within *yourself*.

CHOOSING FRIENDS

Most people feel they have a great deal of latitude in the friends they choose. Easy transportation, telephones, and the spare time available to most Americans would all seem to ease communication among them and, therefore, to permit them a wide range of individuals from whom to choose companions, friends, and lovers. However, the evidence indicates that people usually do not exercise this freedom of choice. In fact, we rarely venture beyond the most convenient methods in making contact with others.

Proximity

Would it surprise you to learn that the single most important factor in determining whether two people will become friends is *physical proximity*—the distance from one another that people live or work? In general, the closer two individuals are geographically to one another, the more

FIGURE 10.10
A set of apartments such as this one was used in a study of friendship choice. It was found that the fewer doors there were between people, the more likely they were to become friends. It seems that "next door" is psychologically closer, because one does not have to pass by any other doors to get there. Also, social rules make one feel more compelled to say "hello" to someone coming out of a door two feet away than to speak to someone twenty feet away. Once people have exchanged hellos, there is at least a chance of their becoming friends.

likely they are to become attracted to each other. And it is more than just the opportunity for interaction that makes the difference.

Psychologists have found that even in a small two-story apartment building where each resident was in easy reach of everyone else, people were more likely to become close friends with the person next door than with anyone else. Psychologists believe that this is a result of the fears and embarrassments most people have about making contact with strangers. When two people live next door to one another, go to the same class, or work in the same place, they are able to get used to one another and to find reasons to talk to one another without ever having to seriously risk rejection. To make friends with someone whom you do not see routinely is much more difficult. You have to make it clear that you are interested and thus run the risk of making a fool of yourself—either because the other person turns out to be less interesting than he or she seemed at a distance or because that person expresses no interest in you. Of course, it may turn out that both of you are very glad someone spoke up.

Reward Values

Proximity helps people make friends, but it does not insure lasting friendship. Sometimes people who are forced together in a situation take a dislike to one another that develops into hatred. Furthermore, once people have made friends, physical separation does not necessarily bring an end to their relationship. What are the factors that determine whether people will like each other, once they come into contact?

One reward of friendship is stimulation. A friend has *stimulation value* if she is interesting or imaginative or if she can introduce you to new ideas or experiences. A friend who is cooperative and helpful, who seems willing to give his time and resources to help you achieve your goals, has

FIGURE 10.11
These two men obviously enjoy each other's company. In addition to having stimulation value for each other, they probably provide considerable utility value: They are able to give each other business advice and exchange information on business opportunities.

utility value. A third type of value in friendship is *ego-support value*: sympathy and encouragement when things go badly, appreciation and approval when things go well. These three kinds of rewards—stimulation, utility, and ego support—are evaluated consciously or unconsciously in every friendship. A man may like another man because the second man is a witty conversationalist (stimulation value) and knows a lot about gardening (utility value). A woman may like a man because he respects her (ego-support value) and because she has an exciting time with him (stimulation value).

By considering the three kinds of rewards that a person may look for in friendship, it is possible to understand other factors that affect liking and loving.

Physical Appearance.   A person's physical appearance greatly influences others' impressions of him or her. An attractive appearance has stimulation value and may also provide ego support. People feel better about themselves when they associate with people others consider desirable. This is true of same-sex as well as opposite-sex relationships. Physical attractiveness influences our choice of friends as well as lovers (Knapp, 1972: 66).

Interestingly, psychologists have found that both men and women pay much less attention to physical appearance when choosing a marriage partner or a close friend than when inviting someone to go to a movie or a party. But neither men nor women necessarily seek out the most attractive member of their social world. Rather, people usually seek out others whom they consider their equals on the scale of physical attractiveness (Levinger and Snoek, 1972).

Approval. Another factor that affects a person's choice of friends is *approval*. All of us tend to like people who say nice things about us because they make us feel better about ourselves—they provide ego-support value.

The results of one experiment suggest that other people's evaluations of oneself are more meaningful when they are a mixture of praise and criticism than when they are extreme in either direction. No one believes that he or she is all good or all bad. As a result, one can take more seriously a person who sees some good points and some bad points. But when the good points come first, hearing the bad can make one disappointed and angry at the person who made them. When the bad points come first, the effect is opposite. One thinks, "This person is perceptive and honest. At first she was critical but later she saw what I was really like" (Aronson and Linder, 1965).

Similarity. People tend to choose friends whose backgrounds, attitudes, and interests are similar to their own. Nearly always, husbands and wives have similar economic, religious, and educational backgrounds.

There are several explanations for the power of shared attitudes. First, agreement about what is stimulating, worthwhile, or fun provides the basis for sharing activities. People who have similar interests are likely to do more things together and to get to know one another better.

Second, most of us feel uneasy around people who are constantly challenging our views, and we translate our uneasiness into hostility or avoidance. We are more comfortable around people who support us. A friend's agreement bolsters your confidence and contributes to your self-esteem. In addition, most of us are self-centered enough to assume that people who share our values are basically decent and intelligent (unlike others we know).

Finally, people who agree about things usually find it easier to communicate with each other. They have fewer arguments and misunderstandings; they are better able to predict one another's behavior and thus feel at ease with each other.

Complementarity. The old saying that opposites attract does not contradict the reward theory of friendship. People who are quite different may be able to fill one another's needs in a special way. A dominant person can satisfy the desire to direct and control things with a person who likes being directed and controlled. An outgoing person makes it easier for a quiet person to meet people, and the quiet person gives the extrovert an audience. A serious individual helps a frivolous one to live up to responsibilities, while the frivolous individual helps the serious one to loosen up and relax.

Psychologist Robert White (1972) provides a good example of how two different personalities complemented each other in the case of the friendship of two adolescent boys:

> Ben, whose school experience had been so unstimulating that he never read a book beyond those assigned, discovered in Jamie a lively spirit of intellectual

inquiry and an exciting knowledge of politics and history. Here was a whole world to which his friend opened the door and provided guidance. Jamie discovered in Ben a world previously closed to him, that of confident interaction with other people. Each admired the other, each copied the other, each used the other for practice.

Psychologists refer to the attraction that often develops between opposites as *complementarity*. Complementary relationships enable both individuals to use their strengths and compensate for their weaknesses, thus expanding their horizons.

MAKING FRIENDS

How does opening a door for a neighbor loaded with packages develop into a lifelong friendship? A glance across a crowded room into a passionate love affair? Two psychologists have identified three stages in human relatedness, each of which represents a step closer to another person (Levinger and Snoek, 1972).

The first step is *awareness*. Some incident makes you aware of a person you hardly noticed before. You're attracted to him because he's good-looking, because he strikes you as interesting or amusing, perhaps because you think he would be a useful person to know. At this point, your knowledge of him is based largely on imagination or implicit personality theory. He may or may not be aware of your interest.

The fact that you are attracted to this person does not necessarily mean that you will look for an opportunity to strike up a conversation, however. It depends on how much you need or want a new person in your life, the current status of your relationships with other people, whether you believe he is accessible, and how you weigh the possible rewards or costs of approaching him. Suppose you decide to speak up and he responds. You begin to greet each other regularly and talk from time to time.

The second stage in a relationship is *surface contact*. Both of you will be somewhat cautious at first. You limit communication to public events (such as exams, politics, or an incident you both observed). You try to create an impression, keeping up your social mask, playing the appropriate social role. So does he. All the while each of you is measuring the other against your expectations. Slight deviations from the social role or the type into which you've cast the person give you a hint of what he is really like—and whether you want to know him better.

Most relationships do not go beyond surface contact. To do so, you or the other person will have to step out of your social roles and indicate a readiness to become friends. This might involve asking the other person out, revealing private opinions or information, or something as trivial as telling a subordinate to call you by your first name.

The third stage in a relationship is *mutuality*. You begin to talk frankly and confidentially about people you both know, about your feelings about yourself, and in time about your feelings toward the other person. You get to know how each other thinks and acts, what you fear and what you dream about. You find yourself considering his feelings and accommo-

FIGURE 10.12
When a relationship reaches the stage of mutuality, two people trust and confide in each other. Another's happiness becomes as important as your own.

dating to his needs—not because you want to impress him, but because your happiness depends in part on his. If this closeness proves rewarding you begin to work out private social rules that apply specifically to your relations with one another—rules for resolving conflicts and maintaining your closeness.

These stages apply to friendships, love affairs and marriages, even to the relationship between parent and child. You might rush through to stage three in a matter of months or spend years on the outer limits of stage two. Progress from one stage to another is far from inevitable. It is just as likely that a relationship will cool off—gradually or abruptly—as that it will continue to grow. The fact that you reach stage three does not mean you will remain there: mutuality is never assured forever.

LOVING

Some years ago, psychologist Zick Rubin (1973) covered the University of Michigan campus with requests for student volunteers. The top line of his posters—*Only dating couples can do it!*—attracted hundreds of students, so many that he had to turn most away. Those who remained—couples who had been going together for anywhere from a few weeks to six or seven years—filled out questionnaires about their feelings toward their partners and their same-sex friends. Their answers verified Rubin's hypotheses about the distinction between liking and loving (see Figure 10.13).

Liking is based primarily on respect for another person and the feeling that he or she is similar to you. Loving is rather different. As Rubin writes, "There are probably as many reasons for loving as there are people who love. In each case there is a different constellation of needs to be gratified, a different set of characteristics that are found to be rewarding, a different ideal to be fulfilled" (pp. 228–229). However, looking beyond these differences, Rubin identified three major components of romantic love: *need, the desire to give,* and *intimacy.*

People in love feel strong desires to be with the other person, to touch, to be praised and cared for by their lover. Whether men and women look to their partners to fill leftover needs that were never satisfied in childhood, as many psychologists suggest, is debatable. But the fact that love is so often described as a longing, a hunger, a desire to possess, a sickness that only one person can heal, suggests the role need plays in romantic love.

Equally central is the desire to give. Love goes beyond the cost-reward level of human interaction. It has been defined as "the active concern for the life and growth of that which we love" (Fromm, 1956: 26); as "that state in which the happiness of another person is essential to our own" (Heinlein, in Levinger and Snoek, 1972: 10). Without caring, need becomes a series of self-centered, desperate demands; without need, caring is charity or kindness. In love, the two are intertwined.

Need and caring are individual experiences. What people in love share is *intimacy*—a special knowledge of one another derived from uncensored

FIGURE 10.13
Rubin's scale items, some of which are shown here, were developed to distinguish between liking and loving in young opposite-sex student couples, but it is interesting to extend the analysis to same-sex relationships, relationships between very old people, people of different ages, and even to relationships that are not strictly human. People form strong likes *and* loves outside the romantic context as well as within it.

Liking

1. *Favorable evaluation.*

   I think that _____ (my boyfriend or girlfriend) is unusually well-adjusted.
   It seems to me that it is very easy for _____ to gain admiration.

2. *Respect and confidence.*

   I have great confidence in _____'s good judgment.
   I would vote for _____ in a class or group election.

3. *Perceived similarity.*

   I think that _____ and I are quite similar to each other.
   When I am with _____, we are almost always in the same mood.

Loving

1. *Attachment.*

   If I could never be with _____, I would feel miserable.
   It would be hard for me to get along without _____.

2. *Caring.*

   If _____ were feeling badly, my first duty would be to cheer him (her) up.
   I would do almost anything for _____.

3. *Intimacy.*

   I feel that I can confide in _____ about almost anything.
   When I am with _____, I spend a good deal of time just looking at him (her).

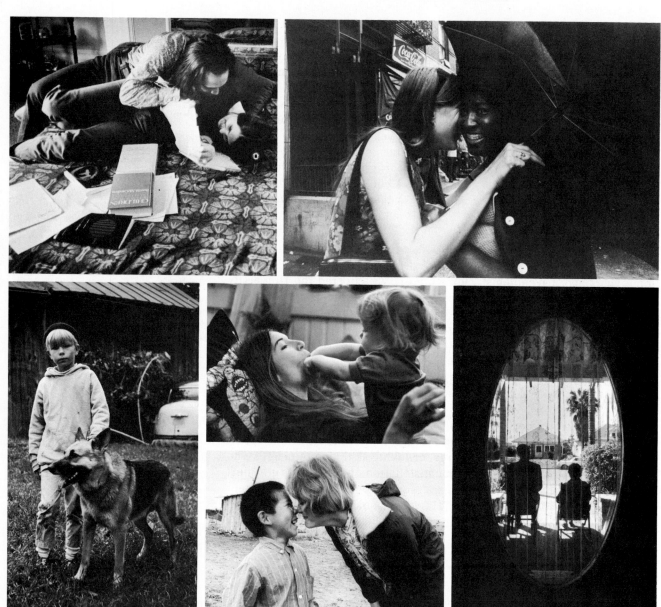

FIGURE 10.14
It is easy to think of love in a narrow context and consider only the sexual relationship that exists between a man and a woman. But this view omits the kinds of love that exist between members of the same sex, between parents and children, between very young or very old people, and between some people and their animals.

self-disclosure. Exposing one's "true self" to another person is always risky. It doesn't hurt so much if a person rejects a role you are trying to play. But it can be devastating if a person rejects the secret longings and fears you ordinarily disguise, or if he or she uses private information to manipulate you. This is one of the reasons why love so often brings out violent emotions—the highs and lows of our lives. In the words of Rollo May: "To love means to open ourselves to the negative as well as the positive—to grief, sorrow, and disappointment as well as to joy, fulfillment, and an intensity of consciousness we did not know was possible before" (1969: 99).

Rubin conducted a number of experiments to test common assumptions about the way people in love feel and act. He found that couples who rated high on his "love scale" did, indeed, spend more time gazing into one another's eyes (while waiting for the experimenter) than other couples did. However, he was unable to prove that lovers sacrifice their own comfort for that of their partners.

Perhaps the most interesting discoveries in "love research" concern the differences between men and women. Rubin found that most couples were equal on the love scale: the woman expressed the same degree of love for her partner as he did for her. However, women tended to *like* their boyfriends—to respect and identify with them—more than their boyfriends liked them. Women also tended to love and share intimacies with their same-sex friends more often than men did with theirs.

This is not surprising. As Rubin suggests, women in our society tend to specialize in the social and emotional dimensions of life. However, the revelation that men are significantly more romantic than women is surprising. Men tended to agree with such statements as "As long as they love each other, two people should have no difficulty getting along together in marriage" but disagree with unromantic statements like "One should not marry against the serious advice of one's parents." Women tended to take practical and social considerations more seriously. A full 72 percent of the women in the study were undecided about whether they would marry someone who possessed all the qualities they looked for in a mate but whom they did not love. In contrast, 65 percent of the men answered this question with a flat no.

A follow-up questionnaire, sent a year after Rubin's original study, indicated that when both a man and woman are romantic, the relationship is likely to progress—that is, they become more intimate and committed to each other. The implication of this finding? That love is not something that happens *to* you; it is something you seek and create.

SUMMARY

1. People vary considerably in their need for social contact and in their desire and ability to be alone. But human beings are social animals, and for most people, prolonged isolation would be torturous.

2. Human interaction begins at birth. This may derive from instinct but is more likely to derive from necessity, as infants and children depend on adults to satisfy their basic needs. As they grow, people continue to seek human contact because it is a learned experience.

3. Social psychologists have found that people need other people most when they are afraid, anxious, unsure of themselves, or want to compare their feelings to the feelings of others.

4. How one should act in a particular situation is governed by generally agreed upon social rules or norms. These rules help people to establish relationships.

5. Communication often takes place on a nonverbal level, through the use of space, body language, and facial expression. The use of space to indicate the closeness of a relationship varies from culture to culture.

6. Body language—gestures, positions, and

movements of the body—communicates information about you. Much of it is unconscious, but many gestures are governed by social rules. Since social rules vary from country to country, body language varies as well.

7. Like professional actors, people play different roles in everyday life. Yet, in all settings people usually feel that they are honest and authentic.

8. Everyone has a self-concept, or "true self," that other people may influence and sometimes help us to change significantly, but it will not be totally replaced.

9. In forming impressions of other people, each person has his or her own implicit personality theory—a set of assumptions about how people behave and what traits or characteristics go together. These theories only have some degree of accuracy and tend to weaken as we develop relationships.

10. The conclusions we draw about people vary according to whether we attribute their actions to personal qualities or to the situation or role in which we find them.

11. The most important factor in determining whether two people will become friends is physical proximity. Psychologists have found that individuals become friends with the people to whom they are close physically.

12. Some of the rewards found in friendships are stimulation, utility, and ego support. These are evaluated consciously or unconsciously in every friendship.

13. Other factors which affect a person's choice of friends are physical appearance, approval, similarity, and complementarity.

14. Psychologists have identified three stages to human relatedness: awareness, surface contact, and mutuality.

15. There are three major components of romantic love: need, the desire to give, and intimacy. Love is not something that happens *to* you; it is something you seek and create.

GLOSSARY

body language: Nonverbal communication through gestures, positions, and movements of the body.

complementarity: The attraction that often develops between opposite types of people because of the ability of one to supply what the other lacks.

ego-support value: The ability of a person to provide another person with sympathy, encouragement, and approval.

implicit personality theory: A set of assumptions each person has about how people behave and what personality traits or characteristics go together.

intimacy: A special knowledge one person has of another, derived from uncensored self-disclosure.

mutuality: Interdependence of attitudes and behavior.

nonverbal communication: The process of communicating through the use of space, body language, and facial expression.

physical proximity: The physical nearness of one person to another person.

reward values: The emotional bonuses obtained from personal interactions with other people, which cause people to develop friendships.

self-concept: The way one believes himself or herself to be: formed by looking at oneself through the eyes of others.

social rule: Any agreement among members of society about how people should act in particular situations; also called a *norm*.

social space: The space between two people which communicates their feelings about one another and defines the relationship.

stereotype: A set of assumptions about people in a given category based on half-truths and nontruths.

stimulation value: The ability of a person or subject to interest or to expose you to new ideas and experiences.

surface contact: Communication that is limited to public events.

true self: A self-concept as experienced from within, which people may influence but which cannot be totally replaced.

utility value: The ability of a person or subject to help another achieve his or her goals.

ACTIVITIES

1. One of the most difficult emotions to define is love. What is your own definition of love? Does this definition apply to love between family members and between friends as well as to romantic love?

2. We may think that stereotyping does not influence us. Watch a television program about (a) a detective, (b) a black family, (c) an independent woman. What character traits does each have? Do we laugh at some of these characterizations when they do not fit the stereotypes? Which stereotypes do we not laugh at?

3. Does your teacher announce test results? When he or she returns a test, watch the reactions of your classmates. How do they respond to any verbal or physical stimuli coming from the teacher?

4. Examine the interactions between members of your family, your friends, or even strangers, paying as little attention as possible to verbal interaction and noting instead proximity, posture, gesture, facial expression, eye contact, relative position, and nonlinguistic verbal cues. Are you able to interpret the body language? Does this nonverbal communication conflict with what people communicate verbally? What happens if you reply verbally to nonverbal messages?

5. How do you analyze new instructors at the beginning of a term? On what do you base your impressions? How do your impressions affect how you behave toward each instructor? Have you ever changed your mind after getting the "wrong impression" about someone?

6. Cut out a variety of pictures of people from magazines. Mount the pictures on plain paper and identify each picture by number. Ask several friends to rate the people in the pictures as potential friends, dates, marriage partners, bosses, co-workers, and so on. Try to identify what characteristics in the pictures people respond to in making these judgments. (Ask your subjects, "What is it that makes you feel this way?") Write a brief summary of your results.

7. Conduct an experiment on body space by going to the library and sitting at a table with another person. After a few minutes begin to "invade" his or her space by placing your books and papers across the imaginary line that divides the space between the two of you. Describe his or her reactions to your encroachments.

8. Have you ever felt like skipping, shouting, or dancing in a crowded public place but refrained because you anticipated social disapproval? Perhaps there was a time when you wanted to engage your parents in a serious discussion but found that they still thought of you as a small child whose thoughts regarding serious, "adult" matters were unimportant. In what other ways do social rules restrict you or keep you from behaving spontaneously?

9. Describe several situations in which you either "put on an act" or disguised your true feeling regarding a person or situation. Did your deception occur consciously or unconsciously?

10. List in detail the main criteria you use in choosing close friends. What are your reasons for rejecting certain people as either close friends or acquaintances?

11. If you knew that you and five other people would be the only survivors on Earth after an atomic holocaust, whom would you choose to be with? Why?

SUGGESTED READINGS

ARONSON, ELLIOT. *The Social Animal.* New York: Viking, 1972. A conversationally written textbook in social psychology. It is excellent reading for the person who wants to go deeper into the ideas presented in this and the next two chapters.

FAST, JULIUS. *Body Language.* New York: Evans, 1970. A good introduction to nonverbal communication.

FROMM, ERICH. *The Art of Loving.* New York: Harper & Row, 1956 (paper). Fromm suggests that there are different types of love and that love is an art that must be learned, just as one must learn any other art form.

HALL, EDWARD T. *The Hidden Dimension.* Garden City, N.Y.: Doubleday, 1966. A thorough and well-written book that describes the bubbles of privacy people carry about them and the purpose of personal space.

——. *The Silent Language.* Garden City, N.Y.: Doubleday, 1959 (paper). Hall suggests that "communication occurs simultaneously on different levels of consciousness, ranging from full awareness to out-of-awareness." An excellent book on nonverbal communication.

HASTORF, ALBERT H., SCHNEIDER, DAVID J., AND POLEFKA, JUDITH. *Person Perception.* Reading, Mass.: Addison-Wesley, 1970. This book provides a brief but comprehensive overview of how people perceive one another. The authors pay special attention to attribution theory and implicit personality theory.

HESSE, HERMANN. *Steppenwolf.* New York: Bantam, 1963 (paper); originally published, 1929. The myriad roles, or personalities, that reside in a single individual are examined in this profound novel.

JOURARD, SIDNEY M. *The Transparent Self.* 2nd ed. New York: Van Nostrand, 1971 (paper). A thorough and straightforward book about the choice between being authentic and playing a series of roles. Jourard contends that honesty "can literally be a health-insurance policy."

LEVINGER, GEORGE, AND SNOEK, J. DIEDRICK. *Attraction in Relationship: A New Look at Interpersonal Attraction.* Morristown, N. J.: General Learning Press, 1972. Levinger and Snoek present their views on how relationships proceed from casual encounters to intimacy. They focus on how the factors leading to attraction and further involvement change as the relationship changes.

RUBIN, ZICK. *Liking and Loving.* New York: Holt, Rinehart & Winston, 1973. In this very readable book Dr. Rubin reviews several major psychological approaches to loving and liking as well as presenting his own study of the factors involved in forming intimate relationships.

BIBLIOGRAPHY

ARONSON, E., AND LINDER, D. "Gain and Loss of Esteem as Determinants of Interpersonal Attractiveness." *Journal of Experimental Social Psychology,* 1 (1965): 156–171.

BOUCHER, JERRY D., AND EKMAN, PAUL. "Facial Areas and Emotional Information." *Journal of Communication,* 15 (1975): 21–28.

BROWN, ROGER. *Social Psychology.* Englewood Cliffs, N.J.: Prentice-Hall, 1970.

DAVIS, KINGSLEY. *Human Society.* New York: Macmillan, 1948.

FREEDMAN, JONATHAN L., CARLSMITH, J. MERRILL, AND SEARS, DAVID O. *Social Psychology.* Englewood Cliffs, N.J.: Prentice-Hall, 1970.

FROMM, ERICH. *The Art of Loving.* New York: Harper & Row, 1956.

GERARD, H. B., AND RABBIE, J. M. "Fear and Social Comparison." *Journal of Abnormal and Social Psychology,* 62 (1961): 586–592.

GERGEN, KENNETH J. *The Concept of Self.* New York: Holt, Rinehart & Winston, 1971.

GOFFMAN, ERVING. *The Presentation of the Self in Everyday Life.* New York: Doubleday, 1959 (paper).

———. *Relations in Public.* New York: Harper & Row, 1971.

HALL, EDWARD T. *The Silent Language.* Greenwich, Conn.: Fawcett, 1959.

———. *The Hidden Dimension.* Garden City, N. Y.: Doubleday, 1966.

HASTORF, ALBERT H., SCHNEIDER, DAVID J., AND POLEFKA, JUDITH. *Person Perception.* Reading, Mass.: Addison-Wesley, 1970.

IZARD, CARROLL E. *The Face of Emotion.* New York: Appleton-Century-Crofts, 1971.

JOHNSON. T. J., FEIGENBAUM, R., AND WEIBY, M. "Some Determinants and Consequences of the Teacher's Perception of Causality." *Journal of Experimental Psychology,* 55 (1964): 237–246.

JONES, E. E., ET. AL. "Internal States or Emotional Stimuli: Observers' Attitude Judgments and the Dissonance Theory–Self-Presentation Controversy." *Journal of Experimental Social Psychology,* 4 (1968): 247–269.

JOURARD, SIDNEY M. *The Transparent Self.* 2nd ed. New York: Van Nostrand, 1971 (paper).

KELLEY, H. H. "The Warm-Cold Variable in First Impressions of Persons." *Journal of Personality,* 18 (1950): 431–439.

KNAPP, MARK L. *Nonverbal Communication in Human Interaction.* New York: Holt, Rinehart & Winston, 1972.

LEVINGER, GEORGE, AND SNOEK, J. DIDRICK. *Attraction in Relationship: A New Look at Interpersonal Attraction.* Morristown, N.J.: General Learning Press, 1972.

MAY, ROLLO. *Love and Will.* New York: Norton, 1969.

MC GINLEY, HUGH, LEFEVRE, RICHARD, AND MC GINLEY, PAT. "The Influence on a Communicator's Body Position on Opinion Change in Others." *Journal of Personality and Social Psychology,* 31 (1975): 686–690.

MEAD, GEORGE H. *Mind, Self and Society.* Chicago: University of Chicago Press, 1934.

RUBIN, ZICK. *Liking and Loving.* New York: Holt, Rinehart & Winston, 1973.

SAMSON, E. *The Perfect Gentleman.* London: Heath, 1956.

SCHACHTER, STANLEY. *The Psychology of Affiliation.* Stanford, Calif.: Stanford, University Press, 1959.

SIFFRE, MICHEL. "Six Months Alone in a Cave." *National Geographic,* 147 (March 1975): 426–435.

VIDEBECK, R. "Self-Conception and the Reaction of Others." *Sociometry,* 23 (1960): 351–362.

WALSTER, E. "The Effect of Self-Esteem on Romantic Liking." *Journal of Experimental Social Psychology,* 1 (1965): 184–197.

WHITE, ROBERT W. *The Enterprise of Living: Growth and Reorganization in Personality.* New York: Holt, Rinehart & Winston, 1972.

WRIGHTSMAN, L. S. "Effects of Waiting with Others on Changes in Level of Felt Anxiety." *Journal of Abnormal and Social Psychology,* 61 (1960): 216–222.

Chapter 11

People in Groups

Each of us feels unique—an individual separate from the rest of humanity. And yet we also have a feeling of being part of something larger than ourselves, of being a member of a class, a profession, a nation, a race, or of humanity. The study of people as members of a larger whole is the study of *groups*.

One of the tasks of psychology is to try to understand how groups work and how they affect their members. What makes people loyal to a group? Why do people in groups sometimes act irrationally? The answers psychologists have tentatively given to these questions are the subject of this chapter.

The study of groups is an important part of the larger field of social psychology. Instead of investigating the *personal* dimensions of behavior, social psychologists focus upon the *interpersonal* aspects, trying to discover regularities in behavior shaped by social expectations.

WHAT ARE GROUPS?

What is the difference between a random aggregate of people and a true group? How is it that three children playing ball and the entire United States Army can both be classified as groups? In general, the features that distinguish a group from a nongroup are *interdependence* and *shared goals*.

Interdependence

All the people in the world who have red hair and freckles make up a category of people, but they are not a group. The people in this collection are not interdependent. Interdependence occurs when any action by one of them will affect or influence the other members or when the same event will influence each member. For instance, in groups of athletes, entertainers, or roommates, each member has a certain responsibility to the rest of the group; if he or she does not fulfill his or her responsibility, the other members will be affected. For the athletes, the consequence may be losing the game; for the entertainers, a bad show; for the roommates, a messy apartment.

In small groups, members usually have a direct influence on one another: One person yells at another, smiles at him, or passes him a note.

FIGURE 11.1

Each of these spectators at a football game displays a card to help spell out messages to the team on the field. The shared sense of excitement and power felt by us when participating in a task that can be accomplished only by a group of people is a sign of how important group membership is in human experience.

255

FIGURE 11.2
Toward the end of a twenty-eight-day mission in space, a Skylab astronaut retrieves some film canisters from outside the module. This precarious situation is an extreme example of the interdependence that can exist between group members. One of the common goals these astronauts share is survival itself.

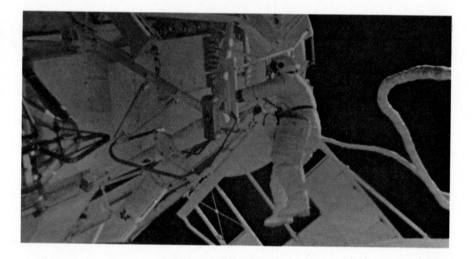

In larger groups, the influence may be highly indirect. The interdependence between you and the president of the United States is not a result of your personal contact with him. Nevertheless, one of the things that makes the people of the United States a group is the fact that the president's actions affect you and that your actions, together with those of many other Americans, affect him.

Common Goals

Group members become interdependent because they see themselves as sharing certain *common goals*. Groups are usually created to perform tasks or to organize activities that no individual could handle alone. Members of a consumer group, for example, share the common goal of working for consumer protection. Members of ethnic and religious groups desire to perpetuate a common heritage or set of beliefs.

The purposes that groups serve are of two general kinds: *task functions*, those directed toward getting some job done; and *social functions*, those that are directed toward filling the emotional needs of the members.

Political parties, teams of surgeons, and crews of construction workers are all task-oriented groups. Although social interactions occur within each of these groups, their main purpose is to complete a project or to achieve some change in the environment. Social functions are emphasized in more informal, temporary groups. When people take walks together, attend parties, or participate in conversations, they have formed a group to gain such social rewards as companionship and emotional support. Nevertheless, in most groups, task and social functions are naturally combined and cannot easily be separated.

HOW GROUPS ARE HELD TOGETHER

The maintenance of cooperative interdependence among group members is not always easy. Athletes may become angry with their teammates or try to distinguish themselves at the expense of a team effort. Members of communes may become disillusioned by difficult work and by conflicts with other members over the division of labor. Soldiers may desert their companies if they lose faith in the army's purposes or in their commander's competence.

Norms

One way in which groups keep their members going in the same direction is by developing group norms. Norms are rules for the behavior and attitudes of group members. These rules are not necessarily rigid laws. They may be more like tendencies or habits. But group members are expected to act in accordance with group norms and are punished in some way if they do not. The punishment may take the form of coldness or criticism from other group members. If the norm is very important to the group, a member who violates it may receive a more severe punishment or may even be excluded from the group.

Psychologists observed the operation of such norms in a group of assembly-line workers. The workers had developed their own norm for the amount of work they should do. Workers who went slower or faster than the prescribed rate endangered the whole group, either by making the management angry because too little work was being done or by giving the management the idea that more work could be done by everyone. The work norm was enforced by "binging." Any worker who saw another worker going too fast or too slow could strike him painfully on the upper arm. "Binging" punished the violator, let everyone else in the group know about the misbehavior, and so preserved the norm (Roethlisberger and Dickson, 1939: 421–423).

Ideology

For a group to be highly cohesive, members must share the group's values. In some cases, people are drawn together because they discover they have

FIGURE 11.3
These men, members of a religious order, radiate a sense of dedication to a common purpose. This, and the sense of membership that is strengthened by their common dress and their shared good feeling, are recognized by psychologists as characteristics that distinguish these men as a group rather than just a collection of people.

common ideas, attitudes, and goals—that is, a common ideology. In other instances, people are attracted to a group because its ideology provides them with a new way of looking at themselves and interpreting events, and a new set of goals and means for achieving them. The civil rights and black power movements, for example, provided an explanation of black oppression in America and the hope that something could be done to change things. Similarly, the women's liberation movement became a focus for female discontent. Leaders, heroes and heroines, rallies, books and pamphlets, slogans, and symbols all help to popularize an ideology, win converts, and create feelings of solidarity among group members.

Commitment

A group's cohesiveness will be high if its members are heavily committed to it. One factor that increases individual commitment is the requirement of *personal sacrifice*. If a person is willing to pay money, endure hardship, or undergo humiliation to belong to a group, he or she is likely to stick with it. For example, college students who undergo embarrassing initiation rites to join sororities or fraternities tend to develop a loyalty to the group that lasts well beyond their college years.

The practice of using personal sacrifices as a method for building group solidarity has a long history. Nineteenth-century utopian communes required personal sacrifice as a basic condition for membership. Social psychologists who studied these communes to better understand the group process found that some groups asked that their members give up such things as wearing jewelry and fine clothes, smoking tobacco, and eating meat. Others required members to renounce all outside ties, including family ones. The communes that required such sacrifices tended to last much longer than ones that did not require sacrifices. The researchers concluded that when membership in a group is costly, it will not be given up lightly (Kanter, 1970). The more one suffers, the more important the reason for suffering must be. (This phenomenon may be explained in terms of the theory of cognitive dissonance, which is described in Chapter 12.)

Another factor that strengthens group commitment is *participation*. When people actively participate in group decisions and share the rewards of the group's accomplishments, their feeling of group membership increases—they feel that they have helped make the group what it is.

Participation in the development of norms, ideology, and goals by all group members makes the group process possible (see Middlebrook, 1974: 552–553). Social psychologists have compared groups of workers who participate in decisions that affect their jobs to workers who elect representatives to decision-making committees and to workers who are simply told what to do. Those who participate have higher morale and accept change more readily than the other workers (Coch and French, 1948).

As these examples show, the processes that hold a group together must work both ways. The individual must be responsive to the norms of the group, subscribe to its ideology, and be prepared to make sacrifices in order to be a part of it. But the group must also respond to the needs of its members. It cannot possibly achieve cohesiveness if its norms are unenforceable, if its ideology is inconsistent with the beliefs of its members, or if the rewards it offers do not outweigh the sacrifices it requires.

This is one reason why so many young blue-collar workers are discontent. Like other American youths, they believe a job should be challenging and provide opportunities for personal growth—as well as a living wage. Working on an assembly line, performing the same tasks over and over, hardly meets this requirement. Lack of opportunity to participate in decisions amplifies the "blue-collar blues" (Yankelovich, 1973; Seashore and Barnowe, 1972).

MEANING OF GROUPS TO THE INDIVIDUAL

An individual's commitment to a group gives that person a source of values and beliefs and a way of defining who he or she is. The groups with which a person identifies are called *reference groups*. Almost everyone uses social groups such as their family, their sex, their race, and their religion as ways of establishing their identities. People also identify themselves with other people who do the same type of work that they do as well as with their country or community. Not all reference groups are so large, however. A person may consider his or her membership in a club, a team, a social crowd, or a gang an important way of defining his or her own values and sense of self.

At times, a group to which people do not belong becomes a powerful reference group for them. Many adolescents, for example, model themselves after the members of an in-crowd in hopes that they will be noticed and accepted by its members. Youth, in general, seems to be a desired reference group for many American adults.

Once a person identifies with a group, his or her actions may be affected by that identification. For example, an individual may defend his or her group to outsiders. To illustrate pride in reference groups, psychologists experimented to see how much pain groups of Jewish and Christian college women would tolerate. A blood-pressure cuff with sharp rubber projections was placed on each woman's upper arm and inflated until she said the pain was intolerable. After this pain limit had been established, the experimenters told the subjects that they would take the measurement again in five minutes. In addition, the experimenters casually mentioned to Jewish subjects that Jews could endure less pain than Christians and told Christian subjects that Christians could endure less pain than Jews. (Neither statement is true.)

When the women were tested again, both Jewish and Christian women let the pressure go higher than they had on their first test. It seems that people tend to interpret "insults" to their religious reference groups as attacks on themselves and are prepared to defend the group publicly, even if doing so causes intense physical pain (Lambert, Libman, and Poser, 1960).

Other experiments have shown that people evaluate themselves in terms of the approval or disapproval they receive from members of their reference groups. Subjects were given a report on what other participants thought of their performance in an experiment. The reports were written by the researchers and bore no relationship to the subject's actual performance. Subjects were then asked to evaluate themselves. Those who were given "bad reports" tended to see themselves in a negative light; most of those who received "high marks" thought they had performed well (Gergen, 1965; Tippett and Silber, 1955). Thus reference groups are a mirror as well as a source of social identity.

INTERACTIONS WITHIN GROUPS

Providing an individual with values and a sense of identity is only one aspect of the group's meaning to him or her. The particular part he or she plays in the group's activities is also important. Each group member has certain unique abilities and interests, and the group has a number of different tasks that need to be performed. The study of the parts various members play in the group, and of how these parts are interrelated, is the study of group structure.

There are many different aspects to group structure: the personal rela-

FIGURE 11.4
A system of categorizing, such as the one shown here, enables psychologists to make detailed analyses of a group's structure and to observe the patterns of interaction among its members. For example, psychologists might observe a particular group in action, say a newspaper staff, and score the behavior of each member according to the twelve categories shown on the chart. The emerging profiles depict each member's role in the structure of the group. For instance, a member who scores high on 5 and 10 and low on 3 might be described as a "maverick," whereas a member who scores high on 1, 3, 8, and 11 could be characterized as "submissive." A person who scores high on 1, 5, and 7 is probably the group leader.

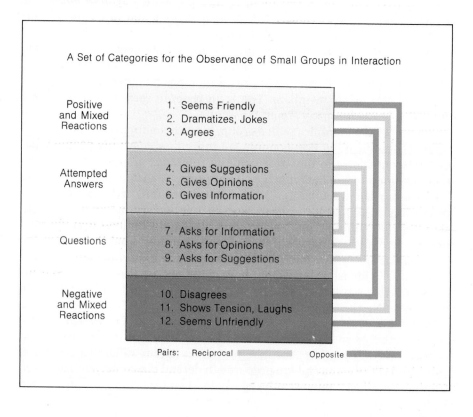

A Set of Categories for the Observance of Small Groups in Interaction

Positive and Mixed Reactions
1. Seems Friendly
2. Dramatizes, Jokes
3. Agrees

Attempted Answers
4. Gives Suggestions
5. Gives Opinions
6. Gives Information

Questions
7. Asks for Information
8. Asks for Opinions
9. Asks for Suggestions

Negative and Mixed Reactions
10. Disagrees
11. Shows Tension, Laughs
12. Seems Unfriendly

Pairs: Reciprocal   Opposite

tionships between individual members, such as liking relationships and trusting relationships; the rank of each member on a particular dimension, such as power, popularity, status, or amount of resources; and the roles various members play. (A few typical group roles are leader, joker, black sheep, and the silent member.)

One technique psychologists use in analyzing group structure is the *sociogram*. Researchers using this device ask all the members of a group to name those people with whom they would like to interact on a given occasion or for a specific purpose, those they like best, and so on. For example, the members may be asked with whom they would like to go to a party, to discuss politics, to spend a vacation, or to complete an organizational task. Their choices can then be diagramed, as shown in Figure 11.5. Sociograms can show a great deal about any one person's status in a group and can help psychologists to predict how that individual is likely to communicate with other group members.

Communication Patterns

Another way to discover the structure of a group is to examine the communication patterns in the group. Who says what to whom, and how often?

An experiment on communication patterns was done by Harold Leavitt in 1951. He gave a card with several symbols on it to each person in a group of five. Then he asked them to find out which symbol appeared on everyone's card. Obviously the group members had to communicate with one another to solve this problem. Leavitt controlled their freedom by putting each person in a separate room or booth and allowing the members to communicate only by written messages. In this way he was able to create the networks shown in Figure 11.6. Each circle represents a person; the lines represent open channels. Subjects placed in each position could exchange messages only with the persons to whom they were connected by channels.

The most interesting result of this experiment was that the people who were organized into a "circle" were the slowest at solving the problem but the happiest at doing it. In this group everyone sent and received a large number of messages until someone solved the problem and passed the information on. In the "wheel," by contrast, everyone sent a few messages to one center person, who figured out the answer and told the rest what it was. These groups found the solution quickly, but the people on the outside of the wheel did not particularly enjoy the job (Leavitt, 1951).

Following the experiment, the members in each group were asked to identify the leader of their group. In the centralized groups (wheel, Y, and chain), the person in the center was usually chosen as the group leader. But in the circle network half the group members said they thought there was no real leader, and those who did say there was a leader disagreed on who that leader was. Thus a centralized organization seems more useful for task-oriented groups, whereas a decentralized network is more useful in socially oriented groups.

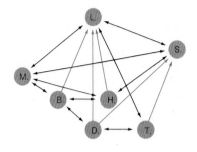

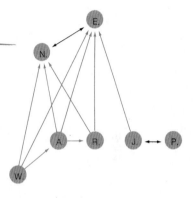

FIGURE 11.5
Patterns of friendship choices within two groups. The blue arrows indicate liking that is not returned; the black arrows indicate a two-way friendship. The more a person is liked, the higher in the pattern he or she appears. Patterns like these are called sociograms. Notice the difference between the two patterns. Whereas the pattern of the bottom group shows a hierarchical structure, with E and N clearly the leaders, the sociogram of the top group indicates strong group cohesiveness with even D and T, the two least-liked members, clearly tied in to the group and having friends who like them.

FIGURE 11.6
Harold Leavitt's communication networks. It is interesting to compare these structures, which were deliberately created by a person outside the group, with those structures shown in Figure 11.5, which spontaneously developed within groups. It is highly unlikely that such uncomplicated patterns as those imposed by Leavitt could develop naturally.

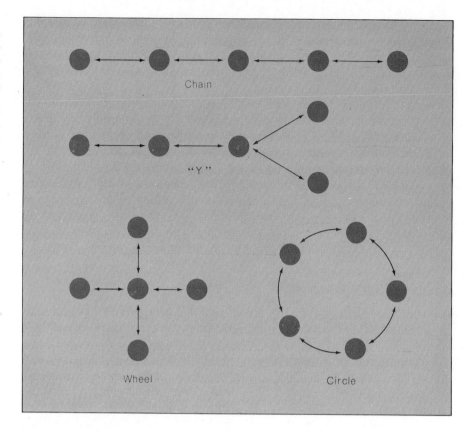

Leadership

All groups, whether made up of gangsters, soldiers, workers, or politicians, have leaders. A leader embodies the norms and ideals of the group and represents the group to outsiders. Within the group, a leader initiates action, gives orders, makes decisions, and settles disputes. In short, a leader is one who has a great deal of influence on the other members of the group.

Most of us think of leadership as a personality trait. To an extent this is true. Leaders tend to be better-adjusted, more self-confident, more energetic and outgoing, and slightly more intelligent than other members of their group (Gibb, 1969). However, the nature of the group in part determines who will lead. Different circumstances call for different kinds of leaders. A group that is threatened by internal conflict requires a leader who is good at handling people, settling disputes, soothing tempers, and the like. A group that has a complex task to perform needs a leader with special experience to set goals and plan strategies for achieving them (Fiedler, 1969).

Within a group there may be two kinds of leaders, then. They are easy to tell apart by the things they say. One kind, the *social leader*, tends to make encouraging remarks, to break any tension with a joke, to solicit the reactions of others to whatever is going on. The other, the *task leader*, takes over when it is time to convey information, give opinions, or suggest how to do something. This leader is bossier and is not reluctant to disagree and press for a particular idea or course of action even if it creates tension in the group. A task leader usually has special knowledge or skills, and so different people may fill this role depending on what the group is doing. The social leader is likely to be the same person, whatever the group does, because the need for promoting cohesion is always there. The social leader usually commands the loyalty of the group (Bales, 1958).

Expertise.   There are many ways in which a person can acquire enough influence to become the leader of a group. One kind of influence comes from being an *expert*. An expert directs the group's activity because he or she has the knowledge that the group needs to achieve its goals. Such a leader is usually someone who has a great deal of experience in the group's tasks. For example, a ship's captain must be someone who knows how to run a ship and how to meet an emergency at sea.

Charisma.   Expertise is not enough by itself, however. Good leaders also possess a strong emotional appeal. Because of this appeal, or *charisma*, their approval or disapproval of other group members has a powerful effect. Nowhere is this kind of influence more apparent than in politics. President John F. Kennedy was a striking example of a political leader with a charisma that aroused strong feelings among both his followers and his enemies.

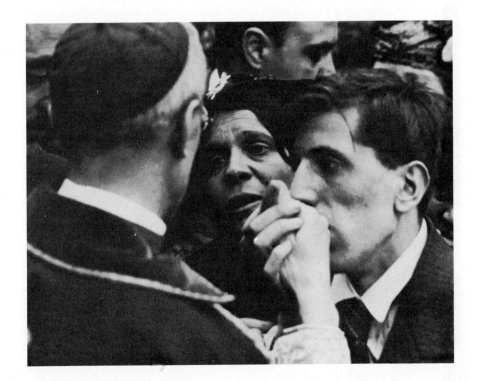

FIGURE 11.7
The Catholic pope is a leader whose influence over millions of people comes from several sources. In addition to the power and charisma inherent in his office, he is considered by Catholics to be the ultimate authority on matters of faith and morals.

Power.   Influence can also come from the power to control the rewards and punishments of group members. A president of a company, for instance, can give raises and promotions and can also fire people or give demotions. He is a leader not because members elected him but because he owns the most shares in the company or because he has been appointed by those who own shares. Similarly, a child who has special toys can influence members of her play group by giving or withdrawing the privilege of playing with her toys. In both cases leadership is determined by the leader's power to grant members the things they want—not by group choice.

Such power is often gained through appointment from outside the group. A person is simply placed in a position of authority and thereby assumes the role of leader. Appointed leaders include teachers, priests, and cabinet members. An appointed leader is usually less permanent and less respected than a leader chosen by the group. In some cases the group may even refuse to recognize that person as the legitimate leader. Obviously, leaders who are elected have potentially more influence than those who are appointed.

Machiavellian Techniques.   Some leaders gain power through *Machiavellian* techniques—tactics based on deceit, emotional manipulation, and the philosophy, "If it works, do it." This type of leader was named for Niccolò Machiavelli, the author of *The Prince*, a classic sixteenth-century book about the differences between people who manipulate and people who are manipulated. Psychologists have found that manipulators are the kind of people who can lie and cheat while still being able to convince people that they aren't lying and cheating. Such individuals feel that most people do not know what is really best for them and that they need to be given some direction. The Machiavellian leader is least influential in situations where he or she cannot be face to face with group members, where there are many rules and regulations for behavior, and where there is little emotional arousal.

For whatever reason a member becomes a leader, the way he or she leads will affect the structure of his or her group and the roles other members play. A powerful leader may make all the important decisions for the group and assign relatively unimportant tasks to other members. A more democratic leader may try to involve as many members as possible in the decision-making process.

GROUP PRESSURE TO CONFORM

Most Americans claim they would never have become supporters of Hitler if they had lived in Germany during World War II. Yet a nation of Germans did. Under pressure from others, individuals at least complied with the prevailing attitudes. Everyone conforms to group pressure in many ways. Have you ever come home and surprised your parents by

FIGURE 11.8
These two cards were shown to subjects in one trial of Asch's experiment on conformity. The actual discrimination involved is easy. Those people not subjected to group pressure chose line 2 as the correct match in 99 out of 100 trials.

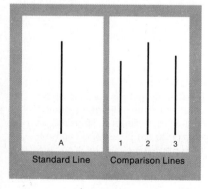

Standard Line   Comparison Lines

wearing the latest fad in clothing? Possibly the conversation that followed went something like this: "How can you go around looking like that?" "But everyone dresses like this."

Psychologist Solomon Asch (1952) designed a famous experiment to test conformity to pressure from one's peers. He found that people may conform to a lie that other people tell, even when they are sure of the truth. The following is what you would have experienced if you had been a subject in this experiment.

You and seven other students meet in a classroom for an experiment on visual judgment. You are shown a card with one line on it. You are then shown another card containing three lines and are asked to pick the one that is the same length as the first line. One of the three is exactly the same length and is easy to determine. The other two lines are obviously different. The experiment begins uneventfully. The subjects announce their answers in the order in which they are seated in the room. You happen to be seventh, and one person follows you. On the first comparison, every person chooses the same matching line. The second set of cards is displayed, and once again the group is unanimous. The discriminations seem easy, and you prepare for what you expect will be a rather boring experiment.

On the third trial, there is an unexpected disturbance. You are quite certain that Line 2 is the one that matches the standard. Yet the first person in the group announces confidently that Line 1 is the correct match. Then, the second person follows suit and he, too, declares that the answer is Line 1. So do the third, fourth, fifth, and sixth subjects. Now it is your

FIGURE 11.9

Photographs taken during Asch's experiment on conformity: Subject 6 is the only real subject; the others are confederates of the experimenter (seen at the right in the first photograph). The subject listens to the others express identical judgments that differ from his own. He is in a dilemma: Does he express the judgment that he knows to be correct and risk being different from the group, or does he conform to the group's judgment?

FIGURE 11.10
Descriptions of the behavior of two subjects in Asch's experiment: one who yielded to the group's judgment and one who remained independent.

Independent	Yielder
After a few trials he appeared puzzled, hesitant. He announced all disagreeing answers in the form of "Three, sir; two, sir." At Trial 4 he answered immediately after the first member of the group, shook his head, blinked, and whispered to his neighbor, "Can't help it, that's one." His later answers came in a whispered voice, accompanied by a deprecating smile. At one point he grinned embarrassedly and whispered explosively to his neighbor: "I always disagree—darn it!" Immediately after the experiment the majority engaged this subject in a brief discussion. When they pressed him to say whether the entire group was wrong and he alone right, he turned upon them defiantly, exclaiming: "You're *probably* right, but you *may* be wrong!" During the experimenter's later questioning, this subject's constant refrain was: "I called them as I saw them, sir."	This subject went along with the majority in eleven out of twelve trials. He appeared nervous and somewhat confused, but he did not attempt to evade discussion at the close of the experiment. He opened the discussion with the statement: "If I'd been first I probably would have responded differently." This was his way of saying that he had adopted the majority estimates. The primary factor in his case was loss of confidence. He perceived the majority as a decided group, acting without hesitation: "If they had been doubtful I probably would have changed, but they answered with such confidence." When the real purpose of the experiment was explained, the subject volunteered: "I suspected about the middle—but tried to push it out of my mind." It is of interest that his suspicion did not restore his confidence or diminish the power of the majority.

turn. You are suddenly faced with two contradictory pieces of information: The evidence of your own senses tells you that one answer is clearly correct, but the unanimous and confident judgments of the six preceding subjects tell you that you are wrong.

The dilemma with which you are faced persists through eighteen trials. On twelve of the trials, the other group members unanimously give an answer that differs from what you clearly perceive to be correct. It is only at the end of the experimental session that you learn the explanation for the confusion. The seven other subjects were all actors, and they had been instructed to give incorrect answers on those twelve trials.

How do most subjects react in this situation? Asch found that almost one-third of his fifty subjects conformed at least half the time. These conformers he called the "yielders." Most yielders explained to Asch afterward that they knew which line was correct but that they yielded to group pressure in order not to appear different from the others. Asch called those who did not conform "independents." They gave the correct answer despite group pressure.

Why so much conformity? Some sociologists argue that cultural forces toward conformist behavior are high in the United States. They contend that Americans are "other-directed." That is, Americans tend to overemphasize the importance of approval from others. At the same time, they fail to develop a strong set of personal values and individual standards. Most American children are taught the overriding importance of being liked and of being accepted. Conformity is the standard means of gaining this approval.

One of the most important findings of Asch's experiment was that if even one other person failed to conform to the group's judgment, the subject was able to adhere to his own perception. It seems that it is hardest to stand alone.

CROWDS AND MOBS

Do people in crowds act less rationally than they would if they were alone? The answer is yes, they often do. The great revolutions and wars of independence in America in 1776, in France in 1789, and in Russia in 1917, for example, were probably possible because of this fact. The marches and protests that changed the American scene in the 1960s were also dependent on the ability of people to find strength in numbers. But in other circumstances group processes go wrong.

Mob Action

The members of the mob believe that they are unanimous in their sentiments: Each individual confirms the feelings of those next to him or her that what they are doing is good and valuable.

Before a crowd can become a mob, its members must go through a slow, aimless *milling behavior*. In the milling process, people drift around transmitting and receiving information between themselves. Thoughts and feelings spread rapidly through the crowd. It is this process that turns the crowd into a collective entity in which each individual feels, thinks, and acts in a way different than he or she would if alone. Because the members of the crowd feel they are "one," they give little individual thought to the consequences of their actions.

People tend to lose their individuality and their sense of responsibility in a mob. Violence and other activities that are prohibited in other settings become *norms* in the mob. Individuals in a mob are anonymous—they do not fear punishment for their behavior. Thus, people in mobs tend to behave similarly, to be prone to violence, and to overreact to their situation without thinking about the outcome. A disgraceful example of mob behavior in this country has been the lynching of black men by whites in many parts of the United States. Although lynchings are rare today, mob violence continues to occur in this and other countries.

Loss of identity weakens the inner controls and social pressures that ordinarily keep aggressive impulses in check. In other words, anonymity can breed violence. This is known as *deindividuation* (Festinger, Pepitone, and Newcomb, 1952). Testing this idea is simple. Take two cars, remove the license plates and leave one on a New York City thoroughfare, another on a street of a small town like Palo Alto, California, where people are likely to know one another. Some researchers left cars like this for sixty-four hours and watched what happened. In New York the car had not been abandoned more than ten minutes when its radio and battery were taken by a well-dressed family. At the end, the car had been nearly demolished by twenty-four separate incidents of vandalism. The car in Palo Alto had not remained untouched, either. Someone lowered its hood to keep the engine dry when rain began to fall. Otherwise it remained as it was for the whole time (Middlebrook, 1974). This quality of deindividuation—the loss of identity and responsibility—is accentuated in a mob, making its members especially prone to rashness and violence.

Diffusion of Responsibility

In some circumstances, being part of a crowd can produce an effect that is just the opposite of mob action but that is equally disturbing. This phenomenon might be called "group paralysis." A famous example occurred in the case of an eighteen-year-old girl who was raped and beaten in her New York office. She temporarily escaped her attacker and rushed out into the street, naked and bleeding. Thirty-eight people looked on, but no one offered to help her and no one prevented the rapist from dragging her back into the building. She was saved only because two policemen happened by.

Why didn't the people act? Psychologists have tried to answer this question by studying artificial crises. In one experiment, college students were asked to wait in individual rooms, where they would soon be participating in a discussion of personal problems. Some of the students were told that they would be communicating with only one other person; others were given the impression that they would be talking with five other people. All communication, the psychologist told each student, was to take place over microphones so that everyone would remain anonymous and thus would speak more freely. Each person was to talk in turn.

In reality, there were no other people—all the voices the subjects heard were on tape. As the discussion progressed, the subject heard one of the participants go into an epileptic-like fit. The victim began to call for help, making choking sounds. The experimenters found that most of the people who thought they were alone with the victim came out of their rooms to help him. But of those who believed there were four other people nearby, less than half did anything to help.

The experimenters suggested that this behavior was the result of *diffusion of responsibility*. In other words, because several people were present, the subjects assumed the others would offer help and so waited. The researchers found that in similar experiments, where people could see the other participants, the same pattern emerged. In addition, bystanders reassured one another that it would not be a good idea to interfere. These findings on diffusion of responsibility suggest that the larger the crowd or group of bystanders, the more likely any given individual is to feel that he or she is not responsible for whatever is going on (Darley and Latané, 1968).

Another influence that inhibits action is the tendency to minimize the need for any response. To act, you must admit that an emergency exists. But you may not know exactly what is going on when you hear screams, for example. You are likely to wait before risking the embarrassment of rushing to help where help is not needed or wanted. It is easier to persuade yourself that nothing need be done if you look around and see other people behaving calmly. Not only can you see that they think nothing is wrong, but you can see that not doing anything is entirely proper. So you are able to minimize the need to act and shift any responsibility to those around you.

GROUPS IN CONFLICT

Conflicts between groups are a fact of everyday life: Some level of hostility exists between women and men, young and old, workers and bosses, blacks and whites, Catholics and Protestants, students and teachers. Why do these conflicts exist, and why do they persist? The main factors contributing to conflict between groups seem to be oppression, stereotyping, prejudice, and discrimination. (We will discuss prejudice and discrimination in Chapter 12.)

Oppression

Often group conflict involves the *oppression* of one group by the other. It is not hard to see how such domination gives rise to feelings of hostility on the part of the oppressed group. In addition, the powerful group hates the oppressed group because it wants to justify its unfair actions and because it wants to stop the oppressed group from fighting back.

This is called a *master-slave* relationship, for obvious reasons. The present relationship between blacks and whites in America is a result of

FIGURE 11.11
These lines from James Baldwin's novel *Nobody Knows My Name* express the impossible dilemma of being black in a white world and the way it feels to try to break free from the roles and stereotypes that are implicit in that situation. Baldwin's lines also point out that roles and stereotypes interlock with each other in such a way that they are self-perpetuating. Baldwin wrote this and several other powerful novels from his own experiences of what it was like to be a black man in Boston and New York during the 1940s and 1950s.
(From James Baldwin, *Nobody Knows My Name.* New York: Dell, 1969, pp. 73, 122–123.)

the fact that at one time blacks were literally the slaves and whites were literally the masters. The oppression of blacks by whites has lessened only gradually. Psychologists are learning that the master-slave relationship exists between other groups, too. The freedom of women has been restricted by men; the freedom of students has been restricted by teachers; and so on.

Stereotypes and Roles

The existence of hostility between groups is strengthened and maintained by the existence of stereotypes and roles. As described in Chapter 10, a stereotype is an oversimplified, hard-to-change way of seeing people who belong to some group or category. Black people, scientists, women, Mexicans, and the rich, for example, are often seen in certain rigid ways without appreciation for individuality. A *role* is an oversimplified, hard-to-change way of acting. Stereotypes and roles can act together in a way that makes them difficult to break down. For example, many whites have a stereotype of blacks. Blacks are believed to be irresponsible, superstitious, unintelligent, lazy, and good dancers. Whites who believe this expect blacks to act out a role that is consistent with a stereotype. Blacks are expected to be submissive, deferential, and respectful toward whites, who act out the role of the superior, condescending parent. In the past, both blacks and whites accepted these roles and looked at themselves and each other according to these stereotypes. In recent years many blacks and whites have tried to step out of these roles and drop these stereotypes, and to some extent they are succeeding.

WAYS TO END GROUP CONFLICT

Psychologists have tried in both experimental and natural settings to analyze group conflicts and to resolve them. Perhaps the most famous of these studies were done with boy campers in the 1950s and with integrated housing projects in the 1940s.

Conflict versus Cooperation

One group of psychologists created a boys' camp for the express purpose of studying intergroup relations. The camp at Robber's Cave offered all the usual activities, and the boys had no idea that they were part of an experiment.

From the beginning of the experiment, the boys were divided into two separate groups. The boys hiked, swam, and played baseball only with members of their own group, and friendships and group spirit soon developed. After a while the experimenters (posing as counselors) brought the groups together for a tournament. The psychologists had hypothesized that when these two groups of boys were placed in competitive situations, where one group could achieve its goals only at the expense of the other, hostility would soon develop. They were right.

Although the games began in a spirit of good sportsmanship, tension mounted as the tournament continued. Friendly competition soon gave way to name-calling, fistfights, and raids on enemy cabins. The psychologists had demonstrated the ease with which they could produce unity within the two boys' groups and hatred between them.

After creating group antagonism, the experimenters then tried to see what might end the conflict and create harmony between the two groups. They tried to bring the groups together for enjoyable activities, such as a movie and a good meal. This approach failed—the campers shoved and pushed each other, threw food and insults, and generally used the opportunity to continue their attacks.

Next, the psychologists deliberately invented a series of "emergencies"

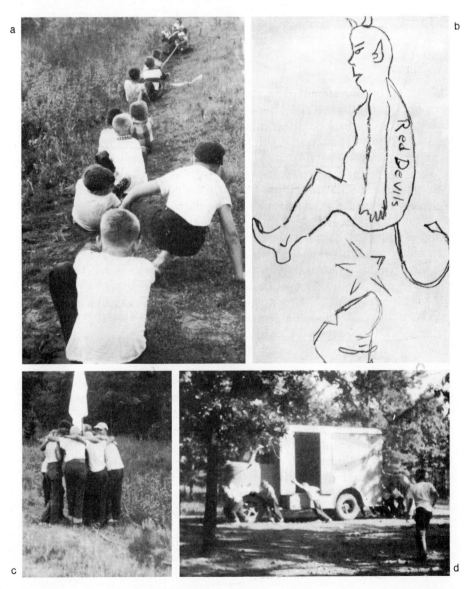

FIGURE 11.12
Scenes from the Robber's Cave experiment, named after the Oklahoma location at which it was conducted. (a) Psychologists posing as camp counselors divided the boy campers into two groups and placed them in competition against one another in such sporting activities as a tug-of-war. (b) Considerable hostility developed between the two groups, the "Bulldogs" and the "Red Devils," which was expressed in drawings like the one shown here. (c) Hostility was also expressed in fights and in raids on enemy cabins. (d) The hostility was eliminated by contrived tasks that had to be performed jointly, such as pushing a heavy truck that supplied food to the camp.

so that the boys would either have to help each other or lose the chance to do or get something they all wanted. For instance, one morning someone reported that the water line to the camp had broken. The boys were told that unless they worked together to find the break and fix it, they would all have to leave camp. By afternoon, they had jointly found and fixed the damage. Gradually, through such cooperative activities, intergroup hostility and tensions lessened. Friendships began to develop between individuals of the opposing groups, and eventually the groups began to seek out occasions to mingle. At the end of the camp period, members of both groups requested that they ride home together on the same bus.

The results of this experiment were striking. A group of boys from identical backgrounds had developed considerable hostility toward each other, simply because they were placed in competition. The crucial factor in eliminating group hostility was cooperation (Sherif et al., 1961).

Integration

The camping experiment demonstrated how easily group hatred can develop. None of the hostility between the two groups could be attributed to former prejudices or discrimination: All the boys were of the same nationality, race, and class. When the campers resolved their hostility by working together to solve a mutual problem, they simply saw themselves as members of a larger group, the camp.

Centuries of racial prejudice in the United States and throughout the world seem to indicate that racial hatred poses a much more complicated problem. One barrier to cooperation between the races is segregation. One group of psychologists created an experiment to test whether racial prejudice could be overcome through desegregation. They reasoned that if people of different races had the opportunity to meet as equals they might come to recognize that their prejudices had no basis.

They interviewed people who had been placed in integrated and segregated buildings of a housing project just after World War II. The results of the interviews showed clearly that the amount and type of contact between black and white neighbors greatly influenced their opinions toward each other.

In the integrated buildings more than 60 percent of the white housewives reported having "friendly relations" with blacks. In the segregated buildings less than 10 percent reported friendships, and more than 80 percent reported no contact at all. In the integrated buildings, two out of three white women expressed a desire to be friendly with blacks. In the segregated buildings only one in eleven expressed such a desire. Similar effects occurred in the attitudes of black women toward whites.

The integrated housing situation gave the housewives a chance to have intimate contact with one another and to interact informally and casually. The housewives were likely to encounter each other in the elevators, hallways, and laundry room. In this informal climate the housewives did not have to worry that trying to strike up a conversation might be misinterpreted. In contrast, contact in the segregated buildings would have to be more deliberate and might be considered suspicious (Deutsch and Collins, 1951).

Similar changes in attitude were observed in an army infantry company that was integrated in 1945—the first of its kind. After living, fighting, and suffering with black soldiers, 64 percent of the white soldiers said they approved of giving blacks combat assignments. In contrast, over 80 percent of soldiers in all-white companies disapproved of integration (Star, Williams, and Stouffer, 1965).

Contact does not always reduce prejudice, however. Studies of schools that were integrated after the 1954 Supreme Court decision show mixed results. While some students became less prejudiced after a semester in an integrated school, others became *more* prejudiced than they had been prior to integration (Campbell, 1958). One exception was a community that voluntarily integrated its schools before the 1954 ruling. Children in that community were significantly less prejudiced than children in a similar community with all-white schools (Singer, 1964).

Why does contact reduce intergroup hostility in some instances but not in others? Several factors seem to be involved. First, the *need to cooperate* forces people to abandon negative stereotypes. This was true for the integrated infantry company as well as for the youngsters in the boys' camp experiment.

Second, contact between people who occupy the same *status* is more likely to break down barriers than contacts between people who do not perceive themselves as equals. Frequent contact with a white landlord is not likely to change a black person's stereotype of whites; nor is the relationship between an upper-class white housewife and a black maid likely to change the white woman's stereotype of blacks. The housewives in the integrated buildings and the soldiers in the integrated company were social equals: They had about the same incomes, lived under similar conditions, faced the same problems, and so on.

Finally, when social *norms* support intergroup cooperation, people are likely to turn contacts into friendships. Presumably the parents and teachers in the community that voluntarily desegregated its schools wanted to break down racial barriers. In accepting integration, the children were conforming to group norms. So were the young people whose communities integrated their schools only after they were required to do so by law. Those whose families and friends approved of integration were open to interracial friendships; those whose families and friends opposed desegregation kept their distance. In the next chapter, we consider in more detail the ways in which reference groups influence people's attitudes.

SUMMARY

1. Groups are aggregates of people who are interdependent—that is, the actions of any one group member will affect or influence other members. Group members become interdependent because they see themselves as sharing common goals.

2. The two primary purposes of groups are to perform task functions and to perform social functions. Most groups serve both functions to some extent.

3. Group interdependence is maintained through the use of group norms that direct the behavior of members. Violation of group norms results in disapproval from other group members.

4. Group cohesiveness is the amount of "we" feeling, or loyalty, among group members. Group cohesiveness depends on individual commitment and is greatest when the members of the group have common norms, adopt a common ideology, each have something to gain from the group, make personal sacrifices to stay in the group, and participate in all group activities.

5. Reference groups are groups with which a person identifies. A reference group provides a set of attitudes and values and a sense of pride for the individual.

6. Group structure is the way in which individuals fit together into a whole unit. The way people interact in a group is studied through the use of sociograms and the analysis of communication patterns. An important element in the group's structure is leadership. A leader is the person who exerts the most influence in a group.

7. There may be different kinds of leaders whose influence may come as a result of expertise, emotional and social appeal, or power. Leadership can also be gained by appointment or by manipulation. One kind of leader, the social leader, deals with group dynamics; the other kind, the task leader, deals with what the group is trying to accomplish.

8. Asch's experiment showed that conformity to pressure from peers may be so strong that people will question or deny their own senses.

9. People in groups often act less rationally than they might as individuals. A crowd becomes a mob when it holds irrational feelings or opinions strongly and unanimously and acts on them. The anonymity of being in a mob makes people prone to be violent, a quality known as deindividuation.

10. Diffusion of responsibility is similar to mob action in that people in a crowd seem to feel they are not responsible for whatever is going on. In a crisis, people often refrain from acting because they minimize the emergency, because they expect other people to act, or because they do not want to be "different."

11. Conflict between groups is usually a result of oppression of one group by another. It is preserved by stereotyping, or perceiving people as belonging to a particular category. People often play the role for which they are stereotyped in order to avoid rejection.

12. The experiment at a boys' camp and studies of integrated housing, infantry companies, and schools suggest that group conflict can be broken down when members of hostile groups need to cooperate; when they come into contact with people of similar status from the other group; and when their reference groups support cooperation.

GLOSSARY

charisma: A leader's strong emotional appeal that arouses enthusiasm and loyalty.

cohesiveness: The degree to which members of groups are closely attached to one another and committed to the group's goals.

deindividuation: Loss of individuality and sense of responsibility that weakens inner controls and social pressures that ordinarily keep aggressive impulses in check.

diffusion of responsibility: The tendency of the

presence of others to lessen an individual's feelings of responsibility for his or her actions or failure to act.

group: An aggregate of people characterized by shared goals and a degree of interdependence.

ideology: The set of principles, attitudes, and defined objectives for which a group stands.

Machiavellian techniques: Techniques of social interaction based on manipulation and extreme pragmatism—so named because they reflect the use of power outlined by Niccolò Machiavelli in his classic book *The Prince.*

norms: Shared standards of behavior accepted by and expected from group members.

reference groups: The groups with which a person identifies.

social functions: In groups, those functions directed toward satisfying the emotional needs of members.

social leader: The leader within a group who promotes group cohesion and commands group loyalty.

sociogram: A diagram representing relationships within a group.

task functions: In groups, those functions directed toward getting some job done.

task leader: The leader within a group who takes over when the group must accomplish something.

ACTIVITIES

1. You probably identify with many groups, including school, religious, work, racial, ethnic, national, political, family, and peer groups. On a chart, indicate the groups that are most important to you and for each record the following: Which ones are the most important? For each, consider: Are you a member of the group? Is it primarily a task-oriented or socially oriented group? What are its goals? What are its values? How does it respond to violations of its norms?

2. Experiments have shown that enforced integration in housing has resulted in less interracial hostility. What is your opinion of legally enforcing racial integration in housing, employment, and schools?

3. Write down the first ten or fifteen words or phrases that come to mind when you ask yourself "Who am I?" Stop. Now, categorize these items as either physical traits, psychological characteristics, or group affiliations. How much of your self-concept is built on your identification with groups?

4. Consider your primary (or most important) group. What sacrifices would you be willing to make in order to remain in the group? What

sacrifices would you be unwilling to make? For what reason(s), if any, would you be willing to sacrifice your life for this group?

5. Do any of the groups to which you belong have rivals—other groups you compete against (for example, a rival team)? If so, what are the people like in the rival group? What information did you use to arrive at an answer to this question?

6. In the groups to which you belong (clubs, your school, and so on) you have undoubtedly had leaders or people with influence over you. Pick a few such leaders and try to analyze the sources of their influence. Are they experts? Do they have charisma? Are they socially attractive? How much power do they have? How have they obtained it?

7. Do you belong to any social or service clubs? Why or why not? Have you ever been rejected by a group you wished to join? Do you know why? What were your feelings on being rejected?

8. Make a list of ten or more nationalities, religions, races, and occupations. Have friends or family members list five things that come to

mind when these groups are mentioned. What are your conclusions?

9. Ask one male and one female to reverse sex roles and discuss the following contentions: (1) Men need liberation as much as women. (2) Men are at least equally as vain as women. (3) Women do not mind being dominated as long as they are loved and cared for. (4) Women can never be as competent as men, or men as women, in which of the following occupations: scientist; child-rearing; politician; construction worker; nurse; airplane pilot?

10. Pick a television program that is based on a set group of characters. Analyze the group by determining what goals the fictional characters share, how they are interdependent, and what maintains their cohesiveness. At the same time, consider what social roles and stereotypes, if any, the program perpetuates.

11. Most groups exercise some control over their members in ways that they are not aware of. Take any group you know well and analyze the controls that exist, the reasons for them, and how they are exercised. Obviously, an analysis of a group to which you belong will be more difficult, but it will also be more interesting.

SUGGESTED READINGS

BENNKS, W. G., ET AL. (EDS.). *Interpersonal Dynamics: Essays and Readings on Human Interaction.* Homewood, Ill.: Dorsey Press, 1973. This set of about forty-five relatively short readings by a very diverse group of authors is held together both by the aim of the editors to broaden our understanding of "our life in others" and by the compelling quality of the writing in most of the selections.

GOLDING, WILLIAM. *Lord of the Flies.* New York: Coward, McCann, 1954 (paper). An absorbing and shocking novel about how the group process runs wild in a bunch of boys stranded on an island.

HOFFER, ERIC. *The True Believer.* New York: Harper & Row, 1951 (paper). Hoffer identifies and analyzes the characteristics of the "true believer"—the person who identifies so much with a group that he or she has no identity away from it.

KINKADE, KATHLEEN. *A Walden Two Experiment.* New York: Morrow, 1973. An account of the efforts of an intentional community—a commune—to start afresh in the ways of living together, with a willingness to experiment and to criticize the experiment relentlessly, seen through the sensitive eyes of the founder of the commune.

KOESTLER, ARTHUR. *Darkness at Noon.* New York: Bantam, 1941 (paper). With personal knowledge and sensitivity, Koestler probes the literal and theoretical consequences of a political doctrine founded on the concept of Machiavellian techniques. A powerful novel.

PARKINSON, C. NORTHCOTE. *Parkinson's Law and Other Studies in Administration.* New York: Ballantine, 1957 (paper). A clever analysis of organizations based on Parkinson's experience in the British civil service. Parkinson's law says that work expands to fill the time available for its completion.

BIBLIOGRAPHY

ASCH, S. *Social Psychology.* New York: Prentice-Hall, 1952.

BALES, R. F. "Task Roles and Social Roles in Problem-solving Groups." In *Readings in Social Psychology,* 3rd ed., edited by E. Maccoby, T. M. Newcomb, and E. L. Hartley. New York: Holt, Rinehart and Winston, 1958, pp. 347–447.

CAMPBELL, E. "Some Social Psychological

Correlates of Direction in Attitude Change." *Social Forces*, 36 (1958): 335–340.

COCH, L. AND FRENCH, J. R. P., JR. "Overcoming Resistance to Change." *Human Relations*, 1 (1948): 512–532.

DARLEY, J. M., AND LATANÉ, B. "Bystander Intervention in Emergencies: Diffusion of Responsibility." *Journal of Personality and Social Psychology*, 8 (1968): 377–383.

DEUTSCH, M. "An Experimental Study of the Effects of Co-operation and Competition upon Group Processes." *Human Relations*, 2 (1949): 199–232.

DEUTSCH, M., AND COLLINS, M. *Interracial Housing: A Psychological Evaluation of a Social Experiment.* Minneapolis: University of Minnesota Press, 1951.

FESTINGER, L., PEPITONE, A., AND NEWCOMB, T. "Some Consequences of Deindividuation in a Group." *Journal of Abnormal Psychology*, 47 (1952): 382–389.

FIEDLER, F. E. "Style or Circumstance: The Leadership Enigma." *Psychology Today*, 2 (1969): 38–43.

GARFINKLE, HAROLD. *Studies in Ethnomethodology.* Englewood Cliffs, N.J.: Prentice-Hall, 1967.

GERGEN, K. "Interaction Goals and Personalistic Feedback as Factors Affecting Presentation of the Self." *Journal of Personality and Social Psychology*, 1 (1965): 413–424.

GIBB, C. "Leadership." In *The Handbook of Social Psychology*, 2nd ed., edited by G. Lindsey and E. Aronson. Reading, Mass.: Addison-Wesley, 1969, vol. 4.

GRIER, WILLIAM H., AND COBBS, P. M. *Black Rage.* New York: Basic Books, 1968.

KANTER, ROSABETH. "Communes." *Psychology Today*, 4 (July 1970): 53–57, 78.

LAMBERT, WALLACE E., LIBMAN, EVA, AND POSER, ERNEST G. "The Effect of Increased Salience of a Membership Group on Pain Tolerance." *Journal of Personality*, 28 (1960): 350–357.

LEAVITT, H. J. "Some Effects of Certain Communication Patterns on Group Performance." *Journal of Abnormal Social Psychology*, 46 (1951): 38–50.

MACKAY, CHARLES. *Extraordinary Popular Delusions and the Madness of Crowds.* New York: Farrar, Straus & Giroux, 1932.

MIDDLEBROOK, PATRICIA NILES. *Social Psychology and Modern Life.* New York: Knopf, 1974.

ROETHLISBERGER, F. J., AND DICKSON, W. *Management and the Worker.* Cambridge, Mass.: Harvard University Press, 1939.

SCHLESINGER, ARTHUR M., JR. *A Thousand Days.* New York: Fawcett World Library, 1965 (paper).

SEASHORE, S., AND BARNOWE, J. "Collar Color Doesn't Count." *Psychology Today*, 6 (3) (1972): 52–54, 80, 82.

SHERIF, MUZAFER, ET AL. *Intergroup Conflict and Cooperation: The Robbers Cave Experiment.* Norman, Okla.: Institute of Group Relations, 1961.

SINGER, D. "The Impact of Interracial Classroom Exposure on the Social Attitudes of Fifth Grade Children." Unpublished study, 1964.

STAR, S., WILLIAMS, R., JR., AND STOUFFER, S. "Negro Infantry Platoons in White Companies." In *Basic Studies in Social Psychology*, edited by H. Proshansky and B. Seidenberg. New York: Holt, Rinehart and Winston, 1965, pp. 680–685.

TIPPETT, J., AND SILBER, E. "Autonomy of Self-esteem: An Experimental Approach." *Archives of General Psychiatry*, 14 (1955): 372–385.

YANKELOVICH, DANIEL, *Yankelovich Youth Study*, © 1973 by the JDR, 3rd Fund.

12 Attitudes and Social Influence

Do you use one brand of aspirin because it is better than the others?

Do you have an opinion about who should be president?

Where did these notions come from? Certainly not from personal knowledge, at least for most of us. We have no way of testing aspirin or presidential aspirants for ourselves. Chances are we rely on an advertiser's word for our choice of aspirin and on the advice of others about our choice of candidates. A lot of our ideas come not from certainty based on personal experience but from what we've been told by others.

This chapter is about how people form attitudes and how these attitudes affect their behavior. It is also about how beliefs, feelings, and actions come to change.

WHERE ATTITUDES COME FROM

An *attitude* is a predisposition to respond in particular ways toward specific things. It has three main elements: (1) a belief or opinion about something; (2) feelings about that thing; and (3) a tendency to act toward that thing in certain ways. For example, what is your attitude toward the senators from your state? Do you *believe* they are doing a good job? Do you trust or distrust them? Would you vote for them?

We have very definite beliefs, feelings, and responses to things about which we have no firsthand knowledge. Where do these attitudes come from? The culture in which you grew up, the people who raised you, and those with whom you associate—your peers—all shape your attitudes.

Culture

Culture influences everything from our taste in food to our attitudes toward human relationships and our political opinions. For example, most (if not all) Americans would consider eating grubs, curdled milk spiced with fresh cattle blood, or monkey meat disgusting. Yet in some parts of the world these are considered delicacies. Most Americans believe eating meat is essential for good health. Hindus consider our relish for thick juicy steaks and hamburgers repugnant.

Almost all Americans would agree that in polygamous societies, where a man is allowed to have more than one wife, women are oppressed.

FIGURE 12.1
Cosmetics advertisements typically offer more than clean skin and hair. The beauty industry spends millions of dollars each year to convince consumers that excitement, love, and happiness can be bought as well.

279

To us, sharing a mate seems unnatural. But women in polygamous societies feel nothing but pity for a woman whose husband hasn't acquired
other wives to help with the work and to keep her company.

Most of us would also agree that parents who interfere in their children's choice of a marriage partner are behaving outrageously and that
a person should be able to marry the person he or she loves. But in India,
parents choose husbands for their daughters, and Indian girls do not
resent this. In fact they are relieved not to have to make such an important
choice:

> "We girls don't have to worry at all. We know we'll get married. When we
> are old enough our parents will find a suitable boy and everything will be
> arranged. We don't have to go into competition with each other. . . . Besides
> how would we be able to judge the character of a boy? . . . Our parents are
> older and wiser, and they aren't deceived as easily as we would be. I'd far
> rather have my parents choose for me" (Mace and Mace, 1960: 131).

The list of culturally derived attitudes is endless. Indeed, it is only by
traveling and reading about other ways of life that we discover how many
of the things we take for granted are *attitudes*, not facts.

Parents

There is abundant evidence that all of us acquire many basic attitudes
from our parents. How else would you account for the finding that 80
percent of a national sample of elementary school children favored the
same political party as their fathers (Hess and Torney, 1967), and 76 percent of high school seniors in a nationwide sample also preferred the same
party as both their parents (Jennings and Niemi, 1968)? Parental influence
wanes as children get older, of course. A sample of college students selected the same party as their father only 50 to 60 percent of the time
(Goldsen *et al.*, 1960). Despite the decline, this study still suggests significant parental influence even after a person has become an adult.

Peers

It is not surprising that parental influence declines as children get older
and are exposed to many other sources of influence. In a now classic
study, Newcomb (1943) questioned and requestioned students at Bennington College about their political attitudes over a period of four years. Most
of the girls came from wealthy, staunchly conservative families. In contrast, most Bennington faculty members were outspoken liberals. Newcomb found that many of the students were "converted" to the liberal
point of view. In 1936, 54 percent of the juniors and seniors supported
F. D. R. and the New Deal—although praising Roosevelt to their families
would have produced about the same reactions as would praising George
Wallace to a group of Black Panthers (Middlebrook, 1974, p. 133). Indeed,
nearly 30 percent of the students favored Socialist or Communist candidates. Newcomb contacted the subjects of his study twenty-five years

FIGURE 12.2
Scenes from Bennington College at the time Newcomb was there. Newcomb himself is shown on the left. Newcomb described Bennington as being suitable for the study of the development of attitudes toward public affairs because it "opened its doors during the darkest days of the depression" and because this was "the period of gathering war clouds in Europe." The Bennington faculty held the conviction "that one of the foremost duties of the college was to acquaint its somewhat oversheltered students with the nature of their contemporary social world." The marked change in reference groups experienced by Bennington students is shown in a remark by one subject that Newcomb quotes: "Family against faculty has been my struggle here."

after they had graduated, and found that most had maintained the attitudes they had acquired in college. One reason was that they had chosen friends, husbands, and careers that supported liberal values (Newcomb et al., 1967).

Newcomb's study underlines a point made in the preceding chapter about reference groups. People tend to adopt the likes and dislikes of groups whose approval and acceptance they seek.

ATTITUDE FORMATION

Having suggested where attitudes come from, we can now look at how they develop. The three main processes involved in forming or changing attitudes are compliance, identification, and internalization (Kelman, 1961).

Compliance

One of the best measures of attitude is behavior. If a man settles back into "his chair" after dinner, launches into a discussion of the merits of women's liberation, then shouts to his wife—who is in the kitchen washing dishes—to bring more coffee, you probably wouldn't believe what he had been saying. His actions speak louder than his words.

Yet the same man might hire women for jobs he has always considered "men's work" because the law requires him to do so. And he might finally accept his wife's going to work because he knows that she, their children, and many of their friends would consider him old-fashioned if he didn't.

People often *comply* with the wishes of others in order to avoid discomfort or rejection and to gain support. As one Bennington student who professed to be a liberal explained,

"It's very simple, I was so anxious to be accepted that I accepted the liberal complexion of the community here. I just couldn't stand out against the crowd . . ." (Newcomb, 1943: 132).

But under such circumstances, attitudes do not really change. Social pressure often results in only temporary compliance. Compliance can have unexpected effects on one's beliefs, as will be seen later in this chapter. In general, however, it takes more than social pressure to change deeply held attitudes.

Identification

One way in which attitudes may really be formed or changed is through the process of *identification*. Suppose you have a favorite uncle who is everything you hope to be. He is a successful musician, has many famous friends, and seems to know a great deal about everything. In many ways you identify with him and copy his behavior. One night, during an intense conversation, your uncle announces that he is an atheist. At first you are confused by this statement. You have had a religious upbringing and have always considered religious beliefs as essential. However, as you listen to your uncle, you find yourself starting to agree with him. If a person as knowledgeable and respectable as your uncle holds such beliefs, perhaps you should, too. Later you find yourself feeling that the atheist view is acceptable. You have adopted a new attitude because of your identification with your uncle.

Identification occurs when a person wants to define himself or herself in terms of a person or group, and therefore adopts their attitudes and ways of behaving. Identification is different from compliance because the individual actually believes the newly adopted views. But because these attitudes are based on emotional attachment to another person or group, rather than the person's own assessment of the issues, they are fragile. If the person's attachment to that person or group fades, the attitudes may also weaken.

Thus one Bennington student ultimately rejected the liberal point of view.

"Family against faculty has been my struggle here. As soon as I felt really secure I decided not to let the college atmosphere affect me too much. Every time I've tried to rebel against my family I've found how terribly wrong I am, and I've very naturally kept to my parents' attitudes" (Newcomb, 1943: 124).

For this student, identification with the college community was only temporary.

Internalization

If you praise a certain film director because everyone else does, you are complying. If you find yourself agreeing with everything a friend you particularly admire says about the director, you are identifying with the friend's attitudes. If you genuinely like the director's work and, regardless of what other people think, regard them as works of brilliance, you are expressing an internalized attitude.

Internalization is the wholehearted acceptance of an attitude: It becomes an integral part of the person. Internalization is most likely to occur when an attitude is consistent with a person's basic beliefs and values and supports his or her self-image. The person adopts a new attitude because he or she believes it to be right—not because he or she wants to be like someone else.

Internalization is the most durable of the three sources of attitude formation or change. Your internalized attitudes will be more resistant to pressure from other people because your reasons for holding these views have nothing to do with other people: They are based on your own evaluation of the merits of the issue.

A Bennington student put it this way:

"I became liberal at first because of its prestige value; I remain so because the problems around which my liberalism centers are important. What I want now is to be effective in solving the problems" (Newcomb, 1943: 136).

As this example suggests, compliance or identification may lead to the internalization of an attitude. Often the three overlap. You may support a political candidate in part because you know your friends will approve, in part because someone you admire speaks highly of the candidate, and in part because you believe his or her ideals are consistent with your own.

ATTITUDES AND PERSONALITY

Suppose you are trying to persuade people to change their minds about something or to accept a new idea. You will find that some people are much more readily persuaded than others. Of course, whether someone will agree or disagree with your ideas is partly determined by the nature of the information you are presenting. But to a considerable extent, a person's readiness to change his or her mind depends on his or her personality.

To be persuaded about something is to admit that another person has more facts, more convincing arguments, greater expertise, or superior command of the issues. Some people are only too willing to make this admission; others are highly resistant.

Some people place a low value on their own opinions and attitudes; consequently, it is not difficult for them to part company with their ideas. They are easily influenced by those around them, both because they have few defenses for their ideas and because their ideas have been of little use to them. Such people often agree with others in order to gain their approval. Because they want to be liked, they do what they think others expect them to do.

At the other end of the spectrum is the person who has an inflated opinion of himself and of his ideas and is thus difficult to influence. Such a person is extremely closed-minded and will stick to his attitudes under all circumstances. He considers any attempt to change his beliefs as an attack on his entire personality. This person clings to his attitudes as a way of defining himself. Without them, he fears loss of identity.

Still other people value their own opinions but, if presented with convincing arguments, may alter their attitudes. This type of person tends to base her attitudes on knowledge rather than on identification or social approval. In fact, she is likely to welcome the chance to examine new ideas and to accept or reject them. Personality factors that seem to influence attitude formation thus include a person's need for social approval, her belief in her own judgment, and the extent of her need to maintain her attitudes.

Prejudice and Discrimination

Prejudice means, literally, prejudgment. It means deciding beforehand what a person will be like instead of withholding judgment until it can be based on his or her individual qualities. To hold stereotypes about a group of people is to be prejudiced about them. Prejudice is not necessarily negative—whites who are prejudiced against blacks are often equally prejudiced in favor of whites, for example.

Shocked by the rise of European fascism in the 1930s, a group of researchers sought to discover the kinds of people who would be attracted to leaders who claimed racial superiority and pledged to destroy those whom they considered inferior.

The researchers found that highly prejudiced people share a number of other personality traits as well. They named this group of traits and attitudes the *authoritarian personality* (Adorno, 1969). Such people tend to have inflexible ideas about themselves and others. Highly conventional, they view differences with suspicion and hostility, and are very attracted to those in authority. They tend to glorify their own qualities and upbringing, overlooking the painful fact that their fathers were inclined to be punitive and exacted obedience and unquestioning loyalty through harsh discipline.

The researchers who originally uncovered the relationships between prejudice, personality traits, and upbringing believed that punitive parents create insecure and hostile children. As adults, these people fear their own aggressiveness and cannot admit their own fears and shortcomings. It is easier to claim that others are inferior than to recognize one's own shortcomings. The authoritarian person falls back on the use of stereotypes about others to keep from facing his or her own inadequacies.

This is not the only interpretation of highly prejudiced people, however. The link may be simpler: Authoritarian parents teach their views to their children. Or perhaps prejudice and authoritarianism may actually be characteristics of lower social standing rather than quirks of personality.

We can see, then, that there are many possible causes for prejudice. Psychologists have found that people tend to be prejudiced against those less well-off than themselves—they seem to justify being on top by assuming that anyone of lower status or income must be inferior. People who have suffered economic setbacks also tend to be prejudiced—they blame others for their misfortune.

Prejudice also arises from "guilt by association." People who dislike cities and urban living, for example, tend to distrust people associated with cities, such as Jews and blacks. Also, people tend to be prejudiced *toward* those they see as similar to themselves and *against* those who seem different.

Whatever the original cause, prejudice seems to persist long afterward. One reason is that children who grow up in an atmosphere of prejudice conform to the prejudicial norm—at first because their parents do and later with the personal conviction that it is the right way to be. Children are socialized into the prejudicial culture of their parents; that is, they encounter numerous forces that induce them to conform to the thoughts and practices of their parents and other teachers, formal and informal.

Prejudice, which is an attitude, should be distinguished from *discrimination*, the unequal treatment of members of certain groups. It is possible for a prejudiced person not to discriminate. He or she may recognize his or her prejudice and try not to act on it. Similarly, a person may discriminate, not out of prejudice, but in compliance to social pressures. *Personal* discrimination may take the form of refusing to rent to black people or allowing only men to frequent a particular bar or paying Mexican-Americans substandard wages.

Many social *institutions* serve to reflect and preserve prejudice and discrimination. For example, many institutions, such as schools and businesses, maintain such discriminatory practices as segregation, unfair hiring, and unequal pay scales. Stereotypes are also preserved in the communications media, which have traditionally portrayed American

FIGURE 12.3
After the assassination of Martin Luther King in 1968, a third-grade teacher gave her students a lesson in discrimination. On the basis of eye color the teacher divided the class into two groups and favored one group (the blue-eyed children the first day) with such privileges as being leaders and having their choice of seats and activities. The next day she reversed the situation, favoring the brown-eyed children. On the day that they were favored, the blue-eyed children reportedly "took savage delight" in keeping "inferiors" in their place and said they felt "good inside," "smarter," and "stronger." On that day, one child drew the picture shown on the right. The next day, the same child, now one of the "inferiors," drew the picture on the left. The children who had felt "smart" and "strong" on their favored day became tense, lacked confidence, and did badly at their work on the day they were discriminated against. They said they felt "like dying" and "like quitting school."

Indians as villains, Italians as greasy gangsters, Jews as misers, and teen-agers as car-crazy, fun-loving rock fans. Many of these stereotypes are changing now, but new ones have replaced them. For example, doctors on television are usually heroes, housewives are charming idiots, and so on. A critical look at television programs and movies reveals a lot about what is widely believed in American society.

COGNITIVE CONSISTENCY AND CHANGING ATTITUDES

Many social psychologists, notably Fritz Heider and Leon Festinger (1957) have theorized that people's attitudes change because they are always trying to get things to logically fit together inside themselves. It is possible for a person to hold two conflicting attitudes, but it is uncomfortable. This is why people often change their ideas when such conflicts occur.

Suppose, for example, that you have always disliked mushrooms. One night you go to a friend's house for dinner and are served a delicious casserole, with flavors you have never before tasted. After the meal, you congratulate your host on the fine dish and ask him what was in it. It turns out that one of the main ingredients was mushrooms. You are now faced with an inconsistency between your antimushroom attitude and your enjoyment of the mushroom casserole. In this case, you are likely to change your attitude and become more of a mushroom eater. In addition, you may be more willing to try new things in the future.

Attitude change is not always this simple. Holding two opposing atti-tudes can create great conflict in an individual, throwing him or her off balance. A pacifist who has been drafted, a doctor who smokes, and a parent who is uncomfortable with children all have one thing in common: They are in conflict.

According to Leon Festinger (1957) people in such situations experience cognitive dissonance. *Cognitive dissonance* is the uncomfortable feeling that arises when a person experiences contradictory or conflicting thoughts, beliefs, attitudes, or feelings. To reduce dissonance, it is neces-sary to change one or both of the conflicting attitudes. A drafted pacifist, for example, is against violence and killing, but he may also feel that he must obey the law, even the draft law. This situation creates cognitive dissonance, and the young man is driven to reduce the conflict. One solu-tion to his problem would be for him to decide that violence is acceptable when it comes to defending one's country. Another would be to decide that certain laws are wrong and should not be obeyed. Or he might at-tempt to convince the draft board that he should be placed in a job that does not involve violence. This solution would not require him to change his attitudes.

Some people attempt to evade dissonance altogether by avoiding situa-tions or exposure to information that would create conflict. For example, they may make a point of subscribing to newspapers and magazines that uphold their political attitudes, of surrounding themselves with people who share the same ideas, and of attending only those speeches and lec-tures that support their views. It is not surprising that such people get

FIGURE 12.4
An example of cognitive dissonance. Mary has a positive attitude
toward Bill and a negative attitude
toward certain clothing styles. She
can maintain both of these attitudes until a situation arises in
which these attitudes are brought
into conflict. Then she is faced with
the same problem mentioned in
the text regarding dislike for
mushrooms. A state of dissonance
exists that can only be reduced
by some change in attitude. For
example, Mary may decide that
she does not care for Bill as much
as she thought; she may decide
that she really does like the new
fashion; or she may resolve the
conflict by deciding that Bill's
"poor taste" is a minor fault compared to his many assets.

quite upset when a piece of conflicting information finally does get
through.

The process of dissonance reduction does not always take place consciously, but it is a frequent and powerful occurrence. In fact, remarkably
long-lasting changes in attitudes were produced in an experiment in
which students were made aware that their high emphasis on freedom
was inconsistent with their indifference to equality and civil rights. The
initial forty-minute session had students rank a number of values in importance to themselves—including the key variables "freedom" and
"equality." They were also asked to express their attitudes toward civil
rights. The students then compared their answers with a table of typical
answers, which was interpreted for them by the researchers. The researchers said that the typical tendency to rank freedom high and equality
low not only showed that students in general are "much more interested
in their own freedom than in other people's" but also that such rankings
are consistent with a lack of concern for civil rights. Finally, students were

asked whether their results left them satisfied or dissatisfied. The control group, who did not receive the researchers' explanation, simply filled out their rankings and went home, oblivious to any inconsistencies in attitude they might have expressed.

Three to five months after the initial test the researchers sent out a solicitation for donations or memberships on NAACP stationery, to test whether students tested would act on the values they expressed. They received many more replies from students in the experimental group than in the control group. They concluded that the test had somehow made the first group of students more receptive to civil rights issues. On tests fifteen to seventeen months later, changes in attitude were much more likely in subjects who had been dissatisfied with what they had been told about the results of their original test than in subjects who had not been dissatisfied. This suggests that cognitive dissonance spurred changes in attitudes toward civil rights.

This is a powerful and lasting impact from a simple forty-minute session and a few follow-up tests. The researcher himself was disturbed by the implications, for "If such socially important values as equality and freedom can be altered to become more important to human subjects, they can surely be altered to also become less important. Who shall decide . . .?" (Rokeach, 1971: 458).

PERSUASION

Persuasion is a direct attempt to influence attitudes through the medium of communication. At one time or another everyone engages in persuasion. When a smiling student who is working her way through college by selling magazine subscriptions comes to the door, she attempts to persuade you that reading *Newsweek* or *Sports Illustrated* or *Ms.* will make you better informed and give you lots to talk about at parties. In return, you might attempt to persuade her that you already subscribe to more magazines than you have time to read. Parents often attempt to persuade a son or daughter to conform to their values about life. And children try to persuade their parents to see their point of view. In each case the persuader's main hope is that by changing the other person's attitudes he or she can change that person's behavior as well. The student hopes you will buy a subscription; you hope she will leave. The parents hope their children will do as they ask; the children hope their parents will stop badgering them.

Types of Persuasion

Persuasion is known by many names—salesmanship, political campaigning, and editorializing, to mention a few. The most familiar and obvious form of persuasion is *advertising*. We will also discuss a subtler form of persuasion, public relations, as well as the very powerful techniques of propaganda.

Advertising.   We are constantly being bombarded by messages from companies that want us to buy their products. A classic example of successful advertising is the Bayer aspirin campaign. There is absolutely no difference between Bayer and other, unadvertised brands of aspirin: All have to meet the same government standards to be called "aspirin." Yet because they are familiar with the name-brands, more people purchase Bayer and other name-brands than unadvertised brands, even though the latter are usually much cheaper.

Public Relations.   This is a form of persuasion largely hidden from view. Public relations is indirect advertising. It involves everything from press releases to "briefings," all-expense-paid trips, gifts, expensive dinners, and other forms of entertainment. The goal is to create favorable attitudes toward a company, interest group (such as physicians), a political candidate, a foreign country, or some other client.

Propaganda.   Nowhere can techniques of persuasion be seen more dramatically than in propaganda campaigns. Propaganda is aimed at inspiring certain thoughts, feelings, and actions in large masses of people by appealing to emotions and prejudice rather than to reason. A talent for swaying large groups of people through such appeals was part of Adolf Hitler's rise to power in Germany. The torch-lit parades, the enormous swastika banners, and the dramatic use of the salute "Seig Heil" chanted in unison were the ritualistic backdrop for speeches that used every tactic of propaganda—appeals to sacred values, invocations of authority, arousal of fears, and denunciation of scapegoat groups, in this case Jews and other non-Aryans (Lee and Lee, 1939). Once in office, Hitler continued his propaganda campaign by subordinating the press, arts, and education to serve the ends of "public enlightenment" (Holborn, 1969).

The Communication Process

As the preceding section suggested, enormous amounts of time, money, and effort go into campaigns to persuade people to change their attitudes and behavior. Some succeed on a grand scale; others seem to have no effect. One of the most difficult questions social psychologists have tried to answer is, What makes a persuasive communication effective?

The communication process can be broken down into four parts. The *message* itself is only one part. It is also important to consider the *source* of the message, the *channel* through which it is delivered, and the *audience* that receives it.

The Source.   How a person sees the source, or originator, of a message may be a critical factor in his or her acceptance or rejection of it. The person receiving the message asks himself or herself two basic questions: Is the person giving the message trustworthy and sincere? Does he or she know anything about the subject? If the source seems reliable and knowledgeable, the message is likely to be accepted.

FIGURE 12.5
Winston Churchill, in a speech to the British House of Commons in 1940. Churchill was able to rouse in the British people a courageous and determined attitude toward the war that probably no other communicator could have roused. His long record as a soldier (in India, South Africa, and in World War I) and as a political leader made him a source whose knowledge and trustworthiness were beyond question by the time he was needed to lead the fight against Hitler.

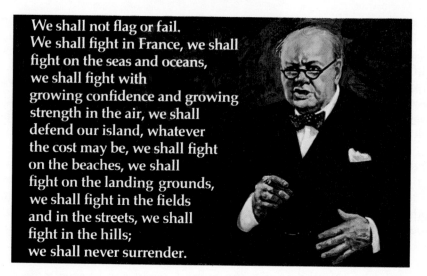

We shall not flag or fail. We shall fight in France, we shall fight on the seas and oceans, we shall fight with growing confidence and growing strength in the air, we shall defend our island, whatever the cost may be, we shall fight on the beaches, we shall fight on the landing grounds, we shall fight in the fields and in the streets, we shall fight in the hills; we shall never surrender.

Suppose, for example, that you have written a paper criticizing a poem for your English class. Your instructor gives you an article that praises the poem and asks you to reconsider your view. The article was written by Agnes Stearn, a student at a state teachers college. You might change your opinion—and you might not. But suppose your instructor tells you that the same positive critique was written by poet T. S. Eliot. The chances are that you would begin to doubt your own judgment. Three psychologists tried this experiment. Not surprisingly, many more of the students who read T. S. Eliot's *expert* than those who read Agnes Stearn's evaluation changed their minds about the poem (Aronson, Turner, and Carlsmith, 1963).

A person receiving the message also asks: Do I *like* the source? If the communicator is respected and admired, people will tend to go along with the message, either because they believe in his or her judgment or because they want to be like him or her. The identification phenomenon explains the frequent use of athletes in advertisements. Football players and Olympic champions are not (in most cases) experts on deodorants, shaving equipment, or milk. Indeed, when an athlete endorses a particular brand of deodorant on television, we all know he or she is doing it for the money. Nevertheless, the process of identification makes these sales pitches highly effective.

Similarly, people are much more likely to respond favorably to a physically attractive source than to one who does not make a good appearance. In the 1960 presidential campaign Richard Nixon apparently lost many votes as a result of his poor appearance on a televised debate with John F. Kennedy. During the 1968 campaign Nixon was coached on how to present a likable image to the camera. His campaign managers filmed him in informal settings, hired people to applaud and crowd around him, encouraged him to joke and smile more often, and even used make-up to erase the shadows that gave many people the impression that he had "shifty eyes" (McGinniss, 1970). Nixon, of course, won that campaign.

However, attempts to be friendly and personal can backfire. When a group of college students who opposed the war in Southeast Asia visited homes in the surrounding community in the hope of persuading townspeople to support their cause, they succeeded in further alienating residents. Why? Apparently the townspeople perceived the students as radicals and resented the invasion of their privacy (Nesbitt, 1972). When people dislike the individual or group that is delivering a message, they are likely to respond by taking the opposite point of view. This is known as the *boomerang* effect.

As the students' failure to persuade townspeople of the wrongfulness of the war suggests, people are more apt to agree with people who are *similar to them* (or who resemble what they would like to be) than to people who seem alien. Suppose you'd read an article by an acknowledged expert who states that taking LSD could be extremely dangerous. A few days later you meet a classmate who says that is nonsense: He's had many fascinating trips on LSD. A friend who is with you agrees. Who would you be more likely to believe—the scientist in his laboratory or your peers?

The Message. Suppose two people with opposing viewpoints are trying to persuade you to agree with them. Suppose further that you like and trust both of them. In this situation the *message* becomes more important than the source. The persuasiveness of a message depends on the way in which it is composed and organized as well as on the actual content.

Should the message arouse emotion? Are people more likely to change their attitudes if they are afraid or angry or pleased? The answer is yes, but the most effective messages combine emotional appeal with factual information and argument. A communication that overemphasizes the emotional side of an issue may boomerang. If the message is too upsetting, it may force people to mobilize their defenses. For example, showing pictures of accident victims to people who have been arrested for drunken driving may convince them not to drive when they've been drinking. But if the film is so bloody that people cannot stand watching it, they may also stop listening to the message. On the other hand, a communication that includes only logic and information may miss its mark because the audience does not relate the facts to their personal lives.

When presenting an argument, is it more effective to present both sides of an issue or only one side? For the most part, a two-sided communication is more effective because the audience will tend to believe that the speaker is objective and fair-minded. A slight hazard of presenting opposing arguments is that they might undercut the message or suggest that the whole issue is too controversial to make a decision about.

People usually respond positively to a message that is structured and delivered in a dynamic way. But a communication that is forceful to the point of being pushy may produce negative results. People generally resent being pressured. If listeners infer from a message that they are being left with no choice but to agree with the speaker's viewpoint, they may reject an opinion for this reason alone.

FIGURE 12.6
Psychologists have found that a message is most effective when it combines an appeal to the emotions with solid facts. This advertisement presents a powerfully emotional picture and headline to shock the readers into attention and to arouse their concern. It then gives some hard facts to further involve them in the subject matter, and finally suggests that the readers subscribe to a certain journal for continuous information on such important matters. Readers might well have ignored the ad if it had simply said, "Doctors need to know about current issues relevant to the medical profession. Subscribe to *Medical World News.*"

The Channel.   Where, when, and how a message is presented also influences the audience's response. In general, personal contact is the most effective approach to an audience. Thus in Ann Arbor, Michigan, 75 percent of voters who had been contacted personally voted in favor of a change in the city charter. Only 45 percent of those who had received the message in the mail, and 19 percent of those who had only seen ads in the media, voted for the change (Eldersveld and Dodge, 1954).

However, as we saw earlier, personal contact may boomerang: People may dislike the communicator or feel that they are being pressured. Besides, you can reach a great many more people through mailings and radio and television broadcasts than you can in person.

There is some evidence that television and films are more effective media of persuasion than printed matter. People tend to believe what they see and hear with their own senses (even if they know the information has been edited before it is broadcast). In one experiment, 51 percent of people who had watched a film could answer factual questions about the issue in question—compared to 29 percent of those who had only seen printed material. And more of the people who had viewed the film altered their viewpoints than did people who had read about the issue (Hovland, Lumsdaine, and Sheffield, 1949). Of course, some people have a distinct distrust of television and are far more likely to believe what they read in newspapers and magazines. Thus the most effective channel depends in part on the audience.

The Audience.   The audience includes all those people whose attitudes the communicator is trying to change. Being able to persuade people to alter their views depends on knowing who the audience is and why they hold the attitudes they do.

Suppose, for example, you are involved in a program to reduce the birth rate in a population that is outgrowing its food supply. The first step would be to inform people of various methods of birth control as well as how and where to obtain them. However, the fact that people know how to limit their families does not mean that they will do so. To persuade them to use available contraceptives you need to know why they value large families. In some areas of the world, people have as many children as they can because they do not expect most babies to survive early childhood. In this case you might want to tie the family-planning campaign to programs for infant care. In some areas, children begin working at odd jobs at an early age and bring in needed income. In this case, you might want to promote an incentive system for families who limit themselves to two or three children.

If the people are not taking advantage of available means of birth control, you will want to know who is resisting. Perhaps men believe fathering a child is a sign of virility. Perhaps women consider motherhood an essential element of femininity. Perhaps both sexes see parenthood as a symbol of maturity and adulthood (see Coale, 1973). Knowing who your audience is and what motivates them is crucial.

One way to maximize the chances for persuasion is to capitalize on the audience's emotional needs. For example, one advertising researcher was able to help the Red Cross collect blood donations from men by analyzing their fears. He thought that men associated loss of blood with weakness and loss of manliness. He suggested that the Red Cross publish ads telling prospective donors how manly they were and offer donors pins

FIGURE 12.7
Audiences change from generation to generation, so the means of persuading them must change, too. Attitudes toward the armed services, for example, have changed markedly since World War II, thus requiring army recruiters to radically alter their approach.

shaped like drops of blood as medals for bravery. The campaign worked: Blood donations from men increased sharply (Dichter, 1964).

The Sleeper Effect

Changes in attitude are not always permanent. In fact, efforts at persuasion usually have their greatest impact immediately and then fade away. However, sometimes more people seem to be persuaded by a message after a period of time has elapsed. This curious *sleeper effect* has been explained in several ways.

One explanation of the delayed action impact depends on the tendency to retain the message but forget the source. As time goes by, a positive source no longer holds power to persuade nor does a negative source undercut the message. When the source is negative and the memory of the source fades, the message then "speaks for itself" and more people may accept it (Kelman and Hovland, 1953).

Perhaps the original message also sensitizes people to subsequent information and events that reinforce the ideas. Repetition is a valuable tool, and the sleeper effect may simply be the result of hearing or reading similar messages from a number of different sources (Middlebrook, 1974).

It may also be that it simply takes time for people to change their minds. As the message "sinks in," attitudes change more. A dramatic example of this was the experiment mentioned earlier in which students who were made aware of inconsistencies in their values concerning civil rights changed their ideas more after fifteen to seventeen months than after three weeks.

The Inoculation Effect

What can you do to resist persuasion? Research has shown that people can be educated to resist attitude change. This technique can be compared to an inoculation (McGuire, 1970). Inoculation against persuasion works in much the same way as inoculation against certain diseases: When a person is vaccinated he or she is given a weakened or dead form of the disease-causing agent, which stimulates his or her body to manufacture defenses. Then, if that person is attacked by a more potent form of the agent, his or her defenses make him or her immune to infection. Similarly, a person who has resisted a mild attack on his or her beliefs is ready to defend himself or herself against an onslaught that might otherwise have overwhelmed him or her.

The inoculation effect can be explained in two ways: It motivates the person to defend his or her beliefs more strongly, and it gives him or her some practice in defending those beliefs. The most vulnerable attitudes you have, therefore, are the ones that you have never had to defend. For example, you might find yourself hard put to defend your faith in democracy or in the healthfulness of beefsteak if you have never had these beliefs questioned.

BRAINWASHING

The most extreme means of changing attitudes involves a combination of psychological gamesmanship and physical torture, aptly called *brainwashing*. Much was made of this technique during the Patty Hearst trials, but exactly what does it involve?

The most extensive studies of brainwashing have been done on Westerners who had been captured by the Chinese during the Korean War and subjected to "thought reform." Psychiatrist Robert Jay Lifton interviewed several dozen prisoners released by the Chinese and, from their accounts, he outlined the methods used to break down people's convictions and introduce new patterns of belief, feeling, and behavior (1963).

The aim in brainwashing is as much to create a new person as to change attitudes. So the first step is to strip away all identity and subject the person to intense social pressure and physical stress. Prison is a perfect setting for this process. The person is isolated from social support, is a number not a name, is clothed like everyone else, and can be systematically surrounded by people who have had their thoughts "reformed" and are contemptuous of "reactionaries." So long as the prisoner holds out, he is treated with contempt or exhorted to confess by his fellow prisoners. He is interrogated past the point of exhaustion by his captors, and is humiliated and discomfited by being bound hand and foot at all times, even during meals or elimination. Any personal information the prisoner uses to justify himself is turned against him as evidence of his guilt.

dehumanize!

At some point, the prisoner realizes that resistance is impossible, the pressures are simply intolerable. Resistance gives way to cooperation, but only as a means of avoiding any more demoralization. The prisoner is rewarded for cooperating. Cooperation involves confessing to crimes against the people in his former way of life.

Throughout the process his cell mates are an integral part of the brainwashing team, berating him at first, then warming to him after his confession. For most of his waking hours, the prisoner is part of a marathon group therapy session built on Marxist ideology. The prisoner is asked not only to interpret his current behavior that way but also to reinterpret his life before capture. Guilt is systematically aroused and defined by Marxist standards. What the prisoner does is to learn a new version of his life, and his confession, provided at first to get some relief from the isolation and pain, becomes more elaborate, coherent, and ideologically based. And with every "improvement" in his attitudes, prison life is made a little more pleasant. Finally, by a combination of threat, peer pressure, systematic rewards, and other psychological means, the prisoner comes to believe his confession. But as one survivor recalled, "it is a special kind of belief . . . you accept it—in order to avoid trouble—because every time you don't agree, trouble starts again" (Lifton, 1963: 31).

These techniques appear to succeed only as long as the person remains a prisoner. Brainwashing seems to be like a magic spell; once the indoctrination stops and the person is in his customary surroundings, the effects wear off.

OBEDIENCE TO AUTHORITY

The influence other people have on your own attitudes and actions is considerable. Sometimes this influence is indirect and subtle, but at other times it is quite direct. Other people may simply tell you what to believe and what to do. Under what conditions do you obey them?

Everyone in this society has had experiences with various authorities, such as parents, teachers, police officers, managers, judges, clergymen, and military officers. Obedience to these authorities can be either useful or destructive. For instance, obeying the orders of a doctor or firefighter in an emergency would be constructive. Psychologists are more interested, however, in the negative aspects of obedience. They know from such cases in history as German Nazism and American atrocities in Vietnam that individuals frequently obey irrational commands. In fact, people often obey authority even when obedience goes against their consciences and their whole system of morality.

Milgram's Experiment

The most famous investigation of obedience was conducted in 1963 by social psychologist Stanley Milgram. The experiment was set up as follows: Two subjects appeared for each session. They were told that they would be participating in an experiment to test the effects of punishment on memory. One of the subjects was to be the "teacher" and the other, the "learner." (In reality, the learner was not a volunteer subject; he was Milgram's accomplice.) The teacher was to read a list of words into a microphone for the learner, who would be in a nearby room, to memorize. If the learner failed to read the list back correctly, the teacher was to administer an electric shock. The alleged purpose of the experiment was to test whether the shock would have any effect on learning. In actuality, however, Milgram wanted to discover how much shock the teacher would be willing to give a fellow human being.

As the experiment began, the learner continually gave wrong answers, and the teacher began to administer the prescribed shocks from an impressive-looking shock generator. The generator had a dial that ranged from 15 volts, which was labeled "Slight Shock," to 450 volts, which was labeled "Danger: Severe Shock." After each of the learner's mistakes, the teacher was supposed to increase the voltage by one level, thus increasing the severity of the shock. The teacher believed that the learner was receiving these shocks because he had seen the learner being strapped into a chair in the other room and had watched electrodes being attached to the learner's hands. In reality, however, the accomplice was receiving no shocks at all from the equipment.

As the experiment progressed, the learner made many mistakes and the shocks became increasingly severe. At 300 volts the learner pounded on the wall in protest and refused to provide any further answers. At this point the experimenter instructed the subject to treat the absence of an answer as a wrong answer and to continue the procedure. The experiment

FIGURE 12.8
Stanley Milgram's experiment on obedience. (a) The fake "shock generator" used by the "teacher." (b) The "learner" is connected to the shock apparatus. (c) Milgram explains the procedure to the "teacher." (d) This subject refuses to shock the "learner" any further and angrily arises in protest. (e) Milgram explains the truth about the experiment.

(©1965 by Stanley Milgram. From the film *Obedience*. Distributed by New York University Film Library.)

ended either when the maximum of 450 volts was administered or when the teacher refused to administer any more shocks.

If at any point the teacher indicated that he wanted to stop, the experimenter calmly told him to continue: "Whether the learner likes it or not," the experimenter asserted, "you must go on until he has learned all the word pairs correctly. So please go on."

Milgram's Results.   The results of the experiment were so startling that Milgram checked with forty psychiatrists in order to get their estimates of what might happen in such an experiment. These experts predicted that most people would not continue beyond the 150-volt level, and that only one in 1,000 would actually give the highest shock. Yet in Milgram's experiments more than half of the forty subjects gave the full shock!

These subjects were not sadists. Many of them showed signs of extreme tension and discomfort during the session, and they often told the experimenter that they would like to stop. But in spite of these feelings, they continued to obey the experimenter's commands. They were ordinary men—salesmen, engineers, postal workers—placed in an unusual situation.

What accounts for this surprisingly high level of obedience? A large part of the answer is that the experimenter represents a legitimate authority. People assume that such an authority knows what he is doing, even when his instructions seem to run counter to their own standards of moral behavior.

Milgram's subjects could have walked out at any time—they had already been paid and had nothing to lose by leaving. Nevertheless, social conditioning for obeying legitimate authorities is so strongly ingrained that people often lack the words or the ways to do otherwise. Simply getting up and leaving would have violated powerful unwritten rules of acceptable social behavior.

Subsequent experiments showed that there were three ways in which subjects could be helped to act more bravely in this situation. One was the removal of the physical presence of the experimenter. Even more effective was putting the subject face to face with his victim. The third and most effective variation of the experiment was to provide other "teachers" to support the subject's defiance of the experimenter (Milgram, 1964).

ATTITUDES AND ACTIONS

Social psychologists have discovered several interesting relationships between a person's attitudes and his actions. Obviously, your attitudes affect your actions: If you like Fords, you will buy a Ford. Some of the other relationships are not so obvious.

Doing Is Believing

It turns out, for example, that if you like Fords but buy a Chevrolet for some reason (perhaps you can get a better deal on a Chevy) you will end up liking Fords less. In other words, actions affect attitudes.

In many instances, if you act and speak as though you have certain beliefs and feelings, you may begin to *really* feel and believe this way. For example, prisoners accused of a crime have, under pressure of police interrogation, confessed to crimes they did not commit. They have confessed in order to relieve the pressure, but having said that they did the deed, they begin to believe that they really *are* guilty.

One explanation for this phenomenon comes from the theory of cognitive dissonance, discussed earlier in this chapter. If a person acts one way but thinks another, he or she will experience dissonance. To reduce the dissonance the person will have to change either the behavior or the attitude. A similar explanation is that people have a need for *self-justification*—a need to justify their behavior.

In an experiment that demonstrated these principles, subjects were paid either $1.00 or $20.00 to tell another person that a boring experiment in which they both had to participate was really a lot of fun. Afterward, the experimenters asked the subjects how they felt about the experiment. They found that the subjects who had been paid $20.00 to lie about the experiment continued to believe that it had been boring. Those who had been paid $1.00, however, came to believe that the experiment had actually been fairly enjoyable. These people had less reason to tell the lie, so they experienced more dissonance when they did so. To justify their lie, they had to believe that they had actually enjoyed the experiment (Festinger and Carlsmith, 1959).

The phenomenon of self-justification has serious implications. For example, how would you justify to yourself the fact that you had intentionally injured another human being? In another psychological experiment, subjects were led to believe that they had injured or hurt other subjects in some way (Glass, 1964). The aggressors were then asked how they felt about the victims they had just harmed. It was found that the aggressors had convinced themselves that they did not like the victim of their cruelty. In other words, the aggressors talked themselves into believing that their defenseless victims had deserved their injury. The aggressors also considered their victims to be less attractive after the experiment than before—their self-justification for hurting another person was something like, "Oh well, this person doesn't amount to much, anyway."

It is this type of self-justification that allows men to go to a country they have never before visited and kill other people they have never before seen. Without self-justification, armies of men would undoubtedly go crazy from guilt—and some war veterans return seriously disturbed for just this reason.

FIGURE 12.9
In communities throughout the People's Republic of China, small discussion groups meet daily to read the thoughts of Chairman Mao Tse-tung. During these sessions, one person is assigned the role of "devil's advocate," which means he or she argues against Mao's statements while others defend them. This exercise strengthens the pro-Mao attitudes of all participants, because it promotes the process of internalization and produces the inoculation effect. The attitudes of the person playing "devil's advocate" are not threatened by his or her acting in opposition to them because he or she is playing a role that everyone expects of him or her.

Self-fulfilling Prophecy

Another relationship between attitudes and actions is rather subtle—but extremely pervasive. It is possible, it seems, for a person to act in such a way as to make his or her attitudes come true. This phenomenon is called *self-fulfilling prophecy*. Suppose, for example, you are convinced that you are a bad cook. Every time you go into the kitchen, you start thinking poorly of yourself. Because you approach the task of baking a cake with great anxiety, you fumble the measurements, pour in too much milk, leave out an ingredient, and so on, and as a result, your cake is a flop. You thus confirm that you *are* a bad cook.

Self-fulfilling prophecies can influence all kinds of human activity. Suppose you believe that people are basically friendly and generous. Whenever you approach other people, you are friendly and open. Because of your smile and positive attitude toward yourself and the world, people like you. Thus your attitude that people are friendly produces your friendly behavior, which in turn causes people to respond favorably toward you. But suppose you turn this example around. Imagine that you believe people are selfish and cold. Because of your negative attitude, you tend to avert your eyes from other people, to act gloomy, and to appear rather unfriendly. People think your actions are strange and, consequently, they act coldly toward you. Thus your attitude has produced the kind of behavior that makes the attitude come true.

Personal Applications

The psychological findings related to self-justification and self-fulfilling prophecy show that there is truth in the saying "Life is what you make it." What you do affects you directly, and it affects the way the world acts toward you. The fact that all people tend to justify their actions by changing their attitudes has several practical consequences. If you give in to pressure and act against your better judgment, you will be undermining your own beliefs. The next time you are in a similar situation, you will find it even harder to stand up for what you believe in because you will have begun to wonder whether you believe it yourself. If you want to strengthen your convictions about something, it is a good idea

"*I will not give in because I oppose it—I do—not my pride, not my spleen, nor any other of my appetites but I do—I!*"

FIGURE 12.10
Sir Thomas More, a respected statesman and lord chancellor of England, defied his friend King Henry VIII and refused to agree to Parliament's Act of Supremacy. This act had given Henry control of the Church of England (so that he could divorce his first wife). More's refusal, based on his determination to be true to his principles, cost him his job, his freedom, and finally his life. These lines are from the play *A Man for All Seasons,* based on More's life.

(From Robert Bolt, *A Man for All Seasons.* In *The New Theater of Europe,* edited by Robert Corrigan. New York: Dell, 1962, p. 111.)

to speak and act on your beliefs at every opportunity. If you do make a mistake and act against your beliefs, you should admit that you are wrong and not try to justify yourself.

The phenomenon of self-fulfilling prophecy shows that the way the world seems to you may be a result of your own actions. Other people, who act differently, will have different experiences and produce different effects. When you find the world unsatisfactory, remember that to some extent, you are creating it. When you find the world a joyful place, remember, too, that it is making you happy partly because you believe that it can.

SUMMARY

1. An attitude is an enduring set of beliefs, feelings, and tendencies to act toward people or things in predisposed ways. Culture, parents, and peers—as well as personal experience—shape a person's attitudes.

2. The processes involved in attitude formation include: compliance (acting as though one has a certain attitude in order to avoid discomfort or rejection and win approval); identification (the adoption of new attitudes as a result of a strong, emotional attachment to another person

or group); and internalization (the incorporation of attitudes into a person's entire belief system).

3. A person's readiness to change his or her mind depends in part on personality. People who need social approval and have little confidence in their own judgment are easily susceptible to persuasion. People whose identities are based on their attitudes are highly resistant to change.

4. Prejudice is judging people on the basis of

stereotypes. Prejudice seems to have a number of causes, and it is perpetuated by social institutions. Discrimination is the unequal treatment of people.

5. People have a need for cognitive consistency—that is, a need to fit their attitudes together into a nonconflicting set of beliefs. People who simultaneously hold two or more opposing attitudes experience cognitive dissonance. In order to reduce dissonance, one or more of the attitudes must change.

6. Persuasion is a direct attempt to change attitudes and behavior through the process of communication. Types of persuasion include: advertising, public relations, and propaganda.

7. Four components of the communication process are the source, the message, the channel, and the audience. For attitude change to occur, the source must be trustworthy and sincere, the message should combine fact and emotional arousal, the channel should be appropriate to the message, and the audience must be receptive.

8. The effects of persuasion are usually short-lived. However, a "sleeper effect," in which attitudes change more as time passes, can occur.

9. People can be educated to resist persuasion by hearing a mild attack on their beliefs. This spurs them to defend their attitudes more strongly and gives them practice in their defense. The inoculation effect helps resist stronger attacks on their beliefs that may follow.

10. The most extreme means of attitude change is called brainwashing. First, identity is crushed and the will to resist is broken. Then intensive indoctrination is combined with rewards for compliance. New attitudes are drilled into the subject. The effects seem to diminish once the prisoner returns to his former life.

11. One of the strongest ways in which social influence is exerted is through authority. Milgram's experiment showed that social conditioning produces such a strong tendency toward obeying legitimate authorities that people may easily be induced to do harm to others against their consciences or better judgment.

12. People's actions affect their attitudes. People often justify actions that go against their beliefs by changing their beliefs. Self-fulfilling prophecy is the phenomenon of acting in such a way as to make one's attitudes come true.

GLOSSARY

attitudes: Predispositions to act, think, and feel in particular ways toward particular things.

audience: In the communication process, the person or persons receiving a message.

authoritarian personality: A personality type characterized by rigid thinking; denial and projection of sexual and aggressive drives onto others; respect for and submission to authority; prejudice regarding people unlike himself—or herself.

boomerang effect: A change in attitude or behavior opposite to the one desired by the persuader.

brainwashing: The most extreme form of attitude change, accomplished through peer pressure, physical suffering, threats, rewards for compliance, manipulation of guilt, intensive indoctrination, and other psychological means.

channel: In the communication process, the means by which a message is transmitted from the source to the audience.

cognitive dissonance: The uncomfortable feeling that arises when a person experiences contradictory or conflicting thoughts, attitudes, beliefs, or feelings.

compliance: A change of behavior in order to avoid discomfort or rejection and gain approval; a superficial form of attitude change.

discrimination: The unequal treatment of individuals on the basis of their race, ethnic group, class, sex, or membership in another category, rather than on the basis of individual characteristics.

identification: The process of seeing oneself as similar to another person or group, and accepting the attitudes of another person or group as one's own.

inoculation effect: A method of developing resistance to persuasion by exposing a person to arguments that challenge his or her beliefs so that he or she can practice defending them.

internalization: The wholehearted acceptance of an attitude because of its consistency with an individual's basic beliefs, values, and self-image; the most enduring form of attitude change.

message: In the communication process, the actual content transmitted from the source to the audience.

obedience: A change in attitude or behavior brought about by social pressure to comply with people perceived to be authorities.

persuasion: The direct attempt to influence attitudes through the communication process.

prejudice: Preconceived attitudes toward a person or group that have been formed without sufficient evidence and are not easily changed.

propaganda: Persuasion designed to help or hinder some cause or group.

public relations: Actions, usually hidden from view, taken to create favorable attitudes towards an individual, group, or cause.

self-fulfilling prophecy: A belief, prediction, or expectation that operates to bring about its own fulfillment. (Also discussed in the Appendix.)

self-justification: The need to rationalize one's attitudes and behavior.

sleeper effect: The delayed impact on attitude change of a persuasive communication.

source: In the communication process, the person or group from which a message originates.

ACTIVITIES

1. Collect magazine ads of ten different brands of cigarettes. Using a scale of 0–10, have subjects rate the cigarettes as being weak or strong—0 being the weakest and 10 being the strongest. Have different subjects rate the same brands on the same scale for masculinity or femininity—0 being the most feminine and 10 being the most masculine. Now average your scores. What conclusions can you draw from your results? (From Sol Gordon, *Psychology and You*, New York: Oxford Book Company, 1972, p. 452.)

2. Collect samples of advertising that depict various techniques of persuasion—identification, social approval, fear of disaster, and so on. Analyze each ad on the basis of effectiveness and what type of person it might appeal to.

3. Do researchers have the right to fool their subjects, even in the name of science? Consider, for example, the effects on Milgram's subjects of believing they had harmed a fellow subject by obliging the order of a stranger. Do you think this experiment was valuable for allowing the subjects to realize the extent of their conformity? If you answered the first question no, and the second, yes, how would you reconcile these two conflicting attitudes?

4. Choose some issue on which you have a strong opinion. If you were given an unlimited budget, how would you go about persuading people to agree with you? Describe the sources you would employ, the channels you would use, the content of your message, and the audience you would try to reach.

5. To what extent does advertising influence

the foods you like? Find several people who prefer butter to margarine. Ask them why they prefer butter. If they say it tastes better, then ask them to participate in an experiment to test their claims. Get several brands of both butter and margarine and spread them lightly on the same kind of crackers or toast. Blindfold your subjects and provide them with a glass of water to rinse their mouths whenever they wish. Ask them to identify the samples. Run through the series about four times, varying the order of presentation. Try similar experiments with people who prefer certain brands of milk, cola, or coffee.

6. Try this experiment to test the effects of self-fulfilling prophecy. Approach someone you vaguely dislike and whom you generally ignore and ask him or her to eat lunch with you, to go to the library, or to do some other socially oriented activity. Make a conscientious effort to get to know the person and see if your attitude of dislike is really justified or if the person's behavior was a function of the way you previously responded to him or her.

7. One of the primary objectives of advertising is to get the viewers/listeners to remember the product. To what extent do you think familiarity with brand names influences your choices in the market? How many television commercials do you find obnoxious? Do you find that you remember the products advertised in "obnoxious" commercials better than you remember products that appear in less offensive advertisements? Do you think there is a possibility that some commercials are deliberately offensive?

8. If any of your attitudes have recently changed, try to pinpoint what made you change your mind. What were the external factors, such as communications, involved? How were the other attitudes you already held involved?

9. Choose a controversial topic, such as abortion, drug abuse, or women's rights, and devise ten questions to measure people's attitudes toward this issue. Give the questionnaire to a number of different people and see whether your results make sense in terms of what you already know about these people. (Psychologists are greatly concerned with devising questionnaires that really tell something about how people tend to act.)

10. Clip editorials from different newspapers or magazines that take opposite sides on an issue. Compare the attitudes expressed and the methods of persuasion used by the different editorial writers.

SUGGESTED READINGS

BEM, DARYL J. *Beliefs, Attitudes and Human Affairs*. Belmont, Calif.: Brooks/Cole, 1970. A well-written and enjoyable book on attitudes and their social implications.

DELLA FEMINA, JERRY. *From Those Wonderful Folks Who Gave You Pearl Harbor*. New York: Simon & Schuster, 1970. A hilarious and insightful look at the world of advertising agencies through the eyes of a creative man with plenty of firsthand experience.

HELLER, JOSEPH. *Catch-22*. New York: Dell, 1961 (paper). One of the saddest and funniest novels ever written about war. But more than that a commentary about social influence—the factors that lead people into double binds, self-fulfilling prophecies, and unwilling obedience.

LIFTON, ROBERT JAY. *Home from the War*. New York: Simon & Schuster, 1973. An interesting account of how veterans of the Vietnam War have had to use self-justification for their wartime actions. Lifton points out that self-justification leads to new and different political consciousness not felt by the men before their overseas experiences.

MCGINNISS, JOE. *The Selling of the President, 1968.* New York: Pocket Books, 1970 (paper). This book shows how advertising people manufacture, package, and market their most lucrative product: the president of the United States. The book is fascinating, frightening, and essential reading for anyone interested in the psychology of advertising and in the ways the public can be manipulated.

ORWELL, GEORGE. *Nineteen Eighty-Four.* New York: Harcourt Brace Jovanovich, 1949. A frightening novel that takes a close look at a future in which attitudes are dictated by a totalitarian government from which there is little hope (or thought) of escape.

ROKEACH, MILTON. "Persuasion that Persists." *Psychology Today,* 5 (September 1971): 68–71. In the experiment reported in this article, subjects were shown that their attitudes toward freedom and equality were somewhat inconsistent; this demonstration by itself greatly changed their attitudes toward certain civil-rights issues. The change persisted for some time, and Rokeach analyzes why.

SHIRER, WILLIAM L. *The Rise and Fall of the Third Reich.* New York: Simon & Schuster, 1960 (paper). A fully detailed and documented account of the dynamics that created and destroyed the most evilly totalitarian political regime in modern history: Nazi Germany. A classic study of propaganda, obedience, and conformity.

VARELA, JACOBO. *Psychological Solutions to Social Problems.* New York: Academic Press, 1971. This book is practically a manual on how to persuade people. It includes a chapter on how to go about correcting social ills.

ZIMBARDO, P. G., AND EBBESEN, E. B. *Influencing Attitudes and Changing Behavior.* Reading, Mass.: Addison-Wesley, 1969. A short introduction to methodology, experimentation, and theory in the field of attitude change. Designed for readers without extensive background.

BIBLIOGRAPHY

ADORNO, T. W., ET AL. *The Authoritarian Personality.* New York: Norton, 1969 (paper).

ALLPORT, GORDON. *The Nature of Prejudice.* Garden City, N.Y.: Doubleday, 1954 (paper).

ARONSON, E., TURNER, J., AND CARLSMITH, M. "Communicator Credibility and Communicator Discrepancy as Determinants of Opinion Change." *Journal of Abnormal and Social Psychology,* 67 (1963): 31–36.

ASCH, SOLOMON. "Effects of Group Pressure upon the Modification and Distortion of Judgments." In *Basic Studies in Social Psychology,* edited by J. Proshansky and B. Seidenberg. New York: Holt, Rinehart and Winston, 1965, pp. 393–401.

BEM, DARYL J. *Beliefs, Attitudes and Human Affairs.* Belmont, Calif.: Brooks/Cole, 1970.

COALE, A. J. "The Demographic Transition Reconsidered." In *International Population Conference,* Liege, 1973.

COHEN, A. R. *Attitude Change and Social Influence.* New York: Basic Books, 1964.

DICHTER, ERNEST. *Handbook of Consumer Motivations.* New York: McGraw-Hill, 1964.

ELDERSVELD, S., AND DODGE, R. "Personal Contact or Mail Propaganda? An Experiment in Voting Turnout and Attitude Change." In *Public Opinion and Propaganda,* edited by D. Katz et al. New York: Dryden Press, 1954, pp. 532–542.

FESTINGER, LEON. *A Theory of Cognitive Dissonance.* Stanford, Calif.: Stanford University Press, 1957.

FESTINGER, L., AND CARLSMITH, J. M. "Cognitive Consequences of Forced Compliance." *Journal of Abnormal and Social Psychology,* 58 (1959): 203–210.

FLACK, R. "The Liberated Generation: An Exploration of the Roots of Student Protest." *Journal of Social Issues*, 23 (1967): 52–57.

GLASS, D. C. "Changes in Liking as a Means of Reducing Cognitive Discrepancies between Self-esteem and Aggression." *Journal of Personality*, 32 (1964): 531–549.

GOLDSEN, R., ET AL. *What College Students Think*. Princeton, N.J.: Van Nostrand, 1960.

HESS, R., AND TORNEY, J. *The Development of Political Attitudes in Children*. Chicago: Aldine, 1967.

HOLBORN, HAJO. *A History of Modern Germany 1850–1945*. New York: Knopf, 1969.

HOVLAND, C., LUMSDAINE, A., AND SHEFFIELD, F. *Experiments on Mass Communication*. Princeton, N.J.: Princeton University Press, 1949.

JENNINGS, M., AND NIEMI, R. "The Transmission of Political Values from Parent to Child." *American Political Science Review*, 62 (1968): 169–184.

KELMAN, HERBERT C. "Processes of Opinion Change." *Public Opinion Quarterly*, 21 (1961): 57–78.

KELMAN, H. C., AND HOVLAND, C. I. "'Reinstatement' of the Communicator in Delayed Measurement of Opinion Change." *Journal of Abnormal and Social Psychology*, 48 (1953): 327–335.

KLAPPER, J. T. *The Effects of Mass Communications*. New York: Free Press, 1960.

LEE, ALFRED M., AND LEE, ELIZABETH. *The Fine Art of Propaganda*. New York: Farrar, Straus, 1939.

LIFTON, ROBERT JAY. *Thought Reform and the Psychology of Totalism: A Study of "Brainwashing" in China*. New York: Norton, 1963 (paper).

——. *Home from the War*. New York: Simon & Schuster, 1973.

MCGUIRE, W. J. "A Vaccine for Brainwash." *Psychology Today*, 3 (February 1970): 36–39, 62–64.

MCGINNISS, JOE. *The Selling of the President 1968*. New York: Pocket Books, 1970 (paper).

MACE, D., AND MACE, V. *Marriage: East and West*. New York: Doubleday, 1960.

MIDDLEBROOK, PATRICIA NILES. *Social Psychology and Modern Life*. New York: Knopf, 1974.

MILGRAM, STANLEY. *Obedience to Authority*. New York: Harper & Row, 1964.

NESBITT, P. "The Effectiveness of Student Canvassers." *Journal of Applied Psychology*, 2 (1972): 252–258.

NEWCOMB, T. *Personality and Social Change*. New York: Dryden Press, 1943.

NEWCOMB, T., ET AL. *Persistence and Change: Bennington College and Its Students after 25 Years*. New York: Wiley, 1967.

REISMAN, D., GLAZER, N., AND DENNEY, R. *The Lonely Crowd*. New Haven, Conn.: Yale University Press, 1953 (paper).

ROKEACH, M. "Long-range Experimental Modification of Values, Attitudes, and Behavior." *American Psychologist*, 26 (1971): 453–459.

ZIMBARDO, P. G., AND EBBESEN, E. B. *Influencing Attitudes and Changing Behavior*. Reading, Mass.: Addison-Wesley, 1969.

UNIT V

Personality and Emotional Life

There are billions of people in this world, and each one is unique. Each individual has not only a unique appearance and genetic endowment, but also a personal way of dealing with the world, of viewing other people, and of viewing him- or herself. You may have noticed that the other Units in this book have for the most part ignored this individuality in order to explore the ways people are alike—in physiological functioning, in mental processes, in growth and development, and in interacting with one another. This Unit, however, focuses on the ways in which people are different—and why.

Chapter 13 presents the theories of several psychologists who have tried to explain why individuals are different from one another. These theorists have addressed such questions as: How is character formed? To what extent can a person know himself? What determines a person's actions? How can a person be happy? Chapter 14 explains the way "normal" or "healthy" individuals adjust to college; to love, marriage, and divorce; to work; to everyday frustrations; and to such natural and man-made problems as tornadoes, war, poverty, and rapid social change. Chapter 15 discusses the problem of people who are so different from everyone else that they are considered abnormal. Such people are often painfully unhappy and are sometimes unable to handle the simplest tasks of everyday life. Chapter 16 focuses on the ways in which such people can be helped to achieve better contact with reality, with others, and with themselves.

13 Personality Theories

FIGURE 13.1
Hippocrates (460–360 B.C.) explained personality in terms of four humors (body fluids): too much black bile produced a melancholic personality (*top left*); a lively or sanguine person had an excess of blood (*top right*); sluggishness resulted from too much phlegm (*bottom left*); and excess yellow bile made a person irritable and aggressive (*bottom right*).

Try to remember the last time you described a friend to someone who had never met her. You may have begun with a few facts—her age, what she looks like, where she lives, what school she attends, how you met her, and so on. Then perhaps you began describing her talents, her likes and dislikes, how she relates to people and reacts to different situations, her moods and quirks. If you knew the person well, you probably found yourself getting caught in contradictions: Susan seems bossy, *but* she's really very shy underneath; Ralph may seem a little dull, *but* wait till you get to know him. Trying to describe and explain yourself is even more difficult—as you know if you've ever had to write an autobiography for a college or job application. Our point, of course, is that human beings are anything but simple.

Speaking loosely, there is something inside people that makes them think, feel, and act differently. And that "something inside" is what we mean by personality. It accounts for both the differences among people and for the consistencies in an individual's behavior over time and in different situations. We use the word "personality" to mean all the things that make a person who they are.

A theory of personality is an attempt to explain human nature, in all its complexity and contradictions. The psychologists and psychiatrists whose insights we will be describing based their theories on what they learned from their own lives; from the patients whose emotional difficulties they helped to ease; and from literature, philosophy, science, and the theories of other psychologists. Directly and indirectly, these theorists have changed the way we think about ourselves.

WHAT PERSONALITY THEORIES TRY TO DO

You might assume that a theory of personality is little more than one person's philosophy of life and speculations about human nature. In fact, personality theories serve a number of very practical functions.

First, personality theories provide a way of organizing the many facts that you know about yourself and other people. You know people may be outgoing or shy, bossy or meek, quick-tempered or calm, witty or dull, fun-loving or gloomy, responsible or lazy.

All these words describe *personality traits,* or general ways of behaving that characterize an individual. Personality theorists try to determine whether certain traits go together and why; why a person has some traits and not others; and why a person might exhibit different traits in different situations. There is a good deal of disagreement among theorists as to which traits are significant, and whether personality traits are stable over time or represent the individual's response to specific circumstances. Nevertheless, all theorists share one common goal: to discover patterns in the ways people behave.

A second purpose of any personality theory is to explain the differences between individuals. In so doing, theorists probe beneath the surface. Suppose a man you know is humble to the point of being self-effacing. When the conversation turns to him, he seems downright embarrassed. He is much happier bustling about, making people comfortable, and asking about their lives than he is talking about himself. A woman you know is just the opposite. She enjoys nothing better than talking about the work she is doing, the people she's met, her plans for the future. When she asks about your life you suspect it's either because she's being polite or because you might be useful to her. You explain their different behaviors in terms of motives: The man's primary goal in life is to please other people; the woman is extremely ambitious. But these explanations are little more than descriptions. How did these two individuals come to have different motives in the first place? A personality theorist might suggest that the man had parents who discouraged any aggressive behavior while the woman's parents encouraged achievement and aggressive behavior.

A third goal of personality theory is to explore how people conduct their lives. It is no accident that most personality theorists began as psychotherapists, attempting to help people overcome emotional problems. In working with people who experienced considerable psychological pain and had difficulty coping with the everyday problems of life, they inevitably developed ideas about what it takes to live a relatively happy, untroubled life. Personality theorists try to explain why such problems arise, and why they are more difficult for some people to manage than for others.

In addition, personality theorists are concerned with determining how life can be improved. It seems obvious that many people are dissatisfied with themselves, their parents, their husbands or wives and children, their home lives. People resign themselves to unrewarding jobs, and there is a widespread feeling that much is wrong with our society and our world. Almost everyone recognizes that we need to grow and change, individually and collectively. But what are the proper goals of growth and change? How can these goals be achieved?

Personality theorists attempt to answer these questions. Each of the theorists we will discuss has a slightly different image of human nature and therefore a different idea of what constitutes improvement. What they have in common is a concern with the quality of life.

SIGMUND FREUD: PSYCHOSEXUALITY AND THE UNCONSCIOUS

Charming, spacious, homelike 1 rm. apts. Modern kitchenette. Hotel service. Weekly rats available.
—from classified advertisement, *The New York Times*

This advertisement was received and typeset by someone at the *Times*. The person who set the ad probably did not leave the "e" out deliberately, but was it just an innocent mistake?

Slips like these are common. People usually laugh at them, even if they are meaningful. But sometimes they are disturbing. Everyone has had the experience of making some personal remark that hurt a friend and has later asked himself, "Why did I say that? I didn't mean it." Yet, when he thinks about it, he may realize that he was angry at his friend and wanted to "get back" at him.

It was Sigmund Freud who recognized that the little slips that people make, the things they mishear, and the odd misunderstandings they have are not really mistakes at all. Freud believed that there was something behind these mistakes, even though people claimed they were just accidental and quickly corrected themselves. Similarly, when he listened to people describe their dreams, he believed that the dreams had some meaning, even though the people who dreamed them could not determine what they meant.

Freud was a physician who practiced in Vienna, Austria, in the early 1900s. As a doctor who specialized in nervous diseases, a great many people talked to him about their private lives, revealing their conflicts, fears, and desires. At that time most people thought, as many people still do, that we are aware of all our motives and feelings. But Freud reasoned that if people can say and dream things without knowing their meaning, they must not know as much about themselves as they think they do. After years of study he concluded that some of the most powerful influences on human personality are things about which we are *not* conscious.

Freud was the first to suggest that every personality has a large *unconscious* component. Life includes both pleasurable and painful experiences. For Freud, experiences include feelings and thoughts as well as actual events. Freud believed that many of our experiences, particularly the painful episodes of childhood, are forgotten or buried in the unconscious. But although we may not consciously recall these experiences, they continue to influence our behavior. For example, a child who never fully pleases his demanding mother or father may feel unhappy much of the time and will doubt his abilities to succeed and to be loved. As an adult, the person may suffer from feelings of unworthiness and low self-esteem, despite his very real abilities. Freud believed that unconscious motives and the feelings people experience as children have an enormous impact on adult personality and behavior.

FIGURE 13.2
Sigmund Freud was nearly forty when he began to formulate the psychoanalytic theories that made him famous. Before that time, he was a medical researcher and practitioner. Then, in the years between 1894 and 1900, he experienced what one writer has called a "creative illness" in which he analyzed his own psychological disturbances and emerged with the basic elements of his theory and a transformed personality. During these years, he wrote his most extraordinary book, *The Interpretation of Dreams*.

The Id, Ego, and Superego

Freud tried to explain human personality by saying that it was a kind of energy system—like a steam engine, or an electric dynamo. The energy in human personality comes from two kinds of powerful drives, the life drives and the death drives. Freud theorized that all of life moves toward death, and that the desire for a final end shows up in human personality as destructiveness and aggression. The life instincts were more important in Freud's theory, however. He saw them primarily as *erotic* or pleasure-seeking urges.

By 1923 Freud had described what became known as the structural components of the mind. These included the *id, ego,* and *superego.* Though Freud often spoke of them as if they were actual parts of the personality, he introduced and regarded them simply as a *model* of how the mind works. In other words, the id, ego, and the superego do not refer to actual portions of the brain. Instead, they explain how the mind functions and how the instinctual energies are regulated.

In Freud's theory the *id* is the reservoir or container of the instinctual urges. It is the lustful or drive-ridden part of the unconscious. The id seeks immediate gratification of desires, regardless of the consequences.

The personality process that is mostly conscious is called the *ego.* The ego is the rational, thoughtful, realistic personality process. For example, if a person is hungry, the id might drive her to seek immediate satisfaction by dreaming of food or by eating all the available food at once instead of keeping some of it for a later time. The ego is the part of the person that would recognize that the body needs real food and that it will continue to need food in the future; it would use the id's energy to preserve some of the food available now and to look for ways of finding more.

Suppose that the ego thought of stealing the desired food from someone else. The part of the personality that would stop the person from stealing is called the *superego.* The id is concerned with what the person *wants* to do and the ego is concerned with what she *can* do; the superego is concerned with what the person *should* do. It is the moral part of personality, the source of conscience and of high ideals. But the superego also can create conflicts and problems. It is sometimes overly harsh, like a very strict parent. The superego, then, is also the source of guilt feelings which arise from serious as well as from the most mild transgressions from what it defines as "right."

The id and the superego frequently come into conflict with each other, and because neither of them is concerned with reality, they may both come into conflict with the necessities of the outside world as well. Freud saw the ego as part of the person that must resolve these conflicts. Somehow, the ego must find a realistic way to satisfy the demands of the id without offending the superego. If the id is not satisfied, the person feels an intolerable tension of longing or anger or desire. If the superego is not obeyed, the person feels guilty and inferior. And if outside reality is ignored, the person suffers such results as starvation or dislike by other people (Freud, 1943).

Defense Mechanisms

The ego's job is so difficult that unconsciously all people resort to a kind of psychological "cheating." Rather than face intense frustration, conflict, or feelings of unworthiness, people deceive themselves into believing that nothing is wrong. Freud called these techniques *defense mechanisms* because they defend the ego from experiencing anxiety about failing in its tasks. Freud felt that these defense mechanisms stem mainly from the unconscious part of the ego, and only become conscious to the individual during psychoanalysis.

To some degree, defense mechanisms are necessary to psychological well-being. They relieve intolerable confusion, help people to weather intense emotional crises, and give individuals time to work out problems they might not be able to solve if they allowed themselves to feel all the pressures at work within them. However, if a person resorts to defense mechanisms all or most of the time, continually lying to himself and others about his true feelings and aspirations, he will avoid facing and solving his problems realistically. A few of the defense mechanisms Freud identified are discussed below.

Displacement.   Displacement occurs when the object of an unconscious wish provokes anxiety. The ego reduces this anxiety by unconsciously shifting to another object. It *displaces* the energy of the id from one object to another, more accessible, object. For example, if you were to hit your kid brother when you really wanted to hit your father, that would be a displacement. Similarly, a husband and father may displace his anger toward his wife onto his child.

Repression.   When a person has some thought or urge that causes the ego too much anxiety, she may push that thought or urge out of consciousness down into the unconscious. This process is called *repression*. The person simply "forgets" the thing that disturbs her. For example, a person who has the impulse to tell a parent or child, "I hate you" may feel so afraid and anxious about having such an impulse that she convinces herself—without realizing what she is doing—that what she feels is not hatred. She replaces the feeling with apathy, a feeling of not caring at all. She says, "I don't hate you. I have no special feelings at all about you." Nevertheless, the feelings of anger and hostility remain in the unconscious and may show themselves in cutting remarks or sarcastic jokes, slips of the tongue, or dreams.

Reaction Formation.   *Reaction formation* involves replacing an unacceptable feeling or urge with its opposite. For example, a divorced father may resent having his child for the weekend. Unconsciously, he feels it is terribly wrong for a father to react that way, so he showers the child with expressions of love, toys, and exciting trips. A woman who finds her powerful ambitions unacceptable may play the role of a weak, helpless, passive female who wants nothing more than to please the men in her life—unconsciously covering up her true feelings.

Projection.   Another trick the ego uses to avoid anxiety is to pretend that impulses coming from within are really coming from other people. For example, a boy who is extremely jealous of his girlfriend but does not want to admit to himself that he is threatened by her independence may claim, "I'm not jealous—she's the one who's always asking where I've been, who was that girl I was talking to. . . ." This mechanism is called *projection* because inner feelings are thrown, or projected, outside. It is a common mechanism, which you have probably observed in yourself from time to time. Many people, for example, feel that others dislike them, when in reality they dislike themselves.

FIGURE 13.3
Some of the defense mechanisms in Freud's theory of personality. Projection is shown by a person seeing ridiculous attributes of his own personality as though they were possessed by others. Repression, which is the unconscious burying of anxiety-causing impulses, is shown by a woman who is not only concealing and restraining a monstrous impulse but also trying to conceal from herself the fact that she is doing so. The displacement of a widow's love from her lost husband and family onto her pets is shown here.

Regression.   *Regression* means going back to an earlier and less mature pattern. When a person is under severe pressure and his other defenses are not working, he may start acting in ways that helped him in the past. For example, he may throw a temper tantrum, make faces, cry loudly, or revert to eating and sleeping all the time the way he did as a small child. If you have ever been tempted to stick out your lower lip and pout when you know that you should really accept the fact that you cannot have your own way, you have experienced regression.

Rationalization.   *Rationalization* refers to an attempt by the ego to make an undesirable action, feeling, or thought acceptable by providing a logical or "reasonable" explanation as its motive. For example, a student might think of all the many events which kept her from studying for a test on which she received a poor grade. Rationalization can be easily identified by the strength with which the arguments are presented.

The recognition of the tremendous forces that exist in human personality and the difficulty of controlling and handling them was Freud's great contribution to understanding human life. After Freud, it became easier to understand why human life contains so much conflict. It is a matter, Freud thought, of a savage individual coming to terms with the rules of society. The id is the savage part, and the superego, the representative of society. In a healthy person the ego, the "I," is strong enough to handle the struggle (see Hall, 1954).

CARL JUNG: ARCHETYPES AND POLARITIES

> It was like a voyage to the moon, or a descent into empty space. First came the image of a crater, and I had the feeling that I was in the land of the dead. The atmosphere was that of the other world. Near the steep slope of a rock I caught sight of two figures, an old man with a white beard and a beautiful young girl.
> —from Carl Jung, *Memories, Dreams, Reflections* (1963)

FIGURE 13.4
Carl G. Jung was a Swiss psychiatrist who formed a close association with Freud after their first meeting in 1906. Later, they split over several differences in opinion as to the direction that psychoanalytic theory should take, and Jung formed his own school of psychoanalytic thought. One of the most mystical and metaphysical of the pioneer theorists, Jung has had, until recently, a wider acceptance in Europe than in America.

If a patient had related this vision to Freud, he would have tried to help the person "translate" the symbols of unconscious wishes and desires into conscious thoughts. (Perhaps the woman represents his mother, the man his father, and the eerie landscape his anxiety over wishing his father would grow old and die.)

Carl Jung saw things differently. To him, the young woman stood for erotic beauty and the old man for wisdom—two things toward which all people yearn. Although he agreed that unconscious motives influence behavior, Jung believed that Freud placed too much emphasis on personal experiences and psychosexual urges. Eventually, his relationship with Freud ended and Jung developed his own personality theory.

Jung believed there is a *collective unconscious* that contains the instincts, urges, and memories of the entire human species. He called these inherited, universal ideas *archetypes*. The same archetypes are present in every person. They reflect the common experiences of humanity with mothers, fathers, nature, war, and so on.

Jung went on to identify the archetypes by studying dreams and visions, paintings and poetry, folk stories, myths, and religions. He found that the same themes—the "archetypes," in Jung's terminology—appear again and again. For example, the story of Jack and the Beanstalk is essentially the same as the story of David and Goliath. Both tell how a small, weak, good person triumphs over a big, strong, bad person. Jung believed that such stories are common and easy to understand because the situations they describe have occurred over and over again in human history and have been stored as archetypes in the unconscious of every human being.

The Polarities of Personality

The discovery that many traditional stories, such as those mentioned above, portray a conflict between opposites led Jung to conclude that human personality includes many polarities.

One pair of opposites that Jung described was *extroversion* and *intro-*

version. These are two different ways of looking at and experiencing the world. Most people, according to Jung, conform to one of these two psychological types. People who are strongly extroverted look outward to the world of things, people, and objects. They are objective, practical, and sociable. Introverted people tend to look inward. They are oriented toward ideas and feelings.

Jung believed that the aim of psychic life was to bring the opposite parts of the person together into a new whole. An extroverted person wants to become more aware of himself and of his own ideals, and an introverted person wants to become more aware of the outside world and of practical realities.

But most people have not achieved these goals. They are fragmented or broken apart. They concentrate on certain parts of themselves and hide certain others. Jung called the process of bringing out various aspects of one's psychological make-up and integrating them into a whole *individuation*. Individuation is a "journey of the soul" that not everyone makes. It means becoming more and more aware of yourself and understanding what parts of yourself you show to the outside world (which Jung called the *persona*) and what parts you hide even from yourself (the *shadow*, in Jung's terminology) (Jung, 1963).

ALFRED ADLER: THE STRUGGLE FOR MASTERY

Like Jung, Alfred Adler was an associate of Freud who left his teacher in the early part of this century to develop his own approach to personality.

Adler believed that the driving force in people's lives is a desire to overcome their feelings of inferiority. Classic examples are Demosthenes, a famous Greek orator who overcame a speech impediment by practicing speaking with pebbles in his mouth; Napoleon, a short man who became conqueror of Europe in the early 1800s; and Glenn Cunningham, an Olympic runner who lost his toes in a fire as a child and had to plead with doctors who wanted to amputate his legs because they thought he would never use them again.

Everyone struggles with inferiority, said Adler. He describes a person who continually tries to cover up and avoid feelings of inadequacy as having an *inferiority complex* (a term he introduced). Children first feel inferior because they are so little and so dependent on adults. Gradually they learn to do the things that older people can do. The satisfaction that comes from even such simple acts as walking or learning to use a spoon sets up a pattern of overcoming inadequacies, a pattern that lasts throughout life. Adler called these patterns *life styles*.

Adler believed that the way parents treat their children has a great influence on the styles of life they choose. Overpampering, in which the parents attempt to satisfy the child's every whim, tends to produce a self-centered person who has little regard for others and who expects everyone else to do what he or she wants. On the other hand, the child

FIGURE 13.5
Alfred Adler's considerable influence on modern psychological theory is often overlooked by many who feel his contributions were overshadowed by the impact of Freud and Jung. Unlike Freud, who had a gift for writing and who was inspired both by Shakespeare and the Greek playwrights, or Jung, whose inspiration came from mystical and religious studies, Adler was an intensely practical man who did not possess the dynamic personality of either of these two contemporaries. Nevertheless, Adler's writings on psychotherapy offer more optimism and practicality than those of Freud or Jung. Futhermore, his intuitive and commonsense approach to human life has greatly affected the thinking of later psychologists interested in the existential approach (presented later in this chapter).

who is neglected by his or her parents may seek revenge by becoming an angry, hostile person. Both the pampered and the neglected child tend to grow up into adults who have a lack of confidence in their ability to meet the demands of life. Ideally, said Adler, a child should learn self-reliance and courage from his or her father and generosity and a feeling for others from his or her mother.

Adler placed great importance on *social interest,* or a feeling for others. He thought that it is proper and natural for people to feel a responsibility toward others and that no one could be happy unless willingly and actively engaged in improving life for everyone, not just for himself or herself (Adler, 1959).

ERICH FROMM: PEOPLE AND SOCIETY

Erich Fromm, too, emphasizes the relationship between the individual and society in his theory of personality. Like Adler, Fromm minimizes the influence of instincts on behavior and stresses the effect of the social environment, especially the economic system. In a sense, Fromm was the first personality theorist to focus on modern people living in industrialized, capitalist societies.

Freedom

In Fromm's view, personality develops around certain basic needs. People need to be *related*—to feel that they are part of humanity by having friends and loved ones. People need to feel that they belong to a family, to a community, and to a church, for example. We need ideals, beliefs, and purposes that give our lives meaning, that suggest the direction we should take. A person also must have a sense of himself as distinctive and unique. Finally a person needs to rise above all the influences life has on him; he needs to have some control over his life, some power to create new things—he needs to be more than an animal.

Modern society allows people to develop their individuality and to transcend their upbringing in a way that traditional societies, where custom rules, generally do not. However, the price people pay for the freedom to be themselves is a growing sense of isolation. Fromm is speaking of emotional and spiritual isolation; of the loneliness that has nothing to do with the presence or absence of other people.

All children face this problem as they grow up and become independent of their family. But the burden of freedom becomes particularly acute in societies where people are expected to "make it on their own." Although crowded together physically, many people are starved for the feeling that they are connected—to someone, some ideal, some purpose. Nothing is more terrifying in Fromm's view.

He suggests that people cope with freedom in one of two ways: by submitting to authority or conforming; or by spontaneously expressing themselves in love and work.

FIGURE 13.6
Erich Fromm has enriched modern personality theory by combining a psychoanalytic perspective with sociological and existential viewpoints. Fromm has been largely influenced by two men: Freud and Karl Marx. Freud explained human personality in terms of unconscious instincts; Marx explained human history in terms of economic pressures. Fromm believes that both factors should be taken into account in explaining and understanding human personality.

Escape from Freedom

The terrible burden of isolation and loneliness makes many people wish to *escape from freedom*. One way for them to escape is to find someone else to do their worrying. They welcome a government or a ruler or a system that tells them just what to do and that looks after them, even though they lose their freedom and the opportunity to be creative.

Fromm points to the success of Nazism in Germany in the 1930s as an example of a mass escape from freedom. The German people had been living in a society in which selfish striving for personal gain took the place of love, brotherhood, and unity. Hitler took advantage of the fact that the German people were, as a result, desperate for something that would guide them and weld them together. He built a society that was unified and purposeful—but based on hatred and fear instead of love.

Although more subtle, conformity is also an escape from freedom. People abandon their individuality to join the crowd. Such individuals are, in Fromm's view, *nonproductive*. They feel that the source of all good in life is outside themselves; that the only way they can get what they need and want is by receiving, taking, or buying it from other people.

Love and Work

The most mature way to overcome the insecurity that accompanies freedom is not through tyranny or conformity, but through love and work. In this way, one can become a part of humankind and nature again, without losing oneself and one's freedom. Fromm says that many people are confused about what real love and work are. They think that owning a person or being owned by one is love. They think of work as a chance to become a company man or woman (a cog in a great machine), or as a chance to enjoy conquering nature. But real love and real work mean a sensitivity and respect for other people and for nature. The object is to join with another person without losing one's own individuality. One should not need to mold oneself, nature, or the person one loves in order to have relationships. Security lies in feeling that the source of what is good in life lies within oneself. People who feel this way are therefore able to be loving, generous, and giving human beings (Fromm, 1941, 1947). Fromm called such people *productive*. In making this distinction, Fromm helped lay the foundations of a new approach to personality theory.

HUMANISTIC PSYCHOLOGY: ABRAHAM MASLOW AND CARL ROGERS

One might look at humanistic psychology as a rebellion against the rather negative, pessimistic view of human nature that, with Freud's leadership, dominated personality theory in the first part of this century. As we have seen, Freud emphasized the struggle to control primitive, instinctual urges on the one hand, and to come to terms with the authoritarian demands of the superego or conscience on the other. In contrast, the humanists stress our relative freedom from instinctual pressures (compared to other animals) and our ability to create and live by personal standards. Freud believed that, in large degree, human beings are enslaved by unconscious desires and moral rules. The humanists disagree.

Humanistic psychology is founded on the belief that all human beings strive for *self-actualization*—that is, the realization of their potentialities as unique human beings. Self-actualization involves an openness to a wide range of experiences; an awareness of and respect for one's own and other people's uniqueness; accepting the responsibilities of freedom and commitment (as Fromm suggested); a desire to become more and more authentic or true to oneself; and an ability to grow. It requires the courage, in Kipling's words, "to trust yourself when all men doubt you. . . . " Humanists view this striving as a basic human instinct and the essence of human dignity.

Abraham Maslow: Growth and Self-actualization

Abraham Maslow, a pioneer in humanistic psychology, became impatient with the amount of time his colleagues devoted to human misery and shame, conflict and hostility.

Maslow devoted much of his career to describing human needs and defining human potential. He believed that people have two kinds of needs, *deficiency needs* and *growth needs*. Deficiency needs are like holes that must be filled. If they are not filled, you get sick. You must have food, water, and shelter, for example. You must also have protection from disaster. If you do not, you will not survive. In addition, you need to feel that you belong, that you are loved, that you are respected; and you need to be able to respect yourself (as Fromm pointed out, in different words). Maslow believed all these needs are basic; you need love and admiration in the same way that you need vitamins and nutrients. Without them you become stunted or sick.

The other kinds of needs, growth needs, are quite different. They are needs to become more and more yourself. Each person wants to develop the abilities and talents he finds in himself; to fulfill his destiny, his fate, or his calling; to know more and more of himself; and to bring the parts of himself into greater harmony, so that he no longer suffers from self-doubt, inner conflict, or confusion.

Maslow pointed out that it is difficult to work on growth needs if you still have deficiency needs. The more energy a person must devote to obtaining food and shelter, to finding love or building up her self-respect, the less she has to devote to self-actualization (Maslow, 1968, 1970).

A person who is uncovering, expressing, and developing her inner nature, a person who is moved by her need to grow, is in the process of self-actualizing. Self-actualization is not a process that has an end; it is a way of being, of continuously becoming more yourself, more human than you are now. In Chapter 14, "Adjustment," we will discuss more fully what Maslow means by self-actualization.

FIGURE 13.7
Abraham Maslow was deeply interested in the study of human growth, or, in his terms, "self-actualization." The work of Maslow, Rogers, and others has helped to create a humanistic orientation toward the study of human behavior by emphasizing the actualization of an individual's full potentialities.

FIGURE 13.8
A representation of Maslow's view of human life as beginning humbly but growing magnificently. Maslow was deeply interested in the ability and need of all human beings to grow toward greater creativity, greater wisdom, and greater devotion to beauty and goodness.

Carl Rogers: Your Organism and Yourself

The people Carl Rogers counsels are "clients," not "patients." The word "patient" implies illness, a negative label that Rogers rejects. As a therapist, Rogers is primarily concerned with the roadblocks and detours on the path to self-actualization (or full functioning, as he calls it). Rogers believes that many people suffer from a conflict between what they value in themselves and what they learn other people value in them. He explains how this conflict develops, as follows.

There are two sides or parts to every person. One is the *organism*, which is the whole of a person, including his or her body. Rogers believes that the organism is constantly struggling to become more and more complete and perfect. Anything that furthers this end is good. The organism wants to become everything that it can possibly be. For example, children want to learn to walk and run because their bodies are built for these activities. People want to shout and dance and sing because their organisms contain the potential for these behaviors. Different people have different potentialities, but every person wants to realize them, to make them real, whatever they are. It is of no value to be able to paint and not to do it. It is of no value to be able to make witty jokes and not to do so. Whatever you can do, you want to do—and to do as well as possible. (This optimism about human nature is the essence of humanism.)

Each individual also has what Rogers calls a *self*. The self is essentially your image of who you are and what you value—in yourself, in other people, in life in general. The self is something you acquire gradually over the years by observing how other people react to you. At first, the most significant other person in your life is your mother (or whoever raises you). You want her approval or *positive regard*. You ask yourself, "How does she see me?" If the answer is, "She loves me. She likes what I am and what I do," you begin to develop positive regard for yourself.

But often this does not happen. The image you see reflected in your mother's eyes and actions is mixed. Whether or not she approves of you often depends on what you do, what you say, what thoughts and feelings you express. In other words, she places conditions on her love: *If you do what she wants, she likes you.* Young and impressionable, you accept these verdicts and incorporate *conditions of worth* into yourself. "When I do this, I am bad." You begin to see yourself as good and worthy only if you act in certain ways. You've learned from your parents and from other people who are significant to you that unless you meet certain conditions you will not be loved.

Rogers's work as a therapist convinced him that people cope with conditions of worth by rejecting or denying parts of their organism that do not fit their self-concept. For example, if your mother grew cold and distant whenever you became angry, you learned to deny yourself the right to express or perhaps even feel anger. Being angry "isn't you." In effect, you are cutting off a part of your organism or whole being; you are only allowing yourself to experience and express part of your being.

The greater the gap between the self and the organism, the more limited and defensive a person becomes. Rogers believes the cure for this situation is *unconditional positive regard*. If significant others (parents, friends, a mate, perhaps a therapist) convey the feeling that they value you for what you are, in your entirety, you will gradually learn to grant yourself the same unconditional positive regard. The need to limit yourself declines. You will be able to accept your organism and become open to *all* your feelings, thoughts, and experiences—and hence to other people. This is what Rogers means by *fully functioning*. The organism and the self are one: The individual is free to develop all his potentialities. Like Maslow and other humanists, Rogers believes that self-regard and regard for others go together, and that the human potentials for good and for self-fulfillment outweigh the potentials for evil and despair (Rogers, 1951, 1961).

FIGURE 13.9
Carl Rogers's theories have had a considerable impact upon modern psychology and upon society in general. His views about personality were the first to seriously rival Freudian theory. Rogers has emphasized the personal experiences of humans rather than their drives and instincts.

FIGURE 13.10
A representation of the two systems that Carl Rogers believes exist in human personality. One is the organism, which values whatever leads to its own growth and perfection. The other is the self, which takes into account the reactions of other people in deciding what is good and bad, and which can therefore be misled.

EXISTENTIAL PSYCHOLOGY: ROLLO MAY AND R. D. LAING

Existential psychologists Rollo May and R. D. Laing have much in common with the humanists. They see personality as a creative process—not as a fixed quantity you acquire in childhood and are more or less "stuck with" for the rest of your life. Like the humanists, they believe that all people need and seek meaningful lives that enable them to discover and express their true feelings and values. Existential psychologists use the word "authenticity" (being genuine) to describe what

Maslow called self-actualization and Rogers, full functioning. They explain this goal somewhat differently, however.

Rollo May: Freedom, Choice, and Responsibility

In *Existential Psychology* (1961) and other works, Rollo May emphasizes freedom, choice, and responsibility. May believes that the individual is free to create his or her identity, values, and life style. This is not to say that a person can be or do anything he or she wants. Opportunity, chance occurrences, other people, and the facts of life to some extent determine how one can live.

In May's view, every action we take, every conversation we have, every explanation we give ourselves or others for our behavior is a choice among alternatives. To achieve authenticity, a person must accept responsibility for these choices—that is, acknowledge that you made a choice that had certain consequences (whether or not things turn out as you anticipated). To say that you had no choice, that "you couldn't help it," that you didn't really mean what you said or did is to deny your true self. Only by accepting freedom and responsibility, by committing ourselves and "playing for keeps," are we able to feel that our lives are *meaningful*. It is a question of living your life, or letting your life live you.

A chief difference between humanist and existential psychologists is that May and others believe the odds are against a person's achieving authenticity. Where the humanists are "eternal optimists," the existentialists are rather gloomy pessimists. In large part this is because they believe society is sick.

We are constantly bombarded with contradictory and empty communications (think of advertisements on television or campaign speeches). We are assigned numbers on the day we are born, and thereby launched into an impersonal, anonymous world. Everything from food to education to entertainment is mass-produced. Things seem out of control: We have little or no influence on the remote forces that push us one way or another.

Given this state of affairs, it takes enormous courage to strive for authenticity. In May's view, most people retreat in self-defense. They lose

 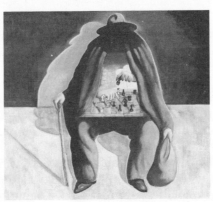

FIGURE 13.11
An interpretation of existential theory. Existentialists emphasize that a person must assume responsibility for his own actions because only through accepting responsibility can he create meaning in his own life. They stress that the individual learn to "control his own chessboard" rather than be a "pawn of fate."

the capacity for involvement, passion, and excitement. They cease to feel and become indifferent and apathetic. May believes that it is the rare and courageous person who pursues authenticity and meaningfulness in our society.

R. D. Laing: Authentic Communication

A psychiatrist who works with severely disturbed people, R. D. Laing believes that many of the people found in mental wards are the victims of families whose members have lost the ability to accept their emotions and communicate honestly. To keep unpleasant facts and feelings from coming to light, they engage in what Laing calls *mystification*. They lie and pretend—to themselves and each other. As a result, the child becomes increasingly confused about what is and isn't real. He or she develops a *false self* system (a self that is radically different from the organism, to use Rogers's terms).

Suppose, for example, a child's parents deny that they feel insecure and afraid sometimes, and ignore him when he expresses these feelings. He may come to believe that he is being controlled by forces beyond his understanding. And in a sense he is right: he is being controlled by an "external and alien" family (Laing and Esterson, 1971). Even if the child avoids such a severe reaction, he will lose his sensitivity to feelings and self-expression.

Laing does not blame the family so much as he does the society that creates and maintains such families, and that treats the people who are able to accept depersonalization and anonymity as "normal." He believes the cure for false self systems is authentic communication—much as Rogers believes the way to close gaps between the organism and the self is unconditional positive regard.

Laing is one of the pioneers in breaking down hospital walls and routines so that patients and staff can live together and help *one another* to work toward authenticity. He takes the position that adjusting to a "sick society" is not necessarily a healthy thing, and that we all have something to learn from people who are unable or unwilling to adjust (Laing, 1967).

THE OBJECTIVE STUDY OF PERSONALITY: B. F. SKINNER AND THE BEHAVIORISTS; RAYMOND CATTELL

The theories of personality we have discussed so far are based on case studies of individuals who sought psychotherapy; observation of people going about their everyday lives; reading about the past; introspection and self-analysis. These theories emphasize the subjective side of personality—that is, the way people experience themselves and their worlds. The theorists we are about to introduce reject this approach. They believe that the proper goal of psychology is to discover laws of human behavior and personality through rigorous application of the scientific method. They

---

seek facts, not insight, and limit themselves to the study of behavior that can be tested and measured.

B. F. Skinner: Behaviorism

Behavioral psychologists maintain that the freedom and dignity the existentialists and humanists seek are illusions. They say that personality is determined by what each person is born with (hereditary characteristics) and what has happened to us since (environmental factors). Unlike the other theorists we've discussed, behaviorists look at the individual objectively, that is, from the outside. Behavioral psychologists are concerned with aspects of human behavior that are dependent upon factors outside the individual's area of control. For this reason, behaviorism takes a deterministic attitude toward human action—that is, it emphasizes that all choice and action are determined by external causes.

This line of reasoning is based on the concepts and principles of learning theory (described in Chapter 2). B. F. Skinner, the most famous living behaviorist, has stated that he objects to the idea of an inner person, or self, that causes one to behave in certain ways. He maintains that people behave as they do because they have been rewarded or punished for their behaviors. Skinner's evidence? The fact that it is possible to change the way people behave—for example, to help a person to overcome an irrational fear of snakes or closed rooms—*without* knowing how or why the individual developed the fear in the first place.

FIGURE 13.12
B. F. Skinner is the most famous living behaviorist. Behaviorism, which emphasizes the development of personality through conditioning and learning, is now a major force in the area of personality theory. Skinner believes that external forces rather than inner choices make people what they are.

Raymond B. Cattell: Trait Theory

Raymond B. Cattell is not a behaviorist, but he shares Skinner's dedication to objectivity. As he states in the introduction to *The Scientific Analysis of Personality* (1965), "In an age when we are investigating everything, how can we shut our eyes to the possibility of scientifically studying personality?" (p. 11)

Cattell believes that in time we will be able to explain and predict human behavior on the basis of a relatively small number of personality traits. Cattell defines a *trait* as a tendency to react to a situation in a way that remains more or less stable over time. He distinguishes between two kinds of tendencies: surface traits and source traits. Surface traits are clusters of behaviors that tend to go together. An example of a surface trait is altruism, which involves a variety of related behaviors such as helping a neighbor who has a problem or contributing to an annual blood drive. Other examples of surface traits are integrity, curiosity, realism, and foolishness. Source traits are the underlying roots or causes of these behavior clusters—for example, ego strength, dominance, or submissiveness. Cattell believes that discovering and learning to measure these traits will enable us to identify those characteristics all humans share and those that distinguish one person from another and make him or her an individual.

How does Cattell approach this task? Unlike the other psychologists we have described in this chapter, whose theories are based on the intensive study of a limited number of people, Cattell uses a variety of tests to reach large numbers of people. He and his associates collect three kinds of data: from life records, from questionnaires, and from objective tests. Life records include everything from descriptions by people who have known an individual for some time to grades in schools and records of automobile accidents. Questionnaire data are the answers individuals give to a series of questions, whether or not they are truthful. (The fact that an individual underrates himself or herself or tries to create a highly favorable impression may be significant.) Objective test data are a person's responses to tests specifically designed to detect or prevent this sort of "cheating."

In collecting all these data Cattell is not simply trying to amass a library on a huge number of individuals. He has made significant progress in analyzing these data with a statistical technique known as multivariate analysis. Simply put, multivariate analysis enables a researcher to examine a collection of data from a number of angles at the same time. (The difference between multivariate and other forms of statistical analysis is like the difference between a three-dimensional model of a chemical molecule and a flat diagram of the same molecule on a blackboard.) In so doing, Cattell is discovering interrelationships among life records, questionnaires, and objective test data. Ultimately, he seeks to establish laws of human behavior.

SUMMARY

1. Personality is that "something" that accounts for the differences among people and for the consistencies in an individual's behavior over time and in different situations.

2. Personality theories provide a way of organizing information about people's thoughts, feelings, and actions; explaining differences between people; exploring the why's of behavior; and determining methods for improving the quality of life.

3. Freudian theory centers around the unconscious and the important role it plays in an individual's personality. Freud believed the mind is like a powerful energy system. Energy from the id, or pleasure-seeking unconscious, is diverted into the ego, or rational part of the self, and superego, or conscience.

4. Defense mechanisms are unconscious solutions to conflict situations. Stress and anxiety are reduced by denial, falsification, or distor-

tion of reality. Some common defense mechanisms are displacement, repression, reaction formation, projection, and regression.

5. Jung believed that personality is made up of opposites such as extroversion and introversion and that the tension between these opposites is the source of mental energy. The collective unconscious is a universally shared inheritance of instincts, urges, and memories called archetypes. Individuation is Jung's term for the process by which the individual integrates various fragments of his or her personality.

6. Adler believed that the main motivating force in the development of personality is the effort to overcome feelings of inferiority. Childhood experiences such as overpampering or neglect set the pattern for adult life styles. The healthy personality is one that is built on an effective life style, which includes a strong social interest.

7. Fromm's theory centers around the need to belong and the loneliness that accompanies freedom. People may react to this by attempting to escape from freedom or by seeking fulfillment in love and work.

8. Humanistic theories of personality emphasize human dignity and potential. Maslow believed that self-actualization involves satisfying deficiency and growth needs.

9. Rogers suggests that full functioning depends on a person's opening the self to include all of the organism, shedding conditions of worth.

10. More pessimistic than the humanists, existentialists May and Laing place heavy emphasis on freedom of choice and responsibility for one's decisions and actions. They believe that authenticity is difficult to achieve in modern society.

11. Other psychologists study personality objectively—that is, from the outside. B. F. Skinner, the leader of the behaviorist school of thought, and Cattell, who is collecting three kinds of data on personality traits for statistical analysis, are examples.

GLOSSARY

archetype: According to Jung, an inherited idea, based on the experiences of one's ancestors, that shapes one's perception of the world.

behaviorism: The school of psychology that holds that the proper subject matter of psychology is objectively observable behavior—and nothing else.

collective unconscious: According to Jung, that part of the mind that contains inherited instincts, urges, and memories common to all people.

conditions of worth: Rogers's term for the conditions a person must meet in order to regard himself or herself positively.

defense mechanisms: According to Freud, certain specific means by which the ego unconsciously protects itself against unpleasant impulses or circumstances.

deficiency needs: According to Maslow, those needs that are basic to survival and freedom from worry, including food, water, shelter, love, and admiration.

displacement: The transference of desires, feelings, or impulses from their proper object to a substitute.

ego: According to Freud, the part of the personality that is in touch with reality. The ego strives to meet the demands of the id and the superego in socially acceptable ways.

existential psychology: The view that human behavior is the result of free choice and is not determined by forces over which the individual has no control.

extroversion: According to Jung, the tendency toward being outgoing, objective, practical, and sociable.

false self system: According to Laing, a distorted self-image a person develops in the absence of authentic communication.

fully functioning person: Rogers's term for an individual whose organism and self coincide, allowing him or her to be open to experience, to possess unconditional positive regard, and to have harmonious relations with others.

growth needs: According to Maslow, those needs that arise from the human desire for self-actualization, including development of abilities, fulfillment of one's unique destiny, and knowledge of self.

humanism: An approach to psychology that stresses the uniqueness of the individual; focuses on the value, dignity, and worth of each person; and holds that healthy living is the result of realizing one's full potential.

id: According to Freud, that part of the unconscious personality that contains our needs, drives, and instincts as well as repressed material. The material in the id strives for immediate satisfaction.

inferiority complex: According to Adler, a pattern of avoiding feelings of inadequacy and insignificance rather than trying to overcome their source.

introversion: According to Jung, the tendency to be inward-directed.

mystification: According to Laing, the process of denying emotions, falsifying feelings, and pretending that occurs in disturbed families.

nonproductive personality: Fromm's term for a person who feels that all that is good in life lies outside himself, and that he can only get what he wants by taking, keeping, or buying from others.

organism: Rogers's term for the whole person, including all of his or her feelings, thoughts, and urges as well as body.

personality: The sum total of physical, mental, emotional, and social characteristics that distinguish one person from another.

positive regard: Rogers's term for viewing oneself in a positive light, because of positive feedback received from interaction with others.

productive personality: Fromm's term for a person who feels that the source of what is good in life lies within himself and who is therefore loving, giving, and generous.

projection: Ascribing one's own undesirable attitudes, feelings, or thoughts to others.

rationalization: An attempt by the ego to make an undesirable action, feeling, or thought acceptable by providing a logical or "reasonable" explanation as its motive.

reaction formation: Replacing an unacceptable feeling or urge with its opposite.

regression: A return to an earlier stage of development or pattern of behavior in a threatening or stressful situation.

repression: The exclusion from conscious awareness of a painful, unpleasant, or undesirable memory.

self: Rogers's term for one's experience or image of oneself, developed through interaction with others.

self-actualization: The humanist term for realizing one's unique potential.

superego: According to Freud, the process of the personality that inhibits the socially undesirable impulses of the id. The superego may cause excessive guilt if it is overly harsh.

trait: A tendency to react to a situation in a way that remains stable over time.

unconditional positive regard: Rogers's term for complete emotional support and complete acceptance of one person by another.

unconscious: According to Freud, the part of the mind that contains material we are unaware of, but that strongly influences conscious processes and behaviors.

ACTIVITIES

1. List the qualities and traits which you think comprise the "healthy" or "actualized" person. If this is done in class you can see how your ideas of health and actualization differ from those of the other class members.

2. What are the key features of your own personality? What are the key features of the personalities of each of your parents? Compare your personality with those of your parents. There will be both similarities and differences.

Because one's parents are necessarily such highly influential forces in a child's development, it may be of greater interest to note the chief differences in personalities. Then try to identify the factors responsible for those differences. For example, what key individuals or events have influenced or redirected the course of your life or changed your habits of living? How have society's institutions affected you?

3. Do some further reading on a particular personality theorist and arrange a class debate. A lively debate would be one between the behaviorists' position and the humanistic or existential approach.

4. The text contains a list of characteristics that Maslow found to be representative of people whom he described as "self-actualized." From among your acquaintances, choose a few whom you especially respect or admire for "doing their own thing," people who achieve satisfaction by being who and what they are. Ask them to list what they see as their distinguishing personality characteristics. Compare their answers and your observations with Maslow's list. In addition, compare this information with Jung's idea of individuation, Fromm's productive person, and Rogers's fully functioning person. Do the theories adequately describe the characteristics you admire? Are they consistent with them?

5. Jung believed that people are unconsciously linked to their ancestral past. Can you think of any evidence for or against the "collective unconscious" Jung described? Which, if any, of your own experiences lend support to or deny this theory?

6. Make a collage that depicts your particular personality, using pictures and words from magazines and newspapers. For example, include your likes, dislikes, hobbies, personality traits, appearance, and so on.

7. Look and listen for "Freudian slips." Write them down and try to determine the reasons for each slip.

8. Listen to conversations of several friends, relatives, teachers, and so on. Try to identify their use of defense mechanisms and write down the circumstances surrounding their use. Try to listen to your own conversations and do the same for yourself. Why do you think people use defense mechanisms?

9. Erich Fromm wrote about specific needs, such as the need to be rooted, to have a frame of reference, to have an identity, and to transcend. What do you think Fromm would say about the current trend for more ethnic courses in high schools and colleges? Do these courses meet these needs? At what expense to the concept of humanity? Are the desires for such courses a result of needs not met? Which ones?

SUGGESTED READINGS

CANNEL, WARD, AND MACKLIN, JUNE. *The Human Nature Industry*. Garden City, N. Y.: Doubleday Anchor, 1974 (paper). Written by a journalist and anthropologist, this book shows in a comical and insightful format how human nature can be manufactured and advertised to create three different images of people.

ELKIND, DAVID. "Freud, Jung and the Collective Unconscious." The *New York Times Magazine*, October 4, 1970, pp. 23–104. This well-written article summarizes much of Jung's principal contributions and includes some revealing anecdotes concerning Freud's relationship to Jung.

FROMM, ERICH. *Escape from Freedom*. New York: Holt, Rinehart & Winston, 1941. In this important work, Fromm explores the problems of freedom and loneliness. He develops the thesis that we can resolve this dilemma through love and work.

GALE, RAYMOND F. *Who Are You?* Englewood

Cliffs, N. J.: Prentice-Hall, 1974 (paper). An excellent summary of humanistic and existential psychology including coverage of Rogers, May, Maslow, and Fromm.

HALL, CALVIN S. *Primer of Freudian Psychology.* Cleveland: World Publishing, 1954 (paper). A good introduction to Freudian theory. The book is clearly written and emphasizes Freud's contributions to the psychology of "normal" people.

JUNG, CARL. *Memories, Dreams, Reflections.* New York: Vintage, 1961 (paper). A beautifully written autobiography that is bound to leave any reader with deep respect and admiration for this highly original thinker and writer.

MASLOW, ABRAHAM. *Toward a Psychology of Being.* New York: Van Nostrand, 1968. Maslow, one of the founders of humanistic psychology, directs current thinking away from its obsession with the "normal" person and focuses on the "healthy" person.

———. *The Farther Reaches of Human Nature.* New York: Viking, 1971 (paper). A collection of Maslow's writings on a wide range of topics including creativity, health and pathology, values and society, and his theory of motivation.

MAY, ROLLO. *Love and Will.* New York: Norton, 1969. May views therapy not as an attempt to cure but as assistance in self-exploration. He emphasizes the forces of love and daimonic—the natural functions that contain vitality and creativity but that also have the power to possess a person. He also emphasizes the will because it contains consciousness, intentionality, and hence, meaning.

ROGERS, CARL. *On Becoming a Person.* Boston: Houghton Mifflin, 1961. Rogers presents a clear and thorough description of the humanistic theory of personality. This is an important work in that it was the first major rival to traditional Freudian theory.

SKINNER, B. F. *Beyond Freedom and Dignity.* New York: Knopf, 1971. Skinner proposes a solution to the world's problems based on the deliberate manipulation of behavior by conditioning techniques.

BIBLIOGRAPHY

ADLER, ALFRED. *What Life Should Mean to You.* New York: Putnam, 1959 (paper).

———. *Problems of Neurosis: A Book of Case Histories.* New York: Harper & Row, 1964.

CATTELL, R. B. *The Scientific Analysis of Personality.* Baltimore, Md.: Penguin, 1965.

FRANKL, VIKTOR. *Man's Search for Meaning.* Boston: Beacon Press, 1962.

FREUD, SIGMUND. *A General Introduction to Psychoanalysis.* Translated by Joan Riviere. Garden City, N. Y.: Garden City Publishing, 1943.

FROMM, ERICH. *Escape from Freedom.* New York: Holt, Rinehart & Winston, 1941.

———. *Man for Himself: An Inquiry into the Psychology of Ethics.* New York: Holt, Rinehart & Winston, 1947.

HALL, CALVIN S. *A Primer of Freudian Psychology.* Cleveland: World Publishing, 1954.

HALL, CALVIN S., AND LINDZEY, GARDNER. *Theories of Personality.* 2nd ed. New York: Wiley, 1970 (paper).

JUNG, CARL G. *Memories, Dreams, Reflections.* Edited by Anna Jaffe. Translated by Richard and Clara Winston. New York: Pantheon, 1963.

LAING, R. D. *The Politics of Experience.* New York: Pantheon, 1967.

LAING, R. D., AND ESTERSON, AARON. *Sanity, Madness, and the Family.* 2nd ed. New York: Basic Books, 1971.

MASLOW, ABRAHAM. *Toward a Psychology of Being*. New York: Van Nostrand, 1968.

——. *Motivation and Personality*. 2nd ed. New York: Harper & Row, 1970 (paper).

MAY, ROLLO. *Existential Psychology*. 2nd ed. New York: Random House, 1961 (paper).

——. *Love and Will*. New York: Dell, 1969 (paper).

ROGERS, CARL. *Client-Centered Therapy*. Boston: Houghton Mifflin, 1951.

——. *On Becoming a Person*. Boston: Houghton Mifflin, 1961.

SKINNER, B. F. *Science and Human Behavior*. New York: Macmillan, 1953.

——. *Beyond Freedom and Dignity*. New York: Knopf, 1971.

14

Adjustment in Contemporary Society

FIGURE 14.1
Starting college involves more than just studying new subjects. Many freshmen have left home for the first time, and all must adjust to new people, greater independence, and pressure to make career choices.

The McCaslins and their five children live in a rural area of eastern Kentucky. The father is a tall, gangly man who broke his back several years ago while working in a local coal mine. He is not able to perform any kind of physical labor and has been unable to find any other kind of work. The coal company refused to give him a disability pension and, probably because he is living at home, his family has been denied welfare. Consequently, the family is forced to survive on garden vegetables and what little food they can buy with some assistance from relatives.

In spite of this hard, meager existence, they all work at maintaining a close, loving relationship with each other. The father has strong ideas, talks a lot, and involves himself with his wife and children. The parents do not touch each other very much in front of strangers or their children, but "they give each other long looks of recognition, sympathy, affection, and sometimes anger or worse. They understand each other in that silent, real, lasting way that defies . . . labels . . ." writes psychiatrist Robert Coles (1971).

Psychologists who study adjustment attempt to understand how people deal with extreme hardship, as well as how they cope with the more ordinary yet stressful experiences of life, such as college, marriage, divorce, and work. Adjusting to each of these experiences involves unique challenges and difficulties. Starting college may involve meeting new people and competing with them in academic subjects you have never studied. Beginning a job may involve learning new skills and performing routine tasks you did not expect to be doing. Even when job opportunities are excellent and people are friendly and helpful, coping with such new experiences can be difficult.

In this chapter, we look at some of the situations most people experience during their lives and how they adjust to them. By *adjustment*, psychologists mean adapting to as well as actively shaping one's environment. When a psychologist says that a person is well-adjusted, she does *not* mean that the individual has managed to avoid problems and conflicts. She means that the person has learned to cope with frustration, disappointment, and loss, and is making the most of himself and his opportunities. In Chapter 15, we suggest why individuals may become unable to cope with everyday life and in Chapter 16, how psychotherapists can help them.

MASLOW'S MODEL OF HEALTHY ADJUSTMENT

When humanist psychologist Abraham Maslow decided to study the most productive individuals he could find—in history as well as in his social and professional circles—he was breaking new ground. Most of the theories of personality we discussed in the preceding chapter were developed by psychotherapists after years of working with people who could not cope with everyday frustrations and conflicts. In contrast, Maslow was curious about people who not only coped with everyday problems effectively, but who also created exceptional lives for themselves, such as Abraham Lincoln, Albert Einstein, and Eleanor Roosevelt.

Maslow found that, although these people sometimes had great emotional difficulties, they adjusted to their problems in ways that allowed them to become highly productive. Maslow also found that these individuals, whom he called *self-actualized,* share a number of traits. First, they perceive reality accurately, unlike most people who, because of prejudices and wishful thinking perceive it rather inaccurately. Self-actualized people also *accept themselves,* other people, and their environments more readily than "average" people do. Most of us engage in a good deal of wishful thinking. Without realizing it, we project our hopes and fears onto the world around us. Often we become upset with people whose attitudes differ radically from our own. We spend a good deal of time denying our own shortcomings and trying to rationalize or change things we do not like about ourselves. Self-actualizing individuals accept themselves as they are.

Secure in themselves, healthy individuals are more *problem-centered* than self-centered. They are able to focus on tasks in a way that people concerned about maintaining and protecting their self-image cannot. They are more likely to base decisions on ethical principles than on calculations of the possible costs or benefits to themselves. They have a strong sense of *identity with other human beings*—not just members of their family, ethnic group, or country, but all humankind. They have a strong *sense of humor,* but laugh with people, not at them.

Maslow also found that self-actualizing people are exceptionally *spontaneous.* They are not trying to be anything other than themselves. And they know themselves well enough to maintain their integrity in the face of opposition, unpopularity, and rejection. In a word, they are *autonomous.* They *value privacy* and frequently seek out solitude. This is not to say that they are detached or aloof. But rather than trying to be popular they focus on deep, *loving relationships with the few people* to whom they are truly close.

Finally, the people Maslow studied had a rare ability to appreciate even the simplest things. They approached their lives with a *sense of discovery* that made each day a new day. They rarely felt bored or uninterested. Given to moments of intense joy and satisfaction, or "peak experiences," they got high on life itself. Maslow believed this to be both a cause and an effect of their creativity and originality (Maslow, 1954, 1971).

As indicated in the preceding chapter, Maslow believed that to become self-actualizing a person must first satisfy his or her basic, primary needs—for food and shelter, physical safety, love and belonging, and self-esteem. Of course, to some extent the ability to satisfy these needs depends on factors beyond the individual's control. A person who grows up in poverty, encounters prejudice, or suffers from a physical handicap has to work harder than someone who is more privileged to attain the same goals. Still, no amount of wealth, talent, beauty, or any other asset can totally shield someone from frustration and disappointment. A certain degree of stress is built into the human condition. The affluent as well as the poor, the brilliant as well as the slow, have to adjust to maintain themselves and to grow.

ADJUSTING TO LIFE'S STRESSES

Stress is the tension or strain you feel when you are unable to satisfy your needs and feel your well-being threatened by forces beyond your control. Stress has many causes.

Sources of Stress

Delay and *frustration* are obvious sources of stress. You have your heart set on going to a particular law school. You take the necessary exams, obtain recommendations, fill out and mail your application. Waiting a month or more for a response can be maddening in itself. You find yourself counting and recounting the days on the calendar and checking your mailbox two or three times a day.

The letter you receive from the school may or may not relieve your tension. You may be rejected because your grades and test scores were not as high as those of other applicants. Suddenly you are confronted with your own limitations. You failed. Why didn't you work harder? Or you may be admitted to the school but not awarded a scholarship. You don't have the money to pay tuition and support yourself so you feel that you can't go anyway.

Adjusting to the effects of either of these letters will be even more difficult if you are under *pressure* to go to that particular law school. The pressure may be internal (you want to prove you're as good as your brother, who went to that school) or external (your parents have made it clear they expect you to get into a top school).

Suppose you are accepted and given a scholarship, but your fiancé has taken a job hundreds of miles away. Going to law school would mean postponing marriage or perhaps risking this relationship. In addition, part of you wants to get married, raise a family, and fulfill the traditional female role. *Conflicts* such as these also create stress because you are forced to make a difficult choice.

Perhaps the hardest thing to adjust to is *loss*—loss of a loved one (through death or separation); loss of a job (being fired or forced to retire); loss of financial security and social standing; loss of self-esteem. Loss is

FIGURE 14.2
Looking for a job is often a stressful, frustrating experience. Inexperienced, former students may find few opportunities in an economy slowed by recession. Many young people must adjust to the idea of postponing or revising their career goals until new opportunities develop.

always disorienting. There is a gaping hole in your emotional life and in your daily routine. Something or someone has been taken from you. You may feel angry or guilty as well as sad.

On occasion, achieving your goals produces stress. Falling in love, going away to college, getting a new job or promotion, moving to a new home, going on the vacation you've dreamed about, and other positive *change*

Table 14.1: Social Readjustment Rating Scale

Rank	Life Event	Mean Value
1	Death of spouse	100
2	Divorce	73
3	Marital separation	65
4	Jail term	63
5	Death of close family member	63
6	Personal injury or illness	53
7	Marriage	50
8	Fired at work	47
9	Marital reconciliation	45
10	Retirement	45
11	Change in health of family member	44
12	Pregnancy	40
13	Sex difficulties	39
14	Gain of new family member	39
15	Business readjustment	39
16	Change in financial state	38
17	Death of close friend	37
18	Change to different line of work	36
19	Change in number of arguments with spouse	35
20	Mortgage over $10,000	31
21	Foreclosure of mortgage or loan	30
22	Change in responsibilities at work	29
23	Son or daughter leaving home	29
24	Trouble with in-laws	29
25	Outstanding personal achievement	28
26	Wife begin or stop work	26
27	Begin or end school	26
28	Change in living conditions	25
29	Revision of personal habits	24
30	Trouble with boss	23
31	Change in work hours or conditions	20
32	Change in residence	20
33	Change in schools	20
34	Change in recreation	19
35	Change in church activities	19
36	Change in social activities	18
37	Mortgage or loan less than $10,000	17
38	Change in sleeping habits	16
39	Change in number of family get-togethers	15
40	Change in eating habits	15
41	Vacation	13
42	Christmas	12
43	Minor violations of the law	11

Reprinted with permission from T. H. Holmes and R. H. Rahe, "The Social Readjustment Rating Scale," *Journal of Psychosomatic Research,* 1967, Table 3, p. 216. ©1967, Pergamon Press Ltd.

force you to readjust. No matter how long you've worked and hoped for this day, not knowing quite what to expect is stressful.

Indeed, one team of researchers believes that change of any kind, good or bad, is the major source of stress (Holmes and Rahe, 1967). The results of a survey they conducted are shown in Table 14.1. Each person was asked to rate items on a list of life changes for impact and difficulty of adjusting. As you can see, respondents considered obvious success (outstanding personal achievement) almost as unsettling as financial problems (foreclosure of a mortgage or loan) and trouble with in-laws.

Alvin Toffler (1970) uses the term *future shock* to describe the effects of the accelerated rate of change in contemporary American society. In his words,

> Future shock is a time phenomenon, a product of the greatly accelerated rate of change in society. It arises from the superimposition of a new culture on an old one. It is [like being an unprepared stranger] in one's own society. But its impact is far worse. For most ... travelers have the comforting knowledge that the culture they left behind will be there to return to. The victim of future shock does not. (p. 11)

Toffler believes an individual can tolerate only so much change in social expectations, economic conditions, technology, and the like, before he or she becomes overloaded.

Responses to Stress

A person may respond to stress in any number of ways. *Crying* may not solve anything, but it does relieve tension. So does pounding it out on a punching bag, going to a lonely place and yelling, or writing a passionate letter you may or may not send.

Talking things out with a friend—telling him or her how much it meant to you, how hard you tried, how rotten you feel—has much the same effect. It releases tension and may elicit the sympathy and emotional support you need. In trying to explain how you feel and listening to the other person's reaction, you may begin to see your situation in a new light. When a person is in a state of utter confusion or extreme emotional pain, he or she may seek professional help from a psychotherapist or clergyman.

Some people prefer to go off and think things through by themselves. *Withdrawing* from ordinary social obligations for a time gives you a chance to come to terms with the new situation and to decide where to go from there.

A few people are able to *laugh* disappointment away. As Maslow suggested, accepting the fact that you cannot always have your way is healthy. However, denying that you feel cheated or sad—even to yourself—is different from admitting and accepting defeat. If, for example, you deny that you were hurt when your girlfriend or boyfriend left you for someone else, you may unconsciously act out your fear of being hurt again by avoiding close relationships or act out your anger by leading new people on and then dropping them, as you were dropped.

Carried to an extreme, any of these responses can be self-defeating. If you cry or become extremely angry every time something goes wrong, friends will begin to consider your behavior manipulative and stop giving you that shoulder to lean on. Talking compulsively to anyone who will listen may be a way of avoiding rather than coming to grips with your problems. Withdrawing can lead to isolation and self-pity. In the preceding chapter we suggested that when an individual uses defense mechanisms (displacement, repression and so on) in rigid and extreme ways, they create more problems than they solve. The same is true here.

The responses we've mentioned are temporary ways of coping. Adjusting to a stressful situation requires *action*. Action is the key word here since it distinguishes adjustment from passive acceptance. Well-adjusted people will go back and try again; decide how to live with only partial satisfaction of their hopes; perhaps change their goals.

Severe and Prolonged Stress.   What happens when things go totally awry? When soldiers are caught under fire with no escape? When an earthquake or other natural disaster literally rips an individual's world apart? When a person realizes that a loved one is dead or that an accident has left him physically handicapped for life?

In all of these situations a person is suddenly faced with a new and bewildering reality. The world is not as it used to be: His house or barracks is suddenly reduced to burning rubble; he can no longer walk or see. According to H. Selye (1969), people respond to disasters and personal tragedies in stages.

When disaster or tragedy hits, people mobilize for "fight or flight." They become exceptionally alert and sensitive to stimuli in the environment. They try to keep a firm grip on their emotions. Selye calls this the *alarm* stage. An example would be people running from an explosion. They don't think about where they are running to—they just run.

In the second stage, which Selye calls *resistance,* people intensify their efforts—denying that the situation is hopeless much as a dying person at first refuses to accept his condition. Thus people caught in a fire will crowd toward the nearest exit, however narrow. They are in too much of a panic to consider alternatives.

In the third stage, people become *exhausted* and disoriented. The classic example of this is a mother sitting in the ruins of a bombed-out house rocking a dead or wounded baby as if nothing had happened. But her eyes are glazed. Soldiers have been known to wander about aimlessly or even fall asleep under fire (Toffler, 1970, pp. 344–346). Selye suggests this is because it is easier for the person to give up than to face the situation and look for solutions. An individual may withdraw completely or experience delusions. A period of prolonged stress due to internal or familial conflicts may have the same effect as a sudden disaster. All efforts to adjust fail and the individual reaches his or her breaking point.

Most people recover their equilibrium and "come back" to reality. This may take time. Studies indicate that people who lose their sight or a limb, their home or their spouse, go through a period of depression and self-pity best described as mourning. But eventually they face their situation, salvage what they can from the past, and begin to restructure their life plans (Cholden, 1954; Parkes, 1972).

Having described sources of and responses to stress in a general way, we now turn to three specific situations which require major adjustments: going to college; falling in love, getting married, and perhaps getting divorced; and going to work.

COLLEGE LIFE

College is not simply an extension of high school. The people and setting, the demands and opportunities, the routines are new and different. For many students, going away to college represents a first step away from their families. They are largely on their own. A decade ago, colleges functioned as surrogate parents. Students were required to live on campus, be in their dormitories by a certain hour, entertain members of the opposite sex in public lounges, and so on. This is no longer the case. College students have to set their own limits. For example, a woman cannot refuse a late-night drive to the lake on the grounds that her parents will get angry or that she will miss curfew. If she says "no," it is on her own authority.

College students are also on their own with regard to when and what they study. Although all colleges have required courses, students have to select a major and choose electives. Their instructors may keep attendance records, but there are no required study halls and few daily home-

FIGURE 14.3
College life makes many demands on students away from home for the first time. Organizing one's time, meeting new people, and confronting ideas which challenge old assumptions all require adjustment.

work assignments. This means it is easier to leave reading and papers until the last moment (which may be too late).

In short, college students are freer than they ever have been or may ever be again. This can be a personally liberating and stimulating experience. But it also requires adjustment. The emotional upheaval many freshmen feel has been called "college shock."

Peter Madison (1969) spent close to ten years collecting data on how several hundred students adjusted to college. Each student provided a detailed life history and kept a weekly journal. Madison had classmates write descriptions of some of the students, and tested and retested some at various points in their college career. The results?

Madison found that many students approach college with high, and often unrealistic, aspirations. For example, Trixie wanted to be an astronomer. She liked the idea of being different, and considered astronomy an elite and adventuresome field. But she didn't know how many long, hard, unadventuresome hours she would have to spend studying mathematics to fulfill her dream. Sidney planned to become a physician for what he described as "humanitarian" reasons. But he had never thought about working in a hospital or watching people sicken and die.

These two students, like many others, based their goals on fantasy. They didn't have the experience to make realistic choices or the maturity to evaluate their own motives and needs. Their experiences during the first semesters of college led them to change both their minds and their images of themselves.

Sources of Change

How does going to college stimulate change? First, college may challenge the identity a student has established in high school. A top student who does extremely well on the College Boards is likely to go to a top college. Nearly everyone there is as bright and competitive as she is. Within a matter of weeks the student's identity as a star pupil has evaporated; she may have to struggle to get average grades. Young people who excelled in sports or drama or student politics may have similar experiences. The high-school president discovers two other high-school presidents in his dormitory alone.

Second, whether students come from small towns or big cities, they are likely to encounter greater diversity in college than they ever have before—diversity in religious and ethnic background, family income level, and attitudes. During his first quarter, Bob dated a Catholic woman, a Jewish woman, and an oriental woman; a history major, a music major, a writer, and a math major. Fred found that the students living in his House ranged from "grinds," who did nothing but study, to "liberals," who were involved in all sorts of causes; athletes, who cared more about physical than intellectual competition; business types, who saw college as a place to get vocational training and make contacts for future use; and guys who just wanted to have a good time.

A student who develops a close relationship with another, then discovers that person holds beliefs or engages in behavior he has always consid-

FIGURE 14.4
After completing a year or two of college, students may find that the career goals they had as high school seniors no longer suit the interests they now have. Adjusting to this realization can be difficult.

ered immoral, may be extremely shaken. If you come from a strict, fundamentalist background, how do you reconcile the fact that a woman you have come to admire drinks heavily on occasion and thinks nothing of sleeping with a man on their first date? You are faced with a choice between abandoning deeply held values or giving up an important friendship. Madison calls close relationships between individuals who force one another to reexamine their basic assumptions *developmental friendships*. He found that developmental friendships in particular and student culture in general have more impact on college students than professors do.

However, if instructors and assigned books clarify thoughts that have been brewing beneath the surface in a student's mind, they can make all the difference. This was true for Sidney. Sidney did extremely well in the courses required for a pre-med student, but found he enjoyed his literature and philosophy classes far more. He began reading avidly. He felt as if each of the authors had deliberately set out to put all his self-doubts into words. In time Sidney realized that his interest in medicine was superficial. He had decided to become a doctor because it was a respected profession that would give him status, security, and a good income—and guarantee his parents' love. The self-image Sidney had brought to college was completely changed.

Coping with Change

Madison found that students cope with the stress going to college creates in several different ways. Some "tighten up" when their goals are threatened by internal or external change—redoubling their efforts to succeed in the field they had chosen and avoiding people and situations that might bring their doubts to the surface. Bob, for example, stuck with a chemical engineering program for three years, despite a growing interest in social science. By the time he realized that this was not the field for him it was too late to change majors. He got his degree, but left college with no idea where he was heading.

Others avoid confronting doubt by frittering away their time, going through the motions of attending college but detaching themselves emotionally.

And some students manage to keep their options open until they have enough information and experience to make a choice. Sidney is an example. In June of his freshman year he wrote in his diary,

> ". . . I must decide between philosophy and medicine. If I have enough confidence in the quality of my thought, I shall become a philosopher; if not, a comfortable doctor." (p. 58)

By June of the following year he had decided.

> ". . . Sitting on a tennis court I had the very sudden and dramatic realization that my life was my own and not my parents', that I could do what I wanted and did not necessarily have to do what they wanted. I think I correlated this with dropping out of the pre-med program. Material values became less and less important from then on." (p. 58)

Madison calls this third method of coping *resynthesis*. For most students this involves a period of vacillation, doubt, and anxiety. The student tries to combine the new and old, temporarily abandons the original goal, retreats, heads in another direction, retreats again—and finally reorganizes his or her feelings and efforts around an emerging identity. Thus Trixie found she was able to combine her desire to be a scientist with her interest in people and changed her major to psychology.

LOVE, MARRIAGE, AND DIVORCE

The idea of love without marriage is no longer shocking. The fact that a couple is developing a close and intimate relationship, or even living together, does not necessarily mean that they are contemplating marriage. Still the idea of marriage without love remains heresy in Western thought. Marrying for convenience, companionship, financial security, or *any* reason that doesn't include love strikes most of us as immoral or at least unfortunate.

And this, according to Zick Rubin (1973) is one of the main reasons why it is difficult for many people to adjust to love and marriage. Exaggerated ideas about love may also help to explain the growing popularity of divorce. Fewer couples who have "fallen out of love" are staying together for the sake of the children or to avoid gossip than did in the past. But let us begin at the beginning, with love.

Love

The very phrase "falling in love" suggests something about the way we conceptualize intimate relationships between members of the opposite sex. Falling in love is like entering a new dimension. Suddenly your whole life revolves around one special person. Just gazing into that person's eyes makes all other thoughts and problems disappear. You share a secret, private world together. The agony you feel when you cannot see each other or when one of you suspects the other of spending time with a rival is certain proof of your feelings. It doesn't matter where the person comes from, what your parents and friends think, or how impossible a future may seem—"Love conquers all." You knew the minute you met that you were made for each other.... Or so most of us are raised to believe and expect. Despite the so-called sexual revolution, Americans—especially American males—are romantics, as suggested in Chapter 10.

The problem is that reality often does not live up to these expectations. As Burgess and Wallin found in extensive interviews, love at first sight is rare (1953). Love affairs that blossom in a matter of days tend to burn themselves out, and marriages conceived in the heat of new romance tend to be ill-conceived. This is not to say that romance is an illusion. But it is only part of love. Many couples who develop a strong attachment soon find themselves disagreeing, getting on one another's nerves, talking to one another and privately to friends about the relationship—and wondering if they are really in love. High expectations and idealized notions of love make it all the more difficult to accept the reality of a close relationship and the other person as he or she really is.

Of course, one of the "prime movers" in the early stages of love is physical attraction. But as Erik Erikson has pointed out, falling in love "is by no means entirely, or even primarily a sexual matter.... To a considerable extent [young] love is an attempt to arrive at a definition of one's identity by projecting one's diffused ego image on another and by seeing it thus reflected and gradually clarified. This is why so much of young love is conversation" (Erikson, 1963, p. 262).

As a result, falling in love may lead to "overidentification" and difficulties in adjusting. You may feel that the self you are discovering depends on the other person, and feel tyrannized by your own feelings of possessiveness and jealousy. Or you may feel trapped. Going out with a number of people who see you differently may feel more comfortable than being with someone who "sees through you." On the other hand, you may become dependent on the image you've formed of your lover and feel threatened when that person reveals sides you had never seen or seems to be changing and growing. What if he or she no longer needs you?

Intimacy involves self-disclosure, and self-disclosure involves risk. Some individuals adjust to this risk by avoiding people and situations that threaten their image of themselves, their mates, and their relationships. Some couples commit themselves to growing together, even though this may someday mean growing apart. Most couples fall somewhere in between.

FIGURE 14.5
Falling in love adds a new, often wonderful dimension to life, yet love too requires adjustment. A couple may have unrealistic ideas about what love should be and may expect too much from the relationship.

Marriage

A couple decides to make a formal and public commitment to one another. They marry. Will they "live happily ever after?" Their chances are good if they come from similar cultural and economic backgrounds, have about the same level of education, and practice (or fail to practice) the same religion. Their chances are better still if their parents were happily married, they had happy childhoods, and they maintain good relations with their families. All of these are good predictors of marital success. Study after study has shown that marital success tends to run in families, and particularly in families whose members marry "their own kind." This is the principle of homogamy: like marrying like (Arkoff, 1968, pp. 467–474). What the statistics do not tell us is *how* couples who report they are satisfied with their marriages adjust to one another's hopes and demands, moods and quirks.

J. F. Cuber and Peggy Harroff (1965) found a wide range of adjustments in the upper-middle-class community they studied. Cuber and Harroff chose to study affluent families for two reasons: first, because they believed that too many marital studies focus on families in crisis; second, because such families represent the American ideal in many respects.

About one in six of the marriages they studied did in fact live up to the ideal. The couple enjoyed one another's company and spent a good deal of time together. At the same time, both husband and wife had a strong sense of individual identity and participated in separate activities. Cuber and Harroff called this a *vital marriage*. In a smaller number of *total marriages*, the husband and wife were deeply involved in one another's careers and hobbies, spent most of their time together, and seemed to live for each other.

FIGURE 14.6
In a vital marriage, couples enjoy each other's company, while still maintaining individual interests outside the home.

More common were what the researchers labeled devitalized and passive-congenial marriages. *Devitalized marriages* had begun with passionate love affairs and high hopes for a life of marital bliss. Over the years the couple had drifted apart, but they still got along well enough to stay together. The couples who had worked out *passive-congenial marriages* had never been deeply involved with one another. For these individuals, marriage was a convenience. Living together and sharing responsibilities made it easier for both husband and wife to pursue individual interests. They had not been looking for a lifelong honeymoon and were content with their relationships.

Cuber and Harroff used the term *conflict-habituated marriage* to describe husbands and wives who spent most of their time fighting. These couples were always at each other's throats. But they did not see their battles as a reason for divorce. Indeed, the fighting seemed to bind them together.

Mirra Komarovsky's study of blue-collar marriages (1964) provides an interesting contrast. Nearly all the couples Komarovsky studied saw marriage as a utilitarian arrangement and had settled into passive-congenial relationships. In general these couples believed that males and females have different needs and interests. They thought it natural for a woman to feel closer to her female friends and relatives than to her husband; a husband, closer to his male friends and relatives than to his wife. So long as the husband filled his role as breadwinner and the wife her role as homemaker and mother, both felt satisfied. There were some exceptions, some vital marriages, in the group studies. Komarovsky notes that the couples who enjoyed one another's company and shared leisure activities had higher levels of education and higher incomes than the other couples she interviewed (See Skolnick, 1973, pp. 238–246).

Both of these studies tend to support Maslow's belief that in order to become self-actualizing, an individual or couple must first fulfill basic maintenance needs. The blue-collar couples Komarovsky studied were struggling to make ends meet. Vital and total marriages, which might be viewed as relationships built around self-actualization, were more common among affluent families who did not have to worry about money. Statistics on the reasons why couples file for divorce reveal a similar pattern. Lower-class couples are more likely to complain of lack of financial support, physical cruelty, or drinking; middle-class couples, of mental cruelty or imcompatibility (Levinger, 1966).

Marital Problems and Divorce

In general, healthy adjustment to marriage seems to depend on three factors: whether the couple's needs are compatible; whether the husband's and wife's images of themselves coincide with their images of each other; and whether they agree on what the husband's and wife's roles in marriage are.

Conflict is likely to develop if the husband or wife has a deep need for achievement but the spouse is content with a leisurely, comfortable, undistinguished life. If a husband sees himself as sensitive and compassionate but the wife considers him crude and unfeeling, they are not likely to get along very well. Problems may erupt when a wife discovers that her husband expects her to quit her job when he finishes school and establishes himself in his career (something they may never have discussed). Similarly, a marriage may founder when a husband finds his wife devoting to their children the attention she once gave to him.

External factors may make it impossible for one or both to live up to their own role expectations. A man who is unemployed cannot be the good provider he wants to be and may take his frustration out on his family, who constantly remind him of this. A woman trying to raise a family in a slum tenement cannot keep the kitchen with a broken sink clean, provide good meals for her family, or keep her children safe. She gives up.

And often couples just grow apart: the husband becomes totally engrossed in his work or in a hobby; the wife, in her career, children, or community affairs. One day they wake up and realize that they stopped communicating years ago (see Arkoff, 1968, pp. 469–487).

Let us suppose they are unable or unwilling to fill one another's needs and role expectations through accommodation or compromise. Perhaps they cannot face their problems. Many people have a taboo about discussing—much less seeking help for—sexual problems, for example. Perhaps they have sought professional help, talked their difficulties out with each other and with friends, and come to the conclusion that they want more from life than their current marriage allows. For whatever reasons, they decide on divorce. What then?

In many ways, adjusting to divorce is like adjusting to death—the death of a relationship. Almost inevitably, divorce releases a torrent of emotions: anger (even if the person wanted a divorce), resentment, fear, loneliness, anxiety, and above all the feeling of failure. Both individuals are suddenly thrust into a variety of unfamiliar situations. A man may find himself cooking for the first time in years; a woman, fixing her first leaky faucet. Dating for the first time in five or ten years can make a formerly married person feel like an adolescent. Friends may feel they have to choose sides. Some may find the idea of giving up on a marriage or being unattached and free to do whatever you like unsettling. One of the biggest problems may be time—the free time a person desperately wanted but now has no idea what to do with.

All of this adds up to what Mel Krantzler (1973) calls "separation shock." The shock may be greatest for individuals who saw divorce as liberation and did not anticipate difficult times. But whatever the circumstances, most divorced people go through a period of mourning that lasts until the person suddenly realizes that he or she has survived. This is the first step toward adjustment to divorce. Resentment of their former spouse and of the opposite sex in general subsides. The pain left over from the past no longer dominates the present. The divorced person begins calling old friends, making new ones, and enjoying the fact that he or she can base decisions on his or her own, personal interests. In effect, the divorcee has begun to construct a new single identity, much as students do after an initial period of "college shock" (Krantzler, 1973, pp. 94–95).

Alternatives to Marriage

It is common knowledge that many young (and not so young) couples are living together openly without getting married. According to a survey of female students at Cornell University, 34 percent had lived with a man to whom they were not married, for at least three months. Surprisingly, perhaps, most of these women did not see cohabitation as a prelude to, or a trial, marriage (Macklin, 1972). Living together is one of many alternatives to traditional marriage.

Open marriage—in which two individuals live together as husband and wife but feel free to engage in intimate relationships with other people—is a second alternative. Those who support open marriage see it as a way to vitalize marriage. Couples who do not draw tight boundaries around their relationship cannot take one another for granted. In a sense, they have to renew their commitment to the marriage daily. (Critics tend to see open marriage as an unwholesome attempt "to have your cake and eat it too" that is based on self-deception and bound to create conflict.)

Communal households offer other options to people who reject traditional marriage. Group marriages, in which three or more people share all the intimacies of traditional marriage, are rare. However, there is a large number of communes that bring single people, unmarried and married couples, and children together in varying combinations. Some are founded on ideological principles and organized around strict rules and regulations; others are largely unstructured. In general, people join com-

FIGURE 14.7
Communal households offer a variety of relationships to people who prefer not to live in a traditional family. On many communes, married and single people have close, familial ties which include sharing the responsibilities for childcare. Living closely with a large number of people, however, often turns out to require adjustments that are difficult to make.

munes because they want to have close, familial relationships with a number of different people—not just a single spouse and their children. However, the number of people in a commune multiplies the number of needs, self-images, and role expectations to which each member must adjust. Quarrels over responsibilities and financial matters, lack of privacy, and jealousy often lead to disillusionment and disengagement.

At the opposite extreme are those individuals who live alone. Not marrying may or may not be a conscious decision. A person may come very close to marrying someone he or she is living with but decide against it. Or a person may remain single because he or she never feels a strong need to settle down and never meets someone who makes marriage look attractive. It seems likely that the number of people who remain single for all or most of their lives will increase in the future—in part because the stereotypes of the fussy bachelor and the old maid are breaking down. Singlehood is gradually changing from a badge of failure to an alternate lifestyle (see Coleman and Hammen, 1974, pp. 292–297).

THE WORLD OF WORK

Nearly all Americans work during at least some part of their lives—including 90 percent of American women. Most people spend as much or more time on the job as they do with their families and friends. This means that deciding what job you want and/or adjusting to the job you get have a decisive impact on your overall happiness.

In many respects, going to work is like getting married. Just as marital success depends on finding a compatible mate and approaching marriage with realistic expectations, satisfaction with a career depends on achieving a realistic match between one's skills and interests and what the job offers.

Attitudes Toward Work

Young people entering the job market today are somewhat more skeptical and demanding than their parents were. According to a nationwide survey, less than half (44 percent) believe that hard work will pay off. Unlike their parents, who by and large were content with good wages and job security, college and noncollege youth are looking for meaningful, challenging work and want to play a role in decisions affecting their jobs. Doing what they're told and collecting their checks isn't enough. Still, the overwhelming majority of young people today believe that a career is a very important part of a person's life, and that it is possible to find self-fulfillment *within* a conventional career (Yankelovich, 1973, 1974). What happens when these young people go to work?

Getting a Job

The kind of job a person gets depends on a number of factors: talents and interests, the level and kind of education he or she has acquired, previous experience, connections with the working world, the impression he or she makes in interviews, and, despite legislation against discrimination, sex, race, and age can still affect one's job opportunities.

Let's focus on the recent graduate. In some cases, a student has trained for a specific career, such as nursing or engineering, teaching or law. More often college students have only general ideas about what they want to do after they graduate. One wants "to work with people"; another, "to go into" business or politics.

Job placement services on campus and employment agencies offer tests that may help the individual to focus his or her interests. For example, the Strong Vocational Interest Blank asks you to indicate whether you like, dislike, or feel indifferent to four hundred items covering everything from academic subjects to hobbies. The results show how much you have in common with successful teachers, architects, forest rangers, etc. The Kuder (Vocational) Preference Record is designed to measure your interest in ten different types of work, ranging from outdoor jobs to scientific, artistic, and "persuasive" careers. These tests are sometimes given before high school or college graduation, to help students select a course of study. Employers may use these or similar tests to evaluate job applicants (a topic we will discuss further in Chapter 17). Of course, the fact that an individual is interested in a particular field does not guarantee that jobs will be available, or that a chosen job or career will fulfill a person's expectations. In work, as in the other areas we have discussed, adjustment to reality is necessary.

Suppose, for example, an English major decides to enter publishing. She may have worked as a camp counsellor, a part-time salesperson or waitress, perhaps as an assistant librarian—but she has no experience in publishing. She finds that the employment agencies are not interested in her opinions on modern poetry. Indeed, a typing course she once took in junior high school counts more than all her classes in literature. She is offered a beginning job as an editorial secretary for a salary that barely pays her rent.

The First Job

For most people, leaving school and getting their first full-time job is the major step into adulthood. It is exciting but also frightening. Most students have vague notions about the world of work, pieced together from hearsay, brief glimpses during interviews, and the employer's sales pitch. The new publishing secretary doesn't know what proofreaders, editors, and others actually do. More important, she doesn't know what will be expected of her. Will other workers accept her? (The fear of rejection will be particularly strong if a well-educated but inexperienced young person is placed in charge of a group of less-educated veterans.) The unknown is always frightening, and the first days and weeks on a job are often stressful. The ex-student finds herself completely exhausted at the end of the day.

Although some individuals receive training in job skills in school, few are taught how to handle office politics, the kinds of trivial problems that

FIGURE 14.8
A young person's first job often requires a long period of adjustment. Hopes for an exciting, interesting job may have to be deferred until after serving an apprenticeship.

make it impossible to do your work, and so on. College tends to teach people to take a long-range view and to approach problems in a rational, calculated manner. This is true of most courses in business management as well as of courses in liberal arts. Work involves "psychological skills" (dealing with people), common sense, and an ability to cope with minor crises on a day-to-day basis. Few students are prepared for this.

The actual tasks a new employee is required to perform may feel like a step down. In college a student was writing papers about the world food crisis and unravelling the symbolism of obscure poets. At work she is typing letters, filling out endless forms, running errands, taking messages, even making coffee. She may get little or no feedback on her performance. (Bosses do not grade subordinates at regular intervals.) A memo she spent hours writing may lie unread on her boss's desk. She dreamed of guiding young authors through their first novel. She discovers that editors are as interested in sales figures as in great literature—if not more so. She rarely meets an author. In short, she finds she is neither growing personally nor making a meaningful contribution to literature. The job falls considerably short of her expectations—in part because they were unrealistic to begin with (Coleman and Hammen, 1974, p. 351).

E. H. Schein (1968) found that half of one class of M.I.T. graduates left their first jobs within three years—in part because they were not prepared for the work, in part because they were disillusioned.

Adjusting to Work

Adjusting to work depends on two factors: what the individual brings to a job and what the job offers the individual (Coleman and Hammen, 1974, pp. 351–354). A knowledge of one's own assets and limitations is essential. Conceivably, some people could talk themselves into a job that requires more skill and experience than they possess. But the strain of "faking it" day after day may prove unbearable. A waitress may dream of becoming an actress. If waiting on tables is the best job she can get, she'll be happier if she pretends to be on stage while working or tries to be the best waitress in the restaurant than if she broods over her situation.

Patience, an ability to tolerate frustration and delay, and a willingness to compromise are also important qualities to bring to a job. As a rule, people do not become stars, editors, or company vice-presidents over night. A young employee may know she could handle things better than her boss does three weeks after taking the job. But if she makes the boss look foolish she is likely to be fired—and lose the opportunity to put her ideas into practice in the future. An aspiring architect may have to compromise his aesthetic principles to fulfill a client's demands more often than an established architect does. In a sense, this is an investment in the future. But the emphasis here is on compromise, on finding a middle road. An employee who blindly follows orders and gives in all of the time is likely to become bitter, detached from his work and to some degree from himself.

Disputes between labor and management in all industries focus on wages, job security, and fringe benefits. As Maslow pointed out, basic maintenance needs come first. Working hard for less than living wages is not likely to produce job satisfaction. But earning a living is not enough, particularly for young people (as suggested above). People want jobs that will hold their interest and satisfy their needs for recognition and achievement.

Sources of Stress.   There are essentially two reasons why the quest for meaningful work has become so difficult. First, the nature of work has changed. Relatively few workers have the satisfaction of producing something they can see and take pride in having made themselves. How can an assembly-line worker, who tightens the same bolts on car after car, day after day, identify with the finished product? Relatively few employees know the names, much less the faces, of the people who make the ultimate decisions about their working lives. The "boss" may be a remote holding company. Big business has reduced workers to anonymous and expendable parts of corporate machines.

Second, expectations have risen. The American Dream promises everyone a chance to find a lucrative and meaningful job—if they work hard and get a good education. The problem is that the number of jobs requiring advanced education has not kept pace with the number of degrees being awarded, and the ratio becomes more unfavorable every year. As a result, jobs that once required a high-school diploma now require a B.A., and an increasing number of graduates are trapped in jobs beneath their level of training. Ph.D.s are driving cabs; engineers are working as salespeople. The individual who can accept so large a gap between education, hopes, and work is rare.

FIGURE 14.9
Doing the same task day after day can be a boring, alienating experience. Assembly line workers cannot feel pride in the finished product and have little say in decisions affecting their working lives.

Methods of Coping. How do people handle anonymity and frustrated hopes? One auto worker told writer Studs Terkel,

"Occasionally one of the guys will let a car go by. At that point, he's made a decision: '[The hell with it.] It's only a car.' It's more important to just stand there and rap. With us, it becomes a human thing. It's the most enjoyable part of the job, that moment. I love it!" (1974, p. xviii)

Contrast this with a fireman who was perhaps the happiest person Terkel interviewed.

"... [T]he firemen, you actually see them produce. You see them put out a fire. You see them come out with babies in their hands. You see them give mouth-to-mouth when a guy's dying.... That's real. To me, that's what I want to be.

"I worked in a bank. You know, it's just paper. It's not real.... You're lookin' at numbers. But I can look back and say, 'I helped put out a fire. I helped save somebody.' It shows I did something on this earth." (p. xxx)

Minority Workers. Members of minorities have a whole additional set of work-related problems to cope with. Whereas almost 80 percent of white youth surveyed in 1973 expressed optimism about their futures, only 56 percent of nonwhite youth were hopeful—with good reason (Yankelovich, 1973). The median income of nonwhite families in this country is slightly more than half that of white families; the unemployment rate for nonwhites, double that for whites.

Women have been subject to the same kind of discrimination. In 1970, women earned 59 percent as much as men did for the same work. One-third of all working women (about nine million) are employed as secretaries. Fewer than 9 percent of full professors, 6 percent of physicians, 5 percent of lawyers, and 1 percent of engineers—the high-prestige professions—are female (Coleman and Hammen, 1974, pp. 361–365).

Women today are in a double bind. On the one hand, they have been raised to think that "a woman's place is in the home." It is difficult to ignore completely the view that a female who does not marry and raise a family is a failure as a woman, and that a wife and mother who works is neglecting her family. On the other hand, the amount of media attention paid to women's liberation and successful career women implies that it is somewhat less than respectable to be a full-time housekeeper. A woman who likes the traditional role may feel somewhat embarrassed about it. Either way—whether she works or not—a woman may feel frustrated.

Legislation against discriminatory hiring practices and ads and TV serials that depict affluent members of minorities may suggest that those who lack opportunities to join the middle class have only themselves to blame. Having the opportunity to get ahead may also be stressful. Many companies are actively looking for nonwhites with higher education—in part to satisfy the laws. In this sense, nonwhites with college degrees may have a slight competitive edge in being hired. But unconscious stereotyping, unthinking remarks, and excessive politeness may make it painfully obvious that many bosses and coworkers are not happy about equal opportunity. A lone black or Spanish worker especially may feel that he or she is on stage all of the time.

Adjusting to these conditions depends on the individual's ability to dispel inner tension by laughing or crying, talking or withdrawing temporarily, to develop strategies for coping with the reality of the situation rather than sinking into bitterness, and to derive a strengthened sense of oneself from the experience.

FIGURE 14.10
An unanticipated side effect of ads depicting affluent black men and women is that they may result in stress and frustration among blacks who have not become financial successes.

SUMMARY

1. Well-adjusted people are able to cope with frustration, disappointment, and loss, and make the most of themselves and their opportunities.

2. After studying highly productive people who fulfilled their capabilities, Abraham Maslow concluded that self-actualized people were not free of emotional problems. Rather, they ad-

justed to their problems in ways that allowed them to become highly productive.

3. Stress is the tension people feel when they can't satisfy their needs or when their well-being is threatened by forces beyond their control. Responses to stress include crying, talking, withdrawing, and laughing. Often these re-

sponses alleviate tension, provide needed sympathy and emotional support, or just provide an opportunity to think and make new decisions. These responses are temporary ways of coping with stress. If they are carried to the extreme, they can be self-defeating and may create even greater problems.

4. People respond to severe or prolonged stress in three stages—the alarm stage, the resistance stage, and the exhaustion stage. Some people are unable to adjust to stress by any means. These people are subject to psychological breakdowns.

5. Students entering college meet people from many different backgrounds and are exposed to new ideas. Many students find that their career aspirations are unrealistic. They may also begin to question their own beliefs and behavior.

6. Some of the ways students cope with the stresses of college life include redoubling their efforts to maintain past choices, avoiding anything or anyone that could foster doubt, detaching themselves emotionally or dropping out, and resynthesizing their feelings and experiences in order to formulate new directions and goals.

7. It is difficult for many individuals to adjust to love and marriage. Exaggerated ideas about love can lead to disillusionment and, perhaps, to divorce.

8. Intimacy involves self-disclosure, and self-disclosure involves risk. Some individuals adjust to this risk by avoiding people and situations that threaten their image of themselves, their mates, and their relationships. Some couples commit themselves to growing together. Most couples fall somewhere in between.

9. Healthy adjustment in marriage depends on at least three factors: whether the couple's needs are compatible, whether their images of themselves coincide with their images of each other, and whether they agree on what their individual roles should be within the marriage.

10. Adjustment to work depends on what a person brings to the job and what the job offers the individual. A knowledge of one's assets, an ability to tolerate frustration and delay, and a willingness to compromise are important qualities to have when beginning a job.

GLOSSARY

adjustment: The process of adapting to and actively shaping one's environment.

conflict-habituated marriage: A marriage in which the partners spend most of their time fighting.

developmental friendship: The type of friendship in which the partners force one another to reexamine their basic assumptions and perhaps adopt new ideas and beliefs.

devitalized marriage: A marriage, originally based on love, in which the partners no longer attempt or expect passion or bliss, but get along well enough to remain together.

future shock: A term used to describe the effects of the accelerated rate of change in society.

passive-congenial marriage: A marriage based on convenience, in which the partners live together and share responsibilities in order to make it easier for each to pursue individual interests.

resynthesis: The process of combining old ideas with new ones and reorganizing feelings in order to renew one's identity.

self-actualized: The term, introduced by Abraham Maslow, to describe a well-adjusted and productive person.

stress: The tension or strain people feel when they are unable to satisfy their needs and feel their well-being threatened by forces beyond their control.

total marriage: A marriage in which the husband and wife are deeply involved in one another's careers and hobbies, spend most of their time together, and seem to live for one another.

vital marriage: A marriage in which the partners enjoy each other's company and spend a great deal of time together. At the same time, each maintains his or her own sense of individual identity, and they participate in separate activities.

ACTIVITIES

1. A basic theme of this chapter has been the disparity between expectation and reality. Somehow, our dreams often manage to be better than what turns out to happen, whether in love affairs, going to college, or starting a new job. Think of an experience you have had where reality turned out more disappointing than you originally thought, and discuss how you adjusted to it.

2. Examine the list of characteristics that Maslow (1971) claims are typical of healthy, adjusted people. Do any of these qualities describe people that you know who you think are successful, self-actualizing individuals?

3. Talk to a few people who went to college and are now pursuing their careers. Ask them if they thought when they were in college that they would be doing what they are now doing or if their goals changed a lot. Ask them how they feel college prepared them for their present careers. How do their answers fit in with what Madison (1969) says about the college experience?

4. The idea of "romantic love" is fostered in fairytales like *Cinderella* and *Sleeping Beauty*, in popular songs, novels, short stories, and TV commercials. Take an example from one or two of these areas and discuss how they express the romantic ideal of falling in love with the perfect stranger.

5. Cuber and Harroff (1965) classify marriages as either vital, total, devitalized, passive-congenial, or conflict-habituated. Think of some of the marriages of people in your family, neighbors, or friends, and discuss why you think they would be classified in one of these five categories.

6. If any of the marriages of people you know ended in divorce, make some notes on why you think this occurred. If some of these people are available, ask them how they adjusted to being divorced and what kind of problems they had.

7. Interview one or two people about their jobs. Ask them how they happened to choose this kind of work; what they feel is wrong with it; if they ever do anything to make it more interesting and enjoyable; what they like about the job. You could also ask them if they ever experience any "peak experiences" in their work.

8. The class could divide into small groups, with females and males in each, to discuss the particular problems of adjustment facing contemporary women. Each group could turn in a list of these problems and then the whole class could discuss them. What did people tend to list most often? What did they leave out? Did groups disagree among themselves on some of these issues?

SUGGESTED READINGS

ARMSTRONG, GREGORY (ED.). *Life at the Bottom.* New York: Bantam Books, 1971 (paper). What adjustment to school, love, marriage, and work means to minority groups in our society is presented in a collection of short statements by the people themselves. A probing introduction by the editor suggests that the adjustment difficulties of ethnic minorities are very similar to those of women, children, students, homosexuals, and the elderly, who are also forced to live at the bottom of the power structure of our society.

BROWN, CLAUDE. *Manchild in the Promised Land.* New York: Signet Books, 1965 (paper). The autobiography of a young man who survived a childhood of extreme poverty, prejudice, gang wars, stealing, and dope pushing on the streets of Harlem to become a law student at one of America's leading universities.

CSIKSZENTMIHALYI, MIHALY. *Beyond Boredom and Anxiety.* New York: Jossey-Bass, 1976. Maslow studied "healthy" individuals and found many commonly have "peak experiences" of intense enjoyment and happiness. Czikszentmihalyi has now made an in-depth study of these experiences, asking surgeons, rock climbers, chess players, dancers, and basketball players what precedes these moments and how they feel during them. The result is an exciting and inspiring picture of healthy adjustment.

FRIEDAN, BETTY. *The Feminine Mystique.* New York: Dell Publishing Co., 1963 (paper). Written with a strong sense of outrage, this well-documented book has become one of the classic treatments of the problems of modern women.

KRANTZLER, MEL. *Creative Divorce.* New York: M. Evans and Co., 1973 (paper). Adjusting to divorce often involves a period of mourning the death of the lost relationship, feeling rejected by old friends, using children as scapegoats for anger at the ex-spouse, and a great deal of loneliness and self-pity. As a specialist in therapy with divorced individuals, the author shows how these difficulties can be avoided so that the experience becomes more liberating and growth enhancing.

ROGERS, CARL. *Becoming Partners: Marriage and its Alternatives.* New York: Delta, 1972 (paper). In this thought-provoking discussion of interpersonal relationships, the lifestyles of many different people are presented in their own words followed by commentaries by the author.

TOFFLER, ALVIN. *Future Shock.* New York: Bantam Books, 1970 (paper). A fascinating picture of how much society has changed since our parents and grandparents were children. This change has been so rapid that many people feel unprepared for the present and even less prepared for the future. The process, like any form of change, requires coping with considerable stress.

TERKEL, STUDS. *Working.* New York: Avon Books, 1974 (paper). A panorama of viewpoints of what Americans from many different walks of life think about their jobs, by a reporter who seemed to ask just the right questions to elicit the most personal and revealing answers.

BIBLIOGRAPHY

ARKOFF, ABE. *Adjustment and Mental Health.* New York: McGraw-Hill, 1968.

BURGESS, E. W., AND WALLIN, P. *Engagement and Marriage.* Philadelphia: Lippincott, 1953.

CHOLDEN, L. "Some Psychiatric Problems in the Rehabilitation of the Blind." *Menninger Clinic Bulletin,* 18 (1954): 107–112.

COLEMAN, JAMES C., AND HAMMEN, CONSTANCE L. *Contemporary Psychology and Effective Behavior.* Glenview, Ill.: Scott, Foresman, 1974.

COLES, R. "Life in Appalachia: the Case of Hugh McCaslin." In G. Armstrong (ed.), *Life at the Bottom.* New York: Bantam Books, 1971, pp. 26–42.

CUBER, J. F., AND HARROFF, P. *Sex and the Significant American.* Baltimore, Md.: Penguin, 1965.

ERIKSON, ERIK H. *Childhood and Society.* New York: Norton, 1963.

HOLMES, T. H., AND RAHE, R. H. "The Social Readjustment Rating Scale." *Journal of Psychosomatic Research*, 11 (1967): 213.

KENISTON, K. "Alienation in American Youth." In A. H. Esman (ed.), *The Psychology of Adolescence: Essential Readings*. New York: International Universities Press, 1975, pp. 434–450.

KOMAROVSKY, M. *Blue-Collar Marriage*. New York: Random House, 1964.

KRANTZLER, MEL. *Creative Divorce*. New York: M. Evans, 1973.

LEVINGER, G. "Sources of Dissatisfaction Among Applicants for Divorce." *American Journal of Orthopsychiatry*, 36 (1966): 803–807.

MACKLIN, E. "Heterosexual Cohabition Among Unmarried College Students." *The Family Coordinator*, 21 (1972): 463–472.

MADISON, PETER. *Personality Development in College*. Reading, Mass.: Addison-Wesley, 1969.

MASLOW, ABRAHAM H. *Motivation and Personality*. New York: Harper & Row, 1954; Viking, 1971.

PARKES, C. M. "Components of the Reaction to Loss of Limb, Spouse, or Home." *Journal of Psychosomatic Research*, 16 (1972): 343–349.

RUBIN, ZICK. *Liking and Loving*. New York: Holt, Rinehart and Winston, 1973.

SCHEIN, E. H. "The First Job Dilemma." *Psychology Today*, 1 (1968): 26–37.

SELYE, H. "Stress." *Psychology Today*, 3 (1969): 24–26.

SKOLNICK, ARLENE. *The Intimate Environment*. Boston: Little, Brown, 1973.

TERKEL, STUDS. *Working*. New York: Avon, 1974.

TOFFLER, A. *Future Shock*. New York: Bantam, 1970.

WILLIAMS, ROBIN. *American Society*. 3rd ed. New York: Knopf, 1970.

YANKELOVICH, DANIEL. *Yankelovich Youth Study*. JDR 3rd Fund, 1973.

——. *Changing Youth Values in the 70s*. JDR 3rd Fund, 1974.

15

Disturbance and Breakdown

A man living off in the Ozark Mountains has a vision in which God speaks to him. He begins preaching to his relatives and neighbors, and soon he has the whole town in a state of religious fervor. People say he has a "calling." His reputation as a prophet and healer spreads, and in time he is drawing large audiences everywhere he goes. However, when he ventures into St. Louis and attempts to hold a prayer meeting on a main street at rush hour, he is arrested. He tells the policemen about his conversations with God and they hurry him off to the nearest mental hospital.

A housewife is tired all the time. The chores keep piling up because she has no energy. Applications for graduate courses and "help-wanted" clippings from the classified ads lie untouched in a drawer. She consults the family doctor, but he says she's in perfect health. One night she tells her husband that she's thinking of seeing a psychotherapist. He thinks this is ridiculous. According to him, all she needs is to get up out of her chair and get busy.

Who is right? The "prophet" or the policemen? The housewife or her husband? It is often difficult to draw a line between "sanity" and "madness," normal and abnormal behavior. Behavior that some people consider normal seems crazy to others. Many non-Western peoples, along with religious fundamentalists in our own country, feel that having visions and hearing voices is an important part of a religious experience. Other people believe these are symptoms of mental disturbance. The man in the example above was interviewed by psychiatrists, diagnosed as "paranoid schizophrenic," and hospitalized for mental illness. Had he stayed home, he could have been considered perfectly okay. Indeed, more than okay—special (Slotkin, 1955).

WHAT IS ABNORMAL BEHAVIOR?

In our example, the man was classified as mentally troubled because his behavior was so different from what other people felt was "normal." Yet the fact that a person is different does not necessarily mean that he or she is insane. Indeed, going along with the crowd may at times be self-destructive. Most readers—and most psychologists—would agree that a teenager who uses heroin because nearly everyone in his social circle does so has problems.

In the case of the housewife, it was she herself who decided that

FIGURE 15.1
Most people feel anxious and alone at times, but sometimes fear, anxiety, and feelings of alienation become overwhelming, as they seem to be in this painting. In this chapter we will consider some of the reasons why people may become seriously disturbed.

she was psychologically troubled, simply because she was so unhappy. Yet unhappiness and even genuine depression are certainly not foolproof signs of psychological disturbance or of impending breakdown. Everyone feels low from time to time.

In short, there is no list of acts and feelings that are abnormal as opposed to normal. How, then, do psychologists distinguish between the two?

There are a number of ways to define abnormality, none of which is entirely satisfactory. We will look at the most popular ways of drawing the line between normal and abnormal: the deviance approach, the adjustment approach, the legal approach, and the psychological health model. We will also consider the criticism that in all these models, people are arbitrarily labeled mentally ill.

Deviation from Normality

One approach to defining abnormality is to say that whatever most people do is normal. Abnormality, then, is any *deviation* from the average or from the majority. It is normal to bathe periodically, to be attracted to the opposite sex, and to laugh when tickled, because most people do so. And because very few people take ten showers a day, or find horses sexually attractive, or laugh when a loved one dies, those who do may be considered abnormal.

This approach is the basis of a number of our assumptions about who is abnormal. For example, the question of whether or not a child is mentally retarded is decided on the basis of how many points the child's IQ score falls below the statistical average of 100. The designation of homosexuality as abnormal also depends heavily on the deviance approach: Most people are interested primarily in the opposite sex; therefore those who are more interested in people of their own sex are judged to be abnormal.

FIGURE 15.2
Does this man strike you as odd? Do you think he should seek help? The photograph, taken in the 1930s, is of an upper-class Frenchman. In his time and place, he might have been considered eccentric, but there would have been no basis for judging him as abnormal or maladjusted. Unusual behaviors that in one context may be signs of disorder may, in another, be only amusing. Defining abnormality, then, is difficult but is of great practical importance.

However, the deviance approach, as commonly used as it is, has serious limitations. If the majority of people smoke cigarettes, are nonsmokers abnormal? If most people cheat on their income tax returns, are honest taxpayers abnormal? If most people are noncreative, was Shakespeare abnormal? Because the majority is not always right or best, the deviance approach to defining abnormality is not a generally useful standard.

Adjustment

Another way to distinguish normal from abnormal people is to say that the normal person is one who is able to get along in the world—physically, emotionally, and socially. He is able to feed and clothe himself, to work, to find friends, and to live by the rules of society. By this definition, an abnormal person is one who fails to *adjust*. He may be so unhappy that he refuses to eat or so lethargic that he cannot hold a job. He may experience so much anxiety in relationships with other people that he ends up avoiding them, living in a lonely world of his own.

The idea of adjustment should not be confused with conformity. The conformist passively accepts his environment and the demands of others. The well-adjusted person, instead, actively shapes his environment and seeks social relationships that are both satisfying and growth-promoting.

The Legal Approach

The terms "sane" and "insane" are not used by psychologists. Rather, they are *legal* distinctions. A person is called legally insane if it is judged that he cannot understand the difference between right and wrong or if he is unable to control his own actions. If normality is defined in terms of sanity, then the normal person is one who is able to exercise a certain amount of judgment; he takes responsibility for his own actions. A person who is unable to judge the rightness or wrongness of his behavior or who cannot control what he does is considered insane, or at least incompetent, in the eyes of the law. He is also considered potentially dangerous and therefore is likely to be institutionalized.

This approach raises many questions, however. How can we account for the many people in mental hospitals who are obviously psychologically disturbed but who are also harmless? How do we distinguish between legal "wrong" and moral "wrong"? And how can we *know* that the individual in question cannot distinguish right from wrong or that his behavior is out of his control?

Psychological Health

The terms "mental illness" and "mental health" imply that psychological disturbance or abnormality is like a physical sickness—such as the flu or tuberculosis. Although many psychologists are beginning to think that "mental illness" is a completely different sort of thing from physical illness, the idea remains that there is some ideal way for people to function psychologically, just as there is physically. Some psychologists feel that

FIGURE 15.3
A still from the film *Who's Afraid of Virginia Woolf?* This powerfully emotional drama (based on Edward Albee's play) portrays one night in the lives of two couples. This play won wide critical acclaim because Albee so accurately (and painfully) exposed the inner conflicts of a "normal" and "stable" marriage to reveal nightmares that are recognizable to millions. What is frightening is that this play is not about "mental illness"—it is about the people next door.

FIGURE 15.4
Psychologically healthy people accept and express their individuality and humanness. Full self-acceptance and the achievement of one's unique potential is called self-actualization.

the normal or healthy person would be one who is functioning ideally or who at least is striving toward ideal functioning. Personality theorists such as Carl Jung and Abraham Maslow (see Chapter 13) have tried to describe this striving process, which is often referred to as *self-actualization.* According to this line of thinking, to be normal or healthy involves full acceptance and expression of one's own individuality and humanness.

One problem with this approach to defining abnormality is that it is difficult to determine whether or not a person is doing a good job of actualizing himself. How can you tell when a person is doing his best? What are the signs that he is losing the struggle? Answers to such questions must often be arbitrary.

The Dangers of Labeling

Indeed, all the current definitions of abnormality are somewhat arbitrary. And this fact has led some theorists to conclude that labeling a person as "mentally ill" simply because his behavior is odd is cruel and irresponsible. The foremost spokesman of this point of view is the American psychiatrist Thomas Szasz (1961).

Szasz argues that most of the people whom we call mentally ill are not ill at all. They simply have "problems in living"—serious conflicts with the world around them. But instead of dealing with the patient's conflict as something that deserves attention and respect, psychiatrists simply label him as "sick" and shunt him off to a hospital. The society's norms remain unchallenged, and the psychiatrist remains in a comfortable position of authority. The one who loses is the patient, who is deprived both of his responsibility for his behavior and of his dignity as a human being. As a result, Szasz claims, the patient's problems intensify. Szasz's position is a minority stand. Most psychologists and psychiatrists would agree that a person who claims that he is God or Napoleon is truly abnormal and disturbed.

The fact that it is difficult to define abnormality does not mean that no such thing exists. What it does mean is that we should be very cautious about judging a person to be "mentally ill" just because he or she acts in a way that we cannot understand. It should also be kept in mind that mild psychological disorders are extremely common. It is only when a psychological problem becomes severe enough to disrupt everyday life that it becomes thought of as "abnormality" or "illness."

THE PROBLEM OF CLASSIFICATION

For years psychiatrists have been trying to devise a logical and useful method for classifying emotional disorders. This is a difficult task, for psychological problems do not lend themselves to the same sort of categorizing that physical illnesses do. The causes, symptoms, and cures for psychological disturbances and breakdowns are rarely obvious or clear-cut.

The main system of classification in use today contains dozens of categories and subcategories of psychological disorders (American Psychiatric Association, 1968). This system has many drawbacks. For example, two psychotherapists may give completely different diagnoses of the same patient. Another problem is that few patients fit neatly into a single diagnostic category. Most disturbed people exhibit behavior typical of several different categories. Nevertheless, this system of classification does permit psychiatrists and psychologists to share information about symptoms and cures and to compare notes on possible causes.

The current diagnostic system distinguishes two main types of disorder: neurosis and psychosis. *Neurosis is a disorder in which severe anxiety reduces a person's ability to deal effectively with reality. Psychosis is a disorder in which a person is often unable to deal with reality at all and withdraws into his or her own private world.* Psychosis is not an advanced stage of neurosis. It is a distinct type of psychological disturbance.

In the following pages we will discuss the symptoms and possible causes of several forms of neurosis and psychosis. We will also examine two other categories of psychological problems: personality disorders and addiction to alcohol and other drugs.

As you read, you will probably feel that some of the descriptions could be applied to you at times. They probably could. But remember, a psychologically disturbed person is one who turns normal human quirks into extreme and distorted *patterns* of thought and behavior. When we speak of psychologically disturbed individuals we are not talking about people who have their normal share of difficulties, but rather people who are hopelessly unhappy, whose minds are confused and chaotic, who have a difficult time doing the simple things in life, or who act in ways that are truly harmful to themselves or to other people.

NEUROSIS

The world of a neurotic person is real but painful. Such a person rarely behaves in an alarmingly unusual fashion, but he is uncomfortable with life and can't seem to resolve his problems. He often has an unrealistic image of himself—feeling unworthy or inferior to those around him. Neurotic individuals are plagued by self-doubt and cannot seem to free themselves of recurring worries and fears. His emotional problems may be expressed in constant worrying, in sudden mood swings, or in a variety of physical symptoms (headaches, sweating, muscle tightness, weakness, fatigue, and the like). He lives a life of continuous anxiety with few periods of true tranquility. Neurotics often have difficulty forming stable and satisfying relationships.

Anxiety

Once in a while, everyone feels nervous for reasons he cannot quite explain; but a severely neurotic person feels this way practically all the time. Neurotic *anxiety* is generalized apprehension—a vague feeling that one

FIGURE 15.5
Anxiety, by Edvard Munch. Munch, probably more than any other artist, expressed in his paintings the emotions and forces studied by psychiatrists and psychologists. Here the vaguely threatening red sky and the tense stark faces serve as the visual image of anxiety, so important in many explanations of neurosis. A biography of Munch reveals that he had a great deal of experience with such disturbed feelings, both in himself and in members of his family.
(Collection, Museum of Modern Art, New York; Matthew T. Mellon Fund.)

is in danger. Unlike fear, which is a reaction to real and indentifiable threats, anxiety is a reaction to vague or imagined dangers.

Where does anxiety come from? Many psychologists believe it is caused by unconscious desires and conflicts that are so disturbing to the individual that he cannot find any satisfying solution. These unresolved conflicts often persist on an unconscious level. The individual lives in a more or less constant state of fear of emotions he doesn't feel capable of handling —his own emotions. When something happens to bring them closer to the surface, the fear becomes intense. For example, a person who is unable to face or express feelings of anger may become tense and fearful when he sees other people arguing or when hostile images flash into his mind, because these things remind him of emotions he is trying to deny. This is what we mean by anxiety. It seems unfounded and irrational because the individual is hiding emotions from himself as well as from others.

Most people are able to cope with occasional bouts of anxiety. However, some individuals find that the tension and uneasiness do not go away. A neurotic person may become so preoccupied with his internal problems that he neglects his social relationships. The people he sees every day recognize that he is nervous and unhappy, but they don't know the source of his problems. He has trouble dealing with his family and friends and fulfilling his responsibilities, and this too begins to worry him, adding to his anxiety. He is trapped in a vicious cycle. The more he worries, the more difficulty he has; the more difficulty he has, the more he worries. If the neurotic person cannot stop this cycle, it may end in a "nervous breakdown." He is temporarily forced to give up his struggle with every-day life and must find other people to look after him until he can sort out his problems (Fenichel, 1945).

Neurotics may develop a number of unusual behaviors in their effort to cope with anxiety—including phobias, obsessions, compulsions, hysteria, and depression. According to learning theory, these behaviors may be seen as the result of conditioning. Or they may be interpreted as extreme forms of the defense mechanisms we discussed in Chapter 13 (displacement, repression, projection, and regression).

Phobias

When severe anxiety is focused on a particular object or situation it is called a *phobia*. A phobia can develop toward almost anything; high places (acrophobia), open spaces (agoraphobia), enclosed places (claustrophobia), darkness (nyctophobia) are a few examples. A person with a phobia has an intense, persistent, irrational fear of something.

Phobic individuals develop elaborate plans to avoid the situations they fear. For example, people with an extreme fear of crowds may stop going to movies or shopping in large, busy stores. Indeed, some reach the point where they will not leave their houses at all.

There are a number of theories about how people develop phobias. In some cases, phobias result from frightening experiences in the past. For example, a person who was locked in a closet as a child (accidentally or as a punishment) may become claustrophobic. She realizes that closets are not harmful, yet feels a distinct dread of enclosed places. Most people have similar feelings about objects and situations associated with past frights.

Neurotic fears, however, do not always have such straightforward explanations. In less clear-cut cases, some psychologists have attempted to explain phobias in terms of projection. What the person really fears is an impulse inside himself: To avoid this fear, he unconsciously projects it onto something outside himself. For example, a person who is terrified of heights may really be afraid of losing control over other wishes or feelings. By concentrating on avoiding heights, he is able to control other disturbing urges and push them out of his consciousness.

FIGURE 15.6
Phobias, or irrational fears, provide the neurotic with an outlet for his anxiety without forcing him to confront the real source of the anxiety. For example, the man in the illustration who is exhibiting a phobia for ladybugs may in fact be frightened of women. By releasing his fear in this way, he avoids facing his real problem. Phobias also serve to command the attention and sympathy that the neurotic person cannot get (or thinks he cannot get) in more direct ways.

FIGURE 15.7
A still from the film *The Caine Mutiny,* in which Humphrey Bogart convincingly portrayed Captain Queeg, an individual who was obsessed with order. Any disruption of Queeg's established routine (as when some strawberries disappeared) sent him into panic and produced the compulsive behavior of continually rolling ball bearings in his hand. Queeg's odd behavior led his officers to label him "mentally ill" and to mutiny against him.

Obsessions and Compulsions

A person suffering from acute anxiety may find himself thinking the same thoughts over and over again, even though he finds them unpleasant. Such an uncontrollable pattern of thoughts is called an *obsession.* Or someone may repeatedly perform irrational actions. This is called a *compulsion.* The neurotic person may experience both these agonies together—a condition called *obsessive-compulsive neurosis.*

A compulsive person may feel compelled to wash her hands twenty or thirty times a day, or to avoid stepping on cracks in the sidewalk when she goes out. An obsessive person may be unable to rid herself of unpleasant thoughts about death, or of a recurring impulse to make obscene remarks in public. And the obsessive-compulsive may wash her hands continually *and* torment herself with thoughts of obscene behavior.

Everyone has obsessions and compulsions. Love might be described as an obsession; so might a hobby that occupies most of a person's spare time. Striving to do something "perfectly" is often considered to be a compulsion. But if the person who is deeply engrossed in a hobby or who aims for perfection enjoys this intense absorption and can still function effectively, he or she is usually not considered neurotic. Psychologists consider it a problem only when such thoughts and activities interfere with what a person wants and needs to do. Someone who spends so much time double-checking every detail of her work that she can never finish a job is considered more neurotic than conscientious.

Why do people develop obsessions and compulsions? Possibly because they serve as diversions from a neurotic person's real fears and their origins, and thus may reduce anxiety somewhat. In addition, compulsions provide a disturbed person with the evidence that she is doing something well, even if it is only avoiding cracks on a sidewalk. Thus there is some logic in this apparently illogical behavior.

Hysteria

Neurotic anxiety can also create a wide variety of physical symptoms with no apparent physical causes. This phenomenon is known as *hysteria.* There are two types of hysteria: conversion reactions and dissociative reactions.

Conversion Reactions. A *conversion reaction* is the conversion of emotional difficulties into the loss of a specific physiological function. Many people occasionally experience mild conversion reactions, as when someone is so scared he cannot move; he is "frozen stiff," as the phrase goes. But neurotic hysteria is not simply a brief loss of functioning due to fright. It persists.

An hysteric experiences a real and prolonged handicap—he literally cannot hear or speak or feel anything in his left hand or move his legs or exercise some other normal physical function. For example, he wakes up one morning and finds himself paralyzed from the waist down. A normal reaction to this would be to become violently upset. However, hysterics often accept their loss of function with relative calm. (This is one sign that a person is suffering from a psychological rather than a physiological problem.) Most psychologists believe that hysterics unconsciously invent physical symptoms to gain freedom from unbearable anxiety. For example, a person who lives in terror of blurting out things that he does not want to say may lose the power of speech. This "solves" the problem.

Hysteria must be distinguished from *hypochondria,* in which a person who is in good health becomes preoccupied with imaginary ailments and blames all his problems on them. Hysteria should also be distinguished from *psychosomatic* illnesses, in which emotional problems have produced real physical damage such as ulcers. Something real has happened to the hysteric, but not physically; once his emotional problems have been solved, his normal functioning is restored. This disorder was rather common in the eighteenth and nineteenth centuries—Freud's first cases were hysterics—but conversion reactions are comparatively rare today.

Dissociative Reactions.   Hysteria may take the form of *dissociative states,* in which the person experiences a loss of memory or identity or exhibits two or more identities. These psychological phenomena fascinate many people, so we hear a good deal about amnesia and "split personalities." Actually, they are very rare—even more so than conversion reactions.

Loss of memory, or *amnesia,* is an attempt to escape from problems by blotting them out completely. The amnesiac remembers how to speak and usually retains a fund of general knowledge. But he does not know who he is, where he lives and works, or who his family is (Levant, 1966).

In *fugue,* another type of dissociative reaction, amnesia is coupled with active flight to a different environment. The individual may suddenly disappear and "wake up" three days later in a restaurant two hundred miles from home. Or she may actually establish a new identity—assume a new name, marry, take a job, and so forth—in whatever place she lands, repressing all knowledge of her previous life. A fugue state may last for days or for decades. However long it lasts, the individual, when she comes out of it, will have no memory of what she has done in the interim. Fugue, then, is a sort of traveling amnesia, and it probably serves the same psychological function as amnesia: escape from unbearable conflict or anxiety.

In *multiple personality,* a third type of dissociative reaction, someone seems to have two or more distinct identities. Eve White, a young woman who sought psychiatric treatment for severe headaches and blackouts, has become a famous example. Eve White was a conscientious, self-controlled, rather shy person. However, during one of her therapy sessions, her expression—and her personality—suddenly changed. Eve Black, as she now called herself, was childlike, fun-loving, and irresponsible—the opposite of the woman who originally walked into the psychiatrist's office. Eve Black was conscious of Eve White's existence, but considered her a separate person. Eve White did not know about Eve Black, however, and neither was she conscious of Jane, a third personality that emerged

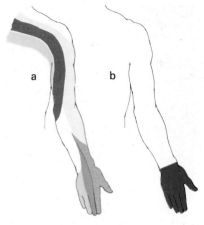

a   b

FIGURE 15.8
A patient who complained to a doctor that his right hand had become numb might be diagnosed either as suffering from damage to the nervous system or as a neurotic suffering from hysteria, depending on the exact pattern of his numbness. The skin areas served by different nerves in the arm are shown in (a). The "glove" anesthesia shown in (b) could not result from damage to these nerves.

FIGURE 15.9
Scenes from a film version of *The Three Faces of Eve.* (a) Eve White, the shy, demure personality that decided to go to a therapist because of frequent headaches and blackouts. (b) Eve Black, the outgoing, fun-loving personality. (c) Jane, the personality that emerged after a long period of therapy.

during the course of therapy. (This case served as the basis for the book and film, *The Three Faces of Eve.*) Psychologists believe that this dividing up of the personality is the result of the individual's effort to escape from a part of himself or herself that he or she fears. The "secret self" then emerges in the form of a separate personality.

Depression

Depression is a pattern of sadness, anxiety, fatigue, insomnia, agitated behavior, and reduced ability to function and interact with others. It ranges from mild feelings of uneasiness, sadness, and apathy to intense suicidal despair. Occasional depression is a common experience. Most of us feel depressed when someone we love dies, for example. And, from time to time, everyone feels "blue" for no apparent reason. However, when depression is chronic (that is, the person never seems to "snap out of it") or especially intense, it is considered a serious psychological problem.

Severe depression may reflect guilt and the need for self-punishment. For example, a person may feel that he or she neglected someone who

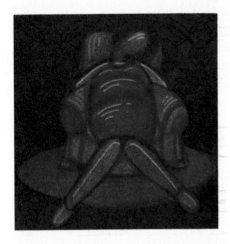

FIGURE 15.10
Neurotic depression frequently takes the form of apathy and withdrawal. The individual in this state simply stops caring about what is going on around him and may spend days or weeks at a time sitting or lying in a darkened room with nothing on his mind but his own feelings of gloom and despair. This state is typically produced by an overreaction to an experience that would be only a minor setback to a nonneurotic individual.

just died and unconsciously hold himself or herself responsible for that person's death. In this case, depression acts as a self-imposed jail term: The person does not allow himself to be active and happy. Depression may also represent displaced aggression. For example, a person who feels that someone she loves has abandoned her, physically or emotionally, may turn her anger on herself. In other cases depression may be an escape from life and its problems—a way of giving up. Consumed by feelings of helplessness, the individual withdraws into mental and physical lethargy. Whatever the source, depression is the most common complaint of people who seek psychiatric treatment.

Suicide

Not all people who commit suicide are depressed, and not all depressed people attempt suicide. But most depressives do think about suicide, and many of them translate these thoughts into action.

People may take their lives for any number of reasons: to escape from physical or emotional pain (perhaps a terminal illness or the loneliness of old age); to end the torment of unacceptable feelings (such as homosexual fantasies); to punish themselves for wrongs they feel they have committed; to punish others who have not perceived their needs (Mintz, 1968). In many cases we simply do not know why the suicide occurred.

But we do know that every year between 20,000 and 30,000 Americans end their lives—about one every thirty minutes. More women than men attempt suicide, but more men than women succeed. Suicide is most common among the elderly, but also ranks as the third most common cause of death among college students. Contrary to popular belief, people who threaten suicide or make an unsuccessful attempt usually are serious. Studies show that about 70 percent of people who kill themselves threaten to do so within the three months preceding the suicide, and an unsuccessful attempt is often a trial run. This implies that a leading cause of suicide is a failure in communication. Most suicidal people are simply not taken seriously enough—a fact that only helps to push them over the edge (Alvarez, 1970).

FIGURE 15.11
A "suicide hotline." The man shown here is one of the many trained volunteers who work at suicide prevention centers throughout the country. Callers are encouraged to talk out their problems and are often referred for psychiatric help.

Anxiety, phobias, obsessions, compulsions, hysteria, depression, and suicide—all are ways people use, in various combinations, to escape problems in themselves or the world in which they live. But, with the obvious exception of suicide, these neurotic reactions do not shut people off completely from daily life. Psychosis does.

PSYCHOSIS

A neurotic person is one who is emotionally crippled by anxiety but continues to slug it out with life as best he or she can. A psychotic person is one whose distorted perceptions and behavior reach such an irrational, fantastic, and fear-laden level that he or she withdraws completely from normal life. One might say that a neurotic dreams in an unreal way about life, whereas a psychotic lives life as an unreal dream.

Like neurosis, psychosis is not a single problem; it has no single cause or cure. Rather, it is a collection of symptoms that indicate an individual has serious difficulty trying to meet the demands of life. Two major categories of psychosis are *schizophrenia* and *affective reactions. Autism* is a psychosis found in children.

Schizophrenia

Approximately half the patients in United States mental hospitals have been diagnosed as schizophrenic (Taube and Rednick, 1973). What distinguishes this disorder from other types of psychological disturbance? *Schizophrenia involves confused and disordered thoughts and perceptions.*

Suppose a psychiatrist is interviewing a patient who has just been admitted to a hospital. The individual demonstrates a wide assortment of symptoms. He is intensely excited, expresses extreme hostility toward

FIGURE 15.12
These paintings were done by a male patient diagnosed as schizophrenic with paranoid tendencies. Both illustrations are characterized by the symbolism of watchful eyes, grasping hands, and the self as subject matter. In the first painting which reflects a subdued emotional state, there is a strong emphasis on the eyes, with a figure watching over the shoulder. The torso of the central figure is surrounded by hands, and the figure in the background is reaching out. Religiosity as well as delusions of persecution and grandeur may be seen in the cross and the Christ-like figure bestowing a wreath. The second painting reflects a more active emotional state. Again there is an emphasis on the eyes and on the hands, represented here as tentacles and claws.

Grammatically sound, but bizarre and jumbled speech is characteristic of schizophrenia. Some psychiatrists consider such speech a kind of secret code through which the schizophrenic effectively isolates himself from the rest of humanity.

"How old are you?"

"Why I am centuries old, sir."

"How long have you been here?"

"I've been now on this property on and off for a long time. I cannot say the exact time because we are absorbed by the air at night, and they bring back people. They kill up everything; they can make you lie; they can talk through your throat."

"Who is this?"

"Why, the air."

"What is the name of this place?"

"This place is called a star."

"Who is the doctor in charge of your ward?"

"A body just like yours, sir. They can make you black and white. I say good morning, but he just comes through there. At first it was a colony. They said it was heaven. These buildings were not solid at the time, and I am positive that this is the same place. They have others just like it. People die, and all the microbes talk over there, and prestigitis you know is sending you from here to another world. . . . I was sent by the government to the United States to Washington to some star, and they had a pretty nice country there. Now you have a body like a young man who says he is of the prestigitis."

"Who was this prestigitis?"

"Why, you are yourself. You can be prestigitis. They make you say bad things; they can read you; they bring back Negroes from the dead."

Source: W. A. White, *Outlines of Psychiatry,* 13th ed. New York: Nervous and Mental Disease Publishing Company, 1932, p. 228.

members of his family, and at the same time claims that he loves them, showing conflicting feelings. One minute he is extremely aggressive, questioning the psychiatrist's motives and even threatening her. The next minute he withdraws and acts as if he does not hear anything she says. Then he begins talking again. "Naturally," he says, "I am growing my father's hair." Although all of the person's other behavior indicates psychological problems, this last statement would be the "diagnostic bell-ringer." It reveals that the man is living in a private disordered reality.

Many schizophrenics experience *delusions* (false beliefs maintained in the face of contrary evidence) and *hallucinations* (sensations in the absence of appropriate stimulation). For example, a paranoid schizophrenic generally believes that others are plotting against him—contriving ways to confuse him, make him look ridiculous, perhaps to get rid of him. People are watching him constantly. His thoughts are being monitored. When he goes to the movies to escape, he finds—to his horror—that the film is all about him. The ticket-taker and the man in the next row are in on the plot. These delusions are usually supported by hallucinations, in which his five senses detect the evidence of the plot. He may taste

FIGURE 15.13
This illustration was painted by a male patient diagnosed as schizophrenic. Schizophrenic art frequently uses intense colors to express the feelings, attitudes, and concerns of the patient. This particular illustration contains biblical allusions and a number of references to sexual organs and sexual functioning, all common themes in psychosis.

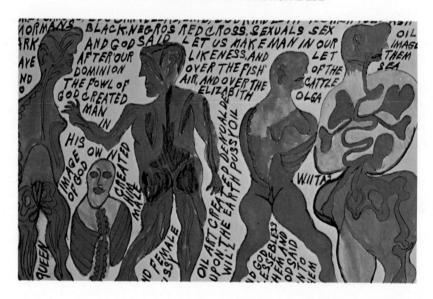

poison in his food, smell gas in his bedroom, or hear voices telling him why he has been singled out or what lies in store for him.

Often, schizophrenics withdraw from other people into a private world of fantasy. In *simple schizophrenia* the person gradually loses interest in what happens around him, becoming increasingly apathetic, listless, and noncommunicative. Such individuals may be able to hold menial jobs or may survive as "drifters," but their interpersonal contacts are few. *Catatonia* is an extreme form of withdrawal in which the person becomes totally unresponsive. He may maintain the same posture for hours, mute and seemingly oblivious to physical discomfort. Periodic flare-ups, when the person becomes violent toward himself or others, may be the only sign of emotional life in a catatonic person.

Other schizophrenics are active and busy, but their behavior and speech are incomprehensible to others. The person may repeat a bizarre gesture, whose meaning is known only to him, over and over. He may express inappropriate emotions—for example, giggling uncontrollably as he relates violent and morbid fantasies. He may invent words, repeat phrases as if they were magical incantations, or talk in rhymes or puns—for reasons known only to himself (Maher, 1972). The result is sometimes what psychologists call "word salad": a jumble of unconnected, irrational phrases.

It is as if the gears in the schizophrenic's mental machinery had slipped and the connections gone haywire. One patient described the experience as losing the ability to focus his thoughts.

"I can't concentrate. It's diversion of attention that troubles me. I am picking up different conversations. It's like being a transmitter. The sounds are coming through to me but I feel my mind cannot cope with everything. It's difficult to concentrate on any one sound."

Another told of being unable to organize his perceptions.

> "Everything is in bits. You put the picture up bit by bit into your head. It's like a photograph that's been torn to bits and put together again. You have to absorb it again. If you move it's frightening. The picture you had in your head is still there but it's broken up" (McGhie and Chapman, 1961).

Affective Reactions

Another common type of psychosis is one in which individuals are excessively and inappropriately happy or unhappy. These *affective reactions* (from the word "affect," meaning mood) may take the form of high elation, hopeless depression, or an alternation between the two.

The *manic*, or highly elated, type is characterized by extreme confusion, disorientation, and incoherence. The person's world is like a movie that is being run too fast so that the people and events are no more than a blur of purposeless activity. The following behavior is typical of acute mania:

> On admission she slapped the nurse, addressed the house physician as God, made the sign of the cross, and laughed loudly when she was asked to don the hospital garb. This she promptly tore to shreds. . . . She sang at the top of her voice, screamed through the window, and leered at the patients promenading in the recreation yard (Karnash, 1945).

In the *depressive reaction,* the individual is overcome by feelings of failure, sinfulness, worthlessness, and despair. We have already described depression as a form of neurosis. Psychotic depression differs from neurotic depression—just as psychosis in general differs from neurosis in general—in that the psychotic has lost contact with reality. The neurotic depressive may feel chronically dejected, but she still knows how to get to the bank, how old her children are, and how to differentiate between fantasy and reality. The psychotic depressive has left reality behind and has moved into a bleak fantasy world constructed out of her despair. She is likely to claim that her children are dead, that she killed them, that the world is coming to an end, that it is all her fault. Furthermore, the psychotic depressive may stop functioning altogether and descend into a stupor, not eating, not speaking, and not moving.

> The patient lay in bed, immobile, with a dull, depressed expression on his face. His eyes were sunken and downcast. Even when spoken to, he would not raise his eyes to look at the speaker. Usually he did not respond at all to questions, but sometimes, after apparently great effort, he would mumble something about the "Scourge of God" (Coleman, 1972).

In some cases, referred to as *manic-depressive psychosis,* a patient will alternate between frantic action and motionless despair. Theorists have speculated that the manic periods serve as an attempt to ward off the underlying hopelessness.

FIGURE 15.14
Among the behaviors typically displayed by autistic children are repetitive movements, echolalia, self-destructive acts, and withdrawal. Persons who attempt to interact with a severely autistic child often feel that, at best, the child acts as though they were objects to be investigated or moved aside and, at worst, as though they were not there.

FIGURE 15.15
An adolescent schizophrenic boy's paintings were made at the request of a therapist who hoped to find a starting place for communication with the withdrawn and unresponsive boy. These paintings illustrate a difficult question that comes up in trying to identify the causes of schizophrenia. Are these paintings bizarre and ominous because of the boy's disorder, or are the paintings sensitive representations of the factors in his family that caused the boy to become schizophrenic? Some theorists would probably say the second alternative was more likely to be true, although they would not deny that schizophrenia involves disorders of perception.

Autism

Autism is a childhood psychosis that seems to be present at birth. From an early age, autistic children are aloof and noncommunicative. Often they do not even cry or coo like other babies. They act as if other people do not exist. Rather than interact with others, they spend their waking hours rocking back and forth, hitting themselves methodically, examining spots on the floor, and the like. They become very upset over any change in their environment. They want things to remain the same.

These children are usually physically healthy—in fact, they are often quite beautiful, and their movements are quick and skillful. Psychologists do not really know what causes autism. Are these children born this way, or are they reacting to rejection by their parents? Do they have some mysterious brain defect? Do their bodies produce too much or too little of certain vital chemicals? Have their families given them some insoluble problem that causes overpowering anxiety?

Causes of Psychosis

A small proportion of the people diagnosed as psychotic are known to have physical brain damage. As for what is wrong with the rest, there are many theories but very few facts. Psychologists think that their problems result from the interaction of several factors, but none of these factors is at all clearly understood.

Hereditary Factors.   There is some evidence that people may inherit a predisposition or tendency to become psychotic. Close relatives of schizophrenics, for example, are much more likely to become schizophrenic than are other people, even if they never come into contact with their schizophrenic relative (Rosenthal *et al.*, 1971; Kety *et al.*, 1971). Just how this predisposition might be transmitted from generation to generation is a matter of speculation. According to one theory, people are born with different kinds of nervous systems. Some respond strongly and persistently to outside stimulation; others respond only weakly and erratically. Some react to new situations extremely quickly; others, more slowly. If a person has inherited an extreme form of nervous system, he may overreact or underreact to stress or conflict and behave oddly as a result. Thus a situation that might be only mildly upsetting to one person might cause a psychotic reaction in an acutely sensitive person. However, if this person is raised in a relatively simple, pressure-free environment, he might never develop psychological problems.

Biochemical Factors.   The proper working of the brain depends on the presence of the right amounts of many different chemicals, from oxygen to proteins. Some psychologists believe that psychosis is due largely to chemical imbalances in the brain. With depression, for example, abnormally low amounts of certain chemicals may disturb the transmission of electrical impulses from one brain cell to another.

Chemical problems may also be involved in schizophrenia. A number of researchers think that the basic problem in schizophrenia is that too much or too little of certain chemicals has "knocked out of kilter" the brain's mechanisms for processing information. As a result, the schizophrenic cannot organize his thoughts. When he tries to keep one thought at the center of his awareness, other thoughts—irrelevant ones—keep pushing in and interfering with his concentration (Litz, 1973). In short, he experiences the kind of thought disturbance reported by the schizophrenic patients quoted earlier in this chapter.

Unusual concentrations of certain chemicals have in fact been found in the bodies of many schizophrenics. However, it is hard to tell whether these chemicals are the cause of schizophrenia or the result of it. They may even be caused by the fact that schizophrenics tend to live in hospitals, where they get little exercise, eat institutional food, and are generally given daily doses of tranquilizers. Living under such conditions, anyone—not just the schizophrenic person—might begin to show chemical imbalances.

The Double Bind. Some theorists believe that many mental problems, particularly those that involve confused thoughts and isolation from other people, result from conflicts in communication. These psychologists believe that a child's ability to think and to communicate with others can be undermined if his parents repeatedly communicate contradictory messages. For example, a mother may resent her child and feel uncomfortable around him, yet also feel obligated to act lovingly toward him. She tells the child how much she loves him, but at the same time she stiffens whenever he tries to hug her. Thus the child is given one message in words and another in action.

As a result, the child is placed in an impossible situation. If he reaches out to his mother, she shows him (in her actions) that she dislikes this. If he avoids her, she tells him (in words) that she dislikes that. He wants very much to please her, but no matter what he does, it is wrong. He is caught in a *double bind.*

According to *double-bind theory*, a childhood full of such contradictory messages results in a person perceiving the world as a confusing, disconnected place and believing that his words and actions have little significance or meaning. Consequently he may develop the kind of disordered behaviors and thoughts we have been describing.

Which of these theories is correct? At this point, we do not know. It may be that each is partially true. Perhaps people who inherit a tendency toward psychological disorders react more strongly to a double bind than others would. Perhaps people who are caught in a double bind are especially vulnerable to chemical imbalances. Or perhaps it takes a combination of all three factors—heredity, biochemical disorders, and conflict—to produce psychotic behavior (Meehl, 1962). Only further research will give us the answer.

PERSONALITY DISORDERS

Personality disorders are rather different from the problems we have been discussing. People with personality disorders generally do not suffer from acute anxiety; nor do they behave in bizarre, incomprehensible ways. Psychologists consider these people "abnormal" because they seem unable to establish meaningful relationships with other people, to assume social responsibilities, or to adapt to their social environment. This diagnostic category includes a wide range of self-defeating personality patterns, from painfully shy, lonely types to vain, pushy show-offs. In this section we focus on the *antisocial personality*, sometimes called the sociopath.

Antisocial individuals are irresponsible, immature, emotionally shallow people who seem to court trouble. Extremely selfish, they treat people as objects—as things to be used for gratification and cast coldly aside when no longer wanted. Intolerant of everyday frustrations and unable to save or plan or wait, they live for the moment. Seeking thrills is their major occupation. If they should injure other people along the way or break social rules, they do not seem to feel any shame or guilt. It's the other person's tough luck. Nor does getting caught seem to rattle them. No matter how many times they are reprimanded, punished, or jailed, they never learn how to stay out of trouble. They simply do not profit from experience.

Many antisocial individuals can get away with destructive behavior because they are intelligent, entertaining, and able to mimic emotions they do not feel. They win affection and confidence from others whom they then take advantage of. This ability to charm while exploiting helped Charles Manson to dominate the gang of runaways whom he eventually led into the gruesome Tate-LaBianca murders.

FIGURE 15.16
This illustration suggests what may happen to a child who is born with a biochemically unusual nervous system, one that reacts very strongly to stimulation. During an early childhood illness that would have no lasting effect on most children, this child has pronounced hallucinations. As he grows older, he tries to understand this experience and integrate it with the rest of his life. He tries to discuss his memories of that time with his parents. Being insecure themselves, they become uneasy and respond in ways that make him feel that he is wrong or bad in some way. His unusual biochemistry causes him to react very strongly to this rebuff, and he thus has further troubling experiences that he needs to make sense of. He now begins to experience a conflict between his need to talk to his parents about his innermost feelings and his fear of their cold response. He is well on the way to becoming psychologically disordered unless the links in this repetitive chain are somehow broken.

378

UNIT V PERSONALITY AND EMOTIONAL LIFE

If caught, the antisocial individual will either spin a fantastic lie or simply insist, with wide-eyed sincerity, that his intentions were utterly pure. Guilt and anxiety have no place in the antisocial personality. A fine example is that of Hugh Johnson, a con man recently caught after having defrauded people out of thousands of dollars in sixty-four separate swindles. When asked why he had victimized so many people, "he replied with some heat that he never took more from a person than the person could afford to lose, and further, that he was only reducing the likelihood that other more dangerous criminals would use force to achieve the same ends" (Nathan and Harris, 1975, pp. 406–407).

How do psychologists explain such a total lack of ordinary human decency and shame? Some researchers explain the development of the antisocial personality as the result of an overindulgent or negligent upbringing. However, it is also possible that the antisocial person is the victim of a faulty nervous system. Experiments have shown that while antisocial people have no trouble learning to perform tasks in order to obtain rewards such as money or cigarettes, they are very slow in learning to perform tasks in order to avoid electric shock. The researchers who conducted these experiments suggest that the nervous system of the antisocial personality does not shoot up to the level of tension that most of us experience when we are in danger and that tells us to do something in order to avoid harm or disgrace. Because of this deficiency, the antisocial personality never experiences the physiological sensation of fear, and consequently he or she never learns to avoid punishment by correcting his or her behavior (Schachter and Latané, 1964).

DRUG ADDICTION AND ALCOHOLISM

In American society, drug abuse has become a major psychological problem. Millions of Americans depend so heavily on drugs that they hurt themselves physically, socially, and psychologically.

Abuse of drugs invariably involves *psychological dependence*. The user comes to depend so much on the feeling of well-being he obtains from the drug that he feels compelled to continue using it. People can become psychologically dependent on a wide variety of drugs, including alcohol, caffeine, nicotine (in cigarettes), opium, marijuana, and amphetamines. When deprived of the drug, a psychologically dependent person becomes restless, irritable, and uneasy.

In addition to psychological dependence, some drugs lead to physiological *addiction*. A person is addicted when his system has become so used to the drug that the drugged state becomes the body's "normal" state. If the drug is not in the body, the person experiences extreme physical discomfort, just as he would if he were deprived of oxygen or of water.

Just as dependence causes a psychological need for the drug, addiction causes a physical need. Furthermore, once a person is addicted to a drug, he may develop *tolerance;* that is, his body may become so accustomed to the drug that he has to keep increasing his dosage in order to obtain

FIGURE 15.17

Heavily carbon-pigmented lung typical of smoker's or coal miner's lung is compared to a normal lung surface. This carbon pigmentation occurs more in urban populations and industrialized countries and appears even in the lungs of non-smokers.

Dependence

Tolerance

Addiction

the "high" that he achieved with his earlier doses. With certain sleeping pills, for example, a person can rapidly develop a tolerance for up to fifteen times the original dose. Whether or not tolerance develops, an addict must have his drug in order to retain what little physical and psychological balance he has left. If he does not get it, he is likely to go through the dreaded experience of withdrawal.

Withdrawal is a state of physical and psychological upset during which the body and the mind revolt against, and finally get used to, the absence of the drug. Withdrawal symptoms vary from person to person and from drug to drug. They range from a mild case of nausea and "the shakes" to hallucinations, convulsions, coma, and death.

The most widely used and abused drug in the United States is clearly tobacco. The nicotine in tobacco is a mild stimulant, like the caffeine in coffee. It can decrease fatigue, increase talkativeness, diminish appetite, and elevate a person's mood. Most users become psychologically dependent on tobacco; they may develop tolerance and become chain-smokers. Unfortunately for these people, cigarettes are toxic—they are poisonous. Smoking can cause respiratory ailments, lung cancer, and heart disease. Both the user and those who inhale the smoke he exhales may be affected. However, because smoking cigarettes is socially acceptable, most people do not recognize nicotine addiction as a psychological problem. (For a discussion of marijuana, which generally is considered a problem, see Chapter 7.)

FIGURE 15.18
The distinctions between drug dependence, drug tolerance, and drug addiction. Dependence is a psychological effect. The drug becomes a significant part of the user's life, and its removal causes him to become irritable or nervous. Tolerance is a physiological phenomenon. To continue reproducing a given effect, the user must take increasingly larger doses. Tolerance may occur with or without addiction. Addiction works more radical physiological changes. The user's metabolism comes to depend on the drug for normal functioning. If the level of the drug in the user's body falls below a certain level, physiological withdrawal symptoms occur.

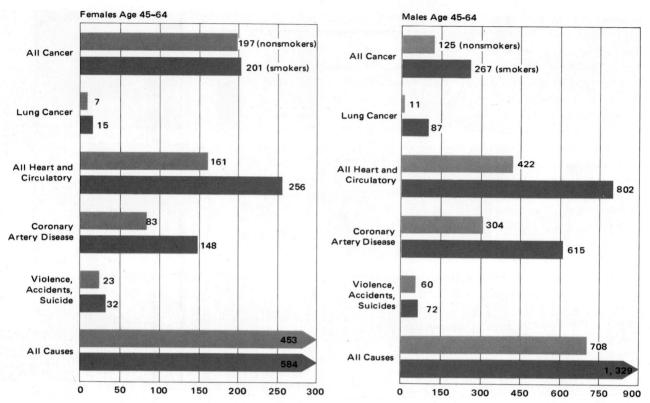

FIGURE 15.19
Death rates of cigarette smokers versus nonsmokers by selected diseases related to smoking (rates per 100,000 person-years).

While nicotine is potentially very damaging to the body, it seems to do very little to the mind (aside from creating dependence). However, three other widely abused drugs—heroin, alcohol, and barbiturates—are extremely dangerous both psychologically and physically. All three are depressants—that is, they slow down the activity of the brain. And all three can easily lead to dependence, addiction, and tolerance. There are other drugs that are equally dangerous (amphetamines, for example), but since these three are widespread enough to pose a serious social threat, it is on them that we will concentrate.

Heroin Addiction

Estimates of the number of heroin addicts in this country run to the hundreds of thousands. Nobody knows for sure how many people abuse this drug. But we do know that its popularity is spreading from big city ghettoes to suburbs and rural areas, to colleges, high schools, and even elementary schools. Hard-drug trade has long been illegal in the United States, but it is so profitable that it is hard to eliminate (Brecher, 1972).

Heroin users claim that they take the drug because it produces a powerful high. However, the price they pay—financially, physically, and psychologically—is even higher. A person who uses the drug frequently soon develops tolerance. And as he increases his dosage, he may easily become addicted. Once this happens, psychological deterioration soon follows. The addict's life becomes centered around getting the drug, through crime, if necessary. And all other considerations—family, friends, school, job, plans for the future—tend to be forgotten.

The reason the drug can control the addict's mind is that it controls his body. If he cannot get enough heroin to satisfy his body's craving, he will go through withdrawal. About ten hours after his last dose the addict begins to feel the first symptoms. He may perspire, yawn, and have a runny nose and watery eyes. A few hours later he falls into a shallow, uncomfortable state of drowsiness. Later, he may develop severe cramps in his arms, legs, and back; nausea, vomiting, and diarrhea; weakness; and gooseflesh ("cold turkey"). These symptoms usually occur forty-eight to seventy-two hours after the last dose. It may take an addict ten or twelve days to recover completely.

Some of the other physical dangers of heroin use are even more severe. The concentration of heroin sold in packets on the streets varies considerably. If a person who is used to fifteen-milligram doses unknowingly purchases and takes a hundred-milligram dose, he may lapse into a coma and die—within minutes. And because people often take heroin with unsterile needles, they may develop hepatitis, infections at the site of injection, and other complications. In 1974, 312 people died from heroin-related causes in New York City alone—most from overdoses.

There is no known cure for heroin addiction. An estimated 90 percent of heavy users who "kick the habit" return to heroin within the year. However, in the last decade doctors have discovered a drug that can effectively be substituted for heroin: methadone (Patch, 1972). Methadone is a synthetic drug with pain-relieving properties similar to those of morphine. Like morphine and heroin, methadone is addictive. However, unlike morphine and heroin, it does not produce a high. In fact, it blocks the high produced by heroin, thereby suppressing the craving for heroin. It also prevents heroin withdrawal.

According to one report, 60 percent of addicts on methadone-maintenance programs give up heroin, drop criminal activities, obtain jobs, and lead relatively normal lives. This figure is strikingly high compared to the low success rates of nonmethadone programs. For example, only 10 percent of the addicts who go through withdrawal at the federal treatment center in Lexington, Kentucky, manage to stay away from hard drugs after leaving the program. However, trading one addiction for another is not necessarily a solution to the problem. Methadone, too, may be abused. (Indeed, some people suggest that we are creating a new generation of addicts—methadone addicts.) Nevertheless, it seems to be the best treatment available to date.

FIGURE 15.20
At Long Beach Memorial Hospital in California, young addicts receive methadone from a registered nurse.

Alcoholism

Although heroin addiction receives more attention, this country's most serious drug problem is alcoholism. As many as nine million Americans—a staggering 5 percent of the population—have a severe drinking problem.

Fifty percent or more of the deaths in automobile accidents each year can be traced to alcohol; in half of all murders either the killer or the victim has been drinking; and some 13,000 people die of liver damage caused by alcohol every year. In addition, the cost in human suffering to the alcoholic and his or her family is impossible to measure.

In small doses, alcohol might be called a social wonder drug. The first psychological function that it slows down is our inhibitions. Two drinks can make a person relaxed, talkative, playful, even giggly. (It is for this reason that many people consider alcohol a stimulant—it is really a depressant.)

As the number of drinks increases, the fun decreases. One by one, the person's psychological and physiological functions begin to shut down. Perceptions and sensations become distorted and behavior may become obnoxious. The person begins to stumble and weave, speech becomes slurred, and reactions—to a stop sign, for example—become sluggish. If enough alcohol accumulates in the body, it leads to unconsciousness—and

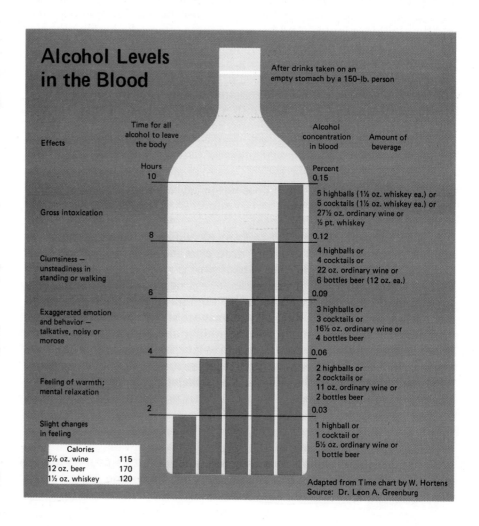

FIGURE 15.21
This chart shows the effects of alcohol on a 150-lb. person. Because alcohol is diluted in the blood, a 200-lb. man can usually tolerate more liquor than a 110-lb. woman.

in some cases coma and death. It all depends on how much and how rapidly alcohol enters the bloodstream—that is, on how big the drinks are and on how quickly a person consumes them (Chafetz, 1967).

Alcohol can produce psychological dependence, tolerance, and addiction. One researcher has outlined three stages of alcoholism. In the first stage, the individual discovers that alcohol reduces his tensions, gives him self-confidence, and reduces social pressures. Drinking makes him feel better. In the second stage, the beverage becomes a drug. The individual begins to drink so heavily that he feels he has to hide his habit. Thus he begins "sneaking" drinks. In this stage he may also begin to suffer blackouts—he is unable to recall what happened during a drinking episode. In the final stage, he drinks compulsively, beginning in the morning. He becomes inefficient at work and tends to go on benders (drinking sprees) that may last for weeks. He is now a thorough alcoholic, drinking continuously, eating infrequently, and feeling sick when deprived of his drug. His health deteriorates rapidly (Jellinek, 1960).

The first step in treating the alcoholic is to see him through the violent withdrawal typical of alcohol addiction, and then to try to make him healthier. He may be given a variety of treatments—from drugs to psychotherapy. Alcoholics Anonymous, an organization run by and for people who have had a drinking problem, has been more successful than most organizations. But there is no certain cure for alcoholism. As many alcoholics return to the bottle as heroin addicts return to the needle. One problem is that our society tends to encourage social drinking and to tolerate the first stage of alcoholism.

Barbiturates

Next to alcohol, the most widely used group of depressants in this country is barbiturates—sleeping pills or "downers." In 1967 alone, drug manufacturers produced over three billion average-size doses (300 mg) of barbiturates. By 1971 this figure had increased to five billion (Lingeman, 1974). There is obviously a heavy demand for the kind of escape that barbiturates provide.

The effects of barbiturates are similar to those of alcohol. They reduce anxiety, slow body functions, and eventually bring drowsiness and sleep. In fact, many people begin taking barbiturates (prescribed by their doctors) to cure insomnia. If taken regularly, however, sleeping pills lose their effectiveness. The person develops a tolerance and slowly increases the nightly dose. In time, she may begin taking a few capsules at stressful times during the day. Eventually, the drug becomes a major focus of her life. Like the advanced alcoholic, the barbiturate addict is unable to function in daily life, gets confused and disoriented, and frequently becomes obstinate, irritable, and abusive. (This behavior is in marked contrast to heroin addicts, who usually become passive and lethargic.)

Barbiturates are dangerous for two reasons. First, the user may knowingly or unknowingly take an overdose. Each year, many people commit suicide by taking barbiturates. Second, barbiturate withdrawal is proba-

FIGURE 15.22
More than ten million Americans use prescription sedatives (barbiturates and tranquilizers) and stimulants (amphetamines). It is estimated that several hundred thousand of these people are drug abusers. The barbiturates ("reds," "blue devils," "rainbows") are physically addicting. A surprisingly large proportion of barbiturate addicts are middle-class housewives who begin using "sleeping pills" but who gradually resort to taking the drug to calm down during the day.

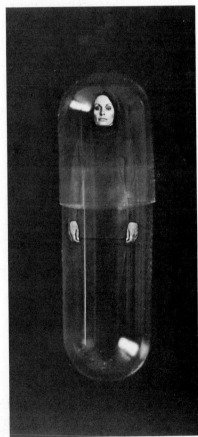

bly more violent than any other form of drug withdrawal. Without medical help, the barbiturate addict trying to kick the habit may easily go from
convulsions to coma to death.

Most psychologists feel that drug abuse reflects an underlying emotional disorder that ultimately would have been expressed in some other
way if the person had not turned to drugs. Individuals who are able to
cope with stresses, conflicts, frustrations, and disappointments of living
are unlikely to become drug abusers.

SUMMARY

1. There is no absolute list of symptoms of mental disorder. Most psychologists define normal behavior as the ability to cope with stress and conflict, and abnormal behavior as the failure to adjust to the stresses of life.

2. Neurosis is a broad category of mental disorders, characterized by chronic anxiety. Severe neurotic anxiety may produce phobias, obsessions, compulsions, various forms of hysteria, and depression.

3. People commit suicide for many different reasons; not all suicidal individuals are depressed. Contrary to popular belief, people who threaten to kill themselves often do so.

4. Psychosis is a second category of mental disorders, characterized by behavior that is so incomprehensible to others as to virtually eliminate the individual's capacity to meet the demands of everyday life.

5. Schizophrenia is a type of psychosis in which a person's thoughts, emotions, and perceptions are confused and disconnected. Schizophrenics may experience delusions and hallucinations, withdraw into fantasies, engage in bizarre behavior, and speak in "word salads."

6. Affective reactions are another type of psychosis. They are characterized by excessive and inappropriate elation (manic behavior) or despair (depressed behavior).

7. Psychosis may be caused by an inherited tendency to become disturbed, by biochemical imbalances, or by exposure to contradictory communications (the double bind), or—most likely—combinations of the three.

8. A personality disorder is an ongoing pattern of maladaptive behavior combined with an inability to establish appropriate relationships with other people and the environment. The antisocial personality is an example.

9. Aside from nicotine (in cigarettes), the three most widely used and abused drugs in this country are alcohol, heroin, and barbiturates. All three of these drugs are depressants, and all are addictive. They may cause psychological dependence, tolerance, physiological habituation, a severe withdrawal reaction, and even death when the individual does not take the drug. Overdoses of heroin and barbiturates may also be fatal.

GLOSSARY

addiction: An altered psychological state in the body that causes physical dependence on a drug.

affective reaction: A type of psychosis in which an individual is subject to excessive and inappropriate mood states of elation or depression.

antisocial personality: A personality disorder characterized by irresponsibility, shallow emotions, and lack of conscience.

anxiety: A vague, generalized apprehension or feeling that one is in danger.

autism: A childhood psychosis characterized by an inability to relate to others and lack of response to attempts at communication.

compulsion: The impulsive and uncontrollable repetition of an irrational action.

conversion reaction: A form of hysteria characterized by the conversion of emotional difficulties into a loss of a specific body function.

delusion: A false belief that a person maintains in the face of contrary evidence.

depression: A pattern of sadness, anxiety, fatigue, insomnia, underactivity, and reduced ability to function and to work with others.

depressive reaction: A psychotic reaction in which a person is overcome by feelings of failure, sinfulness, worthlessness, and despair.

dissociative reaction: A form of hysteria in which a person experiences a loss of memory or identity, or exhibits two or more identities.

double bind: A situation in which a person receives conflicting demands, so that no matter what he or she does, it is wrong.

fugue: A rare dissociative reaction in which complete or partial amnesia is combined with a move to a new environment.

hallucination: Sensations in the absence of appropriate stimulation.

hypochondria: A preoccupation with imaginary ailments, on which a person blames other problems.

hysteria: A form of neurosis in which a person exhibits physical symptoms in the absence of physical causes.

manic reaction: A psychotic reaction charac-terized by extreme elation, agitation, confusion, disorientation, and incoherence.

multiple personality: A rare condition in which one person shows two or more separate consciousnesses with distinct personalities.

neurosis: A psychological disturbance characterized by prolonged high levels of anxiety. Neurotics often suffer from unrealistic self-images and have difficulty forming satisfying, stable relationships.

obsession: An uncontrollable pattern of thoughts.

paranoia: Delusions of persecution, characteristic of some people who are diagnosed as schizophrenic.

personality disorder: A psychological disturbance characterized by lifelong maladaptive patterns that are relatively free of anxiety and other emotional symptoms.

phobia: A form of severe anxiety in which a person focuses on a particular object or situation.

psychological dependence: Use of a drug to such an extent that a person feels nervous and anxious without it.

psychosis: A psychological disturbance characterized by a breakdown in the ability to accurately perceive reality. Psychotics are unable to relate to other people and to function in everyday life.

schizophrenia: A group of psychoses characterized by confused and disconnected thoughts, emotions, and perceptions.

tolerance: Physical adaptation to a drug, so that a person needs an increased dosage in order to produce the original effect.

withdrawal syndrome: The symptoms that occur after a person discontinues the use of a drug to which he or she had become addicted.

ACTIVITIES

1. Formulate a definition of mental illness. Is your definition free of social values, or are values a necessary part of the definition?

2. Many disturbances and breakdowns come about because of some unresolvable conflict. To understand the nature of conflict try the following experiment with several subjects. Materials needed are paper and pencils. Tell each subject to place a pencil point in the middle of the bottom of the paper. They are to draw a line to the upper right-hand corner, or upper left-hand corner whenever you raise your hand on their left or right side. Follow this procedure several times until they become experienced in this activity. Once you are sure the subject is following your directions, raise both hands exactly at the same time. How did each subject handle this conflict?

3. Study a book of paintings and drawings by Vincent Van Gogh. Can you tell which were done when he was mentally healthy and which were done when he was suffering from severe psychological disorder? How?

4. It is thought that one of the conditions that produces mental disorders is overexposure to double-bind situations. Everyone has faced these situations at various times. How many examples from your own experiences can you think of that illustrate various forms of the double-bind situation? How did you resolve the conflicts? Can you see patterns of behavior responses developing?

5. Labeling of mental disorders presents huge problems for patients and therapists. But the problems of labeling are not limited to this area.

Whenever you dismiss certain people as "creeps," for example, you are really saying more about yourself than about the people you are labeling. For example, people who are nervous in social gatherings usually cannot stand other people who are nervous in social gatherings. For a good indication of your own problems, make a list of people you don't like and the reason(s) why you don't like them. Take a hard, honest look at those traits you have written down and see how many of them apply to you as well.

6. Watch television for a week. Keep a journal of programs which have some psychological theme. What examples of mental breakdown are described? How common are they made to appear? Are simple solutions given? How is the psychologist or psychiatrist shown? Does this person have ready answers? What are they?

7. Cut out about fifteen pictures of people from magazines and paste them on a large piece of paper. Include among the pictures several of people with long or mussed up hair and untidy clothes. Ask several friends or classmates if they can determine which of the people in the pictures are mentally ill. How many select the people with unkempt appearances? What conclusions can you draw from this experiment?

8. Discuss how smoking can be considered neurotic behavior.

9. What are you afraid of? Do you fear high places, or water, or maybe snakes or spiders? Try to think back to when you first had these fears. Can you state rationally why you have each of your fears?

SUGGESTED READINGS

ALBEE, EDWARD. *Who's Afraid of Virginia Woolf?* New York: Atheneum, 1962 (paper).

Albee, a famous contemporary playwright, describes the horribly fascinating, extremely neurotic relationship of a husband and wife living in a small academic community in the United States.

ALVAREZ, A. *The Savage God: A Study of Suicide*. New York: Random House, 1970. A well-researched yet highly personal and emotional study of suicide. Alvarez explores the way that thoughts of suicide color the world of creative persons, recounts his own attempt at suicide, and traces the history of myths surrounding the phenomenon.

BARNES, MARY, AND BERKE, JOSEPH. *Mary Barnes: Two Accounts of a Journey Through Madness*. New York: Harcourt Brace Jovanovich, 1971. This book consists of interspersed chapters by Mary Barnes, who went on a journey into and through madness, and by Joseph Berke, the psychiatrist who helped Mary through her "down years" and into her "up years."

GREEN, HANNAH. *I Never Promised You a Rose Garden*. New York: New American Library, 1964 (paper). A moving and compelling story about the terrifying world and successful treatment of an adolescent girl who has been diagnosed as schizophrenic.

KAPLAN, BERT (ED.). *The Inner World of Mental Illness*. New York: Harper & Row, 1964 (paper). A fascinating collection of first-person accounts of what it is like to experience severe mental disturbance. The last section of the book consists of excerpts from literary classics and from the diaries of well-known writers and thinkers.

LAING, R.D. *The Divided Self*. Baltimore: Penguin, 1959 (paper). Laing questions the entire social context that labels a person mentally ill. He believes that psychoses and neuroses make sense if the experience of the person is understood. Presently accepted "normality" is in fact pathological. Psychosis, in a way, is a step toward sanity.

PLATH, SYLVIA. *The Bell Jar*. New York: Bantam, 1971 (paper). An autobiographical novel about a young woman's mental breakdown. Plath is an excellent writer, and the book is especially powerful because she is able to articulate her feelings so well.

RUBIN, THEODORE. *Jordi/Lisa and David*. New York: Ballantine, 1971 (paper). The characters are David and Lisa, two schizophrenic adolescents who have insulated themselves from reality. This is a short, dramatic case history of how their mutual affection became an avenue to recovery.

SZASZ, THOMAS S. *The Myth of Mental Illness*. New York: Dell Publishing Co., 1961 (paper). By drawing philosophical and sociological analyses and by reviewing the history and present-day approaches to what has been termed "mental illness," Szasz argues against the medical model adopted by most psychiatrists. His basic argument is that psychiatrists deal with fundamental problems in human living and human communication, and that these problems cannot be resolved by means of hospitalization and drugs.

BIBLIOGRAPHY

ALVAREZ, A. *The Savage God: A Study of Suicide*. New York: Random House, 1970.

AMERICAN PSYCHIATRIC ASSOCIATION. *Diagnostic and Statistical Manual of Mental Disorders*. 2nd ed. Washington, D.C.: American Psychiatric Association, 1968.

ARIETI, SILVANO (ED.). *American Handbook of Psychology*. 3 vols. New York: Basic Books, 1959.

BATESON, GREGORY. *Steps to an Ecology of Mind*. San Francisco: Chandler, 1972.

BRECHER, EDWARD M., AND THE EDITORS OF *Consumer Reports*. *Licit and Illicit Drugs*. Boston: Little, Brown, 1972.

CHAFETZ, MORRIS E. "Addictions. Ill: Alcoholism." In *Comprehensive Textbook of Psychiatry*, edited by A. M. Freeman and H. I. Kaplan. Baltimore: Williams & Wilkins, 1967, pp. 1011–1026.

COLEMAN, JAMES C. *Abnormal Psychology and Modern Life*. 4th ed. Glenview, Ill.: Scott, Foresman, 1972.

FENICHEL, OTTO. *The Psychoanalytic Theory of Neurosis*. New York: Norton, 1945.

JELLINEK, ELVIN M. *The Disease Concept of Alcoholism*. New Brunswick, N.J.: Hillhouse Press, 1960.

KAPLAN, BART (ED.). *The Inner World of Mental Illness*. New York: Harper & Row, 1964 (paper).

KARNASH, L. J. *Handbook of Psychiatry*. St. Louis: Mosby, 1945.

KETY, S. S., ET AL. "Mental Illness in the Biological and Adoptive Families of Adopted Schizophrenics." *American Journal of Psychiatry*, 128, No. 3 (1971): 302–306.

KISKER, GEORGE. *The Disorganized Personality*. New York: McGraw-Hill, 1964.

KRAMER, M. "Statistics of Mental Disorders in the United States: Some Urgent Needs and Suggested Solutions." *Journal of the Royal Statistical Society*, Series A, 132 (1969): 353–407.

LEVANT, OSCAR. *The Memoirs of an Amnesiac*. New York: Bantam, 1966 (paper).

LINGEMAN, RICHARD R. *Drugs from A to Z*. New York: McGraw-Hill, 1974.

LITZ, T. *The Origin and Treatment of Schizophrenic Disorders*. New York: Basic Books, 1973.

LORENZ, SARAH. *Our Son, Ken*. New York: Dell, 1969 (paper).

MAHER, BRENDAN. "The Shattered Language of Schizophrenia." In *Readings in Psychology Today*. 2nd ed. Del Mar, Calif.: CRM Books, 1972, pp. 549–553.

MC GHIE, A., AND CHAPMAN, J. "Disorders of Attention and Perception in Early Schizophrenia." *British Journal of Medical Psychiatry*, 34 (1961): 103–116.

MEEHL, PAUL M. "Schizotaxia, Schizotype, Schizophrenia." *American Psychologist*, 17 (1962): 827–832.

MINTZ, R. S. "Psychotherapy of the Suicidal Patient." In *Suicidal Behaviors*, edited by H. L. P. Resnik. Boston: Little, Brown, 1968.

NATHAN, P. E., AND HARRIS, S. L. *Psychopathology and Society*. New York: McGraw-Hill, 1975.

PATCH, VERNON D. "METHADONE." *New England Journal of Medicine*, 286 (1972): 43–45.

RABKIN, LESLIE (ED.). *Psychopathology and Literature*. San Francisco: Chandler, 1966.

ROSENTHAL, D., ET AL. "The Adopted-Away Offspring of Schizophrenics." *American Journal of Psychiatry*, 128, No. 3 (1971): 307–311.

SCHACHTER, S., AND LATANÉ, B. "Crime, Cognition, and the Autonomic Nervous System." In *Nebraska Symposium on Motivation*, edited by M. Jones. Lincoln: University of Nebraska Press, 1964.

SHAPIRO, EVELYN (ED.) *PsychoSources: A Psychology Resource Catalog*. New York: Bantam, 1973 (paper).

SILVERMAN, J. "When Schizophrenia Helps." *Psychology Today*, 4 (September 1970): 62–65.

SLOTKIN, J. J. "Culture and Psychopathology." *Journal of Abnormal and Social Psychology*, 51 (1955): 269–275.

SNYDER, SOLOMON H. *Madness and the Brain*. New York: McGraw-Hill, 1973.

STONE, ALAN, AND STONE, SUE. *The Abnormal Personality Through Literature*. Englewood Cliffs, N.J.: Prentice-Hall, 1966.

SZASZ, THOMAS S. *The Myth of Mental Illness*. New York: Harper & Row, 1961.

TAUBE, C. A., AND REDNICK, R. *Utilization of Mental Health Resources by Persons Diagnosed with Schizophrenia*. DHEW Publication No.

(HSM) 72–9110. Rockville, Md.: National Institute of Mental Health, 1973.

VICTOR, MAURICE, AND ADAMS, RAYMOND D. "Opiates and Other Synthetic Analgesic Drugs." In *Harrison's Principles of Internal Medicine*, edited by M. M. Wintrobe et al. New York: McGraw-Hill, 1970, pp. 677–681.

WHITE, ROBERT W. *The Abnormal Personality.* New York: Ronald Press, 1964.

WHEELIS, ALLEN. *The Desert.* New York: Basic Books, 1970.

WOLMAN, BENJAMIN D. (ED.). *Handbook of Clinical Psychology.* New York: McGraw-Hill, 1965.

16

Therapy and Change

FIGURE 16.1

When Sigmund Freud began the practice of psychoanalysis, one patient lay on a couch and spoke, with no one present but the Doctor. Today, it is quite common to find a group of people in a psychotherapy session, although individual therapy and classical psychoanalysis are still preferred by many people.

At certain times of transition and crisis in life, we may feel an urgent need to find someone trustworthy with whom to share our doubts and problems. A parent, relative, or close friend is often helpful in such times of need. But many psychological problems are too bewildering and complex to be solved in this way. When a person becomes dissatisfied or distraught with life and suspects that the reason lies inside himself, he is likely to seek help from someone with training and experience in such matters. People who have been trained to deal with the psychological problems of others include social workers, psychologists, and psychiatrists. The special kind of help they provide is called *psychotherapy*.

This chapter will present some of the major approaches to therapy and will describe what it is like to undergo therapy. It will explore various types of group therapy, probe the current situation in America's mental institutions, and touch on the trend toward community mental health.

WHAT IS PSYCHOTHERAPY?

Psychotherapy literally means "healing of the soul," and in early times psychological disturbances were often thought to represent some sort of moral or religious problem. Madmen were sometimes viewed as being inhabited by devils or demons, and treatment consisted of exorcism—the driving out of these demons by religious ceremonies or by physical punishment. Within the last two hundred years, however, views of psychological disorders have changed. Mental disorders have slowly come to be thought of as diseases, and the term "mental illness" is now popularly applied to many psychological problems.

This medical view of psychological disturbance has helped withdraw some of the stigma associated with such problems, and it has done much to convince society that troubled people need care and treatment. Nevertheless many psychotherapists feel that the term "mental illness" has outlived its usefulness and that, in fact, it may now be doing more harm than good.

The trouble with letting a person think of himself as mentally ill is that he sees himself in a passive, helpless position. He sees his troubles as being caused by forces over which he has no control. By thinking of himself in this way, the person can avoid taking responsibility for his own situation and for helping himself change.

391

One of the functions of psychotherapy is to help people realize that they are responsible for their own problems and that, even more importantly, they are the only ones who can really solve these problems. This approach does not imply that people become disturbed on purpose or that no one should need outside help. People often adopt certain techniques for getting along in life that seem appropriate at the time but that lead to trouble in the long run. Such patterns can be difficult for the individual to see or change. The major task of the therapist, therefore, is to help people examine their way of living, to understand how their present way of living causes problems, and to start living in new, more beneficial ways. The therapist can be thought of as a guide who is hired by the individual to help him find the source of his problems and some possible solutions.

Characteristics of Psychotherapy

There are many different kinds of therapy, only a few of which will be described in this chapter. Each one is based on different theories about how human personality works, and each one is carried out in a different style. Some psychotherapists stick rigorously to one style and consider the others useless. Other psychotherapists pick and choose methods from many different kinds of therapy and use whatever works best. But whatever the style or philosophy, all types of psychotherapy have certain characteristics in common.

The primary goal of psychotherapy is to strengthen the patient's control over his or her life. People seeking psychotherapy feel trapped in behavior patterns. Over the years they have developed certain feelings about themselves as well as behaviors which only reinforce those feelings. Such people lack the freedom to choose the direction their lives will take. Their behavior and feelings make it impossible for them to reach their goals. For example, a man who is severely critical of himself may feel others are equally harsh in their judgments of him. Rather than risk feelings of rejection, he avoids social gatherings. A person who is uncomfortable meeting other people will, no doubt, feel lonely and rejected. His critical feelings about himself will be strengthened, and he may come to feel that he will remain unloved for life.

The aim of psychotherapy for such a person would be to free him of his burden of self-hate. With a more positive self-image, the man would not be locked into the cycle of avoidance, rejection, and despair. For perhaps the first time, he could feel in control of his life. His behavior would be based on *choice,* and not on the necessity that goes with fixed behavior patterns.

In order to change, it is necessary for the patient to achieve some *understanding* of his troubles. One of the first tasks of therapy, therefore, is to examine the patient's problem closely.

The man in our example will, in the course of his therapy, discover the origin of his self-critical, despairing feelings. He may also realize that, although these feelings developed from real situations, perhaps during

FIGURE 16.2
Many people have a mental picture of psychotherapy as taking place with the patient reclining on a comfortable couch while a middle-aged, bearded man sits taking notes in a chair behind the patient. Actually, few therapeutic settings fit this picture nowadays. Therapists are more likely to talk to their patients in a face-to-face position. Furthermore, the therapist is likely to employ a variety of techniques rather than adhere to a strictly psychoanalytic approach. Several of these varied techniques are discussed in this chapter.

his childhood, they no longer apply to his adult capabilities. Gradually the patient's view of himself will become more realistic.

Another major task of therapy is to help the patient find meaningful *alternatives* to his present unsatisfactory ways of behaving. The patient we have been discussing may look for ways to meet new people rather than avoiding them.

One of the most important factors in effective treatment is the patient's belief or hope that he *can* change. The influence that a patient's hopes and expectations have on his improvement is often called the *placebo effect*. This name comes from giving medical patients *placebos*—harmless sugar pills—when they complain of ailments that do not seem to have any physiological basis. The patients take the tablets, their symptoms disappear, and they consider themselves cured.

The placebo effect does not imply that problems can be solved simply by fooling the patient. It does demonstrate, however, the tremendous importance of the patient's attitude in finding a way to change. A patient who does not believe he can be helped probably cannot be. A patient who believes he can change and believes he has the power to change will find a way. Therapy is professional guidance, not a placebo.

What Makes a Good Therapist?

In American society, there are many people who practice psychotherapy. Some, such as psychiatrists and psychoanalysts, are highly trained in psychology and medicine; others, such as counselors and clergymen, have considerably less formal training. The different kinds of professional therapists and the training that each goes through before practicing psychotherapy are shown in Figure 16.3.

Before going to a professional therapist, most people first turn to a friend or other nonprofessional for help and advice. Such nonprofessionals sometimes tell the individual exactly what he wants to hear—"it's not your fault, you couldn't help it." They provide sympathy and an understanding ear. Professional therapists, on the other hand, are more likely to tell the person things he does not want to hear. In the process of therapy, the patient may feel frustrated because he cannot push the burden of responsibility onto someone else the way he can with a friend.

The process of therapy is always difficult and upsetting, and patients often become heavily dependent on the therapist while they are trying to make changes. A patient may become angry or hurt, for example, if his therapist suddenly goes on vacation. The therapist, therefore, has to be careful not to betray the trust that the patient has placed in him. On the other hand, he must not let the patient lean on him or take out his problems on him. Patients often try to avoid their problems by using the therapist as a substitute parent or by blaming him for their misfortunes.

In recent years, some researchers have questioned whether professional psychotherapy really works. They have gathered statistics that seem to bear out their contention that just as many people improve without psychotherapy as with it. Subsequent studies have shown, however, that these original statistics were misleading. A good number of people, it is

FIGURE 16.3

Psychotherapy is practiced by a considerable variety of people with a wide range of training and experience. Just what credentials a psychotherapist should have before he or she can practice is still an open question. What is clear, however, is that the credential is less important than the character of the therapist and the amount of experience he or she has had.

Psychiatrists are medical doctors who specialize in the treatment of mental illness. They generally take a post-M.D. internship in a mental institution. Because of their medical background, psychiatrists tend to be more biologically oriented than psychologists.

Psychoanalysts are psychiatrists who have taken special training in the theory of personality and techniques of psychotherapy of Sigmund Freud, usually from an established psychoanalyst. They must themselves be psychoanalyzed before they can practice.

Lay Analysts are psychoanalysts who do not have degrees in medicine but who have studied with established psychoanalysts.

Clinical Psychologists are therapists with a Ph.D. degree. They are the product of a three-to-four-year research-oriented program in the social sciences, plus a one-year predoctoral or postdoctoral internship in

psychotherapy and psychological assessment.

Counselors generally have a master's or doctor's degree in counseling psychology. They usually work in educational institutions where they are available for consultation about personal problems. They customarily refer clients with serious problems to psychiatrists or psychologists.

Psychiatric Social Workers are people with a graduate degree in psychiatric social work. They generally receive supervised practical training coupled with two years of courses in psychology.

Nonprofessionals include clergymen, physicians, teachers, and others who dispense a great deal of advice despite the fact that they have had no formal training in therapy or counseling. Nevertheless, more troubled people turn to nonprofessionals than to professionals—and they seem to be more satisfied with the therapy they receive.

true, improve whether they see a trained psychotherapist or not, but in most of these cases the person has obtained help from someone else—a clergyman or the family doctor, for example. Furthermore, there is evidence that formal psychotherapy, rather than having no effect, is a powerful experience for good in many cases but has bad effects in some others (Bergin and Garfield, 1971).

Whether psychotherapy will be beneficial to a person depends on both the patient and the therapist. The patients who get the most out of psychotherapy are people with high intelligence, a good education, and a middle-class background. Such people have much in common with most therapists, and this similarity seems to help. In addition, the people who benefit most from psychotherapy are those who have relatively mild problems about which they have considerable anxiety or depression. Severely disturbed, apathetic patients are much more difficult to change. Therapy will also be more effective with people who are introspective and who can withstand frustration. Therapy is neither easy nor fast; it demands as much from the patient as it does from the therapist.

The characteristics that are found in effective therapists are of three kinds: First, a therapist needs to be reasonably *healthy* himself. A therapist who is himself anxious, defensive, and withdrawn will not be able to see his patient's problems clearly. A second important characteristic is a capacity for *warmth and understanding*. Troubled people are usually fearful and confused about explaining their problems. The therapist needs to be able to give the patient confidence that he is capable of caring and understanding.

Finally, a good therapist must be *experienced* in dealing with people—in understanding their complexities, seeing through the "games" they play to trick the therapist and themselves, and judging their strengths and weaknesses. Only by having worked with many people can a therapist learn when to give support, when to insist that the patient stand on his own feet, and how to make sense of the things people say.

KINDS OF THERAPY

Although there are many approaches to psychotherapy (several are included in the suggested readings at the end of this chapter), only the three most influential approaches will be discussed here: traditional psychoanalysis, the human potential movement, and behavior therapy. In addition to these types of individual therapy, several kinds of group therapy will be described.

Psychoanalysis

For a long time *psychoanalysis* was the only kind of psychotherapy practiced in Western society. It was this type of therapy that gave rise to the classic picture of a bearded Viennese doctor seated behind a patient who was lying on a couch.

Psychoanalysis is based on the theories of Sigmund Freud. According to Freud's views, psychological disturbances are due to anxiety about hidden conflicts between the unconscious components of one's personality. (Freud's theory of personality is described in Chapters 8 and 13.) The job of the psychoanalyst, therefore, is to help make the patient aware of the unconscious impulses, desires, and fears that are causing the anxiety. Psychoanalysts believe that if the patient can understand his unconscious motives, he has taken the first step toward gaining control over his behavior and freeing himself of his problems. Such understanding is called *insight*.

Psychoanalysis is a slow procedure. It may take years of fifty-minute sessions several times a week before the patient is able to make fundamental changes in his life. Throughout this time, the analyst assists his patient in a thorough examination of the unconscious determinants of his behavior. This task begins with the analyst telling the patient to relax and talk about everything that comes into his mind. This method is called *free association*. The patient may consider his passing thoughts too unimportant or too embarrassing to mention. But the analyst suggests that he express everything—the thought that seems most inconsequential may, in fact, be the most meaningful upon closer examination.

As the patient lies on the couch, he may describe his dreams, talk about his private life, or recall long-forgotten experiences. The psychoanalyst sits out of sight behind the patient and often says nothing for long periods of time. He occasionally makes remarks or asks questions that guide the patient, or he may suggest an unconscious motive or factor that explains something the patient has been talking about, but most of the work is done by the patient himself.

The patient is understandably reluctant to reveal painful feelings and to examine lifelong patterns that need to be changed, and as the analysis proceeds, he is likely to try to hold back the flow of information. This phenomenon—in fact, any behavior that impedes the course of therapy—is called *resistance*. The patient may have agreed to cooperate fully, yet he finds at times that his mind is blank, that he feels powerless and can no longer think of anything to say. At such times the analyst will simply point out what is happening and wait for the patient to continue. The analyst may also suggest another line of approach to the area of resistance. By analyzing the patient's resistances, both the therapist and the patient can understand how the patient deals with anxiety-provoking material.

Sooner or later, the analyst himself begins to appear in the patient's associations and dreams. The patient may begin feeling toward the analyst the way he feels toward some other important figure in his life. This process is called *transference*.

If the patient can recognize what is happening, transference may allow him to experience his true feelings toward the important person. But often, instead of experiencing and understanding his feelings, the patient simply begins acting toward the therapist in the same way he used to act toward the important person, usually one of his parents.

The therapist does not allow the patient to resort to these tactics. He remains impersonal and anonymous. He always directs the patient back to himself. The therapist may ask, for example, "What do you see when you imagine my face?" The patient may reply that he sees the therapist

FIGURE 16.4
Although the traditional couch has somewhat disappeared from modern psychoanalytic therapy, the phenomena of resistance and transference remain central. Here the patient's resistance is shown in the fact that he is seeing the therapist as a menacing dentist. At the same time, he is transferring: The "dentist" seems to him like an impersonal, frightening mother. Such images arise in the patient's dreams and free associations; the therapist tells the patient to discuss and examine these images and symbols thoroughly.

as an angry, frowning, unpleasant figure. The therapist never takes this personally. Instead, he may calmly say, "What does this make you think of?" Gradually, it will become clear to both patient and therapist that the patient is reacting to the neutral therapist as though he were a threatening father.

Through this kind of process, the patient becomes aware of his real feelings and motivations. He may begin to understand, for example, why he has trouble with his boss at work—he may be seeing his boss, his therapist, and indeed any man in a position of authority in the same way that as a child he saw his father.

The Human Potential Movement

Humanistic and existential psychology have given rise to several new approaches to psychotherapy, known collectively as the *human potential movement*. We discussed these schools of psychology in Chapter 13. To review, humanists and existentialists stress the actualization of one's unique potentials through personal responsibility, freedom of choice, and authentic relationships.

Client-centered Therapy.   Client-centered therapy is based on the theories of Carl Rogers (1951; see Chapter 13). The use of the term "client" instead of "patient" gives one an insight into the reasoning behind Rogers' method. "Patient" may suggest inferiority, whereas "client" implies an equal relationship between the therapist and the person seeking help.

Client-centered therapists assume that people are basically good and that they are capable of handling their own lives. Psychological problems arise when the true self becomes lost and the individual comes to view himself according to the standards of others. One of the goals of therapy, therefore, is to help the client to recognize his own strength and confidence so that he can learn to be true to his own standards and ideas about how to live effectively.

In the course of an interview, the client is encouraged to speak freely about intimate matters that may be bothering him. He is told that what he talks about is up to him. The therapist listens and encourages conversation but tries to avoid giving opinions. Instead, he tries to echo back as clearly as possible the feelings that the client has expressed. He may try to extract the main points from the client's hesitant or rambling explanations. For example, a male client may tell a long story about an incident with his father, and the therapist may respond by saying, "This kind of thing makes you feel very stupid." The client may in turn say, "No, not stupid, angry. It's really he who is being stupid," and the therapist will say, "Oh, I see, you really feel angry at him when he acts this way." Between them, they form a clearer and clearer picture of how the client really feels about himself, his life, and the people around him.

Client-centered therapy is conducted in an atmosphere of emotional support that Rogers calls *unconditional positive regard*. As in psychoanalysis, the therapist never says that he thinks the client or what the client has said is good or bad. But he shows the client that he will accept anything that is said without embarrassment, reservation, or anger. His primary responsibility is to create a warm and accepting relationship between himself and his client.

This acceptance makes it easier for the client to explore thoughts about himself and his experiences. He is able to abandon old values without fear of disapproval, and he can begin to see himself, his situation, and his relationships with others in a new light.

As he reduces his tensions and releases his emotions, the client feels that he is becoming a more complete person. He gains the courage to accept parts of his personality that he had formerly considered weak or bad, and, by recognizing his own self-worth, he can set up realistic goals and consider the steps necessary to reach them. The client's movement toward independence signals the end of the need for therapy—he can assume the final steps to independence on his own.

Existential Therapy.   Like Rogers, all therapists in the human potential movement see their role as helping individuals to achieve self-determination. Rollo May (1969), whose theories we discussed in Chapter 13, emphasizes consciousness. For most, if not all of us, freedom and autonomy are threatening. To acknowledge that you are a unique and independent person is to acknowledge that you are alone. Unconsciously many people avoid this realization, burying their feelings and desires. Rollo May and other existential therapists attempt to help patients overcome the fear of freedom, get in touch with their true feelings, and accept responsibility for their lives.

Viktor Frankl (1970) is also an existentialist, but approaches therapy somewhat differently. After listening to a patient express despair, he might ask, "Why don't you commit suicide?" Frankl is not being cruel or sarcastic. He is trying to help the individual find meaning in life. The patient's answer (whether it is "my husband and children," "my religion," or "my work") provides clues about what the person values.

In Frankl's view, feelings of emptiness and boredom are the primary source of emotional problems.

> ... [M]ental health is based on a certain degree of tension, the tension between what one has already achieved and what one still ought to accomplish, or the gap between what one is and what one should become. Such a tension is inherent in the human being and is therefore indispensable to mental well-being ... What [people] actually need is not a tensionless state but rather the striving and struggling for some worthy goal (1970, pp. 165–166).

Frankl believes a therapist should help to open the patient's eyes to the possibilities in life and guide him or her toward challenges.

Gestalt Therapy

Developed by Fritz Perls in the 1950s and 1960s, gestalt therapy emphasizes the relationship between the patient and therapist in the here-and-now (Perls, Hefferline, and Goodman, 1965). Suppose that toward the middle of a session a patient runs out of problems to discuss and sits mute, staring blankly out the window. Instead of waiting for the patient to speak up, a gestalt therapist would say what he feels. "I can't stand the way you just sit there and say nothing. Sometimes I regret ever becoming a therapist. You are impossible ... There, now I feel better" (Kempler, 1973, p. 272). The therapist is not blowing off steam in an unprofessional method. He does this for a reason—to encourage (by example) the patient to express his feelings, even if it means risking a relationship.

Gestalt therapy is based on the belief that many individuals are so concerned with obtaining approval that they become strangers to themselves. For example, an individual may always defer to authority figures but he may be detached from the part of himself that has fantasies of rebelling. Neither part acknowledges the other. Gestalt therapists attempt to help a person fit the pieces together. (The word "gestalt" comes from the German word for "configuration.")

Transactional Analysis

Introduced by Eric Berne (1964) in the early 1950s, transactional analysis begins with a contract. The individual seeking therapy states how he or she wants to change; the therapist specifies the conditions under which he or she will work. This contract puts them on an equal footing, as professional and client, at the start. The goal of transactional analysis is to help clients to become more flexible by discovering the scripts they play and replay in their lives.

For example, a young woman has problems in her relations with men. On the first date, she makes a point of saying she just wants to be friends. But her seductive gestures and comments on this and other occasions give the opposite impression. She acts "available." Eventually, the man makes a pass. She responds with outrage. Her date may walk out. Or he may go along with her: "You're right; I'm sorry; It won't happen again." Either way, she loses. By exploring her behavior with the therapist the young woman discovers that she is playing a game—in the incidents she described, in her relations with the therapist, and in her reactions to members of a group (if she is also in group therapy). This insight will help her to know when she wants to be "just friends" with a man and when she wants a deeper relationship, and to act accordingly. Thus transactional analysis, like the other therapies we have described, focuses on the individual's assuming responsibility for his or her life (see Holland, 1973).

Behavior Therapy

Psychoanalysis and the human potential movement have sometimes been criticized for being "all talk and no action." In *behavior therapy* there is much more emphasis on action. Rather than spending large amounts of time going into the patient's past history or the details of his dreams, the behavior therapist concentrates on finding out what is specifically wrong with the patient's current life and takes steps to change it.

The idea behind behavior therapy is that a disturbed person is one who

FIGURE 16.5
These photographs illustrate the desensitization of a snake phobia. To overcome her fear, this woman is slowly going through a series of stages in which she learns to be calm in fearful situations. First, she simply observes the snake in the hands of the attendant, who is on the other side of a screen. Just seeing another person handling the snake helps decrease her fear. Next, she gradually gets closer to the snake until she is able to touch it without fear.

has learned to behave in the wrong way. The therapist's job, therefore, is to "reeducate" the patient. The reasons for the patient's undesirable behavior are not important; what is important is to change the behavior itself. To bring about such changes, the therapist uses certain conditioning techniques that were first discovered in animal laboratories. (The principles of conditioning are explained in Chapter 2.)

One technique used by behavior therapists is *systematic desensitization*. This method is used to overcome irrational fears and anxieties that the patient has learned. The goal of desensitization therapy is to teach the patient to associate a pleasant feeling, rather than anxiety, with certain feared objects or events. For example, suppose a student is terrified of speaking in front of large groups of people—that, in fact, his stage fright is so tremendous that he is unable to speak when called upon in class. How would desensitization therapy effectively change this person's behavior?

To begin with the therapist might have the student make a list of all the aspects of talking to others that he finds frightening. Perhaps the most frightening aspect is actually standing before an audience, whereas the least frightening is speaking to a single other person. The patient ranks his fears in order, from the most frightening on down. First, the therapist begins teaching the patient to relax. As he relaxes, the patient tries to imagine as vividly as possible the least disturbing scene on his list. As he thinks about speaking to a single stranger, the student may feel a mild anxiety. But because the therapist has taught him how to relax, the patient is soon able to think about the experience without feeling afraid. The basic logic is that two opposite feelings cannot exist at the same time. The therapist attempts to replace anxiety with its opposite, relaxation.

This procedure is followed step by step by the list of anxiety-arousing events. The patient finally reaches a point where he is able to imagine the situations that threaten him the most without feeling anxiety. Now the therapist starts to expose the person to real-life situations that have previously frightened him. Therapy finally reaches the point where the stage-frightened student is able to get up and deliver an unrehearsed speech before a full auditorium.

Another form of behavior therapy is called _contingency management_. In this method the therapist and patient decide what old, undesirable behavior needs to be eliminated and what new, desirable behavior needs to appear. Arrangements are then made for the old behavior to go unrewarded and for the desired behavior to be reinforced. In its simplest form, contingency management consists of the therapist agreeing with the patient, "If you do X, I will give you Y." This form of agreement is similar to systems of reward that people often use on themselves. For instance, a college student may say to himself, "If I get a good grade on the exam, I'll treat myself to a great dinner." The reward is _contingent_ (dependent) upon getting a good grade.

Contingency management is used in prisons, mental hospitals, schools, and army bases, as well as with individual patients. In these situations it is possible to set up whole miniature systems of rewards, called token

FIGURE 16.6
The behavior therapy approach to the treatment of autism involves the use of contingency management, also known as operant conditioning (see Chapter 2). The therapist is rewarding the child with affection (*left*) and with some food (*top right*) for performing such desirable behaviors as coming toward the therapist and eating and drinking at the table. (*bottom right*) The therapists are introducing two autistic children to the experience of holding hands. If the children find this experience rewarding, they are likely to do it again. The therapists will deliberately ignore such undesirable behaviors as screaming, throwing food, or repetitive hand waving, but may use slaps or even electric shocks to punish such extremely undesirable behavior as the child's beating his head against a wall.

economies. For example, psychologists in some mental hospitals select behavior they judge desirable. Patients are then rewarded for these behaviors with "hospital," or token, money. Thus if a patient cleans his room or works in the hospital garden, he is rewarded with token money. The patients are able to cash in their token money for things they want, such as candy or cigarettes, or for certain privileges, such as time away from the ward. These methods are successful in inducing mental patients, who often sit around doing nothing day after day, to begin leading active lives. They learn to take care of themselves and to take on responsibility instead of having to be cared for constantly.

Rational-emotive Therapy

Rational-emotive therapy (RET) is an action-oriented form of therapy developed by Albert Ellis in the late 1950s (Ellis, 1973). Ellis believes that people behave in deliberate and rational ways, given their assumptions about life. Emotional problems arise when an individual's assumptions are unrealistic.

Suppose a man seeks therapy when a woman leaves him. He cannot stand the fact that she has rejected him. Without her his life is empty and miserable. She has made him feel utterly worthless. He must get her back.

An RET therapist would not look for incidents in the past that are making the present unbearable for this man, as a psychoanalyst would. RET therapists do not probe; they reason. Like a spoiled child, the man is demanding that the woman love him. He expects—indeed, insists—that things will always go his way. Given this assumption, the only possible explanation for her behavior is that something is dreadfully wrong, either with him or with her.

What is wrong, in the therapist's view, is the man's thinking. By defining his feelings for the woman as need rather than desire, he—not she—is causing his depression. When you convince yourself that you need someone, you will in fact be unable to carry on without that person. When you believe that you cannot stand rejection, you will in fact fall apart when you encounter rejection.

The goal of rational-emotive therapy is to correct these false and self-defeating beliefs. Rejection is unpleasant, but it is not unbearable. The woman may be very desirable, but she is not irreplaceable. To teach the individual to think in realistic terms, the RET therapist may use a number of techniques: role-playing (so that the person can see how his beliefs affect his relationships); modeling (to demonstrate other ways of thinking and acting); humor (to underline the absurdity of his beliefs); and simple persuasion. The therapist may also make homework assignments to give the man practice in acting more reasonably. For example, the therapist may instruct him to ask women who are likely to reject him out on dates. Why? So that he will learn that he can cope with things not going his way.

Ellis believes that the individual must take three steps to cure or correct himself. First, he must realize that some of his assumptions are false.

Second, he must see that he is making *himself* disturbed by acting on false beliefs. Finally, he must work to break old habits of thought and behavior. He has to practice, to learn self-discipline, to take risks. Depending on the individual, this may take from five to fifty sessions with the therapist.

Group Therapies

In the forms of therapy described thus far, the troubled person is usually alone with the therapist. In *group therapy*, however, he is in the company of others. There are several advantages to this situation. Group therapy gives the troubled person practical experience with one of his biggest problems—getting along with other people. A person in group therapy also has a chance to see how other people are struggling with problems similar to his own, and he discovers what other people think of him. He, in turn, can express what he thinks of them, and in this exchange he discovers where he is mistaken in his views of himself and of other people and where he is correct.

Another advantage to group therapy is the fact that one therapist can help a large number of people. Most group-therapy sessions are led by a trained therapist who makes suggestions, clarifies points, and keeps activities from getting out of hand. In this way, his training and experience are used to help as many as twenty people at once.

Family Therapy.   Recently therapists have begun to suggest, after talking to a patient, that his entire family unit should work at group therapy. This method is particularly useful because the members of the group are all people of great importance in one another's lives. In family therapy it is possible to untangle the twisted web of relationships that have led one or more members in the family to experience emotional suffering.

Often family members are unhappy because they are mistreating or are being mistreated by other family members in ways that no one understands or wants to talk about. The family therapist can point out what is going wrong from an objective viewpoint and can suggest ways of improving communication and fairness in the family.

Not all group therapies are run by professionals, however. Some of the most successful examples are provided in nonprofessional organizations, such as Alcoholics Anonymous and Synanon.

Alcoholics Anonymous.   The purpose of Alcoholics Anonymous is "to carry the AA message to the sick alcoholic who wants it." According to AA, the only way for an alcoholic to change is to admit that he is powerless over alcohol and that his life has become unmanageable. He must come to believe that only some power greater than himself can help him. The drinker who thinks he can battle out his own problem will not be successful.

Members of AA usually meet at least once a week to discuss the meaning of this message, to talk about the horrors of their experiences with alcohol, and to describe the new hope they have found with AA. Mutual encouragement, friendship, and an emphasis on personal responsibility

FIGURE 16.7
In Alcoholics Anonymous, one of the main emphases is on the alcoholic's responsibility for his actions, both in his personal life and in his efforts to make the organization work. The man at the lectern is recounting his experiences with alcoholism and how his life has improved with the help of AA. All of the people in the room can empathize with his story, and sooner or later they will all tell their stories to the group. This autobiographical storytelling is a technique utilized by AA to build a feeling of cohesiveness and solidarity among group members.

are the main techniques used to keep an individual "on the wagon." Every member must be willing to come to the aid of another member who is tempted to take a drink.

Most psychologists are unable to explain why AA works, but there is no doubt that it is effective: One study showed that of the people who went to seven or more AA meetings 75 percent never took another drink (see Gellman, 1964).

Synanon.   Synanon is an organization that deals with the problem of heroin addiction. Synanon members spend weeks, months, and even years living together in an effort to overcome drug addiction and to create a new and lasting lifestyle.

Synanon is a total experience. During the day everybody works together; in the evenings, members make use of a unique therapeutic device called the "Synanon Game," which all members are required to play. One at a time, members sit in the "hot seat" and receive the harshest possible personal criticism from their fellows. No matter what the target person says or does, he is likely to be fiercely attacked.

These games serve several purposes. They force the individual to see the personal weaknesses that have led him to drug addiction, and they teach him that it is useless to try to defend these weaknesses. He learns that he must overcome them, but he also learns to tolerate and stand up to personal criticism. For many people the game is the first situation in which they learn to respect their own ability to accept criticism and to live with themselves.

For those who can stick with it, the Synanon group is a highly effective method of therapy, but about half the people who try Synanon drop out. Synanon has also been heavily criticized for failing to prepare people to deal with the outside world. But its founder, Chuck Dedrick, sees it as an alternative to traditional American life. "Synanon just happens to be a better way for people to live together, both with themselves and others," he has pointed out (Yablonsky, 1965).

Encounter Groups.   The power of group interaction to affect and change people has given rise to the controversial *encounter group.* Encounter groups are primarily for people who function adequately in everyday life but who, for some reason, feel unhappy, dissatisfied, or stagnant.

The purpose of encounter groups is to provide experiences that will help people live more intense lives. Being in a small group (between five and fifteen people) for this express purpose is bound to teach one something about interpersonal relations. Techniques are often used in groups to overcome the restrictions that people live by in everyday life. A typical

FIGURE 16.8
Carl Rogers is shown here (*on the left, top photograph*) leading an encounter group in front of film cameras. Many encounter group leaders, including Rogers, feel that their role in the group is the same as that of any other member. The only exception is that if the group as a whole or any one of its members gets into trouble, the leader is the person who (as a result of his experience) can perhaps best rescue the situation. Typically, other group members will exhibit leadership or therapeutic skills and the designated leader will remain in the background, letting the group process determine itself but continuing to provide direction when necessary.

exercise requires each person to say something to every other person and at the same time to touch him in some way. Such methods are intended to increase sensitivity, openness, and honesty.

Role playing is another common encounter-group technique. It is a form of theater in which the goal is to help the people expose and understand themselves. A person may try acting out the role of a character in one of his dreams; another person may pretend to be herself as a child talking to her mother, played by another member. By switching roles and placing themselves in each other's situation, group members are better able to see themselves as others see them. Acting out a past experience or playing the role of another person can do much to bring out a person's hidden and true feelings (Back, 1972).

Regardless of the type of therapy, all groups require experienced leaders who are qualified to take responsibility for the group. In a few cases, people who have been unprepared for the intense emotional exposure that occurs in groups have suffered long-lasting psychological distress from the experience. In most of these cases, it has been found that a particular leader was insensitive and misjudged the vulnerability and stability of the group members.

Such casualties are rare, but in general the claims made for the benefits of encounter groups should be carefully examined. There is no doubt that groups can introduce a person to positive aspects of life of which he may have been unaware, but so far there is no guarantee that such experiences will have lasting effects. Groups offer intense and useful experiences, but they are not sure routes to happiness any more than are other new experiences.

PSEUDO-THERAPIES

Since the mid-1970s, thousands of people have become followers of Guru Maharahj Ji, the Perfect Master. Smiling, neatly dressed members of the Christian Unification Church can be found preaching the word of Korean Reverend Sun Myung Moon on street corners in every large city. Over 20,000 Americans have spent about $200 apiece and at least 60 hours in Erhard Seminars Training (est), organized by secular guru Werner Erhard.

In different ways, each of these leaders has offered many of the things individuals seek in psychotherapy: a more effective way of coping with life's problems, increased self-awareness, and relief from emotional pain. Followers of Reverend Moon, like followers of the Maharahj Ji, live and work together. Each hour of their day is planned. They are taught, in daily group meetings, what to think and how to live. Graduates of est spend two weekends or more in crowded halls listening to lectures, watching films and doing exercises borrowed from everything from psychotherapy to fortune telling. The trainers attack them one minute ("You're full of —; all your problems are your own fault"), and tell them they are perfect the next. Thousands have come back for more.

Why are Erhard and the others so successful? If you think back to what

Eric Fromm said about people's attempts to escape from freedom (see Chapter 13) and review the chapter on people in groups, you will begin to understand. These gurus provide an instant community for people who are lonely and dissatisfied with their relationships. They give individuals who feel powerless in their daily lives the feeling of being a part of something greater than themselves. Finally, they promise love, harmony, and freedom—through obedience. The master relieves individuals of the burden of choice. And for some people, the effects are "magical"—at least for a time (Gordon, 1976).

MENTAL INSTITUTIONS

When the demands of everyday life cannot be met, the mentally disturbed person may face the prospect of institutionalization. There are institutions to handle many different social problems: prisons for criminals, hospitals for the physically ill, and mental institutions for people who are considered unable to function in normal society.

Commitment

The process of placing a person in a mental hospital is called *commitment*. About one-half of all mental patients commit themselves voluntarily or have their friends or family commit them. However, many individuals are committed against their will. Involuntary commitment is a controver-

FIGURE 16.9
Phillippe Pinel supervising the unchaining of the inmates of the French insane asylum at La Salpetriere in 1795. Earlier Pinel had obtained permission to unchain the inmates of Bicetre Hospital in the face of such objections from the authorities as: "Why not proceed to the zoo and liberate the lions and tigers?" The conditions depicted here were typical of eighteenth-century asylums.

sial legal and ethical issue. It has been argued that a committed mental patient has fewer rights than a convicted criminal.

Many people have been placed in mental institutions simply because they do not have the money to go elsewhere. People with plenty of money can afford to see a private therapist at fifty dollars an hour. A person with average or below-average income is more likely to go to someone associated with a public institution—a clinic, general hospital, or mental hospital. It is standard procedure at such places to interview potential patients and to commit those who are thought to be seriously disturbed. By this process a poor person may end up in an institution, whereas his rich and equally disturbed counterpart is simply seen by a psycho-therapist four times a week.

Conditions

The quality of care in mental hospitals varies greatly. If the individual can afford it, he can be committed to a private institution with all the comforts of a country club. While paying as much as $150 a day, he can enjoy the use of swimming pools, tennis courts and good food while he considers his problems. But the majority of people go to state mental hospitals or cheaper private institutions. The quality of treatment in these hospitals varies tremendously. It is possible, in fact, for a patient's condition to worsen or remain unchanged because his hospital environment is unconducive to improvement. And because the patient fails to improve, he remains institutionalized year after year. This situation exists because most public hospitals lack funds for adequate nursing staffs, equipment, and trained therapists. In many cases, the patients' day-to-day care is left to attendants who do little more than clean and feed the patients and keep order.

Ideally, a mental hospital should be a place where the patient is tempo-rarily freed from social pressures that he or she cannot bear. Limited and carefully planned demands should be made by a staff capable of under-standing and concern for the individual. Unfortunately, the reality of many state hospitals does not fit this ideal. Patients in a typical public hospital are dressed in dull uniforms, stripped of all individuality. They become molded into a pattern of obedience, dependence, and conformity by a deadening routine of sleep, meals, ping-pong, and other ways of filling time (see Goffman, 1961).

As the patients become increasingly apathetic and resigned, they lose all ties with the outside world. In order to survive the boredom of each day, they rely on fantasy, dreams and sleep, and they stop thinking about returning to outside life. Nevertheless, many patients welcome this routine —they prefer to be taken care of and to avoid the responsibilities of the outside world.

Therapy in Mental Hospitals

Individual and group psychotherapy are provided in mental hospitals, but this type of therapy is slow and expensive, and it does not work well

with people who are often beyond caring whether they improve or not.

Some traditional treatments in mental hospitals are more physical than psychological. A good example is the use of electroconvulsive shock in the treatment of depression. The delivery of an electric current to the brain sufficient to produce convulsions is often effective in reversing severe depression. This result has been compared to the personality changes sometimes seen in people after a bad car accident or a severe physical illness. This treatment is no longer in common use.

Recently, administration of drugs has become the most widely used and most effective form of treatment both in and out of hospitals (Jarvik, 1967). A wide variety of drugs have been developed to deal with specific psychological symptoms. *Tranquilizers* have been remarkably effective in alleviating anxiety, and *antidepressants* have been used successfully with extremely depressed patients. Specific drugs are also given to physically violent patients. It used to be necessary to lock such people in bare rooms, tie them in strait-jackets, or wrap them in wet sheets. Now they can be chemically rather than physically restrained. Drugs do not make any lasting changes in a person, but they can relieve anxiety, depression, or overexcitement. They enable many people to carry on life outside the hospital instead of being confined for months or years.

There are certain dangers inherent in the use of psychiatric drugs. They are often administered to make up for the lack of staff at mental hospitals. In many institutions it is common policy to administer a tranquilizer to every patient early in the morning, so that throughout the day there is very little activity among patients, thus reducing the workload required of an already overworked staff.

Most psychiatric drugs, when given in high doses over long periods, have undesirable side effects, such as extreme lethargy or peculiar losses of coordination. For such reasons, it is not uncommon for mental patients to flush some of their drugs down the toilet.

FIGURE 16.10
These drawings, titled "My Life in the Hospital," were made by a woman considered to be psychotic and depict her self-perceptions during hospitalization. In the first series (*left*) she shows herself as she entered the hospital, bent over and depressed. Then, as she became involved in such activities as cooking and art therapy, she regained a measure of self-confidence, which is reflected in her erect posture and outstretched arms. The series ends with a relapse of the depression and her attempts to deal with questions and fears. The second series of drawings (*right*) initially shows the patient's interaction with the hospital chaplain, who seems to have answered some of her questions and dispelled some of her fears. After the chaplain was transferred to another post, the woman experienced a sense of loss and regression. Once again she shows herself bent over; the rest of the world—her bed and her home—has been crossed out, lost; the last drawing is as the first.

COMMUNITY MENTAL HEALTH

Community mental health programs have been created as an alternative to expensive private therapy and inadequate public institutions. These programs are meant not only to help those who are already troubled and disturbed, but also to change conditions that help to make people this way.

Community Centers

Emotional problems are often caused or made worse by conditions in the community. People who are treated unfairly by police, school authorities, landlords, or shopkeepers feel resentment and anger that cannot readily be expressed. So do people who have trouble feeding and clothing their families.

Conditions that create emotional problems are not confined to slums or ghettoes, however. Colleges create pressures that drive some students to suicide. Suburban homes and schools contain restraints and pressures that can lead to divorce, "delinquency," and severe parent–child conflicts.

The aim of community mental health programs is to provide local centers where personal and community problems can be attacked. Because these centers are community organizations, they can attract people who might never before have dreamed of having psychological help.

The basic idea behind these programs is to establish community clinics staffed by psychiatrists, psychologists, social workers, and trained nonprofessionals who work as a team. Individual patients are charged fees according to their ability to pay. Applicants to a program are evaluated by the entire team. Patients are then assigned to a specially skilled member of the clinic, depending upon their history, needs, and goals. They may receive treatment or counseling or may participate in local group activities (Golann and Eisendorfer, 1972).

Crisis Centers

Crisis centers have been established in many communities to perform services for people who suffer a sudden emotional crisis, such as a death in the family, a divorce, a frightening drug experience, or an urge to commit suicide.

The telephone hotline is a special tool of crisis-center treatment. The hotline is for people who need help but who want to remain anonymous. By calling a local crisis center, a person with suicidal feelings, for example, can receive advice and reassurance that, under regular circumstances, would be almost impossible to obtain.

The crisis center is a preventive measure designed to keep people from acting on their panic. Prevention techniques are also used with entire communities to help people feel that they can become useful and effective in dealing with community problems. For example, a psychologist might teach people to organize and gain some political control over the conditions in their neighborhood.

FIGURE 16.11
A Los Angeles crisis center where trained volunteers are available to receive calls twenty-four hours a day. This telephone emergency service, or hotline, eliminates the long delays and necessity for dealing with authorities that so often frighten people away from seeking help. Note the chart of common drugs in the window on the right: This chart helps the volunteers to identify drugs that have been taken by a caller who has overdosed or is on a bad trip.

Halfway Houses

There are thousands of people who spend time in mental hospitals, prisons, and homes for delinquents and who, when finally released, are psychologically unprepared to return to life in society. They may be able to behave well under structured conditions, but they find the freedom and immensity of society confusing and overwhelming. Such people can ease back into society through halfway houses.

Halfway houses give their inhabitants the support they need in order to build enough confidence to reenter society. Unwritten rules and informal social pressures guide the members in their efforts to readjust to the larger world (Raush and Raush, 1968).

One of the ways in which community mental health programs are changing the way psychotherapy is done in the United States is by recognizing the ability of nonprofessional people to give help. Housewives, policemen, teachers, and nurses are being given short periods of training in psychology. For many of the problems of everyday life, they are just as helpful as a highly trained professional.

Psychotherapy is limited in solving mental problems because human problems are not always limited to individuals, and even an individual's problems are difficult to understand unless his home and neighborhood are well understood. The greatest contribution of community mental health programs is that they recognize the important relation of a community's environment and resources to the emotional well-being of its people.

Community mental health programs have been severely criticized by some psychologists, such as Thomas Szasz, who say these programs are a means of converting social misfits into socially useful citizens with little attention to the person's own psychological needs. These critics point out that such programs are designed to fulfill the goals of the community, not those of the individual. Community mental health programs also suffer from low budgets and understaffing, thus preventing the programs from adequately doing the job they are designed to do.

In conclusion, psychotherapy and treatment of people with psychological problems, whatever the setting they are conducted in, must fulfill two primary goals: They must provide the troubled person with an understanding of his or her problems, and they must help the person find a way to overcome these difficulties and become a responsible, whole person.

SUMMARY

1. Psychotherapy is a method used by social workers, psychologists, and psychiatrists to assist people in dealing with their problems. An important function of psychotherapy is to help people realize that they are responsible for their own lives and that they can solve the problems that have been making them unhappy.

2. The primary goal of all patient–therapist relationships is to strengthen the patient's control of his or her life. In order to change, the patient must achieve some understanding of his or her problems. The therapist helps the patient find meaningful alternatives to the patient's present, unsatisfactory ways of behaving.

3. Effective therapists possess three characteristics: He or she must be a *healthy* individual; he or she must have a capacity for *warmth* and *understanding*; and he or she must be *experienced* in dealing with people.

4. Psychoanalysis is a form of therapy, based on the theories of Sigmund Freud, aimed at making the patient aware of the unconscious impulses, desires, and fears that are causing anxiety. Psychoanalysts believe that if the patient can achieve *insight,* that is, understand his unconscious motives, he can gain control over his behavior and thus free himself of recurring problems.

5. Humanistic and existential psychology have given rise to forms of therapy known collectively as the human potential movement. These forms of therapy include client-centered therapy, existential therapy, gestalt therapy, and transactional analysis. They all stress the actualization of one's potential through personal responsibility, freedom of choice, and authentic relationships.

6. Unlike psychoanalysis and the human potential movement, which emphasize the resolution of conflicts through understanding, behavior therapy focuses on changing specific behaviors through conditioning techniques.

7. Rational-emotive therapy, developed by Albert Ellis, attempts to correct an individual's self-defeating beliefs. Ellis believes that emotional problems arise when a person's assumptions about life are unrealistic. To alleviate emotional problems, the individual must realize his assumptions are false, see that these assumptions are the cause of his disturbance, and work to break old habits of thought and behavior.

8. In group therapy a patient doesn't meet alone with his or her therapist. Instead, a group of people meet with a single therapist. Each group member gains experience with one of his or her biggest problems—interacting with other people. Group-therapy approaches include family therapy, encounter groups, and drug rehabilitation programs, such as Alcoholics Anonymous and Synanon.

9. In recent years thousands of people have been attracted to gurus who promise their followers a better life. This "better life" is achieved by exchanging personal freedom and choice for obedience to the guru.

10. When the demands of everyday life become overwhelming, the mentally disturbed individual may have to be committed to an institution. Treatment in mental hospitals consists of individual and group psychotherapy, or electroconvulsive shock (for severe depression). Drugs, such as tranquilizers and antidepressants, have become the most widely used and effective form of treatment. Such drugs are used with patients out of hospitals as well.

11. Community health programs have been established to help troubled individuals and to change existing social conditions that contribute to people's problems. Community centers are clinics staffed by psychiatrists, psychologists, social workers, and trained nonprofessionals who work as a team. Crisis centers perform services for people who suffer from a sudden emotional crisis. Halfway houses are designed to help people who have been released from a mental institution or prison to gain enough confidence to reenter society.

GLOSSARY

behavior therapy: A form of therapy aimed at changing undesirable behavior through conditioning techniques.

client-centered therapy: A form of therapy aimed at helping the client recognize his own strengths and gain confidence so that he can be true to his own standards and ideas about how to live effectively.

contingency management: A form of behavior therapy in which undesirable behavior is not rewarded, while desirable behavior is reinforced.

encounter groups: A type of therapy for people who function adequately in everyday life but who feel unhappy, dissatisfied, or stagnant; aimed at providing experiences that will help people increase their sensitivity, openness, and honesty.

existential therapy: A form of therapy that helps patients to overcome fear of freedom, get in touch with their true feelings and accept responsibility for their lives.

family therapy: A form of therapy aimed at understanding and improving relationships that have led one or more members in a family to experience emotional suffering.

free association: A method used by psychoanalysts to examine the unconscious. The patient is instructed to say whatever comes into his or her mind.

gestalt therapy: A form of therapy that emphasizes the relationship between the patient and therapist in the here-and-now. The aim is to encourage the person to recognize all sides of his or her personality.

group therapy: A form of therapy in which patients work together with the aid of a group leader to resolve interpersonal problems.

human potential movement: An approach to psychotherapy that stresses the actualization of one's unique potentials through personal responsibility, freedom of choice, and authentic relationships.

placebo effect: The influence that a patient's hopes and expectations have on his or her improvement during therapy.

psychoanalysis: A form of therapy aimed at making patients aware of their unconscious motives so that they can gain control over their behavior and free themselves of self-defeating patterns.

psychotherapy: A general term for treatment used by social workers, psychologists, and psychiatrists to help troubled individuals overcome their problems. The goal of psychotherapy is to break the behavior patterns that lead to unhappiness.

rational-emotive therapy: A form of therapy aimed at changing unrealistic assumptions about oneself and other people. It is believed that once a person understands that he or she has been acting on false beliefs, self-defeating thoughts and behaviors will be avoided.

resistance: The reluctance of a patient to reveal painful feelings and to examine long-standing behavior patterns.

systematic desensitization: A technique used by behavior therapists to help patients overcome learned irrational fears and anxieties. The goal is to substitute pleasant associations for the anxiety connected with feared objects or events.

token economies: A system of rewards in which token money is used to reinforce desirable behaviors; especially useful in mental hospitals.

transactional analysis: A form of therapy aimed at helping clients become more flexible by discovering the scripts they play and replay in their lives.

transference: The process, experienced by the patient, of feeling toward an analyst or therapist the way he or she feels toward some other important figure in his or her life.

unconditional positive regard: In client-centered therapy, the atmosphere of emotional support provided by the therapist. The therapist shows the client that he or she accepts anything that is said without embarrassment or anger.

ACTIVITIES

1. On a sheet of paper draw a large thermometer ranging from 0 to 100 degrees. Think of the most fearful thing you can imagine and write it down at the hundred-degree mark. Write down the least fearful thing you can think of at the zero-degree mark. Continue to list your fears on the thermometer according to their severity. Have several friends make similar lists of their fears. Compare lists, looking for differences and similarities. Do you think any of your fears are based on conditioning? Can you think of a method of reconditioning that would remove the fear or make it less intense?

2. Volunteer your services for a few weeks in a therapeutic nursery, addiction program, or mental hospital. Then write up your impressions about the patients, as well as your own feelings about what you experienced. If given permission by the staff, you could do an in-depth interview and study of one patient with whom you have a good relationship.

3. Find a poverty area and interview people in the community about the kinds of services they feel the community needs. Ask about mental health services, but also ask how they feel housing, employment, and other economic problems affect people's psychological well-being. If there are social service or community mental health centers in the area, visit them and interview some of the staff.

4. When we think about our own lives and about the kind of person we would like to be, there are often certain individuals who stand out as important role models. They could be a parent, a brother or sister, a teacher, or perhaps a good friend. Write a statement about some of your goals in life and discuss how a significant person may have influenced you.

5. Ask several people in different businesses if they would hire someone they knew had undergone psychotherapy. Do their responses indicate to you that society has matured to where it now understands and accepts emotional problems in the same way it accepts medical problems? Do you believe a person should be barred from high public office because he or she has sought psychotherapy?

6. Recommend a treatment for the following problems: compulsive overeating, inability to finish work, severe depression. Think of real examples as much as possible. How do the techniques you suggest resemble the therapies described in this chapter?

7. Find out what program(s) exist in your community to deal with emotional, alcohol, or drug problems. Note how long it takes you to find this information, then ask yourself, "If I really needed this help, would I have found it in time?" If no such programs can be found in your area, how might you help start something of this type?

8. One way to lessen feelings of frustration and hostility is to talk about whatever is disturbing you with a close friend or relative. Think about the last time that you talked out a problem with someone. Did the person sympathize with you? If so, what kind of feelings did that sympathy arouse? Did the person try to help you understand the problem, or did he/she simply uphold your point of view? What approach would have been more helpful?

SUGGESTED READINGS

BRY, ADELAIDE. *Inside Psychotherapy.* New York: Signet, 1972 (paper). Consists of interviews with leading practitioners of psychoanalysis, Jungian therapy, Frommian therapy, gestalt therapy, behavioral therapy, family therapy, group therapy, encounter-group therapy, and nude marathon therapy. An interesting aspect of the book is the response of the different therapists to Bry's question of how each would treat her fear of riding airplanes.

GLASSER, WILLIAM. *Reality Therapy.* New York: Harper Colophon Books, 1965 (paper). A highly influential book, *Reality Therapy* presents Glasser's method of treatment—using concrete, realizable goals, taking responsibility for one's own actions, and formulating a clear "contract" between therapist and patient.

GOFFMAN, ERVING. *Asylums.* Garden City, N.Y.: Doubleday, 1961 (paper). A highly original sociological analysis of institutions by a sociologist who worked as a volunteer in one of them. It presents mental illness as an act played out to fulfill the expectations of institutional custodians.

HALEY, JAY, AND HOFFMAN, LYNN. *Techniques of Family Therapy.* New York: Basic Books, 1967 (paper). This is another good book showing therapy in action. Several well-known practitioners of marriage and family therapy, such as Virginia Satir, Don Jackson, and Carl Whitaker, are first shown conducting sessions with patients and are then interviewed about their philosophies and techniques.

HALL, CALVIN S. *A Primer of Freudian Psychology.* New York: Mentor, 1955 (paper). One of the best introductions to psychoanalysis, this book provides clear summaries of Freud's theory of the unconscious, the defense mechanisms, and his stages of psychosexual development. Each chapter ends with references to Freud's writings for the student who wishes to pursue each topic further.

KESEY, KEN. *One Flew Over the Cuckoo's Nest.* New York: Viking, 1964 (paper). Novelist Kesey worked in a mental hospital and then created a fictional story of a life-loving character who continually challenges the authority of the hospital administration. He gets the other patients to break routines, smuggles in women, and manages to do more for the psychological well-being of the patients than the hospital staff, who try to force everyone to conform to their model of the "adjusted" mental patient.

PERLS, FRITZ. *Gestalt Therapy Verbatim.* New York: Bantam Books, 1971 (paper). This best-known work by the originator of gestalt therapy consists of tape-recorded talks and dramatic passages from therapy sessions. In most of these sessions, Perls uses his method of having individuals role-play parts of their own dreams.

ROAZEN, PAUL. *Freud and His Followers.* New York: Meridian Books, 1971 (paper). A lively history of psychoanalysis showing how the ideas of its most famous figures—Freud, Jung, Adler, Erikson, Reich, Horney, etc.—were often shaped by their own personal problems. In this sense, the author "psychoanalyzes" the psychoanalysts, giving the reader a real feeling for this important school of psychotherapy.

RUITENBECK, HENDRIK M. *The New Group Therapies.* New York: Avon Books, 1970 (paper). Deals with traditional as well as more recent and controversial forms of group therapy, from psychoanalytic group process, theme-centered groups, and psychodrama to weekend marathons, addiction groups, and nude happenings. An unusually well-written and well-documented survey of these different methods.

SCHUTZ, WILLIAM C. *Joy: Expanding Human Awareness.* New York: Grove Press, 1967

(paper). Also *Here Comes Everybody: Everyman's Guide to Encounter.* New York: Harrow Books, 1971 (paper). In his work at the Esalen Institute at Big Sur, California, William Schutz has been famous for his ability to integrate a wide variety of innovative therapy techniques. As a result, these two books provide an exciting view of the many different methods of the human potential movement, giving case examples and an ample list of references.

SZASZ, THOMAS (ED.). *The Age of Madness.* Garden City, N.Y.: Doubleday Anchor Books, 1973 (paper). A large number of personal accounts showing how involuntary commitment to mental institutions works to deny many people the opportunity to get well.

BIBLIOGRAPHY

BACK, KURT W. *Beyond Words: The Story of Sensitivity Training and the Encounter Movement.* New York: Basic Books, 1972.

BERGIN, ALLEN E., AND GARFIELD, SOL L. *Handbook of Psychotherapy and Behavior Change: An Empirical Analysis.* New York: Wiley, 1971.

BERNE, ERIC. *Games People Play.* New York: Grove Press, 1964.

CAPLAN, GERALD. *Principles of Preventive Psychiatry.* New York: Basic Books, 1965.

CORSINI, RAYMOND (ED.). *Current Psychotherapies.* Itasca, Ill.: F. E. Peacock, 1973.

ELLIS, ALBERT. "Rational-Emotive Therapy." In Corsini, *op. cit.*: 167–206.

FITTS, WILLIAM H. *The Experience of Psychotherapy.* New York: Van Nostrand, 1965.

FRANKL, VIKTOR. *Man's Search for Meaning: An Introduction to Logotherapy.* New York: Clarion, 1970.

GELLMAN, I. P. *The Sober Alcoholic: An Organizational Analysis of Alcoholics Anonymous.*

New Haven, Conn.: College and University Press, 1964.

GOFFMAN, ERVING. *Asylums.* Garden City, N.Y.: Doubleday, 1961.

GOLANN, S. E., AND EISENDORFER, C. (EDS.). *Handbook of Community Mental Health.* New York: Appleton-Century-Crofts, 1972.

GORDON, SUZANNE. *Lonely in America.* New York: Simon and Schuster, 1976.

GREENBLATT, MILTON, ET AL. (EDS.). *Drugs and Social Therapy in Chronic Schizophrenia.* Springfield, Ill.: Charles C. Thomas, 1965.

HOLLAND, GLEN A. "Transactional Analysis." In Corsini, *op cit.*: 353–400.

JARVIK, M. E. "The Psychopharmacological Revolution." *Psychology Today,* 1 (May 1967): 51–59.

KEMPLER, WALTER. "Gestalt Therapy." In Corsini, *op. cit.*: 251–286.

LINDNER, ROBERT. *The Fifty-Minute Hour.* New York: Bantam, 1954.

LOWEN, ALEXANDER. *Physical Dynamics of Character Structure.* New York: Grune & Stratton, 1958.

MAY, ROLLO. *Existential Psychology.* 2nd ed. New York: Random House, 1969.

MORENO, JACOB. *Psychodrama.* Vol. 1. Boston: Beacon, 1946.

PERLS, FRITZ, HEFFERLINE, R. F. AND GOODMAN, P. *Gestalt Therapy.* New York: Dell, 1965.

RAUSH, HAROLD L., AND RAUSH, CHARLOTTE. *The Halfway House Movement: A Search for Sanity.* New York: Appleton-Century-Crofts, 1968.

ROGERS, CARL. *Client-Centered Therapy.* Boston: Houghton Mifflin, 1951.

ROLF, IDA P. *Structural Integration.* Available from The Guild for Structural Integration, 1776 Union St., San Francisco, Calif., 1963.

SCHOFIELD, WILLIAM. *Psychotherapy: The Purchase of Friendship.* Englewood Cliffs, N.J.: Prentice-Hall, 1964.

SKINNER, B. F. *Beyond Freedom and Dignity.* New York: Knopf, 1971.

SZASZ, THOMAS. *The Myth of Mental Illness.* New York: Dell, 1967.

——. *The Age of Madness.* Garden City, N.Y.: Doubleday, 1973.

WHEELIS, ALLEN. *Quest for Identity.* New York: Norton, 1958.

YABLONSKY, L. *The Tunnel Back: Synanon.* New York: Macmillan, 1965.

UNIT VI

Psychology and Society

You may know someone who has been in psychotherapy or who has sought professional help during a family crisis. But did you know that psychologists have been evaluating you since the day you entered school and will do so at other times during your life? Psychologists design intelligence, aptitude, and job placement tests as well as personality tests. The chances are that the schools you have attended measured your interests and abilities on numerous occasions.

Psychologists are also helping to solve the problem of alienation on the job and to curb racial and ethnic discrimination in industry. A team of psychologists helped to create the television show Sesame Street, and psychologists continue to advise the producers. Psychologists also work with the courts—not only offering expert testimony on a person's fitness to stand trial, but helping attorneys to select fair juries. These are a few of the examples of *applied psychology* you will be learning about in the next two chapters. In Chapter 17 we will discuss the uses and abuses of intelligence, aptitude, and personality tests. In Chapter 18 we review the work of a number of psychologists who have put their expertise to practical use. We suggest that this is only a start—that we might design a better future if we would take advantage of the information and techniques psychology offers.

17 Psychological Testing

On standardized written intelligence tests, the average scores of black Americans are lower than those of white Americans, and the average scores of poor Americans (white and black) are lower than those of rich Americans. Does this mean that blacks and poor people are naturally inferior intellectually to whites and to rich people?

Psychotics score differently from normal persons on many personality tests. Does this mean that people whose scores are similar to that of the average psychotic should be hospitalized?

Some large corporations use personality tests to screen job applicants. Does this mean that an applicant should be denied a job on the basis of his or her score on a personality test?

These questions only begin to suggest the enormous range and complexity of mental measurement, or testing. Psychologists often disagree strongly about testing. Indeed, perhaps the only point on which most people agree with regard to testing is that our society relies heavily on tests.

Over the years psychologists have devised a wide range of tools for measuring intelligence, interests, skills, achievements, knowledge, aptitudes, and personality patterns. Educators, the military, industry, and mental health clinics depend on these tests. Yet the steady increase in the use of mental measures in recent years has raised numerous ethical questions. This chapter will describe the major types of tests in current use and discuss some of the controversies surrounding psychological testing.

BASIC CHARACTERISTICS OF TESTS

FIGURE 17.1
This woman is taking one subtest of the Wechsler Adult Intelligence Scale. She is being timed while she assembles the cubes to match a pattern in the booklet that stands in front of her. Because testing is one of the principal means psychologists have of quantifying human behavior, tests are used in a great many areas of research as well as for assessing people's capabilities and personalities for purposes of counseling or therapy.

All tests have one characteristic in common that makes them both fascinating and remarkably practical: They promise to make it possible to find out a great deal about a person in a very short time. Tests can be useful in predicting how well a person might do in a particular career; in assessing an individual's desires, interests, and attitudes; and in revealing psychological problems. Psychologists can use some tests to help people understand things about themselves more clearly than they did before.

One of the great dangers of testing, however, is that we tend to forget that tests are merely *tools* for measuring and predicting human behavior. We start to think of test results (for example, an IQ) as things in themselves. The justification for using a test to make decisions about a person's future depends on whether a decision based on test scores would be fairer and more accurate than one based on other criteria. The fairness and usefulness of a test depend on several factors: its reliability, its validity, and the way its norms were established.

Test Reliability

The term *reliability* refers to a test's consistency—its ability to yield the same result under a variety of different circumstances. There are three basic ways of determining a test's reliability. First, if a person retakes the test, or takes a similar test, within a short time after the first testing, does he or she receive approximately the same score? If, for example, you take a mechanical aptitude test three times in the space of six months and score 65 in January, 90 in March, and 70 in June, then the test is unreliable. It does not produce a stable measurement.

The second measure of reliability is whether the test yields the same results when scored by different people. If both your teacher and a teaching assistant score an essay test that you have written, and one gives you a B while the other gives you a D, then you have reason to complain about the test's reliability. The score you receive depends more on the grader than on you. On a reliable test, your score would be the same no matter who graded your paper.

One final way of determining a test's reliability is to find out whether, if you divide the test in half and score each half separately, the two scores are approximately the same. If a test is supposed to measure one quality in a person (for example, reading comprehension or administrative ability), then it should not have some sections on which the person scores high and others on which he or she scores low.

In checking tests for reliability, psychologists are trying to prevent chance factors from influencing a person's score. All kinds of irrelevant

FIGURE 17.2
Two examples of group testing. Examinations and intelligence tests administered under conditions ranging from formal (left) to casual (right) are familiar experiences to students in almost any public school system. Both intelligence tests and regular examinations can be considered psychological tests because both are intended to measure psychological variables (intelligence and knowledge).

matters can interfere with a test. If the test taker is feeling depressed that day, or if the scorer has just received a parking ticket and is annoyed, or if the room where the test is being given is dark and gloomy, all these factors can make the test taker score lower than he would if he and the scorer were feeling relaxed and were working in a cheerful, well-lit room. No test can screen out all interferences, but a highly reliable test can do away with a good part of them.

Test Validity

A test may be reliable but still not be valid. *Validity* is the ability of a test to measure what it is supposed to measure. For example, a test that consists primarily of vocabulary lists will not measure aptitude for engineering. Similarly, a test on American history will not measure students' general learning ability.

Determining the validity of a test is more complex than assessing its reliability. One of the chief methods for measuring validity is to find out how well a test *predicts* future performance. For example, a group of psychologists design a test to measure teaching ability. They ask questions about teaching methods, attitudes toward students, and so on. But do the people who score high on this test really make good teachers?

Suppose the testmakers decide that a good way to check the validity of the test is to find out how much a teacher's students improve in reading in one year. If the students of those teachers who scored high on the test improve more in their reading skills than the students of those teachers who scored low on the test, the test may be considered valid. It identifies good teachers. School boards may then adopt it as one tool to use in deciding whom to hire to teach in their schools.

But what if teachers who are good at improving reading skills are poor at teaching other skills? It may be that this test measures talent for raising reading levels, not general teaching ability. This is the kind of difficulty that psychologists encounter in trying to assess the validity of a test. As the example shows, nothing can be said about a test's validity until the purpose of the test is absolutely clear.

Establishing Norms

Once a test result is obtained, the examiner must translate the score into something useful. Suppose a child answers 32 of 50 questions on a vocabulary test correctly. What does this score mean? If the test is reliable and valid, it means that the child can be expected to understand about 64 percent of the words in a book at the reading level being tested. In other words, the score predicts how the child will *perform* at a given level.

But a "raw" score does not tell us where the child stands in relation to other children at his or her age and grade level. If most children answered 45 or more questions correctly, 32 is a low score. However, if most answered only 20 questions correctly, 32 is a very high score.

The method psychologists generally use to transform raw scores into figures that reflect comparisons with others is the *percentile system.*

FIGURE 17.3
If one were to construct a test of intelligence by measuring head size and equating bigger measurements with higher IQ, one would have a test with high reliability. That is, all the people who independently measure Leonardo's head would come up with much the same results. However, the test would have little validity because large head size simply does not correspond with high IQ in the real world. The tape-measure test would, however, be a valid test for predicting hat size. A test's validity can only be judged on whether it serves the purpose for which it is intended.

FIGURE 17.4

The meaning of percentile scores. The range of possible raw scores on a test is shown in relation to an idealized curve that indicates the proportion of people who achieved each score. The vertical lines on the curves indicate percentiles, or proportions of the curve below certain points. Thus the line indicated as the 1st percentile is the line below which only 1 percent of the curve lies; similarly, 99 percent of the curve lies below the 99th percentile line. Percentiles cluster more closely toward the center of the curve because that is where the majority of raw scores occur.

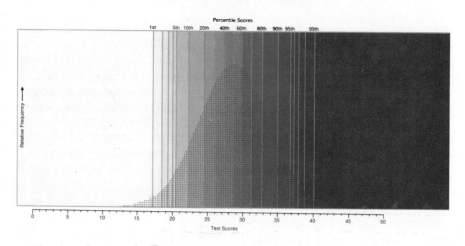

which bears some resemblance to what is called "grading on the curve." In the percentile system the scores actually achieved on the test are written down in order, ranging from the highest to the lowest. Each particular score is then compared with this list and assigned a percentile according to the percentage of scores that fall at or below this point. For example, if half the children in the above example scored 32 or below, then a score of 32 is at the 50th percentile. If 32 were the top score, it would be at the 100th percentile. In the example given in Figure 17.4, a score of 32 correct puts the child in the 75th percentile, since only 25 percent of the children scored higher than she did.

When psychologists are designing a test to be used in a variety of schools, businesses, clinics, or other settings, they usually set up a scale for comparison by establishing norms. The test is given to a large representative sample of the group to be measured—for example, sixth graders, army privates, engineers, or perhaps the population as a whole. Percentiles are then established on the basis of the scores achieved by this standardization group. These percentiles are called the test's norms. Most of the intelligence, aptitude, and personality tests you will encounter have been provided with norms in this way. Your percentile on the College Boards, for example, reflects your standing among people of your age and grade who have taken these exams.

It should be remembered, however, that norms are not really standards—even though a norm group is sometimes misleadingly referred to as a "standardization group." Norms refer only to what has been found normal or average for some group of people. If Johnny can read at the 50th percentile level, that does not mean he has met some absolute standard for ability to read. It only means that he reads as well (or as poorly) as the average American schoolchild of his age.

In summary, when you take a test and obtain your score, you should consider the following questions in evaluating the results: (1) Was the test a reliable one, or could chance factors have influenced the results? If you took the same test or a similar test again, would you receive a similar score? (2) Was this test a valid one? Does your performance on the test reflect your performance in the subject the test is designed to measure? (3) How was the test normed? In other words, what group of people are you being compared to?

INTELLIGENCE TESTING

Among the most widely used and widely disputed tests in America today are those that are designed to measure "intelligence" and yield an "IQ" score. This section will describe some of the major intelligence tests and present some of the issues that surround them.

The Development of Intelligence Tests

Alfred Binet, a French psychologist, was the first to develop a useful intelligence test. In 1904 Binet was asked by the Paris school authorities to devise a means of picking out "slow learners" so they could be placed in special classes from which they might better profit. Binet was unable to define intelligence, but he believed it was reflected in such things as the abilities to make common-sense judgments, to tell the meanings of words, and to solve problems and puzzles. Binet assumed that whatever intelligence was, it increased with age; that is, that older children had more intelligence than younger children. Therefore in selecting items for his test he only included items on which older children did better than younger children. By asking the same questions of many children, Binet was able to determine the average age at which a particular question could be answered. For example, he discovered that certain questions could be answered by most twelve-year-olds but not by most eleven-year-olds. If a child of eleven, or even nine, could answer these questions, he or she was said to have a *mental age* of twelve. If a child of twelve could answer the nine-year-old-level questions but not the questions for ten-year-olds and eleven-year-olds, he or she was said to have a mental age of nine. Thus a slow learner was one who had a *mental age* that was less than his or her *chronological age*.

The Stanford-Binet.   Binet's intelligence test has been revised many times since he developed it. The Binet test currently in widespread use in the United States is a revision created at Stanford University, the Stanford-Binet Intelligence Test (Terman and Merrill, 1973). The Stanford-Binet, like the original test, groups test items by age level. To stimulate and maintain the child's interest, a variety of tasks are included, ranging from defining words to drawing pictures and explaining events in daily life. Children are tested one at a time. The examiner must carry out standardized instructions—at the same time putting the child at ease, getting him to pay attention, and encouraging him to try as hard as he can.

In the final scoring, the mental age indicates how high a level the person has reached. If his performance is as high as the average twelve-year-old's, he has a mental age of twelve. The IQ, or *intelligence quotient*, is called a quotient because it used to be computed by dividing mental age by actual (chronological) age and multiplying the result by 100 to eliminate

FIGURE 17.5
Two tests on the Stanford-Binet Intelligence Test being administered to a little boy. Both these tests are ones that would be easily passed by him unless he were severely retarded. (*top*) The examiner has built a tower of four blocks and has told the child, "You make one like this." The average two-year-old is able to build the tower. Three-year-olds are asked to copy a three-block bridge. (*bottom*) The examiner shows the child the card with six small objects attached to it and says, "See all these things? Show me the dog," and so on. The average two-year-old can point to the correct objects as they are named.

decimals. (A nine-year-old with a mental age of twelve would have an IQ of 133.) Although the term "IQ" has stuck, the actual computation is now made on a basis similar to the percentile system.

The Wechsler Tests.   Two other frequently used intelligence tests are the Wechsler Intelligence Scale for Children, or WISC, and the Wechsler Adult Intelligence Scale, or WAIS (Wechsler, 1958). The Wechsler tests differ from the Stanford-Binet in several important ways. For example, the Wechsler tests place more emphasis on performance tasks (such as doing puzzles) than does the Stanford-Binet, so that individuals who are not particularly skilled in the use of words will not be as likely to receive low IQ scores.

Moreover, in addition to yielding one overall score, the Wechsler tests yield percentile scores in several areas—vocabulary, information, arithmetic, picture arrangement, and so on. These ratings are used to compute separate IQ scores for verbal and performance abilities. This type of scoring provides a more detailed picture of the individual's strengths and weaknesses than a single score does.

FIGURE 17.6

Test items similar to those included in the various Wechsler intelligence scales. (a) A sampling of questions from five of the verbal subtests. (b) A problem in block design, one of the performance subtests. The subject is asked to arrange the blocks to match the pattern on a card that he or she is briefly shown in the notebook. (c) Another example of a performance subtest. The subject is asked to put together puzzle pieces to form a familiar object, such as a duck.

(Test items courtesy The Psychological Corporation, New York.)

a

General Information
1. How many wings does a bird have?
2. How many nickels make a dime?
3. What is steam made of?
4. Who wrote "Paradise Lost"?
5. What is pepper?

General Comprehension
1. What should you do if you see someone forget his book when he leaves his seat in a restaurant?
2. What is the advantage of keeping money in a bank?
3. Why is copper often used in electrical wires?

Arithmetic
1. Sam had three pieces of candy and Joe gave him four more. How many pieces of candy did Sam have altogether?
2. Three men divided eighteen golf balls equally among themselves. How many golf balls did each man receive?
3. If two apples cost 15¢, what will be the cost of a dozen apples?

Similarities
1. In what way are a lion and a tiger alike?
2. In what way are a saw and a hammer alike?
3. In what way are an hour and a week alike?
4. In what way are a circle and a triangle alike?

Vocabulary
"What is a puzzle?"
"What does 'addition' mean?"

Select the missing word by deciding which one of the five words *best* fits in with the meaning of the sentence.

To make you understand my point I must go back a bit and seem to change the subject, but the (   ) will soon be plain.

A correction **B** effect **C** origin **D** controversy
E connection

Choose the correct answer, using scratch paper if necessary.

$\frac{.7}{.05}$ is equal to which of the following?

F $\frac{7}{50}$ **G** $\frac{7}{5}$ **H** 14 **J** 35 **K** None of these

Pick the word or phrase whose meaning is closest to the word in large letters.
induce

A grant **B** prolong **C** mix **D** persuade **E** convict

FIGURE 17.7
Pencil-and-paper tests of intelligence. Items of the type that appear on the School and College Ability Test (SCAT) are shown. The purpose of this test is to estimate high school students' ability to do college-level work. This test provides a measurement similar to that of a general intelligence test; that is, your SCAT score would be about the same as your Wechsler or Stanford-Binet score.

Group Tests. The Wechsler and Stanford-Binet tests, because they are given individually, are costly and time-consuming to administer. During World War I, when the United States Army found that it had to test nearly two million men, and quickly, individual testing was a luxury the Army could not afford. Thus paper-and-pencil intelligence tests, which could be given to large groups of people at the same time, were developed. Current group IQ tests, such as the Army Alpha and Beta tests, have proved to be convenient and effective and are used extensively in schools, employment offices, and many other institutions.

The Uses and Meaning of IQ Scores

In general, the norms for intelligence tests are established in such a way that most people score near 100. Out of one hundred people, seventeen will score above 115 and seventeen will score below 85. About three in one hundred score above 130, and three score below 70. This means that a score of 130 places a person in the 97th percentile; a score of 70, in the 3rd percentile.

What do these scores mean? What do the tests measure? IQ scores seem to be most useful when related to school achievement: They are quite accurate in predicting which people will do well in schools, colleges, and universities. Critics of IQ testing do not question this predictive ability. They do wonder, however, whether such tests actually measure "intelligence." Most psychologists agree that intelligence is the ability to acquire new ideas and new behavior. Is success in school or the ability to take a test a real indication of such ability? Generally, IQ tests measure the ability to solve certain types of problems. But they do not directly measure the ability to pose those problems or to question the validity of problems set by others (Hoffman, 1962). This is only part of the reason why IQ testing is so controversial.

The Controversy over IQ

Much of the debate about IQ testing centers around one question: Do genetic differences or environmental inequalities cause two people to receive different scores on intelligence tests? This controversy around the question becomes particularly heated when researchers consider differences among segments of the population. On the average people from middle-class backgrounds do better on IQ tests than people from poor backgrounds, and whites (more of whom grow up in middle-class environments) do somewhat better than blacks (more of whom grow up in poor surroundings). For years many psychologists assumed that this difference in IQ scores was due primarily to cultural differences—the fact that middle-class white children have better schools, more books, more opportunities to travel, and more encouragement, both from their parents and from their teachers, to use their abilities and "get ahead." It was felt that if lower-class black children were given the same cultural advantages as middle-class children, the black-white IQ gap would be closed. Based on this theory, the federal government instituted such programs as Head Start, designed to enrich the environment of the culturally disadvantaged child.

However, in 1969 psychologist Arthur Jensen published an article questioning all these optimistic assumptions. Jensen claimed that Head Start had *not* succeeded in bringing about any permanent change in the IQ scores of the children in the program. He went on to say that this fact, along with a number of scientific studies, suggested that IQ differences were due primarily to genetic inheritance rather than to environment. Indeed, he argued that fully 80 percent of the difference in IQ scores between individuals was due to genetic difference. And if this were true of IQ differences between individuals, it might reasonably be true of IQ differences between whole races as well. In short, Jensen suggested that the lower IQ average of blacks might be due to genetic disadvantage much more than to environmental disadvantage, and consequently that no amount of "cultural enrichment" programs would ever permit the average black child to keep pace with the average white child on an IQ test.

Needless to say, Jensen's article raised a storm of protest. Some critics pointed out flaws in his methods and calculations. Others argued that it was totally unjustifiable to assume that what was true of individual differences in IQ scores was also true of racial differences in IQ scores. Still others argued that Jensen's conclusions were irrelevant since the standard IQ tests were a completely inadequate measure of intelligence.

From this debate a number of important points emerged, particularly with regard to intelligence tests. In the first place, some of the questions on these tests clearly give middle-class people an advantage. One intelligence test, for example, includes the following question as a test of reasoning ability:

A symphony is to a composer as a book is to what?
paper.   sculptor   author   musician   man

A. Davis (1951) found that 81 percent of children from well-off families, but only 51 percent of children from lower-class families, answered this correctly. When Davis rephrased the question in less "highbrow" terms, using everyday words and common experiences, the gap closed.

A baker goes with bread, like a carpenter goes with what?

a saw   a house   a spoon   a nail   a man

Fifty percent of the children from both income groups answered this question correctly. The first question measured experience in middle-class culture as well as reasoning; the second, reasoning alone.

In addition, there is mounting evidence that poor children do not try as hard as middle-class children on intelligence tests. Why? Because the test itself makes them uncomfortable. They tend to see tests as punishments, as situations designed to make them look bad. Many rush through a test, choosing responses almost at random—just to get it over with. In contrast, middle-class children tend to see tests as an opportunity to prove themselves and to win praise. They work more slowly, making fewer wild guesses and scoring higher. Thus the differences among groups reflect motivation as well as intelligence.

Several researchers have coached disadvantaged youngsters in test-taking—with good results. It seems that many do not fully understand the questions they are being asked or the tasks they are required to perform on the tests. In short, they have not learned the strategies to solve test problems. When they do, their scores improve. This suggests that a person's IQ score also reflects his or her skill and experience in taking tests.

In short, IQ tests are far from perfect measures of intelligence. A variety of factors irrelevant to the question of intelligence affect results and exaggerate differences among groups. This is not to say we should stop using the tests altogether, however. Intelligence tests may be biased in some respects. But they may be less biased than many teachers, whose personal likes and dislikes can easily influence their evaluations of students. And although IQ tests may measure social class, motivation, and experience as well as intelligence, they do in fact test people on the kind of reasoning and problem-solving abilities required for success in school and careers in a complex society. Moreover, by studying the differences in average

FIGURE 17.8
Project SEED (Special Elementary Education for the Disadvantaged) is designed to teach high-level mathematics to disadvantaged elementary school students. Its goal is to teach children that they can be successful in learning and that intellectual work can be rewarding. Another aim is to counter the argument that black children are genetically intellectually inferior to white children. Evaluation studies show that black SEED children score the same as white children of the same age.

IQ among groups, we may find ways to correct inequalities in educational opportunity and experience. To condemn testing would be something like the ancient practice of killing the messenger who brought bad news.

One final and very important point: The fact that *average* IQ scores for lower-class people are somewhat lower than those for middle-class people and that *average* scores for blacks are somewhat lower than those for whites does not tell us anything about *individuals*. The IQ scores of middle-class people and of white people range from a hypothetical zero up to the very rare 200. So do those of poor people and black people. In using the IQ test to place children in classes or adults in jobs, it is the *individual's* score that should matter, not his group's.

MEASURING ABILITIES AND EXPERIENCE

Intelligence tests are designed to measure a person's overall ability to solve problems that involve symbols such as words, numbers, and pictures. Psychologists have developed other tests to assess special abilities and experiences. These include aptitude and achievement tests.

Aptitude Tests

Aptitude tests attempt to discover a person's talents and to predict how well he or she will be able to learn a new skill. The General Aptitude Test Battery (GATB) is the most widely used of these tests. Actually, the GATB comprises nine different tests, ranging from vocabulary to manual dexterity. Test results are used to determine whether a person meets minimum standards for each of a large number of occupations. In addition to the GATB there are aptitude tests in music, language, art, mathematics, and other special fields. Another widely used aptitude test, taken by most prospective college students, is the Scholastic Aptitude Test (SAT), designed to predict success in college.

Achievement Tests

Whereas aptitude tests are designed to predict how well a person will be able to learn a new skill, *achievement tests* are designed to measure how much a person has already learned in a particular area. Such tests not only enable an instructor to assess a student's knowledge, they also help students to assess their progress for themselves.

The distinction between achievement and aptitude tests has become somewhat blurred in recent years. What psychologists had at first thought were tests of aptitude—defined as *innate* ability or talent—turned out to measure experience as well, so that in part they were achievement tests. On the other hand, achievement tests often turned out to be the best predictors of many kinds of occupational abilities, so that they were in some sense aptitude tests. Because of this overlap, psychologists have agreed that the distinction between the two types of tests rests more on purpose than on content. If a test is used to predict future ability, it is

FIGURE 17.9
The General Aptitude Test Battery (GATB) consists of a number of different kinds of tests. Samples of items testing verbal and mathematical skills (*top*) and manual dexterity (*bottom*) are shown here. The results of the GATB might tell a person, for example, that he had the minimum reading comprehension and manual dexterity required to become a typist.

1. Which two words have the same meaning?
 (a) open **(b)** happy **(c)** glad **(d)** green
2. Which two words have the opposite meaning?
 (a) old **(b)** dry **(c)** cold **(d)** young
3. A man works 8 hours a day, 40 hours a week. He earns $1.40 an hour. How much does he earn each week?
 (A) $40.00 **(C)** $50.60 **(B)** $44.60 **(D)** $56.00
4. At the left is a drawing of a flat piece of metal. Which object at the right can be made from this piece of metal?

considered to be an aptitude test; if it is used to assess what a person already knows, it is an achievement test.

PERSONALITY TESTING

The instruments for measuring personality characteristics are fundamentally different from the instruments for measuring abilities. Answers to questions on an intelligence test indicate whether a person can, in fact, do certain kinds of thinking and solve certain kinds of problems. There are right and wrong answers. But the answers to questions on a personality test cannot be right or wrong. The question in personality testing is not "How much can you do?" or "How much do you know?" but "What are you like?"

There are three main types of personality tests: interest tests, objective clinical tests, and projective clinical tests.

Interest Tests

The essential purpose of an *interest test* is to determine a person's preferences, attitudes, and interests. The test taker's responses are compared to the responses given by people in clearly defined groups, such as professions or occupations. The more a person's answers correspond to those of people in a particular occupation, the more likely that person is to enjoy and succeed in that profession.

In constructing the widely used Strong Vocational Interest Inventory, for example, psychologists compared the responses of people who are successfully employed in different occupations to the responses of "people in general." Suppose that most engineers said they liked the idea of becoming astronomers but would not be interested in a coaching job, whereas "people in general" were evenly divided on these (and other)

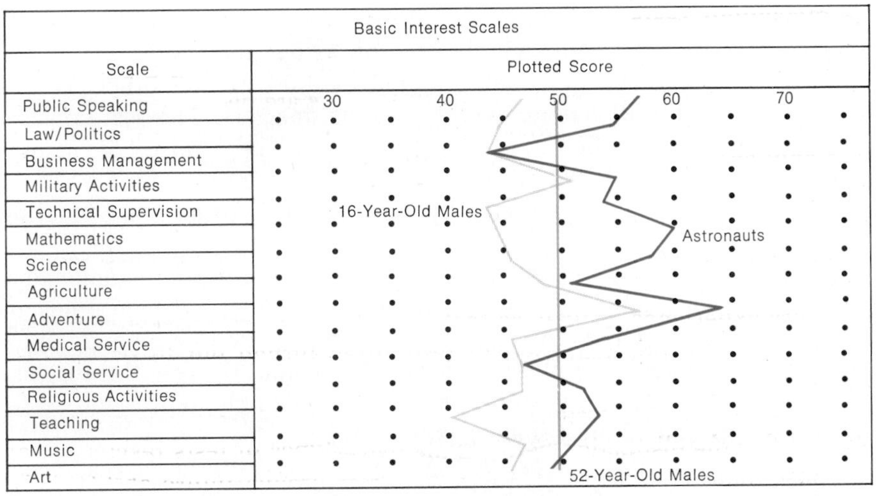

FIGURE 17.10
The Strong Vocational Interest Blank exists in two forms, one for men and one for women. Both forms yield scores on a set of basic interests. Patterns for scores on the male version of the test are shown here. The test is arranged so that a random selection of fifty-two-year-old men provides the standard, or average, against which all other scores are compared. Their scoring pattern appears as the blue line through the 50 mark on every scale. Also shown here are the scoring patterns produced by a group of astronauts and a group of sixteen-year-old males. According to the test, neither of these groups has as much interest in business management as the standard group and both have more interest in adventure. Astronauts appear to be more interested than the sixteen-year-olds in practically every kind of work, particularly mathematics, science, public speaking, and teaching.

Basic Interest Scales	
Scale	Plotted Score
Public Speaking	30 40 50 60 70
Law/Politics	
Business Management	
Military Activities	
Technical Supervision	16-Year-Old Males
Mathematics	Astronauts
Science	
Agriculture	
Adventure	
Medical Service	
Social Service	
Religious Activities	
Teaching	
Music	
Art	52-Year-Old Males

FIGURE 17.11

Items from the Kuder Preference Record (KPR), a test that works similarly to the Strong Vocational Interest Blank. The person taking the test is asked to pick from among three possible activities the one he would most like to do and the one he would least like to do. The test provides numerous sets of such alternatives.

		Most		Least
G.	Read a love story	●	G.	●
H.	Read a mystery	●	H.	●
I.	Read science fiction	●	I.	●
J.	Visit an art gallery	●	J.	●
K.	Browse in a library	●	K.	●
L.	Visit a museum	●	L.	●
M.	Collect autographs	●	M.	●
N.	Collect coins	●	N.	●
O.	Collect butterflies	●	O.	●
P.	Watch television	●	P.	●
Q.	Go for a walk	●	Q.	●
R.	Listen to music	●	R.	●

questions. A person who responded as the engineers did would rank high on the scale of interest in engineering. The Kuder Preference Record, part of which is shown in Figure 17.11, is based on the same principle. The purpose of these measures is to help people find the career that is right for them.

Clinical Tests

Psychiatrists and psychologists use *clinical tests* to assess personality characteristics and to identify problems. Some of these tests are *objective,* or forced-choice—that is, a person must select one out of a small number of possible responses. Other clinical tests are *projective*—they encourage test takers to respond freely, giving their own interpretations of various test stimuli.

Objective Tests.   The most widely used objective personality test is the Minnesota Multiphasic Personality Inventory (MMPI). Like other personality tests, the MMPI has no right or wrong answers. The test consists of 550 statements to which a person can respond "true," "false," or "cannot say." Items include: "I like tall women; I am an agent of God; I wake up tired most mornings; I am envied by most people; I often feel a tingling in my fingers."

The items on the MMPI are designed to reveal habits, fears, delusions, sexual attitudes, religious feelings, social attitudes, and symptoms of mental problems. Although the statements that relate to a given characteristic (such as depression) are scattered throughout the test, the answers to them can be pulled out and organized into a single depression scale. There are ten such clinical scales to the MMPI.

In scoring the MMPI, a psychologist looks for patterns of responses, not a high or low score on all the scales. This is because the items on the test do not, by themselves, identify personality types. In creating the MMPI, the test makers did not try to think up statements that would identify depression, anxiety, and so on. Rather, they invented a wide range of statements about all sorts of topics; gave the test to groups of people already known to be well-adjusted, depressed, anxious, and so on; and retained for the test those questions that discriminated among these groups—questions, for example, that people suffering from depression or from anxiety neurosis almost always answered differently from normal groups (Hathaway and McKinley, 1940). Many of the items on the MMPI may sound like sheer nonsense. But they work, and that's what counts. One unique aspect of the MMPI is that it has a built-in "lie detector." If an individual gives a false response to one statement, he or she is likely to be caught by a rephrasing of the same question at a later point.

The MMPI has proven useful in diagnosing various forms of mental disturbance and in providing data for personality research (Dahlstrom and Welsh, 1960). It has also been used—and misused—in employment offices to screen job applicants. A person who is trying to get a job is likely to give answers he or she thinks the employer would like to see—thereby falling into some of the traps built into the test. Administering the MMPI under such circumstances can produce misleading, even damaging results. Innocently trying to make a good impression, the job applicant ends up looking like a liar instead. As an aid to counseling and therapy, however, it can be a valuable tool.

Projective Tests.   Projective tests are open-ended examinations that invite people to tell stories about pictures, diagrams, or objects. The idea is that because the test material has no established meaning, the story a person tells must say something about his own needs, wishes, fears, and other aspects of his personality. In other words, the subject will project his feelings onto the test items.

Perhaps the best-known and most widely discussed projective measure is the Rorschach Inkblot Test, developed by Swiss psychiatrist Hermann

FIGURE 17.12
Inkblots similar to those used on the Rorschach test. In interpretations of a person's responses to the inkblots, as much or more attention is paid to the style of the responses as is paid to their content. For example, a person's tendency to see the white areas as meaningful or to see the blot as a whole rather than as a collection of parts is considered significant. Formal attempts to establish the Rorschach test's reliability and validity have been failures, but the test remains very widely used.

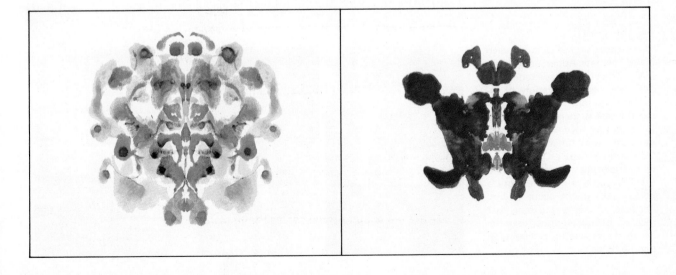

Rorschach. Rorschach created ten inkblot designs and a system for scoring responses to them. To administer the test, a psychologist hands the inkblots, one by one, to the subject, asking the person to say what he or she sees. The person might say that a certain area represents an airplane or an animal's head. This is the free-association period of the test. The psychologists then ask certain general questions in an attempt to discover what aspects of the inkblot determined the person's response.

In evaluating the Rorschach test, a psychologist considers three categories of responses. The first indicates the location or part of the inkblot with which the subject associates each response. The second category relates to whether the subject responds primarily to form, color, shading, or movement. The third category is the content of responses—human, animal, mechanical, and so on (Beck, 1961).

The lack of structure in the Rorschach is both a strength and a weakness. It is a strength in the sense that it provides an opportunity for a person to reveal unconscious aspects of his or her personality that might not emerge otherwise. The disadvantage is that interpretation of responses is left open to the biases of the examiner.

The second most widely used projective measure, the Thematic Apperception Test (TAT), consists of a series of twenty cards containing pictures of vague but suggestive situations. The individual is asked to tell a story about the picture, indicating how the situation shown on the card developed, what the characters are thinking and feeling, and how it will end.

Each TAT story is evaluated on the basis of a standard scoring system. The interpreter focuses on the themes that emerge from the story and the needs of the main characters. Are they aggressive? Do they seem to have needs for achievement, love, or sex? Are they being attacked or criticized by another person, or are they receiving affection and comfort? As with the Rorschach, this "scoring" system leaves room for various interpretations on the part of the examiner.

Other projective tests require a person to draw pictures of people, to construct scenes or stories out of toys or pictures, to make figures out of clay, or to act out social roles. One such measure is the Draw-a-Person Test (DAP), in which the individual is asked first to draw a person and

FIGURE 17.13

Three cards similar to those used in the Thematic Apperception Test (TAT). The scenes depicted in the drawings permit a variety of interpretations, and the person taking the test is therefore assumed to project his own needs, wishes, defenses, and other personality factors into the story. One problem with analyzing the responses to the TAT cards is that the story a person tells might occur to him because of some incident that recently happened rather than because of a basic attitude about life that he holds.

then to draw a person of the opposite sex from the one he or she just drew. The form and content of the drawings—the amount of detail and differentiation between the sexes—provide the psychologist with insights into the subject's personality (Machover, 1949).

SITUATIONAL TESTS

The use of psychological tests for such things as job placement has become extremely controversial in recent years. Is there any direct relation between a person's responses to statements on the MMPI and his everyday behavior? Do a person's perceptions of an inkblot really tell whether she will be able to remain calm under pressure or to give and take orders efficiently? Many psychologists think not. They believe that the closer a test is to the actual situation the examiner wants to know about, the more useful the results will be. A test that measures an individual's performance in terms of emotional, attitudinal, and behavioral responses to "true-life" situations is called a *situational test*. (An example is a test for a driver's license, requiring that the person actually drive.)

One of the first situational tests for job placement was developed by the Office of Strategic Services (OSS) during World War II (Office of Strategic Services Assessment Staff, 1948). The OSS wanted to evaluate

FIGURE 17.14
Using this airplane flight simulator, pilots are trained and tested before they are given the responsibility of flying a real airliner. Emergency situations can be created in the simulator to test how a pilot reacts in a crisis. None of the standard psychological tests described in this chapter could predict accurately whether a pilot would panic in such a situation—that's why this type of test can be extremely valuable.

(United Air Lines photo.)

candidates for assignment to military espionage, which requires a high degree of self-control and frustration-tolerance. In order to judge the candidates, the OSS set up a three-day session of intensive testing during which candidates were required to live together in close quarters and were confronted with a number of complicated and frustrating problems.

In one procedure, a staff member instructed the candidate to build a certain type of cube with the help of two assistants. The helpers were actually psychologists who played prearranged roles. One was extremely lazy and passive, engaged in projects of his own, and offered no advice. The other interfered with the work by making impractical suggestions, harassing the candidate, and asking embarrassing questions. The "assistants" succeeded so well in frustrating the candidates that not one finished the construction. But by placing the candidates in situations similar to those they would encounter as agents, the examiners were able to predict how these men might respond to military intelligence work. Court decisions and federal regulations now stipulate that job placement tests in many professions must be work-related. Consequently, the use of situational tests is likely to increase in the years to come.

THE USE OF TESTS IN WESTERN SOCIETY

As suggested at the beginning of this chapter, tests are used widely in all Western societies. Indeed, testing is probably the biggest single contribution that the science of psychology has made to Western culture.

And to some degree they have been an extremely beneficial contribution, for tests have a number of clear advantages over other evaluation techniques. In the first place, they save time. They enable educators and others to measure large numbers of people in a matter of hours.

Secondly, tests can be extremely efficient. (Indeed, efficiency was the original motivation for the development of IQ testing.) Tests have provided help in identifying people who will and will not do well in school, who will and will not make good mechanics, soldiers, typists, or salespeople. Schools use tests so that they will not waste a brilliant child's time having her read *Dick and Jane* for a year or frustrate a retarded child by forcing him to struggle through algebra books. Businesses use tests so that they will not put clumsy people into jobs requiring great care or highly trained people into jobs that are dull.

A third important advantage is that tests are generally more objective than other forms of evaluation. An individual cannot impress a test by wearing expensive and stylish clothing or by dropping names. A test cannot hear that a person has a foreign accent or see that he has a physical handicap—the sorts of things that might prejudice an interviewer who relies solely on his or her own impressions.

However, all these virtues depend on the accuracy of the tests involved. And as we have seen, psychological testing is far from infallible. Tests do make mistakes. Bright people sometimes get low IQ scores; perfectly sane people sometimes make unusual responses to inkblots; incompetent workers sometimes do well on aptitude tests; and highly disturbed people sometimes show no sign of their problems on a personality test form. Tests usually turn out to measure much less than most people think they do, and they never supply absolutely certain information. *The results of all tests are always a matter of probability.* At best they supply only good clues that should be followed up.

Another drawback of psychological testing is that tests compare an individual with others in his or her society according to accepted social standards. Because psychologists do not agree on exactly what intelligence and emotional disturbance are, they cannot measure them perfectly. What they can do is put together lists of questions that people whom society calls "smart" tend to answer differently from people whom society calls "dumb," or that people whom society calls "stable" tend to answer differently from people whom society calls "crazy." Then when a new person comes along, they can compare his responses to those of the "smart," "dumb," "stable," and "crazy" groups and come up with a judgment of how he stands in relation to these already labeled groups. Test results thus reflect social judgments, and if society is wrong or unfair about something, tests are likely to be, too.

Ethical Problems of Testing

The widespread use of testing raises numerous ethical questions. We would all probably agree that it is appropriate for the law to require that people pass driving tests before taking the wheel alone. But is it appropriate for a business organization to pry into an individual's fundamental beliefs and private fantasies before offering that person a job? Is it right for colleges to use attitude questionnaires in order to select their freshman classes? What does a student's attitude toward her mother or the opposite sex or freedom of the press have to do with whether or not she will be able to pass French 1A or Anthropology 1B?

Such considerations lead to doubts about the use of tests in making major decisions about individual lives. Should people be denied a college education or be confined to a mental institution on the basis of test results? Should people be required to take tests at all, when many find it a traumatic, demanding experience of questionable value? The answers to these questions are not easy. Psychological tests, like other technological advances, have their uses and their limitations. Like automobiles, tranquilizers, and nuclear power, tests can be overused and badly used. But, as is the case with other technologies, they can be used well if people understand them.

SUMMARY

1. All tests are designed to find out a great deal about people in a relatively short time. Test scores are not ends in themselves; they are simply numbers indicating how a person responded to a particular situation.

2. Reliability is the ability of a test to yield the same results under a variety of circumstances. Validity is the extent to which a test measures what it is supposed to measure.

3. The percentile system is a method for ranking scores on a test. Standardization allows a test score to be interpreted in the light of the scores all people in a specified group achieved.

4. The first intelligence test was designed by Alfred Binet as a means of picking out slow learners. The test currently in widespread use is a revision of Binet's test, now known as the Stanford-Binet. The results of this test yield an IQ score that is a measure of "mental age." The Wechsler intelligence tests differ from the Stanford-Binet in that they place more emphasis on performance tasks and yield a number of separate scores for different abilities.

5. IQ tests are good at predicting school performance, but whether they actually measure "intelligence" is difficult to say.

6. The debate over the causes of racial and socioeconomic differences in average IQ scores has called attention to the fact that IQ tests measure social class, motivation, and experience as well as the ability to reason and solve problems.

7. Aptitude and achievement tests are virtually identical in content but serve different purposes. Aptitude tests are used to measure how well a person will be able to learn a new skill; achievement tests measure how much a person has already learned.

8. Personality tests have no right or wrong answers; they attempt to find out what a person is like. Interest tests measure preferences for and attitudes toward different activities.

9. Clinical tests are used primarily as aids to psychotherapy. The MMPI is an objective (forced-choice) clinical test; the Rorschach Inkblot Test, Thematic Apperception Test, and the Draw-a-Person Test are projective (open-ended) clinical tests.

10. A situational test, such as a driver's examination, is designed to measure how well a person performs in specific "real-life" situations.

11. As the most objective measure of intelligence, aptitude or achievement, and personality we have, tests are extremely useful tools. But like any tool, they can be misused.

GLOSSARY

achievement test: An instrument used to measure how much an individual has learned in a given subject or area.

aptitude test: An instrument used to estimate the probability that a person will be successful in learning a specific new skill or skills.

clinical tests: Instruments psychotherapists use to assess personality traits.

intelligence quotient (IQ): Originally, a measure of a person's mental development obtained by dividing his or her mental age (the score achieved on a standardized intelligence test) by his or her chronological age and multiplying by 100; now, any standardized measure of intelligence based on a scale in which 100 is defined to be average.

interest test: An instrument designed to measure a person's preferences, attitudes, and interests in certain activities.

norming: The development of standards of comparison for test results by giving the test to large, well-defined groups of people.

objective clinical tests: Forced-choice clinical tests, in which a person must select an answer from a small number of alternatives.

percentile system: A system for ranking test scores that indicates the percentage of scores lower and higher than a given score.

projective clinical tests: Unstructured clinical tests in which a person is asked to respond freely, giving his or her own interpretation of various ambiguous stimuli.

reliability: The ability of a test to give the same results under a variety of different circumstances.

situational test: A simulation of a real situation designed to measure a person's performance under such circumstances.

validity: The ability of a test to measure what it is intended to measure.

ACTIVITIES

1. Can intelligence be learned? Try the following with two groups of subjects. For one group, give a series of problems like the following example: "Is this statement true or false? If gyuks are jogins and kuulls are jogins, then gyuks are kuulls." For the other group, give the same instructions, but also explain the first example by translating gyuks, jogins and kuulls as cats, animals, and dogs. Then the statement will read, "If cats are animals and dogs are animals, then cats are dogs." The statement is obviously false. You can make up other examples like "If some chairs are made of wood, and some tables are made of wood, then chairs are tables." Experiment with a variety of these statements. Make some true and some false. Compare the results of the two groups. This is a question from an intelligence test. Can people learn to pass intelligence tests? Explain your answer.

2. The chapter discusses a wide range of devices used to measure intelligence, aptitudes, personality traits, and so on. Think about and write down the criteria by which you "test" others. How crucial are these "tests" in determining whether or not you decide to pursue a friendship? Think about the ways in which you "test" yourself. Are the criteria you use for yourself the same as those you use for others? If not, what are the differences?

3. *Barnumisms* are broad generalizations or clinical truisms that apply to nearly everyone (such as "you have a strong need to be liked"). Because they apply to a broad spectrum of any population, they are of little assistance in psychological testing. To become more aware of the various testing techniques, you might consult a college testing service or a clinical psychologist and take one or more of the various psychological tests. While you are taking the test, and with the permission of the person administering the test, jot down any comments regarding the questions and record the numbers of questions you consider to be Barnumisms. Discuss any questions or comments with the test administrator.

4. If you were asked to rate people on an intelligence scale of your own making, what criteria would you use, and how would you make your decision? What roles would such factors as memory, emotional maturity, creativity, morality, and intuition play in formulating your intelligence scale? How would you "test" for these factors?

5. Imagine that you work for an insurance company and are trying to find out how likely it is for people of different ages to be involved in accidents. What criterion do you use? The number of accidents per year? Accidents per thousand miles of driving? Discuss what is right or wrong with these and other criteria.

6. Psychological testing has been considered an invasion of privacy by some people. Defend or refute the use of psychological testing. Discuss this question with your classmates—perhaps you can organize a classroom discussion on the subject.

7. Call or write for one of the questionnaires available from a computer dating service (they usually place advertisements in the classified sections of newspapers). Fill out or just look over the questionnaire. What general categories do the questions seem to fall into? What does the questionnaire seek to measure? Do you think it might be a useful way to obtain meaningful information about people?

SUGGESTED READINGS

AMERICAN PSYCHOLOGIST, 30, No. 1 (1975): 1–50. In this issue of the *American Psychologist* two major review articles are aimed at illustrating the use, misuse, and history of the mental measurement movement in the United States. In the first article some of the major public controversies over mental testing are summarized and in the second the use of mental tests with disadvantaged children is discussed.

FITTS, P. M., AND POSNER, M. I. *Human Performance*. Belmont, Calif.: Brooks/Cole, 1967. A nontechnical book about the differences in human skills and abilities. Especially interesting when read with regard to practical implications for vocational and aptitude testing.

GARCIA, JOHN. "IQ: The Conspiracy." *Psychology Today*, 6 (September 1972): 40–43. A provocative and well-written article about the abuses of IQ testing.

GROSS, MARVIN. *The Brain Watchers*. New York: Random House, 1962. This book is an outspoken and well-written criticism of personality testing as inaccurate and immoral. Worth reading as a signal to the dangers of their excessive and improper use.

HOFFMAN, BANESH. *The Tyranny of Testing*. New York: Collier, 1962 (paper). Hoffman contends that objective tests "reward superficiality, ignore creativity, and penalize the person with a probing, subtle mind." In this readable little book, he criticizes the massive role that tests play in society today.

KAMEN, LEON J. *The Science and Politics of IQ*. Potomac, Md.: Erlbaum, 1974. Kamen not only reviews the history of the mental measurement movement in this country, but also reanalyzes the data Jensen and others have used in arguing for a genetically based interpretation of IQ differences. The author's basic conclusion is that genetics plays no role in the variation of IQ scores and that by making the assumption of genetic influence, dire and unjust political consequences have and will occur.

WILCOX, ROGER (ED.). *The Psychological Consequences of Being a Black American*. New York: Wiley, 1971. A good anthology of articles on testing intelligence in blacks, cultural disadvantages of minority groups, intelligence and achievement, attitudes and emotional characteristics of blacks, and the black psychologist in America.

BIBLIOGRAPHY

ANASTASI, ANNE. *Psychological Testing*. 3rd ed. New York: Macmillan, 1968.

ASH, P., AND KROEKER, L. P. "Personnel Selection, Classification, and Placement." *Annual Review of Psychology*. Palo Alto, Calif.: Annual Reviews, 1975, pp. 481–507.

BECK, SAMUEL J. *Rorschach's Test. Vol. I: Basic Processes*. 3rd ed. New York: Grune & Stratton, 1961.

BUROS, O. K. (ED.). *The Fifth Mental Measurement Yearbook*. Highland Park, N.J.: Gryphon Press, 1959.

CRONBACH, LEE J. *Essentials of Psychological Testing*. 3rd ed. New York: Harper & Row, 1970.

DAHLSTROM, WILLIAM GRANT, AND WELSH, GEORGE S. *An MMPI Handbook: A Guide to Use in Clinical Practice and Research*. Minneapolis: University of Minnesota Press, 1960.

DAVIS, A. "Socio-economic Influences upon Children's Learning." *Understanding the Child*, 20 (1951): 10–16.

FITTS, P. M., AND POSNER, M. I. *Human Performance*. Belmont, Calif.: Brooks/Cole, 1967.

HATHAWAY, STARKE R., AND MCKINLEY, JOHN CHARNLEY. "A Multiphasic Personality Schedule (Minnesota): I. Construction of the Schedule." *Journal of Psychology*, 10 (1940): 249–254.

HERRNSTEIN, RICHARD. "I.Q." *The Atlantic Monthly*, 228 (1971): 43–64.

HOFFMAN, BANESH. *The Tyranny of Testing*. New York: Crowell-Collier Press, 1962.

JENSEN, ARTHUR R. "How Much Can We Boost I.Q. and Scholastic Achievement?" *Harvard Educational Review*, 39 (1969): 1–123.

MACHOVER, KAREN A. *Personality Projection in the Drawing of the Human Figure: A Method of Personality Investigation*. Springfield, Ill.: Charles C Thomas, 1949.

OFFICE OF STRATEGIC SERVICES ASSESSMENT STAFF. *Assessment of Men*. New York: Holt, Rinehart and Winston, 1948.

TERMAN, LEWIS M., AND MERRILL, MAUD A. *Stanford-Binet Intelligence Scale: Manual for the Third Revision. Form L-M*. Boston: Houghton Mifflin, 1973.

TYLER, LEONA E. *The Psychology of Human Differences*, 3rd ed. New York: Appleton-Century-Crofts, 1965.

——."Human Abilities." *Annual Review of Psychology*. Palo Alto, Calif.: Annual Reviews, 1975, pp. 177–206.

WECHSLER, DAVID. *The Measurement and Appraisal of Adult Intelligence*. 14th ed. Baltimore: Williams & Wilkins, 1958.

18 Applying Psychology

At various points in this book we have suggested ways in which psychological knowledge might be put to practical use. (Chapter 16, on therapy and change, is an obvious example.) But our main emphasis has been on understanding human behavior and emotions: Our "heros and heroines" have been research psychologists.

In this chapter we will be introducing you to psychologists who are directly applying the knowledge gained by researchers to the problems of everyday life. Their concerns include improving educational television, matching people to jobs and jobs to people, designing human environments, working in the courts, and developing ways to measure our successes and failures as a society.

If this chapter has a theme or message, it is that psychological expertise may give us new and fresh solutions to social problems we have not been able to solve through intuition and legislation.

THE PSYCHOLOGY OF SESAME STREET

It is a well-known fact that TV is this nation's number one "baby sitter." Nearly every American household has a television set, and most sets are turned on for 40 to 50 hours a week. Youngsters spend more time watching TV than they do at any other waking activity—for a total of 15,000 hours by the time they graduate from high school, compared to 12,000 hours in the classroom (Lesser, 1974, p. 19). It is also a well-known fact that children come away from TV with all sorts of information and misinformation—for example, that eating a particular cereal will turn them into star athletes. Since the mid-1960s there have been several attempts to produce television programs which are both educational and so interesting that children will ask to watch them. But Sesame Street was the first one to succeed on such a large scale. Many subsequent programs for children followed its methods.

As a teacher, TV has drawbacks and advantages. It cannot provide individualized instruction, and it cannot reward a child for learning, the way a live teacher can. On the other hand, TV cannot punish a child for being slow to grasp a point or for not paying attention. This lack of criticism can be an indirect form of positive reinforcement. Children associate TV with fun. The fact that a TV set does not see its viewers frees children from the burden of trying to please others and from the threat of failure

FIGURE 18.1
While satisfying his craving for cookies, Sesame Street's Cookie Monster is also teaching the alphabet to preschool children. With help from psychologists, the creators of this popular television series have successfully combined learning principles with entertainment.

and humiliation. For once, children are in control of the learning situation. They can tune in or out as they please.

What TV can do as well as or better than a live teacher is to provide models—examples of different ways people act in a variety of situations and what happens as a result. Presumably, parents and others will provide positive reinforcement for what children learn by observing and imitating models on TV.

Aware of the need for positive reinforcement of behavior, the Children's Television Workshop (CTW) set out to create a television program that would teach preschool skills to children between three and six.

Harvard psychologist Gerald S. Lesser organized a panel of advisers that included writers and filmmakers as well as educators to establish general goals for the series. The basic idea was to prepare children for school in two ways. The first and most obvious was to lay the foundation for future learning. The second and perhaps more important was to foster confidence by showing children they could learn the kinds of things that impress parents and teachers—and have fun doing so.

The advisers decided that the best way to present information to young children was to use techniques developed for TV commercials: short, fast-paced segments that would not tax a child's attention span; a mix of live characters, puppets, and cartoons; such attention-getting tricks as speeding the film up or running it backwards; catchy rhymes and jingles; music to encourage participation; and a healthy dose of slapstick comedy. They also decided to use a good deal of repetition because studies have found that children are not bored by seeing and hearing the same material over and over, and in fact continue to learn from each repetition. The Sesame Street advisers took a basic concept of learning right out of Pavlovian classical conditioning. They coupled the unconditioned stimulus, in this case TV advertisements, with concepts (conditioned stimulus) of learning such as sequences of numbers. As we discussed in Chapter 2, the UCS plus the CS leads to a conditioned response (CR), in this case the retention of a number sequence, or the alphabet, or concepts in geometry such as squares or circles.

To illustrate the results of this planning: One goal was to teach children to count backwards from ten. (Number sequences were not to go beyond ten: psychologists believed this was as much as a three-year-old could handle.) How did they make this task both memorable and amusing? By showing a rocket countdown over and over, until the sequence became familiar: 10, 9, 8, 7. . . . To prevent boredom and inattention, the producers varied the ending. One time the rocket took off too early; one time it took the rocket launcher with it, his final "onnne" fading off into space; another time the rocket shot down, underground, instead of up. The idea was to encourage children to start counting in anticipation of the surprise.

The next step in putting Sesame Street together was to test programs on children from different socioeconomic backgrounds and from various parts of the country. The CTW hired psychologist Edward Palmer, an experienced child watcher. In each location Palmer created an informal setting, and by using a slide projector that changed pictures every eight seconds, he simulated the distractions a child would be likely to encounter at home. A researcher watched each child constantly, pressing a button when the child was watching TV, releasing it when he or she looked away. In addition, the children were asked questions about the material being presented before and after the pilot show, and again a month later.

As a result of these pretests, a number of segments were revised and some dropped altogether. The researchers discovered that children learn best when a show elicits either physical activity or mental activity, such as having to guess answers or speculate on characters' motives (Lesser, 1974, p. 161). The writers and producers began to depend on the observations and suggestions of Palmer and his associates.

Evaluation did not stop when Sesame Street went on the air in November of 1969. Researchers from the Educational Testing Service were hired to test and retest a cross-section of 1300 children. The results were very encouraging. Disadvantaged children who watched the show regularly scored as high as or higher than middle-class children who watched only infrequently, although their pretest scores had been low. Three-year-olds who became Sesame Street regulars scored higher than "non-regular" five-year-olds—suggesting that small children can learn skills educators have traditionally held back until kindergarten or first grade (Bogatz and Ball, 1971).

Other investigators found that both Sesame Street and a related show, Mr. Rogers' Neighborhood, tend to make children more outgoing (Coates, Pusser, and Goodman, 1976). And white children who saw nonwhites on these shows began to seek out nonwhite playmates in their nursery schools (Gorn, Goldberg, and Kanungo, 1976). The research and planning devoted to Sesame Street paid off in numbers as well. By the end of the first season, no fewer than six million preschoolers had switched from commercial programs to education-made-fun. In all of the shows the CTW has created, testing has become an integral part of production. In Edward Palmer's words, these shows are "an endless experiment—a laboratory on public display."

PSYCHOLOGY IN INDUSTRY

We do not know whether commercial television producers have followed Sesame Street's lead in employing psychologists to design and test new programs. But we do know that other businesses have been hiring psychologists as consultants and full-time employees for years. Like clinical or developmental psychology, industrial psychology is a well-developed subfield, with its own research goals, journals, symposiums, and so on.

Industrial psychologists who work in market research help companies to determine what consumers want, who is likely to buy a given product, and how best to sell it. Other psychologists work in personnel offices. Their main job is to select, administer, and evaluate the tests given to job applicants. Some are hired to design training programs for anyone from machinists to top-level executives. And some are human relations specialists whose main function is to identify and try to resolve conflicts

FIGURE 18.2
The antics of a cat and mouse are used to entertain preschoolers while they learn the word "love." This sequence from Sesame Street also uses repetition, found to enhance learning.

between management and workers, among departments, or within departments.

The literature on the industrial applications of psychology is vast. We have chosen a few examples that illustrate how psychologists are helping business to meet the challenges of a more competitive world market and a more demanding work force.

Fighting Discrimination

Under the pressure of affirmative action programs, or simply from a desire to be fair to minorities, many researchers and others in personnel are trying to make their tests and other evaluative procedures more equitable. For example, a simplified paper-and-pencil intelligence test may select persons who will do well in a job training program, even though the questions on the test may have nothing to do with the type of learning required in the program. Is it fair to use such a test? No, because it does not select people well. The test selects people with a certain kind of aptitude, and those who have that aptitude may also have the aptitude to do well in the program. But others may also have the second kind of aptitude, but may lack the skills to do well on the test. Such a test would not be "culture fair" to some minorities. In a number of court cases such tests have been banned as discriminatory.

This does not mean that testing programs are always discriminatory. Some may truly test for the aptitudes or skills required for a particular job. For example, in a court case the testing program of American Telephone & Telegraph was exonerated (Miner, 1974). In court, data were brought in that showed the tests did well in prediction and tested the right things. Designing fair tests and fair procedures for evaluating job performance and promoting employees is one of the major challenges facing industrial psychologists today.

Job Training Programs

Since the 1960s, industrial psychologists have also been involved in developing job training programs for the "hard-core unemployed." In the late 1960s, two psychologists obtained funds to evaluate the results of a training program for newly hired airline maintenance workers. Nearly all of the 295 men studied were minority group members in their mid-twenties. Fewer than 30 percent had high school diplomas, and 45 percent had criminal records. They were believed to be "unemployable."

The researchers gave each man a standard aptitude test both before and after the eight-week training program. A year later, they obtained job performance ratings (principally rates of lateness and absenteeism) for the men. Surprisingly, those who had done particularly well on the tests and in training had poor performance records. The researchers concluded that this was because the extra attention these men received from training and company staff members had built up their egos and raised their expectations. They had come to believe that they were doing well and would soon move up the job ladder. The fact that they did not created cognitive dissonance (see Chapter 12). They had only two ways to resolve this dissonance: deciding that they were wrong about how well they were doing or that the company was not promoting them fast enough. Most of them chose the second interpretation and grew less conscientious about work in return.

Job Enrichment

With the rise of industrialization, unionization, and automation, the American worker has been both "blessed" and "damned." He now has job security and higher wages through union membership. On the other hand, he no longer identifies with the end-product because most jobs are in large factories where production is often broken down into small tasks that require minimal skills. As a result, jobs are less demanding and less rewarding. Also, workers have better educations today than they did a generation or two ago, and they want jobs that allow them to learn and grow. The result is job alienation—many people work only for the off-the-job benefits. This problem has been augmented by the increased concern with industrial pollution and waste. Job alienation is reflected in high rates of absenteeism, deliberate waste and theft, and even sabotage.

In response to this problem, corporations are inviting psychologists to redesign completely work arrangements to fit the "new worker." The psychologist's approach has been to develop strategies which would lead to job enrichment—a wide range of techniques aimed at making the job more personal. One example is Richard Walton's study (1972). A pet food manufacturer was opening a new plant. Struggling with alienation and

FIGURE 18.3
Psychologists have suggested that alienation would give way to pride if workers could feel responsible for assembling a complete product. As a result, Volvo factory workers no longer work on assembly lines. Instead, a team of people completes each car.

low productivity at other locations, top management did not want to repeat past mistakes. After two years of consultation and debate, they and Walton arrived at the following plan.

Workers are assigned to self-managing teams, rather than to specific tasks. Each team is responsible for a major part of production, and decisions about how to divide the workload and assign tasks are made collectively. In addition, each team solves problems in its area of responsibility, covering for absent workers, selecting and training new workers, and electing team members to serve on committees and task forces. The teams are provided with the economic information necessary to make decisions for themselves. (They may, for example, decide to purchase new equipment or to de-automate a job.)

The company does not hire separate quality-control managers, machine operators, or even janitors. Each team performs its own quality tests, rather than being monitored by outsiders. Each individual is responsible for maintaining the equipment he or she is using and for "housekeeping" chores in the area. Thus no one is forced to do full-time menial work; the most boring tasks are shared. In addition, work assignments are rotated, giving each employee a chance to learn new and more complex skills. Workers are paid according to the number of skills they have mastered. In traditional plants only a limited number of foremen can earn top salaries. In this plant each and every worker can move into the top salary bracket by mastering skills. This encourages workers to help rather than undercut one another.

Finally, the status distinctions between different kinds of workers are minimized. There are no executive parking spaces and the like. Everyone uses the same entrance, the same cafeteria, the same locker rooms. Workers have "conference rooms," just as executives do.

The plan was not perfect: problems developed. Managers in the company headquarters felt that radical change meant they had not been doing their jobs well—an implication many resented. Some feared their jobs would be made obsolete.

Yet Walton believes the benefits of the new design outweigh the costs. The plant is running efficiently with 70 employees, not 110 as originally estimated. Low turnover, reduced absenteeism, and many fewer quality rejects add up to an annual savings of $600,000. Moreover, the new plant has the best safety record in the company.

But the most important benefit has been in human satisfactions. Instead of simply obeying supervisors' orders, the workers now get together and work out for themselves the best way to do the job. They find their work more interesting and meaningful because of this participation.

You may recall Maslow's hierarchy of needs, discussed in Chapter 6. The aim of job enrichment of the kind we have described is to satisfy more than just the lowest needs in this hierarchy by paying a living wage. Workers' needs for social interaction and approval, and for a sense of achievement, must be considered if work is to be meaningful. This in turn will require methods of measuring the psychological quality of work as accurately as we can now measure productivity. We will have more to say about psychological measurement later in this chapter.

FIGURE 18.4
At the Corning Glass Works factory, employees sign their name to a "brag tag" attached to a completed product. Receiving credit in this way is expected to enhance people's pride in their work.

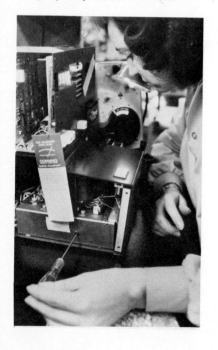

PSYCHOLOGY AND THE COURTS

If you ever follow accounts of trials in the newspapers, you know that selecting a jury can take as long as two or three weeks. This often happens when a case has received widespread coverage in the press prior to the trial, or when the defendant or victim is well known. The court automatically dismisses any potential juror who indicates that he or she has formed an opinion about the case. It also allows both the prosecution and the defense to reject people they consider biased. (The number of potential jurors each may reject is specified in advance.)

Traditionally, lawyers for both sides have based these decisions on direct questioning and on intuitions about how young or old, male or female, poor or well-off jurors will react to the defendant and the evidence. In recent years psychologists have begun to play an increasingly important role in this process. As the examples that follow will illustrate, psychologists are studying the ways juries arrive at decisions. They may help attorneys to select jury members, and often they testify before the court.

Inadmissible Evidence

American law is rooted in the *Bill of Rights*, where a fair trial, protection against self-incrimination, and due process of law are guaranteed. With all these safeguards to a fair trial, there is still one unpredictable element—the jury—who may not understand these principles. A delicate and important point in any trial is inadmissible evidence—evidence which violates the Bill of Rights. Imagine the following case.

A man is on trial for rape. The prosecution begins its case by presenting witnesses who saw the defendant near the scene of the crime, observed he was drunk, and saw him attempt to corner several women on the street. The jury is politely attentive. The next witness is a police officer who testifies that the defendant confessed and described the incident in detail. The jury sits up. However, cross-examination reveals that the officer had not informed the accused of his right to remain silent. The judge rules the officer's testimony inadmissible and instructs the jury to disregard it. The defense produces witnesses who testify that the man was sober on the night of the crime and that the woman was angry at him for ignoring her advances. Both sides rest.

What is the jury to do? Until they heard of the confession, most of the jurors assumed the man was innocent. But they did hear the confession and most now believe he is guilty. If they follow the judge's instruction, they must render a verdict of "innocent" and turn a man they believe to be a rapist free. On the other hand, if they ignore the judge's instruction and deliver a verdict of "guilty," they are violating the law.

Three psychologists presented simulated court cases to "juries" made up of students from college psychology courses to see how such a dilemma would affect them. One group of these subjects read a court transcript in which all of the evidence suggested that the defendant was guilty. A second group was given essentially the same transcript except that an additional piece of evidence which gave conclusive proof of guilt was ruled inadmissible by the judge after it had been presented, as might happen in a real trial. A third group of subjects read a transcript which left considerable room for doubt that the defendant was guilty. And a fourth group read a transcript which was the same as the third group's except that once again an additional piece of evidence strongly suggesting the guilt of the defendant was presented, and then ruled inadmissible by the judge. Thus only the fourth group had to resolve a dilemma like the one described above.

The results were that the fourth group was indeed more likely to find the defendant guilty than was the third group. Jury members had been biased by the inadmissible evidence. The second group, on the other hand, was not biased by the inadmissible evidence, probably because the other evidence they had been given already suggested the guilt of the defendant (Sue, Smith, and Caldwell, 1973).

Whether these findings apply to actual jurors who are dealing with human lives, not hypothetical situations, is debatable. However, the issue cannot be ignored. Psychologists suggested one possible solution to this kind of dilemma—namely to videotape the trial without a jury, cut inadmissible evidence and irrelevant testimony, and only then present the case to the jury. This has been tried in Ohio (Sue, Smith, and Caldwell, 1973).

Jury Selection

Whether jurors obey the court or follow their instincts in cases like the one above depends on a number of factors, including their political attitudes, their level of education, their sex, race, religion, and age. Indeed, most lawyers believe everything depends on who the jurors are. And many are asking psychologists to help them select jurors who will not be biased against their client.

The defense of the "Harrisburg Seven"—one of a number of cases brought against active opponents of the Vietnam War—provides an example. Father Philip Berrigan, Sister Elizabeth McAlister, and five others associated with the Catholic antiwar movement were charged with conspiring to raid draft boards, kidnap Henry Kissinger, and blow up heating tunnels in Washington, D.C. And, while Berrigan was in prison, he and McAlister were also accused of smuggling letters past prison censors. The laws against conspiracy are far from clear, which meant that the jury would have considerable leeway.

The government chose to hold the trial in Harrisburg, Pa., a largely Republican, Protestant city, many of whose citizens work for war-related industries. The cards were clearly stacked against the defense. In theory, the defense could reject prejudiced jurors. But how many people would admit to being anti-Catholic or to considering protest un-American? The defense asked a group of social scientists to help select a jury (Schulman et al., 1973).

The team of experts first conducted a phone survey to gain a general impression of population characteristics in the area, and then personally interviewed a sample of 252 people. The main goal of the interviews was to determine how attitudes that would affect the trial were related to age, sex, religion, education, occupation, and the like. Were women more likely than men to believe that "If the authorities go to the trouble of bringing someone to trial in a court, the person is almost always guilty"? Were white-collar workers more likely than blue-collar workers to think that "The right to private property is sacred"? (The defendants were accused of plotting to destroy property.) Those interviewed were also questioned on their knowledge of the case, and rated for their tolerance of protest.

Some of the results were surprising. For example, in most areas, college-educated people who follow the news media tend to be liberals. In Harrisburg, college-educated people tended to be more conservative than high-school graduates. On the whole, the respondents were usually trusting of government and authority. Many held the "my country, right or wrong" position. But there were variations. Religion proved to be the best measure of a person's openness or lack of openness to evidence.

The psychologists suggested lines of questioning to defense lawyers and sat in on the jury selection proceedings. Each potential juror was rated on a scale of one to five. (The lower the number, the greater the sympathy with the accused.) In the end, the defense was able to place seven of the people who rated 1 or 2 on the jury and minimized risks on the remaining five members.

The results? The jury convicted Father Berrigan and Sister McAlister of smuggling letters, but was unable to agree on a verdict on the conspiracy charges. Ironically, all of the jurors favored acquittal—except two of the defense team's first choices.

Why did this happen? After the trial the defense team realized that they hadn't questioned these two jurors carefully enough. After learning that one juror had two sons who were conscientious objectors, they stopped questioning her. Thus they did not learn about *her* religious convictions, which would have put her in the high-risk category. The other juror told the defense team of his doubts about the war and of his support for activist members of the clergy. (Whether he intentionally misled them is impossible to say.) The defense overlooked the fact that his age, religion, and income conflicted with his views and put him, too, in the high-risk category. Thus in both cases the defense failed to apply the standards they had developed.

If they had rigidly adhered to their criteria, they would have rejected several of the jurors who voted for acquittal. All in all, the interviewing weakened but did not destroy the government's strategy to select conservative jurors. In the words of the defense team, "Without careful screening of prospective jurors, we have every reason to believe that the jury would have consisted of many more individuals who were strongly opposed to the defendants" (Schulman, p. 82).

Informing the Courts

Psychologists Milton Rokeach and Neil Vidmar (1973) are two of many social scientists who have been asked to present expert testimony on jury selection and other matters in court. This particular case involved an Ohio Black Panther who had been charged with murdering a white police officer. In court, Rokeach and Vidmar argued that choosing jurors at random from voting registration lists was likely to produce a biased jury. They used data from a survey to show that it was possible to identify jurors who were likely to be prejudiced against a defendant who was black, poor, politically radical, and charged with murder. For example, the survey had revealed that more men than women are "antipoor," especially men with high incomes. Such data could be used to select more balanced juries.

The prosecutors did not agree.

> Are we to understand from your testimony that the only way to guarantee an impartial trial for this defendant is to select a jury composed of persons who are young, who are single, who are black, who are rich, who are educated, who don't go to church, who don't believe in God, and who are opposed to the death penalty? (p. 24)

No, the psychologists replied.

> Our opinion was that the best way to get an impartial jury would be to select the members in such a way that all biases would be represented, thus cancelling one another so that the final decision would be based on the evidence.... (p. 26)

In more general terms, they were arguing that we should put what psychologists have learned about attitudes, decision making, behavior in small groups, and the like, to work. In this case, the judge did allow the defense to question the jurors much more closely about their prejudices than the prosecution would have liked.

THE EXPERIMENTING SOCIETY

It is no accident that Sesame Street has been such a huge success. As we saw at the beginning of the chapter, members of the Children's Television Workshop not only obtained expert advice in planning the show, they devoted large amounts of time, energy, and money to evaluating the results. Tests and retests, child watching and audience counts provided the CTW with continuous feedback on the effectivenss of different methods of teaching. The CTW took the guesswork out of educational television.

Unfortunately, the CTW is an exception. As Donald T. Campbell, past president of the American Psychological Association, has pointed out, every year government and private agencies spend billions of dollars on experimental programs designed to do everything from convincing people to use litter bags to fighting heroin addiction. But we spend practically nothing on evaluating these programs. We have very little information on whether our social programs actually work, and we are losing the opportunity to learn from our successes and mistakes.

The experimenting society [in Campbell's words] would be one that vigorously tries out solutions to recurrent problems, evaluates outcomes, and keeps good programs or moves on to try out other alternatives. ... [It] is a utopia that makes science its servant, and takes the best of democracy and science as its values: honesty, open criticism, willingness to change in the face of new evidence. (Tavris, 1975, p. 47)

What role might psychologists play in an experimenting society?

Promoting Conservation: A Simple Experiment

Americans use—and waste—more energy than any other people on earth. The fuel crisis of 1974, ad campaigns on the need to conserve energy, and the steadily rising cost of gasoline, oil, and electricity have hardly made a dent in our rate of energy use. How can Americans be persuaded to conserve energy?

Three psychologists attempted to answer this question with an extremely simple experiment (Kohlenberg, Phillips, and Procter, 1976). The demand for electricity tends to peak in the morning and again in the late afternoon, when people take showers and use vacuum cleaners, washing machines, and other electrical appliances. Unlike other forms of energy, electricity cannot be stored. Power companies therefore have to maintain generators that are in full use for only a few hours each day. One solution to the growing demand for electricity is to build more generators. The other solution is to change people's habits, cutting back the peak demand.

Kohlenberg and his colleagues tried three techniques for convincing volunteer families to reduce their electricity use during peak periods. The

FIGURE 18.5
Some people who read this ad may change their habits, but psychologists have found that lowering electric bills now would be more effective than promising future savings.

5 ways to save a billion dollars. Starting tonight.

A large electric plant costs about one billion dollars. If we continue to use electric power primarily during the day and early evening we'll need more power plants. A lot more than if we learn to use electric power at night or—for early birds—early in the morning, or on weekends. It's easy to do, and you'll save money in the long run. Here's how:

1 Turn on bedroom air conditioner when you go to bed—not before!

2 Dishes don't care when they get washed—but a full load's always a good idea.

3 Clothes wash just as clean late at night or early in the morning.

4 And the dryer will work while you're watching the late news or eating breakfast.

5 If you've got a self-cleaning oven, why not be dreaming while it's cleaning?

Put an appliance on the night shift: After 10 p.m. Or be an early bird: Before 10 a.m.

Con Edison conserve energy

first was to provide information. Researchers explained the problem, asked the families to try to cut back, and suggested how they might do so. Monitors installed in each house indicated that his approach had little or no effect. (Considering that all of the families were conservation-minded, this was surprising.)

Next, the researchers tried feedback. A bulb that lit up whenever the family approached peak consumption levels was placed in each house. Immediate and direct evidence of electricity overuse was expected to help the families cut back. Although somewhat more effective than information alone, feedback did not break the families' habits of electricity use.

Finally, the researchers gave the experimental households an incentive. Families would earn twice the amount of their electricity bill if they reduced their peak use 100 percent, the full amount if they cut back 50 percent, and so on. This strategy worked. None of the families reduced their peak use 100 percent, but all did cut back. A follow-up revealed that all returned to their original patterns after the incentive was removed.

What this simple experiment demonstrated was that campaigns to reduce the use of electricity during peak periods are largely ineffective. However, if power companies were to provide incentives—say, reduced rates for families that cut back during the peaks—they might save themselves the cost of building and maintaining partially-used plants.

Crowding and Behavior: Exposing a Myth

Psychologist Jonathan Freedman (1975) tackled a very complex topic that required a number of separate studies extending over a period of years—namely, the effects of crowding on human behavior. At the start, Freedman assumed (as most of us do) that crowding has a negative effect on people. In part this assumption was based on intuition. As he states in the opening of his book on the subject, "Everyone knows that crowding is bad." For centuries people have believed that the high rates of crime, mental illness, and other sicknesses found in cities are the direct result of too many people living in too little space.

Research seemed to support this. In a now classic experiment, John B. Calhoun (1962) showed that when rats are overcrowded some become aggressive and bite other rats; some neglect and even kill their young; some withdraw completely. Reading Calhoun's results, you have the feeling you are reading about an overcrowded city slum.

What Freedman discovered, however, was that Calhoun's findings simply do not apply to people. Study after study showed that we are different. The number of people per square mile, or population density, of a city varies considerably from one neighborhood to the next. So does the amount of space people have in their homes. Freedman selected groups of people who had similar incomes, years of education, and ethnic and religious backgrounds, but who lived in neighborhoods with very different densities. Some might have only five families per acre, while others had hundreds. Some had large homes, while others had less living space. In short, the groups were matched for many characteristics, but were deliberately *mismatched for one*—the density of their neighborhoods and dwellings. Freedman found that crowding was *not* directly related to rates of crime, or physical and mental illness. The researchers then conducted a number of experiments to determine whether groups of people in large rooms with plenty of space perform tasks better than similar groups packed into rooms so small they cannot help bumping into one another. They also wondered whether people in each group would act differently toward one another. Again the results were negative. Crowding did not make people nervous, anxious, or aggressive.

Studies of people who are required to spend relatively large amounts of time in cramped quarters—as astronauts do during training and in space—confirmed this. Indeed, people tend to become friendlier and more cooperative under such conditions.

In the end Freedman concluded that the effects of crowding depend on the circumstances. If the situation is pleasant, crowding makes people feel better; if the situation is unpleasant, crowding makes them feel worse. In other words, being packed together *intensifies* people's reactions, but

FIGURE 18.6
People used to think that high crime rates in urban slums were directly related to high population density. Freedman's research suggests, though, that the effects of overcrowding depend on the *circumstances*. High crime rates are more likely to be found when people live in dense, rundown housing than in dense, but luxurious surroundings.

it does not create feelings of pleasantness or unpleasantness, competitiveness or cooperation, anxiety or ease.

In retrospect, this seems very obvious. Research on early humans indicates that Neanderthal and Cro-Magnon men and women—who had abundant space—chose to crowd together. Relatively small caves often housed as many as 60 people. (In a sense, these caves were the first "apartment houses.") But we needn't go so far back in time. Riding in a subway car, waiting in line, or taking an exam are basically unpleasant experiences—and crowding makes them more so. On the other hand, what is more depressing than watching a sports event or a rock concert in an almost-empty auditorium, or finding that only a dozen people showed up for a party in a large ballroom or apartment? Crowding makes these experiences exciting: the more the merrier!

Freedman's discoveries have obvious implications for city planning. If crowding does not necessarily cause hostility, it makes sense to build high-density housing and leave open spaces where people can congregate or wander by themselves, rather than spread housing out.

Of course, city planners have to take into consideration other aspects. As you recall from Chapter 10, proximity is a major determinant in developing friendships. Row houses allow for neighbors to have more personal and visual contact than do high-rise complexes. Personal contact and people watching out for each other's possessions is a major factor in crime deterrence.

Measuring Ourselves

Some psychologists believe that one of the key functions of the experimenting society is using science to find out what people want. Citizens should be telling the government what to do, not vice versa.

The problem is that often people do not know what they want. Most citizens are upset about crime in the streets, bothered by government red tape, concerned about pollution, resentful of high taxes, sick of traffic jams and inefficient forms of public transportation. They want decent places to live, interesting jobs, good educations for their children, and so on. How do you translate these concerns and desires into specific information? Through psychophysics.

The term psychophysics covers a number of sophisticated techniques for measuring subjective reactions that cannot be measured with any physical instrument. Judgments are based on comparisons. Suppose you want to have your own place and go looking for an apartment. The first one you see is just what you want in terms of location, size, and features, but the rent is three times what you want to pay. The second apartment you see is very cheap, but it's small and dingy and the neighborhood is bad. The third is fairly bright inside and the rent is reasonable—but you can't get the first apartment out of your mind. After some agonizing, you call a friend who is looking for a roommate, and the two of you take the first apartment.

In the course of the afternoon you've made a number of comparisons and established priorities. Privacy and living within your budget are important to you, but so is living in an attractive apartment. In the end you gave the apartment top priority, your budget second place (you're spending a little more than you wanted to), privacy last place. Psychophysics enables researchers to perform similar computations to establish priorities in cases where direct measurement is impossible. (The techniques are far more complex than this example suggests, but the principle is the same.)

Although psychophysics was originally designed to measure perception, psychologists have begun to use scales to measure attitudes and opinions. For example, two researchers gave 569 people—including 38 judges, 286 police officers, and 245 students—21 cards. Each card had a brief description of a crime. Some subjects were asked to rate the seriousness of each crime on a scale of one to eleven (for the most serious offenses). Others were asked to compare offenses, indicating whether one crime was twice, five times, ten times as serious as the first. Surprisingly, perhaps, judges, police officers, and students showed considerable agreement in their ratings (Sellin and Wolfgang, 1964). Data collected on the seriousness of different crimes can give legislators a concrete basis for deciding how much punishment should be given for each offense. This takes the guesswork out of legislation and social planning, much as testing and child watching took the guesswork out of Sesame Street.

Other researchers have used scales to measure religious attitudes, determine the relative prestige of different occupations, even to judge the degree of hostility or cooperation among nations (Stevens, 1972). Such techniques might also be used to evaluate the effectiveness of social programs from the inside—from the schoolchild's or welfare recipient's or taxpayer's point of view.

Looking at the world objectively and learning to measure our reactions to the environment is the essence of applying psychology to solving problems in contemporary society.

SUMMARY

1. The knowledge generated by psychological research has many practical applications.

2. Television, for example, can be a valuable tool for teaching basic skills to preschool children. Television cannot punish children, so it indirectly provides them with positive reinforcement, and because the screen cannot see its viewers, children do not feel they must please others. They also do not face the threat of failure and humiliation. Television also provides models for children by showing different ways people can act in various situations, and what results from their actions.

3. The best methods psychologists have devised to teach young children through television combine the use of short, fast-paced segments—performed by a mix of live characters, puppets, and cartoons—with music, comedy, and attention-getting film tricks. Pretesting is used to calculate the effectiveness of the presentation of certain programs. Psychologists observe children from different socioeconomic backgrounds as they watch selected shows to see how often and when they are distracted. Afterward appropriate revisions in the program's style or content can be made.

4. Industrial psychologists work in market re-

search to help companies determine what consumers want, who is likely to buy a given product, and how to sell it. They also work in personnel departments where their main job is to select, administer, and evaluate tests given to job applicants. Some are human relations specialists whose main function is to identify and resolve conflicts between management and workers.

5. In response to the widespread problem of job alienation, psychologists are being asked by corporations to develop strategies for job enrichment. Some of these strategies involve assigning workers to self-managing teams. Each team shares responsibility for production, and decisions concerning workload are made collectively. The most boring tasks are shared.

6. Psychologists have begun to play an increasingly important role in the process of jury selection. They believe that the knowledge acquired through research concerning attitudes,

decision-making, and behavior in small groups can be used to help select the most impartial jury.

7. Psychologists and other social scientists survey and interview a sample of the population from which the jury will be selected. Characteristics of the population, such as age, sex, religion, education, and occupation are evaluated in terms of the attitudes they tend to foster. The social scientists also suggest questions the defense lawyers can use in court to examine prospective jurors.

8. Although the government and private agencies spend billions of dollars every year on experimental social programs, they spend little on evaluating their effectiveness. Experiments and tests designed by psychologists can be used to determine the usefulness of social programs; those programs that are ineffective can then be revised or discontinued. City and community planning, too, can be aided by the accurate application of psychological research findings.

ACTIVITIES

1. Here is a good excuse to watch Sesame Street or Electric Company. Record the different educational concepts (such as numerical sequences, the alphabet, proper tenses of verbs) you observe in each program. If you were a psychologist, what different concepts would you recommend for high school students who are behind their grade level? You might also try watching a child who is watching these programs. What responses does the child make to the characters? Do those responses seem to help the child learn? Does he or she like or dislike the repetitive nature of some of the sequences? Does the repetition seem to help? Do you think the child learns about different ways of life in a positive manner from watching the programs?

2. In the fall of 1976, television's Mr. Rogers' Neighborhood introduced old people to the

show in order to develop a closer identity between the young and the old. What traits do these people exhibit? In your report compare the people on the show with actual old people you know.

3. In this chapter it was noted that crowding in itself may not make an experience unpleasant, but it does enhance or magnify whatever emotional reactions a person would otherwise have to the situation. Think of situations you have been in that were sometimes crowded and sometimes not. Some examples were given in the chapter, but try to think of personal ones. Was your emotional experience of the situation quite different when you were crowded, or simply intensified?

4. Many people in this country spend much of their lives working at jobs that are inherently

unpleasant. If they were all trained for more interesting kinds of work, how would these jobs get done? A different solution might be to redesign the jobs to make them more tolerable or even challenging, as Walton did in the example given in this chapter. Such redesign will require a good deal of psychological ingenuity. For example, how would you make these jobs interesting: garbage collector; elevator operator; maid; inspector on an assembly line; sales clerk? When you have to do a task that you consider unpleasant, such as washing dishes, how do you try to make it more of a game?

5. Pick a controversial issue or a famous trial. Then organize a "jury" of some sort—perhaps your classmates, or a group of people at a party. First poll your jury members confidentially about their opinions and biases, their social class, religion, and so forth. Then present the details about the issues, or the testimony at the trial (you could use a detailed newspaper account) and get your friends' conclusions about the issue or trial. What aspects of your jury members' personalities would have helped you predict their responses? If a smart lawyer had known this information, what kinds of people would he or she have chosen for the jury?

6. Consider some task you know how to do well. If you were an industrial psychologist, how would you teach someone else to do this job? For example, if you were to create a brief training film, what would you include in the film? In what order? Which points would you convey visually, and which on the soundtrack?

7. Most architects base their designs on their own assumptions about what people are going to do in the spaces they design. C. M. Deasy, in an article in *Psychology Today,* March, 1970, reports on what happens to designs if a psychologist first interviews the future users of the spaces. He found, for example, that the students at a community college didn't really want a student union, at least of the traditional sort. Using the suggestions given in the article, survey the students at your school to see how well its design suits their activities.

SUGGESTED READINGS

HALL, E. T. *The Hidden Dimension.* Garden City, N. Y.: Doubleday, 1966 (paper). SOMMER, ROBERT. *Personal Space: The Behavioral Basis of Design.* Englewood Cliffs, N. J.: Prentice Hall, 1967 (paper). These two paperback books discuss some of the most interesting aspects of the way people behave in various environments. People from different cultures organize their spaces in different ways and keep different distances between themselves and others. Both authors discuss the influence of environmental designs on both the quality and type of social interactions that occur in them. For example, the design of airport waiting areas prevents people from getting acquainted, while the design of bars does the opposite.

KOENIG, PETER. "Field Report on Psychological Testing of Job Applicants: They Just Changed the Rules on How to Get Ahead." *Psychology Today,* 8 (June 1974): 87–96. Describes the history of such testing and what ensued when the courts ruled that most tests were only tests of credentials, and thus discriminatory. New tests may measure job competence instead of vocabulary, and these tests may even become available to those who wish to assess themselves.

LESSER, G. S. *Children and Television: Lessons from Sesame Street.* New York: Random House, 1974 (paper). The author tells the fascinating story behind the creation of "Sesame Street." He includes accounts of the controversies among various psychologists and educators about what kind of educational material should be presented and what would be suitable for the television medium. Lesser also discusses the application of Piaget's theories to educational television.

MILGRAM, STANLEY. "The Experience of Living in Cities." *Science*, 167 (1970): 1461–1468. An analysis of the behavior differences among people living in big cities and those who live in smaller communities. Milgram discusses the essential psychological aspects of the big city that cause these differences. For example, he believes that people in a big city must handle overwhelming stimuli, leading to a kind of "stimulus overload." City dwellers may adapt to this condition by paying less attention to each input. This is why strangers are more likely to be ignored in big cities than in small towns.

STEVENS, A. C. "Here Comes the Electric Company." *American Education*, 7 (November 1971): 18–23. Discusses the extension of the "Sesame Street" concept to a program for older children. Includes an account of the research on the effectiveness of the program in communicating concepts.

VARELA, JACOBO A. *Psychological Solutions to Social Problems*. New York: Academic Press, 1971. More of a handbook than a textbook, this perceptive and ingenious monograph describes applications of many of the principles of psychology covered in previous chapters. Many case histories are given, mostly from business, but with suggestions about applying the ideas elsewhere.

BIBLIOGRAPHY

BOGATZ, GERRY ANN, AND BALL, SAMUEL. "Some Things You Wanted to Know about 'Sesame Street.'" *American Education*, 7 (1971): 11–15.

CALHOUN, JOHN B. "Population Density and Social Pathology." *Scientific American*, 206 (1962): 139–148.

COATES, BRIAN, PUSSER, H. ELLISON, AND GOODMAN, IRENE. "The Influence of 'Sesame Street' and 'Mr. Rogers' Neighborhood' on Children's Social Behavior in Preschool." *Child Development*, 47 (1976): 138–144.

FREEDMAN, JONATHAN L. *Crowding and Behavior*. San Francisco: Freeman, 1976.

GAVIN, JAMES F., AND TOOLE, DAVID L. "Validity of Aptitude Tests for the Hardcore Unemployed." *Personnel Psychology*, 26 (1973): 139–146.

GORN, GERALD J., GOLDBERG, MARVIN E., AND KANUNGO, RABINDRA N. "The Role of Educational Television in Changing Intergroup Attitudes of Children." *Child Development*, 47 (1976): 277–280.

KOHLENBERG, ROBERT, PHILLIPS, THOMAS, AND PROCTOR, WILLIAM. "A Behavioral Analysis of Peaking in Residential Electrical Energy Con-

sumers." *Journal of Applied Behavioral Analysis*, 9 (1976): 13–18.

LESSER, GERALD S. *Children and Television*. New York: Vintage, 1974.

MINER, J. B. "Psychological Testing and Fair Employment Practices." *Personnel Psychology* 27 (1974): 49–62.

ROKEACH, M., AND VIDMAR, N. "Testimony Concerning Possible Jury Bias in a Black Panther Murder Trial." *Journal of Applied Social Psychology*, 3 (1973): 19–29.

SCHULMAN, JAY, ET. AL. "Recipe for a Jury," *Psychology Today*, 6 (May 1973): 37–44.

SELLIN, T., AND WOLFGANG, M. E. *The Measurement of Delinquency*. New York: Wiley, 1964.

STEVENS, A. C. "Here Comes the Electric Company." *American Education* 7 (1971): 18–23.

STEVENS, S. S. *Psychophysics and Social Scaling*. Morristown, N.J.: General Learning Press, 1972.

SUE, S., SMITH, R. E., AND CALDWELL, C. "Effects of Inadmissible Evidence on the Decisions of

Simulated Jurors." *Journal of Applied Social Psychology*, 3 (1973): 345–353.

TAVRIS, CAROL. "The Experimenting Society: To Find Programs That Work, Government Must Measure Its Failures." *Psychology Today*, 9 (September 1975): 46–56.

WALTON, RICHARD E. "How to Counter Alienation in the Plant." *Harvard Business Review*, 50 (1972): 592–608.

ZEITLIN, LAWRENCE. "A Little Larceny Can Do a Lot for Employee Morale." *Psychology Today*, 5 (June 1971): 22–26.

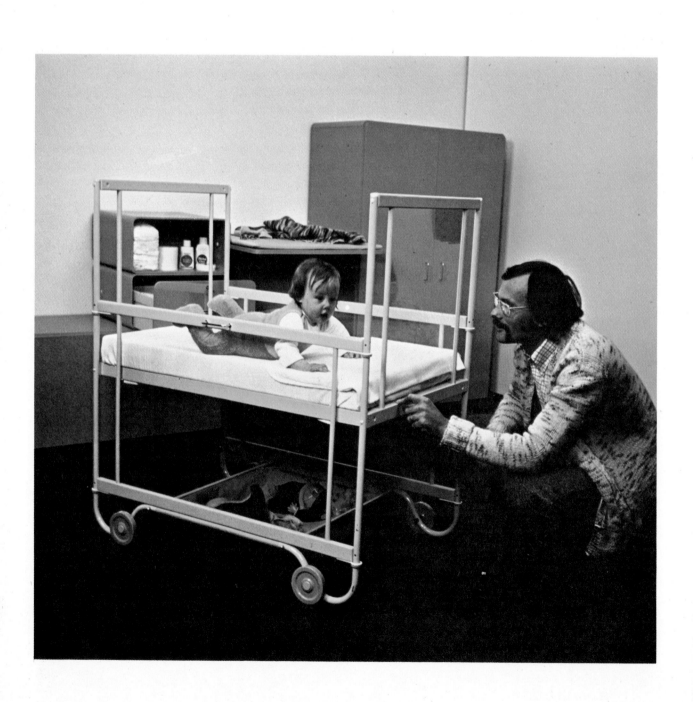

Appendix: How Psychologists Do Research

In this appendix we go behind the scenes to see how psychologists learn about what they don't already know. We poke into laboratories where they are conducting experiments, follow them on surveys, demystify that dreaded word "statistics," and expose some of the problems psychologists have—as researchers, that is.

The surprise is that psychologists do what most people do in everyday life—only better. When you turn on the television and the picture is out of focus, you *experiment* with different knobs and dials until you find the one that works. When you ask a number of friends about a movie you are thinking of seeing, you are conducting an informal *survey*. When you sit down with a pencil and paper to figure out your grade average and see where you stand in relation to your friends and competitors, you are working with *statistics*. Of course, there is more to doing scientific research than turning dials at random or asking friends what they think. Over the years psychologists, like other scientists, have transformed these everyday techniques for gathering and analyzing information into more precise tools.

ASKING THE RIGHT QUESTIONS

You're sitting in the cafeteria with a group of people waiting for your next class. Someone across the table says that she thinks psychotherapy is a waste of time and money. You snap to attention because a friend of yours has been seeing a therapist for some time and, in your opinion, is as mixed up as he was when he started. Before you can say anything, a third person breaks in. He says that his brother has really changed since he entered therapy—he's stopped fighting with their parents, gotten a job, and so on. The person next to you comments that he just needed time to grow up. Someone tells *him* that he's against therapy because he's afraid his girlfriend will leave him if she enters therapy as she's planning to do. "She wouldn't need a therapist if she would move away from her crazy family," he replies somewhat angrily. Another person begins talking about how much he thinks therapy has helped him. The time for class rolls around and you leave feeling more confused about this topic than you were before. Does therapy work or doesn't it?

How would a psychologist go about answering this question? The answer is that a researcher would not tackle such a broad and ill-defined

FIGURE A.1
Observation is one of the primary tools of psychological research. German psychologists found that babies placed in clear-sided beds raised their heads earlier than babies in cribs because they wanted to see what was happening around them. After observing these babies every four weeks, psychologists concluded that at eighteen months the children were more intelligent than two-year-olds who slept in regular cribs.

question. The term "psychotherapy" covers everything from psychoanalysis to token economies, as indicated in Chapter 16. To answer this question you would have to investigate *all* the different kinds of therapy—an enormous task. You might concentrate on one form of therapy, leaving the investigation of other methods of conducting therapy to other researchers. But even then, you would have problems.

Some people see a therapist once a week for a year, some five days a week for six or eight years. Some begin therapy because they want to grow; some because losing their job, getting divorced, or some other crisis has left them confused and unhappy; some because they are hospitalized and cannot function. Some start therapy as children, some in middle age. Some see a therapist of the same sex, some a therapist of the opposite sex. All these factors could make a difference. Whom would you study?

Then there is the question of what you mean by therapy *working*. Do you accept the patient's statement that he feels better about himself and his life, or do you measure success in terms of observable changes in behavior? Suppose the people you question or observe do change during therapy. How do you know the change is due to therapy and not to other events in their lives? That they wouldn't have changed without therapy? That some other form of treatment wouldn't have been more effective? The more you think about this topic, the more questions you ask.

To do research on the effectiveness of psychotherapy a psychologist has to take all these factors into account. And this is why researchers focus on limited, well-defined questions. A psychologist might conduct research on whether people with similar problems and in similar life situations benefit from a specific kind of therapy. But a researcher would not attempt to answer the whole question—"Does Therapy Work?" The answers to big questions come from a great many psychologists researching limited questions in different ways and examining one another's work with respectful skepticism.

The first step, then, in all psychological research is to ask a precise question about the topic one wishes to study. In most cases, the researchers also formulate a *hypothesis*—an educated guess about the relationship between two factors or variables. The hypothesis states what they expect to find, expressed in such a way that it can be proved *or disproved*. An example would be: Hospitalized schizophrenics who participate in a token economy program begin to make intellegible statements to other people sooner than hospitalized schizophrenics who do not participate in such a program. The research project is designed to test this hypothesis. The hypothesis may prove wrong—the researcher may find no difference between the two groups.

GATHERING DATA

How do psychologists collect information about the topic they've chosen to study? The method a researcher uses partly depends on the research topic. For example, a social psychologist who is studying the effects of group pressure is likely to conduct an experiment. A psychologist who is interested in personality theories might begin with intensive case studies of individuals. But whatever approach to gathering data a psychologist selects, he or she must make certain basic decisions in advance.

Samples

Suppose a psychologist wants to know how the desire to get into college affects the attitudes of high school juniors and seniors. It would be impossible to study every junior and senior in the country. There are just too many. Instead, the researcher would select a *sample*, a relatively small group out of the total *population* under study (in this case, all high school juniors and seniors).

Choosing a sample can be tricky. A sample must be *representative* of the population a researcher is studying. For example, if you wanted to know how tall American men are, you would want to make certain that your sample did not include a disproportionately large number of professional basketball players. This sample would be *biased*; it would not represent American men in general.

The editors of *Literary Digest* learned about sample bias the hard way. Before the 1936 presidential election, the magazine conducted a massive telephone survey to find out whether voters favored Franklin Roosevelt or Alf Landon. Based on the results of this poll, the *Digest* predicted that Landon would win by a landslide. However, when the votes were counted on election night, it was Roosevelt who won by a landslide. What went wrong? The magazine had only questioned people who appeared on their subscription rolls or who were listed in the telephone book. In those Depression days, conservatives usually subscribed to this magazine, and only the affluent could afford the luxury of a telephone. And these people tended to be Republicans. In short, the *Digest's* sample did not represent the views of American voters. The sample was biased toward Landon.

There are two ways to avoid a biased sample. One is to take a purely *random sample,* so that each individual within the scope of the research has an *equal chance* of being represented. For example, a psychologist might choose every twentieth name on school enrollment lists for a study of schoolchildren in a particular town. Random sampling is like drawing names or numbers out of a hat while blindfolded.

The second way to avoid bias is to deliberately pick individuals who represent the various subgroups in the population being studied. For example, the psychologist doing research on schoolchildren might select students of both sexes, of varying ages, of all social classes, and from all neighborhoods. This is called a *stratified sample.*

The size of the sample may also be important. If the sample is too small, the results will be meaningless. For example, a pollster who wants to know what Democrats think about a particular candidate will have to question a relatively large number of people. Why? Because Democrats vary considerably in their political attitudes. Northern and southern, rural and urban, male and female Democrats, often disagree. If the pollster only interviews six of the millions of Democrats in the country, the results will not reflect these differences. In most general surveys aimed at large popu-

FIGURE A.2
The sampling problem. An area full of unknowns confronts the researcher. Because he can collect only a limited amount of the information, he must use what he gets to make educated guesses about the rest. In the first frames of this sequence, the researcher obtains misleading information: His first sampling technique produces a biased sample. He then takes a random sample and correctly concludes that most of the unknowns are cubes and spheres. On the basis of the first sample he might have concluded that pyramid shapes were equally as common.

lations, the researcher questions about a thousand people. However, a sample of one hundred may be sufficient *if* those one hundred individuals represent the population as a whole. Indeed, if Democrats were all of one mind it would only be necessary to interview one!

Sampling techniques apply to the collection of data as well as to the choice of subjects for study. A psychologist who wants to learn how children react to their first years at school might observe them every tenth day (a random sample). Alternatively, he or she might spend several weeks observing them when they arrive at school, playing alone and in groups, with and without supervision, at different activities inside and outside—selecting typical school experiences. This would be a stratified sample of observations.

Correlations and Explanations

A researcher may simply want to observe people or other animals and record these observations in a descriptive study. More often, however, researchers want to examine the *relationship* between two sets of obser-vations—say, between students' grades and the number of hours they sleep.

In some cases a psychologist attempts to explain behavior or feelings in terms of *cause and effect*. Scientists use the word *correlation* to de-scribe the degree of relatedness between two sets of data. Sometimes the relationship is quite close. For example, there is a *positive correlation* between IQ scores and academic success. High IQ scores tend to go with high grades; low IQ scores tend to go with low grades. On the other hand, there is a *negative correlation* between smoking cigarettes and living a long, healthy life. The more a person smokes, the fewer years he or she may live. In this case, a high rank on one measure tends to go with a low rank on the other.

Establishing a correlation is useful because it enables scientists to make relatively accurate *predictions*. Knowing that there is a positive correla-tion between IQ and academic success, you can predict that a person with a high IQ will do well in school. You won't be right all of the time: Some people with high IQs do poorly in school. But you will be right most of the time. Similarly, knowing that there is a negative correlation between smoking and good health enables you to predict that a person who smokes heavily will not live as long as someone who does not smoke. Again, you will make a few mistakes but you will be right most of the time.

Often people confuse correlations with explanations. Instead of looking at a correlation as a comparison of two things, they think of it as a cause-and-effect relationship. Some years ago, for example, medical researchers discovered a high correlation between cancer and drinking milk. It seemed that the number of cancer cases was increasing in areas where people drink a lot of milk (such as New England) but that cancer was rare in areas where they do not (such as Ceylon). These data suggested to many people that milk causes cancer.

However, when researchers analyzed these data further they found a third factor was involved. Cancer usually strikes people in middle age or later. As a result, cancer is more common in places where people enjoy a high standard of living and live longer than in places where people tend to die at an earlier age. Thus drinking milk is related to cancer, but only because they are both related to a high standard of living. Milk does not cause cancer, but they may be correlated.

As this example illustrates, a correlation between two things may or *may not* indicate a cause-and-effect relationship. To test their hypotheses about cause-and-effect relationships, researchers turn to experiments.

Experiments

Why would a reseacher choose experimentation over other research methods? Becasue it enables the investigator to *control* the situation and to eliminate the possibility that unnoticed, outside factors will influence the results.

This is why, for example, social psychologists Kenneth Gergen, Mary Gergen, and William Barton (1973) put groups of six and seven student

FIGURE A.3
This series of drawings depicts a correlation between the woman's sadness and the man's anger. But is one causing the other? Not necessarily. Correlation does not imply causation. It is possible that the woman's sadness is causing the man's anger; it is possible that his anger is causing her sadness; and it is also possible that they are both responding to a third factor.

volunteers who did not know each other in a dark room for an hour, told them they could do whatever they liked, then photographed their activities with infrared cameras and recorded their conversations. What was the purpose of this experiment? To test the hypothesis that a group of strangers left alone in a dark room will do and say things they would not do and say in a lighted room. Darkness provides a cloak of anonymity. The researchers thought that if people can't see each other, they won't worry about being recognized after the experiment and so will be uninhibited. The experiment was designed to prove or disprove this hypothesis. This is the main purpose of psychological studies and experiments—to develop a hypothesis or refine and test previous ones.

In designing and reporting experiments, psychologists think in terms of *variables*—that is, conditions and behaviors that are subject to variation or change. In the experiment we are describing, the two significant variables were the amount of light in the room and the amount of conversation, movement, and touching in each of the groups. There are two types of variables: independent and dependent. The *independent variable* is the one experimenters deliberately control so that they can observe its effects. Here, the independent variable is darkness. The *dependent variable* is the one that researchers believe will be affected by the independent variable. Here, conversation, movement, and touching were the dependent variables. The researchers thought that darkness would influence these behaviors.

Of course, there is always a chance that the very fact of participating in an experiment will change the way people act. For this reason, Gergen, Gergen, and Barton put similar groups of students in a lighted room, told them they could do whatever they liked, and photographed and recorded their behavior. Subjects such as these, who are exposed to all elements of the experiment *except the independent variable* (here, darkness), form the *control group*. The subjects who *are* exposed to the independent variable are called the *experimental group*.

A control group is necessary in all experiments. Without it, a researcher cannot be sure that the experimental group is reacting to what he or she thinks it is reacting to—the independent variable. By comparing the way control and experimental groups behaved in this experiment, the researchers could determine whether darkness did in fact influence behavior and how.

What were the results of this experiment? In the lighted room students

FIGURE A.4
The experimenters hypothesized that darkness would encourage strangers to relax social inhibitions. The experimental group was placed in a dark room (darkness is the independent variable), and the amount of talking, moving, and touching was recorded. A control group was placed in an identical room, but with normal light. Again talking, moving, and touching were measured. See the text for the results of this experiment.

remained seated (about three feet apart) for most of the hour and kept up a continuous conversation. No one touched anyone else. In the dark room, the students moved around. Although conversation tended to slack off after a half-hour or so, there was a great deal of touching—by accident and on purpose. In fact, half of the subjects in the experimental group found themselves hugging another person. Thus the researchers' hypothesis was supported. Anonymity does to some extent remove inhibitions against letting conversation die out and against touching, even hugging a stranger.

Replication. The results of this experiment do not constitute the final word on the subject, however. Psychologists do not fully accept the results of their own or other people's studies until they have been *replicated*—that is, duplicated by at least one other psychologist with different subjects. Why? Because there is always a chance that the subjects in the experimental group were atypical. Here, they might have been unusually outgoing; the subjects in the control group might have been inhibited.

One example will illustrate why replication is so important. In the mid-1960s, Neal Miller and Leo DiCara (1967) stunned the psychological and medical world by reporting that they had trained rats to control their heart rates. For a brief time, doctors had hopes of controlling high blood pressure and preventing heart attacks and strokes by teaching patients to regulate their pulse. But all attempts to replicate Miller and DiCara's study failed—including their own. What went wrong? To date, no one has found the answer.

Sometimes, a second researcher purposely changes one or more variables of the original study. For example, he may use middle-aged people instead of college students as subjects. The goal is to find out whether the conclusions drawn from the original study apply to people in general, not just to one segment of the population.

Often, experimentation is impossible for practical or ethical reasons. Suppose a psychologist suspects that normal visual development in humans depends on visual experience as well as on physical maturation. An ideal way to test this hypothesis would be to raise an experimental group of infants in total darkness, thus depriving them of visual experience, and a control group of infants under similar conditions but with normal lighting. Such an experiment would be impossible, of course. A researcher might conduct this kind of experiment with animals, but in many instances the behaviors and feelings psychologists want to study do not occur in animals. Language is an obvious example. In addition, psychologists need information about the way people and animals behave naturally, when they are not conscious of being the subjects of an experiment. To obtain such information a psychologist would use *naturalistic observation*.

Naturalistic Observation

One of the most direct ways to learn about psychology is to listen and watch—observing how humans and animals behave, without interfering.

FIGURE A.5
Naturalistic observation is a method comparable to making large numbers of case studies. By observing the behavior of many individual pairs of sticklebacks, ethologist Niko Tinbergen was able to give the general description of stickleback mating behavior illustrated here. (*reading from top left to bottom right*) In apparent response to the zig-zag dance of a red-bellied male, the female swims directly toward him. He then turns to lead her to the nest he has previously built. She follows, and when he points his head into the nest, she enters it. Then, touching her abdomen, the male trembles, and the female spawns. Finally the male ejaculates to fertilize the new eggs.
(After Tinbergen, 1951.)

For example, a social psychologist might join a commune or participate in a therapy group to study how leadership develops in these settings. A developmental psychologist might position himself or herself behind a two-way mirror to watch youngsters at play. Ethologists (scientists who specialize in studying animal behavior) often spend years observing members of a species before even considering an experiment. Niko Tinbergen, who investigated the mating dance of the stickleback, is an example (see Figure A.5).

The cardinal rule of naturalistic observation is to avoid disturbing the people or animals you are studying, by concealing yourself or by acting as unobtrusively as possible. Otherwise, you may observe a performance produced for the researcher's benefit rather than natural behavior.

Case Studies

A *case study* is an intensive investigation of an individual or group. Many case studies focus on a particular disorder, such as schizophrenia, or a particular experience, such as being confined to prison. And most combine long-term observation (by one or more researchers), self-reports (such as diaries, tapes of therapy sessions, or perhaps artwork), and the results of psychological tests.

In the hands of a brilliant psychologist, case studies can be a powerful research tool. Sigmund Freud's theory of personality development, discussed in Chapter 13, was based on case studies of his patients. Jean Piaget's theory of intellectual development, described in Chapter 8, was based in part on case studies of his own children. By itself, however, a case study does not prove or disprove anything. The sample is too small, and there is no way of knowing if the researcher's conclusions are correct. For example, a researcher might conduct intensive case studies of families that include an individual diagnosed as schizophrenic. On the basis of these studies she might conclude that a particular kind of interaction produced schizophrenia. However, unless she studies families that do *not* include schizophrenic individuals and finds they interact differently she has no way of proving her conclusion. In other words, what is missing from case studies is a control group. The researcher might study a million families that include a schizophrenic person and find similar patterns. But unless she compares these families to others, she cannot prove a cause-and-effect relationship.

What, then, is the value of case studies? They provide a wealth of descriptive material that may generate new hypotheses that researchers can test under controlled conditions with comparison groups.

Surveys

Surveys may be impersonal, but they are the most practical way to gather data on the attitudes, beliefs, and experiences of large numbers of people. A survey can take the form of interviews, questionnaires, or a combination of the two.

Interviews allow a researcher to observe the subject and modify ques-

FIGURE A.6
Jean Piaget's theories of intellectual development stemmed partly from case studies of his own children. Here, Piaget observes children playing in a park near his home.

tions if the subject seems confused by them. On the other hand, questionnaires take less time to administer and the results are more uniform. Questionnaires also eliminate the possibility that the researcher will influence the subject by unconsciously frowning at an answer he or she does not like. Of course, there is always a danger that subjects will give misleading answers in order to make themselves "look good." One way to detect this is to phrase the same question in several different ways. A person who says yes, she believes in integration, but no, she would not want her child to marry someone of another race, is not as free of prejudice as the first answer implied.

Perhaps the most famous survey of recent times is the Kinsey report. Alfred Kinsey and his staff questioned over 10,000 men and women about their sexual attitudes and behavior—a radical thing to do in the 1940s. The results shocked many people, much as Masters and Johnson's observational studies of human sexual behavior did in the late 1960s.

Longitudinal Studies

Longitudinal studies cover long stretches of time. The psychologist studies and restudies the same group of subjects at regular intervals over a period of years to determine whether their behavior and feelings have changed, and if so, how. For example, Lewis Terman followed over a thousand gifted children from an early age to adulthood. He found that they were generally taller, heavier, and stronger than youngsters with average IQ's. In addition, they tended to be active socially and to mature faster than average children. (So much for the stereotype of the skinny, unpopular bookworm.) As adults, they were less likely than people with average intelligence to become involved in crime, to depend on alcohol or drugs, or to develop severe mental illnesses. Some people have said that geniuses are crazy. This study indicates that they are more adaptive, creative, and adjusted than people of normal intelligence.

Longitudinal studies are time-consuming and precarious; subjects may disappear in mid-study. But they are an ideal way to examine consistencies and inconsistencies in behavior over time.

Cross-cultural Studies

Cross-cultural studies are just what the term suggests: comparisons of the way people in different cultures behave, feel, and think. The primary purpose of such research is to determine whether a behavior pattern is universal or reflects the way children are raised and the experiences adults have in a particular culture. For example, Lawrence Kohlberg, who was studying the development of moral reasoning, presented American, Mexican, and Taiwanese boys age seven and older with a series of dilemmas. (For example, if a man's wife is dying, should he steal a drug that he cannot afford to save her life?) He found that some children in all three societies progress through six stages of moral awareness, from fear of punishment to an inner sense of justice. However, the percentage of those in each society who reached stage six varied. Thus although certain values appear to be universal, cultural differences do affect the development of moral reasoning.

All the methods for gathering information we've described have advantages and disadvantages. No one technique is better than the others for all purposes. The method a psychologist chooses depends on what he or she wants to learn; on what hypothesis is being tested.

TRAPS IN DOING PSYCHOLOGICAL RESEARCH AND HOW TO AVOID THEM

In describing the methods and statistical techniques psychologists use, we have made research appear much simpler and much more straightforward than it actually is. Science is a painstaking, exacting business. Every researcher must be wary of numerous pitfalls that can trap him or her into mistakes. In this section we look at some of the most common problems psychological researchers confront and how they cope with them.

The Self-fulfilling Prophecy

Psychologists are only human, and like all of us they prefer to be right. No matter how objective they try to be in their research, there is always a chance that they will find what they want to find, unwittingly overlooking contrary evidence. This is what we mean by the *self-fulfilling prophecy*.

Researchers have shown how the self-fulfilling prophecy works in an experiment with experimenters (Rosenthal and Rosnow, 1969). The task was to administer the Wechsler Intelligence Scale for Children to twelve youngsters. Each child was tested by two experimenters, one of whom administered the odd-numbered questions, the other the even-numbered questions. With each child, one of the experimenters was told beforehand that the subject was above average in intelligence. The other was told the subject was below average. The results? The youngsters scored an average of 7.5 points higher on the half of the test administered by the experimenter who had been told they were bright than they did on the other half of the test. Thus the experimenters found what they expected to find. The prophecy that a given child would achieve a relatively high score was self-fulfilling.

The Double-blind Procedure

One way to avoid the self-fulfilling prophecy is to use the double-blind technique. Suppose a psychologist wants to study the effects of a particular tranquilizer. She might give the drug to an experimental group and a placebo (a harmless substitute for the drug) to a control group. The next step would be to compare their performances on a series of tests. This is a *single-blind* experiment. The subjects are "blind" in the sense that they do not know whether they have received the tranquilizer or the placebo.

As a further guarantee of objectivity, the researcher herself doesn't know who takes the drug or the placebo. (She may ask the pharmacist to number rather than label the pills.) *After* she scores the tests she goes back to the pharmacist to learn which subjects took the tranquilizer and which took the placebo. This is a *double-blind* experiment. Neither the subjects nor the experimenter know which subjects received the tranquilizer. This eliminates the possibility that the researcher will unconsciously find what she expects to find about the effects of the drug.

FIGURE A.7
The Red Queen's fatalistic attitude is likely to be confirmed if she behaves in this way. This common phenomenon is called self-fulfilling prophecy.

Observer Effects

Psychologists, like everyone else, are complex people, with attitudes, feelings, and ideas of their own, and their reactions to different subjects may distort the results of a study. Researchers may, unknowingly, react quite differently to male and female subjects, short and tall subjects, subjects who speak with an accent or who remind them of someone they particularly like or dislike. These attitudes, however subtly expressed, may influence the way subjects behave.

Another experiment with experimenters showed just how subtle this sort of influence may be. A group of graduate students administered the Rorschach test to a number of subjects. Half the students were led to believe that it would reflect favorably on them if people they tested saw more animals than humans on the inkblot cards. These students obtained one-third more descriptions of animals than the other students. Yet tape recordings of the test sessions revealed that they had not coached the subjects in any way, and the subjects themselves were not aware that the students had reacted more favorably to animal than human responses (Masling, 1965).

In addition, subjects may behave differently than they would otherwise just because they know they are being studied. The presence of an ob-

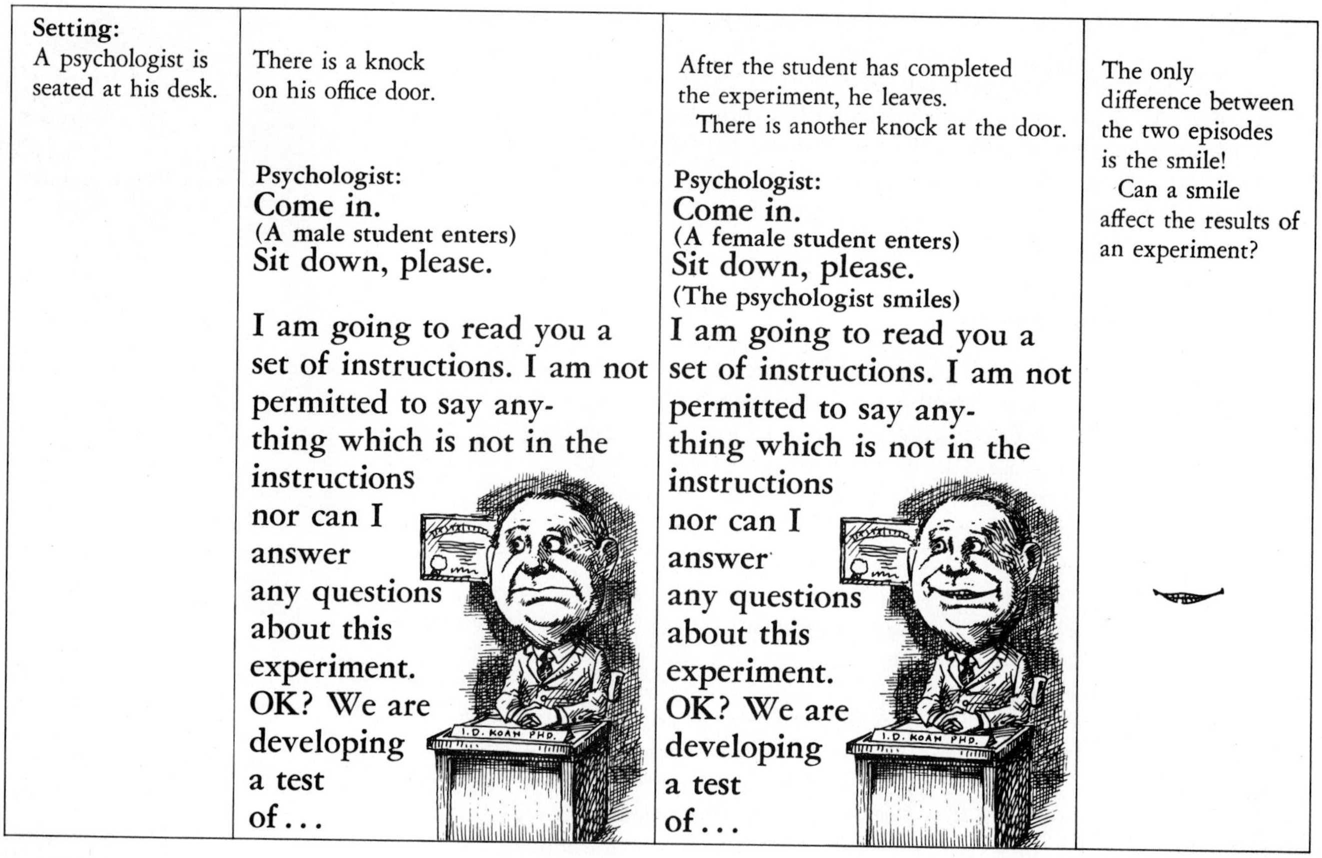

| Setting:
A psychologist is seated at his desk. | There is a knock on his office door.

Psychologist:
Come in.
(A male student enters)
Sit down, please.

I am going to read you a set of instructions. I am not permitted to say anything which is not in the instructions nor can I answer any questions about this experiment. OK? We are developing a test of . . . | After the student has completed the experiment, he leaves.
    There is another knock at the door.

Psychologist:
Come in.
(A female student enters)
Sit down, please.
(The psychologist smiles)
I am going to read you a set of instructions. I am not permitted to say anything which is not in the instructions nor can I answer any questions about this experiment. OK? We are developing a test of . . . | The only difference between the two episodes is the smile!
    Can a smile affect the results of an experiment? |

FIGURE A.8

Yes, and so can any number of other factors that may have escaped the researcher's attention. Not surprisingly, this researcher will probably find that females are more friendly and cooperative than are males. Other researchers, even when working with animals, have obtained the results they anticipated by unconsciously handling the animals in ways that produce the expected behaviors.

server may cause them to change their behavior, just as the presence of a photographer can transform a bunch of unruly children into a peaceful, smiling group. Under observation, people are apt to try to please or impress the observer—to act as they think they are expected to act. The use of a control group helps to correct for this, but does not totally eliminate the "observer effect."

Finally, a researcher may not have the equipment to study a subject adequately. For example, it was perfectly reasonable to assume that the earth was the center of the universe—until the invention of the telescope and other advances in astronomy proved otherwise. Psychology is a relatively young science, and the tools and techniques psychologists possess may not be equal to the questions they ask.

INTERPRETING DATA: USING STATISTICS

The last stage of psychological research is often the most difficult one. The researcher's desk is piled high with notes and tapes from a case study, questionnaires, test scores, or whatever he or she has collected. By themselves, the *data* (the results of a study) mean little. Think back to the experiment with groups of students who were put in light and dark rooms.

Results: Observations of behavior in the experimental chamber:

	Black Room	White Room
Movement	50% change of position every five minutes.	10% change of position during whole session.
Verbal communication	High during first half-hour, then low	High throughout session.

Percent of subjects reporting selected behaviors and experiences in questionnaire:

	Black Room	White Room
Talked small talk	96	100
Introduced self by first name	92	100
Laughed or giggled	80	100
Felt close to other person	92	75
Felt suspended—beyond normal time and space	80	65
Touched accidentally	100	5
Felt sexually aroused	75	30
Lay on floor	64	50
Found self in middle of room	84	10
Touched purposefully	88	0
Hugged	48	0
Prevented self from being touched	16	0

FIGURE A.9
The results of the experiment conducted by Gergen, Gergen, and Barton. Note that the results given here are summaries of the data, not a list of every behavior of every subject observed and recorded by the experimenters.

Suppose the researchers found that Subject A sat by the wall for a time, got up to explore, bumped into Subject B, burst out laughing, sat down again, talked to Subjects C and D, then fell silent. Subject B began exploring the room immediately. Subject C stood around—and so on. What does this information mean?

Psychologists nearly always collect data in the form of specific measurements. For example, Gergen, Gergen, and Barton measured the amount of time subjects spent sitting and moving about, talking and being silent. They also asked the subjects to fill out a questionnaire and counted the number of times individuals recalled bumping into someone, hugging another person, preventing contact, and the like. Then they converted this information into *statistics*, which are mathematical summaries of raw data. Statistics are a concise form of data that can be evaluated and reported.

Descriptive Statistics

The term *descriptive statistics* applies to a range of techniques psychologists use to summarize the scores obtained in a study, so that they are easier to read and interpret.

To illustrate: A psychologist is studying anxiety in different occupa-

FIGURE A.10
Examples of statistical distributions and averages. (a) The distribution of the scores from an imaginary group of gas station attendants on an imaginary questionnaire. (b) The distribution of the scores of an imaginary group of dentists on the same test. Note that these distributions are similar in range but different in their averages.

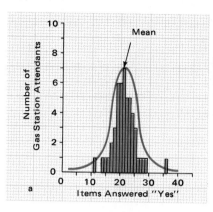
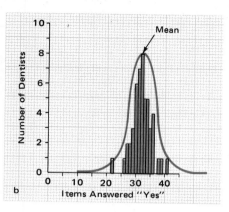

tional groups. He asks a sample of fifty gas station attendants to answer "Yes, I do worry about this" or "No, I never worry about this" to 40 questions. Then he adds up each of their scores. One of the attendants seems quite anxious: He worries about 29 of the items. Another is extremely cool: She only worries about 11 of the items. But most of the subjects fall somewhere in between: Their scores were (starting from the least anxious): 11, 13 14, 15, 17, 17, 18, 18, 18, 19, 19, 19, 19, 19, 19, 20, 20, 20, 20, 20, 20, 21, 21, 21, 21, 21, 21, 21, 22, 22, 22, 22, 22, 23, 23, 23, 23, 23, 24, 24, 24, 24, 24, 25, 25, 25, 26, 27, 28, and 29. Now you can see why descriptive statistics are so useful. It is difficult to try to make any sense out of this list of scores. However, a summary turns this list into a manageable figure. By adding up the total scores and dividing by the number of subjects, the psychologist can calculate the average, or *arithmetic mean,* for the whole group—in this case, 21.

The psychologist then presents the same questions to a group of dentists, and calculates *their* average score. It seems that as a group, they are somewhat more anxious than gas station attendants: The arithmetic mean for dentists is 32 worried responses. As this indicates, calculating the arithmetic mean can be extremely useful when a psychologist wants to compare the overall performances of different groups. But psychologists are also interested in variations within groups.

Distributions. Both the gas station attendants and the dentists in the example above showed a *normal distribution* of scores. A few subjects scored quite low, a few high, but most of the scores fell somewhere between the extremes. This is sometimes referred to as a "bell curve," because when a normal distribution of scores or data is plotted on a graph, it makes a neat curve (see Figure A.10).

However, scores do not always fall into the normal distribution pattern, and when they do not, the arithmetic mean is misleading. For example, the mean salary at a small plastics company is $9,200, but how are salaries distributed? The president earns $40,000 a year. He pays three executives $30,000 a year; four junior executives, $20,000. There are six managers who earn $15,000 and six salesmen who earn $10,000. The company pays ten of its machine operators $5,000 and twenty of them $2,500. Given this

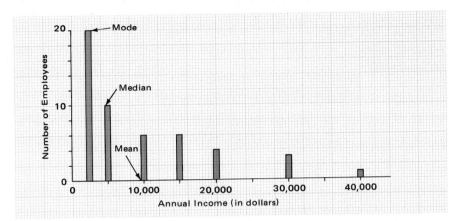

FIGURE A.11
The distribution of incomes in an imaginary plastics company. Note that the shape of this distribution is completely different from the shapes in Figure A.10. Note also how the locations of the mean, median, and mode vary in this distribution.

uneven distribution, the arithmetic mean paints a highly distorted picture of earnings. No one in the company earns exactly $9,200; some employees earn substantially more, while 60 percent earn considerably less than that amount.

In this example, a more accurate representation of income distribution would be the *median*—the figure that falls exactly in the middle of the distribution. The median income at the factory is $5,000. An even more revealing figure would be the *mode*—the figure that appears most frequently. For salaries at this company, the mode is $2,500 a year—rather a comedown from $9,200 (the mean).

Variability and Standard Deviation.   The mean, median, and mode are three ways of summarizing the central trend in a set of figures. But they do not tell you how much *variation* there is in scores. Figure A.12 shows the scores two groups of students received on a history test. The mean for the two groups is the same: 58. But in Class A the scores are clustered together. Nearly everyone passed (assuming 58 is the passing grade). In Class B, there is a much wider range of scores. A relatively large number of students did poorly, and an almost equal number achieved better than average scores.

Psychologists express variability in terms of the *standard deviation*—a number that indicates the extent to which, on the average, figures in a given set of data vary from the mean. You find the standard deviation by calculating a special kind of average of the deviations of all the scores from the group mean. If you know, for example, that the mean of a set of scores on a history quiz is 58 and the standard deviation is small—say, 2—then you can expect almost all the scores to be very close to 58. About two-thirds of the scores will be within 2 points of the mean, so most of the scores will be between 56 and 60. Suppose, however, that the scores are widely spread, with a standard deviation of 17, for example. Now, although there are more scores around 58 than anywhere else, scores much higher and lower than this figure are common, too. By knowing the mean, you know what score a person was most likely to have obtained; by knowing the standard deviation you know whether to expect the actual scores to vary from the mean a little or a lot.

FIGURE A.12
Two imaginary distributions of the history-quiz scores of fifty students. Note that these two distributions have the same average but different ranges. The standard deviation of the distribution for Class B is *larger* than that of the Class A distribution.

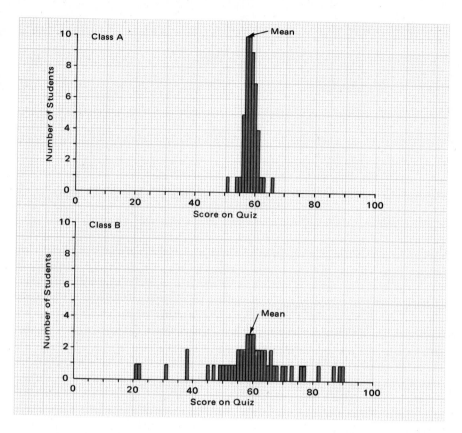

Inferential Statistics

As the term suggests, *inferential statistics* involve mathematical inferences based on descriptive statistics. Psychologists use these calculations to determine how much confidence they can place in the results of a study and whether the scores their sample achieved apply to the population as a whole.

The most important question in this regard is, Might these results be due to chance or do they show a significant pattern or relationship? To answer this, psychologists turn to *probability theory*. Although probability theory is highly sophisticated, the basic principles are quite simple. If you toss a coin in the air, the chance of getting heads is 50 percent. The odds are even. What are the chances of getting ten heads in a row? Probability theory gives a definite answer. It is possible to calculate that there is a little less than one chance in a thousand. If you actually get ten heads in a row, you would undoubtedly suspect that something is wrong with the coin.

This is exactly the logic behind inferential statistics. Suppose a psychologist is conducting an experiment on ESP. The plan is to have subjects guess which of five symbols appears each time the experimenter turns over a card in another room. For each card, the chances are one in five that a subject will guess correctly. If the investigator gives each subject a hundred cards, the rules of probability dictate that each will get roughly twenty cards right out of the hundred. Some will get a few more; others, a few less. The question is, How many more correct answers than twenty does a subject have to get before the psychologist can conclude he has ESP? Could he get thirty by chance? fifty? He *could* get any number. But the rules of probability indicate that while it is possible to guess thirty cards correctly fairly often, it is highly *im*probable that a person would make fifty correct guesses.

Such unusual results are called *significant differences*—a difference that is so unlikely it is probably not due to chance alone. In the ESP experiment, the researcher could reasonably conclude that there is a significant difference between a person who guessed fifty cards correctly and the other subjects, who guessed about twenty cards correctly. (Real ESP experiments never produce such extreme results, but the logic is the same.)

Inferential statistics are thus mathematical calculations of the odds against something happening by chance. If the pattern of results differs significantly from the pattern that would be expected to occur by chance, a psychologist is encouraged to continue that line of research and to try to verify the results.

CONCLUSIONS

What distinguishes psychologists and other scientists from nonscientists is nagging skepticism. Scientists do not believe that they have any final answers, or that they ever will. But they do believe they can learn more about feelings and behavior if they persist in asking questions and studying them systematically. Do people actually behave like that? Does this method work? Does that way of thinking help? When the answer is yes, scientists do not stop asking questions. It is always possible that the next answer will be no, or that it is yes for some people and no for others. Hence it is essential for researchers to *invite* criticism by publishing detailed accounts of their methods as well as their results.

The reason why *students* of psychology need to understand research methods is really quite simple. You wouldn't vote for a political candidate simply because she promised to do something you agreed with. You'd want to know whether she had delivered on past campaign promises, whether she was indebted to special-interest groups, and whether she was an effective bargainer in the legislature. You wouldn't buy a new brand of soap because the company claimed that "tests prove" it is good for your skin. You'd want to know what the tests were, who conducted them, and why other companies make the same claim.

By the same token, you shouldn't accept what you read about psychology in magazines, newspapers, or for that matter this text just because a psychologist says so. (The "experts" can and often do disagree.) To evaluate psychological studies for yourself and weigh the evidence for conflicting views, you need to understand research methods. Thus the goal of this appendix has been to make you more informed "consumers" of psychology.

SUMMARY

1. The first step in psychological research is generating testable ideas. Usually these take the form of a hypothesis: a statement about what a researcher expects to find, put in such a way that it can be proved or disproved.

2. The next step is to select a sample of the population relevant to a study. A random sample (the equivalent of picking subjects while blindfolded) or stratified sample (one that mirrors variations in the population as a whole) helps a researcher avoid bias.

3. Although some research is purely descriptive, more often studies are designed to investigate the degree of association or correlation between two phenomena. But neither a positive nor a negative correlation should be mistaken for a cause-and-effect relationship.

4. Psychologists often use experiments to test hypotheses about cause-and-effect relationships. The researchers observe the effects of the independent variable (the condition they manipulate) on the dependent variable (the condition they think will change) in an experimental group. They then compare the reactions of the experimental group to those of a control group that has not been exposed to the independent variable.

5. Psychologists do not accept the results of an experiment until it has been replicated by another researcher using different subjects.

6. Other methods for gathering data on behavior and feelings include:
   a. naturalistic observation—watching and recording behavior without intruding on the actors
   b. case studies—intensive investigations of individuals or groups that convey the quality of behavior and experiences

   c. surveys—gathering data from a large number of people through face-to-face interviews or questionnaires
   d. longitudinal studies—studying and restudying the same group of subjects over a period of years
   e. cross-cultural studies—comparing the way people from different cultures behave and feel

7. Psychological research is full of traps. The self-fulfilling prophecy (which the double-blind procedure is designed to eliminate), observer effects, and inadequate tools may distort the results.

8. Statistics are the mathematical computations researchers perform on the data they collect by one of the methods in number 6.

9. Descriptive statistics are used to summarize the distribution of responses in groups. The average score for a group may refer to the mean (the sum of all the scores divided by the number of subjects); the median (the score that falls exactly in the middle of the distribution); or the mode (the score that occurs most frequently in the distribution). The standard deviation is a statistic that indicates how much variability there is in a set of scores.

10. Inferential statistics are used to draw conclusions about a population from a sample, and to calculate the odds against something happening by chance. Odds are figured according to probability theory. A significant difference is one that is so unlikely that it must mean something.

11. Careful collection and analysis of data do not provide "final answers," however. Science is based on insatiable curiosity and persistent questioning.

GLOSSARY

case study: An intensive investigation of an individual or group, usually focusing on a single psychological phenomenon.

control group: In an experiment, a group of subjects that is treated in the same way as the experimental group, except that the independent variable is not applied.

correlation: The degree of relatedness between two sets of data.

cross-cultural studies: Acquiring comparable data from two or more cultures for the purpose of studying cultural similarities and differences.

dependent variable: In an experiment, the factor that is not controlled by the experimenters but changes as a result of changes in the independent variable.

descriptive statistics: The statistical methods used to reduce masses of data to more manageable and understandable forms.

double-blind technique: A research technique in which neither the subjects nor the experimenter know which subjects have been exposed to the independent variable.

experimental group: In an experiment, the group of subjects to which the independent variable is applied.

hypothesis: An educated guess about the relationship between two variables.

independent variable: In an experiment, the factor that is deliberately manipulated by the experimenters to test its effect on another factor.

inferential statistics: Computations performed on descriptive statistics that are designed to answer questions about the meaning of the statistics and the degree of certainty about results.

longitudinal studies: Repeatedly gathering data on the same group of subjects over a period of time for the purpose of studying consistencies and change.

mean: A numerical average computed by dividing the sum of a set of scores by the number of scores in the set.

median: In a set of scores ranked from low to high, the score that has half the scores above it and half below.

mode: In a set of scores, the score that occurs most frequently.

naturalistic observation: Studying phenomena as they occur in natural surroundings, without interfering.

negative correlation: A correlation indicating that a high value for one variable corresponds to a low value for the other variable, and vice versa.

normal distribution: A bell-shaped distribution of data, with most scores falling in the middle and few scores at the high and low ends of the curve.

population: The total group of subjects from which a sample is drawn.

positive correlation: A correlation indicating that a high value for one variable corresponds to a high value for the other variable.

probability theory: The branch of mathematics concerned with the calculation of odds, chances, and the like.

random sample: A sample that gives an equal chance of being represented to every piece of data within the scope of the research.

replication: Repetition of an experiment and achievement of the same results.

sample: The small portion of data, out of the total amount available, that a researcher collects.

self-fulfilling prophecy: A belief, prediction, or expectation that operates to bring about its own fulfillment.

significant difference: A difference that is unlikely to be due to chance alone.

standard deviation: A number that indicates the

extent to which figures in a given set of data vary from the mean.

statistics: The branch of mathematics concerned with summarizing and making meaningful inferences from collections of data.

stratified sample: A sample that includes representatives of subgroups or variations of the population being studied.

survey: A relatively large sampling of data, obtained through interviews and questionnaires.

variable: In an experimental situation, any factor that is capable of change.

ACTIVITIES

1. Measurement is the assignment of numbers to observations. Psychologists face many problems in trying to measure behaviors and feelings. For example, how might the following factors be measured? (1) the number of people in a room; (2) height; (3) the proportion of votes a candidate will receive; (4) hunger; (5) love; (6) liberty. What makes each phenomenon difficult or easy to measure? What can you predict from this exercise regarding the difficulties of measuring such things as personality and intelligence?

2. With a pad of paper and pencil, watch television commercials for several evenings, paying particular attention to those advertising such products as toothpaste, headache remedies, detergents, and others that claim their product has been "proven more effective." Take notes as you watch, jotting down the "statistics" the advertisers use to support their claims. Often, the statistics used in advertising have been manipulated in various ways to present a distorted version of the facts. How many fallacies can you spot in the commercials you watch? Compare and discuss your results with others in your class.

3. You wish to determine whether or not a young child can be taught to love cauliflower. Would you use the method of simple observation or would you need to design an experiment? What would your independent and dependent variables be? What controls would you use? Could you develop a theory from this experiment, if it turned out to be valid? How far could you generalize your findings?

4. Several theories are presented below. How could you attempt to disprove each one? Are there any that could not be disproved?
   a. A person will remember an unfinished task.
   b. Love reduces hate.
   c. You can raise blood pressure by making a subject anxious.
   d. Motivation increases learning.
   e. Making a rat hungry will cause *it* to require less training to find its way through a maze.

5. Select a particular area of psychological investigation that is of interest to you. Go to a main branch or university library and by utilizing the card catalog, bibliographical references, and journals or magazines, see how far your research takes you. You may find that, like looking up a word in the dictionary, one thing leads to another, which leads to another, and so on.

6. Look through a popular magazine such as *Time, Newsweek,* or *Psychology Today.* Read an article about a scientific experiment and try to determine if the results presented correspond to the data given. What approach to obtaining data was used? Did the experiment contain a control group? What were the dependent and independent variables?

7. Based on the information provided in this chapter, design your own research experiment. If you should decide to carry out your design, write up a research report according to the style presented in the chapter and present your findings to the class.

8. Using the mean, median, and mode, devise some fake "statistics." Present your "facts" to family members, classmates, and friends (who are not taking a psychology class). Did your classmates spot the fallacies more quickly than the other subjects?

9. Take ten pennies, a sheet of paper (graph paper, if you have any), and a pencil. Put the numbers 0 through 10 along the bottom of the sheet, spaced evenly apart. Then toss the coins, all at once. Count the number of heads and make a mark (or fill in a square) above the appropriate number on the paper. Toss the coins again and again (fifty to one hundred times), each time making another mark or filling in another square to indicate how many heads came up. In this way, you will generate a distribution. Does your distribution show a normal curve?

10. Using a watch with a second hand, or a stopwatch if you have one, count how many seconds it takes for different people to tell you what they were doing exactly twenty-four hours ago. Plot the results in the same manner as you did for the coins. Try to get scores for as many people as the number of times you tossed the coins, then compare the two distributions.

SUGGESTED READINGS

AGNEW, NEIL, AND PYKE, SANDRA. *The Science Game: An Introduction to Research in the Behavioral Sciences.* Englewood Cliffs, N.J.: Prentice-Hall, 1969. A nontechnical book for the introductory student or curious layman about "the continuity between everyday truth-seeking activities and the methods of science."

DETHIER, VINCENT. *To Know a Fly.* San Francisco: Holden-Day, 1963 (paper). This book is a personal and witty description of the author's research on the appetites of houseflies. This book describes the experience of obtaining those results.

DUSTIN, DAVID S. *How Psychologists Do Research: The Example of Anxiety.* Englewood Cliffs, N.J.: Prentice-Hall, 1969. Designed for beginners in psychology, this book discusses how a number of psychologists—each representing a different approach—do different kinds of research on the same topic—anxiety. Each chapter describing a particular line of research is followed by a chapter evaluating the contribution of that research to solving the problem.

HUFF, DARRELL. *How to Lie with Statistics.* New York: Norton, 1954. An easy-to-read and thoroughly enjoyable book about how people use statistics to "prove" anything they want to prove. This book is loaded with useful and practical information—and lots of surprises.

KOESTLER, ARTHUR. *The Case of the Midwife Toad.* New York: New American Library, 1971 (paper). Koestler presents a well-documented account of the mystery surrounding a highly respected Austrian scientist's suicide, committed when his findings of half a lifetime of research were being harshly questioned. A fascinating and revealing description of the little-known inner world of scientific investigation.

SABIN, THEODORE, AND COE, WILLIAM. *The Student Psychologist's Handbook: A Guide to Sources.* Cambridge, Mass.: Schenkman, 1969. A practical guide to the gathering of resources and the presentation of research papers. Excellent material on how to use the library.

WHALEY, DONALD, AND SURRATT, SHARON. *Attitudes of Science.* Behaviordelia, Inc., P.O. Box 1044, Kalamazoo, Michigan 49005. Although the information in this manual is presented in a highly clever and humorous manner, it is nevertheless designed to teach the scientific method to serious students of psychology. Strongly recommended for those who plan to continue the study of psychology.

BIBLIOGRAPHY

BACHRACH, A. J. *Psychological Research: An Introduction.* 2nd ed. New York: Random House, 1965.

EDITORS OF THE *Literary Digest.* "Landon, 1,293,669; Roosevelt, 972,897."*Literary Digest,* 122 (October 31, 1936): 5–6.

GERGEN, KENNETH J., GERGEN, MARY M., AND BARTON, WILLIAM H. "Deviance in the Dark." *Psychology Today,* 7 (October 1973): 129, 130.

HAYS, WILLIAM L. *Statistics for Psychologists.* New York: Holt, Rinehart and Winston, 1963.

KINSEY, ALFRED C., POMEROY, WARDELL B., AND MARTIN, CLYDE E. *Sexual Behavior in the Human Male.* Philadelphia: Saunders, 1948.

KINSEY, ALFRED C., ET AL. *Sexual Behavior in the Human Female.* Philadelphia: Saunders, 1953.

KOHLBERG, L., AND KRAMER, R. "Continuities and Discontinuities in Child and Adult Moral Development." *Human Development,* 12 (1969): 93–120.

MASLING, J. "Differential Indoctrination of Examiners and Rorschach Responses." *Journal of Consulting Psychology,* 29 (1965): 198–201.

MILLER, NEAL E., AND DICARA, LEO. "Instrumental Learning of Heart Rate Changes in Curarized Rats: Shaping and Specificity to Discriminative Stimulus." *Journal of Comparative and Physiological Psychology,* 63 (1967): 12–19.

MILLER, NEAL E., AND DWORKIN, B. R. "Visceral Learning: Recent Difficulties with Curarized Rats and Significant Problems for Human Research." In *Contemporary Trends in Cardiovascular Psychophysiology,* edited by Paul A. Obrist *et al.* Chicago: Aldine-Atherton, in press.

ROSENTHAL, ROBERT. *Environmental Effects in Behavioral Research.* New York: Appleton-Century-Crofts, 1966.

ROSENTHAL, R., AND ROSNOW, R. L. (EDS.). *Artifact in Behavioral Research.* New York: Academic Press, 1969, pp. 210–211.

SCOTT, WILLIAM, AND WERTHEIMER, MICHAEL. *Introduction to Psychological Research.* New York: Wiley, 1962.

SNELLGROVE, L. *Psychological Experiments and Demonstrations.* New York: McGraw-Hill, 1967.

TERMAN, LEWIS M. *The Measurement of Intelligence.* Boston: Houghton Mifflin, 1916.

TERMAN, LEWIS M., AND MERRILL, MAUD A. *Measuring Intelligence.* Boston: Houghton Mifflin, 1937.

Index

(Italic numbers refer to illustrations and captions. Glossary terms and the names of authors listed in Suggested Readings sections are indicated by asterisks.)

Credits and Acknowledgments

Chapter 1
2, 5 — Michal Heron; 6 — Howard Saunders; 9 — Dr. Burton L. White; 10 — Werner Kalber/Busco-Nestor; 13 — *Puddles* by M. C. Escher, Escher Foundation-Haags Gemeentemuseum, The Hague.

Chapter 2
22 — Burk Uzzle/Magnum; 24 — Karl Nicholason; 25 — John Dawson; 28 — (*top left*) Steve McCarroll, (*bottom right*) Bill Boyarshy; 31 — John Dawson, after J. B. Wolfe, 1935; 32 — Steve McCarroll; 33 — Howard Saunders; 37 — Bob Quittner/Photophile; 40 — Robert Isaacs; 43 — Michal Heron.

Chapter 3
52 — Martha Swope; 52 — (*top) Eye Movements and Vision*, Plenum Press, 1967, (*bottom*) From J. P. Guilford and R. Hoepiner, *The Analysis of Intelligence*, McGraw-Hill, 1971; 55 — Doug Armstrong; 58 — John Dawson; 59 — Doug Armstrong, after D. Elkind and J. Flavell (eds.), *Studies in Cognitive Development, Essays in Honor of Jean Piaget*, © 1969, Oxford University Press, with permission; 60 — Doug Armstrong; 62 — Gillian Theobald, after Edward De Bono, *New Think: The Use of Lateral Thinking in the Generation of New Ideas*, © 1967, 1968 by Edward De Bono, published by Basic Books, Inc.; 64 — (*top*) Werner Kalber/PPS; 65 — John Dawson; 66 — (*top left*) Gillian Theobald, after Edward De Bono, *New Think: The Use of Lateral Thinking in the Generation of New Ideas*, © 1967, 1968, by Edward De Bono, published by Basic Books, Inc., (*right*) John Dawson, (*bottom left*) Werner Kalber/PPS.

Chapter 4
74 — Howard Sochurek/Woodfin Camp & Associates; 76 — John Dawson; 77 — Doug Armstrong/John Dawson; 78, 79, 80 — John Dawson; 83 — (*top*) James Olds, (*bottom*) Steve McCarroll; 84 — John Dawson; 86 — (*left*) Courtesy Neal Miller; 88 — Doug Armstrong; 91 — John Dawson; 92 — (*top*) Thomas McAvoy, © Time, Inc., (*bottom*) John Dawson; 94 — John C. Fentress.

Chapter 5
100 — Stephen Rudley; 105 — John Dawson; 106 — (*top*) Reproduced by permission of the author of the Dvorine Color Plates, distributed by Harcourt Brace Jovanovich, Inc., N. Y., (*bottom*) Tom Suzuki; 107, 108, 109, 110 — John Dawson; 111 — (*right*) After R. F. Street, *Teachers College Contributions to Education*, No. 481, Columbia University, N. Y., 1931, (*top*) Courtesy of Jerome Kagan, (*bottom*) John Dawson, after R. Held and A. Hein, "Movement Produced Stimulation in the Development of Visually Guided Behavior," *Journal of Comparative and Physiological Psychology*, 1963, Vol. 56, pp. 872–876, © 1963 APA and reproduced with permission; 114 — Steve McCarroll; 116 — Philip Clark; 117 — Photo by Robert Berger, reprinted with permission of *Science Digest*, © The Hearst Corporation.

Chapter 6
124 — Chris Bonington/Woodfin Camp & Associates; 126 — Michal Heron; 127 — Darrel Millsap; 128 — Adapted from D. N. Jackson, *Personality Research Form Manual,* © 1967 by Research Psychologists Press Inc.; 129 — Harry Crosby; 134 — Reproduced from *Darwin and Facial Expressions*, Paul Ekman (ed.), Academic Press, 1973, with permission from Paul Ekman and Silvan Tomkins; 137 — Photo by Bill Call; 138 — Everett Peck, quote from Magda B. Arnold, *Emotion and, Personality*, Columbia University Press, 1960, Vol. 1, p. 180.

Chapter 7
144 — *The Sleeping Gypsy* by Henri Rousseau. Collection The Museum of Modern Art, New York. Gift of Mrs. Simon Guggenheim; 153 — The Bettmann Archive, Inc.; 154 — John Dawson; 155 — Werner Kalber/Busco-Nestor; 156 — Reproduced from *Triangle*, The Sandoz Journal of Medical Science, Vol. 2., No. 3, 1955; 158 — Werner Kalber/Busco-Nestor.

Chapter 8
166 — Helena Frost; 168 — Ken Heyman; 169 — (*left*) Bill MacDonald, (*right*) Jason Lauré; 170 — (*top left, center, bottom left, bottom center*) Bill MacDonald, (*top right, center left, bottom right*) Steve McCarroll, (*center right*) Pamela Dalton; 171 — Jason Lauré; 172 — George Zimbel/Monkmeyer Press Photos; 173 — (*top*) George Zimbel/Monkmeyer Press Photos, (*bottom*) Bill MacDonald; 175 — Steve Wells; 178 — R. A. and B. T. Gardner; 180 — (*top*) Thomas McAvoy, Time-Life Picture Agency, © Time, Inc., (*bottom*) Harry F. Harlow, University of Wisconsin Primate Center; 181 — Harry F. Harlow, University of Wisconsin Primate Center; 183 — Myron Papiz; 186 — (*top left*) Steve McCarroll, (*top right*) Bill MacDonald, (*bottom left*) Robert Smith/Black Star, (*bottom right*) Charles Harbutt/Magnum; 188 — Courtesy of Albert Bandura from A. Bandura, D. Ross, and S. A. Ross, "Imitation of Film-Mediated Aggressive Models," *Journal of Abnormal and Social Psychology*, 1963, p. 8; 189 — Jane Brown.

Chapter 9
198 — Michal Heron; 200 — Charles Gatewood; 202 — John Oldenkamp; 204 — Michal Heron; 205 — Courtesy, Lee, Inc.; 209 — Courtesy of Vista; 212 — © 1976 Helena Rubinstein Inc.; 215 — Henri Cartier-Bresson/Magnum; 216 — Charles Gatewood; 218 — Joan Liftin/Woodfin Camp & Associates; 219 — Marvin E.